MW01004435

A Companion to Walt Whitman

Blackwell Companions to Literature and Culture

This series offers comprehensive, newly written surveys of key periods and movements and certain major authors, in English literary culture and history. Extensive volumes provide new perspectives and positions on contexts and on canonical and post-canonical texts, orientating the beginning student in new fields of study and providing the experienced undergraduate and new graduate with current and new directions, as pioneered and developed by leading scholars in the field.

Published

1. *A Companion to Romanticism* Edited by Duncan Wu
2. *A Companion to Victorian Literature and Culture* Edited by Herbert F. Tucker
3. *A Companion to Shakespeare* Edited by David Scott Kastan
4. *A Companion to the Gothic* Edited by David Punter
5. *A Feminist Companion to Shakespeare* Edited by Dympna Callaghan
6. *A Companion to Chaucer* Edited by Peter Brown
7. *A Companion to Literature from Milton to Blake* Edited by David Womersley
8. *A Companion to English Renaissance Literature and Culture* Edited by Michael Hattaway
9. *A Companion to Milton* Edited by Thomas N. Corns
10. *A Companion to Twentieth-Century Poetry* Edited by Neil Roberts
11. *A Companion to Anglo-Saxon Literature and Culture* Edited by Phillip Pulsiano and Elaine Treharne
12. *A Companion to Restoration Drama* Edited by Susan J. Owen
13. *A Companion to Early Modern Women's Writing* Edited by Anita Pacheco
14. *A Companion to Renaissance Drama* Edited by Arthur F. Kinney
15. *A Companion to Victorian Poetry* Edited by Richard Cronin, Alison Chapman, and Antony H. Harrison
16. *A Companion to the Victorian Novel* Edited by Patrick Brantlinger and William B. Thesing

17–20. *A Companion to Shakespeare's Works: Volumes I–IV* Edited by Richard Dutton and Jean E. Howard

21. *A Companion to the Regional Literatures of America* Edited by Charles L. Crow
22. *A Companion to Rhetoric and Rhetorical Criticism* Edited by Walter Jost and Wendy Olmsted
23. *A Companion to the Literature and Culture of the American South* Edited by Richard Gray and Owen Robinson
24. *A Companion to American Fiction 1780–1865* Edited by Shirley Samuels
25. *A Companion to American Fiction 1865–1914* Edited by Robert Paul Lamb and G. R. Thompson
26. *A Companion to Digital Humanities* Edited by Susan Schreibman, Ray Siemens, and John Unsworth
27. *A Companion to Romance* Edited by Corinne Saunders
28. *A Companion to the British and Irish Novel 1945–2000* Edited by Brian W. Shaffer
29. *A Companion to Twentieth-Century American Drama* Edited by David Krasner
30. *A Companion to the Eighteenth-Century English Novel and Culture* Edited by Paula R. Backscheider and Catherine Ingrassia
31. *A Companion to Old Norse-Icelandic Literature and Culture* Edited by Rory McTurk
32. *A Companion to Tragedy* Edited by Rebecca Bushnell
33. *A Companion to Narrative Theory* Edited by James Phelan and Peter J. Rabinowitz
34. *A Companion to Science Fiction* Edited by David Seed
35. *A Companion to the Literatures of Colonial America* Edited by Susan Castillo and Ivy Schweitzer
36. *A Companion to Shakespeare and Performance* Edited by Barbara Hodgdon and W. B. Worthen
37. *A Companion to Mark Twain* Edited by Peter Messent and Louis J. Budd
38. *A Companion to European Romanticism* Edited by Michael K. Ferber
39. *A Companion to Modernist Literature and Culture* Edited by David Bradshaw and Kevin J. H. Dettmar
40. *A Companion to Walt Whitman* Edited by Donald D. Kummings

A Companion to Walt Whitman

EDITED BY DONALD D. KUMMINGS

Blackwell Publishing

© 2006 by Blackwell Publishing Ltd
except for editorial material and organization © 2006 by Donald D. Kummings

BLACKWELL PUBLISHING
350 Main Street, Malden, MA 02148-5020, USA
9600 Garsington Road, Oxford OX4 2DQ, UK
550 Swanston Street, Carlton, Victoria 3053, Australia

The right of Donald D. Kummings to be identified as the Author of the Editorial Material in this Work has been asserted in accordance with the UK Copyright, Designs, and Patents Act 1988.

All rights reserved. No part of this publication may be reproduced, stored in a retrieval system, or transmitted, in any form or by any means, electronic, mechanical, photocopying, recording or otherwise, except as permitted by the UK Copyright, Designs, and Patents Act 1988, without the prior permission of the publisher.

First published 2006 by Blackwell Publishing Ltd

1 2006

Library of Congress Cataloging-in-Publication Data

A companion to Walt Whitman / edited by Donald D. Kummings.
p. cm.—(Blackwell companions to literature and culture ; 40)
Includes bibliographical references and index.
ISBN-13: 978-1-4051-2093-7 (hardcover : alk. paper)
ISBN-10: 1-4051-2093-2 (hardcover : alk. paper)
1. Whitman, Walt, 1819–1892—Criticism and interpretation—Handbooks, manuals, etc. I. Kummings, Donald D. II. Series.

PS3238.C57 2006
811′.3—dc22

2005017017

A catalogue record for this title is available from the British Library.

Set in 11 on 13pt Garamond
by SPI Publisher Services, Pondicherry, India
Printed and bound in Great Britain
by TJ International Ltd, Padstow, Cornwall

The publisher's policy is to use permanent paper from mills that operate a sustainable forestry policy, and which has been manufactured from pulp processed using acid-free and elementary chlorine-free practices. Furthermore, the publisher ensures that the text paper and cover board used have met acceptable environmental accreditation standards.

For further information on
Blackwell Publishing, visit our website:
www.blackwellpublishing.com

To Jeremy, Jill, William, and Eamon

Contents

Notes on Contributors

Harold Aspiz, Professor Emeritus of English at California State University, Long Beach, has authored many studies of nineteenth-century American literature, particularly on Walt Whitman, including two pioneering books – *Walt Whitman and the Body Beautiful* (1980) and *So Long! Walt Whitman's Poetry of Death* (2004).

Brett Barney is Research Assistant Professor at the University of Nebraska-Lincoln's Center for Digital Research in the Humanities. He is also Project Manager for the Walt Whitman Archive (www.whitmanarchive.org), where his current project, "An Edition of All Known Whitman Interviews," will be published.

Sherry Ceniza, Associate Professor Emeritus at Texas Tech University, now lives in Brooklyn, New York. She is the author of *Walt Whitman and 19th-Century Women Reformers* (1998).

Robert Leigh Davis is Associate Professor of English at Wittenberg University, Springfield, Ohio. An award-winning teacher, Professor Davis teaches courses on nineteenth- and twentieth-century American literature and directs Wittenberg's First-Year Seminar Program. His book on Whitman's career as a Civil War nurse, *Whitman and the Romance of Medicine* (1997), was published by the University of California Press.

James Dougherty is Professor Emeritus of English at the University of Notre Dame, Indiana, and editor of *Religion & Literature*. He has written *Walt Whitman and the Citizen's Eye* (1992), *The Fivesquare City* (1980), and essays on twentieth-century poets and on the city as a symbol in literature, painting, and architectural design.

Gregory Eiselein is Professor of English at Kansas State University, where he teaches American literature and cultural studies. His books include *Literature and Humanitarianism in the Civil War Era* and two editions of the works of nineteenth-century American poets, *Emma Lazarus: Selected Poems and Other Writings* and *Adah Isaacs Menken: Infelicia and Other Writings*. With Anne Phillips, he edited *The Louisa May Alcott Encyclopedia* and the Norton Critical Edition of *Little Women*.

Ed Folsom is the editor of the *Walt Whitman Quarterly Review*, codirector of the Whitman Archive, and editor of the Whitman Series at the University of Iowa Press. Carver Professor of English at the University of Iowa, he is the author or editor of numerous books and essays on Whitman, including *Walt Whitman's Native Representations*, *Whitman East and West*, *Walt Whitman: The Centennial Essays*, and (with Gay Wilson Allen) *Walt Whitman and the World*.

Amanda Gailey is a doctoral candidate in nineteenth-century American literature and digital text editing at the University of Nebraska. Her article, "How Anthologists Made Dickinson into a Tolerable Woman Writer," is forthcoming in *The Emily Dickinson Journal*.

Ted Genoways is the author of one book of poems, *Bullroarer* (Northeastern University Press, 2001), winner of the Samuel French Morse Poetry Prize, and editor of six books, most recently, *Walt Whitman: The Correspondence, Vol. VII* (University of Iowa Press, 2004). He is editor of the *Virginia Quarterly Review* at the University of Virginia, for which he edited a special issue of essays on the 150th anniversary of *Leaves of Grass*.

Walter Grünzweig is Professor of American Literature and Culture at Universität Dortmund and Adjunct Professor at University of Pennsylvania, SUNY Binghamton, and Canisius College. Beyond his reception study *Constructing the German Walt Whitman* (1995), he is mainly interested in literary and cultural relations between the US and German-speaking Europe.

Eldrid Herrington is a Professor of English Literature at University College Dublin. She is a National Endowment of the Humanities Fellow and a Government of Ireland Fellow and has taught at the University of Cambridge and Boston University. She has published widely on nineteenth-century British and American literature, and her book, *Civil War, Revision, and Self-Representation*, is forthcoming.

Andrew C. Higgins teaches American literature at Louisiana Tech University in Ruston, LA. He has written articles on Whitman and other topics, focusing on nineteenth-century American poetry. He is currently at work on a study of Henry Wadsworth Longfellow.

Tyler Hoffman is Associate Professor and Director of Graduate Studies in the Department of English at Rutgers University in Camden. His book, *Robert Frost and the Politics of Poetry*, published in 2001, received the South Atlantic Modern Language Association Studies Book Award. He has published essays on a range of modern American poets and their poetics, and is editor of the electronic Whitman Studies/American Studies journal *The Mickle Street Review* and associate editor of *The Robert Frost Review*.

Andrew Jewell received his PhD in American literature from the University of Nebraska-Lincoln in August 2004. He has published on Whitman, Mark Twain, and Willa Cather and has served as an editorial assistant on the Walt Whitman Archive since 2001. He currently works at the University of Nebraska's Electronic Text Center as part of the Initiative for Digital Research in the Humanities.

M. Jimmie Killingsworth, Professor of English at Texas A&M University, is the author of many books and essays on American literature, rhetoric, and culture. His publications include three books on Whitman: *Whitman's Poetry of the Body: Sexuality, Politics, and the Text* (1989), *The Growth of Leaves of Grass: The Organic Tradition in Whitman Studies* (1993), and *Walt Whitman and the Earth: A Study in Ecopoetics* (2004).

Martin Klammer is Professor of Africana Studies and English at Luther College, Decorah, IA. His publications include *Whitman, Slavery, and the Emergence of Leaves of Grass* (Pennsylvania State University Press, 1995) as well as essays on Whitman and Frederick Douglass.

Joann P. Krieg is a Professor at Hofstra University, Department of English. She is the author of *Whitman and the Irish* (University of Iowa Press, 2000), *A Whitman Chronology* (University of Iowa Press, 1998), and of many articles. She edited *Walt Whitman, Here and Now* (Greenwood Press, 1986), as well as a number of volumes in American Studies. She is currently writing a study of Whitman and opera.

David Kuebrich is an Associate Professor of English at George Mason University. His previous writings on Whitman include *Minor Prophecy: Walt Whitman's New American Religion* (1989).

Donald D. Kummings is a Professor of English at the University of Wisconsin-Parkside. A recent publication is the entry on "American Poetry" in *The Oxford Companion to United States History* (2001). His work on Whitman includes three books: *Walt Whitman, 1940–1975: A Reference Guide* (1982), *Approaches to Teaching Whitman's "Leaves of Grass"* (1990), and (with J. R. LeMaster) *Walt Whitman: An Encyclopedia* (1998). In 1990, his collection of poems, *The Open Road Trip*, was awarded the Posner Poetry Prize by the Council for Wisconsin Writers. In 1997, the Carnegie Foundation for the Advancement of Teaching named him Wisconsin Professor of the Year.

Kerry C. Larson is currently Associate Professor of English and Senior Associate Dean of the Rackham Graduate School at the University of Michigan. His publications include *Whitman's Drama of Consensus* (University of Chicago Press, 1988) and articles on Emerson and Whitman in *Raritan*, *ELH*, *Nineteenth-Century Literature*, and *Nineteenth-Century Prose*. His current project analyzes the cultural impact of equality on antebellum American literature.

J. R. LeMaster grew up in Ohio, graduated from Defiance College, and then received his MA and PhD from Bowling Green State University. LeMaster taught English at Defiance College for 15 years before moving to Baylor University in Texas where he has taught for the past 27 years. LeMaster's research interests are varied, including the Kentucky writer Jesse Stuart, Walt Whitman, and Mark Twain. With Donald D. Kummings, LeMaster edited *Walt Whitman: An Encyclopedia*, published by Garland in 1998.

Stephen John Mack teaches Advanced Writing and American Literature at the University of Southern California where he received his PhD. He is the author of *The Pragmatic Whitman: Reimagining American Democracy.*

Luke Mancuso teaches English at St John's University in Collegeville, Minnesota. He has contributed to Whitman studies with *The Strange Sad War Revolving: Walt Whitman, Reconstruction, and the Emergence of Black Citizenship, 1865–1876* (Camden House, 1997), as well as essays, reviews, and *Walt Whitman Encyclopedia* entries. Mancuso is currently writing an academic memoir.

Maire Mullins serves as coeditor and poetry editor of the journal *Christianity and Literature* and teaches in the Social Action and Justice Colloquium at Pepperdine University, California. Her articles on Walt Whitman have appeared in *Tulsa Studies in Women's Literature*, *The Walt Whitman Quarterly Review*, *The Walt Whitman Encyclopedia* (Garland Press, 1998), *Tohoku Journal of American Studies* (Sendai, Japan), and *The American Transcendental Quarterly.* She has also written articles on Willa Cather, Hisaye Yamamoto, Isak Dinesen, and William Butler Yeats, and published in the journal *Academic Leader.*

Martin G. Murray is an independent researcher and founder of the Washington Friends of Walt Whitman. He has written and lectured extensively on Whitman for both academic and nonacademic audiences. He has been published in the *Walt Whitman Quarterly Review*, the *Yale University Library Gazette*, *Washington History*, and the *Walt Whitman Encyclopedia*, as well as on The Classroom Electric and Walt Whitman Archive websites. His contributions include the discovery of several pieces of uncollected prose journalism, biographical annotations of soldiers appearing in Whitman's *Memoranda During the War*, and a biography of Whitman's companion Peter Doyle. An economist by profession, Murray has a graduate degree from The George Washington University, and is employed by the Commodity Futures Trading Commission, a federal regulatory agency.

Howard Nelson teaches at Cayuga Community College in Auburn, New York. He is the author of *Robert Bly: An Introduction to the Poetry* (Columbia University Press) and editor of *Earth, My Likeness: Nature Poems of Walt Whitman*, recently reissued in an expanded edition (Heron Dance/herondance.com).

Douglas A. Noverr is a Professor and Chairperson in the Department of Writing, Rhetoric, and American Cultures at Michigan State University and a member of the core faculty in the American Studies Program. He is the coauthor of *The Relationship of Painting and Literature: A Guide to Information Sources* (1978) and *The Games They Played: Sports in American History, 1865–1980* (1983) as well as author of numerous book chapters and articles on nineteenth- and twentieth-century American literature, sports and culture, film, and popular culture. He served as one of the two associate editors of *The Journalism*, volumes I and II in *The Collected Writings of Walt Whitman* (1998, 2003). His current research focuses on American literature dealing with Mexico and on globalization.

Steven Olsen-Smith is an Associate Professor of English at Boise State University, Idaho, where he teaches courses on early American and antebellum literature. Along with research on Walt Whitman, he has published extensively on Herman Melville, and he is General Editor of *Melville's Marginalia Online*.

William Pannapacker is Assistant Professor of English and Towsley Research Scholar at Hope College in Holland, Michigan. He is the author of *Revised Lives: Walt Whitman and Nineteenth-Century Authorship* (2004) and is currently writing a book entitled *Walt Whitman's American Cities*.

Kenneth M. Price is Hillegass Professor of American literature at the University of Nebraska-Lincoln and codirector of the Walt Whitman Archive. He is the author of *Whitman and Tradition: The Poet in His Century* (Yale University Press, 1990) and *To Walt Whitman, America* (University of North Carolina Press, 2004).

Kathy Rugoff is an Associate Professor of English at the University of North Carolina at Wilmington. She has published in such areas as American poetry and twentieth-century history and American poetry and music, including an essay in *Walt Whitman and Modern Music* (2000), edited by Lawrence Kramer.

William J. Scheick is the J. R. Millikan Centennial Professor at the University of Texas at Austin. His books include *The Slender Human Word: Emerson's Artistry in Prose*; *The Half-Blood: A Cultural Symbol in Nineteenth-Century American Fiction*; *Fictional Structure and Ethics: The Turn-of-the-Century English Novel*; and *The Ethos of Romance at the Turn of the Century*.

M. Wynn Thomas is Professor of English and Director of CREW (Centre for Research into the English Literature and Language of Wales), University of Wales Swansea. A

Fellow of the British Academy, he has published some 20 books, in English and Welsh, on American literature and the literatures of Wales. Of his many studies of Whitman, the latest is *Transatlantic Connections: Whitman US–Whitman UK* (2005).

Jim Warren is S. Blount Mason, Jr. Professor of English and Chair of the English Department at Washington and Lee University, Lexington, VA. He has published articles and books on Whitman, Emerson, Thoreau, and other nineteenth-century American authors. His current work is in the field of American environmental writing. He has a new book, *John Burroughs and the Place of Nature*, forthcoming (from University of Georgia Press).

Edward Whitley is an Assistant Professor in the English Department at Lehigh University, Bethlehem, Pennsylvania. His essays on Walt Whitman and American poetry have appeared in *The Walt Whitman Quarterly Review* and *Melus*. He also created an online version of the British editions of Whitman's poetry for the Walt Whitman Hypertext Archive.

Gary Wihl is Dean of Humanities at Rice University, Houston, TX, and Francis Newman Moody Professor of the Humanities. He is the author of *Ruskin and the Rhetoric of Infallibility* (Yale University Press 1985) and *The Contingency of Theory* (Yale University Press 1994). He is currently completing a book on literature and liberalism that includes studies of George Eliot, Walt Whitman, E. L. Doctorow, and Milan Kundera.

Illustrations

Abbreviations of Standard Whitman Works

LG	*Leaves of Grass, Comprehensive Reader's Edition*, ed. Harold W. Blodgett and Sculley Bradley. New York: New York University Press, 1965.
LG Var.	*Leaves of Grass, A Textual Variorum of the Printed Poems*, ed. Sculley Bradley, Harold W. Blodgett, Arthur Golden, and William White, 3 vols. (vol. I: 1855–56; vol II: 1860–67; vol III: 1870–91). New York: New York University Press, 1980.
EPF	*The Early Poems and the Fiction*, ed. Thomas L. Brasher. New York: New York University Press, 1963.
PW	*Prose Works, 1892*, ed. Floyd Stovall, 2 vols. (vol. I: *Specimen Days*; vol. II: *Collect and Other Prose*). New York: New York University Press, 1963, 1964.
DBN	*Daybooks and Notebooks*, ed. William White, 3 vols. (vol. I: Daybooks, 1876–November 1881; vol. II: Daybooks, December 1881–1891; vol. III: Diary in Canada, Notebooks, Index). New York: New York University Press, 1978.
NUPM	*Notebooks and Unpublished Prose Manuscripts*, ed. Edward F. Grier, 6 vols. (vol. I: Family Notes and Autobiography, Brooklyn and New York; vol. II: Washington; vol. III: Camden; vols. IV, V, VI: Notes). New York: New York University Press, 1984.
Corr.	*The Correspondence*, ed. Edwin Haviland Miller (vols. 1–6) and Ted Genoways (vol. 7), 7 vols.: vol. I: 1842–67; vol. II: 1868–75; vol. III: 1876–85; vol. IV: 1886–89; vol. V: 1890–92; vol. VI: A Supplement with a Composite Index; vol. VII: A Second Supplement with a Calendar of Letters to Whitman. Vols. 1–6: New York: New York University Press, 1961 (I, II), 1964 (III), 1969 (IV, V), 1977 (VI); Vol. 7: Iowa City: University of Iowa Press, 2004.
Jour.	*The Journalism*, ed. Herbert Bergman, with Douglas A. Noverr and Edward J. Recchia, 2 vols. (vol. I: 1834–46; vol. II: 1846–48). New York: Peter Lang, 1998, 2003.

Introduction

Donald D. Kummings

Over the years, Walt Whitman has been called many things: literary agitator, ultimate democrat, proponent of sexual liberation, paterfamilias of the tribe of American poets, shamanistic role-player, the Great Cataloguer, a presiding spirit of American cultural history, the bard of death, a kosmos, and *hombre contradictorio,* just to mention a few. Recently he has been called a maximalist and contrasted with minimalist Emily Dickinson. In an article in the *New York Times*, Charles McGrath (2005) declares that Americans "believe with equal fervor in artistic self-effacement and artistic self-aggrandizement. We like tiny well-made stuff and also great sprawling messes; art that is full of feeling and also art that aspires to a kind of icy perfection." Maximalist Whitman, perpetrator of "sprawling messes," is now known worldwide as the author of *Leaves of Grass*, and his reputation seldom has been larger than it is today.

Signs of that reputation are visible in the numerous special events that took place in 2005, a year that marked the 150th anniversary of the first edition of *Leaves of Grass*. Celebrations occurred at the University of Nebraska in Lincoln; the Walt Whitman Birthplace on Long Island, New York; the Seaport Museum in New York City; Columbia University; the College of New Jersey; the University of Iowa; and the University of Paris in France, as well as other, less prominent sites. Among the commemorative events were the presentation of scholarly papers, lectures, classical concerts, jazz performances, poetry readings (both standard and marathon), poetry contests, radio interviews, multimedia presentations, book exhibits, and special issues of journals, the most notable of these being the vibrant and visually stunning "Whitman's *Leaves of Grass* at 150" issue of *The Virginia Quarterly Review*. In addition to these occurrences, the University of Nebraska Press issued a collection of conference essays on Whitman, the University of Iowa Press came out with M. Wynn Thomas's *Transatlantic Connections: Whitman U.S., Whitman U.K.*, and Oxford University Press published several books on Whitman, including David S. Reynolds's "150th Anniversary Edition" of the 1855 *Leaves*.

Even if somewhat belatedly, *A Companion to Walt Whitman* hopes to contribute to the excitement and energy generated by sesquicentennial activities. With its in-depth analyses of a writer often deemed quintessentially American, and with its emphasis on social and political as well as literary issues, the *Companion* reveals that the poet's writings contain many ideas relevant to the ideological debates – indeed, to the culture wars – currently dominating American society. Beyond question, that society has been and is being transformed by the shocking events of September 11, 2001. To many observers, especially those in foreign countries, the United States is now profoundly troubled, a country in crisis. For instance, consider the view of the US articulated by Andrew O'Hagan, who, in New York City in August 2004, covered the Republican National Convention for *The London Review of Books*:

> Confounded in Iraq, isolated from its traditional allies, shamed over Abu Ghraib, soaked in corporate corruption and the backwash of environmental harm, sustaining an uninherited budget deficit while preparing more tax rewards for the rich, as dismissive of the unhealthy as the foreign, as terrified of the unfolding truth as of mailed anthrax, [America] is a society made menacing by a notion of God's great plan. America is tolerance-challenged, integrity-poor, frightened to death, and yet, beneath its patriotic hosannahs, a country in delirium before the recognition that it might have spent the last three years not only squandering the sympathy of the world but hot-housing hatreds more ferocious than those it had wished to banish forever from the clear blue skies. (O'Hagan 2004: 6)

Though Walt Whitman died well over a century ago, his poetry and prose continue to speak to the condition of an anxious and divided United States.

For the most part, *A Companion to Walt Whitman* depicts the poet as a creature of his own time and place. Often, though, what Whitman said of his era has a surprising applicability to the present era. For example, in a poem entitled "To the States, To Identify the 16th, 17th, or 18th Presidentiad," he reacted with impassioned scorn to the inept administrations of Presidents Millard Fillmore, Franklin Pierce, and James Buchanan:

> Why reclining, interrogating? why myself and all drowsing?
> What deepening twilight – scum floating atop of the waters,
> Who are they as bats and night-dogs askant in the capitol?
> What a filthy Presidentiad! (O South, your torrid suns! O
> North, your arctic freezings!)
> Are those really Congressmen? are those the great Judges?
> is that the President?
> Then I will sleep awhile yet, for I see that these States sleep,
> for reasons;
> (With gathering murk, with muttering thunder, and lambent
> shoots, we all duly awake,
> South, North, East, and West, inland and seaboard, we will
> surely awake.)
>
> (*LG*: 278–9)

Many readers will find this poem relevant to today's political scene, and to the George W. Bush administration in particular.

Yet one more example of Whitman's pertinence to the twenty-first century involves comments he made in *Democratic Vistas* (1871), a book published during a period of time that came to be known as the Gilded Age. Named after a satirical novel published in 1873 by Mark Twain and Charles Dudley Warner, the Gilded Age was notable for its government corruption, corporate malfeasance, huge disparities in the distribution of wealth, "conspicuous consumption," and the American middle class's obsession with getting rich. That era, as recent social critics have pointed out, bears strong resemblances to the present day. Thus when Whitman excoriates his own time he also seems to censure ours:

> The depravity of the business classes of our country is not less than has been supposed, but infinitely greater. The official services of America, national, state, and municipal, in all their branches and departments, except the judiciary, are saturated in corruption, bribery, falsehood, mal-administration; and the judiciary is tainted. The great cities reek with respectable as much as nonrespectable robbery and scoundrelism. In fashionable life, flippancy, tepid amours, weak infidelism, small aims, or no aims at all, only to kill time. In business (this all-devouring modern word, business), the one sole object is, by any means, pecuniary gain. The magician's serpent in the fable ate up all the other serpents; and money-making is our magician's serpent, remaining to-day sole master of the field. (*PW*, II: 370)

Designed to appeal to upper-level students, postgraduates, both specialist and non-specialist faculty, and readers among the literate public, *A Companion to Walt Whitman* brings together 35 original essays. Because many of these are 8,000 words in length, the volume is ambitious. It aims to provide a comprehensive guide to the study of the poet. Moreover, it tries to include information representing the best and most current thinking in Whitman scholarship. The essays are arranged under four sections: "The Life," "The Cultural Context," "The Literary Context," and "Texts," with the final section divided into "Works of Poetry" and "Prose Works." Although excellent and at least somewhat comparable anthologies of criticism are already available to students of the poet – *The Cambridge Companion to Walt Whitman* (1995), edited by Ezra Greenspan, and *A Historical Guide to Walt Whitman* (2000), edited by David S. Reynolds, to mention a couple – none matches the scope and depth of coverage of this book in Blackwell's Companions to Literature and Culture series.

Appropriately, the book's first essay is a compact biography of Whitman. Written by Gregory Eiselein, the account provides information on all the principal phases of the life, including Whitman's birth in 1819, and humble beginnings on Long Island; his jobs as a schoolteacher; his writing of conventional short stories and a temperance novel; his work as a journalist in Brooklyn and Manhattan; his occasional forays into politics; his publication, in 1855, 1856, and 1860, of the extraordinary early editions of *Leaves of Grass*; his countless visits to Washington, DC army hospitals; his activities in post-Civil War Washington; and his nearly two decades in Camden, New Jersey, which concluded with the publication of the so-called Deathbed edition of the *Leaves* (1891–2). Though brief, Eiselein's biography contains abundant detail.

Following the biography is "The Cultural Context," the 20 essays of which comprise the largest section of the *Companion*. These essays stress those aspects of nineteenth-century society and culture that Whitman absorbed and transformed in his creation of *Leaves of Grass*. Opening the section is Douglas A. Noverr, who shows how Whitman's experience in journalism – especially at the New York *Aurora* and Brooklyn *Daily Eagle* – contributed in fundamental ways to his development as a poet. William Pannapacker convincingly argues that Whitman's poetry and prose were even more decisively shaped by his immersion in urban life than by his encounters with Nature. Illustrating Whitman's lifelong love of ordinary workers, both male and female, M. Wynn Thomas maintains that Whitman is "the great Homeric poet of American labor." Gary Wihl concentrates on Whitman's complex notions of individualism, concluding that his political writings must be understood in the context of nineteenth-century liberalism and Romanticism. J. R. LeMaster demonstrates that Whitman was deeply impressed by oratorical culture in nineteenth-century America – that is, by preachers, stump speakers, social reformers, lyceum lecturers, and so on – and drew on their principles and techniques in crafting his poems. In close readings of key passages, Martin Klammer clarifies Whitman's apparently contradictory attitudes toward the issue of slavery and the future of black persons in the United States. These six essays reveal much about the sources of the first edition of *Leaves*.

The middle group of "Cultural Context" essays explores a wide range of topics: nation and identity, the concept of democracy, imperialism, sexuality, gender, religion, and science and pseudoscience. Noting that Whitman's literary project begins with the yoking of "America" and "I," Eldrid Herrington proceeds to show that the words *nation* and *identity*, which the poet uses throughout his career, are far more multivalent than readers have supposed. Stephen John Mack declares that democracy is the central concern of Whitman's literary vision, and that his contributions to democratic theory are profoundly innovative and yet largely unappreciated. Looking at the poet from the perspective of readers outside the United States, Walter Grünzweig sees Whitman's writings as paradoxical, containing elements of both imperialism and internationalism. Maire Mullins reveals how Whitman, in a society resistant to any published utterance involving sexuality, nevertheless extended the boundaries of discourse by incorporating throughout *Leaves of Grass* images of heterosexual, homosexual, autoerotic, and bisexual desire. Sherry Ceniza claims that not only did Whitman develop a theory of gender; he was also "reaching beyond the binaries of male/female, seeing identity as more accountable to a being's spirit than contemporary gender theorists posit." Taking seriously Whitman's avowed religious intentions, David Kuebrich reads *Leaves of Grass* as an attempt to found a post-Christian faith that (1) emphasizes human divinity, and (2) fits the conditions of America's emerging scientific and democratic culture. In a richly detailed account, Harold Aspiz surveys the various sciences (such as anatomy, astronomy, geology, and chemistry) and pseudosciences (such as phrenology, physiognomy, and mesmerism) that influenced Whitman's thinking.

The remaining essays in the "Cultural Context" section begin with an examination of nineteenth-century popular culture, in which Brett Barney finds fascinating connections between Whitman's poetry and plebeian entertainments such as the circus, P. T. Barnum's American Museum, and the moving panorama. Kathy Rugoff probes the subject of music, revealing, among other things, that Whitman strongly admired both "art music" (such as opera) and "heart music" (such as the sentimental songs of Stephen Foster or of the Hutchinson family). Ed Folsom indicates how developments in visual culture, particularly in photography and realistic painting, helped Whitman create his democratic poetry. Concentrating on the historical essays of "Brooklyniana" and the poems of *Drum-Taps* and *Sequel to Drum-Taps*, Luke Mancuso points out how Whitman's responses to the Civil War often involve nostalgic representations of nation, home, and memory. Jimmie Killingsworth looks at Whitman through the lens of ecopoetics and finds his writings concerned with both "wide open spaces" and "special places," that is, with representations of nature that are both universal and regional. Whitman's poems, William Scheick declares, reflect his century's preoccupation with death, his own misgivings relating to mortality, and his deliberate effort to create in his culture "a right understanding" of dying. Focusing not on the nineteenth but the twentieth century, Andrew Jewell and Kenneth M. Price trace the evolution of Whitman's image in the mass media – specifically, in advertising, magazines, popular music, television, mass-market paperbacks, and the internet.

"The Literary Context" section contains five essays. In the first of these, Tyler Hoffman discusses something that deeply interested Whitman and that has long been viewed as one of the most revolutionary aspects of *Leaves of Grass* – language. James Perrin Warren analyzes Whitman's style, finding there, from 1855 to 1892, a "pattern of persistent innovation, marked by constant reinvention and refashioning." Joann Krieg surveys the contacts or connections that Whitman had with American writers (such as Bryant, Poe, Emerson, Thoreau, Longfellow) and with British and Irish writers (such as Rossetti, Swinburne, Symonds, Tennyson, Wilde). Amanda Gailey has written an engrossing publishing history of the six distinct editions of *Leaves of Grass* – those editions Whitman released in 1855, 1856, 1860, 1867, 1871–2, and 1881–2 – and she has appended to this history a groundbreaking set of tables on "*Leaves of Grass* Titles." Finally, Andrew C. Higgins recounts some 150 years of reaction to Whitman and his work, from the early remarks of Ralph Waldo Emerson and Rufus W. Griswold to the recent responses of June Jordan and Jorie Graham.

"Texts," the concluding section of *A Companion to Walt Whitman*, is devoted to analyses of specific works of poetry and prose. Edward Whitley writes on the first edition of *Leaves of Grass*, exploring fully the implications of the fact that this volume of poems was published in conjunction with the Independence Day celebrations of 1855. Writing on "Song of Myself," Whitman's longest and perhaps greatest poem, Kerry C. Larson looks afresh at an old subject – the theme of equality. James Dougherty regards "Crossing Brooklyn Ferry" as one of Whitman's best works and asserts that it can be interpreted in at least four ways: a poem in the Romantic tradition, an urban poem, a poem about poetry itself, and a poem about Whitman's continuing "presence." Mindful of the work's technical artistry, Howard Nelson connects "Out of the Cradle Endlessly Rocking" to opera, to the Long Island seashore of Whitman's youth, to the lost love laments of the "Calamus" poems, and to the powerful theme of death. Steven Olsen-Smith clarifies issues of autonomy and interdependency among three impressive works: the original, separate sequence known as "Live Oak, with Moss" and the two larger poem clusters entitled "Calamus" and "Children of Adam." Focusing on the "Drum-Taps" and "Memories of President Lincoln" clusters, Ted Genoways finds that their depictions of the Civil War fall into five groups: recruiting poems, realistic sketches, poetic portraits of the common soldier, hospital poems, and tributes to Abraham Lincoln.

Whitman's prose is the concern of the final three essays of the *Companion*. In a lively critique of *Democratic Vistas*, arguably Whitman's most important prose work, Robert Leigh Davis comments on several key issues but considers mainly the aims, implications, and ambitious scope of the poet's "culture programme." Granting that *Specimen Days* is cobbled together and improvisational, with its genealogical reminiscences, Civil War memoranda, and nature notes, Martin G. Murray nevertheless shows that this "autobiography of sorts" was Whitman's "last sustained treatment" of major themes. Last is a first-of-its-kind bibliography in which I list and annotate all consequential critical comments on Whitman's prose writings, not just on *Democratic Vistas* and *Specimen Days* but also the short stories, *Franklin Evans*, the journalistic articles, *An American Primer*, the 1855 Preface, and so on.

To undertake a project of the magnitude of this collection of essays is to contract many debts. I am grateful first of all to Literature Editor Andrew McNeillie, formerly with Blackwell Publishing, now with Oxford University Press. McNeillie's enthusiasm and encouragement were most instrumental in my decision to assume the responsibilities of editing the *Companion*. There are others at Blackwell to whom I am grateful: Jennifer Hunt, Senior Publishing Coordinator; Emma Bennett, Commissioning Editor; Astrid Wind, Publishing Coordinator for Literature; Karen Wilson, Editorial Controller; Lisa Eaton, Production Controller; and Laura Montgomery, Marketing Manager. Finally, I greatly appreciate the sound and meticulous work of freelance copyeditor Jenny Roberts.

Thanks are due to Gregory Eiselein, Ezra Greenspan, and George B. Hutchinson, as well as several anonymous readers, for their endorsement of my Blackwell prospectus. For expert advice and timely recommendations I am beholden to Kenneth M. Price and Ed Folsom. Others in the community of Whitman scholars to whom I owe thanks – for assistance of various kinds – include Betsy Erkkila, Jimmie Killingsworth, Sherry Ceniza, Marina Camboni, and M. Wynn Thomas. Finally, I am under many obligations to the contributors to this volume, each of whom interrupted his or her busy schedule to take on a demanding assignment.

The University of Wisconsin-Parkside is deserving of recognition for financial support from the Department of English and the Committee on Research and

Creative Activity, for invaluable clerical support provided by Program Assistant Kathy Caskey, and for the tonal graphite drawings created by Art department printmaker Doug DeVinny. The DeVinny pieces were executed expressly for the Whitman *Companion*.

Finally, I am pleased to extend my appreciation to the following family members: Laura and Keith Stummer, Diana and Saunders Kohn, Eric Larsen and Debra Zaionc, Wanda and Todd Stingley, and Sharon and John Kummings. For many years now these individuals have made possible the conditions under which one can accomplish such things as a large-scale literary project. To my wife, Patricia, for her resilience, unflagging support, and love, I proclaim my unbounded gratitude.

References

McGrath, Charles (2005). "The Souped-Up, Knock-Out, Total Fiction Experience." *The New York Times*, 17 April, Section 4: 16.

O'Hagan, Andrew (2004). "The God Squad." *The London Review of Books*, 23 September, 26 (18): 6–9.

PART I
The Life

1
Whitman's Life and Work, 1819–92

Gregory Eiselein

Childhood and Adolescence, 1819–36

With its free verse form that abandoned traditional metrical systems and regular patterns of rhyme, *Leaves of Grass* dramatically altered the history of poetry in English and made Walt Whitman the most famous and influential poet in American literature. The facts of his early life may not immediately announce the arrival of one who would reshape literary history, but Whitman saw in his boyhood – especially in "the locality itself" (*PW*, 1: 10), Long Island – the genesis of a poet.

Born on May 31, 1819, in West Hills, Long Island, Walter (later Walt) Whitman, Jr. was the second child of Walter Whitman, Sr. (1789–1855) and Louisa Van Velsor Whitman (1795–1873). Married in 1816, the couple had their first child, Jesse, in 1818. After two boys, Louisa gave birth to two girls, Mary Elizabeth (1821–99) and Hannah Louisa (1823–1908), and a child who died in infancy and was never named. The next three boys were named after American presidents: Andrew Jackson (1827–63), George Washington (1829–1901), and Thomas Jefferson (known as Jeff, 1833–90). At the age of 40, Louisa gave birth to her last child, Edward (1835–92), who lived with significant mental and physical disabilities.

Walter, Sr.'s English ancestors had lived on Long Island since the seventeenth century, though the previously well-off Whitmans were in economic decline by the nineteenth century. A large man and a heavy drinker, Walter Sr. could be serious, private, and angry. He worked as a farmer and later a house builder in Brooklyn, but his financial instability forced the family to move several times. The poet was never close to his father, yet Walter, Sr.'s admiration of freethinkers and radicals left an unmistakable influence on his namesake's early intellectual development.

Walter, Jr. deeply loved his mother and thought of her as "a perfect mother" (*LG*: 15). She never appreciated his poetry, yet he saw her as the primary influence on his work, saying, "Leaves of Grass is the flower of her temperament active in me" (Traubel

1906–96, 2: 113). She was born on the Van Velsor's Long Island homestead to a family of Dutch ancestry. A homemaker with no formal education, Louisa was a lively, hard-working woman. Walt took pride in his mother's "Quaker lineage" (Traubel 1906–96, 1: 78) and believed it shaped his own life.

A few days before Walter, Jr.'s fourth birthday, Walter, Sr. moved the family to Brooklyn where he hoped to purchase empty lots, build houses on them, and sell them at a profit. Never quite successful in this business, he moved the family several more times to various addresses throughout Brooklyn. Walter, Jr. attended the city's public elementary school, though he does not seem to have excelled in his studies.

School may not have left a strong impression, but Whitman's childhood encounters with the Marquis de Lafayette and Elias Hicks became enduring memories. At six, Whitman was among a group of schoolchildren who welcomed the Revolutionary War hero at an Independence Day celebration. Lafayette picked up Whitman and gave him a hug and kiss before setting him back down to watch the ceremonies. For a boy whose family so admired the young nation's heroes, this memory merged personal affection with a celebration of democratic independence. Four years later, he joined his parents to hear Quaker minister Elias Hicks whose powerful eloquence moved the boy deeply that night. For decades, he remembered Hicks for his willingness to stand by unpopular convictions and his strong belief in individual divine inner light.

At 11, Whitman left school to work as an errand boy for a lawyer named James Clark. It was not, however, the end of Whitman's education. Clark's son, Edward, provided Whitman with a library membership, which allowed him to read and revel in the *Arabian Nights* and Walter Scott. After working as an office boy for a local doctor, Whitman took his first job with a newspaper, the *Long Island Patriot*, where he learned typesetting and wrote his first published work. The education in printing led to a succession of newspaper jobs and a lifelong appreciation for the materiality of printed pages. Whitman worked for a printer named Erastus Worthington in 1832, before moving on to a position as a compositor for the *Long Island Star*, where he stayed for almost three years. As he honed his printing skills, the rest of his family, struggling financially, moved back to the country. Employed and on his own, Whitman developed an interest in theatre, joined debating societies, and read voraciously. In 1835, as an experienced compositor who occasionally wrote for various newspapers, he moved across the East River to work in Manhattan. His career seemed set, when a fire swept through New York's printing district in August and left Whitman unemployed. He returned to rural Long Island in May 1836 and rejoined his family.

Early Adulthood, 1836–48

A month after his return, Whitman began a second career and became, out of financial necessity, a schoolteacher for villages across Long Island. His first position was in East Norwich in the summer of 1836, but he moved on to teach in Babylon when his parents moved there that autumn. In 1837, he was teaching in Long Swamp during the spring and in Smithtown by the fall.

Whitman took a hiatus from teaching in 1838 and started his own newspaper, the *Long-Islander*. He purchased a printing press and hired his brother George to help. This enterprise kept Whitman out of the classroom and provided him the pleasure of delivering newspapers on horseback. He enjoyed his new work but left the *Long-Islander* after about 10 months. In August 1839, he joined the *Long Island Democrat*. Its editor, James Brenton, appreciated Whitman's literary talents and published his articles and poems – rhymed, metrical pieces that often took death as their theme.

After this return to newspapers, Whitman was again teaching, in Flushing Hall for six months and then in Little Bay Side at the end of 1839, moving from teaching post to teaching post. In the spring of 1840, he moved to a position in Trimming Square. He then taught at Woodbury, before going to Whitestone in 1841. In May, however, Whitman gave up teaching, a profession he never really enjoyed. He was not a careless, mean, or unskilled educator. Rejecting rote memorization and corporal punishment, he preferred the pedagogical use of activities, games, and conversations. Still, the life of a country schoolteacher with its low pay, long hours, and numerous students did not suit Whitman; and the pupils, their parents, and these rural communities annoyed him. "I am sick of wearing away by inches," he wrote to a friend, "here in this nest of bears, this forsaken of all Go[d]'s creation; among clowns and country bumpkins, flat-heads, and coarse brown-faced girls, dirty, ill-favoured young brats, with squalling throats and crude manners" (*Corr*, 7: 2).

Seizing a chance to leave teaching, Whitman re-entered New York's newspaper world in 1841. In May, he started work as a compositor for the *New World*, a weekly owned by Rufus Griswold and Park Benjamin. He also continued his efforts on behalf of the Democratic Party. In 1840 on Long Island, he had worked for Martin Van Buren in his unsuccessful bid for a second presidential term. The following summer in Manhattan, Whitman delivered a speech at a Democratic Party rally in City Hall Park.

He also began writing and publishing fiction. His first published piece was an educational reform story, "Death in the School-Room" (1841). Like most of the two dozen stories Whitman published from 1841 to 1848, "Death in the School-Room" has a loosely autobiographical relationship to his own life. "Wild Frank's Return" (1841) takes place in rural Long Island and dramatizes the conflict between a young man and his family, while "Bervance" (1841) tells the story of an eccentric second son committed to an insane asylum by his callous and unloving father. Written in 1836, "My Boys and Girls" (1844) focuses on his siblings. Whitman's final piece of short fiction – "The Shadow and the Light of a Young Man's Soul" (1848) – recounts his experience of leaving New York to teach at a country school.

Whitman's best-selling work and only novel, *Franklin Evans*, first appeared as an extra to the *New World* in 1842. A temperance novel that sold some 20,000 copies, *Franklin Evans* tells the story of an orphan whose drinking initiates a chain of horrible events. Whitman later dismissed the novel as "damned rot," claiming he wrote it in three days "with the help of a bottle of port" (Traubel 1906–96, 1: 93). *Franklin Evans* was not, however, Whitman's only foray into temperance literature. Three earlier stories – "The Child's Champion" (1841), "Reuben's Last Wish" (1842), and "Wild Frank's Return" – depict the fatal results of heavy drinking. Whitman also explored temperance themes after *Franklin Evans*, starting but never finishing a novel called *The Madman* and eventually incorporating temperance discourse into *Leaves of Grass*.

In 1842, Whitman became a writer and editor for the *Aurora*, a patriotic daily that allowed Whitman to cover politics, society, theatre, and music. By May, he had moved to the *Evening Tattler*, though he remained only through the summer. Living in boarding houses and writing for various periodicals, Whitman worked for several different New York newspapers in the early 1840s, including the *Daily Plebeian*, the *Sunday Times & Noah's Weekly Messenger*, the *Subterranean*, the *New York Sun*, and the *New Mirror*. He took a position as editor of the *Statesman*, a Democratic Party paper, for a short time in 1843 and served another short editorship for the *New York Democrat* in 1844, before being turned out by conservative party members.

Although he moved from job to job, Whitman published journalism and short fiction on a regular basis. For the *Columbian*, Whitman wrote sentimental stories such as "Dumb Kate" (1844) and "The Little Sleighers" (1844). More exotic fiction became his focus in 1845, as he contributed stories on American Indians, the Holy Land, and a mutiny in the British Navy for the *Aristidean*. Whitman also produced sensationalistic, reform stories, including "The Boy Lover" (1845), which revisited temperance themes, and "Revenge and Requital" (1845), which echoed his opposition to capital punishment. In August 1845, however, a financially strapped Whitman returned to Brooklyn and moved in with his family again.

In Brooklyn, Whitman wrote theatre and music articles for the *Long Island Star*. With no permanent position but enjoying all that Manhattan and Brooklyn had to offer, the freelancing Whitman penned an essay titled "Art-Music and Heart-Music" for the *Broadway Journal*, edited by Edgar Allan Poe, whom Whitman remembered as a quiet Southerner. Although this piece protested Europe's influence on American music, Whitman was actually developing a fascination with opera, particularly Italian opera. He took in Verdi and Donizetti, became an enthusiastic fan, wrote reviews, and started to attend the opera regularly when the Astor Place Opera House opened in 1847.

In March 1846, Whitman assumed editorship of the *Brooklyn Daily Eagle*, a Democratic Party paper, and held the position for two years. He wrote editorials, reviews, and articles on a wide variety of topics. He even contributed a couple of conventional poems during his tenure at the *Eagle*, though he had also started to experiment with prose poetry. National topics, like the Mexican War and slavery, also drew Whitman's attention. A critic of radical abolitionism but proponent of the war in Mexico, Whitman used the *Eagle* to back a Free Soil position on slavery – that is, opposition to slavery's extension into the western territories. His boss, Isaac Van Anden, probably fired Whitman in January 1848 because of his support of the Wilmot Proviso, proposed legislation to exclude slavery from the territories. Whitman was again out of a job.

Wandering and Experimenting, 1848–55

The next month, J. E. "Sam" McClure, part-owner of the *New Orleans Daily Crescent*, met Whitman at a Broadway theatre and offered him and his brother Jeff a chance to work for his newspaper. With $200 from McClure, the Whitman brothers left New York two days later and traveled by train, stagecoach, and riverboat to New Orleans, arriving on February 25. Though at times lonely, Jeff was happy to make five dollars a week as an office boy and amazed by New Orleans's sights and sounds. Walt supervised the *Crescent*'s small staff, wrote articles, and compiled news that appeared in newspapers from around the country. New Orleans was Whitman's first opportunity to travel beyond his two-island home of Manhattan/Long Island. In this diverse and lively city, he took walks in the French Quarter and wandered through the city's markets, theatres, saloons, hotel lobbies, and bars. He also witnessed slave auctions, an experience that he later represented in *Leaves of Grass*. By the end of May, however, the *Crescent*'s owners began to reveal "a singular sort of coldness" (Loving 1999: 134) toward Whitman. Whether the chill was over money or a conflict between the Whitmans' Free Soil views and the paper's proslavery stance, Whitman and the *Crescent* parted ways. On May 27, Walt and Jeff were on a steamboat headed north.

Back in Brooklyn on June 15, Whitman looked for work and perhaps some direction in his life. In August, the Free Soil Party selected Whitman as a delegate to the state convention in Buffalo. Upon his return, he began to edit Brooklyn's Free Soil newspaper, the *Freeman*. Although a fire destroyed the newspaper's offices the day after his first issue, the paper and its editor were back in business with a second issue in November. Whitman had not yet found his calling, however. He tried to run a bookstore-stationery shop but eventually abandoned that enterprise and gave up the *Freeman* as well in September 1849. In July, perhaps in an effort to learn about himself and his future, Whitman had visited phrenologist Lorenzo Niles Fowler to have his skull examined, a then popular way of analyzing personality and destiny. Fowler wrongly predicted an early marriage for his client, but rated him high in Friendship, Sympathy, Self-Esteem, and Caution. The analysis also revealed Whitman's capacity for Adhesiveness (same-sex love), Amativeness (opposite-sex love), Combativeness, and more. Whitman seems to have accepted the report as a reliable picture of himself and found in phrenology a vocabulary to describe the kinds of love he later celebrated in *Leaves of Grass*.

During the early 1850s, Whitman still had no permanent newspaper position. He did, however, contribute four poems to the *New York Evening Post* and the *New York Tribune* in 1850. These poems celebrated revolution, expressed dismay and anger over the political compromises surrounding slavery, and revealed an increasingly radical antislavery position. One of these poems, "Resurgemus," was later included in the first edition of *Leaves of Grass*, the only previously published poem in the volume. Thus these poems are clues to Whitman's changes as a writer during the early 1850s – the moment in which this intermittently employed journalist, printer, and author of conventional short fiction remade himself into "The American bard" (*PW*, 2: 446). Biographers know relatively little about Whitman's life in this period. He worked as a printer, house builder, and occasional journalist. He delivered a lecture on art at the Brooklyn Art Union in 1851, visited the Crystal Palace Exhibition in 1853, and attended the opera. None of these facts quite explain this most remarkable change, however. Indeed, the transformation seems so radical that some have suggested that Whitman must have had a mystical experience that accounts for the ecstasies, insights, and revelatory nature of a poem like "Song of Myself." But mystical experiences are difficult to document. What biographers do know is that Whitman thought about politics (especially slavery) and popular culture, took notes toward a never-completed study of language, experimented with words in his notebooks, and wrote poems.

Leaves of Grass, 1855–61

In 1855, Whitman pulled together 12 of these untitled poems, composed a prose preface, and applied for a copyright. With the help of Andrew and James Rome, Whitman printed his new book at the Rome Brothers shop in Brooklyn. The homemade, self-financed volume appeared for sale around July 4 with Fowler & Wells, publishers of phrenology titles, as its distributor. Whitman turned out 795 copies of the 95-page, oversized volume and bound them in a green cover with gold lettering that read "Leaves of Grass," a cover that resembled Fanny Fern's best-selling *Fern Leaves from Fanny's Portfolio* (1853).

During the month that followed, the poet experienced emotional lows and highs. A failing Walter, Sr. died on July 11. Ten days later, Ralph Waldo Emerson wrote to acknowledge the copy of *Leaves of Grass* that Whitman had sent. Full of appreciation for Whitman's achievement, the letter opened: "I am not blind to the worth of the wonderful gift of 'Leaves of Grass.' I find it the most extraordinary piece of wit & wisdom that America has yet contributed" (*Corr*, 1: 41). The praise elated Whitman, who carried the letter with him for the rest of the summer, published it in the *New York Daily Tribune*, and added to the spine of the next edition of *Leaves of Grass* an excerpt that read: "I greet you at the beginning of a great career. R. W. Emerson." Emerson followed with a visit to Brooklyn in December. Other writers and critics publicly praised the book as well, including Edward Everett Hale in the prestigious *North American Review* and the widely read Fanny Fern. Whitman even wrote a few anonymous reviews himself.

Despite the positive press, hostility and neglect were common responses to the poems. The book sold few copies, and some critics wrote savage reviews. In the *Criterion*, for example, his former boss Rufus Griswold openly wondered "how any man's fancy could have conceived such a mass of stupid filth" (Griswold 1983: 25).

Poor sales and negative reactions did not deter the poet, who soon began writing new poems, while contributing articles to *Life Illustrated* and working on a political tirade called "The Eighteenth Presidency!" By September 1856, a second edition of *Leaves of Grass* had arrived, complete with poem titles and 20 new poems, including "Sun-Down Poem," later titled "Crossing Brooklyn Ferry." The new edition sold poorly, perhaps worse even than the first. Whitman continued to draw literary admirers, however, including Bronson Alcott and Henry David Thoreau that fall.

From 1857 to 1859, Whitman worked for the *Brooklyn Daily Times*, writing reviews and editorials. Upset with how Fowler & Wells handled the distribution of the first two editions, Whitman made plans for a third edition, a project he saw as "*The Great Construction of the New Bible*" (*NUPM*, 1: 353). By June 1857, he had written about 68 new poems, though he hadn't yet located a publisher.

During this period, Whitman was spending time at Pfaff's, a restaurant-saloon in Manhattan, and socializing with literary bohemians – editors John Swinton and Henry Clapp, daring feminist celebrities Ada Clare and Adah Isaacs Menken, famous humorist Artemus Ward, and writers Thomas Bailey Aldrich, Fitz-James O'Brien, and Edmund Clarence Stedman. Pfaff's was perhaps also the place where Whitman met Fred Vaughn, a young, working-class Irish-Canadian with whom he had a romantic relationship in the late 1850s. Vaughn may have been the inspiration for "Live Oak, with Moss," a 12-poem sequence that details the speaker's affection for his unnamed male lover, his powerful delight in their relationship, and his reflections on their bond. Whitman never published the poems as a series but folded them into the "Calamus" cluster that emerged in the next edition of *Leaves of Grass*. Another of his memorable pieces from this period appeared as "A Child's Reminiscence" (later "Out of the Cradle Endlessly Rocking") in the December 24, 1859, issue of the *Saturday Press*, the literary journal edited by Pfaff's regular, Henry Clapp. A deeply moving piece about love, death, and poetic creation, "A Child's Reminiscence" recounts a memory of a mockingbird couple along a Long Island beach and a boy's first encounter with death.

In February 1860, Whitman received an unexpected offer from Boston publisher Thayer & Eldridge to publish a new edition of *Leaves of Grass*. The parties quickly negotiated a contract, and Whitman went to Boston to oversee the printing. Thayer & Eldridge released the book in May 1860. To the previous poems, Whitman added 146 new poems, altered earlier ones, and revised titles. He also began placing poems into distinct, thematic clusters, a sign of increased attentiveness to the organization of *Leaves of Grass*. The volume's principal themes are religion, democracy, and love, and "Calamus" brings together all three. The "Calamus" poems focus on love between men, but Whitman insisted they were political. He imagines in these poems of homoerotic affection a spiritualized comradeship, which he imagines as the basis for democracy. The third edition is also darker and more melancholy than previous editions. In contrast to the confident "I" of the opening poem in the 1855 edition or the "Poem of the Road" in 1856, the disconsolate speaker in 1860 often expresses sadness, woe, and painful uncertainty about relationships, personal identity, national destiny, and metaphysical order.

The well-publicized third edition received more attention and critical acclaim than previous editions, and it sold far more copies. The contemporary reviews were mostly positive, and a number of women expressed their enthusiasm. Menken, for example, declared him "centuries ahead of his contemporaries" (Menken 1860: 1). The book's new sense of structure, all of the new poems, its wider readership, and the critical praise, made it one of Whitman's most successful books.

Unfortunately, Thayer & Eldridge went bankrupt in January 1861. Whitman had received about $250 in royalties, which abruptly stopped. During the bankruptcy, the book's plates were transferred to Boston publisher Richard Worthington who began printing pirated editions.

The Civil War, 1861–65

Shortly after war broke out in April 1861, Whitman's 31-year-old brother George joined the Union army and relocated to the Washington-Baltimore area with his regiment. Like many Americans, George, Walt, and their mother were hoping the conflict would pass quickly. Not regularly employed and not finished with *Leaves of Grass*, Walt continued to write poetry and journalism. Following Union defeat at the First Bull Run in July, he began to compose poems with martial images and patriotic tones, "Beat! Beat! Drums!" and "Eighteen Sixty-One," among others. Articles on Brooklyn and a series called "City Photographs" occupied Whitman journalistically in 1861–2, as did visits to the wounded and sick soldiers at the New York Hospital and at Fort Hamilton in Brooklyn. He had been visiting injured stage drivers in the years leading up to the war, and these hospital calls were a continuation of that work and an expression of the poet's concern for ordinary, working-class men. Whitman and his mother regularly checked newspapers for information about the war. On December 16, 1862, three days after the battle of Fredericksburg, they were alarmed to come across the name "First Lieutenant G. W. Whitmore" (Allen 1985: 281) listed among the wounded, and worried it was a misprinting of George's name. George had written a letter that very day to let them know he was "safe and sound" (Whitman 1975: 75) except for a cheek wound, but Walt had already left to find his brother.

On his way to the Washington army hospitals, Walt had his money stolen in Philadelphia. George, moreover, seemed to be in none of those hospitals. Luckily, Walt stumbled upon an abolitionist he had met in Boston while preparing *Leaves of Grass*, William Douglas O'Connor, who now worked for the federal government. O'Connor lent him money, and Walt left for Falmouth, Virginia, to look for his brother among the Union soldiers camped there. When he arrived, a disturbing sight greeted him – dead bodies covered with blankets and "a heap of amputated feet, legs, arms, hands, &c." (*PW*, 1: 32). The mental picture stayed with him for years, shaping his attitude toward the war and images in his letters, poems, and nonfiction. Finding his "dear brother George . . . alive and well" (*PW*, 1: 62), Walt stayed with the army through the holidays.

Whitman had returned to Washington by January. He was living in a small bedroom in O'Connor's apartment, looking for a job, drafting poems, and visiting the sick and wounded in the army hospitals. With a daypack full of paper, stamps, tobacco, candy, cookies, fruit, and other small items, he distributed gifts to soldiers and offered consolation and cheer in whatever ways he could, writing letters for them, reading to them, sitting by them, talking, and listening. With some soldiers, he developed close, loving relationships. Lewis Brown, for example, cherished Whitman's picture and longed to be with him again after they parted, saying in his letters, "I feel quite lost without you hear [sic]" (Shively 1989: 124). To such expressions, Whitman responded with emotion and reassurance, "O Lewy, how glad I should be to see you, to have you with me" (*Corr*, 1: 121).

To continue his unpaid hospital work, Whitman took a position in the Army Paymaster's Office. As he settled into his job and new circle of friends that included O'Connor and the naturalist John Burroughs, his family underwent a series of crises. His brother Jesse, struggling with deep emotional problems, had become violent, while Andrew grew seriously ill with tuberculosis and alcoholism. In November 1863, Walt returned to Brooklyn for a month-long stay; shortly after the visit ended, Andrew died. Even with multiple family problems, a new job, and hospital visitations, Whitman worked on a prose project about his wartime experiences and pitched the idea to James Redpath, publisher of Louisa May Alcott's *Hospital Sketches* (1863). He was also developing a collection of poems about the war. The stress of these multiple demands, long hours in the hospitals, and ongoing anxiety about the war and family led to a collapse in Whitman's health in June 1864. At the urging of friends and physicians, Whitman moved back to Brooklyn to recover and to finish his new book of poems. Although Brooklyn provided him with a much-needed break from Washington and the war, hospital visits and family problems continued to preoccupy him. During the course of 1864, Jeff and Walt arranged for an increasingly unmanageable Jesse to be committed to a lunatic asylum. George, moreover, had disappeared, captured by Confederate troops in September 1864, though the anxious family heard no news about him until the following January. These wartime stresses and maladies eventually left the once hearty Walt in poor health for the rest of his life.

Whitman returned to Washington in January 1865 and, with O'Connor's help, landed a position as copyist at the Interior Department's Bureau of Indian Affairs. Because of poor health, Whitman visited area hospitals less frequently but continued such trips nonetheless, bringing gifts and writing letters for soldiers long after the war ended.

In February or March, as a passenger on a horsecar, Whitman met a 21-year-old former Confederate soldier turned conductor named Peter Doyle. The two fell in love almost immediately. Years later, Doyle remembered their first meeting vividly:

> He was the only passenger, it was a lonely night, so I thought I would go in and talk with him. Something in me made me do it and something in him drew me that way. He used to say there was something in me had the same effect on him. Anyway, I went into the car. We were familiar at once – I put my hand on his knee – we understood. He did not get out at the end of the trip – in fact went all the way back with me. (Shively 1987: 116)

Whitman often joined Doyle on his streetcar, and the regular passengers soon became well-known acquaintances as well. The two took long walks together, went out for drinks, and talked at great length about everything from music and literature to stars and animals and presidents and politics.

Soon after their relationship began, Whitman returned to Brooklyn to see George (no longer a prisoner of war) and finish his new book, *Drum-Taps*. On April 1, 1865, he signed a contract with New York printer Peter Eckler for five hundred copies of the new book. On April 14, while Whitman was in Brooklyn, John Wilkes Booth shot President Lincoln during a performance at Ford's Theatre, which Doyle happened to have been attending. Because Whitman had so intensely admired Lincoln, saying at one point, "After my dear, dear mother, I guess Lincoln gets almost nearer me than anybody else" (Traubel 1906–96, 1: 38), his death had a profound impact. Some copies of *Drum-Taps* were bound and distributed, but the poet realized that his book needed something on Lincoln's death. Delaying further distribution, Whitman began work on a *Sequel to Drum-Taps*. These 18 new poems included one of his most highly regarded pieces, "When Lilacs Last in the Dooryard Bloom'd," and perhaps his most famous and most memorized poem, "O Captain! My Captain!" By October, Whitman had finished the sequel totaling 24 pages and bound it with the previously printed pages from *Drum-Taps*.

Post-War Washington, 1865–73

The Bureau of Indian Affairs promoted Whitman on May 1, 1865, shortly after his return to Washington. Two months later, Whitman was fired. Purging his department of employees who possessed questionable moral character, Interior Secretary James Harlan discovered at Whitman's desk a book he thought obscene, *Leaves of Grass*. The unemployed Whitman went for help to O'Connor, who quickly found his friend a copyist position in the Attorney General's office, a job Whitman held until 1874. Though all seemed put right, O'Connor remained outraged about Harlan's narrow-minded judgment – so outraged that he composed a passionate, 46-page apology, *The Good Gray Poet* (1866), that defends Whitman as a patriotic, humane, healthy-minded, and misunderstood poetic genius who could hardly have intended anything filthy. While it did nothing to change Harlan's views or the opinions of conventional critics, the pamphlet helped transform Whitman's reputation and make his poetry acceptable to mainstream audiences.

Other public defenses of Whitman ensued. Burroughs published an insightful essay titled "Walt Whitman and his 'Drum-Taps'" (1866) in the *Galaxy* and followed up with *Notes on Walt Whitman as Poet and Person* (1867). In England, Moncure Conway published in 1866 an essay that openly endorsed Whitman's poetic achievements. William Michael Rossetti followed in 1867 with his own essay on "Walt Whitman's Poems," before putting together a British edition of the *Poems of Walt Whitman* in 1868. Rossetti's edition paved the way for an expanding appreciation of Whitman's work throughout the British Isles and into Europe.

Nevertheless, just as Whitman's reputation was improving, his poetic powers and productivity declined. After a decade of remarkable literary output that would change the history of poetry, Whitman added just six new poems to the fourth edition of *Leaves of Grass* (1867). The oddly patched-together book collected under one cover four separate volumes: a re-edited version of *Leaves of Grass*, *Drum-Taps*, *Sequel to Drum-Taps*, and *Songs Before Parting*, a new section made up of previous poems.

In several respects, Whitman turned his attention not to poetry but prose after the war. In response to a Thomas Carlyle critique of democratizing cultural developments, Whitman authored an essay called "Democracy" (1867). "Personalism" (1868) and a never published piece called "Orbic Literature" followed. He eventually combined and revised these prose pieces on democracy and individualism into *Democratic Vistas* (1871). In this examination of American culture and ideology, Whitman scrutinizes the conflict "between democracy's convictions, aspirations, and the people's crudeness, vice, caprices" (*PW*, 2: 363). Not always smoothly articulated, his hope-filled solution in *Democratic Vistas* is not so much political as spiritual, cultural, and artistic.

Whitman continued to write poems, however, though they were only rarely as inspired and powerful as his 1855–65 verse. A fifth edition of *Leaves of Grass* appeared in 1871, or, rather, versions of it started to appear. Printed in New York, the first issue was a 384-page volume with 10 new poems. A 504-page version published in Washington emerged in 1872; it included a separately paged "Passage to India" section of 24 new poems and 51 older ones. A third version published in 1872 added another supplement titled "After all, Not to Create Only." The final 1872 issue appended one more separate "book" of poems, "As a Strong Bird on Pinions Free," which included seven new poems and a preface. This succession of issues and supplements suggests that Whitman was not entirely certain about the shape, organization, and direction of *Leaves of Grass* in the 1870s. The fifth edition also demonstrates that Whitman was not finished as a poet: he started seeing new creative possibilities for *Leaves of Grass* and cultivating "the ambition of devoting yet a few years to poetic composition" (*PW*, 2: 459).

In postbellum poems like "A Carol of Harvest, For 1867," and "A Passage to India" (1870), Whitman celebrates modernity and technological progress – which is also the theme of "After all, Not to Create only" (1871), later retitled "Song of the Exposition" after the American Institute's Industrial Exhibition, where he first recited it. "After all" was the first of the occasional pieces Whitman presented publicly during Reconstruction. In June 1872, he traveled to Dartmouth College to read a commencement poem, "As a Strong Bird on Pinions Free" (retitled "Thou Mother with Thy Equal Brood"). A couple of years later, a convalescing Whitman wrote a second commencement poem, "Song of the Universal" (1874), and had it read on his behalf for the graduates at Tufts.

Despite this public recognition and professional success, Whitman's personal life became increasingly sad and difficult. Jeff and his family had moved to St Louis in 1868. Later that same year, a nephew died in a cart accident while playing in the street. An institutionalized Jesse passed away in the winter of 1870. Whitman also worried at times that his feelings for Doyle were not entirely mutual. Someone was deeply in love with Whitman, however. Anne Gilchrist, a widowed mother of three and devoted defender of Whitman in England, was sending him letters expressing her desire to be his bride and wife. Whitman's responses were affectionate, but they attempted to redirect her feelings away from hope for a conventional marriage.

Whitman then had the worst year of his life. In the summer of 1872, high blood pressure exacerbated Whitman's already poor health. That fall, he and O'Connor had an angry dispute (probably about African American suffrage) that led to an estrangement in which the two would not talk to each other for 10 years. In January 1873, Whitman suffered a stroke that paralyzed the left side of his body and forced him eventually to give up his clerkship at the Attorney General's office. The experience was deeply frustrating: "it [is] so slow, so aggravating, to be disabled, so feeble, cannot walk nor do any thing" (*Corr*, 2: 208), he wrote to his mother. Around this time, his close friend John Burroughs left Washington for New York. It had been a terrible series of months, and then in the spring, on May 23, 1873, his mother died. Her passing devastated Whitman, who called it "the great dark cloud of my life" (*Corr*, 2: 242).

Camden, 1873–84

In mourning, in poor health, and unable to work, Whitman moved to Camden, New Jersey to live with his brother George and George's wife, Lou. After a succession of painful losses, he now found himself also separated from his beloved, Peter Doyle, who remained in Washington. From Camden, he wrote Doyle almost cheerful letters of consolation that talked of reunion but revealed real sorrow. Whitman never moved back to Washington, and the two gradually saw less of each other. He felt "*very lonesome*" (*Corr*, 2: 267). Whitman's "Prayer of Columbus" (1874) portrays the explorer as "A batter'd, wreck'd old man, / Thrown on this savage shore, far, far from home" (*LG*: 421) – an image of Whitman himself during his first sad, sad year in Camden.

Ill throughout 1874, he suffered another stroke in the winter of 1875, this one paralyzing his right side. Yet he did his best to carry on with his work. He returned to his Civil War notebooks and produced *Memoranda During the War* (1875), a 68-page prose account of his war experiences. He also planned a two-volume set that included a "Centennial Edition" of *Leaves of Grass*, a reissue of the fifth edition, and an extraordinary new book titled *Two Rivulets*. Mixing poetry and prose and experimenting with page layout, *Two Rivulets* collected Whitman's postbellum writings – poems, prefaces, *Democratic Vistas*, *Memoranda During the War*, and more. This two-volume complete works appeared in 1876. Expensively priced at 10 dollars a set, it still sold relatively well because of Whitman's growing reputation and a perception that he was in financial need. Sales were brisk and provided some income to the poet.

In September 1876, despite Whitman's attempts to discourage her plans and matrimonial hopes, Anne Gilchrist and her children arrived in the United States. The Gilchrists rented a house in Philadelphia and provided the poet with his own room. Although it became clear a marriage would not work, Whitman and the Gilchrists became close friends and remained so, even after the Gilchrists returned to England in 1879.

During this period, Whitman met Harry Stafford and began an intense relationship with the moody young man. The two became friends during the preparation of the "Centennial Edition," as Whitman oversaw the printing process and Stafford worked as an errand boy for the printer. Whitman became the Staffords' regular guest at the family farm, Timber Creek, south of Camden. The war, family troubles, and poor health had devastated Whitman; but these visits from 1876 to 1884 and his relationship with Harry brought him back to life. He told Harry:

> I realize plainly that *if I had not known you* – if it hadn't been for you & our friendship & my going down there summers to the creek with you – and living there with your folks, & the kindness of your mother, & cheering me up – I believe *I should not be a living man to-day.* (*Corr*, 3: 215)

He loved the open air, the Stafford family, and especially Harry. Despite the great affection each had for the other, the two sometimes quarreled. Harry was self-confessedly "lovin, but bad-tempered" (Shively 1987: 151). Whitman gave him a ring, which was repeatedly returned and regiven, as their relationship went through its emotional ups and downs. Stafford married in 1884, but the two remained friends.

During the late 1870s and early 1880s, as his health improved, Whitman's public and social life expanded again. He lectured on Tom Paine in Philadelphia in 1877 and then developed a lecture on the "Death of Abraham Lincoln" that he later delivered at various venues along the east coast from 1879 to 1890. In it, using Doyle's first-hand account, Whitman depicts the assassination with dramatic immediacy and imagines Lincoln's murder as a sacrificial event that heals the nation's conflicts. He typically ended these evenings with a reading of "O Captain! My Captain!" These lectures provided the poet with income and deepened in national memory the association of Whitman with the dead President.

Canadian physician Richard Maurice Bucke came to Camden in 1877 to see the poet and began his long friendship with Whitman. Writers from England also began to call. Edward Carpenter – a champion of Whitman's work in England and author of works on same-sex love and democracy – visited in 1877 and again in 1884. Oscar Wilde dropped by in 1882, and Whitman described him to Stafford as "a fine large handsome youngster" (*Corr*, 3: 264).

By 1879, Whitman felt well enough to travel again. As the guest of former antislavery advocates in Kansas, he journeyed west to St Louis, Kansas City, Lawrence, through Kansas as far as Denver. On the return trip, he stayed with his brother Jeff and family in St Louis, extending his visit by a few months for health reasons. In January 1880, a healthier Whitman returned to Camden and made plans for a second journey, this time to Canada to see Bucke in June. During the trip to Canada, the two discussed Bucke's plans for a biography of Whitman, visited the London, Ontario asylum that Bucke oversaw, and traveled through Ontario to Québec. Bucke returned to America in 1881 and traveled to Long Island with Whitman to see the poet's childhood haunts.

In 1881, Whitman was working on a new edition of *Leaves of Grass* with Boston publisher James Osgood. In a massive restructuring, Whitman created five new clusters, shifted and regrouped poems, included 17 new ones, deleted 39 previous pieces, and edited or tinkered with most of the others. Always concerned with the material look and feel of his books, he traveled to Boston to oversee the printing that summer. With a respected publisher behind it, the new 382-page edition seemed to have a promising future and soon sold 1,500 copies. When faced with possible prosecution for distributing obscene literature, however, Osgood discontinued the volume. During the ensuing controversy that generated a great deal of interest in the book and stirred ardent denunciations and defenses of the poems, Whitman found a new publisher – Rees, Welsh of Philadelphia (David McKay would later acquire the rights). On July 18, 1882, the first Philadelphia printing of 1,000 copies was completely bought up within the first day; the second printing took just a week.

Later that year, Rees, Welsh published a companion volume titled *Specimen Days & Collect* – a volume that contained a fragmentary autobiography and other prose pieces. Bucke's biography, *Walt Whitman* (1883), appeared the following summer. In many respects, with a full-length biography and comprehensive editions of his poetry and prose published, Whitman's career seemed complete.

Mickle Street, 1884–92

In the period following publication of these volumes, Whitman felt at times that he lacked direction but kept writing poetry, memoirs, and criticism. Impeded periodically by summer heat or his own poor health, he still published his writings in a number of venues, and by 1886 he was at work on a new book titled *November Boughs*.

His brother George and family moved from Camden in 1884, leaving the poet with instructions to find a new place before April when new tenants would arrive. Refusing to leave the city and without family, Whitman bought a two-story house at 328 Mickle Street. Mary Davis moved in the following year as his housekeeper and later brought her foster son, Warren Fritzinger, who became Whitman's nurse. Gifts from all over – money, furniture, home furnishings – arrived at Mickle Street to help the poet settle into his new surroundings. Thirty well-wishers chipped in to buy him a horse and buggy, and a young man named Bill Duckett soon became Whitman's companion and driver on these excursions.

From Mickle Street, Whitman received and added to his circle of friends and disciples, including journalist/editor Talcott Williams and lawyers Thomas Harned, Thomas Donaldson, and Robert Ingersoll. Whitman had also generated a following in England, and English disciples such as John Johnston and J. W. Wallace made pilgrimages to see Whitman at Mickle Street. One of Whitman's British readers, the poet John Addington Symonds, had been asking for years about the "Calamus" cluster and its portrayal of homosexual love. In an 1890 letter, Whitman responded to what he called Symonds's "morbid inferences" (*Corr*, 5: 72–3) with an outrageously unconvincing story of having fathered six children. Whitman also circulated in these years among artists, some of whom wanted to capture his image: John W. Alexander, for instance, asked Whitman to sit for a portrait in 1886, sculptor Sidney Morse created a bust in 1887, and Thomas Eakins finished a portrait in 1888. During Whitman's final years, however, Horace Traubel proved to be his steadiest friend. From March 1888 until the moment of the poet's death, Traubel visited Whitman daily and recorded their conversations in astounding detail.

In 1887–8, a flurry of new work appeared in *McClure's*, the *Critic*, *Lippincott's*, and the *New York Herald*. By the fall of 1888, Whitman had finished *November Boughs*, a 140-page book of prose pieces written over the 1880s with a preface titled "A Backward Glance O'er Travel'd Roads" and a new poem cluster called "Sands at Seventy." A stroke in 1888 left Whitman feeble and quite dependent, though another collection of prose and verse titled *Good-Bye My Fancy* appeared in 1891. Even as he drew up his will in 1888, made arrangements for a tomb in Camden's Harleigh Cemetery in 1890, and struggled with pneumonia in the winter of 1891–2, Whitman continued to write and to prepare a final, "Deathbed" edition of *Leaves of Grass*. The final version of his democratic epic consisted of the 1881–2 edition along with two "annexes" of poems, "Sands at Seventy" and "Good-Bye My Fancy," plus the "Backward Glance" preface as a prose finale. Despite his poor health and declaration that *Leaves of Grass* was complete, he worked on further poems, including "A Thought of Columbus," his final poem, authored in December 1891.

Ten days after giving this last poem to Traubel, Whitman died, taking his last breath at 6.34 p.m. on March 26, 1892, and Traubel held his hand as he passed away. On the day of the poet's funeral, thousands turned out. The poet's brother George attended the funeral, as did Peter Doyle, who came and left by himself. Harned, Bucke, and Ingersoll spoke at the funeral, but Traubel did not. At the tomb itself, no words were shared, though, according to Traubel, "Birds sang" (Traubel, Bucke, and Harned 1893: 438).

References and Further Reading

Allen, Gay Wilson (1985). *The Solitary Singer: A Critical Biography of Walt Whitman*. Chicago: University of Chicago Press.

Asselineau, Roger (1999). *The Evolution of Walt Whitman: An Expanded Edition*. Iowa City: University of Iowa Press.

Griswold, Rufus W. (1983). Review of *Leaves of Grass*. In James Woodress (ed.), *Critical Essays on Walt Whitman*. Boston: G. K. Hall, pp. 25–6.

Kaplan, Justin (1980). *Walt Whitman: A Life*. New York: Simon & Schuster.

Krieg, Joann P. (1998). *A Whitman Chronology*. Iowa City: University of Iowa Press.

LeMaster, J. R. and Kummings, Donald D. (eds.) (1998). *Walt Whitman: An Encyclopedia*. New York: Garland Publishing.

Loving, Jerome (1999). *Walt Whitman: The Song of Himself*. Berkeley: University of California Press.

Menken, Adah Isaacs (1860). "Swimming Against the Current." *Sunday Mercury*, June 10: 1.

Reynolds, David S. (1995). *Walt Whitman's America*. New York: Knopf.

Shively, Charley (ed.) (1987). *Calamus Lovers: Walt Whitman's Working Class Camerados*. San Francisco: Gay Sunshine Press.

Shively, Charley (ed.) (1989). *Drum Beats: Walt Whitman's Civil War Boy Lovers*. San Francisco: Gay Sunshine Press.

Traubel, Horace, Bucke, Richard Maurice, and Harned, Thomas B. (eds.) (1893). *In re Walt Whitman*. Philadelphia: David McKay.

Traubel, Horace (1906–96). *With Walt Whitman in Camden*, 9 vols.: vol. 1 (1906) Boston: Small, Maynard; vol. 2 (1908) New York: Appleton; vol. 3 (1914) New York: Mitchell Kennerley; vol. 4, ed. Sculley Bradley (1953) Philadelphia: University of Pennsylvania Press; vol. 5, ed. Gertrude Traubel (1964) Carbondale: University of Southern Illinois Press; vol. 6, ed. Gertrude Traubel and William White (1982) Carbondale: University of Southern Illinois Press; vol. 7, ed. Jeanne Chapman and Robert MacIsaac (1992) Carbondale: University of Southern Illinois Press; vols. 8–9, ed. Jeanne Chapman and Robert MacIsaac (1996) Oregon House, CA: W. L. Bentley.

Whitman, George Washington (1975). *Civil War Letters of George Washington Whitman*, ed. Jerome M. Loving. Durham, NC: Duke University Press.

Whitman, Walt (1963). *Early Poems and Fiction*, ed. Thomas L. Brasher. New York: New York University Press.

Whitman, Walt (1980). *Leaves of Grass: A Textual Variorum of the Printed Poems*, ed. Sculley Bradley, Harold W. Blodgett, Arthur Golden, and William White, 3 vols. New York: New York University Press.

PART II
The Cultural Context

Walt Whitman. Inspired by a photograph taken by Alexander Gardner (1864?). Tonal graphite drawing by Doug DeVinny.

2
Journalism

Douglas A. Noverr

As an individual working in the printing business, Whitman inaugurated his career in 1831 at age 12 when he began an apprenticeship under Samuel E. Clements, the editor of the *Long Island Patriot* and a job contract printer. Whitman later recalled that he wrote bit pieces for the *Patriot* and even managed to place some of his earliest work in the New York City *Mirror.* Between the ages of 12 and 19 he moved through the standard training of printer's "devil" to "journeyman" printer to compositor or typesetter. After a period of working as a compositor in New York City, he returned to Long Island and launched his own weekly newspaper in Huntington in June of 1838. With a hand press and type he had bought in New York, and with money from financial backers, he began a largely one-person operation and delivered the papers on horseback to a circuit of small Long Island villages. However, his initial dedication to issuing a weekly paper of about 200 circulation waned, and the paper began to be issued irregularly (Bergman 1971a: 196). This experience with writing and printing a country paper at age 20 was important in the sense that it directly connected the editor-writer-producer to his readers in the region where he was born and raised, and Whitman had the satisfaction of seeing his readers pleased at the delivery of local news and features suited to a rural and agricultural audience. He remembered that he was received with "hospitality, nice dinners, occasional evenings" (*PW*, 1: 287). This pleasant experience ended in May 1839 when a new proprietor took over the *Long Islander* and Whitman sold his interest. Whitman then moved on to a position of setting type for the *Long Island Democrat* and contributing his first sustained series of 10 essays titled the "Sun-Down Papers – From the Desk of a Schoolmaster." In No. 9 (of which there are two versions) Whitman celebrated "loaferism" and jokingly proposed an "entire loafer kingdom" (*Jour.*, 1: 28). He also struck a serious note for the social and moral value of "kindness":

> I would have men cultivate their disposition for kindness to all around. I would have them foster and cherish the faculty of love . . . It is a faculty given to every human soul, though in most it is dormant and used not. It prompts us to be affectionate and gentle

> to all men. It leads us to scorn the cold and heartless limits of custom, but moves our souls to swell up with pure and glowing love for persons and for communities. It makes us to disdain to be hemmed in by the formal mummeries of fashion, but at the kiss of a sister or a brother, or when our arms clasp the form of a friend, or when our lips touch the cheek of a boy or girl whom we love, it proves to us that all pleasures of dollars and cents are dross to those of loving and being loved. (*Jour.*, 1: 29–30)

This philosophical observation is prompted by the writer's suddenly encountering "a man with whom I was bitterly at variance" and with whom there "was an impassable gulf" due to an earlier argument. Here Whitman's later "amativeness" can be seen, which goes against customs and fashion and which originates in the soul and finds expression in the human contact of lips and bodies. The faculty of love "moves our souls to swell up with pure and glowing love for persons and for communities." Thus it is individual and collective. Sun-Down Paper No. 10 concludes the series with the description of a boat trip of a party of 15 men that featured group singing, an individual's oratory, a bath in the ocean surf, and good-natured jokes and stories. The sketch concludes "that we returned home perfectly safe in body, sound in limb, much refreshed in soul, and in perfect good humor and satisfaction one with another" (*Jour.*, 1: 32). The "Sun-Down Papers" are important since, in many ways, they represent the collective experience of Whitman's early life on Long Island and the early formation of his character and social personality. In No. 7 (dated September 29, 1840) the "Schoolmaster" stated:

> I think that if I should make pretensions to be a philosopher, and should determine to edify the world with what would add to the number of those sage and ingenious theories, which do already so much abound, I would compose a wonderful and ponderous book. Therein should be treated on, the nature and peculiarities of men, the diversity of their characters, the means of improving their state, and the proper mode of governing nations . . . Who should be a better judge of a man's talents than a man himself? I see no reason why we should let our lights shine under bushels. Yes: I *would* write a book! And who shall say that it might not be a very pretty book! Who knows but that I might do something very respectable? (*Jour.*, 1: 21–2)

By 1842 Whitman was in New York working as a printer in the pressroom of the *New World* and finding places to publish fiction, stories, and sketches.

He came to a world and work of journalism that, except for the basic work of the compositor, was undergoing rapid and dramatic changes. By 1835 the introduction of the rotary steam press brought the capability of printing 3,000 copies in an hour. Benjamin Henry Day's New York *Sun* reached a circulation of 20,000 copies per day by 1837 (Huntzicker 1999: 165–6). The penny press, of which the *Sun* dominated, had a combined circulation of 44,000 copies daily of the top three competitors (Huntzicker 1999: 166). The penny press thrived by creating its own market and readership of mechanics, tradesmen, artisans, immigrants, day laborers, and shopkeepers. This commercial push and expansion of the newspaper market was based on the presentation of the sensational news created by a booming metropolis and its people of all ranks and conditions. The penny press capitalized on such things as murders, disappearances, frauds, corruption, fires, rows, accidents, lawsuits, and other exciting news that commanded popular attention. Editors like James Gordon Bennett, James Watson Webb, and Park Benjamin emerged as personalities and public figures who quickly figured out that their circulation battles and rivalries could be profitably exploited through name-calling, slights, and vituperation against each other in their papers. Businesses saw that advertising in these penny papers could be profitable for their consumer goods, products, and services. Purveyors of popular entertainments or patent medicines were also pulled into advertising. The penny papers were "hawked" by newsboys and girls who took the product to the streets and delivered to subscribers. These products coexisted with the commercial and business newspapers and weekly literary news journals like the *New Yorker*, established by Horace Greeley and Jonas Winchester in 1834, which in three years reached a circulation of 9,500 subscribers.

Another significant development involved the establishment of political or party newspapers, either dailies or weeklies. The rise of the national Whig Party after 1836 introduced new political dynamics at the national, state, and local levels, with prominent Whig leaders like Henry Clay and Daniel Webster emerging. In New York the Loco-Foco faction split off from the Democratic Party and broke ranks with the Tammany Hall Democrats. The Loco-Focos focused their opposition on the chartering of state banks and other forms of monopoly and privilege as well as calling for the legal protection of labor unions. By 1838 this faction had been taken back into the Democratic Party, but only after forcing changes in key issues. Later, in 1848 the Free-Soil Party was formed, with its focus on opposing the extension of slavery into the national territories. The Free-Soil Party ran candidates for President in 1848 and 1852. Newspapers like William Cullen Bryant's *New York Evening Post* aligned themselves with the Democratic Party and supported Andrew Jackson and Martin Van Buren, while newspapers like the *Daily Whig* and the *Log Cabin* were sponsored and funded by the local and state Whig leaders. Some political party papers were campaign organs and disappeared after elections. The political dynamics of the nation, the state of New York, and New York City were rapidly changing with issues of economic power, wealth, property, and labor emerging (including free labor as well as slave labor). Partisan and political party newspapers fueled these issues but also brought more citizens into the political process.

After serving as a freelance writer for the New York *Aurora*, a penny paper distributed Monday through Saturday, Whitman became the chief editor in March 1842. Although his terms as editor of the *Aurora* lasted less than two months, Whitman experienced marked success as its chief writer. The paper had been established as an independent publication that advocated "democratic" principles and broad "Americanism." As Whitman wrote in his April 19, 1842 editorial with regard to immigration:

> We would see no man disfranchised because he happened to be born three thousand miles off. We go for the largest liberty – the widest extension of the immunities of the

> people, as well as the blessings of the government. Let us receive these foreigners to our shores, and to our good offices. (*Jour.*, 1: 124)

In the same edition Whitman stated that the "cheap papers have influence with this mass," which consists "of men [comprising] the governing power, 'the people' " (*Jour.*, 1: 124). Earlier, on March 24, 1842, Whitman had called the penny press "these mighty engines of truth" that are read by the "lower and middling classes" as well as are "found in the houses of the rich" (*Jour.*, 1: 74). In establishing his role and public voice as editor, Whitman wrote an editorial titled "We" on April 9, 1842.

> We glory in being *true Americans*. And we profess to impress Aurora with the same spirit. We have taken the high American ground – not the ground of exclusiveness, of partiality, of bigoted bias against those whose birthplace is three thousand miles from our own – but based on a desire to possess a republic of a proper respect for itself and its citizens, and of what is due its own capacities and its own dignity. There are a thousand dangerous influences operating among us – influences whose tendency is to assimilate this land in thought, in social customs, and, to a degree, in government, with the moth eaten systems of the old world. Aurora is imbued with a deadly hatred of all these influences; she wages open, heavy, and incessant war against them. (*Jour.*, 1: 106)

In columns written in a spirited and earnest tone, Whitman asserted that his paper promoted the common good of a republic and its citizens (present and future) by its pro-immigration and anti-aristocracy stance. To Whitman, this was not the journalism of party partisanship or cheap, sensational entertainment. As he stated on April 1, 1842, "We have a lofty sense of what the press should be. We desire to stir up men's minds – to move the waters of the fountains of thought; and for these objects we shall never flinch from the expression of opinion – never hold back when honor waves us onward" (*Jour.*, 1: 89).

In his *Aurora* writings Whitman advocated for the value of public school education, the inculcation of public morals and the democratic spirit by those responsible for this, a decrease in the number of laws, charity and sympathy for the suffering or the poor, and the sacred value of fostering happiness and love. He also took his columns into the streets and described visits to and observations of a gymnasium, Jewish synagogue, flower shops, Broadway, fires, schools, a market, political halls, parks, and theatres. He covered local controversies, and took what was, for a time, a sharply antagonistic position against the Catholics and Irish who wanted to establish a separate school system with state funding. He insulted Bishop Hughes, the leader of this movement, and referred to the Irish "mobs" that thronged the streets at night. He drew a sharp contrast between the "foreigner" Irish and "free born American citizens" and expressed outrage at the "insolence" of the Irish. In a series of volatile and undoubtedly inciting articles Whitman tried to deal with the facts of the growing political power of Irish immigrants and their own determination to shape their culture and society in New York City.

In the April 18, 1842 issue of the *Aurora* Whitman began his editorial with short clips from the previous day's New York *Mercury* and New York *News*. In the first the *Aurora* was cited for "roaring very loudly and ably, though somewhat savagely, on behalf of the Native Americans, during the past week." The *News* quote called for a "Native American party" as a "remedy" to dangers and "our only safeguard." However, Whitman's column stated, "we repudiate such doctrines as have characterized the 'Native American' party" (*Jour.*, 1: 124). In his editorials and reportage on the "Catholic rows" Whitman carried out his pledge to wage "open, heavy, and incessant war" against "dangerous influences" that tended "to assimilate this land in thought, in social customs, and to a degree, in government, with the moth eaten systems of the old world" and to "never flinch from the expression of opinion." Whitman believed in the assimilation of immigrants into American institutions and identity as citizens, and for him, a public, not a parochial, education was the pathway to the immigrants' separation from the Old World and incorporation into American society. It may well have been that the "Irish issue" and Whitman's columns on it caused the paper's owners, Anson Herrick and John F. Ropes, to terminate Whitman as editor (Bergman 1971a: 200), and it may be that Whitman's sharp criticisms of Tammany Hall exercised too much freedom. However, it was also clear that Whitman had brought a certain dash and spirit to this penny daily with a circulation of 5,000, and that his articles connected the paper to the streets and the people with a sense of immediacy and a spirit of independent position.

Whitman then moved on to write for various New York papers from 1842 to 1846, occasionally assuming editorial duties. Before he became chief editor of the Brooklyn *Daily Eagle* in March, 1846, Whitman's most sustained period of work involved writing over 50 articles for the Brooklyn *Evening Star* in an eight-month period in 1845–6. In certain ways these articles represent his disconnection from New York City and his reconnection to Brooklyn and Long Island. In his article of February 5, 1846 for the *Star*, titled "Vulgarity of Newspaper Quarrels," Whitman commented on the "warfare of abuse" in "more than half the political journals of New York" and their use of columns to fight the "editors' personal quarrels." He stated:

> Our citizens are universal readers of newspapers, which give a general tone to moral and social affairs. How unhappy then, must be the effect of such spiteful and vulgar quarrels, as disgrace the American press! 'Reform it altogether', gentlemen. It is as high and noble trait to be distinguished for urbanity in your literary intercourse as in that which you carry on by word of mouth. (*Jour.*, 1: 251)

Whitman responded to slights in New York papers directed to Brooklyn and Long Island with articles that defended their beauty, smaller scale living, civic improvements, independence, and connections to the rural country and seashore in contrast to New York City.

In early March of 1846, Whitman became a "principal editor" or "chief editor" of the leading paper in a growing city. Brooklyn did not feature a Wall Street, theatres, a

Broadway, the sharp contrasts of upper-class luxurious dwellings and lower-class tenements and slums, a growing diversity of population, or the spirited and rancorous competition of the penny press. The *Eagle* had a daily circulation of less than 500, but it was a fertile and promising opportunity for Whitman with a different readership. In his "Ourselves and the 'Eagle'" column for June 1, 1846, he stated:

> With all and any drawbacks, however, much good can always be done, with such potent influence as a well circulated newspaper. To wield that influence, is a great responsibility. There are numerous noble reforms that have yet to be pressed upon the world. People are to be schooled, in opposition perhaps to their long established ways of thought . . . and each paper, however humble, may do good in the ranks. (*Jour.*, 1: 392)

In a series of *Eagle* articles Whitman regularly called for a daily press that demonstrated "depth, force, power, and solidity" and for editors who "write to bear on the light of great principles and truths." Whitman believed that the editor who "manifested a disposition to discuss questions in the light of great principles" or who "refused to listen to the whispers or moved at the beck of cliques and factions" was met with rejection and "hostility and contempt" (*Jour.*, 2: 70–71). Whitman laid the blame on society not demanding and expecting more from journalists and settling instead for entertainment and novelty. In assessing the state of affairs, Whitman saw political parties utilizing journalism for the purpose of securing office holding and furthering party partisanship. For Whitman, the newspaper and editor could advance the cause of the republic and democratic principles of equality and freedom. American writers of literature also had this high calling. In his "Honest Opinions Forever!" article of September 4, 1846, Whitman asked:

> When will American writers, even the best of them, learn to be true to the souls and thoughts God has given them? – When will they cast the slough of the imitation of the conventionalities of other people? – the slough not only of the past, with its mummery, its iron foolishness, and its paralytic influence on natural truth – but of the present, coming to them at second-hand, and having the same degenerating effect in the moral world as continued breeding in-and-in has in the physical. (*Jour.*, 2: 49)

In his June 15, 1846 "Very Excellent News!" Whitman described the signing of the Oregon Treaty between the United States and England, which was received "over the Magnetic Telegraph this morning!" (*Jour.*, 1: 423). As Blondheim (1994: 51–5) notes, 1846 was a key year when the various separate telegraph lines underwent a combination into a network, and a common telegraphic news dispatch over the Magnetic line created a national wire service. In this way Whitman could gain access to news from Washington, DC, Albany, and across the country. While most of Whitman's *Eagle* columns focused on matters related to Brooklyn, the paper also covered national issues: the Mexican War and calls for annexation of Mexico, relations with England, public lands, the national tariff, free trade, sessions of the national Congress and its legislation, issues in the national territories, party politics, the establishment of new states, currency, and regional developments. Whitman also gleaned information from other newspapers about national developments and turned them into articles. As editor, he demonstrated remarkable resourcefulness in gathering news and stories at all levels and enriching the paper with book notices and reviews. He brought a concern for needed relief of suffering in Ireland and Scotland to his readers in the same way that he covered the need for clean streets and streetlights in Brooklyn. He regularly wrote columns about Long Island and its villages and people, viewing them as an extension of his Brooklyn readership.

For Whitman, one particular national issue emerged that pulled him back into the political arena: the question of the possible extension of slavery into the new territories that would eventually become states in the Union. The Mexican War, which Whitman had vigorously supported in his editorials, brought this issue to the forefront. Whitman supported the Wilmot Proviso that sought to maintain the territories for free laborers and settlers who had no need for slaves. In his April 22, 1847 "New States: Shall They Be Slave or Free?" Whitman disavowed any connection with the " 'abolitionist' interference with slavery in the southern states" and asked "Is *this* the country, and *this* the age, where and when we are to be told that slavery must be propped up and extended?" (*Jour.*, 2: 254). Whitman saw free land and free labor in the new territory as parts of the same equation of a democratic republic. For him, the Northwest Ordinance of 1787 was as central a document as the Constitution because the Ordinance secured freedom in the new national lands and forbade slavery. As he stated in "American Workingmen, versus Slavery" on September 1, 1847,

> Experience has proved, (and the evidence is to be seen now by any one who will look at it) that a stalwart mass of respectable workingmen, cannot exist, much less flourish, in a thorough slave state.... Slavery is a good thing enough, (viewed partially,) to the rich – the one out of thousands; but it is destructive to the dignity of all who work, and to labor itself. (*Jour.*, 2: 318–19)

A month later Whitman would refer to "the plague spot of slavery, with its taint to freemen's principles and prosperity" (*Jour.*, 2: 347). For Whitman, slavery was an "evil" threatening freedom and its natural spreading to new lands. In moving to clear and consistent support of the Wilmot Proviso, Whitman had crossed politics with the *Eagle's* publisher, Isaac Van Anden, who was a conservative Democrat favoring political compromise or accommodation on the question of the extension of slavery into the territories. As a result Whitman was dismissed for his radical editorial positions. Under Whitman's editorship the *Eagle* had expanded its circulation and garnered praise from New York papers for being a quality publication. In the end Whitman had learned, however, that an editor's position was insecure as long as others owned and managed the paper and as long as their politics and political connections had to be reflected in the paper. Unlike Horace Greeley and William Cullen Bryant, Whitman never held any financial interest or shares in the papers he worked for, and while Greeley's and Bryant's respective editorships of the New York *Tribune* and the New York *Evening Post* survived political turmoil and crises and were long-lasting as well as nationally prominent, Whitman's personal politics were costly in terms of longevity.

After a brief period in early 1848 of working for the New Orleans *Crescent*, Whitman returned to Brooklyn and edited the Brooklyn *Freeman* (at first a weekly and then a daily) from September 1848 through early September 1849. As a radical Free-Soil paper, the *Freeman* was intended to challenge the Whigs and conservative Democrats (Old Hunkers) in Kings County. The national election in 1848, however, saw the Whigs claim the White House. The Free-Soil candidate, former President Martin Van Buren, received 10 percent of the popular vote, and pulled enough votes from the Democratic Party candidate, Lewis Cass (whose position was to let the residents in the territories decide on whether slavery would be allowed), to hand the election to General Zachary Taylor. With the *Daily Freeman* Whitman worked in a compatible and supportive political environment, but the work of editing a low circulation penny daily in competition with two established Brooklyn papers must have been too much for Whitman and he announced his withdrawal from the paper.

Whitman's last significant connection with a Brooklyn newspaper was with the *Daily Times* in the period of early 1857 until the spring of 1859. However, as Loving has carefully argued (1999: 227–9), Whitman's connection to the *Daily Times* and to its conservative editorials and social viewpoints is definitely questionable in terms of documentation. It is entirely possible that the *Times* editorial pieces have almost no connection to Whitman and that his contributions were restricted to informational and local feature articles or to arrangement of the paper's format by integrating materials taken from other papers or the wire services. Earlier, Whitman had worked for the Brooklyn *Evening Star*, a Whig Party paper, so there was precedent for his working for a conservative newspaper, even one diametrically opposed to his own radical democratic principles. These two instances occurred when Whitman was hard pressed to make a living and when his own status and identity as a productive free laborer were in doubt. But his *Star* contributions were relatively short and did not touch on political or controversial topics. As Loving also notes, the problem of attributing Brooklyn *Daily Times* articles to Whitman and representing accurately and fully what views he may have expressed in the paper is one that must be dealt with carefully, based on full, scholarly, accurate texts (Loving 1999: 230–1). The earliest collections and reprintings of Whitman's work in *The Gathering of the Forces*, edited by Cleveland Rodgers and John Black (1920), and in *I Sit and Look Out: Editorials from the Brooklyn Daily Times*, edited by Emory Holloway and Vernolian Schwarz (1932), organized and presented the articles in a topical format, abstracted from the newspaper's daily and sequential context, and as Loving demonstrates with regards to the *I Sit and Look Out* editorials: "Comparison of the editorials selected for *I Sit* with their originals in the *Times* reveals inaccurate transcriptions as well as silent omissions" (Loving 1999: 230). Loving (pp. 230–2) illustrates how the "silent omission" of two paragraphs from the May 6, 1858, "Prohibition of Colored Persons" by Holloway and Schwarz results in an incomplete text that does not represent Whitman's "conflicted" view on black people and racial relations.

While Whitman continued to write articles for various Brooklyn and New York newspapers as well as literary magazines after his voluntary disconnection from the Brooklyn *Daily Freeman* in 1849, it seems that his faith in the newspaper editor as an agent of reform and general uplifting waned, especially as national developments turned to compromise and expediency over the issue of the extension of slavery into the territories. In 1859 Whitman published 17 "Paragraph Sketches of Brooklynites" in the Brooklyn *Daily Advertiser*, followed 10 years later by "Brooklyniana: A Series of Thirty-Nine Local Articles, on Past and Present" (Bergman 1971b: 436). Whitman's avid interest in local history never waned, and as Brooklyn grew as a city he recorded its history in the same way as he had done earlier in connection with Long Island and New York City. Whitman never stopped writing for newspapers during the Civil War and in the 1870s and 1880s.

Over the course of time he developed his own style and treatment of the historical or social sketch, the information piece, feature article, travel observation piece, and "inside" or "behind the scenes" article. In his Brooklyn *Daily Eagle* editorial for June 1, 1846 Whitman had stated that a "true editor" should have "a fluent style" without "elaborate finish" and "His articles had far better be earnest and terse than polished; they should ever smack of being uttered on the spur of the moment, like political oratory" (*Jour.*, 1: 391).

This sense of fluent spontaneity and natural public talk was, of course, Whitman's ideal and not possible to attain or maintain on a consistent level due to the demands of deadlines and the need to feed written texts to the compositors and then proofread and edit their typeset texts before the press run. The work was one of a constant flow once the composition began, with turnaround time tight. At his best moments as an editor and chief writer, Whitman loved this printing culture and took great pride in his ability to bring favorable notices and praise to the papers on which he worked. He knew that the writerly qualities he brought to newspapers increased circulation, and he loved to hear directly from the readers of what they found interesting and engaging in the daily paper. He was particularly adept at bringing a surge of interest and readership to a paper by changing its "public face" in terms of composition, mix of news and features, tone and outlook, selection of reading material from other sources, and ongoing or recurring stories or editorials on certain topics. Like Horace Greeley, Whitman believed that the penny press could elevate and instruct the readership, by adhering to a standard focused on high moral, political, and social principles and providing direction on the issues of the day. This may have been too high an expectation for the public press and for the influencing position of the editor, given the commercial and political party connections of journalism, but Whitman held to this standard even when it pushed him in the direction of taking political stances that opposed or contradicted those of the paper's owner or business manager.

Estimations of the quality and contributions of Whitman's journalism generally recognize its competence, earnestness of tone and purpose, and its variety or range of topics and interests. In terms of style, Rubin and Brown, in commenting on Whitman's work for the New York *Aurora*, stated:

> Whitman's *Aurora* prose reveals more of his native character – his individuality or eccentricity of style, his intuitive rather than logical presentation of thought, his broadly impressionistic reception of facts and ideas, his sentimentality. . . . Some of his early prose mannerisms would be carried over into his later poetry: his ejaculatory style, his long catalogues, his ignoring of conventional syntax, and the use of the dash. (1972: 11)

Earlier, Fausset observed that Whitman saw writing as "incidental to life" and "not, save in a minor degree, an art to be mastered." Fausset stated further: "But when his passion for humanity was roused, his sympathy for suffering, his hatred of cruelty and injustice, or his love of common people and things, his prose could develop a life and rhythm of its own, that contain the promise of the later poet" (Fausset 1942: 54). In his book-length study of Whitman's writing for the Brooklyn *Daily Eagle*, Brasher found little that presaged the 1855 poet of *Leaves of Grass*.

> Walter Whitman went about his daily work as editor and reporter, enjoying his task of schooling the citizens of Brooklyn (and himself) in conventional language on conventional topics, little suspecting that in a few years he would shock and amuse many of those Brooklynites by suddenly revealing himself to their incredulous eyes as "Walt Whitman, a kosmos" – "he who would assume a place to teach or to be a poet here in the States." (Brasher 1970: 229)

Others, like Loving in his richly detailed and balanced biography, see a strong connection between the journalist and poet.

> Whitman was already assuming as journalist the role he would take up as Emerson's poet – the representative singer of *all* the voices. [. . .]
>
> As the poet's *Star* editorials have suggested, this picture restores the immediacy and character of Whitman's revelations and pronouncements as he applied the ideals of both Jefferson and Jackson to the immediate political and cultural developments of the 1840s. If a whaling ship was Melville's Harvard and Yale, Brooklyn and newspaper work were this poet's university. (Loving 1999: 66, 102)

The issue of the significance and impact of Whitman's journalism on his development as a poet is central to the scholarship and biography ranging from Holloway's 1926 portrait to Loving's 1999 profile. Like Brasher, Kaplan (1980) and Zweig (1984) found the journalism relatively unremarkable and distinguished by nothing that would suggest the eventual emergence of poetic genius or a distinctive voice. Zweig stated that Whitman was "a man so undistinguished from the swarm of his colleagues that it is almost impossible to tell how many of the newspaper articles attributed to him he actually wrote, they are so completely expressions of the age at its lowest and most ordinary" (Zweig 1984: 4). This sweeping and blanket dismissal of the journalism serves two purposes. The first is to separate the poet and the genesis of *Leaves of Grass* from the prosaic and commonplace work of the journalist and to argue that the poet had to emerge from other sources and influences. The "long foreground somewhere" that Emerson stated in his famous July 21, 1855 letter to Whitman "must have" existed prior to the "beginning of a great career" did not, then, according to this view, include Whitman the columnist and editor. The second purpose is to show that Whitman's expression, whatever its potential or distinguished characteristics, was wasted and even "dragged down" by a journalistic world that was confined to common expression and low aims. This view diminishes and marginalizes the burning national issues of the times and Whitman's struggle to deal with them in both personal and political terms.

In her 1985 study, Fishkin daringly asserted: "His success as a poet came only when he stopped trying to be 'artistic' and circled back to the subjects, style, stance, and strategies he had first developed as editor of the *New York Aurora*" (p. 15). Fishkin saw a direct connection of subjects and themes as well as innovations with Whitman's early journalism. In showing how Whitman transformed and vitalized subjects treated in the *Aurora* articles, Fishkin demonstrates how breathing, inhaling and exhaling, and absorbing become the animating life force of the ordinary and commonplace and elevate them into symbolic unity. What were earlier subjects for journalistic description become animated and infused with "a new sense of radiance and wonder." Occupations, the vital process of work as an expression of self, the new social patterns and relationships established by work and exchange of services and products – all anchored the poetry in the density of sensations, reactions, sights and sounds, observed movements, and meaningful looks or contacts. In this way the flow of life becomes a shared transcendence or a new zone of meanings or "signifiers" that become the democratic universals. The underlying unities are revealed in the very moment of their perception and experience as activities. Fishkin's contribution is to connect "the material and method that characterized Whitman's early journalism" and to show how these are artistically transformed by the creative process of sympathetic engagement and fresh revelation. She argues that "on occasion Whitman's [journalistic] reports differ significantly from those of his competitors" (Fishkin 1985: 19). Further, she believes that "Whitman's experience as a journalist made him aware of how unexamined conventions, narrow perspectives, misleading appearances, and all varieties of the counterfeit could interfere with the accurate perception and interpretation of one's world" (p. 23). Fishkin provides some specific examples of how scenes described earlier from an editorial viewpoint are brought into new contexts of meaning in *Leaves of Grass*, such as section 34, which deals with the Goliad massacre of 412 American soldiers by the Mexicans. Poetically, the horror and brutality of war become immediate and visual, memorialized by the "tale of a jet-black sunrise."

In his study of language and style in *Leaves of Grass*, Hollis provided a chapter titled "The Journalistic Background" and examined "the language of the profession he had trained himself for, journalism" (1983: 205). Hollis examined how Whitman modified journalistic devices such as neologisms, verb forms, mix of Romance-Latinate words, noun forms and clusters, adjectival compounding, and other rhetorical features to create a "prophetic poetry." Combined with the "easy confidence, sometimes the poetic boldness" of the persona established in the 1855 "Song of Myself," the "journalistic devices and practices are more eye-catching and attention-getting" (p. 225). Hollis contended that Whitman made unusual and "new use of the old rhetorical rules" to create a unique discourse, most notably in the early major poetry. In this sense the experience of the journalism was embedded, Hollis argues, in the poetry so that any separation of journalistic prose and "prophetic poetry" is impossible.

The work of Fishkin, Hollis, and Loving has served to connect what some have claimed were two different Whitmans or two different careers, or two only loosely and generally related careers. The full and complete scholarly texts of Whitman's journalism (newspaper and magazine contributions), now being realized with the publication of the first two volumes edited by Bergman, may not settle this argument or bridge this division. The plain fact is that "Song of Myself" and *Leaves of Grass* were "let out" and that Whitman set much of the type for the 1855 edition in a small printing shop, supervised its printing and binding, and designed its cover. Fausset has a speculative description of 11-year-old Walt learning the work of a compositor in the printing establishment of the *Long Island Patriot* from its foreman printer William Hartshorne:

> Even one who has no special knowledge of the craft can imagine the effect such a training must have had upon a young apprentice with expansive impulses who had now continually to focus his eyes on an immediate foreground. Certainly the three years he spent learning the trade were to give him a sense of the anatomy of words which all the subsequent years of fluent journalism could not dissipate. (Fausset 1942: 19)

As Walt set the type for the 1855 *Leaves*, he must have seen a new "anatomy of words" set in a new anatomy of lines and poetic space. Appropriately, the book was advertised for sale in a New York newspaper, and in his famous letter Emerson said "I did not know until I last night saw the book advertised in a newspaper that I could trust the name as real and available for a post-office" (quoted in Fausset 1942: 102). In the physical creation of the first edition of *Leaves of Grass*, its setting in type by an experienced craftsman and its arrangement into lines and pages, the printer and poet were one.

References and Further Reading

Bergman, Herbert (1971a). Walt Whitman as a Journalist, 1831–January, 1848. *Journalism Quarterly*, 48: 195–204.

Bergman, Herbert (1971b). Walt Whitman as a Journalist, March, 1848–1892. *Journalism Quarterly*, 48: 431–7.

Blondheim, Menahem (1994). *New Over the Wires: The Telegraph and the Flow of Public Information in America, 1844–1897*. Cambridge, MA: Harvard University Press.

Brasher, Thomas L. (1970). *Whitman as Editor of the Brooklyn Daily Eagle*. Detroit: Wayne State University Press.

Fausset, Hugh l'Anson (1942). *Walt Whitman: Poet of Democracy*. New York: Russell & Russell.

Fishkin, Shelley Fisher (1985). *From Fact to Fiction: Journalism & Imaginative Writing in America*. Baltimore: Johns Hopkins University Press.

Hollis, C. Carroll (1983). *Language and Style in Leaves of Grass*. Baton Rouge: Louisiana State University Press.

Holloway, Emory (1926). *Whitman: An Interpretation in Narrative*. New York: Alfred A. Knopf.

Huntzicker, William E. (1999). *The Popular Press, 1833–1865*. Westport, CT: Greenwood Press.

Kaplan, Justin (1980). *Walt Whitman: A Life*. New York: Simon & Schuster.

Loving, Jerome (1999). *Walt Whitman: The Song of Himself*. Berkeley: University of California Press.

Rodgers, Cleveland and Black, John (eds.) (1920). *The Gathering of the Forces by Walt Whitman: Editorials, Essays, Literary and Dramatic Reviews and Other Material Written by Walt Whitman as Editor of the Brooklyn Daily Eagle in 1846 and 1847*, 2 vols. New York: G. P. Putnam's Sons.

Rubin, Joseph Jay and Brown, Charles H. (eds.) (1972). *Walt Whitman of the New York Aurora: Editor at Twenty-Two*. Westport, CT: Greenwood Press.

Zweig, Paul (1984). *Walt Whitman: The Making of a Poet*. New York: Basic Books.

3
The City
William Pannapacker

Whitman lived in cities nearly all of his adult life. He worked as a carpenter, journalist, fiction writer, and editor in New York and Brooklyn from the mid-1830s through the early 1860s (excluding a few months with the New Orleans *Crescent* in 1848). He moved to Washington, DC, in 1862 and volunteered as a hospital aide during the Civil War, supporting himself by working as a clerk for the Department of the Interior. In 1873, after suffering a stroke, Whitman went to live with his brother in Camden, New Jersey, near Philadelphia. He remained there, surrounded by a circle of friends and admirers, revising his poetry and consolidating his reputation, until his death in 1892.

Like his American contemporaries Ralph Waldo Emerson and Henry David Thoreau, Whitman valued solitary encounters with Nature. Such moments occur frequently in Whitman's poetry in works like "Out of the Cradle Endlessly Rocking" and "When I Heard the Learn'd Astronomer." But, alone among well-known American Romantic writers of his era, Whitman chronicled and celebrated urban life as well, seeing the city as complementary with the country rather than in opposition to it. "New-York loves crowds – and I do, too," he writes, "I can no more get along without houses, civilization, aggregations of humanity, meetings, hotels, theaters, than I can get along without food" (*PW*, 1: 354). Though Nature was a major theme in his poetry, Whitman disliked rural isolation and looked to the city as the future of American democracy. In doing so, he countered a growing American mistrust of cities as sites of moral decadence and revolutionary violence, and he complicated the Romantic nostalgia for a pre-industrial, pastoral existence that precluded urban life, and most of all city people, as a source of inspiration:

> When I pass to and fro . . . beholding the crowds of the great cities, New York, Boston, Philadelphia, Cincinnati, Chicago, St. Louis, San Francisco, New Orleans, Baltimore – when I mix with these interminable swarms of alert turbulent, good-natured, independent citizens, mechanics, clerks, young persons – at the idea of this mass of men, so fresh and free, so loving and so proud, a singular awe falls upon me. (*PW*, 2: 388)

Instead of looking to the past for mythic heroes, Whitman looked at the average American of his time, whose activities he sketches in his many poetic catalogues. Increasingly, these people were city-dwellers, seeking freedom and opportunity, and, for Whitman, their collective, mutually reinforcing energy sustained the ideal America that was the larger subject of his visionary poetry.

An American *Flâneur*

Though Whitman's writing transcends regional categorization, the intellectual, cultural, and political ferment of antebellum New York provided the setting for many of the experiences that went into the first edition of *Leaves of Grass* in 1855. Indeed, many passages in Whitman's extensive journalistic writings about urban life from the 1830s to the 1850s are transcribed, almost verbatim, into his poetry. This link between Whitman's poetry and urban spectatorship supports a view of Whitman as an American version of the *flâneur*. "Whitman not only knew the flaneur," writes Dana Brand, "he was a flaneur" (Brand 1991: 159).

Best embodied in the contexts of Paris and London by Baudelaire and Dickens, the *flâneur* guides his presumably middle-class reader away from the familiar arcades, avenues, and boulevards into the labyrinthine and subterranean passageways of the metropolis, highlighting its most notable human spectacles: the high and low, the beautiful and the ugly. The *flâneur* relishes the extremes of behavior in the city on which he comments with the ironic detachment and conspiratorial superiority of the highly cultured urbanite. The oldest surviving daguerreotype of Whitman from the early 1840s makes it easy for viewers to imagine him as a *flâneur*, an American boulevardier, sauntering through the urban spectacle. More significantly, the tone of Whitman's early journalism frequently echoes European *flanerie*, as in this passage from "Life in a New York Market," written for the *Aurora* in 1842:

> A heterogeneous mass, indeed, are they who compose the bustling crowd that fills up the passage way. Widows with sons, boys of twelve or fourteen, to walk with them for company; wives, whose husbands are left home to "take care of the children;" servant women; cooks; old maids (these are the especial horror of every salesman in the market;) careful housewives of grades high and low; men with the look of a foreign clime; all sorts and sizes, kinds, ages, and descriptions, all wending, and pricing, and examining, and purchasing. (*Jour.*, 1: 56)

The *flâneur* does not participate in the spectacles he describes, preferring to look and comment, as if the city and its people were a series of department store windows prepared for his visual, consumerist delight. The *flâneur* seeks to distinguish himself from the urban mass rather than to merge with it. Whitman, for example, mocks the "servant women; cooks; old maids" from a position of class and gender superiority, expressing his sympathy for the middle-class "salesmen." Nevertheless, along with

Plate 3.1 Walter Whitman, daguerreotype, early 1840s. Photographer unknown. Courtesy Gay Wilson Allen.

the affected tone of *flanerie*, Whitman's prose already demonstrates the catalogue rhetoric – the syntactically parallel lists of human types – that would later distinguish his poetry.

While the persona of the *flâneur* is an apt characterization of Whitman as a journalist in the early 1840s, it is, however, an inadequate description of the persona he presents in *Leaves of Grass*. In *Leaves* Whitman represents himself as the average American, not only in the famous frontispiece illustration of him as a laborer, but in numerous places in the text: "What is commonest, cheapest, nearest, easiest is Me" (*LG*: 41). Whitman's poetic catalogues of people and sights attempt to represent more than mere spectacles for the middle-class voyeur; they are an almost operatic panorama of simultaneous human action in which all apparent differences – the urban and the rural, the past and the future, the observer and the observed – are dissolved:

> The Missourian crosses the plains toting his wares and his cattle,
> As the fare-collector goes through the train he gives notice by the jingling of loose change,
> The floor-men are laying the floor, the tinners are tinning the roof, the masons are calling for mortar,
> In single file each shouldering his hod pass onward the laborers;
> Seasons pursuing each other the indescribable crowd is gather'd, it is the fourth of Seventh-month, (what salutes of cannon and small arms!)
> Seasons pursuing each other the plougher ploughs, the mower mows, and the winter-grain falls in the ground; [. . .]
> And these tend inward to me, and I tend outward to them,
> And such as it is to be of these more or less I am,
> And of these one and all I weave the song of myself.
>
> (*LG*: 43–4)

According to Walter Benjamin, the *flâneur* retains his individuality, even in the midst of a crowd, which he regards with some contempt (Benjamin 1973: 54). The moment in which Whitman proclaims his solidarity with the urban crowd (and, by extension, one with his imagined America) is the moment at which the persona of the *flâneur* is complicated by what a contemporary reviewer called a "compound of New England transcendentalist and New York rowdy" (quoted in Reynolds 1995: 106).

For some critics, centrifugal and centripetal catalogues such as the above are visions of universal, transcendent oneness; they are laudable expressions of Whitman's democratic populism. For others, Whitman's poetry reflects a scopophilic, imperial gaze that seeks to control difference and promote a vision of American exceptionalism and Manifest Destiny. "Whitman, like others of his time," writes Brand, "was unable to turn toward the crowd a gaze that could accept the reality of its otherness, that desired to reduce it to neither insubstantiality nor coherence" (Brand 1991: 185). According to Michel de Certeau, the stance of the *flâneur* is practically inevitable because any act of urban representation is an effort to contain the unlimited proliferation of meanings (Certeau 1984: 91–110). Why, for example, does Whitman introduce Independence Day into his cycling of the seasons? Why does Whitman's vision seem limited to the United States?

Why does Whitman presume that his persona can encompass everything he sees? Arguably, Whitman's catalogues of occupations reduce individuals to types who cannot challenge his particular vision of America. In such passages as the above, and in other poems like "Pioneers! O Pioneers!," Whitman seems to position the United States – and himself as its representative poet – outside history, absolving his America of responsibility for the host of injustices that accompanied its economic growth and geographic expansion. If Whitman attempted to abandon the persona of the *flâneur* in his poetry, there are, nevertheless, substantial reasons to question the perfect authenticity of his merger with the urban crowd on its own terms. As Whitman writes in "Song of Myself," "I teach straying from me, yet who can stray from me?" (*LG*: 85).

"The Mighty Labyrinth"

One of the most durable themes of American urban writing – beginning at least as early as Benjamin Franklin's *Autobiography* (1791) – is that the city represents the freedom to escape the limitations of one's origins. Relative anonymity allows one to experiment with identity, to reinvent oneself, and to choose one's own affiliations. The city offers economic opportunity, the chance to rise, as Franklin put it, "from the Poverty and Obscurity in which I was born and bred, to a State of Affluence and some Degree of Reputation in the World" (Franklin 1987: 1307). In proportion to their size, cities enable professional specialization, creating opportunities for the painters, poets, and entrepreneurs who, in a different context, might have worked as sign-painters, printers, and tallow-chandlers. In this sense, the American city came to represent internally what the New World represented externally to prospective immigrants, and nineteenth-century American literature is disproportionately populated by the success narratives of parvenus like Franklin who "made it" in the big city.

The dream of urban success, however, is counterbalanced by the probability of failure. Personal failure is the subject of few autobiographies but many cautionary works of fiction such as Whitman's sensationalist temperance novel, *Franklin Evans* (1842):

> Yes, here I had come to seek my fortune! A mere boy, friendless, unprotected, innocent of the ways of the world – without wealth, favor, or wisdom – here I stood at the entrance of the mighty labyrinth, and with hardly any consciousness of the temptations, doubts, and dangers that awaited me there. Thousands had gone on before me, and thousands were coming still. Some had attained the envied honors – had reaped distinction – and won princely estate; but how few were they, compared with the numbers of failures! (*EPF*: 148)

It is almost unnecessary to describe the fate of this new arrival in the city; the achievements of Whitman's Franklin will not parallel those of his namesake. Novels like *Franklin Evans* provided a counternarrative for the seductive, capitalist myth of the self-made man. The city may become a utopia for the upwardly mobile, but there is an equally pervasive dystopian vision of the American city as a "labyrinth" into which innocent young people are lured and destroyed. The city is portrayed as a place from which one must ultimately escape, like Nineveh or Sodom, in order to retain one's virtues as an ideal American, who is, almost by definition, not a city-dweller. As Thomas Jefferson put it, "Those who labor in the earth are the chosen people of God" (Jefferson 1984: 290). If Whitman eventually became known as a poetic celebrator of urban life, his prose writing reflects ambivalence about the city that is characteristic of nineteenth-century American culture as it transitioned from an agricultural to an industrial economy.

The market-orientation of cities such as New York – founded and conducted primarily as money-making enterprises – often creates a culture in which everything seems to be judged on economic terms. Human beings become commodities. Slaves, prostitutes, and exploited factory workers populate the dark side of the nineteenth-century city of opportunity. The arts become empty signifiers of class position; treasured sites of meaning are destroyed in the name of efficiency. The freedom to give up the past is paid for by feelings of anonymity, isolation, and anomie. As Whitman writes in "Song of the Open Road" (1856), "Smartly attired, countenance smiling, form upright," the urban go-getter endures "death under the breast-bones, hell under the skull-bones" (*LG*: 158). The excitement of crowds, the openness of the streets, and the prospect of sexual adventure, are stalked by fears of madness, crime, violence, disease, and death.

In the middle of the nineteenth century, large parts of New York were expanding beyond the capacity of the government to maintain much more than the semblance of civilization. By 1850 nearly half of New York's population was foreign-born, most of them crowded into ramshackle tenements. Streets were piled high with garbage, dead animals, and excrement. The rivers were poisoned by industrial chemicals. A woman, unaccompanied by a man, could not walk the streets safely. Respectable gentlemen carried knives, pistols, and heavy canes for self-defense. Ethnic neighborhoods were policed by violent gangs that shaded off into corrupt political machines. Everyone feared transgressing the shifting boundaries of urban geography. Immigrant and nativist gangs fought pitched battles with each other for dominance over neighborhoods. "Gotham," foremost among American cities, was a powder keg of ethnic, racial, and religious hatreds; it intermittently teetered on the brink of mass violence, anarchy, and revolution. For all his famous celebration of New York, Whitman also described it as one of "the most crime-haunted and dangerous cities in all of Christendom" (quoted in Reynolds 1995: 109).

Middle-class reformers, along with sensationalist writers like the young Whitman, descended like urban explorers into immigrant neighborhoods such as the Five Points, where the Irish, African Americans, Eastern European Jews, scavengers, prostitutes of all kinds, criminals, addicts, and the variously disabled and diseased formed an animated Whitmanian catalogue of middle-class anxieties. "Darkest Africa and the polar regions are becoming familiar," writes the Rev. Walter Rauschenbusch later in the century, "but we now have intrepid men and women who plunge for a time into the life of the lower classes and return to write books about this unknown race" (quoted in Boyer 1978: 127). For readers eager for such adventures, Whitman played the "urban guide," who denounces the vice he describes with such gusto: "Every kind of wickedness that can be festered into life by the crowding together of a huge mass of people is here to be found" (*Jour.*, 1: 165). In his poem "The Sleepers" (1855) Whitman lists the familiar faces of nineteenth-century urban degeneracy in a manner that suggests the new mug books created by urban police departments: "The wretched features of ennuyés, the white features of corpses, the livid faces of drunkards, the sick-grey faces of onanists" (*LG*: 424).

Whitman's dark poems such as "The Sleepers" and "I Sit and Look Out" (1860) are more typical of urban writing in his era than celebratory poems such as "Mannahatta" (1860) or "A Broadway Pageant" (1860). Often posing as guides to moral reform, the genre somewhat reductively called "urban plunge literature" revels in the wickedness, sensation, and mystery of the city. Typical works in the genre include Joseph Holt Ingraham's *The Miseries of New York* (1844), E. Z. C. Judson's *The Mysteries and Miseries of City Life* (1849), George Foster's *New York Naked* (1850), George Lippard's *The Empire City* (1850) and *New York: Its Upper Ten and Lower Million* (1853). Typically, plunge literature, like *flânerie*, affirms the moral superiority of the middle-class reformer while condemning the profligate rich and ignorant poor.

Though some of Whitman's writing – particularly his early fiction and journalism – suggest the plunge genre, it is, nevertheless, more common in Whitman's poetry for the shadowy side of urban life to be presented as part of a larger panorama in which even apparent evil is good when viewed from a wide enough perspective: "Agonies are one of my changes of garments," he writes (*LG*: 67). Whitman's use of the rhetorical style of the evangelical reformer in "Song of Myself," for example, does not affirm moral distinctions so much as present them as a challenge to equality: "The kept-woman, sponger, thief, are hereby invited / The heavy-lipp'd slave is invited, the venerealee is invited; / There shall be no difference between them and the rest" (*LG*: 46). If Whitman's poetry contains some of the scenes and characters of urban plunge literature, it frequently has the effect of destabilizing the social hierarchies on which this literature was based. The city was a labyrinth, but even its darkest corners and most despised denizens were latent with sacred meanings for the poet of *Leaves*.

The Country and the City

Whitman said that *Leaves of Grass* "arose out of my life in Brooklyn and New York from 1838 to 1853, absorbing a million people, for fifteen years with an intimacy, an eagerness, an abandon, probably never equaled" (quoted in Reynolds 1995: 83). Whitman enjoyed the varied cultural life of the city: "going everywhere, seeing everything, high, low, middling – absorbing theatres at every pore" (Traubel [1906] 1961: 455). In addition to "Plays and Operas," in *Specimen Days and Collect* (1882) Whitman dwelled on three other specific memories of antebellum New York that appeared in his poetry: "My Passion for Ferries," "Broadway Sights," and

"Omnibus Jaunts and Drivers" (*PW*, 1: 16–21). As David Reynolds demonstrates, Whitman encountered many of the cultural fads that swept through New York: phrenology, free love, male purity, vegetarianism, hydrotherapy, to name only a few. As a young man, Whitman boarded around, met all kinds of people, and knew about their private lives as well as their public ones. Whitman, as much as anyone of his time, was well suited by experience to produce an epic poem about the cultural currents of a great American city.

As a reporter for such papers as the *Aurora*, the *Evening Tattler*, the *Statesman*, the *Democrat*, and the *Mirror*, Whitman learned to extract meaning from the apparent chaos of the urban scene. His writing for a mass audience in the penny papers was a form of cultural work, educating citizens on the progressive issues of his time such as public education, immigration policy, public health, and sanitation, and slavery. The newspapers for which Whitman worked were an important means of consolidating otherwise disconnected and inchoate communities. The advertisements and want-ads – the economic reason for the existence of papers – were a crucial element in creating a vision of the city as a network of reciprocal needs and shared interests. As Whitman writes in the Long Island *Star*, newspapers forge "intellectual and moral association" and "maintain civilization" (quoted in Conrad 1984: 10). It is significant that the preface to the first edition of *Leaves* was set in columns like a newspaper; the content, form, and unifying vision of *Leaves* was, in large part, an outgrowth of Whitman's years of experience as an urban journalist.

With few exceptions, Romantic writers other than Whitman turned their backs on the city, as if urban life recapitulated the Fall of Man and Nature offered the possibility of spiritual rebirth. In the 1800 Preface to the *Lyrical Ballads*, Wordsworth and Coleridge define Romanticism, in part, as a solitary encounter with Nature. Romantics sought what they regarded as the simplicity and authenticity of country life as opposed to the complexity and artificiality of life in the city. Romantics crave solitude, but cities are full of people. Wordsworth's sonnet, "Composed upon Westminster Bridge" (1802), for example, celebrates the natural beauty of the city before the population awakens. Nature is present in the absence of people, and the city is most beautiful when the streets are empty.

The antiurban tendencies of European writers were magnified in the American context. In general, American Romanticism did not look for ways to improve urban life; rather, it advocated escaping alone to the woods, the sea, or the frontier. "The great vice in Thoreau's composition," according to Whitman, was "his disdain of cities, companions, civilization" (Traubel 1982: 201). The cabin at Walden Pond was less a utopian experiment than it was a rejection of the possibility of an urban civilization. William Cullen Bryant, who lived most of his life in New York City, almost never mentions urban life in his long career as a poet. One exception, "The Crowded Street" (1843), presents New York – for all its human variety – as anonymous and alienating: "Each, where his tasks or pleasures call, / They pass, and heed each other not." City people are only capable of being held together in the mind of God: "There is who heeds, who holds them all, / In His large love and boundless thought" (Lounsbury 1912: 58).

Large cities were so repellent to Romantic sensibilities that antebellum American painters almost never represented urban life in realistic terms. American Romantics tended to view the city in light of Edward Gibbon's *Decline and Fall of the Roman Empire* (1788) and the Terror that followed the French Revolution. When cities were depicted in Romantic paintings, they were typically ruins or classical cities on the eve of their inevitable destruction (see, for example, Thomas Cole's *The Course of Empire: Consummation*, 1835–36, or John Martin's *The Fall of Babylon*, 1831). The city was dangerous; it was the condenser of revolutionary mobs and moral decadence; and, ultimately, like the tower of Babel, all cities were symbols of the vanity of human wishes: populations are fragmented by internal strife, the barbarians (internal or external) arrive, the city burns, and nothing remains but picturesque, moonlit ruins. Nature triumphs over the greatest capitals in the end, just as it does in Cole's series of paintings in which the *Consummation* is succeeded by *Destruction* and *Desolation*.

Romantic poets in general offered the literate middle and upper classes an armchair escape from the seeming chaos and uncertainty of urban life. The refreshment of a train trip to the Catskills could be simulated midweek by reading Bryant's poetry or by viewing the pastoral paintings of the Hudson River School. New rural cemeteries such as Mt Auburn in Cambridge and Greenwood in Brooklyn provided middle-class city-dwellers with orderly, albeit elegiac, landscapes before the existence of public parks. Similarly, the middle-class home, with its books, plants, paintings, curios, pets, and proprieties could become a museum of preurban simplicity, displaying, most prominently, the women and children who were sheltered from the urban chaos of industry, immigration, and simmering discontent that gathered around them before new modes of transportation enabled the middle classes to pursue the ongoing pastoral ideal into the suburbs and countryside.

The mature Whitman, however, was a lifelong city-dweller, but as a poet who sought to represent all of America, he often embraced the rural and pastoral in ways that reflected the abstract concept of "Nature" celebrated by his Romantic contemporaries. "Song of Myself" begins with the poet stripping away the superficial constraints of civilization, going to "the bank by the wood," and standing "undisguised and naked" like Adam. He proposes to speak "Nature without check with original energy" (*LG*: 29). Nature, for Whitman, is a source of foundational, even prelapsarian, knowledge and a means of spiritual rejuvenation. As such, Nature is a central element in many of Whitman's most notable poems: "Crossing Brooklyn Ferry," "Song of the Broad-Axe," "Out of the Cradle Endlessly Rocking," and "When Lilacs Last in the Dooryard Bloom'd." Whitman's poetic visits to the rural Long Island of his childhood parallel the efforts of poets such as Wordsworth to find solace in an Edenic, formative experience prior to the confusions and ambiguities of adult life, which parallel the anxieties of urban growth in the industrial era.

Whitman, however, differs from his Romantic contemporaries in his view of the city as complementary with the country: "not Nature alone is great in her fields of freedom and the open air, in her storms, the shows of night and day, the mountains, forests, seas," Whitman writes, "but in the artificial, the work of man too is equally great" (*PW*, 2: 371). Correspondingly, Whitman makes numerous efforts in his poetry to present the city and the country as parts of a larger, organic whole. Frequently, he pairs them, as if balancing an equation: "The city sleeps and the country sleeps," "Sounds of the city and sounds out of the city," "To the cities and farms I sing" (Whitman *LG*: 44, 56, 166). He often blurs the line between the urban and rural entirely in the deliberate randomness of his lists of occupations in *Leaves*: "contralto . . . carpenter . . . children . . . pilot . . . mate . . . duck-shooter . . . deacons . . . spinning-girl . . . farmer . . . lunatic . . . printer . . . surgeon . . . quadroon girl . . . machinist" (*LG*: 41–2). Whitman's poetry de-essentializes the arbitrary, imagined distinction between urban and rural modes of existence that, as Raymond Williams (1973) observes, seemed to be pulling farther apart in Whitman's century. The various occupations of the city and country interconnect with each other in a larger economic system that functions within a still larger spiritual economy.

Whitman's poetry tries to view the city from an ever wider perspective, not just from an elevated position above it, but from a God's-eye view, encompassing all of time as well as a place in a moment of history. In 1842 Whitman writes, "New York is a great place – a mighty world in itself," and he often presents New York as a microcosm of his vision for America (*Jour.*, 1: 44). In this sense, Whitman's poetry paralleled contemporary exhibitions that sought to show the unity of the city through panoramas just as the city was becoming increasingly difficult to comprehend in a single image. *Edward Burkhardt's Panorama of New York*, 1842–5, had eight sections providing a circular panorama from the steeple of the North Dutch Church. John Bachman's *New York and Environs* (1859) attempted to encompass the whole of the city with a circular, fish-eye view that seemed to make New York City into the equivalent of the globe. In 1845–6, E. Porter Belden, aided by nearly 150 artists, built a scale model of the city, more than 20 feet square, that included 200,000 buildings, 30,000 trees, and 5,000 ships (Kelley 1996: 44). The extravagance of the details of this project – the statistical sublime – echoed the astounding scale of the city's development in those years. No doubt these images and models of the city provided the illusion of stability, order, and controllability. Some critics, such as de Certeau, would view projects like these – along with Whitman's poetry – as panoptic efforts to attribute an "all-seeing power" to a state equipped with new regulatory technologies (Certeau 1984: 92). The expansion of the urban grid to the line of the horizon creates the impression of the inevitability of rational, technological power and presents the city as the point from which the empire radiates.

Whitman's efforts to create a panoramic view of the city and the nation in his poetry is matched by his comprehensive vision of time in poems such as "Crossing Brooklyn Ferry" (1856): "What is the count of the scores or hundreds of years between us? / Whatever it is, it avails not – distance avails not, and place avails not" (*LG*: 162). The voyage from Brooklyn to New York represents not only Whitman's personal experiences on the Fulton Ferry, but the journey to the New World, the dream of an American Jerusalem, the voyage from life to death, the link between the body and the soul, the

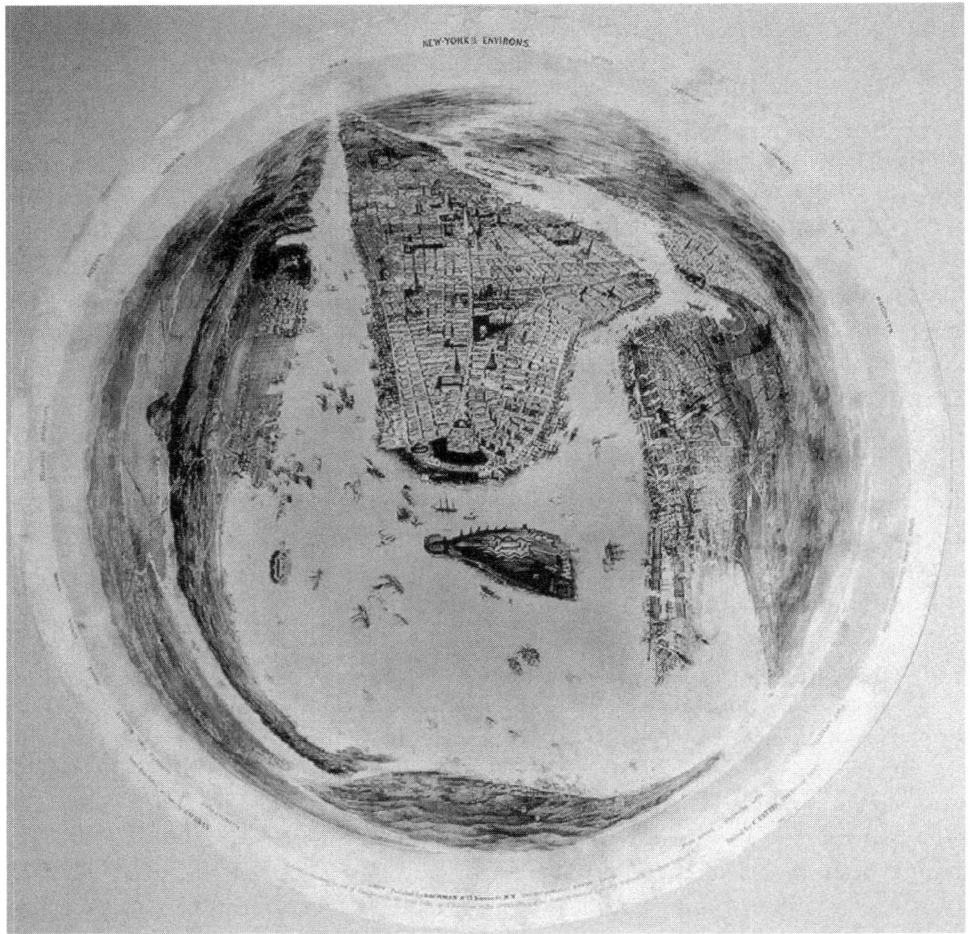

Plate 3.2 (John) Bachman, "New York & Environs" (1859). Courtesy New York Public Library.

gulf between the observer and the observed, the poet and the reader, and a future in which the illusory distinction between the urban and the pastoral is erased. In "Brooklyn Ferry," the City of Man becomes identical with the City of God, and Whitman reveals himself as an illuminator of the urban millennium in which all can participate if they share his vision: "Diverge, fine spokes of light, from the shape of my head, or any one's head, in the sunlit water!" (*LG*: 165). Whitman's transcendent vision undoes the Fall, so closely associated with urban life, by representing himself – and, by extension, the people around him and his readers – as "Christs" crossing on Brooklyn Ferry.

"Crossing" concludes with a passage described by William Chapman Sharpe as an "urban-pastoral synthesis, the prosperous, industrialized garden of the West" (Sharpe

1990: 98). The foundry chimneys, which "cast red and yellow light over the tops of the houses," are not the "dark Satanic mills" of William Blake's "Jerusalem" but a natural part of Whitman's panoramic view of human progress. Industry is no less worthy of poetry than the sunset he describes: "Thrive, cities! bring your freight, bring your shows, ample and sufficient rivers." He addresses the ferries, buildings, and people of the city as "dumb, beautiful ministers"; "Great or small, you furnish your parts toward the soul" (*LG*: 165). If all things are appearances behind which lie greater, spiritual truths, then there is, at bottom, no difference between the country and the city, between Nature and humanity.

"This is the City and I am One of the Citizens"

Whitman is not a systematic thinker; he is, as he admits, often contradictory. Though he depicts the city and the country as complementary or undifferentiated, it is clear that, overall, Whitman personally prefers urban life. He would often describe himself as a specifically urban poet in *Leaves:* "This is the City and I am One of the Citizens," he writes in "Song of Myself" (*LG*: 77). Whitman sometimes disliked the extremes of the city, but he seems to have loathed rural isolation even more. His earliest surviving letters, written when he was working as a teacher on Long Island, express manifest disdain for country people: "Now is the season for what they call 'huckleberry frolicks.' – I had the inestimable ectasy [sic] of being invited to one of these refined amusements" (*Corr.*, 7: 1). Whitman then describes the denizens of rural Woodbury, New York, as "bumpkins, flat-heads, and coarse brown-faced girls, dirty, ill-favored young brats, with squalling throats and crude manners, and bog-trotters, with all the disgusting conceit of ignorance and vulgarity" (p. 2). Whitman never overcame his dislike of the remote country and the mental narrowness he believed went with it. After his youthful experiences as a teacher, Whitman never resided in the country again, aside from vacations, even when his friends encouraged him to do so late in life for the sake of his health.

While "Crossing" attempts to unify the urban and the pastoral, "Give Me the Splendid Silent Sun" (1865) is a decisive manifesto of the importance of the city over the country so valued by Romantic poets. The poem opens with a pastoral idyll: "Give me juicy autumnal fruit, ripe and red from the orchard; / Give me a field where the unmow'd grass grows; / Give me an arbor, give me the trellis'd grape." Whitman then supplies an Eve for this Eden: "Give me for marriage a sweet-breath'd woman, of whom I should never tire; / Give me a perfect child – give me, away, aside from the noise of the world, a rural, domestic life" (*LG*: 312). Though Whitman contrasts the "primal sanities" of country life with the "shows" and "phantoms" of the city, his naïvely descriptive pastoralism is a Romantic cliché that is constructed to be rejected in the second half of this two-part poem.

Just as a child must abandon innocence, so the poet must accept the world as it is, rather than as he – or his fellow Romantics – would hope it to be: fallen but capable of redemption through contact with fellow human beings. The poet rejects the previous image of exclusive, isolated domesticity; instead, he celebrates the more varied and expansive scope of urban erotic encounters: "Give me interminable eyes! give me women! give me comrades and lovers by the thousand! / Let me see new ones every day! let me hold new ones by the hand every day!" Rural life, as Whitman knew by experience, was not congenial to unfettered fellowship; it was devoid of the sexual energies – the promiscuous attractions of all people towards each other – that Whitman believed were the essence of the democratic spirit. For this reason, in the final lines of the poem, Whitman rejects the country: "Keep your splendid, silent sun; / Keep your woods, O Nature, and the quiet places by the woods; / Keep your fields of clover and timothy, and your corn-fields and orchards." Instead, Whitman embraces the life of the city: "O such for me! O an intense life! O full to repletion, and varied! / The life of the theatre, bar-room, huge hotel, for me! . . . Manhattan crowds, with their turbulent musical chorus – with varied chorus, and light of the sparkling eyes; / Manhattan faces and eyes forever for me" (Whitman *LG*: 313–14). Salvation – the larger union with God that lies at the heart of much of Whitman's poetry – was not to be found in the country, for all its rejuvenating power, but in the arms of lovers so readily found in the city.

Whitman recognized that people go to cities for sexual adventure as well as to gratify their professional ambitions. In 1841 Whitman may have been tarred and feathered and run out of town on a rail by the "bumpkins" of Woodbury for a sexual transgression with a student (Reynolds 1995: 71–3). Such an event would help to explain Whitman's antagonism towards rural life; it also explains the attraction of the city for a man with homoerotic inclinations: anonymity, relative tolerance, and the scale of population needed to create distinct sexual subcultures. Though it is problematic to regard Whitman as a "gay" poet when modern sexual identities were still being constructed, it is clear that the sexual freedom of the city – alluded to in both "Crossing Brooklyn Ferry" and "Give Me the Splendid Silent Sun" – is central to Whitman's understanding of the purpose of his larger poetic project. Whitman sees sexual energy as a binding force that gives unity and vitality to the city. Cities facilitate sexual relationships between people with radically different backgrounds. In time, these relationships lead to the erasure of physical and cultural differences, creating, in Whitman's vision, a new race of "Americans."

Whitman celebrates heterosexual "amativeness," but he places no less value on homosocial and homosexual "adhesiveness." In the "Calamus" poems (1860), written on the eve of the Civil War, Whitman asserted this principle in "For You O Democracy": "I will make inseparable cities with their arms about each other's necks, / By the love of comrades, / By the manly love of comrades" (Whitman *LG*: 117). Undoubtedly, Whitman's experiences of comradeship with the wounded soldiers in the hospitals of Civil War Washington, DC confirmed his belief in the importance of loving relationships between men. He expanded on this point in the preface to *Leaves* in 1876:

> In my opinion, it is by a fervent, accepted development of comradeship, the beautiful and sane affection of man for man, latent in all the young fellows, north and south, east and west . . . that the United States of the future, (I cannot too often repeat,) are to be most effectually welded together, intercalated, anneal'd into a living Union. (*PW*, 2: 471)

Though the Union was preserved and slavery ended, Whitman would increasingly rely on his belief in comradeship, as well as the spiritual interconnection of all people, as the means by which cities like New York could sustain a sense of order and community.

"A Complex Order"

Even after the abolition of slavery and the preservation of the Union, the "Immigrants arriving, fifteen or twenty thousand in a week," initially celebrated by Whitman in "Mannahatta" (1860), increasingly became for him a class of seemingly unassimilable, impoverished, and dangerous outsiders (*LG*: 475). In the 30 years before the Civil War, the population of New York grew from about 200,000 to 800,000, but by 1900 the population had swelled to 3.4 million (Boyer 1978: 67, 123). Whitman's middle class of skilled workers ("mechanics of the city, the masters," who had the habit of "looking you straight in the eyes") were gradually replaced by extremes of poverty and wealth with implacable hatreds on both sides. The supposedly welcoming town of Whitman's youth ("A million people – manners free and superb – open voices – hospitality – the most courageous and friendly young men") had become a metropolis of foreign-born, non-English-speaking strangers. As the middle classes began to flee major cities for the emerging suburbs, the urban fabric was ripped apart by the struggles of unregulated capital and impoverished labor. By the end of Whitman's life, the American city – the "Mannahatta" of his memory – had grown, like the nation as a whole, almost beyond any reasonable belief in the capacity of his poetry to comprehend it or assuage its tensions.

As M. Wynn Thomas observes in *The Lunar Light of Whitman's Poetry*, Whitman's "future hopes are raised as much on the grounds of disenchantment with the urban present as on his mistaken faith in its potential for growth" (Thomas 1987: 166). In 1863, during the New York City Draft Riots, Whitman began to yield to the despair that his poetry was, in part, an effort to forestall: "So the mob has arisen at last in New York – I have been expecting it," he wrote to his mother, "We are in the midst of strange and terrible times" (*Corr.*, 1: 117). If *Leaves* could be seen as a means of building community in the antebellum era, the work, for all its ongoing revisions, seemed increasingly inadequate for American cities during the Gilded Age. The Draft Riots would be followed by showdowns between labor and capital at Haymarket in 1877 and Homestead in 1892. The regional conflict that led to the Civil War had been succeeded by a struggle between rich and poor, in which the principal battle-ground would be the American cities in which Whitman had once placed so much hope. After the Civil War, as Malcolm Andrews writes, "the city of his poems was an anachronism," or at least, at times, it must have seemed so (Andrews 1988: 190).

Antebellum Brooklyn and New York had been, in Williams's term, "knowable communities," relative to what they became after the Civil War. But even as a young journalist, Whitman had lamented the relentless speed with which the economic logic of the city was uprooting the village of his memories:

> The beautiful large trees that stood so long on Dr. Hunt's old place, corner of Concord and Fulton streets, were cut down the other day, to gain a few inches more room, to build brick and lime walls on . . . we pity and denounce the taste of the Brooklyn Savings' Bank directors, which achieved this work of death . . . It is perhaps expecting too much of those who new-come or new-buy in Brooklyn, that they should look upon such things with the regard of love or sorrow. *They* never played under them in childhood. (*Jour.*, 1: 464)

Whitman disliked the city's tendency to tear down history; to base everything on money. A writer in *Harper's Monthly* in 1856 described New York as "the largest and least loved of any of our great cities." Anyone over 40 "finds nothing, absolutely nothing, of the New York he knew" (quoted in Barth 1980: 31). The older parts of the city had been replaced by new construction. The hills had been leveled and the streams covered over. The organic flow of older streets had been tamed and gridded for maximum efficiency and profit. The era of the "walking city" was over; the scale of New York, like other major American cities, was becoming seemingly too large and diverse to consolidate through even the most visionary poetic project.

Whitman visited New York many times after 1862, but he never lived in the city again. His poetry assumed an increasingly elegiac tone: romanticizing antebellum New York, recording Civil War Washington, and mythologizing Abraham Lincoln and himself in revised and supplemented editions of the book that grew originally out of youthful experiences in a city and a neighboring countryside that no longer existed as he remembered them.

Some of Whitman's disciples, such as Horace Traubel, urged him towards a more radical position. The lives of the working poor were not going to be improved by Whitman's poetic notion of "comradeship" unless it was in support of labor unions and, possibly, social revolution. Before the end of the nineteenth century, Whitman's desire for frankness and gritty representation in poetry seemed tepid compared to the realism of emerging photographers such as Jacob Riis, the muckraking journalism of Ida Tarbell and Upton Sinclair, and literary naturalism of Stephen Crane and Jack London. Whitman put his hopes in the native goodness of the American people – their inchoate genius, like the order of a flock of birds – rather than in systematic ideologies. Activists like Emma Goldman would admire Whitman's poetry, but he would never support any specific political movement after the Civil War, and his principled inclusiveness increasingly seemed like an affirmation of the status quo.

Nevertheless, Whitman's development was not an entirely linear path towards disillusionment with the city and its future. There were reasons for optimism; change was inevitable, and the older Whitman had his eye on posterity rather than on the present. Moreover, as Brand observes, Whitman was always conflicted about the city, and he compartmentalized his views within different modes of interpretation: "his 'moral telescope' never showed him the same city as he saw with 'spiritual' or 'poetic' ones" (Brand 1991: 217). The labyrinthine city was balanced by the openness of the country; the isolation of the country was balanced by the messy vitality of the city. And, in a larger sense, there was no difference between the two.

But even as Whitman was denouncing the corruption of the American character in the anguished prose of *Democratic Vistas* (1871), he was composing his finest short poem on urban experience. "Sparkles from the Wheel" (1871) represents the poet as an observer of an ordinary street scene:

> By the curb, toward the edge of the flagging,
> A knife-grinder works at his wheel sharpening a great knife;
> Bending over he carefully holds it to the stone, by foot and knee,
> With measur'd tread, he turns rapidly, as he presses with light but firm hand,
> Forth issue then in copious golden jets,
> Sparkles from the wheel.
>
> (*LG*: 390)

"Sparkles" draws a correspondence between the poet – "a phantom, curiously floating" – and a knife-grinder, a "sad sharp-chinn'd old man with worn clothes." Both are anachronisms in the industrial age, and yet both preside over a spectacle of creation, "showers of gold" that draw the rapt attention of onlookers without defining the meaning of these "Sparkles." The poem recalls the line from "Song of Myself": "there is no object so soft but it makes a hub for the wheel'd universe" (*LG*: 86). Even as his prosaic view of the city darkened, Whitman's poetic vision of the city retained a Romantic sense of the immanence of the divine in ordinary Americans that could not be reduced to a specific political program.

No doubt, Whitman's work reflects a scopophilic drive; his sources of knowledge are primarily visual. On the basis of this, he often presumes to know not only his own mind, but the minds of everyone through all of time. This tendency towards imperial generalization offended D. H. Lawrence in his *Studies in Classic American Literature* (1923), and several more recent critics, most notably Brand in *The Spectator and the City* (1991), who writes, "however much enthusiasm Whitman may have had for the city, he had little of substance to say about it" (Brand 1991: 159). Thomas offers a more judicious critique of Whitman's method in *The Lunar Light of Whitman's Poetry* (1987):

> [Whitman's] approach has the strengths of its considerable weaknesses. It makes no attempt to consider the underlying structure and internal character of an urban society full of growing divisions and conflicts, but it is admirably suited to the uninhibited evocation of the excited and exciting surface of contemporary life. And yet Whitman

> never really participates in the unpredictable turbulence. He remains an impassioned observer, sustained by the conviction that this disorder is more apparent than real (Thomas 1987: 151)

Nevertheless, the impact of Whitman's vision of the city, for all its arguable shortcomings, remains vast. The urban writer is a subjective interpreter of the city as a "text," but, over time, the work of the urban writer can change the meaning of that urban text. Whitman's vision of the city extends, for example, beyond literature and the arts and into professions such as urban planning. The winning arguments of Jane Jacobs, struggling against the so-called slum clearance projects of Robert Moses in New York in the 1960s, often echo Whitman's language, and, more importantly, his conception of the hidden harmonies of diverse people interacting in a complex, organic urban space:

> Under the seeming disorder of the old city, wherever the old city is working successfully, is a marvelous order for maintaining the safety of the streets and the freedom of the city. It is a complex order. Its essence is the intricacy of sidewalk use, bringing with it a constant succession of eyes. This order is all composed of movement and change, and although it is life, not art, we may fancifully call it the art form of the city and liken it to the dance – not a simple-minded precision dance with everyone kicking up at the same time, twirling in unison and bowing off en masse, but to an intricate ballet in which the individual dancers and ensembles all have distinctive parts which miraculously reinforce each other and compose an orderly whole. (Jacobs [1961] 1993: 65)

Jacobs's *The Death and Life of American Cities* ([1961] 1993) and the influence it has had on contemporary urban life, perhaps better than any work of literature or art, represents the enduring, pervasive impact of Whitman's vision of the city.

Whitman realized that poetry can capture the amplitude of urban life – the way that a city is an imagined community, an idea preserved over time, even in the midst of contending groups – more than a cluster of changing, unrelated physical spaces. Constructed over many years by countless people, the city is like an archive, a repository of memories, or a palimpsest in which the writing of previous years remains legible beneath the inscriptions of today. Whitman's poetry reveals the hidden connections of city life, the ways in which strangers over many generations are linked together by common experiences. As Whitman writes in "Song of the Answerer" (1855), the poet "is the joiner, he sees how they join" (*LG*: 168). His poetry presented the cohesive energies of the city as a means by which the many divisions of his time and place might be reconciled. No doubt, Whitman struggled to find a means of ordering an increasingly diverse urban population, but he also recognized that apparent disorder is one of the chief delights of the city and its greatest source of progressive energy.

References and Further Reading

Andrews, Malcolm (1988). Walt Whitman and the American City. In Graham Clarke (ed.), *The American City: Literary and Cultural Perspectives*. New York: St. Martin's Press, pp. 179–97.

Barth, Gunter (1980). *City People: The Rise of Modern Culture in Nineteenth-Century America*. Oxford: Oxford University Press.

Baudelaire, Charles ([1863] 1964). *The Painter of Modern Life and Other Essays*, trans. Jonathan Mayne. London: Phaidon.

Benjamin, Walter (1973). *Charles Baudelaire: A Lyric Poet in the Era of High Capitalism*, trans. Harry Zohn. London: Verso.

Boyer, Paul (1978). *Urban Masses and Moral Order in America, 1820–1920*. Cambridge, MA: Harvard University Press.

Brand, Dana (1991). *The Spectator and the City in Nineteenth-Century American Literature*. Cambridge, UK: Cambridge University Press.

Burrows, Edwin G. and Wallace, Mike (1999). *Gotham: A History of New York City to 1898*. New York: Oxford University Press.

Certeau, Michel de (1984). "Walking in the City." In *The Practice of Everyday Life*, trans. Steven Randall. Berkeley: University of California Press, pp. 91–110.

Clarke, Graham (1991). "'The Sleepers': Whitman's City of Dreadful Night." In *Walt Whitman: The Poem as Private History*. London: Vision, pp. 99–126.

Conrad, Peter (1984). *The Art of the City*. Oxford: Oxford University Press.

Franklin, Benjamin (1987). *Essays, Articles, Bagatelles, and Letters, Poor Richard's Almanack, Autobiography*. New York: Library of America.

Jacobs, Jane ([1961] 1993). "The Uses of Sidewalks: Safety." In *The Death and Life of Great American Cities*. New York: Modern Library, pp. 37–96.

Jefferson, Thomas (1984). *Autobiography, Notes on the State of Virginia, Public and Private Papers, Addresses, Letters*. New York: Library of America.

Johnson, John H. (1984). *The Poet and the City*. Athens: University of Georgia Press.

Kelley, Wyn (1996). *Melville's City: Literary and Urban Form in Nineteenth-Century New York*. Cambridge, UK: Cambridge University Press.

Kouwenhoven, John A. (1953). *The Columbia Historical Portrait of New York*. Garden City: Doubleday.

LeMaster, J. R. and Kummings, Donald D. (eds.) (1998). *Walt Whitman: An Encyclopedia*. New York: Garland Publishing.

Lounsbury, Thomas R. (ed.) (1912). *Yale Book of American Verse*. New Haven, CT: Yale University Press.

Machor, James L. (1987). *Pastoral Cities: Urban Ideals and the Symbolic Landscape of America*. Madison: University of Wisconsin Press.

Newcomb, John Timberman (2004). "'The Housetop Sea': Cityscape Verse and the Rise of Modern American Poetry." *American Literature*, 76 (2): 275–306.

Reynolds, David S. (1995). *Walt Whitman's America: A Cultural Biography*. New York: Knopf.

Sharpe, William Chapman (1990). *Unreal Cities*. Baltimore: Johns Hopkins University Press.

Thomas, M. Wynn (1987). *The Lunar Light of Whitman's Poetry*. Cambridge, MA: Harvard University Press.

Trachtenberg, Alan (1996). "Whitman's Lesson of the City." In Betsy Erkkila and Jay Grossman (eds.), *Breaking Bounds: Whitman and American Cultural Studies*. New York and Oxford: Oxford University Press, pp. 163–73.

Traubel, Horace ([1906] 1961). *With Walt Whitman in Camden*, vol. 1. New York: Rowman and Littlefield.

Traubel, Horace (1982). *With Walt Whitman in Camden*, vol. 6, ed. Gertrude Traubel and William White. Carbondale: University of Southern Illinois Press.

Voorsanger, Catherine Hoover and Howat, John K. (2000). *Art and the Empire City: New York, 1825–1861*. New York and New Haven, CT: Metropolitan Museum of Art and Yale University Press.

Weimer, David R. (1966). *The City as Metaphor*. New York: Random House.

Whitman, Walt (1972). *New York Dissected*. Folcroft, PA: Folcroft Library.

Wilentz, Sean (1984). *Chants Democratic: New York City and the Rise of the American Working Class, 1788–1850*. New York: Oxford University Press.

Williams, Raymond (1973). *The Country and the City*. London: Oxford University Press.

4
Labor and Laborers

M. Wynn Thomas

As a youthful contributor to *The New York Democrat*, Walt Whitman gave expression to what was to become his lifelong creed: "labor creates real wealth. It is to labor that man owes every thing possessed of changeable value. Labor is the talisman that has raised him from the condition of the savage" (*Jour.*, 1: 197). It followed that, as he put it two years later in a piece for *The Brooklyn Eagle*, "There is hardly anything on earth, of its sort, that arouses our sympathies more readily than the cause of a laborer, or a band of laborers, struggling for a competence" (*Jour.*, 1: 303). He was writing from personal experience. Throughout much of Whitman's childhood and youth his father had worked in the building trade, as later did his brother Andrew, and so the family had suffered (and no doubt also benefited) at first hand from the dramatic changes in the life of the working population that had been effected by the United States's transition to a new phase of capitalist activity. But in using the word "competence," the young Whitman was using the vocabulary of a past period and betraying his origins in a time when workers could still expect to control their own livelihood.

Nor was it only the urban workforce with which Whitman felt a strong sense of solidarity. In *Specimen Days*, his friend John Burroughs, writing to Whitman's dictation, observed of the poet's farming ancestors on Long Island that "both sexes labor'd with their open hands – the men on the farm – the women in the house and around it" (Whitman 1982: 694). And those sections of *Specimen Days* in which Whitman recalls his earliest years on the island he affectionately called "Paumanok" are full of fond, detailed references to the ordinary workers, farmers, and fishermen. Moreover, the passion of Whitman's identification with the workers never really waned – neither when he himself became a successful middle-class journalist; nor when he became an explosively controversial poet; nor in his old age, when an instinctive faithfulness to his earliest experiences prevented him from ever appreciating the real character of working life in the America of the Gilded Age, polarized between corporate power and an increasingly unionized labor movement.

So ingrained was Whitman's sense that his own creativity, even as writer, was continuous with the "creativity" of labor ("a framer framing a house is more than the equal of all the old-world gods," Whitman 1982: 74) that he instinctively turned to his family's trade (his father was primarily a carpenter) for images of creative self-construction: "Sure as the most certain sure, plumb in the uprights, well entretied, braced in the beams / [. . .] / I and this mystery here we stand" (Whitman 1982: 28); "My foothold is tenoned and mortised in granite" (Whitman 1982: 46). But equally significantly, and no doubt equally unconsciously, he also conceived of himself (and of every person) as not to be limited by the constraints of any such traditional trade identity. By declaring "Unscrew the locks from the doors! / Unscrew the doors themselves from their jambs!" (Whitman 1982: 50), he was in effect declaring for a new liberty of personal development, as unimaginable as it was unavailable to an earlier society in which personal fulfillment was achievable only through the performance of an ascribed social role. As such, Whitman was the typical product of the new society of individual, and individualizing, opportunity being produced by the new economic order that had replaced the working world of his own childhood and youth. Yet he simultaneously continued to prize the values of that largely disappeared artisanal order, for the continuation of which his father and his generation of workers had fought so bitterly during the 1820s and 1830s – indeed Whitman's very insistence on the labor theory of wealth was a conscious reaffirmation of that older politics in the face of the new world's demonstration of the primary wealth-creating powers of money, in the form of capital and its powers to profit quite unscrupulously from any "band of laborers, struggling for a competence."

Prefabricated buildings – a typical product of the postartisanal period – helped put Whitman's father out of work. And when he asks "Who learns my lesson complete?" and answers "Boss and journeyman and apprentice" (Whitman 1982: 341) he is compressing into a single phrase the incompatible features of the artisanal and postartisanal orders. "Boss" was a term that entered New York English (from the Dutch *baas*) in the 1820s to describe a new kind of social and economic phenomenon which involved not the old master–apprentice relationship of the craft world but a new relationship of employers to labor. So when Whitman elsewhere, speaking ecstatically of his rapport with the dreams of sleepers, exclaims "I am their boss" (Whitman 1982: 108), he is doing what he repeatedly did in the early editions of *Leaves of Grass*. He is trying to reform the new emergent socioeconomic order by refashioning the key terms of its vocabulary and hence redefining its governing concepts. Time and time again, from the 1855 Preface onwards, the terms of profit, loss, speculation, gain, spending, and the like are employed by him in senses designedly contrary to their current usage in his time: "What is commonest and cheapest and nearest and easiest is Me, / Me going in for my chances, spending for vast returns" (Whitman 1982: 38). And even his stance as a loafer, fundamental to the working of "Song of Myself," was in part an act of dissent, a conscious opting out of a world in which, increasingly, time meant money. Thus did Whitman conduct, on the field of language, a guerilla action against the new capitalism. But if he mounted a counterattack, he never intended a counterrevolution. Whitman was never disaffected with capitalism *per se*, as were the socialists. On the contrary, he thrived on the vitality, the energy, the variety, the inventiveness, of the very new world of labor and capital whose values he in other ways so deeply distrusted.

And radically divided as he thus was in his sympathies – between the new individualistic, laissez-faire libertarianism and an older collectivist, collaborative ethos – he found in poetry a unique medium that offered him the indispensable means of reconciling these two otherwise incompatible systems of value. So, in claiming that "Neither a servant nor a master am I" (Whitman 1982: 89), he seeks to place, and thus define, himself as existing outside the social categories produced by, and in turn producing, the emergent economic order. Similarly, when he states that "I take no sooner a large price than a small price" (ibid.) he is substituting the notion of a "fair" price for that of "market value," in a gesture that is implicitly a criticism of the whole system of values promoted by a new capitalism.

It was in the guise – or, in one important sense, in the disguise – of an ordinary worker that Whitman first studiedly introduced himself as a poet. Whereas earlier visual images represent him as a fashionable successful urbanite, in the famous frontispiece engraving which served in lieu of an author's name in the first (1855) edition of *Leaves of Grass* he chose to appear in the jauntily angled hat and unfashionably informal (un)dress of an ordinary worker. And while the self-portrait was in part a literary allusion – a kind of paradoxically fashionable act of homage to the cult of the carpenter created by George Sand – there was behind this affectation a sincere sense of his role as the voice of the largely silenced class that had produced him. This was, in turn, his authority to release "... many long dumb voices, / Voices of the interminable generations of slaves, / Voices of prostitutes and deformed persons, / Voices of the diseased and despairing, and of thieves and dwarfs" (Whitman 1982: 50). It was indeed his authentic right, his birthright as child of the working class, to act as spokesperson for the suppressed and the dispossessed; and for examples both of prostitution (the modern term "hooker" actually derives from Whitman's New York, from the red-light district of the Hook, on the East River, frequented by sailors, stevedores, and workmen) and of psychological deformity he needed to look no further than his immediate family, still largely working-class in its struggling character, with whom Whitman chose to continue living for most of his years as working journalist and emergent poet.

"The floormen are laying the floor – the tinners are tinning the roof – the masons are calling for mortar, / In single file each shouldering his hod pass onward the laborers" (Whitman 1982: 41): when Whitman records the world of work he does so with all the respectful inwardness of understanding, all the loving care and wondering attention, that characterize the jeweled miniatures of contemporary life captured by monkish scribes in the lunettes of medieval manuscripts. They are his hymns to creation – the creation of more than wealth, the creation of a plenitude of artifacts, through the scrupulous, satisfying exercise of trade skills and craft skills. But as such they are also his unacknowledged elegy for a lost world; the artisanal world of small masters, craftsmen, skilled workers and apprentices. It was an arrangement he retrospectively idealized; "masters" could be as tyrannical as bosses, and there was no great satisfaction to be gained from being subject, as farmer's son or daughter, to omnipotent patriarchal power.

So when he builds his great celebratory structures of praise of the working world he seems to model his rhetoric on the visual rhetoric of the pageants organized by the self-promoting artisans in their erstwhile pomp, when they marched behind the proud emblems of their respective trades – the chairman's chair, the schooner of the shipwrights, the arm-and-hammer of the General Society:

> Manufactures . . . commerce . . . engineering . . . the building of cities, and every trade carried on there . . . and the implement of every trade,
> The anvil and tongs and hammer . . . the axe and wedge . . . the square and mitre and jointer and smoothingplane;
> The plumbob and trowel and level . . . the wall-scaffold, and the work of walls and ceilings . . . or any mason work
>
> (Whitman 1982: 95)

In passages such as this he implicitly affirms the labor theory of value, in the face of the reality of contemporary capitalism, representing products as the end-product of the creative process of skilful work. He also succeeds, by a sleight of rhetoric, in making a world which is co-operative merely in the sense of temporally coactive seem co-operative in the ethical sense. He thus substitutes collaboration for competition as the motor of the new economy and the new society:

> Where the triphammers crash . . . where the press is whirling its cylinders;
> Wherever the human heart beats with terrible throes out of its ribs;
> Where the pear-shaped balloon is floating aloft . . . floating in it myself and looking composedly down;
> Where the life-car is drawn on the slipnoose . . . where the heat hatches pale-green eggs in the dented sand.
>
> (Whitman 1982: 60)

Through parataxis, work activities are cunningly humanized by being linked metaphorically to human metabolism (the rhythmic repetitive crash of triphammers is associated with the beatings of the heart), and they are also naturalized as creative acts by being treated as part of the cosmic process of procreation ("where the heat hatches eggs in the dented sand"). The same rhetorical device of juxtaposition is used elsewhere to suggest that in the world of labor Whitman actually heard America singing: "The pure contralto sings in the organloft, / The carpenter dresses his plank . . . the tongue of his foreplane whistles its wild ascending lisp" (Whitman 1982: 39). The Whitman who yearned for an indigenous form of American musical theatre found it in precisely such moments. It is no accident that Whitman's exclamation "I hear the chorus . . . it is a grand-opera . . . this indeed is music!" occurs in "Song of Myself" at exactly the point of transition between his relish of "The heav'e'yo of stevedores unlading ships by the wharves, the refrain of the anchor-lifters" and a tenor's aria, "The orbic flex of his mouth is pouring and filling me full" (Whitman 1982: 54). It is therefore appropriate that the poem "I hear America singing" turns out to be entirely about working America:

> The mason singing his [carol], as he makes ready for work, or leaves off work,
> The boatman singing what belongs to him in his boat, the deckhand singing on the steamboat deck,
> The shoemaker singing as he sits on his bench, the hatter singing as he stands.
> (Whitman 1982: 174)

No hint there of the discords caused by New York's headlong laissez-faire capitalism.

Those artisanal pageants were, however, in some ways at their most impressive during the very period – the period of Whitman's childhood and youth – when the artisanal order was making its last stand, desperate to demonstrate how central it still was to the maintenance of republican values. Whitman's writing remained steeped in these values, even as he welcomed not only the new freedoms of the postartisanal society but also the plethora of new products made available by the bounty of commercial capitalism – in his early journalism he typically waxes lyrical over "rare specimens of art" in the form of the false teeth crafted by Dr Jonathan W. Dodge, "such as would almost tempt a man to knock out his own and have some from Dr D instead" (*Jour.*, 1: 225). But while he delighted in celebrating in his poetry the newest devices for revolutionizing the world of work (the Singer sewing machine is featured as soon as it appears on the market), he can also declare "No labor-saving machine / . . . have I made / [. . .] / But a few carols vibrating through the air I leave, / For comrades and lovers" (Whitman 1982: 182).

Whitman was certainly imaginatively excited by the new capitalism's exuberant inventiveness. In particular, he reveled in its incomparable powers to accomplish transformations, miraculous acts of metamorphosis. "Materials here under your eyes shall change their shape as if by magic," he declared (Whitman 1982: 345), and, as "Song of the Broad Axe" shows, he saw human progress in American capacity, if not to beat swords into ploughshares, then at least to change the barbarous weapons of Europe's feudal past into the all-conquering axe that enabled the American frontiersman and settler to hew fertile ground out of wilderness. It was through work – emblematized by the axe – that the United States would build a new, democratic society, the eventual site of which would be not the established cities of the East but the as-yet "virgin lands" of the West (once the aboriginal inhabitants had finally died out, as Lamarckian evolution decreed that they must). Meanwhile, Whitman celebrates the labor, country-wide, that is setting this final work in progress, sensuously envisaging "The flexible rise and fall of backs, the continual click of the trowels striking the bricks" and "The brisk short crackle of the steel driven slantingly into the pine, / The butter-color'd chips flying off in great flakes and slivers, / The limber motion of brawny young arms and hips in easy costumes" (Whitman 1982: 333).

Such a passage is a revelation not least of how sensuous, not to say sexual, was Whitman's homoerotic response to the world of masculine work, and how correspondingly sensitive he was to the way in which the new socioeconomic order, which crammed men in their young physical prime together into boarding-houses, had created what historians have called an intensely "homosocial city," ripe with opportunities for sexual intimacy (Burrows and Wallace 2000). Same-sex relations – "homosexual" did not yet exist either as a term or a concept – were usually viewed with relative indulgence by the civic authorities. Most of Whitman's own friendships were with young working-class men like Thomas Sawyer and Pete Doyle, friendships that were undoubtedly passionately intimate and that may have found sexual expression. In this sense, Whitman's "Calamus" poems, with their celebration of "the need for comrades," their commendation of the "salute" of manly kissing, and their memories of a youth glimpsed "among a crowd of workmen and drivers in a barroom around the stove late of a winter night" (Whitman 1982: 283), capture – albeit with a singular anguished intensity and complexity of ambivalent feeling – a defining feature both of his own experience and of the New York labor scene: "I am enamoured of. . . . / Men that live among cattle or taste of the ocean or woods, / Of the builders and steerers of ships, of the wielders of axes and mauls, of the drivers of horses" (p. 38). Yet Whitman openly professed himself dismayed at the limited vocabulary of feeling among the "muscular classes," at their aversion to thus admitting their "passionate fondness for their friends." "Calamus" may therefore be read as a deliberate attempt to extend that vocabulary, to develop a proper language of love, to demonstrate to them a language for "their most ardent friendships," and thus to enrich the consciousness of the working class that it was "where the real quality of friendship is always freely to be found" (Traubel [1904] 1987: 15).

Whitman was very conscious that his poetry was as much a product of this new society of labor as was "the ring on your finger . . . the lady's wristlet" (Whitman 1982: 96) and other manufactured artifacts which he also viewed as the product of creative acts. In those passages of his late prose work *Specimen Days* in which he offers his own account of "the growth of a poet's mind" – so different from boyhood in the Lake District, the locale in which Wordsworth experienced the fair seed-time of his soul – he recalls roaring out lines from Shakespeare above the din of city streets while riding the top deck of one of the horse-drawn "stages" whose drivers became his close friends; and he lists the names of the most colorful of those drivers, now long dead, as if they were Homeric heroes: "George Storms, Old Elephant, his brother Young Elephant (who came afterward), Tippy, Pop Rice, Big Frank, Yellow Joe" (Whitman 1982: 703). Whitman relished the tang of their names every bit as much as he loved the ripeness of their "largely animal" characters.

One of the greatest gifts of the laboring world to Whitman was that of language – including slang, the sign of the imaginative vitality of working life; the inventive new language of the teeming streets, bred of the mingling of peoples and races in a city. Slang was "lawless," Whitman declared exultantly, and he reveled in the "powerfulness" of its transgressive expressions. His ear was attuned to "the recitative of fish-pedlars and fruit-pedlars . . . the loud laugh of workpeople at their meals" (Whitman

1982: 54) – the inflections of speech every bit as much as its grammar and vocabulary ("pronunciation is the stamina of language," as Whitman vividly noted, Traubel 1987: 2). Working America was a language experiment, just like *Leaves of Grass* itself, and in places slang seems to erupt spontaneously out of Whitman's mouth – "I do not snivel . . . / That life is a suck and a sell" (p. 45); "The blab of the pave . . . the tires of carts and sluff of bootsoles" (p. 33); "Washes and razors for foofoos . . . for me freckles and a bristling beard" (p. 48); "The spotted hawk swoops by and accuses me . . . he complains of my gab and my loitering. / I too am not a bit tamed . . . I too am untranslatable, / I sound my barbaric yawp over the roofs of the world" (p. 87).

But it was not just in slang that Whitman the poet delighted, welcome evidence though it was, like leaves of grass, of the heedlessly rank abundance of life, and of the procreant urge of the world. The American world of labor was a verbal cornucopia of new possibilities which were also new necessities – words born of the need to articulate new experiences, new processes, new products, new businesses, new developments, new inventions: "shipping, steam, the mint, the electric telegraph, railroads . . . Mines – iron works – the sugar plantations of Louisiana . . . all these sprout in hundreds and hundreds of words, all tangible and clean-lived, all having texture and beauty" (Traubel [1904] 1987: 3). If words were always for Whitman "magic" they were also "acts" and "things," and he was confident that the United States would prove equal to the challenge of producing a "renovated English speech," adequate to the articulation of a vast new world of work experience – "Words of Modern Inventions, Discoveries, engrossing Themes, Pursuits, . . . Words of all kinds of Building and Constructing" (Traubel [1904] 1987: 27) – because its English was "enriched with contributions from all languages, old and new."

It was the same process of mixing, of hybridization, that characterized the new forms of popular entertainment that thrived in the famous working-class district of the Bowery where "a full-blown working-class entertainment strip" had developed (Burrows and Wallace 2000: 486). In some ways, nothing more clearly demonstrates how Whitman, whose family had in any case always tended towards the "respectable" end of the working-class spectrum, had become middle-class in outlook than the reservations he expressed at such raucous popular forms of entertainment as the circus. And nowhere does he mention the rat fights of the Bowery. Moreover, while he can include the "brothels, porter-houses, oyster houses, dance halls, and gambling dens" of the district in his poetic panoramas, it was to the Bowery Theatre that Whitman was in fact primarily drawn, as much as to the colorful street theatre that was the district's everyday "performance." And while he idolized the great contrasting tragedians Booth and Forrest, he also mentioned seeing popular entertainers such as "Daddy Rice." It is an interesting reference, because it was Thomas Dartmouth "Daddy" Rice who brought burlesques, in the form of "Negro" (blackface) songs and dances, to the Bowery stage in the late 1820s. "Guised in blackface, the artist could safely mock elites, snobs and condescending moralists" (Burrows and Wallace 2000: 489) and Whitman evidently warmed to such broad, subversive humor. Out of such materials Rice was to fashion the "minstrel" shows. In one respect an appalling travesty of black experience and of indigenous black entertainment, minstrelsy was also "an exercise in creative cultural amalgamation, something for which New York would become famous. It blended black lore with white humour, black banjo with Irish fiddle, African-based dance with British reels" (Burrows and Wallace 2000: 490). As such, it anticipated, and perhaps encouraged, Whitman's own turn to "hybridity" in "Song of Myself," a poem that bewilderingly mixes genres and changes registers, and whose vocabulary switches constantly from racy street-talk to biblical sonority to dignified discourse.

And when a contemporary reviewer described the Whitman of the first edition of *Leaves of Grass* as "a compound of the New England transcendentalist and New York rowdy," the latter epithet again perceptively placed the poet in the context of the working-class culture of the Bowery, one of whose most dominant and colorful specimens of character was the "Bowery B'hoy." In social reality, the "B'hoy" was a product of the gangland culture of working-class New York, a swanking thug but also a cultural conglomerate; "a multiethnic construction, part native American rowdy, part Irish 'jackeen,' part German 'younker' " (Burrows and Wallace 2000: 753). By the time that Whitman came to model his persona, in the original "Song of Myself," on "one of the roughs" of this kind, something interesting had happened to the B'hoy. He had come to be represented by popular, best-selling middle-class writers like George Foster as the quintessential American: a free spirit, impulsive, warm-hearted, brave, strong, and high-spirited; the urban equivalent of the trapper of the Rockies. And the B'hoy hated financiers, bosses, businessmen, and all the types that the new capitalist culture had spawned. The B'hoy and his G'hal belonged to "the great middle class of free life under a republic of which they are the types and representatives" (Foster 1850: 109). Whitman found this kind of idealizing aggrandizement of the New York laborer irresistible, and in many ways his persona in "Song of Myself" – "one of the roughs, large, proud, affectionate, eating, drinking, and breeding" (Whitman 1982: 50) – is modeled on such middle-class romances of the working class as this. Moreover, Foster sentimentally claims that when the B'hoy and his G'hal ostentatiously drive along fashionable Broadway (the Bowery's near neighbor but class opposite), differences of class are "Macadamized" (i.e., leveled and smoothed) like the avenue itself. "Song of Myself" is a similar dream of social integration, Whitman's attempt to reconcile the two halves of a world in which, in actual fact, the laboring class, from which he had himself in a sense derived, was tensely opposed to the middle class of owners, businessmen – and journalists (albeit their in some ways ambivalent social position) such as Whitman himself

In some ways, it was a relish for language, as typical of a streetwise journalist as it was of a poet, that led him to haunt the Bowery B'hoy's working-class culture. Not for nothing had coarse invective traditionally been dubbed "billingsgate," after the London fish-market; the working world had always been renowned for its ability to spawn "vulgar" expletives. It is therefore appropriate that a Whitman who relished "coarseness, directness, live epithets, expletives, words of opprobrium, resistance," and who took "pleasure in the use, on fit occasions, of traitor, coward, liar, shyster, skulk, doughface, trickster, mean, curse, backslider, thief, impotent, lickspittle" (Traubel [1904] 1987: 16), most vigorously exercised his talents for words aggressively "whirled like chain-shot rocks" (p. 14) in his unpublished 1856 pamphlet, "The Eighteenth Presidency!" Addressed to the workingmen and workingwomen of the United States, this squib, intended to influence the outcome of the presidential elections of that year, gave final, and fullest, expression to the radical politics of labor that Whitman had originally derived from his father, Walter Whitman, Senior. During the 1820s and 1830s the crisis in the craft system had steadily deepened, as the old master-journeyman-apprentice system changed into a new socioeconomic system central to which was the relationship between entrepreneurial employers and unskilled wage earners, a relationship governed strictly by market forces. New political alignments appeared in response to this stratification and degradation of labor, a process accelerated by the surge in the power of New York capital in the wake of a boom in building railways and the opening up of western markets. Walter Whitman, Snr. was interested in the radical solutions offered by figures such as Fanny Wright, Robert Dale Owen, and William Leggett, all of whom advocated economic and political programs specifically designed to promote social egalitarianism and based on respect for the primary wealth-creating power of labor. The Democratic Party itself developed a radical "Loco-Foco" wing, in an attempt to contain labor agitation within the established mainstream of contemporary politics. One lasting outcome of these labor movements was the democratization of the press through the publication of new cheap "penny" papers aimed at a mass market. Walt Whitman was to spend many years editing such newspapers, as he was also to account himself a "Loco-Foco" for the whole of his writing life. He shared the movement's hatred of business monopolies, paper money, banks, the exploitation of female labor, and all the other social ills it attributed to a political system in which government (deeply mistrusted by the Loco-Focos) had been usurped by an un-American monied class.

In many ways, "The Eighteenth Presidency!" is a Loco-Foco tract updated to take account of the 1856 political situation. An unremittingly scurrilous attack on the corrupt contemporary political system ("dough-faces, office-vermin, kept-editors," Whitman 1982: 1309), alienated as it had become from the interests of the masses, it calls upon the authentic representatives of democracy, the working people, to assert their power and so to bring a truly egalitarian, authentically American, society into being. The workers particularly favored by Whitman are those of the new western territories, since it is from there that he expects a new political force, "a new race," to appear. This will embody "the young genius" of America and will revolutionize the old, Europeanized, and thus corrupted, societies of the seaboard states. It is also from there that he imagines a Redeemer President will emerge, a figure strikingly prefigurative of Abraham Lincoln as Whitman was later to view him: "some heroic, shrewd, fully-informed, healthy-bodied, middle-aged, beard-faced American blacksmith or boatman [will] come down from the West across the Alleghanies, and walk into the Presidency, dressed in a clean suit of working attire" (Whitman 1982: 1308).

The future of the West is, in fact, the focal concern of "The Eighteenth Presidency!" Whitman was a convinced Free Soiler, believing that the states being formed out of the western territories should be kept free of slaves so as to be reserved exclusively for white labor. Indeed, such was the passion of his belief that a truly democratic America could be developed only in and through the new western societies, that upon the outcome of the Free Soil issue hung, for him, the very future of democracy in the United States – and hence the very future of that vanguard of democracy, the laboring classes. But in allowing a newly formed state to decide for itself whether it should be "slave" or "free," the 1854 Kansas-Nebraska Bill had turned the midwest into the bloody cockpit of political struggle for the future of America. The Bill led to the shattering of the established system of political parties, out of which was formed the Republican Party which Whitman implicitly supports in "The Eighteenth Presidency!" and which was for him to continue to be the truest party of labor throughout the turbulent years ahead.

What the pamphlet clearly shows is how Whitman's devotion to the working class limited his human and social sympathies quite as much as it served to promote them. On the one hand, his repeated insistence on explicitly including "workingwomen" amongst his target audience as well as "workingmen" is a reminder of his substantially enlightened attitudes on gender issues – although nowhere visible in his work are black washerwomen. He was particularly fond of Mattie, the wife of his favorite brother, Jeff. She made shirtfronts for a local manufacturer, and thus helped Whitman gain personal insight into the working conditions of the army of seamstresses, milliners, dressmakers, and other female outworkers, mill-workers, and piece-workers in mid-century New York who are given "bit parts" in his poetic panoramas ("The spinning girl retreats and advances to the hum of the big wheel," Whitman 1982: 39). Their working conditions were frequently dismal, "too confining for health and comfort" as Whitman somewhat euphemistically put it in *Democratic Vistas* (1982: 966). As for their pay, it was often short of bare subsistence and could leave them at starvation level. Some – including his brother Andrew's wife, Nancy – turned to prostitution to augment their income, and Whitman's sympathy with "hookers" may well be partly rooted in his awareness of their social situation. "Not till the waters refuse to glisten for you and the leaves to rustle for you, do my words refuse to glisten and rustle for you," he writes in a poem which is deliberately structured on a customer's making of an "appointment" to meet "A Common Prostitute" (Whitman 1982: 512).

When it came to recognizing and honoring black American labor, however, Whitman was altogether less defiantly outspoken. Even as, in the 1855 "Song of Myself," he was becoming "the hounded slave. . . . I wince at the bite of the dogs" (Whitman 1982: 65), he was insisting in "The Eighteenth Presidency!" that fugitive slaves should be returned to their southern masters, and throughout that pamphlet slavery is consistently represented, not as an inherent evil, but purely as a threat to the interests of white labor. Whereas securing the future of white "democracy" in America demanded urgent immediate action, the abolition of slavery was deferred by Whitman to some future period and was left to the cold care of "progress." Nor did he spare very much space in his poetry for free black labor, although in saluting both the "drudge of cottonfields and emptier of privies" (p. 72) he did implicitly recognize that the plight of New York's blacks (to whom were largely entrusted only menial jobs, like the nightly emptying of privies) might be little better than that of southern plantation workers. Because they were menials, they had to compete with the newly arrived immigrants to scrape a living in such trades as drayage, construction, and domestic service. When Whitman eulogizes the physical beauty of the black carter – "I behold the picturesque giant and love him" (Whitman 1982: 37) – he does not recognize the fact that in New York blacks were debarred from all the better work for cartmen that required a municipal license. And little would one realize from his poetry that the "free" blacks of his city were a ghettoized underclass, that there was constant tension between them and white workers, and that they went in fear of "blackbirders" who snatched free blacks in New York for bounty offered by Southern slave-owners.

But then, it would be unwise ever to trust to Whitman's poetry for an accurate representation of working life in his America. As Alan Trachtenberg has wisely observed, "Whitman's laborer tends to be a person in the condition of potentiality: not so much a social figure but, like America and democracy, a literary figure, a trope of possibility" (1994: 123). One needs to turn to his journalism for a more faithful mapping of the contemporary world of the working classes – the concept of a single unified white "labor" force, opposed to the interests of capital, appeared in fledgling form in the 1830s but was consolidated only during the class-torn and correspondingly class-conscious postwar period. His newspaper articles and editorials do exist on the same plane as such social realities as the Five Point slums, the opium dens, the race riots, and all the other disturbing and disfiguring features of mid-century New York. When these occur in the poetry, as they do in parts of "Song of Myself" and "The Sleepers," they are offered more as distressing aspects of the dynamics of urban experience than as sites and occasions for remedial action. But in his editorials Whitman campaigned for reforms. He deplored the hold of liquor over working people's lives, argued for reduction in transport costs (particularly ferry charges), demanded that clean drinking water be supplied, and pleaded for the provision of decent housing.

One other salient fact is also registered much more bluntly in the journalism – that the majority of the New York workforce was in fact not American but immigrant. In his editorials, Whitman was more than capable of railing against some of the socio-political consequences of this – the campaigns of Bishop John Hughes in the early 1840s for separate Catholic schools provoked the poet to verbal attacks on the Irish as a threat to American values, attacks so vehement that he found himself publicly defending his writing against the charge that it was nativist and xenophobic. For a variety of reasons – partly a wish to avoid ethnic tensions in the face of the political power of nativism in 1855, and partly because, for all the sincerity of his repeated affirmations of welcome, he could himself be disconcerted by the obstinacy with which foreigners remained perplexingly attached to their foreignness – Whitman downplayed in his poetry the fact that the New York workplace was overwhelmingly immigrant in character. Instead, he devised a grammar of integration, writing, for instance, of "Mechanics, Southerners, new arrivals" (Whitman 1982: 91). Indeed, with regard to the world of labor, Whitman's purpose in his poetry was almost always to mediate it through a rhetoric of integration, thus occluding the extent to which, in historical reality, it was a social space riven by class and ethnic divisions – by 1855 the massive ethnic enclave of Kleindeutschland on Manhattan's Lower East Side alone, with its tens of thousands of non-English-speaking foreigners, was the largest German city in the world apart from Berlin and Vienna.

Whitman's real constituency was white America, and his favorite constituents by far were the working-class "boys" and "comrades" who, for him, constituted the best hope of a future American democracy. Tragically, however, the fullest confirmation of his grounds for trust in them was to come not in peace but in war and in the form of his experiences nursing the desperately wounded in the great hospitals of Civil War Washington. Whitman saw that war not as one to liberate the slaves, and not even as one between North and South, but as a "class war" of sorts. He believed it was fought between the Northern rural and urban working class, that for him represented true American democracy, and the class of owners (in which Southern slave-owners were allied with Northern businessmen) who oppressed not only the blacks but also the white working population of both the Northern and the Southern states. Some 600,000 lives were lost as the United States tried to solve its labor problems. It was in these terms that the Civil War was, for him, a war for "democracy"; for social, political, and economic egalitarianism. And it was the workingmen who won that struggle, as much through their powers of suffering and endurance as through their military prowess.

From beginning to end, Whitman's Civil War collection, "Drum-Taps," is his highly idealistic memorial tribute to the ordinary soldiers. It is they who, when war is declared, spring voluntarily and enthusiastically to arms, leaving "the houses . . . and the workshops, . . . / The mechanics arming, (the trowel, the jack-plane, the blacksmith's hammer, tost aside with precipitation, . . . / The driver deserting his wagon in the street" (Whitman 1982: 416–17). And it is they who, at war's end, return peacefully to their task of building a better society. In the heat of battle, it is the "tan-faced prairie boy" and his urban counterpart who distinguish themselves through their bravery, not least when they are brought to hospital. The greatest heroes, wrote Whitman, were "working on farms or at some trade before the war – unaware of their own nature" (Whitman 1982: 739). In their transformation he found final evidence of the heroic potential of American democracy. When he saw them en masse "it fell upon me like a great awe." When he encountered them as the young inarticulate illiterates he nursed in hospital wards he devoted himself to their service, not least by writing simply worded letters on their behalf. And Lincoln he regarded as an embodiment of their stalwart working-class qualities, as those had been further Americanized, and thus more perfectly democratized, in the West, the real, capitalist nature of which Whitman never confronted. In his great elegy for Lincoln, "When Lilacs Last in the Door-yard Bloomed," it is to the world of work that he turns to find the dead president's lasting memorial – to "pictures of growing spring and farms and homes," and "the city at hand with dwellings so dense, and stacks of chimneys, / And all the scenes of life and the workshops, and the workmen homeward returning" (Whitman 1982: 462).

How cruelly, however, was Whitman to be disappointed in that vision of a postwar America in which labor, and with it democracy, came into its own. In the event, the war ironically made possible, through the huge boost it had given industrialization, the ways in which it had fostered a centralization of economic and political power, and its creation of a disciplined class of aggressive leaders, a society deeply divided along class lines, and a business culture in which financially bloated industrial tycoons and predatory corporations thrived. In response, an alienated labor force turned in self-defense to weapons, such as unionism and strikes, which Whitman regarded as un-American and of which he deeply disapproved. For him, prose was better suited than poetry to wrestle with such conditions, and in works like *Democratic Vistas* he struggled to keep faith with his vision, focusing on the belief that the social jungle of the Gilded Age would evolve into a society in which all workers would be property owners. But even his most affirmative writing seems now shadowed by darkness. Unable to confront his anxieties directly – to have admitted the depth of his uncertainty about the future of working-class America would have been to begin to doubt the purpose of that hideously destructive war in which he had watched so many young working men die – he found alternative means of expression. In his late, obsessive, passion for Jean François Millet's heroic picture of labor, "The Sower," may be detected both a nostalgia for a lost world of work and perhaps an unspeakable sympathy with the social radicals of the French Revolution. He was particularly shaken by what he called "the tramp and strike question," those worrying symptoms of serious social disorder. Meeting a homeless family on the road, he fails to make out the woman's features under her large bonnet, almost as if he were unwilling to look such suffering in the face. Analogously, he finds it increasingly difficult in his postwar poetry actually to home in on those telling details of working life that, in his prewar poetry, had been incandescent with his belief in the immanent potential of the American laboring classes. Then he had been writing "the evangel-poem of comradeship and love" (Whitman 1982: 179).

He did, however, continue to write a poetry of work, one that tended to be as vague in its rhetoric as it was strident in its optimistic affirmations. Also, by attaching the annexes *Passage to India* and *After All, Not to Create Only* to the postwar (1871) edition of *Leaves of Grass* he continued to try to find means of integrating the best qualities of the old artisanal order with the inventiveness of the new ruthlessly productive economy. Perhaps his most ambitious attempt to spiritualize the postwar nation's frenetic materialism was his commissioned piece for the 1871 National Industrial Exposition, where the Muse is addressed, with somewhat cumbersome irony, as if she were an illustrious immigrant. She is reduced to a gawking visitor awed by the assembled evidence of the New World's superiority to the Old and discerning in it the westward march of civilization. Among the amazements on offer are "the Hoe press whirling its cylinders, shedding the printed leaves steady and fast, / The photograph, model, watch, pin, nail, shall be created before you" (Whitman 1982: 345). But for all its ostensible celebration of modern mass-production, the text occasionally betrays its origins in Whitman's artisanal sympathies, as when he claims the function of the

Exposition is "to teach the average man the glory of his daily walk and trade . . . " (p. 347). And in a reversal of the Cinderella story of old Europe, Whitman amusingly declares that the Muse "is here, installed amid the kitchen ware!" (p. 343)

Behind all this boosterism, however, lie darker imperatives, evident when Whitman uses the Exposition to banish the nightmare of the recent carnage ("Hence from my shuddering sight to never more return that show of blacken'd, mutilated corpses," Whitman 1982: 346). It becomes clear that in the Exposition Whitman finds comforting evidence of the triumph of the democratic United States, a workers' collective, as emblematized by the Union flag ("But I have seen thee, bunting, to tatters torn upon the splinter'd staff," p. 350). And the poem further confesses its origins in anxiety when Whitman hopefully represents the Exposition as a site for reconciliation between polarized classes: "The male and female many laboring not / Shall ever here confront the laboring many / With precious benefit to both, glory to all, / To thee America, and the eternal Muse" (p. 346).

Another interesting, if neglected, instance of Whitman's postwar poetry of labor is "Outlines for a Tomb," which may be briefly described as a recycling of his great elegy to Lincoln in the form of an elegy addressed to that unlikely subject, for Whitman, a businessman. One sign of Whitman's postwar disorientation was his (reciprocated) admiration, in old age, for that hammerer of labor, Andrew Carnegie. But it is to the memory of a businessman of a quite different character, the millionaire philanthropist George Peabody who founded museums at Yale and Harvard, that the poem is dedicated. In a rhetorical turn that repeats the way in which Whitman had imagined decorating the walls of Lincoln's tomb, he here imagines scenes for Peabody's mausoleum. And, as in the case of Lincoln, what he comes up with are scenes from working life – "among the city streets a laborer's home appear'd, / After his day's work done, cleanly, sweet-air'd, the gaslight burning, / The carpet swept and a fire in the cheerful stove" (Whitman 1982: 506). "All, all the shows of laboring life" are conjured up as tribute to the millionaire who had so kindly supplied all the wants of labor, with a magnanimity equal to that of nature itself: "From thee such scenes, thou stintless, lavish giver, / Tallying the gifts of earth, large as the earth, / Thy name an earth, with mountains, fields and tides" (p. 507).

It is a remarkable poem, embarrassing in its effusions if placed next to the great, "Loco-Foco" poetry of the earlier Whitman. But what it represents is an aging man's attempts to believe, in the face of such dire evidence to the contrary as the great railroad strike of 1877 and the Chicago Haymarket riots (1886), that a humane alliance between business and labor was still possible and that in it lay the hope for progress towards a truly democratic American society. Yet as ever Whitman's prose starkly and faithfully registered an altogether different reality, and warned "of the unjust division of wealth-products, and the hoggish monopoly of a few, rolling in superfluity, against the vast bulk of the working people, living in squalor" (Whitman 1982: 1065). Moreover, in 1871 Whitman had included a new section entitled "Songs of Insurrection" in his new edition of *Leaves of Grass* as a protest against "the more and more . . . insidious grip of capital" (*NUPM*, 2: 932).

There was also another disappointment evident towards the end. Whitman had not only wished to write *of* American labor, he had wished to write *for* American labor. But American labor had plainly shown that it was not listening. While Whitman was heartened by the evidence of appreciation that came from such British lower-middle-class supporters of his work as the members of the Bolton Group (who succeeded in creating a public labor day in honor of Whitman that continued to be observed for much of the twentieth century), he was not to live to see how much his poetry would come to matter to Eugene Debs and other leaders of labor in the United States. Nor was he ever to know how important he was to become for several figures influential within the Socialist movement in the British Isles.

Yet, for all his disappointment and bewilderment, Whitman's concern not just for the condition but for the *cause* of labor and the laboring classes never really slackened, alienated though he had become, by the end of his life, from the (to him un-American) forms that the politics of labor had taken, and baffled though he was, at the end, by the class polarities within his society. The writer who, in the 1855 Preface to *Leaves of Grass*, had praised "the noble character of the young mechanics and of all free American workmen and workwomen . . . the general ardor and friendliness and enterprise – the perfect equality of the female with the male . . . the large amativeness" (Whitman 1982: 8) was still reaffirming that vision, that faith, in the very last years of his life:

> Without yielding an inch the working-man and working-woman were to be in my pages from first to last. The ranges of heroism and loftiness with which Greek and feudal poets endow'd their god-like or lordly born characters – indeed prouder and better based and with fuller ranges than those – I was to endow the democratic averages of America. I was to show that we, here and today, are eligible to the grandest and the best – more eligible now than any times of old were. (Whitman 1982: 668)

And if that had been his intention, then such, too, had been his achievement. For all his shortcomings and blindnesses Whitman remains the great Homeric poet of American labor. It is certainly too much to claim, adapting a phrase from that early statement of his in *The New York Democrat*, that "it is to labor that [he] owe[d] everything." But there is surely some truth in the assertion that but for "the democratic averages" he might well not have been a poet at all.

References and Further Reading

Burrows, Edwin G. and Wallace, Mike (2000). *Gotham: A History of New York City to 1898*. Oxford: Oxford University Press.

Erkkila, Betsy (1989). *Whitman the Political Poet*. Oxford: Oxford University Press.

Foster, George G. (1850). *New York by Gas-Light: With Here and There a Streak of Sunshine*. New York: Dewitt & Davenport.

Hodges, Graham (1992). Muscle and Pluck: Walt Whitman's Working-Class Ties. *Seaport*, 26: 32–7.

Lawson, Andrew (2003). "Spending for Vast Returns": Sex, Class and Commerce in the First *Leaves of Grass*. *American Literature*, 15 (2): 335–65.

Thomas, M. Wynn (1987). *The Lunar Light of Whitman's Poetry.* Cambridge, MA: Harvard University Press.

Thomas, M. Wynn (1994). Whitman and the Dreams of Labor. In Ed Folsom (ed.), *Walt Whitman: the Centennial Essays*. Iowa City: University of Iowa Press, pp. 133–52.

Trachtenberg, Alan (1994). The Politics of Labor and the Poet's Work: A Reading of "A Song for Occupations." In Ed Folsom (ed.), *Walt Whitman: The Centennial Essays*. Iowa City: University of Iowa Press, pp. 120–32.

Traubel, Horace ([1904] 1987). *An American Primer by Walt Whitman.* Stevens Point, WI: Holy Cow! Press.

Whitman, Walt (1982). *Whitman: Poetry and Prose*, ed. Justin Kaplan. New York: The Library of America.

Wilentz, Sean (1984). *Chants Democratic: New York City and the Rise of the American Working Class, 1788–1850*. Oxford: Oxford University Press.

5
Politics
Gary Wihl

Walt Whitman's *Democratic Vistas* (1871), a gathering of three essays on voting rights, individualism, and political rhetoric, is one of the most important and overlooked works of American political thought. Comparable to Jefferson's *Notes on the State of Virginia* (1782), Thoreau's *Walden* (1854), or John Dewey's *Freedom and Culture* (1939), it is a passionate vision of American liberty and struggle. Written in a tone of idealism, in the belief that the American political order offers unprecedented, true conditions for citizenship, *Democratic Vistas* is a book about democracy at the level of doctrine. But its reasoning is subtle, complex, and original. Scholars have tried in various ways to reconcile Whitman's expression of democratic doctrine with the issues of slavery and abolition (Higgins 2002, Klammer 1995), tolerance for sexual differences and women's rights (Ceniza 1998), and with strong sentiments about human solidarity across class and social status (Erkkila 1989). Whitman's poetry and journalism offer evidence of his interest in these issues, but not a definitive political position. To get at the heart of Whitman's politics, and its foreshadowing of contemporary political debates about individualism and community, his political writings need to be placed in the canon of nineteenth-century liberalism and Romanticism. The endurance of his political thought rests in his definition of individualism, or personalism, which draws upon the liberal debates of his time, but frames these debates in the language of romantic recollection, sentiment, and imaginative vision. The status of the individual, as a bearer of rights, liberties, and the source of our culture's rich pluralism, continues to be at the center of much contemporary political theory. Whitman anticipates many of these debates and is relevant to contemporary reformulations of the issues of individualism in modern democracy.

Whitman's prescience is remarkable. He focuses upon fundamental problems of an emerging democracy, not only in his concern that citizens learn to appreciate the full implications of becoming enfranchised but in his grasp of the basic principle of individualism. The "basic structure of future literature and authorship" in a democracy is:

> the origin-idea of the singleness of man, individualism, asserting itself, and cropping forth, even from the opposite ideas. But the mass, or lump character, for imperative reasons, is to be ever carefully weigh'd, borne in mind, and provided for. Only from it, and from its proper regulation and potency, comes the other, comes the chance of individualism. The two are contradictory, but our task is to reconcile them. (*PW*, 2: 373)

Much of *Democratic Vistas* is an unfolding of the meaning of this dense quotation, as Whitman tracks back and forth between the political capacity of individualism to sweep away all the customs and traditions of the literary past, yet find itself confronted with uncertainty, instability, and an edge of social chaos. More than his contemporaries like Matthew Arnold, Whitman never abandoned faith in the individual, never reducing it merely to egoism or self-interest or "doing as one likes" (see Weisbuch 1986, McGuire 2001). Rather, he maintains a clear focus on the need to reconstruct a different political order, one that has yet to be imagined:

> I submit, therefore, that the fruition of democracy, on aught like a grand scale, resides altogether in the future. As, under any profound and comprehensive view of the gorgeous-composite feudal world, we see in it, through the long ages and cycles of ages, the results of a deep, integral, human and divine principle . . . so, long ages hence, shall the due historian or critic make at least an equal retrospect, an equal history for the democratic principle. (*PW*, 2: 390)

Every aspect of Whitman's politics rests on his projection of democratic individuality. The main barrier to its realization is its sheer originality, and the commentators who have taken on that problem of that originality, George Kateb and Richard Rorty, have offered the best insights into Whitman's politics. Whitman's capacity to imagine a new political order, working through all the paradoxes of individuality, may appear to be an abstract exercise, removed from the more immediate political pressures of Reconstruction exploitation, of poverty, of irregular voting practices, or of ongoing racism and gender inequality. In his journalism, diaries, and in other prose writings and passages, Whitman chooses to write about very concrete problems. As a poet, he most often expresses frustration with "hacks" and "blatherers," who tear down the fabric of democracy with cynicism:

> It is the fashion among dillettants and fops . . . to decry the whole formulation of the active politics of America, as beyond redemption, and to be carefully kept away from. See you that you do not fall into this error. America, it may be, is doing very well upon the whole, notwithstanding these antics of the parties and their leaders . . . (*PW*, 2: 399)

In large part, the contribution of the poets and novelists to a democracy consists in raising the level of speech about liberty, personality, and shedding the limitations of the feudal past. The lofty tone of Whitman's own rhetoric and poetry is a conscious effort to displace political slogans and the manipulation of public opinion. On this topic, he is equally prescient about the risks contained in democratic speech – as evident in today's political discourse as it was in Whitman's time. But for Whitman the rhetorical battle over democratic values returns to the imaginative grasp of the wholly original meaning of the democratic individual. His politics cannot be understood apart from the poetic expression of individuality, and individuality, as a fragile political concept, finds some of its most practical formulations in the vocabulary of sentiment, natural beauty, and personal dignity.

George Kateb's essays on Walt Whitman (collected and revised in his book *The Inner Ocean*) serve as an excellent point of departure for assessing the fate of individualism today and for seeing how it is intertwined with Romanticism and liberalism. It is fair to say that Kateb is the most forceful exponent of individualism among contemporary political philosophers. Far from retreating from a strong position on individual rights, Kateb argues, we have barely begun to grasp the meaning of rights in the lives of individuals and the forms of association that may arise from individuals in a democracy. Kateb writes:

> To speak, therefore, of individualism is to speak of the most characteristically democratic political and moral commitment. It would be a sign of defection from modern democracy to posit some other entity as the necessary or desirable center of life. There is therefore nothing special (much less, arbitrary) in assuming that the doctrine of the individual has the preeminent place in the theory of democracy... Any philosophical consideration of the individual (or the person or "subject") which does not take this contribution [of the work of Emerson, Thoreau, and Whitman] into account simply ignores the richest set of ideas belonging to the field. (Kateb 1992: 78)

Kateb believes that we have not yet absorbed the complexity of Emerson, Thoreau, or Whitman into discussions of democracy.

To see how individuality becomes a political way of life, the best means of insuring justice and freedom, and to see what Kateb means by the project of individualism and its episodic nature, we have to turn back to the poetry and prose of Whitman. In Whitman, we have the imaginative portrayal of the state of individuality, but this imaginative portrayal raises questions and issues that touch on the topic of "adhesion" or free association between individuals at the level of collective action. At the level of abstract individuality, or "composite" individuality as Whitman says in the 1872 Preface to *Leaves of Grass*, care is required for the correct interpretation of expressions of fulfillment and personal growth. Is an abstract, poetical expression of composite individuality sufficiently robust to compete with the political discourse of cultural solidarity and collective expressions of virtue and religious belief? What are the positive attributes of composite individualism?

As we look more carefully at Kateb's definition of individuality within a democratic society, three categories of expression emerge. These expressive categories ultimately refer to the Romantic structure of the great poems that Whitman wrote between 1855 and 1860, his peak of poetic creativity, during which time he produced three editions of *Leaves of Grass*. The poems that mark Whitman's greatest expressions of individuality include "As I Ebb'd With the Ocean of Life" (1860), "Crossing

Brooklyn Ferry" (1856), "By Blue Ontario's Shore" (1856), and "Out of the Cradle Endlessly Rocking" (1859). These poems express the multiplication of selfhood and identity characteristic of Whitman's most complex poetry, but contain this multiplicity with reference to the task of expressing one's individuality. These poems stand as great poetic achievements, the aesthetic equal of some of the greatest British Romantic lyrics written by Wordsworth or Shelley.

For the comparison to Wordsworth, scholars of Whitman are indebted to the work of Harold Bloom (Bloom 1976). As the leading interpreter of English Romantic verse of his generation, Bloom has made a convincing case that Whitman is best read against the background of the Wordsworthian lyric. Whitman does not need the comparison to Wordsworth in order to claim the canonical status of the American poet of democracy, but Bloom's comparison reinforces Kateb's intuition that there is a complex movement of self-expression in Whitman's poetry. The work of Bloom and other literary critics make the Romantic strain within those lyrical movements clearer. The Romantic, specifically Wordsworthian, context illuminates the categories that Kateb uses to read Whitman. Kateb's expressive scheme of individualism bears a certain resemblance to the structures of the Romantic lyric as it has been mapped by M. H. Abrams and Harold Bloom.

Individualism's dialectic of withdrawal, concentration of self, and openness to the plenitude of human being also have affinities with the Romantic sources of liberalism as they have been mapped by Nancy Rosenblum (Rosenblum 1987). Whitman, Emerson, and Thoreau have slowly emerged as the canonical voices of individualism, at the center of a distinct American tradition, the voices of exceptional commitment, who fascinate other students of liberal Romanticism, such as Judith Shklar or Stanley Cavell. But we need to keep Bloom's perspective on these writers in mind. Canons are made from other canons. Whitman had to appropriate certain features of Romanticism, to take over the structure of the Romantic lyric, in order to achieve what now stands out as his clearest expression of individualism as the foundation of American democracy. A key component of Kateb's formulation of democratic individuality is the poetical loss of self in Whitman, or impersonality, which is the most democratic moment of self, in its capacity to see the spectrum of humanity in oneself through the lens of equality, captured in Whitman's line "I contain multitudes" (*LG*: 88). Whitman holds the poetical vision of citizenship.

Whitman refers to Mill's *On Liberty* in the opening paragraphs of his greatest prose tract on democracy, *Democratic Vistas*, but Kateb believes that Whitman went astray at that moment. Whitman's best insights into composite individuality have little to do with Mill's defense of eccentricity:

> Mill's grand (third) chapter on individuality may contaminate Whitman's thinking . . . an individual should try not to acquire or retain an identity (in the wrong spirit). I mean that a democratic individual, if he or she is to be true to the spirit of democracy, should not (on the one hand) aspire to become a shaped presence, like a work of art . . . or (on the other hand) try to disclose one's true "genius." (Kateb 1992: 257)

Strangely enough, this is a very good reading of Whitman. I want to emphasize the justness of Kateb's emphasis. He is right to quip that no one, even in 1855, was particularly interested in Walt Whitman the person. "Song of Myself," in its earlier versions, contained very little autobiographical interest for its readers. Similarly, Kateb is right to assert that Whitman works in an area of literature far away from the novelist, the writer of story and character: "He is not a novelist or a sponsor of novelists whose ultimate reality is well-rounded characters" (Kateb 1992: 246).

The great lyrics and many sections from "Song of Myself" refer to a soul, a real me, an infinite multiplicity of selves, what could be fairly called a democratic genius. About the time that Whitman composed *Democratic Vistas* he was immersed in reading German idealist philosophy. More of his writings on Kant, Fichte, Schelling, and Hegel are coming to light even today. These writings back up Rorty's claim, in *Achieving Our Country* (Rorty 1998: 14–32), that Whitman is the great secularist of American cultural politics, the author who displaces God in the American Transcendental tradition with a fully articulated concept of secular humanist individualism. More than any other contemporary reader of Whitman, Rorty argues for a fully secularized politics, even finding secularism at the heart of some of Whitman's most mystical sounding utterances (see also Mack 2002). Rorty writes, "Whitman and Dewey were among the prophets of this civic religion. They offered a new account of what America was ... The most striking feature of their redescription of our country is its thoroughgoing secularism" (1998: 15). By secularism Rorty means no source of authority outside human politics, no reference to the God's eye point of view over human affairs, and as a consequence, no sense of shame, fault, or guilt that would impede the search for dignified coexistence. In the spirit of Whitman's individualism, Rorty suggests that we embrace democracy as the capacity for self-improvement, unimpeded by traditional concepts of punishment, retribution, and as a continuous testing of new forms of self-expression. He writes, following Whitman, "To say that the United States themselves are essentially the greatest poem is to say that America will create the taste by which it will be judged. It is to envisage our nation-state as both self-creating poet and self-created poem" (p. 29). The newness of political freedom, the fact that is not fully felt, preoccupies Rorty as much as it did Whitman in *Democratic Vistas*. The failure of democracy is quite literally a failure of imagination.

The problem is that Whitman's real me, like the Hegelian spirit, never settles on one type of individual but rather hovers over or enters into the laborer, farmer, sailor, husband, wife, the lover's physical body, or the crowd on the streets of Brooklyn or Manhattan. It has no real shape but is rather best seen in the pattern of its development. What is this abstract level of impersonal, secular, Romantic selfhood referred to by Whitman's poetry? How does Whitman's poetry of individualism work so well despite its high level of abstraction? How can these powerfully secular, impersonal elements in the poetry be joined to paradigms of Romantic expression? And would this joining restore the necessary robustness to the liberal definition of individuality? Whitman's great lyric poems sustain the initial hypothesis that abstract, or composite, individualism may be capable of a robust formulation after all. Individualism cannot be reduced to personality, psychology, or atomism. By the same token, to stick to the vocabulary of soul, infinite inwardness, the great potential of each and every human being, produces a rather flat, empty-sounding political discourse.

Nancy Rosenblum, one of Kateb's most astute students, tries to make political sense of this play of voices and roles. She is particularly interested in how the liberal self is developed from an array of relations in diverse spheres that is part and parcel of Romanticism. By casting Romanticism as the precursor of contemporary pluralism, Rosenblum rebuilds Kateb's concept of the democratic individual in Whitman's writings. Instead of experiencing different kinds of concentration or interiority of self, democratic individuality, coming jointly out of a Romantic splitting of the self and a liberal respect for the self, produces an array of spheres of attachment, what Rosenblum calls involvements among plural spheres. Neutrality and detachment retain their importance in legal definitions of the individual's rights, and they remain in play in procedural and institutional settings. But with the whole idea of spheres suddenly in focus, there is room enough for neutral legal procedures and a variety of poetic figures of selfhood.

Romanticism is a vast topic, but there is a definite congruence between Kateb's democratic individual, Rosenblum's Romantic self caught up in distinct political spheres, and Harold Bloom's extraordinary interpretation of the Romantic strain in Whitman going back to Wordsworth. At this critical juncture, where all these lines of investigation converge on Whitman's poetry, the devil is in the details. Only careful attention to the poetry itself can determine the ultimate shape of these variously reconstructed liberal-Romantic canons.

Rosenblum's emphasis on the intersection between Romanticism and liberalism is essential to our understanding of Whitman's politics today. She goes much further than Kateb in assessing the play of Romantic and liberal elements in writers such as Humboldt, Mill, Constant, or Hegel. Her frame of analysis is much wider than Kateb's, who sticks closely to the exceptional elements of the American tradition of liberalism. Rosenblum takes us back into the world of character and personality, which Kateb purposefully limits, in order to get at the essence of democratic individuality. Multiple attachments, competing but separate spheres of social life, a generous and tolerant pluralism, are where she situates the best examples of Romantic and liberal thought. It is a powerful and impressive synthesis of two traditions. But how well does it help us understand Whitman? The truly abstract nature of individualism needs to be worked through before it can be remade as a feature of modern-day democratic pluralism. The terms of Romanticism and liberalism need to be broken down and recombined. As traditions, they point the discussion in the right direction. As terms that modify and correct the triad of voices in a Whitman poem, be it Bloom's or Kateb's, they are too broad to engage the poetic material. The poetic language of abstraction imposes very special burdens of interpretation that cannot be captured in psychology of character. Whitman's sort of poetry is a good place to look for that vocabulary.

For the sake of economy, I'm going to analyze a pair of poems: Wordsworth's "Composed upon Westminster Bridge, September 3, 1802" and Whitman's "Crossing

Brooklyn Ferry." This pairing, however, can be and should be extended to other examples where Whitman appears to be responding to or rewriting some of the dominant tropes of Wordsworthian Romanticism. Other examples for future analysis would include Wordsworth's "Ode. Intimations of Immortality from Recollections of Early Childhood," the paradigmatic Romantic crisis poem, and Whitman's "Out of the Cradle Endlessly Rocking," portions of *The Prelude* and "Song of Myself" and "By Blue Ontario's Shore."

In Wordsworth's sonnet, composed upon Westminster Bridge, the city lies sleeping before the poet as the sun rises. The beauty of the poem, of the early morning scene of London, lies in the stillness of everything. The "Ships, towers, domes, theatres, and temples lie / Open" just as "the very houses seem asleep / And all that mighty heart is lying still." The conceit of the poem is to compare the turbulent, busy cityscape to a powerful natural impression, an organic image of circulation, sleep, and tranquility. Many of the typical elements of Wordsworthian Romanticism are present in this neat little poem. The use of a specific time and place as a moment of spiritual revelation in stillness; a mirroring of inner and outer states which crisscross each other (the whole city is like one person, with one mighty heart, even as the poet speaks in his own proper person when he writes "Ne'er saw I, never felt, a calm so deep!"); a shifting perspective from visual impression to a depth of feeling connected to "soul." The expression of depth of feeling among the elements of a broad social vista was a device that Wordsworth perfected. It defines one of the major conventions of English Romantic verse in its sincerity, tranquility, and attachment to ordinary, common experience. What the poet feels, anyone could feel: "Dull would he be of soul who could pass by / A sight so touching in its majesty." This kind of poem is one of the sources of that transparency of self, concentration of self (though not connected to Thoreau here), and impersonality that fascinates liberal theorists. Wordsworth speaks of an I, of a soul, of a God in this poem and all of these terms stand in a smooth relationship to each other. The revelation of depth within the individual is the main theme of the poem and it occurs in very specific moments that balance between stillness and spontaneity, this moment, this day, this bridge. A great deal of scholarship has gone into deciphering the delicate components of Romantic verse that set it apart from earlier genres, such as its individuality and concreteness and its effort to share the experience of depth of feeling. After all, it is the beauty of London, its vast scale of activity, that contains and builds that mighty heart. But beyond the figural exchange of inner depth and outer stillness, a powerful trope of Romantic verse, what more can we say about the first person voice of the poem? In achieving its depth, presumably that feature that it has in common with all other not dull souls, the poet has done his work.

If we were to call this poem democratic, it could only be in the vague sense in which we assume that everyone has the potential for depth of feeling. Everyone has the capacity to experience beauty in the ordinary, because the object of admiration here is not some special aesthetic object, some Grecian urn, but simple, clear sensation.

In Whitman's "Crossing Brooklyn Ferry," the Wordsworthian tropes are reassembled. Whitman's poem could not have been written without the conventions invented by Wordsworth. But there is a radical shift of emphasis. Whitman's poem is explicitly democratic, most important of all in the terms attached to the poetic I. Where Wordsworth empties the scene to capture depth in tranquility, Whitman crams the scene of the ferry crossing the Hudson to Manhattan with crowds of people. The burden of the poetic I in Whitman's verse is to absorb and reflect the crowds, not to transcend them for the sake of some higher vision of soul. Like Wordsworth, Whitman writes a poem in celebration of a joyful, emotional vision. Like Wordsworth, Whitman includes in his poem a picture of beautiful commerce and urbanization. Looking upon the ferries crossing the Hudson, Whitman sees a blending of waves, reflected sunlight, and geometric patterns, the tremulous whirl of steamboat wheels, round masts, swinging hulls, slender serpentine pennants, thick-stemm'd steamboat pipes. But every stanza is suffused with the masses: men and women of generations, the living crowd, the ties between the me and the them, or, most abstractly, others who will be hence fifty or a hundred years from the writing of the poem, the similitude of the past and the future. So there is a fairly huge rhythmical motion to the poem, involving commercial activities, human masses, the motion of the river and sunlight, and a glittering array of sights that signal continuity between past and future. The combination of delight, acceptance of the masses, and prosperity and growth are distinctly optimistic themes; as in his prose writings, Whitman's poetry asserts a belief in progress. The assertion of progress is a deliberate rhetorical tactic, aimed against the cynics, political frauds, and hacks, who, Whitman believed, posed a real threat to the fledgling democratic institutions of his day. Whitman's explicit intention was to overcome the publicity of degradation, pessimism, and humiliation – which he saw as the evils of republican discourse. (In this respect he exerts a great influence on a more contemporary poet of democracy, Robert Penn Warren.) But what has he put together, as poet, that bears complex scrutiny? What stamps the poem as a complex scenario, capable of articulating in fine terms the legitimacy of the democratic individual?

Whitman's poem works because it defines in rather precise, *nongeneric* terms, degrees of fit between fundamentally distinct individuals. That articulation could not be sustained strictly on the level of formal rhythm or in a poetic form found in Wordsworth. When Whitman personifies nature, as in the line that describes the spokes that radiate from reflections of the human face upon the river, the spokes do not recall a greater stage of personhood, but merely the lines of connection to other, equal persons. The labor of the poem is to reach a sufficient degree of formal coherence without resort to a generic vocabulary of singular democratic soul. The combination of compressed coherence of statement with an ever-shifting, nongeneric depiction of individual relationships joins poetic expression to a democratic, political purpose. Whitman's is the voice of nongeneric, emergent individuality that expresses itself in a multitude of relationships that cannot be determined at some final resting point but must be redetermined, over and over again. This point is quite crucial to the way the poetry works. Consider this selection of lines from the poem:

> It is not upon you alone the dark patches fall,
> The dark threw its patches down upon me also,
> The best I had done seem'd to me blank and suspicious,
> My great thoughts as I supposed them, were they not in reality meagre? [. . .]
> I too knitted the old knot of contrariety [. . .]
> Refusals, hates, postponements, meanness, laziness, none of these wanting [. . .]
> The same old role, the role that is what we make it, as great as we like,
> Or as small as we like, or both great and small
> [. . .]
> Play the old role, the role that is great or small according as one makes it!
> Consider, you who peruse me, whether I may not in unknown ways be looking upon you.
> (*LG*: 221–2, 224)

These lines are rather vague in meaning but can be adapted to a broad spectrum of readers; more than that, they will be reshaped and redefined by new sets of readers. To the extent that this sort of poetry is capable of being refined rather than summarized, it does the work for which it was intended. Part of the work of realizing multiple forms of social coherence involves this sort of poetic articulation of various points of resemblance and difference. The vocabulary is abstract, nonreferential, but capable of being used to point to various combinations of social recognition. Whitman's name for that fluctuating but precise project of recognition is democracy. Kateb rightly calls it an episodic project, and rightly sees that it works at some level beyond personality. In asking the reader to determine over and over again the relative coherence of individuals, Whitman makes it difficult to equate democratic individuality with one intrinsic property of human beings, say for example their depth of soul, or reflective consciousness. Individuation is difficult work; it is not a given state that can be described or defined in one set of ethical terms.

In the discipline of literary criticism, the merits and interpretive complexity of poems and other formally complex genres of writing do not equate with concrete descriptions of facts. Description itself is one category of language, often in play with rhetoric, narrative conventions, devices of sound, and the visual *mise en page*. When the interpretive stakes are very high, as in poetry that claims political relevance, or in poets like Whitman who belong to debates about key political concepts of individualism, it is tempting to go back to the primacy of description. My point is that Whitman may not be describing one thing called the liberal individual, but rather using formal poetic devices to capture the work of individuation that is much closer to the robust individualism that liberals like Kateb and Rosenblum defend. Whitman may show us that the weakest defense would be to turn the individual into a generic term for a set of innate human properties or legal fiction of complete disinterestedness. Literary criticism can further the project of liberalism by adding depth to the definition of individualism without turning it into metaphysics. Here Rorty's contribution to Whitman studies fits in.

A quotation from Steven Knapp's book, *Literary Interest* (Knapp 1993), may clarify the sort of democratic project contained in Whitman's poetry. Knapp is particularly helpful in connecting the insights of literary analysis to the best features of the liberal, democratic project. Knapp writes:

> There may be another way . . . to explain why a single complex scenario [a shorthand term for a work of literature] should seem to possess an unusual moral interest. A number of philosophers have recently denied that ethical claims are grounded either in an objective moral reality or in necessary conditions of practical reasoning; instead, these philosophers argue, the only plausible ground of ethical values is "people's dispositions" . . . if dispositionalists are right, then our values derive from dispositions that can go wrong only by conflicting with other, stronger (or perhaps deeper) dispositions . . . Perhaps, then, the moral benefit of literary interest lies not in any capacity to tell us which values are the right ones, but far more modestly, in the way it helps us find out what our evaluative dispositions are. Perhaps a complex scenario sets up a kind of experiment in which we test not the moral worth of one scenario against another one . . . but the relative strengths of our own responses to the alternative scenarios. (Knapp 1993: 100)

There are many strands of argument in this dense quotation. Knapp believes we are more or less thrown into a world of competing values and beliefs and gradually acquire the dispositions that enable us to live in a "modern, Western, liberal, quasi-democratic form of life." Which is not to say that values are randomly significant, or randomly dropped or acquired, but rather that they are not self-evident or intrinsically valuable. Having the disposition to fight slavery or colonialism or legal injustice has something to do with the way you are put together as a specific person. Entering the arena of moral or political conflict, therefore, is part of tracing and developing the central values that define the individuals that we are.

> The kind of person we happen to value – by no means the kind of person valued at every time in every human society – is the kind that wants to check itself out, know how it feels, be aware of its inconsistencies, whether or not fixing them is either possible or desirable. Whether or not its particular choices and actions are the right ones from some external perspective, we might just say that such a person fits in better with our . . . quasi-democratic form of life. (Knapp 1993: 101)

The task of reading literature is placed upon the task of fitting oneself to a democratic form of life, and that task cannot be articulated in generic terms; it can only be articulated as contradictions, inconsistencies, particular choices, beliefs, and convictions. Knapp's account of the moral function of literature fits very well with the kind of poetry Whitman writes and with the kind of liberalism that it supports.

References and Further Reading

Adolph, Robert (1995). Whitman, Tocqueville, and the Language of Democracy. In Donald E. Morse (ed.), *The Delegated Intellect: Emersonian Essays on Literature, Science, and Art in Honor of Don Gifford*. New York: Peter Lang, pp. 65–88.

Beach, Christopher (1996). *The Politics of Distinction: Whitman and the Discourses of Nineteenth-Century America*. Athens: University of Georgia Press.

Bloom, Harold (1976). American Poetic Stances. In *Wallace Stevens: The Poems of our Climate*. Ithaca, NY: Cornell University Press, pp. 1–26.

Cavell, Stanley (1994). *This New Yet Unapproachable America: Essays after Emerson after Wittgenstein (Frederick Ives Carpenter Lectures, 1987)*. Albuquerque, NM: Long Batch Books.

Ceniza, Sherry (1998). *Walt Whitman and Nineteenth-Century Women Reformers*. Tuscaloosa, AL: University of Alabama Press.

Erkkila, Betsy (1989). *Whitman the Political Poet*. New York: Oxford University Press.

Higgins, Andrew C. (2002). Wage Slavery and the Composition of *Leaves of Grass*: The "Talbot Wilson" Notebook. *Walt Whitman Quarterly Review*, 20: 53–77.

Kateb, George (1992). *The Inner Ocean. Individualism and Democratic Culture*. Ithaca, NY: Cornell University Press.

Klammer, Martin (1995). *Whitman, Slavery, and the Emergence of Leaves of Grass*. University Park: Pennsylvania State University Press.

Knapp, Steven (1993). *Literary Interest. The Limits of Anti-Formalism*. Cambridge, MA: Harvard University Press.

Mack, Stephen John (2002). *The Pragmatic Whitman: Reimagining American Democracy*. Iowa City: University of Iowa Press.

McGuire, Ian (2001). Culture and Antipathy: Arnold, Emerson and *Democratic Vistas*. *Symbiosis*, 5: 577–84.

Rorty, Richard (1998). American National Pride: Whitman and Dewey. In *Achieving Our Country: Leftist Thought in Twentieth-Century America*. Cambridge, MA: Harvard University Press, pp. 1–38.

Rosenblum, Nancy (1987). *Another Liberalism. Romanticism and the Reconstruction of Liberal Thought*. Cambridge, MA: Harvard University Press.

Warren, Robert Penn (1975). *Democracy and Poetry*. Cambridge, MA: Harvard University Press.

Weisbuch, Robert (1986). *Atlantic Double-Cross*. Chicago: University of Chicago Press.

6
Oratory

J. R. LeMaster

In an article entitled "Whitman's Voice in 'Song of Myself': From Private to Public," Donald D. Kummings (1971) compares "Song of Myself" in the 1855 edition of *Leaves of Grass* to the same poem as printed in the 1891–2 edition and maintains that the later version became more oratorical than poetic. Citing earlier work by such people as Roger Asselineau and Roy Harvey Pearce, Kummings concludes, "[A] decided oratorical element finds its way into the Deathbed version of 'Song of Myself'" (p. 11). Further, says Kummings, in the later edition Whitman offers the reader "a mythic, cosmic self" (p. 13). However, he senses a conundrum and writes, "The difficulty in dealing with Whitman is that no matter what thesis one proffers or advances, evidence to the contrary may be found" (p. 15). And he is right. Reading Whitman is like reading the Bible. There are about as many interpretations as there are interpreters.

In the case of oratory (Whitman's lifelong interest in and use of), much has also been written, the best and the most of which written in the twentieth century was by C. Carroll Hollis. Hollis's book *Language and Style in "Leaves of Grass"* (1983) is a masterly treatment of the subject, as are such of his articles as "The Oratorical Stance and Whitman's Early Poetry," "Rhetoric, Elocution, and Voice in *Leaves of Grass*: A Study in Affiliation," and "Is There a Text in This Grass?," the latter a response to an article by Mark Bauerlein entitled "The Written Orator of 'Song of Myself.'" The chief difference between the two seems to be over whether Whitman was a fake or true prophet, not over Hollis's speech act theory or the issue of oratory in general.

Like Ralph Waldo Emerson, Whitman tried to move away from the rigid conventions of classical oratory – to loosen it up and make it democratic. Politicians were doing it, churchmen were doing it, social reformers were doing it, and there was no reason why poets should not do it. It was happening in theatre, in music, and in the other arts. Whitman was enamored with a powerful platform performance, as indicated by everyone who has written on Whitman and oratory since Thomas B. Harned, who wrote the first manuscript study of Whitman's interest in oratory. In his "Emerson's Stylistic Influence on Whitman," Donald Ross writes,

"A common stylistic base . . . affected both Emerson's essays and Whitman's verse: mid-nineteenth-century American *oratory.* Emerson made his living by giving speeches. Whitman heard Emerson lecture . . . and hoped to be an orator during the mid-1850's" (1975: 47). For a more detailed discussion of how both Whitman and Emerson were children of their times, as well as how Emerson influenced Whitman, see Jerome Loving's (1982) book *Emerson, Whitman, and the American Muse.* David Warren Shawn's 1998 Boston University dissertation "The Transformation of Oratory in Antebellum America: Democrats, Demagogues, and the Quest for Citizenship" provides evidence of what happened to oratory in the early part of the nineteenth century. Illuminating commentary can also be found in James Perrin Warren's (1999) book *Culture of Eloquence: Oratory and Reform in Antebellum America.* Finally, for abundant evidence concerning the changing estate of oratory, see Gregory Clark and S. Michael Halloran's *Oratorical Culture in Nineteenth-Century America: Transformations in the Theory and Practice of Rhetoric* (1993).

A recent writer who has influenced my thinking about Whitman, and therefore about oratory, is the philosopher Richard Rorty. In his book *Contingency, Irony, and Solidarity,* Rorty writes about Sigmund Freud, "He has provided us with a moral psychology which is compatible with Nietzsche's and Bloom's attempt to see the strong poet as the archetypal human being" (1989: 34). Suffice it to say that Whitman – in the 1855 preface, in *Democratic Vistas* (1871), and in numerous poems and prose pieces – does the same thing. Rorty paraphrases from Michael Oakeshott's book *On Human Conduct* (1975): "We can keep the notion of 'morality' just insofar as we can cease to think of morality as the voice of the divine part of ourselves" (Rorty 1989: 59). Rorty's world, of course, is a postmodern one; Whitman's was not. Considerable evidence suggests that Whitman was not ready to discard the idea of the divine, nor was he willing to discard the idea of morality. As for Rorty's "strong poet," one must keep in mind Rorty's commitment to a liberal society in a postmodern world, which is not the same as nineteenth-century liberalism. Nevertheless, I do see similarities between Rorty's "strong poet" and Whitman's "poet-prophet."

Was Whitman a poet-prophet? The "poet" part obviously does not need an answer. The "prophet" part, however, does. In "Is There a Text in This Grass?," C. Carroll Hollis questions Mark Bauerlein's contention in "The Written Orator of 'Song of Myself'" that Whitman either was a prophet or at least thought of himself as one. In his article Bauerlein writes, "Whitman desires his readers to view him as the 'bard' amalgamating society through the exhilarating attraction of inspired oration" (1986: 3). Bauerlein, contends Hollis, sees Whitman as "true prophet," but Hollis, of course, does not. The latter writes:

> Although Walt admired the passionate directness and intensity of Elias Hicks and Rev. Edward Taylor (Melville's Father Mapple), he wanted to imitate their outward illocutionary style and not their inward convictions. I find nothing in Whitman's life to indicate that he was a true prophet. But there is much, both in the workbooks and in the poetry, to show that he wanted to sound like one. (Hollis 1986: 17–18)

The implication of Hollis's conclusion here seems to be that Whitman was a con artist – a trickster. I would add, however, that as far as Whitman's oratory is concerned the issue is not whether Hollis sees him as a prophet, but rather how Whitman views himself. I agree with Hollis that there is much in the notebooks and the poems to demonstrate that Whitman wanted to sound like a prophet – like Elias Hicks or Edward Taylor, both of whom Whitman admired greatly, and to a large extent because they were great orators. On the other hand, I do not agree that this precludes Whitman from considering himself a "poet-prophet." On the contrary, the tone of his many writings on oratory – including those in Harned's "Walt Whitman and Oratory" – as well as the tone of poems in *Leaves of Grass* and the tone of the prose pieces collected in volume two of *Prose Works 1892* all point to the fact that he did. I simply do not believe that any one who wrote as much as Whitman, and for as long as Whitman, can sustain the seriousness of tone that Whitman maintained merely to deceive people.

Much has been written on Whitman and oratory, and much that has been written has been repeated. Here I would like to avoid such issues as how much Whitman borrowed from other sources to incorporate into his manuscript notes on oratory. For this issue one can see William L. Finkel's (1950) "Walt Whitman's Manuscript Notes on Oratory." I would also like to avoid a detailed analysis of Whitman's speech acts, including the illocutionary, Whitman's use of negation, and other such devices as metaphor and metonymy. Hollis has done a thorough job on these in his book *Language and Style in "Leaves of Grass."* Nor do I want to take up what Hollis calls Whitman's use of "dots" to mark rhetorical pauses in his poems, and how the dots gave way to commas as Whitman's poems became less "speech based"; that is, when the early poems, what Hollis calls the "platform poems," gave way to poems written for publication. Hollis also handles these things well in "Rhetoric, Elocution, and Voice in *Leaves of Grass*." However, not all who have written about Whitman's poetry agree with Hollis's assessment that oratory gave way to poetry after the 1860 edition of *Leaves of Grass*, or even after the Civil War. As I pointed out earlier, Donald D. Kummings compares the 1855 and 1891–2 editions of "Song of Myself" and declares the latter edition more oratorical than poetic. If Kummings's observation is true of the other poems in the 1891–2 edition, one must question Hollis's observation. Bauerlein seems not to agree, at least not entirely. He says that Whitman uses "open addresses" to "inject his speaking presence into the poem" (1986: 5). Whether Bauerlein is right or not, and I think he is, the critics generally agree that something happened to Whitman around the time of publication of the 1860 edition to cause him to shift his emphasis from oratory to poetry.

Let us turn at this point to Thomas B. Harned's essay "Walt Whitman and Oratory," the first treatment of the topic. Harned's observations have been discussed ever since they were published in volume five of *The Complete Writings of Walt Whitman* in 1902. Over the years I have read suggestions that Harned, as a friend and disciple of Walt Whitman, could not be expected to be objective. I have also read suggestions to the contrary. This should not be surprising since people who write about Whitman have very different views of Whitman the man and Whitman the poet. Some rely heavily upon biography to assess the poems, and some rely heavily upon the poems to assess the man. Vincent J. Bertolini (2002) discusses this issue as it relates to sex, sexuality, and homosexuality, for example, in a well-researched and brilliantly written article entitled "'Hinting' and 'Reminding': The Rhetoric of Performative Embodiment in *Leaves of Grass*."

Harned said Walt Whitman possessed "many of the attributes of a great orator" (1902: 244). Then he lists those things that he said qualified Whitman to be successful on the platform:

> His build, his commanding stature, his exceptional health of mind and body, his highly developed moral and emotional nature, his courage, firmness, and resolution, his creative imagination, the grace of his movements and gestures, the magnetism of his presence, the cheery, ringing, clarion voice, his sense of harmony, his freedom from conventions, his originality of thought and statement, his sympathy with humanity, the personal conviction that he had an important message to convey to the American people, and his determination that he should be heard. (Harned 1902: 244)

This is indeed an impressive list of characteristics that one would wish on any orator. As generally recognized by Whitman scholars and students, however, there were people who attended the few lectures that Whitman actually gave who greatly disagreed with Harned's assessment of Whitman's qualifications to be a platform speaker.

The issue of Whitman's performance as a platform speaker, for some scholars, has colored their assessment of his written work. One thing in the above quotation on which scholars seem to agree is that Whitman believed he had an important message he needed to communicate to the American people – and that he was determined he would be heard. Harned continues by saying that Whitman produced many notes and suggestions on oratory, that early on he studied public speaking, and that he proposed to present his "message" from the platform – and this all before his plan to reach his audience through print (1902: 244). Harned maintains that he himself obtained his material from a sheaf marked "Oratory" and that "[t]hese notes constitute a text-book of more than common comprehensiveness upon the subject of public speaking" (p. 245). Then for some 15 pages Harned produces selected quotations from Whitman's notes. For example, in an apparent allusion to himself as orator, Whitman notes, "Washington made free the body of America for that was first in order. Now comes one who will make free the American soul" (quoted p. 245). About the relationship of the speaker and his listener, Whitman writes, "The place of the orator and his hearer is truly an agonistic arena. There he wrestles and contends with them – he suffers, sweats, undergoes his great toil and ecstasy. Perhaps it is a greater battle than any fought for by contending forces on land and sea" (quoted pp. 245–6). Harned quotes extensively on the matter of gesture, in a small fragment of which Whitman declares: "Restrain and curb gesture. Not too much gesture. Animation and life may be shown in a speech by great feeling in voice and look. Interior gesture, which is perhaps better than exterior gesture" (quoted

p. 246). Harned also quotes Whitman on the use of the face and other parts of the body in communicating with a listening audience: "Animation of limbs, hands, arms, neck, shoulders, waist, open breast, &c. – the fullest type of live oratory – at times an expanded chest, at other times reaching forward, bending figure, raised to the fullest height, bending way over, low down &c" (quoted p. 247). On the matter of style, Whitman writes "[T]here should be no hasty thrusting of one word or thought before the preceding words or thoughts have had time to alight and remain upon all the hearers." In the same quotation Whitman says that it is a critical thing in oratory "to preserve a style as if held by a strong hand, a determined, not hurried, not too pouring style of vocalism, but yet animated and live with full swelling, serious life" (quoted p. 247). Before he is through, Harned selects quotations from Whitman's notes addressing all the concerns a successful orator could possibly raise. In his study of oratory Whitman attended plays, operas, public lectures, concerts, singings, and many other events making use of the voice. Furthermore, he wrote about the voices of his favorite actors, opera singers, and others, including popular singers – searching for "the perfect voice." According to Harned, Whitman also studied the Greek masters, such as Pericles, about whom he also wrote (pp. 256–7).

The point here has not been to claim that Whitman was a great orator. He was not. At least on the platform before an audience he was not. It is, nonetheless, to assert that Whitman knew oratory – the principles and conventions of oratory – that he would utilize in writing his poems and his prose, with the 1855 preface of *Leaves of Grass* serving as an excellent example, at least until the 1860 edition, and in many cases far beyond. Whether Whitman was merely posing as a serious orator in his poems, or actually being one, is open to debate. I agree with those who contend that Whitman could not write traditional verse. At least I agree that, for whatever reason, he did not – except for a few early newspaper pieces. I prefer to think that the traditional meter and rhyme used by many of his contemporaries did not suit his purposes – partially because they were too European, and he exerted considerable effort to distance America from Europe, declaring that our language, including that of our poetry, should spring from native soil. In 1858 – which was only three years after the first edition of *Leaves of Grass* and two years before the 1860 edition – Whitman was still saying such things as this about American oratory: "It seems to me called for a revolution in American oratory . . . to make the means of the grand modernized delivery of live modern orations, appropriate to America, appropriate to the world" (quoted in Harned pp. 257–8). He had not given up on the power of oratory, and he would not abandon it.

One last point in Harned's study deserves attention. In his book *Language and Style in "Leaves of Grass,"* C. Carroll Hollis basically questions Whitman's morality. Eloquence was a large issue in nineteenth-century rhetoric, and much has been written about it. Whitman's notes in Harned's essay address this issue:

> The eloquent man is natural. His manner, his tones, his style, his argumentation, his feeling, his flight of fancy are all spontaneous results of his mind being fully occupied

> with his subject and with nothing else for the time being. A manner studied and artificial, tones that rise not from and correspond not with, the sentiments he utters; a style that attracts attention to itself and is not the transparent vehicle of his thoughts; reasoning that is far-fetched and fantastic, pathos that tends to start no tear because it finds no sympathy; and figures that neither elucidate nor adorn, constitute a mere parody of oratory, and fitted to provoke the mirth of wise men, if their disgusts did not stifle their laughter. (quoted in Harned 1902: 258)

In another note Whitman writes, "An eloquent man must be earnest and honest. His heart's desire is to communicate with the mind of his audience, to lay hold of it and wield it for some cherished purpose" (quoted p. 259). I remind the reader that this is Walt Whitman addressing the issues of eloquence and morality. False eloquence was widely practiced during Whitman's time, and he abhorred it.

Roy S. Azarnoff, in his article "Walt Whitman's Concept of the Oratorical Ideal," discusses the many roles of Whitman's "ideal orator," but he makes other worthwhile observations. He says, for example, that Whitman not only practiced his oratory in his youth in Brooklyn and as a schoolteacher in Long Island (Azarnoff 1961: 171), but that he had a life-long interest in oratory. He also speculates that Whitman sustained his interest in oratory because he "thought that he might not 'get delivered' as a poet and therefore stressed oratory as an alternative or co-equal path" (p. 169). Contrary to what Whitman might have expected, he did "get delivered" as a poet, but not on anyone's grand scale in his lifetime. He went to his grave bemoaning the fact that his poems had not been embraced by the American people. Hollis writes that Whitman wrote "a new kind of poetry" (1983: x), a kind that changed as Whitman changed: "[H]e not only wrote a different sort of poetry but also tried to change the original poetry as well" (ibid.). Hollis's contention is that poems written after the Civil War did not contain the "oral features" of those written before the Civil War. The "prophetic posture" of early poems, says Hollis [and I take the word "posture" to mean "faked"], simply did not last, and the result was that Whitman shifted his emphasis from orality to poetry (1983: 64, 79). Hollis recognizes that Whitman, in a document found around the time of his death, affirms his seriousness about lecturing (p. 13), but he also argues that Whitman's accumulating numerous notes on oratory does not mean that he wanted to fuse the rules of oratory and eloquence. Hollis agrees with Roger Asselineau, who rejects the influence of oratory on Whitman's poems, declaring that for Whitman oratory and poetry were two separate things. Hollis goes back to F. O. Matthiessen, saying that the idea that *Leaves of Grass* originated in oratory, which Matthiessen claimed, has largely been abandoned. Of course, my response to that is that Matthiessen took Whitman seriously – and not as one faking the voice of a prophet in order to be accepted.

The issue here is not what Whitman intended, but rather what happened. Did the oratorical principles Whitman knew and practiced find their way into his poems? Hollis obviously supports Bruce McElderry's idea that Whitman progressed from "bardic inflation" in the first poems to "lyric perfection" in the latter (Hollis 1983: 4).

However, scholars continue to write articles to the effect that oratory is not missing in either the late or early poems. Jake Adam York takes up the issue in "When Time and Place Avail: Whitman's Written Orator Reconsidered." In his article York proposes to read Whitman's poem "Crossing Brooklyn Ferry" in terms of oral and textual expression as they existed in nineteenth-century American rhetoric. In order to do this he draws an analogy between Daniel Webster's 1825 address at the dedication of the Bunker Hill Monument and Whitman's poem. He sees the Bunker Hill Monument as both evoking memory and remaining as a sign and argues that Whitman's poem in a book does likewise. Further, he criticizes Derridean readings by such as Mark Bauerlein and Tenney Nathanson. He is also critical of C. Carroll Hollis, insisting, "[T]here is more to oratory than cadence, than style, than persona. There is argument, the large form, and there are theatrical and public gestures written in the liturgies within which addresses were made. And some of these items seem to explain both Whitman's hope for a written orality and his attempts to produce it" (York 2001: 92). In short, Hollis's definition is too narrow, explaining that the boundaries between speech and writing in Whitman's time were not as restricting as they are now. York concludes that Whitman – even after the 1860 edition, I presume – was trying to publish his *Leaves of Grass* "as printed speech and so imply an oral genesis, or to project a text that would move fluidly into speech, drawing on the grammar of oratorical publication" (p. 94). As for "Crossing Brooklyn Ferry," York argues that Whitman "repeats Webster's translation of speech and writing" in it (p. 94). Conveying knowledge, according to York, does not depend on "mutual presence, but rather upon the strength of both the conveyor's and the recipient's effort" (p. 98), and a book may be superior to mere oration. In nineteenth-century oratory, York continues, "[T]he text is established as an effective structure of delay that does not radically diminish the content of the communication.... Thus in Whitman's practice, oration and publication become fused, and print publication becomes no longer an addition to the oratorical moment but a part of it instead" (p. 99). York's argument is both intricate and convincing. Admitting that no evidence exists proving that Whitman ever read Webster's 1825 address, York concludes with the following:

> Whitman, it seems, like Webster, found the notion of a fusion of speech and writing useful. Whitman, like Webster, seems to have developed both a functional theory about the ideal relation between speech and writing and a practice whereby to realize that relation. And it is this we must look for, this we must keep in mind when we read to understand Whitman's practice. (York 2001: 104)

I would like to underscore three or four observations made by York: that *Leaves of Grass* is printed speech, that a "mutual presence" is not a prerequisite, that in nineteenth-century oratory print was simply an instrument of delay, and that Whitman fuses speech and writing, which is just the opposite of Hollis's idea that he kept them separate. In this regard, Neil Schmitz, in his article "Our Whitman," makes a significant distinction:

> Our Whitman is a writer, not the speaker. . . . The post-modernist Whitman calls attention to his writing. . . . The nineteenth-century reader of *Leaves of Grass* read the speech, looked to the person of the speaker, and either discounted the writer or happily found a way to justify Whitman's errant form and style. (Schmitz 1984: 16–17)

If I understand Schmitz, he is saying that the nineteenth-century reader looked through or beyond the text to a speaker. He is quite right. Nor have I lost sight of the fact that "The post-modernist Whitman calls attention to his writing." The difference is that the nineteenth-century listener/reader often heard the speech or lecture and then read the text. The postmodern reader – more often than not – encounters only the text from which the foreground is missing. Furthermore, readers spend as little time with the text as possible, maintaining distance from it. If we did not, we might find the body of a speaker in it. In short, for Whitman to communicate himself as orator through a speaking/writing act, both the speaker/writer and the listener/reader have to make a considerable effort. Otherwise, what Whitman called "magnetism," that thing (self) that he thought could be communicated through a "magnetic influence," could never be realized.

Earlier in the chapter I referred to Vincent J. Bertolini's "'Hinting' and 'Reminding.'" I don't know much about pragmatics, the branch of semiotics that deals with the relation between signs (linguistic expressions) and their users, but in his effort to explain Whitman's erogenous language Bertolini, it seems to me, is engaging in an exercise in pragmatics. As far as oratory is concerned, what Bertolini does is draw upon what C. Carroll Hollis treats as the illocutionary act. Apparently disconcerted by what he calls "gay identitarian readings," Bertolini sets out to demonstrate their inadequacy. After reminding us that Whitman warned his readers that his poems were not his autobiography, that understanding his poems and himself were two different things, Bertolini writes, "In the more stringently gay identitarian version of these readings, the historical author of the *Leaves* is identified with the speaking and self-representing persona of the lyric, and Whitman's poetry is constructed as a species of gay confessional" (2002: 1047). Bertolini prefers a different tack from that of the gay identitarian group, and he immediately recognizes two things that are extremely important to his case.

First, Whitman was a reformer. To substantiate this he quotes extensively from Betsy Erkkila's (1989) book *Whitman the Political Poet*. Erkkila writes, "In his editorials for the *Eagle*, Whitman placed himself at the center of these reformist energies and political struggles" (quoted in Bertolini 2002: 1076 n.16). She also enumerates the many causes that Whitman supported. Of course, Whitman was a liberal, and Bertolini feels it necessary to distinguish the liberalism of Whitman from that of someone like de Tocqueville, who believed in freedom of the individual over that of the democracy. Whitman, by contrast, fused them, and found them compatible (Bertolini 2002: 1079 n.33). Second, we do not know a lot about some aspects of Whitman's life. Before he died, he destroyed all papers that he did not want to become documentation for his life. Drawing his information from the first two volumes of Horace Traubel's *With Walt Whitman in Camden*, Bertolini makes clear that any papers which might have lent credence to reading Whitman's poems as autobiography no longer exist.

Using what Bertolini calls a "rhetoric of embodied performativity," Whitman communicates, or rather has his persona communicate, his wishes. Arguing for what he calls "the rhetorical ethico-politics of subjectivity operating in Whitman's text" (p. 1048), Bertolini explains:

> [E]ven as the author of *Leaves of Grass*, who has his speaker name himself "Walt Whitman," continually tempts the reader to identify the speaking "I" of his lyric with him, he also repeatedly deflects those identifications, inviting the reader instead to see the self gaining expression in the poetry as "being realized" – being instantiated, rendered real, brought into being – through the reader's participatory agency. (Bertolini 2002: 1048)

So there are two selves, as Bertolini explains, but they are compounded – the abstract "you," which is the reader, and the "lyric persona," which is the speaker. The two selves are brought together into one, nonetheless, through "hinting," "reminding," and "translating." Bertolini quotes from Robert K. Martin's Introduction to *The Continuing Presence of Walt Whitman: The Life After the Life*: "[T]he response to Whitman is mediated through a host of factors including race, history, class, nationality, gender, and sexuality" (Martin 1992: xvii). Martin concludes that "[w]hat Whitman seems to have provided for readers of varied backgrounds and allegiances is a sense of *enablement*" (p. xvii). The language, asserts Bertolini, is abstract, by which he does not mean "in the familiar agglomerative and 'kosmic' sense . . . but in the sense of Whitman's attempting at moments to vocally perform a lyric self devoid of embodied, historically marked concreteness, to be understood as empty form to be filled with content by the reader" (Bertolini 2002: 1053). In other words, these are abstract bodies.

Bertolini uses two 1860 poems – "So Long" and "Full of Life" – to illustrate what it means to use "the transformative power of lyric reading as resulting from the displacement of the speaker by a newly powerful, embodied reader" (2002: 1053). He hearkens back to "Song of Myself" and to Whitman's idea that the reader most honors him by destroying the teacher (*LG*: 84). Bertolini reads Whitman's lines as saying that readers are most affected through "dematerialization" of the speaker. He clarifies: "The speaker . . . removes himself from the text, troping himself as definitively departing the volume, as if his words were a space of physical encounter with the reader from which he absents himself" (Bertolini 2002: 1053). "As if" seems to be the key. There is an encounter of sorts, but it is not between physical speakers and physical listeners. Nor in the case of a written text is it between a persona (especially the writer as persona) and a reader. No, these are abstract bodies, as Bertolini explains: "As Whitman's conjunction between abstract bodies and empty styles indicates, the curious status of poetic communication in his text has much to do with the notion of his speaker being metaphorically rematerialized in the embodied subjectivities of his readers" (p. 1053). This strikes me as very important to explaining Whitman's oratory, and especially after 1860. The speaker is "metaphorically rematerialized" in the mind of the reader – as a body among the embodied subjectivities in the reader's mind. Thus the idea that a platform situation involving the presence of a speaker and a listener is duplicated in a text makes sense. The speaker of the text and the reader of the text meet in the reader's mind. Whitman, using what Bertolini calls "conventional liberal Enlightenment abstractions" (p. 1054), is "frontally deploying, and not unreflectively reiterating, the abstract conceptual materials of his Enlightenment inheritance with particular ethical and political purposes in mind" (p. 1055). It is in this sense that Whitman's concept of oratory applies not just to a platform situation, but to his written poems as well.

Bertolini's article is quite long and quite intricate and complicated. I have tried to avoid his detailed analyses of Whitman's poems "So Long" and "Full of Life," but hope the reader can appreciate how Whitman, through use of a certain "oratorical method," with which he experimented in his early journals (Bertolini 2002: 1059), came to "break down the barrier between words and the world" (p. 1062).

In his book *The Reenchantment of the World* (1981), Morris Berman explains that "mind" is characteristic of human beings, but "Mind" is comparable to "God." Emerson put it another way in *Nature*: "The currents of the universal Being circulate through me; I am part or parcel of God" (1903a: 10). This was the Transcendental view of God. Berman makes other observations essential to reading Whitman. For example, there lingers the question of how to account for both sensuality and sensuousness in Whitman's poems – especially as they relate to the "Children of Adam" and "Calamus" poems. Are not many of the images coming from those poems an exercise in pure voyeurism? I think not. Berman writes, "The 'secret' that lies at the heart of the occult world view, with its sense of everything being alive and interrelated, is *that the world is sensual at its core*; that this is the essence of reality" (Berman 1981: 177, my italics). In his chapter "Eros Regained," Berman discusses Wilhelm Reich's rejection of the Cartesian paradigm – which recognizes a mind/body split. This is the soul/body split that Whitman addresses in "Song of Myself" (*LG*: 32–3, 82–9). But the Cartesian paradigm or worldview also introduced a split between the individual and the world outside the individual. Still relying on Wilhelm Reich, Berman begins with a child in the womb and traces the development of that child, stressing the importance of "touch" between mother and child, until it can be said of that child "that it is an 'I,' an ego at odds with the world (to some extent), and to the interpretation that the world might place upon it. Dualistic consciousness is now an irrevocable fact" (Berman 1981: 162).

The above exercise in child care has to do with the importance of tactile stimulation as the beginning of knowing, a matter of epistemology. The child first "knows" the world through its mouth. Berman explains "holistic" cognition in terms of child development:

> The entire surface of its body is an agent of sense, and its relationship to its surroundings almost completely tactile. Its entire body, and thus its entire world, is sensualized.

> For more than two full years, then, a fundamental realization is fostered in the body, or unconscious mind, of all of us, a foundation that can never be uprooted: *I am my environment*. (Berman 1981: 158)

Although Whitman never heard of "holism" (a word coined by Jan Christian Smuts and first used in his book *Holism and Evolution* in 1926), and although he may not have known anything about child care, he obviously did know that we learn through our senses. Why else does he use those long catalogues beginning with "I see," "I feel," "I hear"? (For examples, see "Salut Au Monde," *LG*: 144–45). The "I" of the poem is not taking into himself the words of the poem. On the contrary, he is taking into himself images of the things named and thereby creating reality – an awareness, perhaps, that he, the "I," and the things named make up one reality (see *LG*: 139–41, section four of "Salut Au Monde," for example). In other words, the "I" of the poem is doing exactly what Bertolini suggests happens in Whitman's poems. He is breaking down the barrier "between words and the world" (Bertolini 2002: 1062), and in doing so, he is breaking down the barrier between himself and the "world."

We don't know why Whitman saw another world – one other than our Cartesian one – but he did, and the evidence is plentiful in both his poems and his prose. First, consider section six in "Starting from Paumanok":

> The soul,
> Forever and forever – longer than soil is brown and solid – longer than water ebbs and flows.
> I will make the poems of materials, for I think they are to be the most spiritual poems,
> And I will make the poems of my body and of mortality,
> For I think I shall then supply myself with the poems of my soul and of immortality.
> (*LG*: 18)

As for the idea of the "One," Whitman writes,

> And a song make I of the One *form'd out of all,*
> The fang'd and glittering One whose head is over all,
> Resolute warlike One *including and over all,*
> (However high the head of any else *that head is over all.*)
> (*LG*: 19, my italics)

This is obviously a recognition of what we call "holism."

The next quotation is essential to understanding Whitman's interest in a new religion – as well as his three primary concerns and his overall reform mission.

> Know you, solely to drop in the earth *the germs of a greater religion,*
> The following chants *each for its kind I sing.*
> My comrade!
> For you to share with me two greatnesses, and a third one rising inclusive and more resplendent,
> The greatness of *Love* and *Democracy*, and the greatness of *Religion*.
> (*LG*: 21, my italics)

Consider one more quotation from "Starting from Paumanok":

> I will not make poems with reference to parts,
> But I will make poems, songs, thoughts, with reference to ensemble,
> And I will not sing with reference to a day, but with reference to all days,
> And I will not make a poem nor the least part of a poem but has reference to the soul,
> Because having look'd at the objects of the universe, *I find there is no one nor any particle of one but has reference to the soul.*
>
> (*LG*: 23, my italics)

Here is Whitman's worldview – the one with the new man, the new morality, the new democracy, the new religion, and the new oratory.

The lines taken from "Starting from Paumanok" come as close to reconfiguring the God of the Hebrews as Whitman ever came – also to reconfiguring what we call "reality." Consider as well some lines in "Song of Myself": From section 7, for example, "I pass death with the dying and birth with the new-wash'd babe, and am not contain'd between my hat and boots" (*LG*: 35); in section 22: "Partaker of influx and efflux, I, . . . " (p. 50); in section 24: "Divine am I inside and out, and I make holy whatever I touch or am touch'd from" (p. 53); section 40: "Behold, I do not give lectures or a little charity, / When I give I give myself" (p. 73). These last two lines are essential to understanding Whitman's concept of the oration as performance as well as Bertolini's explanation of "embodiment" and "disembodiment" in the written poems. In section 48 the speaker says, "I have said that the soul is not more than the body, / And I have said that the body is not more than the soul" (p. 86). In section 50, the "I" of the poem first says, "There is that in me – I do not know what it is – but I know it is in me" (p. 88). The speaker adds, "I do not know it – it is without name – it is a word unsaid, / It is not in any dictionary, utterance, symbol" (p. 88). Then at the end of section 50 the speaker concludes, "It is not chaos or death – it is form, union, plan – it is eternal life – it is Happiness" (p. 88). Suffice it to say that these passages point toward holism, and Whitman's attempt to name the unnamable reminds one of Emerson's Universal Being: "I am part or parcel of God" (1903a:10).

But how does all of this relate to Whitman's mission to usher in a new age – an age of Love, Democracy, and Religion? And how does this relate to his wish for a new oratory? What about morality? The answers, I think, need not be long or difficult. I say this fully aware that near the beginning of my essay I agreed with Donald D. Kummings's assertion that one can support almost any thesis concerning Whitman's work by selecting the appropriate passages. However, I have selected passages, as few as they are, which express Whitman's overarching concerns – the concerns which, in my opinion, shape his worldview.

I don't want to mount a moral defense of Walt Whitman. For the most part, modern critics have made much of his alleged homosexuality and sometimes have labeled him immoral – relying largely on evidence of their own choosing. For a different view, I recommend two sources: Jan Christian Smuts's *Walt Whitman: A Study in the Evolution of Personality* and a PhD dissertation by John Lee Jellicorse entitled "The Poet as Persuader: A Rhetorical Explication of the Life and Writings of Walt Whitman." Written in 1895, Smuts's book has much to say about "man and God," revealing his ideas on *Eenheid* (a Dutch word meaning unit or unity), which he later published in a book entitled *Holism and Evolution*. Smuts traces the development of Whitman's personality through four stages in his much-neglected book, and I highly recommend chapters six ("Period of Spiritualism, 1866–1873") and seven ("Period of Pure or Religious Spirituality, 1873–1892"). Smuts saw Whitman as "the complete man." John Lee Jellicorse, in his lengthy dissertation, reaches a similar conclusion in the longest and most heavily documented single-author work on Whitman I have ever seen. Arguing that Whitman's primary purpose was to establish a "Religious Democracy" in America, he agrees with and cites Basil De Selincourt's conviction that for Whitman the poem was to fulfill "spiritual needs" (quoted in Jellicorse 1967: 84). Jellicorse also agrees with J. Middleton Murry that Whitman's greatest achievement was the founding of Democracy on religious revelation, a process of "spiritualization," the process "which alone can save Democracy from moral disaster" (quoted p.107).

Was Whitman literally a utopian dreamer, faking his moral and spiritual condition merely to draw attention to himself? In spite of much that has been written to support that position in the past 50 years, I think not. His appropriating the oratorical techniques of Elias Hicks and Reverend Edward Taylor, especially as those techniques apply to their "outward evolutionary styles," should count for something. After all, oratory was the rage during the first half of the 1850s. Whitman could have appropriated the oratory of any number of politicians, orators, singers, and social reformers, and to some extent he did. But he could not let go of the Quaker idea of the "inner light," and of oratory as a medium for addressing the moral and spiritual condition of his fellow human beings.

References and Further Reading

Azarnoff, Roy S. (1961). "Walt Whitman's Concept of the Oratorical Ideal." *Quarterly Journal of Speech*, 47 (2): 169–72.

Bauerlein, Mark (1986). "The Written Orator of 'Song of Myself': A Recent Trend in Whitman Criticism." *Walt Whitman Quarterly Review*, 32: 1–14.

Berman, Morris (1981). *The Reenchantment of the World*. Ithaca, NY: Cornell University Press.

Bertolini, Vincent J. (2002). " 'Hinting' and 'Reminding': The Rhetoric of Performative Embodiment in *Leaves of Grass*." *ELH*, 69: 1047–82.

Clark, Gregory and Halloran, S. Michael (eds.) (1993). *Oratorical Culture in Nineteenth-Century America: Transformations in the Theory and Practice of Rhetoric*. Carbondale: Southern Illinois University Press.

Emerson, Ralph Waldo (1903a). *Nature*. In *Nature; Addresses and Lectures, vol.* 1 of *The Complete Works of Ralph Waldo Emerson*, 12 vols. Boston: Houghton, Mifflin, *pp.* 1–77.

Emerson, Ralph Waldo (1903b). "Man the Reformer." In *Nature; Addresses and Lectures, vol.* 1 of *The Complete Works of Ralph Waldo Emerson*, 12 vols. Boston: Houghton, Mifflin, and Company, pp. 225–56.

Emerson, Ralph Waldo (1903c). "The Method of Nature." In *Nature; Addresses and Lectures, vol.* 1

of *The Complete Works of Ralph Waldo Emerson*, 12 vols. Boston: Houghton, Mifflin, and Company, pp. 189–224.

Erkkila, Betsy (1989). *Whitman the Political Poet*. New York: Oxford University Press.

Finkel, William L. (1950). "Walt Whitman's Manuscript Notes on Oratory." *American Literature*, 22: 29–53.

Harned, Thomas B. (1902). "Walt Whitman and Oratory." In *The Complete Prose Works of Walt Whitman Vol. 5*. New York: G. P. Putnam's Sons, pp. 244–60.

Hollis, C. Carroll (1970). "The Oratorical Stance and Whitman's Early Poetry." In Lester F. Zimmerman (ed.), *Papers on Walt Whitman*. Tulsa: University of Tulsa Press, pp. 56–79.

Hollis, C. Carroll (1983). *Language and Style in "Leaves of Grass."* Baton Rouge: Louisiana State University Press.

Hollis, C. Carroll (1984). "Rhetoric, Elocution, and Voice in *Leaves of Grass:* A Study in Affiliation." *Walt Whitman Quarterly Review*, 2 (2): 1–21.

Hollis, C. Carroll (1986). "Is There a Text in This Grass?" *Walt Whitman Quarterly Review*, 32: 15–22.

Jellicorse, John Lee (1967). "The Poet as Persuader: A Rhetorical Explication of the Life and Writings of Walt Whitman." PhD Dissertation. Northwestern University. Washington, DC: Charles E. Feinberg Collection, Library of Congress, Box 75.

Kummings, Donald D. (1971)."Whitman's Voice in 'Song of Myself': From Private to Public." *Walt Whitman Review*, 17: 10–15.

Loving, Jerome (1982). *Emerson, Whitman, and the American Muse*. Chapel Hill: University of North Carolina Press.

Martin, Robert K. (1992). "Introduction." In Robert K. Martin (ed.), *The Continuing Presence of Walt Whitman: The Life After the Life*. Iowa City: University of Iowa Press, pp. xi–xxiii.

Mason, John B. (1998). "Oratory." In J. R. LeMaster and Donald D. Kummings (eds.), *Walt Whitman: An Encyclopedia*. New York: Garland Publishing, pp. 489–90.

Rorty, Richard (1989). *Contingency, Irony, and Solidarity*. Cambridge, UK: Cambridge University Press.

Ross, Donald (1975). "Emerson's Stylistic Influence on Whitman." *American Transcendental Quarterly*, pt.1: 41–50.

Schmitz, Neil (1984). "Our Whitman." *Parnassus: Poetry in Review*, 12 (1): 4–19.

Smuts, Jan Christian (1973). *Walt Whitman: A Study in the Evolution of Personality*, ed. Alan L. McLeod. Detroit: Wayne State University Press.

Warren, James Perrin (1999). *Culture of Eloquence: Oratory and Reform in Antebellum America*. University Park: Pennsylvania State University Press.

York, Jake Adam (2001). "When Time and Place Avail: Whitman's Written Orator Reconsidered." *Walt Whitman Quarterly Review*, 19: 90–107.

7
Slavery and Race

Martin Klammer

Slavery was the most important issue facing the United States in the mid-nineteenth century and no one wrote about American slavery in more powerful, imaginative, and self-contradictory ways than Walt Whitman. In *The Poetry of Slavery: An Anglo-American Anthology, 1764–1865*, a 700-page collection including the works of Blake, Coleridge, Wordsworth, Wheatley, Dickinson, and Melville, the editor Marcus Wood states simply: "Whitman's poetry is the most important writing in this book" (Wood, 2003: 626). The anthology includes the best known of Whitman's passages on black Americans, both slave and free, from the 1855 *Leaves of Grass,* including three famous passages from "Song of Myself": the "runaway slave" aided by the speaker, the "hounded slave" with whom the speaker identifies ("All this I feel or am"), and the Negro drayman, for whom the speaker professes love. In the context of dozens of antislavery poems in England and the United States, Whitman's poetry is singularly original and compelling.

Yet Whitman's attitudes toward race and slavery continue to mystify his readers. For the poet who cheerfully admits "I contradict myself" appears no more self-contradictory than on the contentious issue of slavery and the future of black persons in the United States. Whitman projects a deep, humanitarian empathy for blacks in the 1855 *Leaves of Grass*, yet he consistently opposed the extension of slavery not out of concern for black persons but rather for white laborers whose economic opportunities and dignity he felt would be harmed by the presence of slaves. Whitman celebrated the beauty and dignity of black persons, yet he never argued for their inclusion in a democratic America. He famously asked in an 1858 editorial: "Who believes that the Whites and Blacks can ever amalgamate in America?" (Whitman 1932: 90).

This essay argues that far from being mystifying or self-contradictory Whitman's attitudes toward slavery and black persons remained remarkably consistent among all genres of his writing and throughout his career. Like the vast majority of whites in the nineteenth century, Whitman felt blacks to be distinct from and inferior to whites and hoped that America's future would be for whites only. Whitman's 1840s Free Soil journalism identifies the white (male) laborer as the symbol and hope of American democracy and champions his freedom over against the possibility of slavery in the new territories. At no point until the 1855 *Leaves of Grass* does Whitman display any concern, much less awareness of, the suffering of black slaves, and at no point does he seriously challenge the status quo of slavery in the South. (Whitman opposed not slavery, but the *extension* of slavery.) Whitman's striking and empathetic portrayal of blacks in 1855 emerged from a distinct coalescing of circumstances never again to be repeated: a radicalized North after the passage of the 1854 Kansas-Nebraska Act and controversial enforcements of the 1850 Fugitive Slave Law and Whitman's own dramatic development as a poet, evident from notebooks and manuscripts dated 1853–5. Even at its most radical, Whitman's poetry about slavery sought to produce a poetics of Union that would bring together Northern and Southern *whites*. Whitman's poetry argues for the humane treatment of slaves (especially fugitive slaves) but projects a future where whites and blacks would exist apart. After 1855 Whitman whitens his *Leaves* by deleting previous passages about black persons, just as he hoped that black persons (and American Indians) would eventually "filter through in time or gradually eliminate & disappear" (Price 1985: 205). No matter how self-liberating his poetry projects himself to be, Whitman could never liberate himself from the hard grip of antebellum American racism.

When Whitman first wrote about slavery in the 1840s, the idea of an exclusively white America was embedded in the national consciousness. According to historian Joseph Ellis, during the revolutionary era none of the founders "contemplated, much less endorsed, a biracial American society" (Ellis 2002: 101).[1] In the nineteenth century, whites both North and South continued to share Thomas Jefferson's belief that "the real distinctions that nature has made" between blacks and whites prohibited racial integration (Jefferson 1964: 132). Whitman himself consistently championed a form of white nationalism rooted in freedom and opportunity for white laborers. The most pressing slavery issue for Whitman was not its persistence in the South, but whether slavery would be permitted in the new territories. This issue came to a head in 1846 when a vast new territory for settlement was opened up by the results of the Mexican War. In August 1846, Representative David Wilmot of Pennsylvania introduced an amendment to an appropriations bill stating that slavery was to be excluded from any territory acquired in the war with Mexico. Despite the eventual failure of the "Wilmot Proviso" in the Senate, the issue gave rise to the "free soil" sentiment that would lead in 1848 to the formation of the Free Soil Party (Klammer 1995: 29).

In contrast to abolitionists, Free Soilers cared almost exclusively about the freedoms and rights of whites. Free Soilism in fact became popular among a segment of the North in part because of what historian George Fredrickson calls its "overtly Negrophobic or exclusionist" element. Most Free Soilers opposed "the presence of Negroes on any basis whatsoever," giving expression to a deep desire for a "future America that would be all white, or nearly so" (Fredrickson 1971: 130–40). The Free Soil movement's approach to slavery attracted more Northerners than did abolitionists, and marked what Eric Foner has called a "vital turning-point" in antislavery, making opposition to the *extension* of slavery a "truly mass movement in the North" (Foner 1980: 72, 93).

Whitman supported the Wilmot Proviso and "Free Soil," arguing, as did Free Soilers in Congress, that the introduction of slavery would discourage, if not prohibit, white men from settling in the new territories because white labor could not economically compete with slave labor and would also be "degraded" by association with black slaves. His position was that of Wilmot, who said when he introduced the proviso: "I would preserve for free white labor a fair country, a rich inheritance, where the sons of toil, of my own race and color, can live without the disgrace which association with negro slavery brings upon free labor" (quoted in Klammer 1995: 30–1).

In his Free Soil editorials at the *Brooklyn Eagle* in 1846–7, Whitman consistently invoked white working-class solidarity. In a September 1847 editorial titled "American Workingmen, versus Slavery," Whitman defines the issue as one between "*the grand body of white workingmen, the millions of mechanics, farmers, and operatives of our country*, with their interests, on one side – and the interests of the few thousand rich, 'polished,' and aristocratic owners of slaves at the south, on the other side" (original emphasis). He is concerned about the threats to whites' economic interests and to their moral character. Slavery is "destructive to the dignity and independence of all who work, and to labor itself," he writes, and the white freeman "will not comfortably stand such degradation." Whitman worries that slavery's extension may lead white freemen to become like Southern commoners: "a miserable, ignorant, and shiftless set of beings" (*Jour.*, 2: 318–19).

In these editorials Whitman rarely shows concern for slaves, or even mentions them.[2] Whitman's contact with black persons, like that of most Northerners, was limited. Both sides of his family had been slave-owners for more than a century, and near the end of his life Whitman remembered " 'Old Mose,' one of the liberated West Hills slaves. He was very genial, correct, manly, and cute, and a great friend of mine in childhood" (Whitman 1982: 1174). "Old Mose" may have been the only black "friend" Whitman ever had. Most black persons in Brooklyn were employed as coachmen, gardeners, and cooks, and the school that Whitman attended as a boy was segregated by race on each floor. And while black persons in Brooklyn established churches, mutual aid societies, and abolitionist groups, they led separate lives from whites, and Whitman likely had no more than a passing acquaintance with them (Reynolds 1995: 47–8, Klammer 1995: 24).

Whitman's first representation of a black person is of the Creole slave Margaret in his 1842 temperance novel *Franklin Evans*. In the novel the narrator Franklin, a young, alcoholic Northerner, becomes sexually obsessed with Margaret during his visit to a Virginia plantation. In a fit of drunkenness Franklin has her manumitted and marries her, only, upon sobering, to feel disgusted at his actions. The novel climaxes when Margaret murders a white rival for Franklin's affections and then commits suicide. In this brief and melodramatic sequence, Whitman adapts the voluptuous "tragic mulatto" archetype from abolitionist fiction, representing her not, however, as a victim unfairly sold into slavery, but as a sexually aggressive murderess – unstable, violent, and unfit for freedom.[3] This early work, then, reproduces some of the most conventional and racist images of blacks.

Whitman may have derived this stereotype of Margaret from "blacks" he saw in minstrel shows. Whitman took an avid interest in "Ethiopian" minstrel troupes that proliferated in the 1840s and early 1850s, watching white performers such as T. D. Rice "blacken up" and parody black dress, dance, speech, and song. Whitman confessed a weakness for "nigger singers," saying later in life that "the wild chants were admirable" (*Brooklyn Eagle,* April 28, 1847, Whitman 1982: 1290). Yet while minstrel shows played to the crudest fictions of white racism, according to Marcus Wood many songs came at issues of race and slavery "in pungent ways." Some songs went "deeply into the horror of slave experience," including narratives of a slave husband sold down the river when his wife stopped producing children, or a slave denied his freedom and contemplating suicide (Wood: 685–6). Whitman's later poetic images of slaves – both stereotypical and sublime – may have been influenced by these shows.

On the political front, Whitman continued to support Free Soilism, even losing his job at the *Brooklyn Eagle* in 1848 because of his position on slavery. After a four-month stint at the *New Orleans Crescent*, Whitman returned in June 1848 to head the *Brooklyn Freeman*, a Free Soil newspaper, until he resigned in September 1849. Then in 1850 Congress began to consider a series of slavery compromises that would galvanize Whitman and other Free Soilers. The bills included a provision that would organize some western territories without restrictions on slavery and a fugitive slave law that would compel local citizens to assist federal marshals in the return of fugitive slaves. Whitman turned to poetry to express his outrage, publishing three anticompromise poems in New York newspapers from March through June of 1850. The poems were scathing in their denunciation of Northerners whom Whitman felt had sold out to Southern interests. Yet only one, "Blood-Money," considers the slave's experience, likening the fugitive slave's suffering to that of Jesus:

> Again they surround thee, mad with devilish spite;
> Toward thee stretch the hands of a multitude, like vultures' talons,
> The meanest spit in thy face, they smite thee with their palms;
> Bruised, bloody, and pinion'd is thy body,
> More sorrowful than death is thy soul.
>
> (*EPF*: 48)

Whitman demonstrates for the first time an attempt to imagine the brutality of the slave's experience, one of the hallmarks of his writing about black persons in the 1855 *Leaves of Grass*. Yet Whitman employs this rhetoric in the service of a specific political agenda: in depicting a *fugitive* slave, he appeals to a coalition of abolitionists and Free Soilers without offending either (a strategy he will employ in the 1855 poetry) (Klammer 1995: 79).

The passage of the Compromise in Fall 1850 frustrated Whitman, though many Free Soilers hoped it would preserve the Union by ending "agitation of the slavery question" (Foner 1980: 89). Whitman aired his anger that Fall in three letters for the Free Soil journal *National Era*, predicting "slavery must go down. It may be years yet; but it must go" (quoted in Silver 1948: 303). That was the last to be heard from him on slavery – or just about any issue–until 1854. Whitman himself provided few clues to this period of his life, saying only that he was "occupied in house-building in Brooklyn" (Whitman 1982: 705).

Yet in 1854 two national events radically altered Northern attitudes about slavery, suddenly providing Whitman with an audience that would be receptive to his antislavery views. The passage of the Kansas-Nebraska Act in May infuriated many Northerners because the bill repealed the 1820 Missouri Compromise ban on slavery north of 36'30. The repeal seemed to reserve Nebraska for freedom and Kansas for slavery, violating the fragile trust between North and South established by the 1850 Compromise. Public meetings were held in every Northern state to denounce the bill, and, according to Allan Nevins, the Free Soil press "spoke with an energy for which the history of American journalism had no parallel" (Nevins 1947, 2: 125). Yet despite Northern opinion the bill passed, bitterly dividing the country along sectional, rather than party, lines (Klammer 1995: 102–3).

A short time later Northern anger was further galvanized when Anthony Burns, an escaped slave from Virginia, was arrested in Boston and placed under federal guard. An attempt to rescue Burns failed, and federal troops were called in to ensure Burns's return. This spectacle was unparalleled in the short history of the Fugitive Slave Law, with more than 20,000 people jeering the police escort. In other Northern cities crowds numbering in the thousands stood vigil to protect escaped slaves from federal arrest. The Kansas-Nebraska Act and the Anthony Burns episode together created what one historian has called "a wholly altered Northern attitude" (Nevins 1947, 2: 152).

In other words, Whitman's attitudes toward slavery had not changed, but those of his potential *readers* had. In this profoundly new context he wrote his first poem in four years, "A Boston Ballad," satirizing the supposed apathy of Boston's citizens to the Burns affair. The poem narrates how "bandaged and bloodless" phantoms of revolutionary war heroes return from the dead to protest Burns's arrest (Whitman 1982: 264). When the phantoms level their crutches like muskets at the escort to show the course of action required, the speaker understands this merely as a senile gesture, and urges instead a proper respect for federal power. Horrified at citizens' indifference, the revolutionaries retreat. The speaker then realizes "the one thing that belongs here," convincing the mayor to send for the corpse of King George III to be crowned in Boston (ibid., p. 265). Whitman's sardonic point is that the Fugitive Slave Law should be resisted solely to protect Northern white communities from an invasive federal power. Anthony Burns does not appear in the poem.

At the same time, however, Whitman was beginning to develop new ways of representing black persons and slavery in his notebook poetry experiments.[4] In the context of a nation increasingly imperiled by divisions over slavery, Whitman begins to see his poetic vocation as a mediator and unifier:

> I am the poet of the body
> And I am the poet of the soul
> Thus the slaves are mine and the masters are equally mine
> And I will stand between the masters and the slaves,
> And I enter into both, and both shall understand me alike.
>
> (*NUPM*, 1: 67)

Whitman begins to develop images of black persons that are increasingly nuanced, humane, and real – but also unthreatening. One of his first attempts, in late 1853 or early 1854, is an experimental poem he titled "Pictures." Among its 150 randomly ordered "pictures" are four images of black persons that largely reinforce racialist stereotypes, such as an old black man begging on a street corner, or "my slave gangs . . . clumsy, hideous, black, pouting, grinning, sly, besotted, sensual, shameless" (*NUPM*, 4: 1302). Yet one image stands out as innovative and bold:

> And this black portrait – this head, huge, frowning, sorrowful, –
> Is Lucifer's portrait – the denied God's portrait.
> But I do not deny him – though cast out and rebellious,
> He is my God as much as any.
>
> (*NUPM*, 4: 1300)

For the first time Whitman seeks to capture something of the complex humanity of a black person – his social status ("cast out"), political response ("rebellious"), and emotional state ("frowning, sorrowful"). The stunning analogy of the black man as "Lucifer" – the name traditionally given to the proud archangel who sought equality with God but was cast down – suggests how Whitman is finding compelling new language to represent the lives of enslaved black persons.

These poetic experiments show Whitman to be especially interested in narrating the experience of *fugitive* slaves. An early fragment tells how "The slave that stood could run no longer," stung by buckshot and bleeding while clutching a fence. A later version revises the personal pronoun from "He" to "I" ("I am the hunted slave"), suggesting how Whitman now seeks to enter the slave's suffering, not unlike abolitionist tracts and slave narratives, and certainly useful in a context where, as one Northerner wrote in June 1854: "We went to bed one night old fashioned, conservative Compromise Union Whigs & we waked up stark mad Abolitionists" (quoted in Pease and Pease 1975: 43).

How Whitman came to such new and surprising language about enslaved black persons is beyond explanation. His desire to create a poetic persona capable of embracing all people; his passion for freedom as the primary American ideal; his calculation of negotiating a politics of union by mediating without offense between all forces (including abolitionists and slaveholders) – all these played a part. Yet

Whitman, like the nation he loved, was also rife with contradictions about slavery and race. And perhaps it is Whitman's *contradictory* impulse toward black persons – as fellow humans part of the divine "Myself," yet "less than" whites and a troublesome presence – that ignites such astonishing language.

In the 1855 *Leaves of Grass* Whitman pushes himself and his readers toward understanding that one's humanity depends upon recognizing the humanity of others, especially those most distant from Whitman's readers: black persons. And yet none of Whitman's poems threaten his white readers with the notion that blacks and whites will some day live equally together in America. Whitman's project, then, is to imagine a future free of both slavery *and* blacks.

Whitman's first poem in the 1855 *Leaves of Grass*, later titled "Song of Myself," dramatizes black persons in three vignettes. These passages demonstrate both the importance of blacks in the movement of the poem and the contradictions inherent in Whitman's racial project. The movement of "Song of Myself" is toward complete merger of self and other, ignited by the speaker's sexual self-union of "my soul" and "the other I am" in section 5. Shortly after this, the speaker comforts a runaway slave:

> The runaway slave came to my house and stopped outside,
> I heard his motions crackling the twigs of the woodpile,
> Through the swung half-door of the kitchen I saw him limpsey and weak,
> And went where he sat on a log, and led him in and assured him,
> And brought water and filled a tub for his sweated body and bruised feet,
> And gave him a room that entered from my own, and gave him some coarse clean clothes,
> And remember perfectly well his revolving eyes and awkwardness,
> And remember putting plasters on the galls of his neck and ankles;
> He staid with me a week before he was recuperated and passed north,
> I had him sit next me at table... my firelock leaned in the corner.
>
> (Whitman 1982: 35–6)

The speaker's actions are not just broadly humanitarian, but intimate and physical, as if extended by a loving comrade. And in extending himself the white speaker merges his identity with that of the fugitive slave. Karen Sanchez-Eppler notes that while the slave remains outside of the house, the speaker "retains the fixed integrity of an observing 'I' clearly distinct from what it observes." But once the speaker tends to the slave, the speaker relinquishes the "I" as his identity is gradually absorbed by the body of the slave. The repetition of "And" connects the speaker and slave in space and time and in their common humanity. Only after the fugitive passes north does the speaker reassert his "I," suggesting that at least for the time of intimate contact "the differentiations of identity" were held in abeyance (Sanchez-Eppler 1993: 76–7).

Yet the passage contains its own contradictions by inscribing what George Fredrickson calls the "romantic racialist" notion of blacks as helpless, docile children, an idea popularized by Harriet Beecher Stowe's *Uncle Tom's Cabin* (1852). Blacks were seen at this time, like women, to possess the "natural Christian" attributes of "gentleness" and the "facility of forgiveness." In fact, the "feminine" conception of blacks contributed to "a revived interest in black expatriation or colonization in the 1850s," as the ascribed differences in character between blacks and white (male) Americans implied that "American blacks should return to the environment where their special potentialities could be most fully realized" (Fredrickson 1971: 111–15). Thus Whitman's portrayal of the runaway slave as "limpsey and weak," a feminized, passive recipient of the speaker's actions, works both to model a white response of humanitarianism toward slaves and to demonstrate such differences between speaker and slave that a more permanent union is out of the question.

This merger of speaker and slave lasts only a week but propels the poem toward fuller, more complete merger of self and other in the poem. In the next sections, the "twenty-ninth bather" merges with 28 men and the speaker merges with the "butcher-boy" and the "blacksmiths," but in all cases only through imaginative sexual desire. Complete merger becomes possible only when Whitman offers the dramatic image of a handsome, powerful, and autonomous black man:

> The negro holds firmly the reins of his four horses . . . the block swags underneath on its tied-over chain,
> The negro that drives the huge dray of the stoneyard . . . steady and tall he stands poised on one leg on the stringpiece,
> His blue shirt exposes his ample neck and breast and loosens over his hipband,
> His glance is calm and commanding. . . . he tosses the slouch of his hat away from his forehead,
> The sun falls on his crispy hair and moustache . . . falls on the black of his polish'd and perfect limbs.
> I behold the picturesque giant and love him. . . . and I do not stop there,
> I go with the team also.
>
> (Whitman 1982: 37)

The body of the "runaway slave" bruised and broken by slavery here becomes perfect and whole in freedom. The black man is "steady and tall," with "ample neck and breast" and "polish'd and perfect limbs." His autonomy begets impressive power: he holds "firmly the reins of his horses," is "poised on one leg," and "His glance is calm and commanding." At the end of the passage the speaker declares his "love" for the man and joins him in driving the team. The gesture is striking; Whitman does nothing less than merge "himself, his poem, and his idealized country with a black man," the ultimate Other in antebellum America (Outka 2002: 315). Yet even this loving merger is problematic, for the description of the drayman matches the "dress and posture" of Whitman *himself* on the title page of the 1855 *Leaves* (Sanchez-Eppler 1993: 55). If the Other can only be imagined as a blacker version of the self, one might ask, is it really merger?

The final portrait of a black person in "Song" completes the speaker's quest to become fully human through merger. Yet this passage even more than others has raised questions about the ease of the speaker's sympathetic identification. In the long middle of the poem (section 33) the self enters into the suffering of martyrs through episodes of increasing violence: soldiers at battle, a widow viewing the body of her drowned husband, and a mother burnt as a witch in front of her children (Whitman 1982: 64). The speaker says: "I am the man.... I suffered... I was there" (ibid.). Then as the cosmic self expands through suffering, it makes the final leap from self to other as America's signal martyr, the "hounded slave":

> The hounded slave that flags in the race and leans by the fence, blowing and covered with sweat,
> The twinges that sting like needles his legs and neck,
> The murderous buckshot and the bullets,
> All these I feel or am.
>
> I am the hounded slave... I wince at the bite of dogs,
> Hell and despair are upon me... crack and again crack the marksmen,
> I clutch the rails of the fence... my gore dribs thinned with the ooze of my skin,
> I fall on the weeds and stones,
> The riders spur their unwilling horses and haul close,
> They taunt my dizzy ears... they beat me violently over the head with their whip-stocks.
>
> Agonies are one of my change of garments;
> I do not ask the wounded person how he feels...
> I myself become the wounded person,
> My hurt turns livid upon me as I lean on a cane and observe.
>
> (Whitman 1982: 65)

The imaginative self-projection of the speaker (and by implication, of Whitman's readers) into the "Hell and despair" of the fugitive slave marks one of the most radical passages in "Song" about slaves, slavery, and the moral obligations of whites. To understand the slave's experience, Whitman is saying, one must seek to imaginatively enter it: "I do not ask the wounded person how he feels... I myself become the wounded person."

Yet critics have long taken issue with the seeming ease of Whitman's sympathetic identification, the claim that "Agonies are one of my change of garments." Most famously, D. H. Lawrence argued in *Studies in Classic American Literature* (1923) that what Whitman achieved in identifying with the slave was not sympathy but appropriation: "If Whitman had truly sympathized, he would have said: "That negro suffers from slavery. He wants to free himself. His soul wants to free him... If I can help him I will: I will not take over his wounds and his slavery to myself" (Lawrence 1986: 184). More recently, Sanchez-Eppler has asserted that Whitman's claim to "inhabit another's body" is a "failed poetic ideal." Whitman's line, "All these I feel or am," applies not only to the fugitive slave, she writes, but to the fence, buckshot, and bullets, thus undermining the authority of his assertions. Moreover, Whitman's "odd doubleness" of presenting himself as both subject and object (as he leans on his cane and observes) "retains the distance and difference of the observer" (Sanchez-Eppler 1993: 79–80).

If Whitman's claim of identification with the slave seems insincere or self-aggrandizing, it was precisely what his contemporary Frederick Douglass asked for.

In *The Narrative of the Life of Frederick Douglass* (1845), Douglass writes that if the reader is to understand his "most painful situation" in the North, he or she must either "experience it, or imagine himself in similar circumstances" (Douglass 1968: 111). And in a long sentence describing his predicament ("without home or friends – without money or credit," etc.), Douglass three times urges his reader to "place himself in my situation" (ibid.). According to William Andrews, the "imaginative self-projection of the reader into the text" was Douglass's solution to the "central rhetorical problem of the slave narrative – how to build a bridge of sympathetic identification between the diametrical points of view of the northern white reader and the southern fugitive slave" (Andrews 1986: 138). In "Song of Myself," Whitman not only "places himself" in Douglass's situation; he places the *reader* there as well. As the reader merges with the speaker in the poem ("what I assume you shall assume") and the speaker merges with the "hounded slave," the reader also becomes "the wounded person."

Two other major 1855 poems extend the pattern of Whitman claiming a merger of identity with black persons when enslaved but not when freed. In "The Sleepers," Whitman strikingly gives voice to a slave's rage, at once representing the depths of human suffering and pointing to alienation so extreme as to argue for permanent separation of the races. The poem narrates the psychic drama of a cosmic self, wandering through the night and encountering "the sleepers," whose dreams he enters. Midway through the poem the speaker descends into visions of separation and death, including that of George Washington as a Revolutionary War general weeping at "the slaughter of the southern braves" in the battle of Brooklyn (Whitman 1982: 112) and the visit of a "red squaw" to the "old homestead," where she develops a love for the speaker's mother. The "Lucifer" passage follows in dramatic fashion, articulating the slave's rage and naming the forced separations of his family as the *depth* of human anguish.

> Now Lucifer was not dead . . . or if he was I am his sorrowful terrible heir;
> I have been wronged . . . I am oppressed . . . I hate him that oppresses me,
> I will either destroy him, or he shall release me.
>
> Damn him! How he does defile me,
> How he informs against my brother and sister and takes pay for their blood,
> How he laughs when I look down the bend after the steamboat that carries away my woman.
>
> Now the vast dusk bulk that is the whale's bulk . . . it seems mine,
> Warily, sportsman! Though I lie so sleepy and sluggish, my tap is death.
>
> (Whitman 1982: 113)

One critic calls this "one of the most powerful and evocative passages about slavery in American literature" (Folsom 2000: 51). This "heir" of "Lucifer" is no longer "frowning, sorrowful" as in the earlier notebook poem, but vengeful and explosive.[5] The combustible heat of his anger expresses itself in a curse against the slave-master ("Damn him!"), anguished repetition ("I have been wronged," "I am oppressed," "I hate him," etc.), and narration of injuries. The slave suffers not from violence but from separation from those he loves: a brother and sister, fugitive slaves turned in by a paid informer, and "my woman" carried away by steamboat. In depicting this emotional torment, Whitman, like Douglass and other slave narrators, builds a powerful bridge between white readers and the "black" narrator.

In the passage's complex and unusual final trope, the slave imagines himself as the "vast dusk bulk" of the whale vowing deathly revenge. The image may have been adapted from Melville's "mysterious and demonic White Whale," according to Christopher Beach: in both texts the whales are "unnaturally large," will kill when driven "by attack or injury," and are identified by color (Beach 1996: 57). Yet the passage's power is achieved not only from Whitman's innovative coalescing of metaphors (heir of "Lucifer" and the "whale's bulk"), but also from its first-person perspective, emotive range, familial narrative, and the slave's direct threat to the slave-master (and, implicitly, to the reader).

By imagining a slave imagining *himself* as the "whale's bulk," Whitman portrays the slave internalizing his degradation and agonizing over his alienation from human community. The adjectives the slave uses to describe himself also name prejudices about blacks that Whitman's readers would have had. He is "sleepy and sluggish," an undifferentiated mass of black humanity, huge, unknowable, and imminently violent. (It is not clear whether Whitman is controlling the irony of a black man identifying himself by whites' perspectives or if Whitman is *himself* ironically controlled by the stereotypes from which he hopes to liberate the slave.) In the abrupt resolution to "The Sleepers," the speaker is restored to wholeness through immersion in nature, prompting a return for all peoples to health and home – in the case of the slave, to the plantation: "The call of the slave is one with the master's call . . . and the master salutes the slave." Thus, at risk of alienating white readers with the threat of slave revolt or race war, Whitman dissipates the slave's anger and safely retreats to an idealized master–slave relationship.

In "I Sing the Body Electric," Whitman in a similar fashion compels his white readers to recognize their common humanity with enslaved black persons but then removes those black persons to foreign soil. The poem celebrates the sacredness of the human body, climaxed by a cataloguing of the wondrous body of a slave man at auction.

A slave at auction!
I help the auctioneer . . . the sloven does not half know his business.

Gentlemen look on this curious creature,
Whatever the bids of the bidders they cannot be high enough for him,
For him the globe lay preparing quintillions of years without one animal or plant,
For him the revolving cycles truly and steadily rolled.

In that head the allbaffling brain,
In it and below it the making of the attributes of heroes.

Examine these limbs, red black or white . . . they are very cunning in tendon and nerve;
They shall be stript that you may see them.

Exquisite senses, lifelit eyes, pluck, volition,
Flakes of breastmuscle, pliant backbone and neck, flesh not flabby, goodsized arms and legs,

> And wonders within there yet.
> Within there runs his blood . . . the same old blood . . the same red running blood;
> There swells and jets his heart . . . There all passions and desires . . all reachings and aspirations:
> Do you think they are not there because they are not expressed in parlors and lecture-rooms?
>
> (Whitman 1982: 123)

At first glance, by appropriating the auctioneer's role the speaker seems to collaborate in the very dehumanization he decries. But the speaker sings the slave's true value, where the bidders cannot possibly fathom that for this man all time and creation "steadily rolled." As in the "negro drayman" section of "Song," the speaker praises the black man not only, as the bidders might, for his body ("Flakes of breastmuscle, pliant backbone and neck," etc.), but also for his "allbaffling brain" and his "pluck, volition." In the man's blood, heart, and "passions and desires" the speaker finds the basis of commonality between slave and master, and between black slaves and white readers. He asks: "Do you think they are not there because they are not expressed in parlors and lecture-rooms?"

Yet despite the "same old blood" running between black and white, the future of Whitman's "curious creature" is not in America, but elsewhere:

> This is not only one man . . . he is the father of those who shall be fathers in their turns,
> In him the start of populous states and rich republics,
> Of his countless immortal lives with countless embodiments and enjoyments.
>
> (Whitman 1982: 123)

For Whitman, even the radical equality of the body does not lead to democratic inclusion. Rather, blacks are destined to start their own "populous states and rich republics." The logic of the poem thus summarizes Whitman's racial thinking, balancing his compelling images of the dignity and humanity of slaves with the comforting revelation to whites that the destiny of America's slaves is not with them. In this way Whitman captures and capitalizes on what George Fredrickson has called "a general resurgence in Northern humanitarian circles" in the 1850s of an interest in black repatriation to Africa (Fredrickson 1971: 116). Two of the "basic principles of Northern white nationalism," according to Fredrickson, were that whites and blacks "could not live together in equality and that each was biologically suited to inhabit a different region" (p. 151). By the mid-1850s such thinking was bolstered by the pseudo-science of an emerging "American school of ethnology" which held that "the races of mankind had been separately created as distinct and unequal species" (p. 74). A new "climactic racial determinism" also stated that blacks were better suited to warmer climates and so the American race problem could be solved "by establishing colonies in Central America or the Caribbean" (p. 149). (President Lincoln sought in 1862–63 to establish a colony for blacks in Central America, but the idea proved impractical.) Fredrickson writes that white "racial nationalism" was significant to Free Soil thinking in the 1850s, as whites expected that they would expand "into every corner of the nation" and the Negro would disappear through "planned colonization, unplanned migration, or extermination through 'natural' processes" (pp. 145–7).

Whitman's own scheme for colonization in "I Sing the Body Electric" describes how "rich republics" will be populated by the wondrous procreative potential of slaves, especially the female slave, "the teeming mother of mothers":

> A woman at auction,
> She too is not only herself.... she is the teeming mother of mothers,
> She is the bearer of them that shall grow and be mates to the mothers.
> Her daughters or their daughters' daughters . . who knows who shall mate with them?
>
> (Whitman 1982: 124)

Whitman's emphasis on eugenics – the strong mating with the strong – is like that of slaveholders, with the exception that he hopes not for stronger slaves but for "heroes" of "populous states" who will take their own place in history.

Whitman's "colonization" of blacks becomes clear the following year in his poem "Salut au Monde!" – significantly, the only one of 20 new poems in the 1856 *Leaves of Grass* which addresses race. The poem extends Whitman's project from embracing America's diversity to embracing the world's diversity: its geography, nations, and peoples. Yet in the final four sections (10–13) Whitman's universal embrace – "I salute all the inhabitants of the earth" (Whitman 1982: 294) – is qualified by an evolutionary eugenics. For while "Each of us [is] here as divinely as any is here," some are not quite yet "here." In section 12 Whitman catalogues those who will "come forward in due time to my side" – Africans, Asians, and Latin Americans (Whitman 1982: 296). And in the very process of describing these persons he reinforces the stereotypes which whites believed placed such peoples "away back there" to begin with: the "woolly-hair'd hordes" of the "Hottentot" (Khoisan of southern Africa); the "Austral negro, naked, red, sooty, with protrusive lip, groveling, seeking your food!"; "plague-swarms in Madras, Nankin, Kaubul, Cairo!"; and the "benighted roamer of Amazonia" (ibid.). As Dana Phillips notes, the speaker's confidence in racial progress for these peoples is "inversely proportional to the abject barbarity" he ascribes to them. The speaker meets and greets them enthusiastically precisely *because* they are "away back there" and "do not threaten him" (Phillips 1994: 300).

Whitman's representation of "Africans" among more than 30 other peoples in section 11 is especially telling:

> You dim-descended, black, divine-soul'd African, large, fine-headed,
> nobly-form'd, superbly destin'd, on equal terms with me!
>
> (Whitman 1982: 294)

The line summarizes Whitman's thinking about black persons: they are innately inferior ("dim-descended"), spiritually gifted ("divine-soul'd"), and physically – but not intellectually – developed ("fine-headed, nobly-form'd"). Black persons are "superbly destin'd" and "on equal terms" with the speaker not because they share a future together in America, but because the black person is where he or she belongs for Whitman – in Africa.

Such colonizationist thinking helps us understand what is generally regarded as Whitman's most racist and surprising writing about black persons. In an 1858 *Brooklyn Daily Times* editorial supporting the proposed Oregon constitution which would forbid "colored persons, either slave or free, from entering the State," Whitman wrote:

> Who believes that Whites and Blacks can ever amalgamate in America? Or who wishes it to happen? Nature has set and [sic] impassable seal against it. Besides, is not America for the Whites? And is it not better so? As long as Blacks remain here, how can they become anything like an independent or heroic race? There is no chance for it. (Whitman 1932: 90)

The editorial, which has vexed Whitman's readers, is perfectly consistent with his general thinking about black persons and his specific ideas about colonization. Whitman shared with his culture the fundamental convictions that blacks were different from (and likely inferior to) whites, that white prejudice was ineradicable, and therefore that blacks and whites could not live together in America. In the 1858 editorial Whitman hopes that "the colored race" might find "some secure and ample part of the earth" where they could form "a race, a nation" and take their place among the peoples of the world. But this, "or anything toward it, can never be attained in the United States" (quoted in Loving 1999: 231).

In each succeeding volume Whitman whitens *Leaves of Grass* by dissipating the presence of blacks. While nine of 12 poems in 1855 include at least one reference to black persons, few do in succeeding editions: seven of 20 in 1856, and nine of 135 in 1860. Black persons in the new 1860 poems are docile, happy, even at home in slavery. The longest passage depicts healthy, busy blacks at work in the South:

> Deep in the forest, in the piney woods, turpentine and tar dropping from the incisions in the trees – There is the turpentine distillery,
> There are the negroes at work, in good health – the ground in all directions is covered with pine straw;
> In Tennessee and Kentucky, slaves busy in the coalings, at the forge, by the furnace-blaze, or at the corn-shucking;
> In Virginia, the planter's son returning after a long absence, joyfully welcomed and kissed by the aged mulatto nurse . . .
>
> ("Chants Democratic 4," later titled "Our Old Feuillage," Whitman 1961: 162–3)

Whitman's cheerful plantation romance is clearly his response to the historical moment. With the nation on the verge of civil war, Whitman urgently wished to "make a song of the organic bargains of These States – And a shrill song of curses on him who would dissever the Union" ("Proto-Leaf," Whitman 1961: 10). Thus the angry "heir" of Lucifer, still extant in "The Sleepers," is now countered by the image of the mulatto nurse "joyfully" welcoming home the master's son with a kiss. The "free range and diversity" (p. 159) Whitman claimed to celebrate in 1860 would not include black persons or "red aborigines" (p. 20), who "melt" and "depart" (p. 20) leaving the "land and water with names" (p. 20). The "divine average" was for whites only (p. 194).

Wynn Thomas describes Whitman's writings between 1855 and the start of the Civil War as the "rhetoric of conciliation." Whitman's racialist prose and reactionary poetics, Thomas says, were driven by his desire to preserve not only the Union but also a free and democratic West for the masses of laboring whites. Whitman hoped to achieve this double aim by conciliating Southern opinion on slavery without compromising his Free Soil principles (Thomas 1994: 137–9). Whitman's racially charged "conciliatory discourse" is especially evident in "The Eighteenth Presidency!," the unpublished screed written around 1856 which, as a decade earlier, interprets the slavery conflict as the interests of "three hundred and fifty thousand masters" pitted against the "true people" of the North and the South, "the millions of white citizens, mechanics, farmers, boatmen, manufacturers, and the like" (Whitman 1982: 1311). Whitman continued to employ images of slavery to dramatize his concerns for white laborers, even though as a rhetorical strategy it had long outlived its political usefulness (Roediger 1991: 85). In this instance, white laborers are oppressed by a minority of masters (slaveholders and corrupt Northern politicians) who deny them the right to form state governments in the new territories "unless they consent to fasten upon them the slave-hopple, the iron wristlet, and the neck-spike" (Whitman 1982: 1311).

Whitman seeks to make *Leaves of Grass* as white as he hoped the new territories would be not only by limiting but even *eliminating* black persons through revisions of the 1855 poems. In "To Think of Time," for example, Whitman writes that in time's inevitable passage "The perpetual succession of shallow people are not nothing as they go" (Whitman 1982: 105). Among these "shallow people" in 1855 are "The barbarians of Africa and Asia," followed by what Whitman might consider American "barbarians": "A zambo or a foreheadless Crowfoot or a Comanche" (Whitman 1982: 105). The passage certainly denigrates blacks and Indians through racist diction ("zambo" or "sambo") and supposed physical difference ("foreheadless Crowfoot"). But even these problematic references are dropped in 1856, leaving only *non-American* "barbarians" (Africans and Asians), thus cleansing the poem of Americans who are not white.

In "I Sing the Body Electric" the slaves whom Whitman celebrates for their humanity become in 1856 something less than human. Whitman revises "A slave at auction!" to "A man's body at auction," thus objectifying the man as "body." Whitman further objectifies the slave by changing "him" to "it": "Whatever the bids of the bidders they cannot be high enough for it [him]" – and deleting the personal possessive "his" ("Within there runs [his] blood," and "There swells and jets a [his] heart," Whitman 1982: 129). The gutting of Whitman's racial polemic is completed by two changes at the end of the poem. First, Whitman removes the concluding couplet with its implicit critique of slavery: "Who degrades and defiles the living human body is cursed, / Who degrades or defiles the body of the dead is not more cursed" (Whitman 1982: 130). Second, he adds a final section of more than 30 lines, enumerating the myriad features of his *own* body to be celebrated and so reducing the emphasis on the sacred bodies of slaves.

By the time of the Civil War, race had little if anything to do with the conflict for Whitman and for most other white Americans. In fact, the kind of American nationality for which the North was fighting could be fully achieved, according to George Frederickson, "only by the removal of the Negro" (1971: 151). None of Whitman's "Drum-Taps" poems published during the war included a single image of a black person, slave or free. Whitman interpreted the war as "a violent expression of the persistent conflict between democratic and broadly antidemocratic tendencies within the one 'identity' of American republicanism," writes Wynn Thomas (1987: 178). That "one identity" was white. Whitman must have known black soldiers from his hospital visits, but the only marker of color in "Drum-Taps" occurs when the speaker in "Reconciliation" reflects on the dead enemy beside him, bends down, and touches "lightly with my lips the white face in the coffin" (Whitman 1982: 453). While "white" indicates the pallor of death, it also indicates the race for which Whitman and most Northern whites believed the war was fought.

Whitman's only other poem featuring a black person was the curious 1867 work "Ethiopia Saluting the Colors," which in 1881 he included in "Drum-Taps." The poem recounts an old black woman greeting General Sherman's army in 1865 marching through her Carolina town on its way to the sea. The speaker, one of the soldiers, cannot understand who this old woman is, or why she rises to greet the troop's colors. The poem is written in surprisingly conventional form: five stanzas of three lines each, with internal and end rhyme. Ed Folsom notes that "Whitman tended to embrace conventional metric and rhyme schemes when he felt acute social instability," in this case, the "period of massive transition" as both Whitman and the nation "struggled to figure out how they would reconstruct" themselves after the Civil War (Folsom 2000: 53–4).

The most telling issue, of course, was whether or to what extent black persons would figure in that reconstruction. The language and images of Whitman's poem clearly mark the woman as unsuited for American citizenship. Indeed, every detail in the poem marks the woman as Other to the soldier: her "hardly human" nature (mentioned twice), "woolly-white and turban'd head," and especially her unusual speech. The soldier's persistent questioning of the woman (five of his seven sentences are questions) suggests that he simply does not understand her and cannot perceive her relationship to him. He asks, "Why rising by the roadside here, do you the colors greet?" The soldier may simply be asking, "What are you doing here?" But the question can also be read as accusatory: "What do you *think* you are doing here?" The woman responds with a brief narrative:

> *Me master years a hundred since from my parents sunder'd,*
> *A little child, they caught me as the savage beast is caught,*
> *Then hither me across the sea the cruel slaver brought.*
>
> (Whitman 1982: 451, original italics)

Her story answers his question indirectly by intimating that she recognizes the connection between her enslavement as a child with her liberation by the soldier. But this "ancient" woman's story *stops* at precisely the moment she is brought to America. She is frozen in time as African, and not a century of her life and labor as a slave makes her any more of an American to the soldier – or to Whitman. Her turban is of African colors (yellow, red, and green), and the American colors she greets are "strange and marvelous." Moreover, her awkward language reinforces her alien status: her syntax is backward and, as Ed Folsom points out, she "literally cannot speak an 'I' " (Folsom 2000: 67). A hundred years on American soil has not given her American voice or subjectivity. The guidons move by, but the life of this "fateful woman" does not move with them.[6]

"Ethiopia's" distance from the soldier (and the reader) marks Whitman's distance from the idea of an integrated America. While Whitman advocated emancipation before the war, after the war "the very nature of that freedom became the problem" (Folsom 2000: 76). As Congress was passing the first Reconstruction Act in 1867, Whitman was already anxious about a new black presence: "Washington is filled with darkies – the men & children & wenches swarm in all directions – (I am not sure but that the North is like the man that won the elephant in a raffle)" (*Corr.*, 1: 323). Elsewhere he describes blacks at a parade "yelling & gesticulating like madmen – it was very comical, yet very disgusting & alarming in some respects – They were very insolent, & altogether it was a strange sight – they looked like so many wild brutes let loose" (*Corr*, 2: 34–5).

Whitman never advocated black suffrage, even after Congress passed the 15th Amendment in 1870. In "Democracy," the first essay in *Democratic Vistas* (1871) and intended as a rejoinder to Thomas Carlyle's harangue against multiracial America in "The Nigger Question," Whitman vows not to "gloss over" the question of black suffrage, but he does precisely that. It is a "stunning avoidance," Folsom writes, adding that Whitman admitted in a footnote he had "once been in the like mood" of seeing "persons and things" in the same light as Carlyle (Folsom 2000: 79–80). The following year Whitman angered his friend William Douglas O'Connor by saying blacks were unfit for voting (Loving 1978: 95). Black suffrage was in fact supported by only a "small minority in the North" until the persistent refusal of Southern whites to assent to even the smallest Northern demands provided the impetus to extend voting rights to black persons (Frederickson 1971: 183–4). Blacks were seen to be loyal to the Union, though at no point did Northern whites believe in "the black man's capacity for intelligent citizenship" (ibid.).[7] Whitman once claimed to "favor the widest opening of the doors" regarding suffrage, but elsewhere worried that "we have now infused a powerful percentage of blacks, with about as much intellect and caliber (in the mass) as so many baboons" (*PW*, 2: 762).

"Madmen," "wild brutes," "baboons" – Whitman's language shows that for him the presence of free blacks was not just an annoyance but a threat to the very foundations of white democracy. In *Memoranda During the War* (1875–76), Whitman asks: "Did the vast mass of the blacks, in Slavery in the United States, present a terrible and deeply complicated problem through the just ending century? But how if the mass of blacks in freedom in the U.S. all through the ensuing century, should present a yet more terrible and deeply complicated problem?" (*PW*, 1: 326). The answer to this "terrible and deeply complicated problem" was not, for Whitman, political and social equality. Whitman predicted, and perhaps hoped, that "the blacks must either filter through in time or gradually disappear, which is most likely though that termination is far off, or else must so develop in mental and moral qualities and in all the attributes of a leading race, (which I do not think likely)" (Price 1985: 205). Whitman's hope for blacks' disappearance is not as strange as might first appear. Many Northerners believed after the war that "blacks would not survive emancipation" (Fredrickson 1971: 236). Some felt that black persons would be pushed out by an "unequal economic struggle." Others, echoing Darwin's *Origin of Species* (1859), believed in the "inevitable extinction of the weaker race by the stronger." Even liberal Unitarian minister Theodore Parker wrote that the "law of nature" is that "the stronger replaces the weak," and so "the white man kills out the red man and the black man" (quoted in Frederickson 1971: 154–8).

For his part, Whitman continued to make blacks "gradually disappear" in his writings. At Lincoln's second inauguration Whitman noted the presence of black soldiers "with raised faces, well worth looking at themselves, as new styles of physiognomical pictures" (Bandy 1984: 25). But by the mid-1870s, with Reconstruction failing in the eyes of many Northerners, Whitman dropped all references to blacks in the text: "[T]he inauguration had come to be for Whitman an all-white affair" (Folsom 2000: 57). More significantly, Whitman removed the angry "heir" of Lucifer from *Leaves of Grass* after 1871, thus eliminating the most potent, and perhaps for him most problematic, of his slave images. "Lucifer's cry against slavery seemed less and less relevant to the postwar concerns of the nation," Folsom writes, "when Lucifer's cry had changed to a demand for citizenship and civil rights." Folsom goes on to emphasize that Whitman "creates no black characters, not a hint of representation that offers a place or role for the freed slaves in reconstructed America" (p. 52). The deletion of "Lucifer," like other of Whitman's erasures, leaves only a black *African* presence in "The Sleepers": the "Asiatic and African are hand in hand" and separate from the "European and American . . . hand in hand" (Whitman 1982: 550). In this way, Whitman takes blacks out of America *and* America out of blacks.

"Ethiopia" in Whitman's poem thus bears her name because she is African, not American, for Whitman – as African as the nation for which she is named and to which she must now return. She is like one of the Ethiopian minstrels Whitman saw perform, a player on America's racial stage whose drama was now over. In his later years Whitman's language evinced a squeamishness about blacks bordering on abhorrence. In 1875 he called the migration of blacks from South to North "the black domination," to be viewed as "temporary, deserv'd punishment" for the South because of its "Slavery and Secession sins," but in the North "as a permanency of course is not to be consider'd for a moment" (*PW*, 1: 326). When in 1888 Horace Traubel asked about racial amalgamation, Whitman responded: "I don't believe in it – it is not possible. The nigger, like the Injun, will be eliminated: it is the law of history, races, what-not: always so far inexorable. Someone proves that a superior grade of rats comes and then all the minor rats are cleared out" (Traubel 1908: 283). In the final year of his life Whitman said that "the horror of slavery was not in what it did for the nigger but what it produced of the whites," and he theorized that the reasons "niggers are the happiest people on earth" is "because they're so damned vacant" (Traubel 1996: 439). Ed Folsom notes that Whitman worked "very cautiously when he put on record anything about his views of race or emancipation." Many of Whitman's statements on race are "parenthetical or in small print in notes at the end of texts" or offhand comments to Horace Traubel (Folsom 2000: 83). Yet they provide evidence not only of Whitman's deepest fears during Reconstruction, but of views we now see he held his entire life.

The stunning, even brilliantly conceived images of blacks in the 1855 *Leaves of Grass* are a crucial part of Whitman's poetry and legacy. But black persons held no place for Whitman in his vision of America. After 1855 they were largely written out of the picture or frozen in time as slaves. Whitman's own identity, his democratic vision, and his deepest affections were always and only white. He wrote late in life in an unpublished fragment: "I do not wish to say one word and will not say one word against the blacks – but the blacks can never be to me what the whites are. Below all political relations, even the deepest, are still deeper, personal, physiological and emotional ones." He concludes: "the whites are my brothers & I love them" (*NUPM*, 6: 2160).

Notes

1 When the Continental Congress in 1776 asked Thomas Jefferson, Benjamin Franklin, and John Adams to design a national seal, they produced one "depicting Americans of English, Scottish, Irish, French, German, and Dutch extraction," writes Ellis. "There were no Africans or Native Americans in the picture" (2002: 101).

2 In a March 1846 *Eagle* editorial Whitman decried the illegal slave trade, voicing anger at "the crowding of a mass of compact human flesh" on slave ships and asking his readers to "Imagine" the suffering of the slaves. And yet he is excoriating not slavery but the slave *trade* – already illegal and practiced openly only in Brazil. Indeed, Whitman justifies slavery itself as natural. "It is not ours to find an excuse for slaving, in the benighted conditions of the African," he writes. "Has not God seen fit to make him, and leave him so?" (*Jour.*, 1: 288–9)

3 For further discussion of the novel, see Martin Klammer (1995: 7–22).

4 A critical finding in Whitman scholarship is Andrew Higgins's revelation that Whitman's famous notebook fragment, "I am the poet of slaves and the masters of slaves," was not written around 1847, as has long been thought, but rather falls within the period of late 1853 and 1854. Scholars had followed the lead of Edmund Grier, editor of Whitman's *Notebooks and Unpublished Prose Manuscripts*, who suggested that literary work in the "Talbot Wilson" notebook begins in 1847. Higgins's finding of a later date dispels some of the more vexing problems in Whitman scholarship – for example, why Whitman would focus on slaves in his poetry experiments while he was omitting them from his late 1840s Free Soil editorials (Higgins 2002: 55).

5 Folsom notes that one definition of "Lucifer" in dictionaries of the time was an ignitable match, first manufactured in the 1830s. The "Lucifer-matches" were also known as "Loco-Focos," the name given to the radical wing of the Democratic Party (Folsom 2000: 49).

6 One other interesting historical detail – which Whitman may or may not have known about – suggests the exclusion of the black woman. On January 16, 1865, General William Tecumseh Sherman *himself* issued a famous Special Field Order Number 15, setting aside "the Sea islands of South Carolina and Georgia and a coastal area for thirty miles inland for exclusive settlement by Negroes, who were given temporary 'possessory' titles to the land." The Order, which was not carried out, would have separated the black and white populations and may have "drastically altered, for better or worse, the future history of the region," according to George Fredrickson (1971: 175). The black woman's gesture of saluting Sherman's troops thus carries an added irony.

7 Fredrickson notes the double standard embodied in the 1868 Republican Party platform which sought to impose black suffrage throughout the South while allowing Northern states to determine their own suffrage requirements (1971: 186)

References and Further Reading

Andrews, William (1986). *To Tell a Free Story: The First Century of Afro-American Autobiography, 1760–1865*. Urbana: University of Illinois Press.

Bandy, W. T. (1984). "An Unknown 'Washington Letter' by Walt Whitman." *Walt Whitman Quarterly Review*, 2: 23–7.

Beach, Christopher (1996). *The Politics of Distinction: Whitman and the Discourses of Nineteenth-Century America*. Athens: University of Georgia Press.

Douglass, Frederick (1968). *Narrative of the Life of Frederick Douglass*. New York: New American Library.

Ellis, Joseph J. (2002). *Founding Brothers: The Revolutionary Generation*. New York: Vintage.

Folsom, Ed (2000). "Lucifer and Ethiopia: Whitman, Race, and Poetics before the Civil War and After." In David S. Reynolds (ed.), *A Historical Guide to Walt Whitman*. New York: Oxford University Press, pp. 45–95.

Foner, Eric (1980). *Politics and Ideology in the Age of the Civil War*. New York: Oxford University Press.

Fredrickson, George M. (1971). *The Black Image in the White Mind: The Debate on Afro-American Character and Destiny, 1817–1914*. New York: Harper and Row.

Higgins, Andrew C. (2002). Wage Slavery and the Composition of *Leaves of Grass*: The "Talbot Wilson" Notebook. *Walt Whitman Quarterly Review*, 20 (2): 53–77.

Jefferson, Thomas (1964). *Notes on the State of Virginia*. New York: Harper and Row.

Klammer, Martin (1995). *Whitman, Slavery, and the Emergence of Leaves of Grass*. University Park: Pennsylvania State University Press.

Lawrence, D. H. (1986). *Studies in Classic American Literature*. New York: Penguin Books.

Loving, Jerome (1978). *Walt Whitman's Champion: William Douglas O'Connor*. College Station, TX: Texas A & M University Press.

Loving, Jerome (1999). *Walt Whitman: The Song of Himself*. Berkeley: University of California Press.

Nevins, Allan (1947). *Ordeal of the Union*, 2 vols. New York: Scribner's.

Outka, Paul H. (2002). "Whitman and Race ('He's Queer, He's Unclear, Get Used to It')." *Journal of American Studies*, 36: 293–319.

Pease, Jane H. and Pease, William H. (1975). *The Fugitive Slave Law and Anthony Burns*. Philadelphia: J. B. Lippincott.

Phillips, Dana (1994). "Nineteenth-Century Racial Thought and Whitman's 'Democratic Ethnology of the Future.'" *Nineteenth-Century Literature*, 49 (3): 289–320.

Price, Kenneth (1985). "Whitman's Solutions to 'The Problem of the Blacks.'" *Resources for American Literary Study*, 15: 205–8.

Reynolds, David S. (1995). *Walt Whitman's America: A Cultural Biography*. New York: Alfred A. Knopf.

Roediger, David (1991). *The Wages of Whiteness: Race and the Making of the American Working Class*. New York: Verso.

Sanchez-Eppler, Karen (1993). *Touching Liberty: Abolition, Feminism, and the Politics of the Body.* Berkeley: University of California Press.

Silver, Rollo G. (1948). "Whitman in 1850: Three Uncollected Articles." *American Literature*, 19: 301–17.

Thomas, M. Wynn (1987). *The Lunar Light of Whitman's Poetry.* Cambridge, MA: Harvard University Press.

Thomas, M. Wynn (1994). "Walt Whitman and the Dreams of Labor." In Ed Folsom (ed.), *Walt Whitman: The Centennial Essays*. Iowa City: University of Iowa Press, pp. 133–52.

Traubel, Horace (1908). *With Walt Whitman in Camden*, vol. 2. New York: Appleton.

Traubel, Horace (1996). *With Walt Whitman in Camden*, vol. 8, ed. Jeanne Chapman and Robert MacIsaac. Oregon House, CA: W. L. Bentley.

Whitman, Walt (1932). *I Sit and Look Out: Editorials from the Brooklyn Daily Times*, ed. Emory Holloway and Vernolian Schwarz. New York: Columbia University Press.

Whitman, Walt (1961). *Leaves of Grass by Walt Whitman: Facsimile Edition of the 1860 Text*, introduction Roy Harvey Pearce. Ithaca, NY: Cornell University Press.

Whitman, Walt. (1982). *Complete Poetry and Collected Prose*, ed. Justin Kaplan. New York: Library of America.

Wood, Marcus (ed.) (2003). *The Poetry of Slavery: An Anglo-American Anthology, 1764–1865*. New York: Oxford University Press.

8
Nation and Identity

Eldrid Herrington

In the first sentence of his new writing life as "Walt," Whitman contrasts memory and development; the political remembrance of feudal past is a buried corpse. Feudalism has to be carried; America stands on its own:

> America does not repel the past or what it has produced under its forms or amid other politics or the idea of castes or the old religions.... accepts the lesson with calmness... is not so impatient as has been supposed that the slough still sticks to opinions and manners and literature while the life which served its requirements has passed into the new life of the new forms... perceives that the corpse is slowly borne from the eating and sleeping rooms of the house... perceives that it waits a little while in the door... that it was fittest for its days... that its action has descended to the stalwart and wellshaped heir who approaches... and that he shall be fittest for his days. (1855 preface, *LG*: 709)

"America" is the first name celebrated in the first edition of *Leaves of Grass* in a sentence that announces his and his nation's preference of futurity over feudalism. This is in prose; the first word of Whitman's poetry was "I": "I celebrate myself." "America" and "I" are yoked together and held at the same level: nation and self-identity inaugurate Whitman's writing life and describe the ambition of the scale he sings, a range he makes an equation.

"Nation" and "identity" are precisely the contrast in scale and the range of paradoxes Whitman explores in his poetry: the integration of the collective and the individual, captured in the name "United States" (not "United State"; compare "United Kingdom," not "Kingdoms"). I investigate Whitman's claim to represent the nation by examining the kinds of things he meant by identity itself and by examining his picture of the United States. One of Whitman's most astonishing achievements is his claim for the ultimate abnegation of both, at the very moment that he commits himself passionately to each. He turned to advantage the uncertainties within the state of the nation, and showed how there could be ecstasy in the loss of self and hope in the seeming dissolution of the nation. The selfish operation of the self that Tocqueville predicted for America has its acme in Whitman. But in another way, Whitman is the most unegotistical of writers; his imagination is singularly willing to abnegate and anonymize identity. Wai Chee Dimock's phrase about this forgetful equivalence is beautifully exact about its *range*; she speaks of Whitman's "cosmic tenderness" (Dimock 1996: 115). Whitman's self disappears, for example at the end of "Song of Myself"; his "sex" poems explore erotic self-abandonments; within his poems he lists competing versions of selves; he hopes for an internationality which would do away with national identifications. This apparent "contradiction" is inherent to his vision, and one way in which he "contain[s] multitudes." Critics who have sought to make Whitman purely anti-individualist or purely individualist miss his conviction about a paradox which is political and personal: state/nation; self/aggregate. This inflects his style: he rarely mentions the word "identity" in *Democratic Vistas* without pairing it with "aggregate." In this, he adheres to a grammatical pattern of paradox marrying the many and one, for example, "divine average." When he speaks of "the word En Masse" (printed both with and without a hyphen) (*LG Var.*, 1: 30), he knows that there are two words to "En Masse."

Politics

Civil war and national identity

> I consider the war of attempted secession, 1860–65, not as a struggle of two distinct and separate peoples, but a conflict (often happening, and very fierce) between the passions and paradoxes of one and the same identity – perhaps the only terms on which that identity could really become fused, homogeneous and lasting. ("Origins of Attempted Secession," PW, 2: 426–7)

The poles of individual and nation were an extension of a perennial paradox within the United States itself: the constitution of separate states within a federal system. One of Whitman's favorite names for the nation was "these States," a name that underscores the plurality of national identity and also its augmentative identity, where the political status of the accumulation was at issue for half Whitman's lifetime. The Civil War tested this American system; from well before the date that Whitman began to write, the coherence of the United States was in question. He lived in a nation highly self-conscious about its identity because of its sense of imminent disintegration, a fact which makes his pose of being hopeful an even braver one than it would be today, in more settled times. When he writes of the "nation one and indivisible, whatever happens" in the "Blue Book" revisions, he demonstrates his greater belief in the theory of the States, the fact that its true identity had not yet been achieved. The political outcome and national continuance in many ways was immaterial; in the middle of the war, uncertainty was an extension of the extant disjunction between the "one nation, indivisible, with liberty and justice for all" and generations of Americans living without liberty.

Whitman believed that with the Union struggle came the true existence of the United States; with the Union struggle, his poems also lived again. When he says that his book and the war are one (with a pun on "victory" in "one") (*LG*: 5), he is referring to *Leaves of Grass*, not "Drum-Taps." His positive interpretations of the conflict bear witness to a plurality of humanity on the battlefield and in the hospitals; the very soldiers he grieves give him hope in the national character, to be reborn at the end of the war. This view was not just personal and poetical but political; Whitman would have held with Hegel that the United States had its full elaboration of ideas and ideologies only on the dissolution of the subject; civil war was the only way in which the identity of the States could become "fused, homogeneous, and lasting" (*PW*, 2: 427).

Whitman makes his understanding of the identity of his poetic self necessary to the identity of the nation. The provisional identity of the States continues after the war and requires correction and a role for the poet, as stated in his prose work *Democratic Vistas* (1871) – a lovingly tough, resoundingly rough criticism of the United States in Reconstruction. The Constitution and founding documents of the United States, the "compact," for Whitman, comprised not merely words but their interpretation (an important judicial point crucial to understanding of the Civil War). His damning treatise on the greed in Reconstruction paints a nation refusing to fulfill its potential and shaming its past (despite a past full of shame). One of the central points he makes in *Democratic Vistas* is that the letter of the law is not enough; the spirit of a nation must be interpreted rightly. The poet, he believes, best expresses the nation, including its laws. What is necessary – the spirit – cannot be legislated; therefore the unacknowledged nonlegislator, the poet, is the best chance for the nation. Making poetics, above and beyond politics, crucial to a nation might seem somewhat undemocratic, but Whitman extends this back to the national, as Richard Rorty notes: "Whitman thought that we Americans have the most poetical nature because we are the first thoroughgoing experiment in national self-creation: the first nation-state with nobody but itself to please – not even God" (Rorty 1998: 22).

Issues of equality fought out in the Civil War in particular demonstrated that the ways in which America represents itself to itself and the world do not necessarily accord with historical fact. Whitman's insistence on interpretation of the laws and on "spirit" recognizes this whitewashing, but also recognizes the power of that belief for good as well as ill. The States never were a nation of freedoms during Whitman's lifetime, yet they had the framework to become that.

Race and American identity

"For to democracy, the leveler, the unyielding principle of the average, is surely join'd another principle, equally unyielding, . . . individuality, the pride and centripetal isolation of a human being in himself – identity – personalism" (*Democratic Vistas*, *PW*, 2: 391).

Never a committed abolitionist, Whitman gave precedence to national coherence over the emancipation of blacks; with Lincoln, he gave precedence to nation over the rights due to one American racial identity. He habitually countered others' arguments for abolition with his own desire for universal male suffrage. There are limits and problems with Whitman's presentation of race: he patronizes the "Koboo" and "Plague-swarms in Madras, Nankin, Kaubul, Cairo" who "will come forward in due time to my side" (*LG Var.*, 1: 174). When his racial categories are emptied, it is implicit that he or she is white (in "Drum-Taps" "the soldier's face is white as a lily"). But Whitman's understanding of identity also runs counter to his more nineteenth-century presentations of race. Identity is not racialism for Whitman: it is pitted against religious, gender, and ethnic identity, and American nationality itself had appropriate vagueness with regard to these categories.

Whitman's manifestations of his era's views of race have a strong answer in his own poetry. His celebration of races, genders, sexualities, classes, and so forth, places the excluded on a leveling social plane that was not politically realized for at least a generation after his death; in particular, racial identifications we think of as distinctively and wholly American today were not considered American during Whitman's lifetime. Rorty cautions against mistaking Whitman's inclusion of diversities for present-day multiculturalism; instead Whitman "wanted competition and argument between alternative forms of human life" (Rorty 1998: 24). He is not a conservative, social conservationist of ossified identifications; he liked competition between ethnic identities because only then could new identities emerge.

The fact that Whitman includes various races, genders, and religions in his lists of identities is part of his Americanness. Michael Walzer contends that "American" was never an ethnic identification (despite attempts within Whitman's lifetime):

> The adjective "American" named, and still names, a politics that is relatively unqualified by religion or nationality or, alternatively, that is qualified by so many religions and nationalities as to be free from any one of them. It is this freedom that makes it possible for America's oneness to encompass and protect its manyness. (Walzer 1990: 598)

The plurality of presentation is part of Whitman's fundamental point about identity itself: it cannot be reduced to a race. Not only is American nationality not predicated on such group identities, but it is as though Whitman understands the contradiction and tautology in the ways in which we use the word "identity" – one that Philip Gleason teases out: "identity is what a thing is!" and so "how are we to understand identity in such expressions as *ethnic identity, Jewish identity,* or *American identity*?" (Gleason 1992: 124).

Toni Morrison has shown persuasively that one powerful operation within white American writers' imaginations is the act of constituting white identity in their works by predicating it on what they believe it is not: black (and blackness invested in myth) (Morrison 1992: 3 and *passim*). Whitman turns Morrison's playing in the dark to positive ends, equalized across races: he at once identifies these people and shows how close "myself" is to them, and then insists on the differences too. His acts of identity with outcasts are audacious, and then, when he enumerates these identities and acts, he says that "they are not the Me myself" (*LG Var.*, 1: 5), and he does not predicate this separate identity on an invented racial difference. Such immeasurable identity is not exclusion but a mystery of existence even to the self itself. He imagines identities against the pattern of extant national enfranchisement and suffrage: the runaway slave, the lower classes, women, and so on. He makes racial identifications that were not accepted national ones for half his life. The minute Whitman names himself in the 1855 *Leaves of Grass*, he lists the disenfranchised, those who do not participate in the nation; when he mentions democracy, he mentions people not considered part of the nation. This is not to distinguish "Walt Whitman" from the demos but to ally them (*LG*: 52).

There is something dispassionate and cursory about Whitman's identifications: he imagines himself in the situation of a slave or upper-class woman, and then moves on to yet another identification. The restlessness of identifications might seem callous, but it should be remembered that there are dangers to "identifying with" someone else that ought to be resisted. In holding the self responsible for itself only, Whitman contends that there is one available field for equality at a national level: identity by itself. To that end, what is commonly seen as Whitman's egomania is a curious absence or anonymity of identification that serves this shifting identity, fundamentally an identity of futurity. His method of presenting identity provides difficulty for memory in the drive for *divestment* of all associations: immemorial but also unmemorable and anonymous. There remains something intangible: myself, the nature of which will always remain a mystery. The self is a mystery to itself; in the end, identity is unidentifiable, as the self cannot say what the "Me myself" is. To this end, Whitman's identifications are frequently dispassionate, moments when he is merely there, observing as a presence, not presuming to "identify with." (In *Studies in Classic American Literature*, D. H. Lawrence chooses to misread these moments with an exuberant, teasing cynicism about a tenderness he respects.) These moments register the mysterious, distinctive difference of the self instead of disclosing an indifference to that self. The speaker of "Song of Myself" "note[s] where the pistol has fallen" by the side of the suicide (*LG*: 36).

Whitman's lesson looks like a recipe for Jeffersonian happiness: do not be frightened by shifting national identity and by the bewildering plurality of identities around you: these *are* our national identity. Contradictions within identity constitute virtues for Whitman, where identity is not permitted to be a denigrating action formed by morbidity; comparatives are positive and equalizing. There is joy in identity chaos, which is never a crisis. He insists on the "mere fact consciousness" (*LG Var.*, 2: 468), enjoining people not to ask "Who am I?" or "who am I not?" and to "be not curious about God" and death (*LG Var.*, 1: 79). Most things do not happen; this one will.

Justice and plural identity

Krishan Kumar argues that greater political freedom of a society increases width and facility of association within it (Kumar 2003: 202). The width of possible identity in Whitman is intended to correlate with this political width of possibility; this has particular consequences for a democratic notion of justice. Dimock shows how closely Whitman parallels John Rawls's notion of distributive justice, as witnessed in the poet's elimination of kinds of luck that induce invidious distinctions. Anonymity as well as chance (hazard) are the field for freedom; Whitman believes in having a chance in life, in the sense of "field of risk" and "opportunity for success."

In one of the finest lines on justice, from the 1855 preface to *Leaves of Grass*, Whitman states that the poet "judges not as the judge judges but as the sun falling around a helpless thing" (*LG*: 713). Justice is constituted through anonymity and indifferent witness – an absence of judgment, in fact. The ability of the self to care about itself is paramount; caring on behalf of someone else is feudal, futile, and patronizing. This self-contained nature is a moral and national lesson: be happy with your self-image. Just egotism is the basis for caring about others; only in self-love is love for others possible. The danger of such width and facility of association is vacuity, but Whitman empties his own self in order to make room for the extreme selfhood of others. He also uses extreme specificity and particularity in his descriptions, creating a seeming contradiction in scale.

The combination of anonymity and particularity seems to be a paradox in that local caring and foundational nationalism appear to operate at a distance from each other, but as the urban historian Richard Sennett shows in *The Uses of Disorder* (1970: 120), cohesion at a small scale is necessary for national development. He argues that disorder can benefit both civic identity and self-identity; conflictual encounter is vital to city life because it avoids the puritanized uniformity of communities such as those found in suburbs (where there is actually more violence, especially in racially uniform groups). Representation, the act of listing to shadow a greater list, the total tally, also has the function of movement, change through a city and across a country. Allen Ginsberg thought Whitman's lines resembled city streets; Whitman himself said that "The movement of his verses is the sweeping movement of great currents of living people" (Whitman [1855] 1996: 31). The free verse of "Song of Myself" enlists reading order to display disorder, variety, and random encounter. Its disordered particularity bridges progress *through* a city with progress *of* a city. This messy disorder essential to development of cultural and national adulthood happens at a local level. Sennett praises curiosity as the touchstone for graspable images on a human scale:

> "caring about" . . . is closely related to a simple, creature-like curiosity, but a curiosity about graspable images, that is, individualized images. The more individual, the more particular the thing or person cared about becomes, the more men are able and willing to care about it . . .
>
> Socially, this kind of caring would be hostile to any abstract notion of humanity or brotherhood – hostile to any ideology, for a universalized notion of humanness is impossible for limited creatures like ourselves to grasp, and therefore to care about. (Sennett 1970: 48)

Sennett's claims have their parallel in Whitman's modernity of style that chimes with his democratic project. Disorder is a way of asserting that disconnection of individualism. It prevents universalizing and therefore is human; it becomes in Whitman not just reflective poetics but a hope for growth. Deferring order defeats omnipotent plans and returns people to the human. Think of those instances in "Song of Myself" where the abstract universalized is humanized or naturalized, as, for example, in the ending of section 5, where the soul and body merge incestuously. Philippians 4.7 ("And the peace of God, which passeth all understanding, shall keep your hearts and minds through Christ Jesus") is brought back to earth, as "elderhand" (in the 1855 edition) distills into "elder, mullein, and pokeweed" (*LG Var.*,1: 6). The insistence on range is at once an ambition and a statement about the States themselves: "And nothing, not God, is greater to one than one's self is" (*LG*: 86).

Whitman's present vision is an aspiration: America is not the land of the free. Whitman makes uncertain identity a virtue; groping for tentative and experimental associations for him constitutes hope. Nation and self are not "settled" in all senses. In his presentation of plural equality, Whitman presents a prospective view of his nation; it is not accurate of his own present day but more true to a democracy not yet in place.

Whitman celebrates through paradox, contradiction, and opposites which give him range as well as freedom (he can shrug his shoulders at logic): US, world; country, city; country, industry; city, individualism. Whitman's diction habitually turns feudal, class-sodden words on their heads: "average" and "common" are words of highest praise. His altruism of vision suits an idealist view of the world, but Whitman, hymnodist of the democratic real, pictured a utopia of the ordinary and saw the flawed and quotidian as glorious. The "average" is "divine." Whitman's vision is emphatically *not* idealism but an optimism about the real and the equalities the real can provide. This is what William James praised in him: the ability to see ordinary things and have that be enough.

"The best of America is the best cosmopolitanism"

" . . . my dearest dream is for an internationality of poems and poets binding the lands of the earth closer than all treaties or diplomacy" (To Dr John Fitzgerald Lee, December 20, 1881, *Corr.*, 2: 259).

Whitman is keen to recognize and extend the reach of identities within the United States, and the range of identity outside the nation. In registering the diversity of his nation, he is one of few nineteenth-century writers with a sense of the continent of "America" as part of the identity of the "United States." His choice of Spanish, French, and Native American words and names recognizes past colonialisms and extant cultures that contributed to the identity of the present-day United States. The dominant memory of American history forgets that the oldest city within the country is a Spanish foundation; Whitman's "Americanos" registers the continental reach of the "English" name, "American."

There are oddities and problems with this, though: as Louise Pound (1926) points out, the word "camerado," for example, is from Sir Walter Scott. When it was pointed out to Whitman in 1887 that "Yonnondio" did not mean "lament for the aborigines" but rather named a white governor in Canada, he still continued to print the poem with the same title and subtitle. Whitman greets the world in the languages of that world – "Salut au Monde!" – but much of this language is knowingly made up. Henry James's reported regret at Whitman's "too extensive acquaintance with foreign languages" pokes fun at the fact that Whitman's "internationality" of diction is actually an internally idiosyncratic language. This rewriting of language is a deliberately paradoxical move: the range of the world is transformed by the self. Whitman makes the range from local- and self-based scales to international, cosmopolitan ones and claims there is no scale.

Whitman was predictive in his hope for diversity of individuals' participations in his nation and in the world, a diversity limited within his own time. His forward-looking definitions of the nation in which identity is aspirational accords with one distinguishing mark of American national identity: its "future orientation" (Gleason 1980: 33). Such pride in the nation is vaunting, but one consequence of this pride is the disappearance of the country, its utter transformation from the present state. Betsy Erkkila, notably among critics, is right to identify Whitman's drive to empire (see Erkkila 1989, particularly chapter V), but this is counterbalanced by the extreme competition that Rorty identifies in Whitman's attitude to diversity. Whitman hoped for a day in which America's relationship to the world would mean the disappearance of national identity into global cosmopolitanism; in celebrating a cosmopolitanism that is neither isolationist nor aristocratic, Whitman makes an audacious claim for a demotic global culture that would eclipse the States of his time.

Style

Style: personal and political

Whitman's style reflects an ongoing and growing nation of nascent identity; his predictive claims but also the nation itself suit a poetry of beginnings. When he asks of his own poetry in one of his self-reviews, "is it any more than a beginning?" (Whitman [1855] 1996: 13) his verse form happily imitates this claim. Beginnings are at times grammatically identical, but endings resolutely refuse rhyme. The States were always in the process of becoming, and Whitman's identifiable style was intended to mirror his perception of his nation. There is the name, "Walt Whitman," but a shifting presence; there are the lines, always a beginning, never a unified termination. As I have argued above, chaos becomes representative as well as heroic (catalogues can be either), relating the particularity of mess to the responsibilities of the mass. Disordered technique is intended to imitate the foundations of democratic justice and equality. The disparate lists have a consequence for memory that would fix identity. They progress relentlessly in order to register disconnection and surprise, not connection and predictability, involving the action of forgetting, restless identifications. Larzer Ziff notes that "Democratic practice did bring together all men into a featureless mediocrity," which leads Whitman to vivify individuals (Ziff 1981: 249). His changeful identities reflect geographical and political realities about the shifting nature of the States.

The paradoxical poles of identity and nationality inflect Whitman's distinctive technique of open-ended "freedom" from rhyme. For Whitman, the uncertainty so many fear is actually the virtue of futurity. The lines of Whitman's poems celebrate this lack of finish; the self is still in process in a country still in process. Even the closing lines of "Song of Myself" constitute a challenge not to close; this is helped in 1855 by the fact that there is no period to end the poem (*LG*: 89).

Diction

Whitman plays with "foreign" words and with the "renovated English speech in America" (*DBN*, 3: 732), the linguistic register of different national conditions. Rhyme can register or aid identification of a national accent, but even in this unrhymed verse there is a place for a national accent to sound itself out. Using the merits of an American accent, Whitman masks the myth of the first man, transposing his name to the word "atom," one of many constituent physical minutiae: "And every atom belonging to me as good belongs to you" (*LG*: 28). Each tiny, anonymous part is as important as Adam. The smallest unit within a human being sounds out the name of the first human being.

"Equal" is one of Whitman's preferred words, encompassing the possibility of being "equal to" anything as well as the "equal of" anything, as in the title, "Thou Mother With Thy Equal Brood." Equality is the basis of taking on challenges. In "America," that Americentric poem, Whitman shows how individuals within a "self-poised Democracy" ("To Other Lands," *LG Var.*, 2: 417) are themselves "in the middle, well-pois'd" ("A Broadway Pageant," *LG*: 245), "well entretied" ("Song of Myself," *LG*: 31). It is as though Whitman puns on the word "fair," meaning "beautiful" as well as "egalitarian." The pun on "center" indicates internal identity, a self-centered "selfishness," with "center" and "equal" as equivalents. "Center" embodies the balance invoked, the physical political balance. America is the "center of equal daughters, equal sons" who are equals of one another but also "equal to" themselves, equal to challenges.

Poem structure

One danger of such extreme self-reliance is isolation, very much a threat the Romanticists felt in their notion of the self: their view raised the specter that anything outside the self might not be real. Whitman recognizes this disconnection in "A Noiseless Patient Spider" (*LG*: 450) and explores the nature of isolated identity through play on extant poetic techniques. The poem is composed of two sets of five lines, each a sentence; the pause between them perfectly enacts the difficult poise between ostensive and internal identity. The bridge between two creatures is the noiseless space between stanzas, at once separating and connecting "my soul" with the spider. The poem pictures loneliness, but pairs two beings through its typography. Diction echoes between the "stanzas": "Surrounded, detached" in line 7 picks up "isolated" and "surrounding" at the endings of lines 2 and 3. Metaphor, that literary bridge, also ties the spider and soul together. Apposition and assonance unite them immediately in the first two lines: "A noiseless patient spider / I . . . ." The "I" does not just "mark" – see – the spider but *is* the spider. Metaphor, grammar, diction, poem structure, all work against the painful doubt in the poem that there is no other being out there with whom to share the world.

Beautifully, grammar effects this typically deliberate Whitmanian incertitude. The first stanza is a sentence, but the second stanza is an incomplete sentence – there is no main verb, and the sentence is wrapped up in its subject, starting with "you O my soul" and ending with "O my soul." It is an exhortation to self-sufficiency carried in a self-sufficient manner. It waits, as the ending of "Song of Myself" waits, for connection with another to complete it. Conditionality tinges the grammar: the last line does not read "Till the gossamer thread you fling *catches* somewhere" but "Till the gossamer thread you fling *catch* somewhere, O my soul." "Fling catch" is a beautiful picture of the thin space needed for connection, a minute typographical distance pointing out a vast gap, a void in relations that needs to be bridged.

The identity of soul and spider lives in the poem's structure, and in its claims: the very moment a bridge is asked for, the bridge (metaphor) is there. Whitman's deliberate incertitudes about identity are most frequently carried through direct contradictions, here between sentiment and sentence: the poem form and manner work against what is being said and claim an answer to the loneliness depicted.

Time and identity

Whitman undertakes myth making of the future, not of the past, supplanting the traditional view of *history* as the site of national identity. To this end, historical events are made anonymous, from the Goliad massacre to John Paul Jones's battle. Futurity characterizes the American sense of identity as a belief in destiny.

History is no longer famous events and people but ordinary events and identities, a move that Whitman extends to the demotion of time itself. The erasure of time is part of the equalizing nature, the democratic leveling of "Crossing Brooklyn Ferry." The poem is not about transfer of identity but a crossing of identity, "crossing" in the sense of "paralleling" and "transferring." Temporal identity becomes contemporary identity in "Crossing Brooklyn Ferry," which still speaks to the people of today – this is the "eternity" of the poem. It is only a poem of temporality in that the openness of identity ("you" being general) leaves poetry alive to pluralities not yet known to the poet, combining mysteries of new identities together with the certainty of identity itself. In time, a new nation unknown to Whitman will exist, and it does not terrify him. Time is irrelevant because the self-same experiences can happen to separate selves, and several selves, even when living several generations and centuries apart. The same plane of space unites them. Again the bare fact of identity is not a mere fact. Whitman does not strip each being of identity, individualism, but states that the general experience of individualism will remain the same for all human beings. "I too had receiv'd identity by my body" (*LG Var.*, 1: 221): the materiality of this experience is the same even if the bodies are different living in different times; this is not a poem of transubstantiation or transference of the soul. Jochen Achilles sees this disintegration in social terms:

> The danger of fragmentation lurking behind the nonetheless fascinating heterogeneity of the urban situation, from which James recoils in *The American Scene*, poses no threat for Whitman. He sees himself and others – "everyone disintegrated yet part of the scheme" – as elements of a cityscape whose very shiftiness is redeemed by a transindividual and transhistorical perceptual unity, as unshakeable sense of identity which is, in the last analysis, founded on the metaphysicization of physical existence: "I too had receiv'd identity by my body, / That I was I knew was of my body, and what I should be I knew should be of my body." (Achilles 2000: 106–7)

The open spaces of Central Park are a threat to Henry James in *The American Scene* but the open space and time of the East River between Manhattan and Brooklyn, between Whitman and the future reader, are not recoiled from but reveled in. Shiftiness *is* redemption within the poem; Whitman has sufficient and generous imagination to register that his present identity will not last into the future, but refuses morbidity; someone else will take its place, and he welcomes the change.

Geographic national identity

In "Crossing Brooklyn Ferry" the identity of bodily presence is transposed to an other-body experience, but the physical for Whitman is not only an urban experience. He looked to the material identity of the nation for parallels with the style of his poetry. When he saw Platte Canyon, he said it was as rugged as his verse, creating an identity between his poetry and the physical characteristics of his land. Though he loved the principle of variety, surprise, he chose the Plains as representative of Americanness, perhaps because of democratically flat sameness, the Midwest average. He at once makes a great case for national literature, and also identifies it with other things: "The United States themselves are essentially the greatest poem" (*LG*: 709).

Whitman's cosmopolitan vision seems to be at odds with his biography: he only traveled outside the States when he went to Canada; he lived in New York and in Camden, across the river from Philadelphia, ranging from the northeastern United States. But there is another way in which this can be read as appropriate: his cosmopolitanism was crucially founded in the imagination and did not need physical verification of the common humanity of the globe.

Self

The abnegation of selfhood and nation

This biographical fact about Whitman's limited physical vision of the world is appropriate to a poet who believed that his nation contained all other nations already (and specifically Manhattan: "city of the world! (for all races are here)," *LG Var.*, 2:

490). In his definition of his own identity and in the first moment he names himself, Whitman gives an impossible vista of selfhood. The progress and parallel from "Whitman, a kosmos," to "of Manhattan the son" traces an isolation and a connectedness. Whitman suggests that he contains a world inside himself, a world indebted to his birthplace. No man is an island, unless he is a populous and cosmopolitan island, a world within an urban world.

Whitman set up a mystery about his presence, at once material and immaterial; Emerson had trouble identifying him – literally. Again this presents an identity-paradox: Whitman is anonymous and bodily; he is present and absent. There is the temptation to believe his claim that he does talk about himself in "Song of Myself." The self, in the end, cannot be represented, is a mystery even to itself; this accounts for the "anonymity" of Whitman's great poem of the self, "Song of Myself," which had a variety of title-identities over its lifetime. The changes to the title should be warning and indication enough, from no title in 1855 to "Poem of Walt Whitman, an American" in 1856 to "Song of Myself" in 1881 – in other words, from anonymous to eponymous to generalized (another kind of anonymity). The final title of the poem abnegates a claim for universality; in the vagueness of reference ("myself"), anyone could be designated.

Whitman's fine line of egotism bears re-explaining. He desires people to exercise just pride as against vaunting ego or shame. His presentation of the self is at once egotistical and emptied, identifying and unidentifiable. Whitman's act of putting the self on record is separate from identity with other selves, a confusion Lawrence makes. "Song of Myself" finishes with a bravura encouragement to the reader to try to find him, but also to try to find what the self is. Readers confuse the "I" with ego, ignoring the knowingness of Whitman's pose; as Randall Jarrell (1996) pointed out, Whitman knows it when he overdoes it. His statements about the self are obvious, declaratory, but the self is anonymous. The nature of the self that represents remains mysterious but the nature of representation itself is transparent.

Whitman is willing to abnegate his own identity in favor of others'. He lets go of omniscience in favor of an unknown future. He lets go of the national in favor of the international. Part of the charge of this loss is deeply erotic: section 11 of "Song of Myself" registers an ecstasy and loss of self through the absence of pronouns that might identify the gender of the onlooker ("she," "he"). This is about what happens during eroticism. For Whitman, sex is the human activity that enacts "losing" ego (see sections 5 and 11 of "Song of Myself" particularly); love for others, selflessness, carries sexual charge. Critics focus on homosexuality to assert this, but Whitman has sufficient imagination to apply this to heterosexuality as well. His style is deliberately disobedient when describing sexual abandonment of identity: grammar breaks down. At the end of "The Dalliance of the Eagles," the eagles separate, "their separate diverse flight, / She hers, he his, pursuing" (*LG Var.*, 3: 685). Whitman writes "flight" instead of "flights" because their identities are still entwined through sex, though they are physically separate.

The way in which self gives self up to another and to pleasure chimes with the retreat to happiness at the end of "Song of Myself":

> Failing to fetch me at first keep encouraged,
> Missing me one place search another,
> I stop somewhere waiting for you.
> (*LG Var.*, 1: 83)

The passionate identifications insisted upon throughout the poem actually take a different direction from the one that you might suppose. A latent pun informs this end: at the close of the poem Whitman invites the reader to get close. And after all, how could you close a poem like this? Only by saying that there is no close. Identification, at the end, is elusive, illusory; if anything, "Song of Myself" has shown what "myself" is not. Anonymity fits with the futurity and welcome of beginning this end heralds. "I" waits to be filled by "you" – someone else. Keats identified this lack of identity as the role of the poet:

> What shocks the virtuous philosop[h]er, delights the camelion Poet. It does no harm from its relish of the dark side of things any more than from its taste for the bright one; because they both end in speculation. A Poet is the most unpoetical of any thing in existence; because he has no Identity – he is continually in for – and filling some other Body. (Keats to Richard Woodhouse, October 27, 1818, Keats 2002: 148)

It is as if Whitman had read this (and read it sexually); he said of himself in one of his self-reviews, "If health were not his distinguishing attribute, this poet would be the very harlot of persons" (Whitman [1855] 1996: 36).

Susan Sontag notes that Whitman's paradox is the way in which egotism is every ego, a seeming indifference to individualism. In this he importantly reverses one foundational method of American identity: if you want to define yourself, assert what it is you are not:

> In the mansions of pre-democratic culture, someone who gets photographed is a celebrity. In the open fields of American experience, as catalogued with passion by Whitman and as sized up with a shrug by Warhol, everybody is a celebrity. No moment is more important than any other moment; no person is more interesting than any other person. (Sontag 1977: 23)

In this light, it is surprising that Whitman is taken to be an egotistical writer; as Randall Jarrell says, "Whitman is often written about . . . as if he were . . . the hero of a de Mille movie about Walt Whitman" (1996: 97). "Song of Myself" is the first poem about the self in American literature, and it is also not about himself. It is no autobiography, no Wordsworthian *Prelude* for American literature.

Whitman's changeful identity of self, of politics, looks like an evolutionary adaptability to future conditions. The provisionality of identity is a freedom of spirit and a flexibility of nationality that assures pre-eminence, though perhaps not in the same national form. Uncertainty of identity is made a virtue across all ranges of life, from self to geography to politics to the world. The poet also claims that there is no range at all, that self and world are as large as each other. This vast scale and possibility for selfhood as well as its fluidity are essential to democracy. Whitman's understanding of identity renders the traditional range from nature to nation to self insignificant; he demands an American identity divested of genuflection: "nothing, not God, is greater to one than one's self is." Whitman invites people of any nation to join in this ostensive identity; his own poem about self-identity has its first word as "I." Its last word is "you."

References and Further Reading

Achilles, Jochen (2000). Men of the Crowd: The Challenge of Urbanization and Negotiations of National Identity in Antebellum Short Stories. In Roland Hagenbüchle, Josef Raab, and Marieta Messmer (eds.), *Negotiations of America's National Identity*, vol. 2. Tübingen: Stauffenburg, pp. 104–30.

Carlisle, E. Fred (1973). *The Uncertain Self: Whitman's Drama of Identity*. East Lansing: Michigan State University Press.

Clarke, Graham (ed.) (1994). *Walt Whitman: Critical Assessments*, 4 vols. Robertsbridge, UK: Helm Information.

Dimock, Wai Chee (1996). *Residues of Justice*. Berkeley, CA: University of California Press.

Erkkila, Betsy (1989). *Whitman the Political Poet*. New York: Oxford University Press.

Erkkila, Betsy and Grossman, Jay (eds.) (1996). *Breaking Bounds: Whitman and American Cultural Studies*. Oxford: Oxford University Press.

Gleason, Philip (1980). American Identity and Americanization. In Stephan Thernstrom, Ann Orlov, and Oscar Handlin (eds.), *The Harvard Encyclopedia of American Ethnic Groups*, Cambridge, MA: Belknap Press, pp. 31–85.

Gleason, Philip (1992). *Speaking of Diversity*. Baltimore: Johns Hopkins University Press.

Greenspan, Ezra (1990). *Walt Whitman and the American Reader*. Cambridge, UK: Cambridge University Press.

Jarrell, Randall (1996). *Poetry and the Age*. London: Faber.

Jehlen, Myra (1998). Multitudes and Multicultures. In Hans Lofgren and Alan Shima (eds.), *After Consensus: Critical Challenge and Social Change in America*. Goteborg, Sweden: Acta Universitatis Gothoburgensis, pp. 155–69.

Keats, John (2002). *Selected Letters*, ed. Robert Gitting. Oxford: Oxford University Press.

Killingsworth, M. Jimmie (1992). Tropes of Selfhood: Whitman's "Expressive Individualism." In Robert K. Martin (ed.), *The Continuing Presence of Walt Whitman: The Life After the Life*. Iowa City: University of Iowa Press, pp. 39–52.

Kumar, Krishan (2003). *The Making of English National Identity*. Cambridge, UK: Cambridge University Press.

Lawrence, D. H. (1986). *Studies in Classic American Literature*. New York: Penguin Books.

Martin, Robert K. (1994). Whitman and the Politics of Identity. In Ed Folsom (ed.), *Walt Whitman: The Centennial Essays*. Iowa City: University of Iowa Press, pp. 172–81.

Morrison, Toni (1992). *Playing in the Dark*. Cambridge, MA: Harvard University Press.

Pound, Louise (1926). Walt Whitman and the French Language. *American Speech*, 1: 421–30.

Rorty, Richard (1998). *Achieving Our Country*. Cambridge, MA: Harvard University Press.

Sennett, Richard (1970). *The Uses of Disorder*. New York: W. W. Norton.

Sontag, Susan (1977). *On Photography*. New York: Farrar, Straus and Giroux.

Thomas, M. Wynn (1981). Whitman and the American Democratic Identity Before and During the Civil War. *Journal of American Studies*, 15 (1): 73–93.

Walzer, Michael (1990). What Does It Mean to be an "American"? *Social Research*, 57 (3): 591–613.

Whitman, Walt (1996). Walt Whitman and His Poems. *United States Review*, 5 (September 1855), 205–12. In Kenneth M. Price (ed.), *Walt Whitman: The Contemporary Reviews*. Cambridge, UK: Cambridge University Press, pp. 8–14.

Ziff, Larzer (1981). *Literary Democracy*. Harmondsworth, UK: Penguin.

9
A Theory of Organic Democracy

Stephen John Mack

In section 24 of "Song of Myself," Walt Whitman's most paradigmatic poem, the poet-narrator dramatically identifies himself and the scope of his literary mission: "Walt Whitman, a kosmos, of Manhattan the son" (*LG*: 52). Discussions of Whitman often begin with this central metaphor, his equation of the individual self with the entire social and material universe: "every atom belonging to me," he declares, "as good belongs to you" (*LG*: 28). But if the safest thing we can say about Whitman's own "kosmic" identity is that it really means everything, then perhaps the most important thing we can say about that *everything* is that it defines – and is defined by – democracy. Nine lines after he names himself (and all selves) the ultimate microcosm, he qualifies the claim by adding, "I speak the pass-word primeval, I give the sign of democracy."

It is not surprising that Whitman made democracy the central concern of his literary vision. He was, in a sense, a political operative long before he became an innovative poet. His father was an enthusiast of the Democratic Party who claimed to his son to have been a friend of Thomas Paine. At the age of 21 Whitman campaigned for Martin Van Buren, the handpicked successor of the great democrat of Whitman's time, Andrew Jackson. And his education as a writer came largely as a result of his work for, and editorship of, several highly partisan New York newspapers from 1841 to 1849. Indeed, so intense were Whitman's political sentiments that a few critics speculate that his turn to the more distant environs of visionary poetry in 1855 reflected some deep disillusionment with real-world politics as a vehicle of social change. If so, it is clear that visionary writing did nothing to alleviate his polemical instincts. In 1856, shortly after publishing his second edition of *Leaves of Grass,* he wrote "The Eighteenth Presidency!," a model of passionate political prose. In this unpublished tract, Whitman castigates the entire political class of the United States for its impotent attempts to confront the slavery crises, taking special aim at Millard Fillmore and Franklin Pierce, presidents who:

> have shown that the villainy and shallowness of great rulers are just as eligible to These States as to any foreign despotism, kingdom, or empire – there is not a bit of difference. History is to record these two Presidencies as so far our topmost warning and shame. Never were publicly displayed more deformed, mediocre, sniveling, unreliable, false-hearted men! (Whitman 1982: 1310)

It would be misleading, however, to suggest that Whitman's choice of democracy as poetic material derived merely from a preoccupation with politics. In the early nineteenth century, the curiosity of democracy was a widespread concern. It inspired nearly as much popular discussion as democratic politics. And to discuss democratic theory was to discuss America. When Whitman wrote that he used "America and democracy as convertible terms," he was articulating an assumption widely shared in both the United States and Europe. When Alexis de Tocqueville visited America in the first decades of that century he was but the most famous and insightful of what one historian refers to as the "stream of European visitors," who came to discover whether "masterless men in a structureless society" could work (Wiebe 1995: 41). Though sometimes sympathetic, these "amateur scientists" "carefully compiled field reports" about "a strange new world" in which greed, uncouth manners, and hostility to class-based social hierarchy were creating a nation of ungovernable barbarians (1995: 42). To these observers, America was a problem because democracy was a problem. Both seemed the death knell of civilized life. But both also had its apologists – and Whitman was certainly among them. Thus as he nears the end of "Song of Myself," the great poem that metaphorically yokes self and society within a democratic cosmos, he asks "Do you see O my brothers and sisters? / It is not chaos or death – it is form, union, plan – it is eternal life – it is happiness" (*LG*: 88).

The significance of Whitman's most startling metaphor, however, transcends whatever small role it may have played in the debate over the virtues of practical democracy. More important is the way the metaphor itself enabled him to make a series of unprecedented – if underappreciated – contributions to democratic theory. In particular, Whitman's imaginative formulation joins his two most useful theoretical innovations. First, Whitman's democracy essentially erases the boundary between other democratic theories that traditionally compete with one another. Broadly speaking, notions of democracy divide into two camps: classical liberal theories that conceive the individual as a rights-bearing autonomous being, and, alternatively, a host of other theories that either define the individual in essentially social terms or subordinate individuals to some notion of civic good. There are, of course, cross-fertilizations; but generally democratic ideas name either individualist or collective values as foundational and, therefore, those most necessary for the state to protect. By imaginatively erasing the distinction between the self and the social, however, Whitman denies privileged status to either loci of concern. Consequently, he advances a view of democracy that redefines the traditional interests of both the individual and the collective in ways that make them identical.

The second innovative contribution to democratic theory suggested by Whitman's "kosmic" metaphor is its comprehensive scope. For Whitman, the universe, with all its conflicts and contradictions, is an organic whole – and democracy its defining quality and animating principle. This is to say that democracy names a variety of interdependent conditions and processes, none of which can be properly understood in isolation from the others. For example, the political process – arguably the central concern of most democratic theories – is for Whitman only one feature of *total democracy*; elections, he argues, are the political manifestation of a logic that operates throughout the universe. A full appreciation of democracy, then, requires an accounting of the ways the democratic processes of physical nature inform or parallel democratic social, political, economic and cultural practices – and, just as importantly, how our insights into the interrelation of those practices can guide our construction of the institutions that support democratic life.

Democracy and Nature

Whitman's complete vision of democracy developed in stages throughout his poetic career, finally maturing with the publication of *Democratic Vistas* in 1871. His democratic ontology, however – his vision of a free and natural self – was fully articulated in the first edition of *Leaves of Grass* in 1855. Like many of the European political philosophers who precede him – most famously, Hobbes, Locke, and Rousseau – Whitman derives his notion of the political self from a conception of nature. But while it is true that each of the aforementioned philosophers constructed significantly different versions of the "state of nature," Whitman's conception of nature marked a radical, and instructive, departure from the entire tradition. In Western political thought, nature is typically evoked as a useful fiction, a hypothetical set of precivil conditions tailor-made to explain whatever version of the "social contract" a particular writer thinks ideal. Social contract theories generally legitimize state power either by stabilizing natural conditions thought desirable, or insulating human life from nature's brutalizing vagaries. In all cases, social contracts function to separate human beings from their natural condition. But for Whitman, there was no separation. He regards human beings as thoroughly and inescapably *natural beings*. Hence the ideal state, the true state – the democratic state – is the one that most faithfully mirrors those qualities of nature Whitman regards as essential.

The significance of Whitman's view of nature is especially striking when contrasted with the ideas of John Locke, the thinker who exerted the most influence on Jefferson and thus on American political doctrine. For Locke, original nature was essentially placid, static, and bountiful. But in essence, it was also something different and apart from humankind – and this condition lays the foundation for his conception of political rights. In the *Second Treatise on Government,* Locke writes "God gave the World to Men in Common; but since he gave it to them for their benefit, and the greatest Conveniences of life they were capable to draw from it, it cannot be supposed he meant it should always remain common and uncultivated" (Locke 1988: 291). The implication here is that nature is something external and *ownable,* not so much something that includes human beings but a resource that is available to them. And indeed, ownership is essential to Locke's political conception of nature. Starting from the assumption that individuals own their own bodies and labor, Locke reasons that anything they remove from nature to develop and use "with the labour that was mine" must axiomatically become their property as well (p. 289). Further, since the enjoyment of property rights generally requires collective security arrangements, we are compelled to form civil societies. Thus – and to put the point more instructively – since civil society is established in order to protect natural property rights, then the political rights that attend civil society should also be thought of as properties of the individual.

There is no equivalent doctrine of rights in Whitman's democratic theory. To be sure, he assumed that all human beings enjoyed political rights and quite likely regarded them as both fundamental and inalienable. But unlike Locke, Whitman's view of nature was not motivated by a need to legitimate individual liberty or governments organized to protect it. By Whitman's time the notion of popular sovereignty was so well entrenched that, as Alexis de Tocqueville put it, "it was not even permissible to struggle against it any longer" (1969: 59). So the nature Whitman imagines is quite different from Locke's; consequently, his vision of individual selfhood – including the political aspects of selfhood – is also substantially different. For Whitman, nature is an all-encompassing, ever-changing, integrated whole. Human beings are not the beneficiaries of nature, but aspects of it. As such, we are composed of the same material substance pervasive throughout the rest of the universe. In section 31 of "Song of Myself," for example, he writes "I find I incorporate gneiss, coal, long-threaded moss, fruits, grains, esculent roots, / And am stucco'd with quadrupeds and birds all over" (*LG*: 59). This insistence on humanity's fundamental materiality is ubiquitous in Whitman and is often linked to his understanding that nature is characterized by change. He refers to a nameless corpse in section 49 of "Song of Myself" as "good Manure," and to "Life" itself as "the leavings of many deaths" (*LG*: 87). This is not a vision of humanity possessing nature or being invested with entitlements or rights. If anything, humanity is subordinated to nature and its processes. The only "natural law" Whitman recognizes is that of eternal regeneration through death.

Liberty, Equality, and Process

If Whitman's construction of nature does not lead to a notion of rights as individual property, it does, nevertheless, integrate three fundamental expressions of democratic experience: (1) a bias for open, process-oriented systems over closed, rigidly ordered and hierarchical systems; (2) the belief that individual liberty is an absolute value; (3) a faith that when democracy is fully implemented it will inevitably lead to social equality.

The first of these, the bias for process-oriented systems, is the political version of his "open-road" philosophy in which he imagines the self as the product of a lifetime of freely embraced experiences – a developmental process. This philosophy was itself the psychological analogue of Whitman's larger conception of nature as a place of infinite size and continuous change:

> I open my scuttle at night and see the far-sprinkled systems,
> And all I see multiplied as high as I can cipher edge but the rim of the farther systems.
> Wider and wider they spread, expanding, always expanding,
> Outward and outward and forever outward.
> My sun has his sun and round him obediently wheels,
> He joins with his partners a group of superior circuit,
> And greater sets follow, making specks of the greatest inside them.
> There is no stoppage and never can be stoppage.
>
> (*LG*: 82)

This is not just motion; it is creative change. Because the universe is constantly expanding, it is constantly remaking itself. It, along with everything in it, is the product of its own processes of self-invention. Thus he can write, "I believe a leaf of grass is no less than the journey-work of the stars" (*LG*: 59). Thus, too, he can embark on his own path of self-creation as he does in "Song of the Open Road."

> Afoot and light-hearted I take to the open road,
> Healthy, free, the world before me,
> The long brown path before me leading wherever I choose.
>
> (*LG*: 149)

Along the poet's journey of self-creation he affirms the shaping value of all that is new and unconventional: "You paths worn in the irregular hollows by the roadsides! / I believe you are latent with unseen existences, you are so dear to me" (*LG*: 150). Further, he knows that accessing the creative power of the unconventional means becoming wary of the conventional – in effect, asserting critical governing authority over his own developmental process:

> From this hour I ordain myself loos'd of limits and imaginary lines,
> Going where I list, my own master total and absolute,
> Listening to others, considering well what they say,
> Pausing, searching, receiving, contemplating,
> Gently, but with undeniable will, divesting myself of the holds that would hold me.
>
> (*LG*: 151)

Here, as elsewhere, Whitman finds in nature both a warrant and model for personal governance. In so doing he does not imagine governance as a conservative force employed merely to stabilize life; he views it as the process of harmonizing with nature's own dynamic powers of creation – not only tolerating the destabilizing aspects of nature, but exploiting them. Importantly, though, he makes it clear that this process is not just personal, but social as well. The poem concludes, characteristically, with Whitman's invitation to his readers:

> Camerado, I give you my hand!
> I give you love more precious than money,
> I give you myself before preaching or law;
> Will you give me yourself? Will you come travel with me?
> Shall we stick by each other as long as we live?
>
> (*LG*: 159)

Affirming the "democratic process" has become a rhetorical cliché in the United States. Whitman, however, understood the radical implications of the emphasis on process. For one thing, rather than privileging stability, order, the known, it renders them targets of habitual suspicion. As a social value, process elevates inventiveness, experimentation, *becoming* – and the likely chaos associated with both – over stasis and tradition. It also elevates the unknowable future over secure past: "Thus," he writes in *Democratic Vistas*, "we presume to write, as it were, upon things that exist not, and travel by maps yet unmade and a blank" (*PW*: 391).

A preference for the notion of becoming over being also has obvious implications for the problem of national identity. Whitman famously embraced the idea of America as a "teeming nation of nations," as he phrased it in the 1855 "Preface" (*LG*: 711). The foregoing passage (and others like it throughout *Leaves of Grass*) illustrates how this view of national identity functions – and also distinguishes his view of national identity from that found in another great democratic theorist, Jean-Jacques Rousseau. By inviting his readers to join him – love and the adventure of self-definition his only lures – Whitman implicitly repudiates (though it was probably not his intention) Rousseau's version of the social contract. Here Whitman suggests that disparate people become a nation, a collective entity, by choice. That choice, moreover, is motivated and maintained by love, not necessity. And further, the meaning of their association, the particular ways they might characterize their own national identity, is always subject to change and renewal. For Rousseau (as for others, as we have seen), the social contract was not so much a continuation of nature but a correction of it. People unite, he asserts, because the resources at the disposal of individuals for their maintenance in the state of nature are no longer sufficient. Nature presents "obstacles" to survival. In joining together, then, they surrender those individual resources in order to avail themselves of the greater resources of the group. But this is a conundrum for Rousseau because the most important resource to be surrendered is individual liberty: "the force and liberty of each man, being the primary instruments of his own self preservation." This suggests that being in a group means being a slave to the group. Rousseau accepts this condition, but reasons that it is permissible because it is an equally shared condition. The single most important clause of the social contract demands

> the total alienation of each member, with all his rights, to the community as a whole. For, in the first place, since each gives himself entirely, the condition is equal for all;

> and, since the condition is equal for all, it is in the interest of no one to make it burdensome to the rest. (Rousseau 1986: 15)

In this scheme, sovereign authority rests with what Rousseau famously calls the "general will," so that in place of the individual personality, the act of association creates a collective body, a common identity by which it gains its life and will (Rousseau 1986: 25–6). The problem with this construction, as so many of Rousseau's critics have pointed out, is that it is so removed from the actual interests and desires of the people it would claim to empower that it is as much a source of tyranny as collective will. The coercive potential of Rousseau's general will becomes even more apparent when he writes of the legislator's responsibility to make stable and perfect the new institutions he creates by "annihilating" the "natural resources" that enable individuality (pp. 41–5). Whitman, by contrast, imagines precisely those natural resources as the necessary material of collective identity formation. Hence it is not surprising that he would imagine human sociality as a function of nature, not its alienation. Likewise, it is not surprising that, until he writes *Democratic Vistas*, Whitman makes almost no attempt to theorize social institutions. The purpose of stabilizing institutions is to arrest change and Whitman regarded change as a creative force of life.

Whitman's treatment of liberty, like his view of creative process, emerges as something like an existential condition. He regards freedom as a fact of nature before it is a social or political utility. In this, too, Whitman differs somewhat from the Western political tradition. Unlike John Milton, that is, he did not feel obliged to defend liberty on the grounds that it permitted ideas to be tested and truth validated. And although he was clearly sympathetic with laissez-faire-oriented writers such as Thomas Paine, he did not seem to feel obligated to rationalize a faith in freedom – particularly freedom from restrictive government – by arguing that it unleashed the natural forces by which society regulates and reconstitutes itself (Paine 2000: 167). Whitman thought of freedom as simply a fact of nature. It was self-evident to him that nature is infinite and self-directed, beyond the reach of some anterior authority. Freedom in nature did not need arguing for; sometimes it was sufficient to acknowledge that one's own freedom and power were gained by harmonizing with nature: "My ties and ballasts leave me," he announces at the start of an especially spirited catalogue in "Song of Myself," "my elbows rest in sea-gaps, / I skirt sierras, my palms cover continents, / I am afoot with my vision" (*LG*: 61).

Whitman's conception of a free and infinite universe does, however, have social and political implications. It would have to, of course, for whatever characterizes the essential qualities of nature must also characterize humanity itself. Thus he writes in the "Preface" to the 1855 edition of *Leaves of Grass* "the idea of political liberty is indispensable." But because liberty is already justified by its grounding in nature, Whitman apparently feels no need to argue for it. In the discussion that follows this pronouncement, he does not bother to make the case for liberty by, for example, pointing out the material benefits of living in a free society. Rather, he is far more concerned to stress the importance of preserving liberty. Indeed, at one point he even reverses the logic by which freedom is justified by the material gain it enables: "Liberty is poorly served by men whose good intent is quelled from one failure or two failures or any number of failures." That is, we should not value freedom because it is the means to material success; rather, the argument for material success (or at least, the avoidance of failure) is that it leaves one psychologically emboldened to fight for freedom. Freedom is not a utility. "Liberty relies upon itself, invites no one, promises nothing, sits in calmness and light, is positive and composed, and knows no discouragement." Perhaps most basically, Whitman treats the wish for freedom as an innate human motivation that precedes and informs the particular ways cultures define it and the political arrangements societies devise to further it. As such, it cannot be defeated until "all life and all the souls of men and women are discharged from any part of the earth – then only shall the instinct of liberty be discharged from that part of the earth" (*LG*: 722–3).

Whitman's view of equality also owes much to his conception of nature. And to be sure, no single term has inspired more controversy among democratic theoreticians than equality. Earlier, Enlightenment-era theorists used the word to describe the way identical political rights were grounded in nature and thus protected individuals as they engaged in the unavoidably unequal pursuit of private gain. The social democrats who followed them, however, used the term more prescriptively, to denote nature's mandate of social and economic parity. These later democrats would often reread Jefferson's famous assertion that "all Men are created equal" as, at worst, a grand lie or, at best, an expression of the utopian essence of America's national mission. (Jefferson himself, of course, saw no contradiction in proclaiming equality on the one hand and then, on the other, arguing to John Adams that the best form of government is that which cultivates the "natural aristocracy" of virtuous and talented men.) Whitman's view of equality bridges these approaches. He fully accepted the Jeffersonian and Enlightenment stress on the individual. In one of the short poems titled "Thought," he reflects "Of Equality – as if it harm'd me, giving others the same chances and rights as myself – as if it were not indispensable to my own rights that others possess the same" (*LG*: 277).

Even if nature does not provide the legal precondition for a conception of individual rights, the fact that we are all equally composed of the same material substances – the "gneiss, coal, long-threaded moss, fruits, grains" – was enough to disprove the notion that nature was biased in favor of hierarchical distinctions. For Whitman, the salient political truth about human beings, however, does not concern their common material origins but their distinction as individuals. "Births have brought us richness and variety," he writes in "Song of Myself" (*LG*: 80). And the variety he affirms is the uniqueness of individual human identity – something he treats as a thing acquired after birth, not a derivative of our material composition. "I too," he writes in "Crossing Brooklyn Ferry," "had receiv'd identity from my body" (*LG*: 162). That is to say, identity – particularly, the reception of it from the body – is a physical process. We are a function of sensory and social experience: "Is this then a touch?

Quivering me to a new identity," he asks in the famous autoerotic section 28 of "Song of Myself" (*LG*: 57). Whitman did not conflate political equality with sameness. Hence, his belief in political equality did not undermine the high value he placed on individual differences or the contribution such differences make to a rich social life.

This is not to say, however, that Whitman was sanguine about social inequality. An idea such as Jefferson's "natural aristocracy" in which the most talented in society were rightfully promoted to positions of leadership is deeply antithetical to Whitman's essential faith in human potential. More pointedly, it violated the moral implications of democracy itself. Still, Whitman was slow to regard social inequality as a problem requiring political reform. In his early work, inequality is represented as unethical elitism, an attitude to be scorned – not an intractable social fact. In the middle of one of the great catalogues of "Song of Myself," for example, the poet sharply comments on invidious class distinctions by the way he juxtaposes the disparate people he subsumes in his collective identity:

> The bride unrumples her white dress, the minute-hand of the clock moves slowly,
> The opium-eater reclines with rigid head and just-open'd lips,
> The prostitute draggles her shawl, her bonnet bobs on her tipsy and pimpled neck,
> The crowd laugh at her blackguard oaths, the men jeer and wink to each other,
> (Miserable! I do not laugh at your oaths nor jeer you;)
> The President holding a cabinet council is surrounded by the great Secretaries,
> On the piazza walk three matrons stately and friendly with twined arms, . . .
> (*LG*: 43)

As the voice of the moral ideal that defines a democratic people, the poet's parenthetic embrace of the prostitute is a strong rebuke to class snobbery. And by bringing the impatient bride, the opium-eater, the prostitute, the laughing crowds, and the three matrons together on equal footing with the President and his cabinet, he challenges us to think of them as equal. But he does not make them equal or explain why they're not already so.

In the economically explosive, socially unstable, and politically corrupt years that followed the Civil War, Whitman would come to regard inequality as a cancer on democracy that needed curing. Unlike the primarily European thinkers of the social democratic tradition, however, he continued to work within the individualist framework. In *Democratic Vistas* he articulates a "programme of culture" to remediate inequality. He begins by responding to those critics of popular democracy who claim that social inequality merely reflects the unequal distribution of talents and abilities meted out by nature itself. Such writers as Thomas Carlyle (whom Whitman specifically addresses) had argued for some time that the effort to empower the lower classes was reckless because it ignored their innate deficiencies. Whitman's retort was that such analyses fail because they have not been informed by "a fit scientific estimate and reverent appreciation of the People – of their measureless wealth of latent power and capacity" (*PW*: 376). For Whitman, the problem is not that vast numbers of people are fated for underclass status because of some natural limitations; rather, they have been subordinated by the feudal values encoded in elitist culture. Aristocratic literature in particular has deprived them of the psychic and cognitive tools necessary to achieve full and equal selfhood. Whitman's approach was to call for a new democratic literature. Such a literature would remedy inequality (and a host of other unsavory behaviors characteristic of underclass life) by privileging fundamentally democratic models of being, what he calls a "democratic ethnology of the future" (*PW*: 396). In short, Whitman is not interested in promoting a standardized personality type; rather, he singles out those physical attributes of common people he most admires – the "wealth of latent power" that enables them to govern their own bodies – and urges that they be translated into cultural and political terms. Such a literature, he believes, would inevitably foster a nation of people both intolerant of, and able to resist, any attempt to subjugate them.

Democratic Culture

Whitman's "programme of culture" was a significant amendment to his democratic thought. It wove connections among the multitude of meanings Whitman ascribed to democracy. It also reconciled the more descriptive, "laissez-faire," democratic vision of the 1855 and 1856 editions of *Leaves of Grass* with the more activist and revolutionary vision of his later work. That earlier vision is characterized by Whitman's famous optimism – a euphoric faith that the democratic processes of nature would, like Adam Smith's invisible hand, order a just society. Indeed, Whitman's trademark invention of "free verse" is the stylistic manifestation of that vision of perfect freedom. But in 1859, Whitman's well-documented psychosexual crisis compelled him to develop a more personal (and perhaps more conventional) application of his poetic style. In his "Calamus" poems (particularly in the earliest versions of those poems), Whitman uses his verse to remediate his own psychic turmoil. In effect, he incorporates into his poetics a kind of stylistic agency by which he does not so much passively describe the superhuman processes of nature, but instead tries to manage the natural emotional forces raging uncontrollably within himself. The political and democratic significance of this stylistic alteration is twofold: first, since much of his democratic theory is an expression of his style, a change in style implies a change in vision; second and more immediately, it positioned him, as the bard of democracy, to creatively engage the twin failures of democracy in his generation: the Civil War and the orgy of corruption that followed it.

The tragedy of the Civil War did not undermine Whitman's essential belief that democracy was the social and political expression of nature, but it did leave him open to the notion that human intelligence and agency were nature's indispensable tools for creating equitable social life. The nature he imagined before the Civil War was so benign and human-friendly that he was willing to end his greatest poem by "bequeath[ing] myself to the dirt to grow from the grass I love" (*LG*: 89). But by the war's midpoint, when Lincoln's army was suffering some of its worst losses,

Whitman apparently lost his confidence in nature as a cosmic guarantor of human success. In "Year That Trembled and Reel'd Beneath Me" he writes:

> Year that trembled and reel'd beneath me!
> Your summer wind was warm enough, yet the air I breathed froze me,
> A thick gloom fell through the sunshine and darken'd me,
> Must I change my triumphant songs? said I to myself,
> Must I learn to chant the cold dirges of the baffled?
> And sullen hymns of defeat?
>
> (*LG*: 308)

When the Union eventually did prevail, Whitman was still unable to return to the innocent faith that nature alone, absent human intervention, was a sufficient agent of democracy. In a number of passages throughout *Democratic Vistas* he struggles with what appears to be evidence of nature's deficiencies. In particular, "general humanity... has always, in every department, been full of perverse maleficence, and is so yet. In downcast hours the soul thinks it always will be – but soon recovers from such sickly moods" (*PW*: 946).

Whitman can recover from his "sickly" despair because he concludes that such deficiencies are more of an aberration of nature than an example of its proper functioning. For centuries, the instruments of feudal culture (especially feudal literary models and motifs) had sustained aristocratic hierarchies by promoting the values of servility and dependence. Whitman argues that this cultural indoctrination has eviscerated the people's natural capacity for self-governance. "The great poems," he writes, "Shakspere included, are poisonous to the idea of the pride and dignity of the common people, the life-blood of democracy. The models of our literature, as we get it from other lands, ultramarine, have had their birth in courts, and bask'd and grown in castle sunshine; all smells of princes' favors" (*PW*: 388). The problem, and thus the solution, was culture. In the Victorian era, however, culture meant "high culture," a reservoir of elitist knowledge and values that social critics from the ruling class hoped would educate and thus control the increasingly powerful working classes. Whitman repudiated the antidemocratic values implicit in such an approach, but he did embrace the idea of culture as education:

> I do not so much object to the name, or word, but I should certainly insist... on a radical change of category.... I should demand a programme of culture, drawn out, not for a single class alone, or for the parlors or lecture-rooms, but with an eye to practical life. (*PW*: 396)

In this context, "practical life" may be read as all that is natural in everyday life – the complex flow of emotion and thought, labor and leisure that beat out the rhythms of human experience. In his mature political thinking, then, Whitman attempts to retheorize the concept of culture by reconnecting it to nature; in effect, he attempts to translate the democratic aspects of nature into a model of human sociality. So reconceived, educative culture can be used as a program for democratic reform.

Whitman's notion of democratic culture takes full advantage of the transitive verb "cultivate." Self-government requires individuals "properly train'd in sanest, highest freedom" (*PW*: 374). To achieve this education in freedom, he calls for the development of a "New World Literature" – a new kind of literature that would promote democratically oriented archetypes, narratives, and other imaginative constructs that refuse to "recognize a theory of character grown of feudal aristocracies, or form'd by merely literary standards." Truly democratic literature, he insists, "sternly promulgates her own new standard" of personal identity (*PW*: 402). Whitman elaborates this model in his theory of "personalism," which he sees as a complement to the more social dimension of democracy. He argues that both democratic society and the individuals within that society are products of a three-part developmental process. For the individual, the process begins with the cultivation of a "clear-blooded, strong-fibered physique," the primary manifestation in nature of the principle of self-sufficiency and thus an appropriate analogue of higher forms of self-governance. The same value of self-sufficiency informs his discussion of the second dimension of his model, the "mental-educational" aspect. Third, he underscores the importance of cultivating the "simple, unsophisticated Conscience, the primary moral element." Whitman identifies this moral element as an expression of an "all penetrating Religiousness," but is careful to distinguish it from the contamination of "churches and creeds." Protected from such institutional influences the spiritually sensitive individual may "enter the pure ether of veneration, reach the divine levels, and commune with the unutterable" (*PW*: 397–9).

Whitman believes that religion is *politically* important, a necessary quality of full democratic selfhood, because it provides the means and motive for connecting to others. Democracy may certainly depend on the development of strong individuals; but strong individuality, however essential, also tends to alienate people from one another. Whitman was troubled by this tendency, for he placed great value in social cohesion. The idea of social unity clearly resonated with his conception of cosmic integration. It was also the thing that made democratic cooperation possible – and life in general rewarding. For a democratic society to thrive, then, it needed some mechanism for counterbalancing the fragmenting effects of the same individualism it necessarily cultivates. Religion, especially the mystical experience of "communing with the unutterable," promises just such a mechanism: anticipating William James's assertion that the ecstatic experience reflects a common psychological need to sense that one's own consciousness is "*continuous with a* MORE *of the same quality, which is operative in the universe outside of him*," Whitman's notion of religion permits democratic individuals an imaginative experience in which (despite evidence to the contrary) they are part of something larger than themselves (James 1977: 774, italics and upper case in original). In a democracy, a proper religious sensibility is an emotional state whereby individuals sense themselves folded into a seamless social whole.

Fittingly then, religiousness is not only the third stage of his scheme for personality; it is also the third stage of his theory of democratic society. Indeed, the earlier stages receive comparatively little attention: he regards democratic political arrangements like the "rights of immense masses of people" that are secured by the Federal Constitution and the Declaration of Independence as merely the first stage of democratic development. Such legal structures are obviously necessary – but what makes them so valuable is the role they play in fostering democratic personality and culture. "Political democracy," he writes "... supplies a training school for making first-class men. It is life's gymnasium" (*PW*: 385). Similarly, he treats his second stage of democratic social evolution, the "material prosperity, wealth," and the widely distributed fruits of economic development, as a reasonable expectation of democratic life, but not its definitive quality. It is the third stage he emphasizes, "without which the other two were useless," "a sublime and serious Religious Democracy" (*PW*: 409–10). The profound function of religion for Whitman is that it weds the private and public spheres. As he puts it in the "Preface 1872 – As a Strong Bird on Pinions Free":

> As there can be, in my opinion, no sane and complete Personality – nor any grand and electric Nationality, without the stock element of Religion imbuing all the other elements, (like heat in chemistry, invisible itself, but the life of all visible life,) so there can be no Poetry worthy the name without that element behind all. The time has certainly come to begin to discharge the idea of Religion, in the United States, from mere ecclesiasticism, and from Sundays and Churches and church-going, and assign it to that general position, [...] inside of all human character. [...] The People, especially the young men and women of America, must begin to learn that Religion, (like Poetry,) is something far, far different from what they supposed. It is, indeed, too important to the power and perpetuity of the New World to be consigned any longer to the churches, old or new, Catholic or Protestant – Saint this, or Saint that. It must be consigned henceforth to Democracy *en masse,* and to Literature. It must enter into the Poems of the Nation. It must make the Nation. (*LG*: 745)

Whitman's theory of democracy is, at least in part, a theory of democratic culture – and there is nothing new about the notion of cultural democracy. In the most famous statement on democracy to emerge from the ancient world, for example, the funeral oration Thucydides attributes to Pericles at the start of the Peloponnesian war, the primary focus is Athenian democratic culture, not political organization. "Because we are governed for the many and not for the few," he says, "we go by the name democracy." Then Pericles teases out the social behavior and values such a democratic purpose implies: "We are generous towards one another," he claims, and refuse to "get angry at our neighbor if he does as he pleases." Moreover, democratically minded Athenians are inclined to obey all laws, especially those "meant to relieve victims of oppression," even when they are "unwritten" and enforced only by "penalty of shame" (Thucydides 1998: 73). It is not unreasonable to read such optimistic sentiments as prefiguring Whitman's insistence that "intense and loving comradeship, the personal and passionate attachment of man to man," is the emotional core of democratic life

(*PW*: 414). But what distinguishes Whitman's democratic theory from its ancient (and modern) precursors is its totality and dynamism. Whitman is not content merely to describe an idealistic version of the ideas and values that may accompany democratic life; he sees democratic culture as the ideological blood of a humane and organic social life.

Indeed, for Whitman, democratic life is humane precisely because it is organic. The ideological polarities that have inspired the Western world's most bloody conflicts – self and society, nature and culture, religion and science – have no champion in Whitman because each names some vital element in his interrelated vision of democracy. To tease out the implications of that web of relations is to lay the imaginative foundations of future human progress. He makes the point directly by answering a rhetorical question in *Democratic Vistas*:

> Did you, too, O friend, suppose democracy was only for elections, for politics, and for a party name? I say democracy is only of use there that it may pass on and come to its flower and fruits in manners, in the highest forms of interaction between men, and their beliefs – in religion, literature, colleges, and schools – democracy in all public and private life. (*PW*: 389)

So conceived, Whitman's democracy is far more ambitious, far more demanding, than anything the eighteenth-century founders of American democracy imagined. It is also a democracy he rightly assumes to be "at present in its embryo condition" (*PW*: 392).

References and Further Reading

Agard, Walter R. (1942). *What Democracy Meant to the Greeks*. Chapel Hill: University of North Carolina Press.

Erkkila, Betsy (1989). *Whitman the Political Poet*. New York: Oxford University Press.

Folsom, Ed (1998). "Democracy." In J. R. LeMaster and Donald D. Kummings (eds.), *Walt Whitman: An Encyclopedia*. New York: Garland, pp. 171–4.

James, William (1977). "Conclusions [to *The Varieties of Religious Experience*]." In *The Writings of William James: A Comprehensive Edition*, ed. John J. McDermott. Chicago: University of Chicago Press, pp. 758–82.

Jefferson, Thomas (1959). Letter to John Adams: October 28, 1813. In *The Adams-Jefferson Letters; the Complete Correspondence Between Thomas Jefferson and Abigail and John Adams*, vol. 2, ed. Lester J. Cappon. Chapel Hill: University of North Carolina Press, pp. 387–92.

Kateb, George (1990). Walt Whitman and the Culture of Democracy. *Political Theory*, 18: 545–600.

Kaufman-Osborn, Timothy V. (1994). The Politics of the Enlightenment: A Pragmatic Reconstruction. In Lyman H. Legters, John P Burk, and Arthur DiQuattro (eds.), *Critical Perspectives on Democracy*. Lanham, MD: Rowman & Littlefield, pp. 21–43.

Lakoff, Sanford (1996). *Democracy: History, Theory, Practice*. Boulder, CO: Westview Press.

Larson, Kerry C. (1988). *Whitman's Drama of Consensus*. Chicago: University of Chicago Press.

Lipson, Leslie (1964). *The Democratic Civilization*. New York: Oxford University Press.

Locke, John (1988). *Two Treatises of Government*, ed. Peter Laslett. Cambridge, UK: Cambridge University Press.

Mack, Stephen (2002). *The Pragmatic Whitman: Reimagining American Democracy*. Iowa City: University of Iowa Press.

Paine, Thomas (2000). Rights of Man, Part II. In *Political Writings*, ed. Bruce Kuklick. Cambridge, UK: Cambridge University Press.

Parker, Hershel (1996). The Real "Live Oak, with Moss": Straight Talk about Whitman's Gay Manifesto. *Nineteenth Century Literature*, 51: 145–60.

Rosenblum, Nancy L. (1990). Strange Attractors: How Individuals Connect to Form Democratic Unity. *Political Theory*, 18: 576–85.

Rousseau, Jean Jacques (1986). *The Social Contract*. In *Political Writings*, ed. and trans. Frederick Watkins. Madison: University of Wisconsin Press, pp. 3–155.

Thomas, M. Wynn (1997/98). Weathering the Storm: Whitman and the Civil War. *Walt Whitman Quarterly Review*, 93: 87–109.

Thucydides (1998). *The Peloponnesian War*, ed. Walter Blanco and Jennifer Tolbert Roberts. New York: Norton.

Tocqueville, Alexis de (1969). *Democracy in America*, trans. George Lawrence, ed. J. P. Mayer. New York: Harper & Row.

Whitman, Walt (1982). The Eighteenth Presidency! In *Whitman: Poetry and Prose*, ed. Justin Kaplan. New York: Library of America, pp. 1307–25.

Wiebe, Robert H. (1995). *Self-Rule: A Cultural History of American Democracy*. Chicago: University of Chicago Press.

10
Imperialism

Walter Grünzweig

Walt Whitman's "international" quality has long been noted as an exceptional feature of his work. If, on one level, his poetry is considered to be quintessentially American and he, biographically, as *the* American bard, he is also seen by many readers, especially, but not exclusively, abroad, as *the* poet of the world, of internationalism, of an earth-spanning fraternity.

European and international readers, especially on the far left of the political spectrum, attempting to overcome the limitations of the exploitative nation-state and the destructive ideologies and practices of nationalism, celebrated Whitman's call to the peoples and nations around the world as an unparalleled project of poetic solidarity. Indeed, it seems as though Walt Whitman's *Leaves* were read by many leftists – from the European '48ers such as Ferdinand Freiligrath, a German revolutionary poet and friend of Marx, to the first Soviet commissar of education, Anatoly Lunacharsky, to many representatives of the institutionalized international communist movement up to 1989 – as the lyrical correlative to Karl Marx's *Communist Manifesto* published merely seven years before the first edition of *Leaves* and calling for the "Working Men of all countries, [to] unite!" (see Grünzweig 1996, especially pp. 241–5). "From early on," Ed Folsom summarizes this appeal, "Whitman has been read in other cultures as a poet of revolution, and his influence has been notably cross-cultural, as writers from one nationality export or import him with ease into another" (Folsom and Allen 1995: 4).

Born out of an international resistance to the social democratic acquiescence to, and support of, World War I which resulted in a nationalist coalition of capitalists and workers' movements in virtually every country, the communist "Third International" had the internationalist discourse virtually written into its birth documents. Whitman's poetry, which was an important emotive force above the battlegrounds from 1914 through 1918, culminating in the international celebrations of Whitman's centennial in 1919, was readily available to give this internationalist feeling both aesthetic and propagandistic expression and has been used by Marxist-Leninists ever since (see Grünzweig 1991, especially pp. 100–18, and Grünzweig, 1995, especially pp. 149–60).

Poems such as "Salut au Monde!," seemingly greeting "all the inhabitants of the earth" from the "Frenchman of France" to the "Tartar of Tartary" without discrimination, or "Song of Myself," with its geographical catalogues, were supremely equipped to address the world in its entirety and, beyond the competition of nation-states, to initiate a dialogue with peoples, ethnic minorities, and other groups on the geopolitical periphery. Later poems such as "Passage to India" developed this internationalist discourse into a vision which hailed the emergence of a global culture, the birth of all humanity as a single organized entity.

Marxist criticism of Whitman has praised this quality of the poet programmatically. The Soviet-American Whitman critic Maurice Mendelson, in his Whitman book published in the bicentennial year of 1976, proclaimed: "Walt Whitman, the poet of the revolutionary struggle for freedom and the solidarity of working people, was a true internationalist; and although some of Whitman's parallelisms may sound monotonous, the internationalist ideas of the author of 'Salut au Monde!' are not merely ideas, but often take the form of living images" (p. 177). The astute critical mind of the USSR's best-known Americanist obviously noted the aesthetic deficit but did not see any attending flaws in the message. Rather, the artlessness seemed a necessary evil which needed to be accepted in the interest of the cause. In fact, this "monotony" seemed to guarantee the egalitarian internationalist message: "In 'Salut au Monde!', the uniform syntactical organization of the verses conveys the idea of the equality of all human beings with maximum poetic force" (p. 177).

One of the heroes of international Marxist criticism, George Lukács, even included Whitman in a canon of world literature with an explicitly anti-imperialist orientation, claiming that "great literature has a powerful historical function, a pioneering role in the true aspiration of the people, in the establishment of a true democracy. From Walt Whitman to Anatole France, from Ibsen to Shaw, from Tolstoy to Gorki, the leading writers of freedom-loving peoples have fulfilled their mission in the age of imperialism" (Lukács 1975: 140).[1] And on the occasion of the centennial of *Leaves*, in 1955, when Whitman's book was used in an extensive political campaign by the World Peace Council in the midst of the Cold War, a GDR critic wrote that in *Democratic Vistas*, Whitman "found that the growing hyena of monopolism and imperialism had almost completely destroyed democracy. . . . Thus, his emphasis shifted from national ideals to the ideal of a general fraternization of all peoples" (Findeisen 1955: 504).

In the most convincing political interpretation to date of Whitman's life and work, Betsy Erkkila, describing Whitman as a revolutionary, similarly praises Whitman's international vision. "Passage to India" to her is a "vision of a world united in a common democratic culture by means of modern advances in communication and transportation" (Erkilla 1989: 266), a "manifesto poem that adumbrates the religious and spiritual orientation of Whitman's later work" (p. 273). In spite of the obvious celebration of the techno-commercial achievement of the age, Erkkila sees an "increased emphasis on the spiritual world [which] was in part a reaction against Gilded Age America" (p. 273).

In a contribution for a French–German symposium on the "American Empire" in 1990 and in two articles in the course of the 1990s designed to refine and enlarge this argument (Grünzweig 1996, 1997), not to mention an entry on "Imperialism" in the Walt Whitman *Encyclopedia* (Grünzweig, 1998), I have hesitantly attempted to correct that image – hesitantly because as a "Whitmanite" I did not want to question what so many voices around the world hailed as one of the poet's major achievements. While I noted a large-scale consensus on Whitman's internationalism, I pointed to a relatively little-known book by Mexican critic Mauricio Gonzáles de la Garza, *Walt Whitman: Racista, Imperialista, Antimexicano*, which formulated some very fundamental attacks against Whitman based on the American's enthusiastic support of the Mexican War, which might be labeled colonialist rather than imperialist but which definitely follows an imperialist logic. It is interesting, however, that Gonzáles de la Garza does not condemn Whitman wholesale. Rather, he took up Whitman's famous self-estimate when he called him "un hombre contradictorio" (a contradictory man), noting "la discrepancia entre su vida y su poesia" (the discrepancy between his life and his poetry) (1971: 9).

What Gonzáles de la Garza is referring to is the discrepancy between Whitman's journalistic support of the War in contributions such as the Brooklyn *Daily Eagle* and the poetry, where he recognizes an alternative discourse. In support of his thesis, Gonzáles de la Garza quotes some of the most fiery journalistic statements by Whitman such as that of May 11, 1846 where he formulated a call to arms reminiscent of some of the less guarded statements of the administration of George W. Bush: "Let our arms now be carried with a spirit which shall teach the world that, while we are not forward for a quarrel, America knows how to crush, as well as how to expand!" (quoted from Gonzáles de la Garza 1971: 182).

Gonzáles de la Garza does make an attempt to explain this discrepancy: "Aunque es cierto que en ocasiones expresó el sentimiento del internacionalismo, estaba convencido – tal vez con razón – de que Estados Unidos era el único escenario para el drama de la democracia, y de que los americanos eran los únicos capaces y dignos para actuarla" (Even though it is certain that at times he expressed the feeling of internationalism, he was convinced – perhaps with good reason – that the United States were the only stage for the drama of democracy and that the Americans were the only ones able and worthy to act it out) (p. 10). Thus, de la Garza, in a line of argument well-known in the political criticism of "American imperialism" in the twentieth century, provides an apology for this policy (ostensibly conducted in the interest of democracy) which is turned into a new criticism – namely the charge that the country is on an exceptionalist, and hence unjustified and ultimately false, sense of mission.

In my 1990 contribution, I attempted to show that Whitman's "expansionism [. . .] is really an early version of imperialism" (p. 164) and that it was read as such. I quoted a 1907 letter of Felix Schelling, professor of English at the University of Pennsylvania, to Horace Traubel, which I had found in the Traubel papers at the

Library of Congress. In that letter, Schelling stressed how Penn's English department had taken up Whitman's cause in a very specific way:

> It may interest the members of the Walt Whitman Fellowship to know that the students of the University have been lectured to specifically on Walt Whitman every year for the last ten years, that they have been instructed fully to recognize the importance of Whitman from a historical point of view and for the intrinsic nobility of his opinion and liberal art.
>
> Of late I think we have laid especial stress on the fact that Mr. Kipling in his imperialism, his sense of expansion and his large treatment of large issues is, when all has been said, a disciple of Walt Whitman.
>
> It was the contemporaneousness of Whitman that made him the man that he was and will long remain. It was a great truth to be told that in literature we must not dwell wholly in the past. (quoted in Grünzweig 1990: 155)

As this quotation impressively shows, this was a time when imperialism could be attributed to an author with the intention of paying him respect and giving praise rather than as an expression of political condemnation. If Whitman by 1907 had been taught for the "last ten years," this would roughly coincide with the new, imperialist era the United States had entered with the start of the Spanish–American War. Whitman, whose reputation was then largely under the guardianship of his leftist friend Horace Traubel, was obviously used in order to offset the anti-imperialist activities of an outspoken author such as Mark Twain, vice-president of the Anti-Imperialist League, who stated, in reference to the Philippines:

> You ask me about what is called imperialism. Well, I have formed views about that question. I am at the disadvantage of not knowing whether our people are for or against spreading themselves over the face of the globe. I should be sorry if they are, for I don't think that it is wise or a necessary development. [. . .] we have got into a mess, a quagmire from which each fresh step renders the difficulty of extrication immensely greater. I'm sure I wish I could see what we were getting out of it, and all it means to us as a nation. (from interview in *The New World*, October 14, 1900, in Twain 1992: 59)

Twain is asking an interesting question which goes beyond political and economic motivations and focuses on the identity, the self-definition, of the country – "what it means to us as a nation." His criticism is as valid today as it was when it was written a century ago.

The situation is puzzling. Are Whitman (or rather his construction as an imperialist poet) and Twain antagonists in the fight over the "imperialist" development of the country? Is Whitman's global vision grossly misrepresented, and indeed, abused, by those advocating a global political role for America? Recent studies such as those by Malini Johar Schueller (1998) or Irene Ramalho Santos (2003) further qualify and explain this paradox, but finally accept it as at least partially built into the American experiment as a whole.

In hindsight, my own use of Schelling's letter is not altogether clear to me. On the one hand, it certainly *is* an apology (to Whitman? to my readers? to myself, who otherwise dealt with Whitman in such an enthusiastic way? to or for the United States?) especially in view of the accusations made against some of his best-known poetry. On the other hand, it was obviously also an initial attempt, beyond my political positioning, to understand the multifaceted and contradictory quality of "Empire" which would unfold in the course of the post-1989 world and which was so brilliantly analyzed by Michael Hardt and Antonio Negri in their monumental study of that same title. In the present contribution, then, I am trying to suggest that, yes, Whitman was an imperialist, but in a forward-looking (progressive?) fashion and that he initiated a way of thinking about global development which has only become apparent in the last decade and a half. While this will neither "vindicate" Whitman (if that were necessary), nor completely explain or "solve" the paradox, it will position his work in the complex and contradictory context of the discussion of "Empire" itself.

The most influential (and probably far-reaching) statement on imperialism was made by Vladimir Ilyitch Lenin in his groundbreaking analysis entitled *Imperialism: The Highest Stage of Capitalism,* written in 1916 while he was in Swiss exile. Whereas Lenin provides a severe and very systematic criticism of imperialism as capitalism in the age of the monopolies and trusts, his most scathing words are reserved for those critics of imperialism who view it as an aberration from otherwise civilized modes of political behaviors:

> In the United States, the imperialist war waged against Spain in 1898 stirred up the opposition of the "anti-imperialists," the last of the Mohicans of bourgeois democracy. They declared this war to be "criminal"; they denounced the annexation of foreign territories as being a violation of the Constitution, and denounced the "Jingo treachery" by means of which Aguinaldo, leader of the native Filipinos, was deceived (the Americans promised him the independence of his country, but later they landed troops and annexed it). [. . .] But while all this criticism shrank from recognizing the indissoluble bond between imperialism and the trusts, and, therefore, between imperialism and the very foundations of capitalism; while it shrank from joining up with the forces engendered by large-scale capitalism and its development – it remained a "pious wish." (Lenin 1939: 111)

This was not only an expression of the hatred for the type of "bourgeois" reformism represented, for example, by Twain. Rather, imperialism was not entirely unwelcome to Lenin, because it seemed to foretell the end of the capitalist system as a whole: "From all that has been said in this book on the economic nature of imperialism, it follows that we must define it as capitalism in transition, or, more precisely, as moribund capitalism" (p. 126). More radically, he implicitly suggests that imperialism provides the tools for an eventual overthrow of capitalism (see pp. 115f.).

In their groundbreaking study of *Empire*, Michael Hardt and Antonio Negri, while bringing their analysis up to date, acknowledge Lenin's vision:

> Lenin saw imperialism as a structural stage in the evolution of the modern state. He imagined a necessary and linear historical progression from the first forms of the modern European state to the nation-state and then to the imperialist state. [...] Lenin recognized finally that, although imperialism and the monopoly phase were indeed expressions of the global expansions of capital, the imperialist practices and the colonial administrations through which they were often pursued had come to be obstacles to the further development of capital. [...] Imperialism actually creates a straitjacket for capital – or, more precisely, at a certain point the boundaries created by imperialist practices obstruct capitalist development and the full realization of its world market. (Hardt and Negri 2000: 232–4)

In their analysis, Hardt and Negri follow the global development from imperialism to "Empire" which, unlike imperialism, is "characterized fundamentally by a lack of boundaries: Empire's rule has no limits" (p. xiv). Unlike some of the critics of "globalization" – but in Lenin's spirit – they

> claim that Empire is better in the same way that Marx insists that capitalism is better than the forms of society and modes of production that came before it. Marx's view is grounded on a healthy and lucid disgust for the parochial and rigid hierarchies that preceded capitalist society as well as on a recognition that the potential for liberation is increased in the new situation. (Hardt and Negri 2000: 43)

It is thus wrong "to claim that we can (re)establish local identities that are in some sense *outside* and protected against the global flows of capital and Empire" (p. 45). Rather, alternatives must be found within Empire which open up possibilities for resistance.

I am arguing here that Whitman's poetry does constitute a version of imperialism but that its lyrical representation points beyond the repressive nature of this social and cultural formation in the sense that Hardt's and Negri's "Empire" does. What is offered here is a parallel reading of Whitman's globalist poetry and Hardt and Negri's analysis which will help to overcome the "imperialist" problem or paradox with Whitman's poetry pointed out earlier. Although this is not a historical reading of texts published almost one and a half centuries before the emergence of the term "Empire" in this sense, it is also neither ahistorical nor antihistorical. Rather than as a pseudomimetic reflection of an "external reality," Whitman's poetry can be read as a *simulation* of a speeded-up development of a globalizing world. In his poetry, he was examining the consequences of processes he saw by modeling them in his poetry – much like the future behavior of substances and products is studied by subjecting them to conditions simulating long-term use.

At first glance, "Salut Au Monde!" (1856) seems indeed an internationalist poem. Its charm lies in the direct address of the reader abroad ("And I salute all the inhabitants of the earth," *LG*: 145), the immediate apostrophe from the American poet everybody can supposedly hear – and feel – and the detailed listing of these addressees: "You Sardinian! you Bavarian! Swabian! Saxon! Wallachian! Bulgarian!"

(p. 146). Even the inhabitants of those niches of the world not represented in Whitman's lyrical atlas will well be able to imagine that their place *might* have been included had the author only added a few more lines. The basic open-endedness of sections 3 through 11 vouch for the sincerity of Whitman's ardent wish to include "You whoever you are!"

However, this optimistic reading remains on the surface. The critical interrogation of the poem does not need to be concerned with questions of a "politically incorrect" terminology, although the description of the "Hottentot with clicking palate" living in "wooly-hair'd hordes!" (l. 199) or the "Austral negro, naked, red, sooty" (l. 204) are somewhat troubling. The problem is, already in 1856, the imperialist vision:

> I see the tracks of the railroads of the earth,
> I see them in Great Britain, I see them in Europe,
> I see them in Asia and Africa.
> I see the electric telegraphs of the earth,
> I see the filaments of the news of wars, deaths, losses, passions, my race.
> (*LG*: 141)

The truly innovative quality of these lines derives not from the mention of railroad, telegraph, and news media, but from their globalized *presentation*. The first railroad in Africa, from Cairo to Alexandria, had only just been built in 1855 and the first line in India two years earlier. Yet Whitman envisions these railroads as a network across and around the earth, in analogy to the telegraph (which, in Egypt, started in 1856). It is the globalized representation which creates the modern impression of these lines as well as the haphazard arrangement, say, of the news that is transmitted filament style, much like Whitman's poetry.

But the impressive modernity of this passage should not obscure its basic exploitative quality. These railroads are not owned by the global community, and the "Hottentots" are not riding the trains. Rather, these are colonial, and indeed imperial, achievements and technologies which are introduced at the expense of the global community – in the interest of, as Whitman ignores or wants to ignore, the international capital or the industrializing, colonizing world.

As I pointed out in my 1990 article, the catalogue lines themselves are highly problematical, as they present different and highly differentiated cultures in an isolated way, one line per culture, "much in a way modern tourism markets one peculiar aspect of a given culture, out of context, at the expense of a more complex understanding" (Grünzweig 1990: 161). From such a perspective, the railroads of the earth exist mainly to ship and sell these products.

Moreover, in spite of the seeming equality in this multicultural poem, there are groups of people and human qualities which at least *appear* to be labeled as superior:

> I see the constructiveness of my race,
> I see the results of the perseverance and industry of my race
> (*LG*: 145)

Even though other cultures are presented in different terms, it is obvious that it is the "constructiveness" and "industry" of the WASPs (or whichever "race" is Whitman's in this case) which has brought about this state of global progress and connectedness.

However, the charge of imperialism really falls short here, mainly because of the complete lack of boundaries which Hardt and Negri consider characteristic of the postimperialist world of Empire. By the 1850s, the atlas Whitman used showed clear political dividing lines not just in Europe but also in Africa and Asia. In contradistinction, one of the dominant themes in "Salut Au Monde!" is the *lack* of such divisions, political or otherwise:

> Such join'd unended links, each hook'd to the next [...]
> I see ranks, colors, barbarisms, civilizations, I go among them, I mix indiscriminately [...]
> All you continentals of Asia, Africa, Europe, Australia, indifferent of place!" [...]
> "Each of us limitless – each of us with his or her right upon the earth.
> (*LG*: 137, 145, 147)

Thus the catalogued groups often do not fit into any specific national territory. Instead, the "straightjacket" of the national boundary and its imperialist sphere of interest is transcended in favor of a global distribution. Whereas the collection of workingmen, and workingwomen, living along German rivers – "the Rhine, the Elbe, or the Weser" (l. 173) – provide at least a cross-section of Germany (at that time not yet united), the line listing Sardinians, Bavarians, Swabians, Saxons, Wallachians, and Bulgarians moves from the Mediterranean northward up into the Alps, to the Southeast of Germany into the Balkans, to Transylvania and southward. The logic to this line is precisely the lack of political coherence and, especially, the nonapplicability of the category of the national state.

Hardt and Negri emphasize that the resistance, rebellion, or insurrection in the age of Empire is different from the internationalist movement in the nineteenth and the early and middle parts of the twentieth centuries:

> We ought to be able to recognize that this is not the appearance of a new cycle of internationalist struggles, but rather the emergence of a new quality of social movements. We ought to be able to recognize, in other words, the fundamentally new characteristics these struggles all present, despite their radical diversity. First, each struggle, though firmly rooted in local conditions, leaps immediately to the global level and attacks the imperial constitution in its generality. Second, all the struggles destroy the traditional distinction between economic and political struggles. The struggles are at once economic, political and cultural – and hence they are biopolitical struggles, struggles over the form of life. They are constituent struggles, creating new public spheres and new forms of community. (Hardt and Negri 2000: 56)

It is amazing to what extent Whitman's "Salut Au Monde!" fits this characterization of "Empire." First of all, we recognize what has been little noted, namely, that the catalogues in this supposedly exuberant poem are not just celebrations but also list grievances and injustice, albeit expressed in novel ways. Whereas this is made explicit in the case of "You women of the earth subordinated at your tasks!" or "You own'd persons dropping sweat-drops or blood-drops!" it is less explicit, but nevertheless present, in "You mountaineer living lawlessly on the Taurus or Caucasus!" or "You olive-grower tending your fruit on fields of Nazareth, Damascus, or lake Tiberias" (*LG*: 146, 147). But what unites them is a global perspective, in spite of the frequent regional groupings. In view of the global epidemics of our last few decades, especially in the developing world, the address to "You plague-swarms in Madras, Nankin, Kaubul, Cairo!" (*LG*: 147) is eerie indeed.

What Whitman is doing, then, in this poem, is making global connections of various groups throughout the world. He declares himself as seer in whom this global outlook is created, but in effect, it is the 226 lines of the poem, seemingly disparate as they are, that make up that globality. It is the task of the reader to "make sense" of this disparateness and to create connections, affinities and, in the end, solidarities, where there appear to be none. This indeed creates "new public spheres and new forms of community." Negri's and Hardt's notion of the connection of the political, economic, and cultural in the world of Empire explains the curious mixture of ethnic/national features, work and occupation, and the various forms of domination and hegemony.

The speaker of the poem, raising "high the perpendicular hand," "mak[ing] the signal," even though he does so "in America's name" (*LG*: 148), makes the many different groups of his text aware of their existence as global entities and of their work as global phenomena, of their suffering, their similar condition in one global system. Given the centralized quality of much of the leftist world since 1848, with its struggles for leadership and dictatorship in the various movements, its central committees, its politbureaus, and its philosophy of democratic centralism, it is not surprising that leftist readings of the poem have often focused on the bilateral relationship between the various groups and the poetic voice in the center. From a multilateral reading, the voice of the bard becomes a way to make known the global situatedness that all human beings find themselves in. Solidarity is not a function of the soothing, benevolent voice of an American bard but the emergence of a global consciousness as a result of reading/hearing the poem.

The questions put to the speaker, "Walt Whitman," are questions about the nature of a world that has become limitless, although its inhabitants have not yet become aware of it. The initial voice knows that the world is no longer fixed and stable but "gliding wonders" (l. 2) characterized by global interconnectedness: "Each answering all, each sharing the earth with all" (l. 4). The nine questions concluding section 1, which will be answered in the course of the poem, are necessary for the emergence of an awareness of this situation. The knowledge about the global production of goods and cultural artifacts, the global rendering of services, which are highlighted in the poem, provides a prerequisite for such an awareness. Then, and only then, can the "multitude" (a key term in Hardt and Negri and, of course, a key term in Whitman's poetry) "establish [itself] as a properly political subject" (Hardt and Negri 2000: 395). Whitman's poetry establishes the "multitude" as a subject which will learn how to act in the social formation of "Empire."

But does Whitman's poetry in any way *empower* the imperial subjects beyond helping them recognize their situation? I believe it does. Hardt and Negri emphasize that one way the exploited people in the formation of Empire (re)gain their agency and power is through their constitution as a "mobile multitude" (p. 398):

> Through circulation the multitude reappropriates space and constitutes itself as an active subject [. . .] by geographical mythologies that mark the new paths of destiny. These movements often cost terrible suffering, but there is also in them a desire of liberation that is not satiated except by reappropriating new spaces, around which are constructed new freedoms. (Hardt and Negri 2000: 397)

This is the grand theme of Whitman's "Passage to India" (1871). Whereas the global vision of "Salut" was brought about by the enumeration of parallel multitudes around the world, "Passage" emphasizes their growing together, their movement towards and into each other.

The Suez Canal, the establishment of the transcontinental railroad and the telegraph provide a starting point for a celebration of a new kind of movement around the world. This "Passage to India," which Henry Nash Smith in his *Virgin Land* has identified as one of the central myths, or narratives, of American culture, is presented as a telos written into the destiny of humankind:

> Passage to India!
> Lo, soul, seest thou not God's purpose from the first?
> The earth to be spann'd, connected by network,
> The races, neighbors, to marry and be given in marriage,
> The oceans to be cross'd, the distant brought near,
> The lands to be welded together.
>
> (*LG*: 412)

No matter how much truth the society of the Gilded Age might have found in such lines, no matter how much readers of the first half of the twentieth century may have seen their own situation as a fulfillment of this vision – the possibility of a much more literal reading of these lines has only become apparent in the final decades of the twentieth century. Whereas "connection by network" was essentially metaphorical in the case of the telegraph and highly individualized in the case of the telephone, it has become much more real (albeit not necessarily more authentic) through email and digital communication. The marriage of "races," certainly a demographic reality in the melting pot, has taken on a new meaning as a result of the ceaseless migration between developing countries and between the developing and the developed world. The vision is, indeed, not that of a highly internationalized but separated world, but one where these separations have been overcome, indeed, where "All these separations and gaps shall be taken up and hook'd and link'd together" (l. 109):

> Europe to Asia, Africa join'd, and they to the New World,
> The lands, geographies, dancing before you, holding a festival garland,
> As brides and bridegrooms hand in hand.
>
> (*LG*: 416)

Whereas many explications, including my own, have interpreted the teleological vision, which in the poem is strongly connected with that of the "Admiral," Columbus, as a version of American manifest destiny, the present reconsiderations point to the progressive vision of a unified earth as a result of technological and economic development.

Similarly, the metaphysical orientation of the poem needs to be reconsidered in the context of "Empire." The poem has frequently been read as a "striving for a transcendent state" (Mason 1998), as an attempt to provide a metaphysical superstructure for modern technological and commercial society. Instead, I would suggest turning the argument around. As we have seen, Whitman's teleology is a divinely ordained movement toward an integrated, universalized world, which means that the culmination of that spiritually, metaphysically underwritten world is the here and now. The globalized *lebenswelt* itself is the fulfillment of the divinely ordained plan:

> The whole earth, this cold, impassive, voiceless earth, shall be completely justified,
> Trinitas divine shall be gloriously accomplish'd and compacted by the true son of God, the poet, [. . .]
> Nature and Man shall be disjoin'd and diffused no more,
> The true son of God shall absolutely fuse them.
>
> (*LG*: 415, 416)

The earth remains cold, impassive, and voiceless until the voice of the poet has "joined" it – nature, whose geographical, ethnic, political, and other dividing lines separate human beings from it and each other, and humanity, are restored to each other, "absolutely fuse[d]."

The soul, then, addressed from section 7 onward, is an expression of the "mythology of reason that organizes the biopolitical reality of the multitude" (Hardt and Negri 2000: 407), a version of what Hardt and Negri describe in their visionary and speculative final pages as the "posse," the potential of humankind for liberation. It is, however, a "metaphysical term [which] became a political term. Posse refers to the power of the multitude and its telos, an embodied power of knowledge and being, always open to the possible" (p. 408). The global, indeed cosmic, flight of Whitman's "soul" in "Passage" locates the metaphysical in the material, and translates the initial steps toward world integration described in the first part of the poem into a vision of the voyage to get to the final stage of a globalized world:

> Joyous we too launch out on trackless seas,
> Fearless for unknown shores on waves of ecstasy to sail
>
> (*LG*: 418)

The vagueness of this journey is not surprising for a poem written at the beginning of the Gilded Age, but Hardt and Negri too do not have any more concrete models to offer. But they do insist, at the end of their volume, that a "joyous life" is the prerequisite for a revolution turning the "Empire" into an equitable, just, and sustainable society.

Whitman's imperialism, then, is one which looks beyond, which implies, and indeed includes the forces and tools which will help overcome it. This does not mean that he is free from American (i.e., US) visions of manifest destiny. Obviously, his imperial vision is closely connected with his own country, but then again, given the developments between 1871 and our own time, his foresight was justified. In his finest moments, as for example in "A Broadway Pageant," anticipating "Passage" as early as 1860, he refers to a "Libertad of the world" (*LG*: 245) which goes beyond the confines of "America." And, towards the conclusion of *Democratic Vistas*, he warns of the "cost," "the proportionate price" of trying to be the "empire of empires" (Whitman, 1982: 990f.).

The integration of the world, as we see now, albeit under capitalist and late capitalist, exploitative and aggressive, conditions, is a prerequisite for solving its problems – and not the helplessly retrospective, if not reactionary, yearning for the divided past. This analysis might be rather troubling in view of current imperial interventions around the globe. But, as we have seen, Empire does not negate but enables the agency of human individuals and groups – and Whitman's poetry certainly has provided a blueprint for the self-organization and self-management of the "multitudes." This analysis corresponds to Whitman's statement published in his dedication for the first German book-length translation of *Leaves* (1889) which identifies poetry as a transnational force:

> Indeed, as conceited as this statement may seem, I did not only have my own country in mind when composing my work. I wanted to take the first step toward bringing to life a cycle of international poems. The main goal of the United States is the mutual benevolence of all humanity, the solidarity of the world. What is lacking in this respect perhaps may be supplied by the art of poetry, by songs radiating from all countries in the world (quoted from Grünzweig 1995: 29).

Note

1 Translations from German texts are my own.

References and Further Reading

Erkkila, Betsy (1989). *Whitman: The Political Poet.* New York, Oxford: Oxford University Press.

Findeisen, Helmut (1955). Gedenktag der Weltfriedensbewegung: "Grashalme" – der weltweite Siegeszug einer Dichtung. Zum 100. Jahrestag der Erstveröffentlichung von Walt Whitman's berühmten Gedichten. *Börsenblatt für den deutschen Buchhandel*, 9 July: 504–5.

Folsom, Ed and Allen, Gay Wilson (1995). Introduction: "Salut au Monde!" In Gay Wilson Allen and Ed Folsom (eds.), *Walt Whitman and the World*. Iowa City: University of Iowa Press, pp. 1–10.

Gonzáles de la Garza, Maurico (1971). *Walt Whitman: Racista. Imperialista. Antimexicano*. Mexico City: Colección Málaga.

Grünzweig, Walter (1990). Noble Ethics and Loving Aggressiveness: The Imperialist Walt Whitman. In Serge Ricard (ed.), *An American Empire: Expansionist Cultures and Policies, 1881–1917*. Aix-en-Provence: Université de Provence, pp. 151–65.

Grünzweig, Walter (1991). *Walt Whitman: Die deutschsprachige Rezeption als interkulturelles Phänomen*. Munich: Fink.

Grünzweig, Walter (1995). *Constructing the German Walt Whitman*. Iowa City: University of Iowa Press.

Grünzweig, Walter (1996). "For America – For All the Earth": Walt Whitman as an International(ist) Poet. In Betsy Erkkila and Jay Grossman (eds.), *Breaking Bounds: Whitman & American Cultural Studies*. New York and Oxford: Oxford University Press, pp. 238–50.

Grünzweig, Walter (1997). The New Empire Grander Than Any Before: 19th-Century American Versions of a Democratic Imperialism. In John G. Blair and Reinhold Wagnleitner (eds.), *Empire: American Studies*. Tübingen: Gunter Narr, pp. 243–50.

Grünzweig, Walter (1998). Imperialism. In J. R. LeMaster and Donald D. Kummings (eds.), *Walt Whitman: An Encyclopedia*. New York and London: Garland, pp. 304–5.

Hardt, Michael and Negri, Antonio (2000). *Empire*. Cambridge, MA and London: Harvard University Press.

Jung, Kyunghoon (2002). How To Do with the Absolute Other: Signifier, Subject, and Other in Lacan, Levinas, Whitman, and Duncan. PhD dissertation, State University of New York at Buffalo.

Lenin, V. I. (1939). *Imperialism: The Highest Stage of Capitalism. A Popular Outline*, rev. translation. New York: International Publishers.

Lomas, Laura Anne (2001). American Alterities: Reading Between Borders in José Martí's "North American Scenes." PhD dissertation, Columbia University.

Lukács, Georg (1975). *Kurze Skizze einer Geschichte der neueren deutschen Literatur*. Darmstadt and Neuwied: Luchterhand.

Mason, John B. (1998). "Passage to India" (1871). In J. R. LeMaster and Donald D. Kummings (eds.), *Walt Whitman: An Encyclopedia*. New York and London: Garland, pp. 507–9.

Mendelson, Maurice (1976). *Life and Work of Walt Whitman. A Soviet View*. Moscow: Progress.

Ramalho Santos, Irene (2003). Atlantic Poets: Fernando Pessoa's Turn in Anglo-American Modernism. Hanover, NH: University Press of New England.

Schueller, Malini Johar (1998). *U.S. Orientalisms: Race, Nation, and Gender in Literature, 1790–1890*. Ann Arbor: University of Michigan Press.

Smith, Henry Nash (1950). *Virgin Land: The American West as Symbol and Myth*. Cambridge, MA: Harvard University Press.

Twain, Mark ([1900] 1992). Mark Twain on American Imperialism. *The Atlantic Monthly*, 269 (4, April): 49–65.

Whitman, Walt (1982). *Complete Poetry and Collected Prose*. New York: Library of America.

11
Sexuality
Maire Mullins

> Without shame the man I like knows and avows the deliciousness of his sex,
> Without shame the woman I like knows and avows hers.
>
> ("A Woman Waits for Me," ll. 9–10)

Sexuality is one of the most complex and challenging concepts in the life and work of Walt Whitman. Whitman incorporated heterosexual, homosexual, autoerotic, and bisexual desire throughout *Leaves of Grass*, but the kinds of sexuality he expresses in the poetry cannot be defined by these terms alone. Eve Kosofsky Sedgwick offers this more general definition of the word "sexuality": "the array of acts, expectations, narratives, pleasures, identity-formations, and knowledges, in both women and men, that tends to cluster most densely around certain genital sensations but is not adequately defined by them" (Sedgwick 1990: 29). Sexual themes in *Leaves of Grass* have been interpreted transhistorically, outside their historical context. Sexual themes in the poetry have also been considered as part of the contemporary discourses of nineteenth-century America – social, political, religious, and economic – and thus as inflected and shaped by these forces, in a place and at a time where the cultural constraints against including sexual themes in public discourse were formidable. Indeed, given the contemporary resistance to any published utterance that included sexual overtones, it is remarkable that Whitman was able to carry out his poetic project at all – and to do so over the course of several decades and six editions of *Leaves of Grass*. In conversations with Horace Traubel near the end of his life Whitman offered this seemingly simple explanation of *Leaves of Grass*: "Sex is the root of it all. Sex – the coming together of men and women: sex: sex" (Traubel 1914: 452–3). Yet he also told Edward Carpenter in 1884, "I think there are truths which it is necessary to envelop or wrap up" (Carpenter 1906: 43). Whitman realized that he could not speak directly about the "truths" of sex and sexuality in the late nineteenth century, so he used poetic language to celebrate first his own male body and its many erogenous zones, and then widened that celebration to include the bodies, the desires, and the sexualities of others. These "truths" he could utter using the slant language of poetry.

Whitman's striking, provocative pose in the opening page of the first edition (1855) of *Leaves of Grass* declares a considerable and formidable masculine physical presence before the reader knows who the writer of these poems is. Thus Whitman places his body at the forefront of his work, even before he has named himself as the author of this text. The image the reader must come to terms with is that of a healthy, muscular, attractive, youthful-but-not-young, bearded male, whose gaze both engages and challenges. Whitman sustains this erotic conversation with the reader throughout the 12 poems of the first edition, writing his (male) body into the text, and offering himself as an image of male beauty and desire at once breathtaking and magnetic, as well as working class, "one of the roughs" ("Song of Myself," Whitman 1959: 48). Andrew Lawson notes, however, that "Whitman's working-class identity is not as straightforward as it may seem, even in his own self-representations. . . . As a journeyman printer who worked variously as a teacher, carpenter, journalist, and government clerk, Whitman belonged to a Jacksonian lower middle class undergoing the transition from an agrarian, artisan culture to an urban, market economy" (Lawson 2003: 335–6). The anxiousness that this transition induced in the members of these classes is evident in Whitman's hypermasculinized, assured posture. In the poems, Whitman merges sexuality with the project of nation building even as the debate about slavery in the antebellum United States and its new territories was coming to a fragmenting climax. The virility and confidence Whitman espouses in the pose he includes in the first edition of *Leaves of Grass* thus conceals and reveals wider cultural anxieties and tensions having to do with sexuality, gender, race, and class. His gaze in this portrait both challenges the onlooker and draws him or her in, inviting further scrutiny yet setting boundaries around it.

The nineteenth-century American reading public did not readily embrace *Leaves of Grass* partly because of the explicitness of its sexual themes. One contemporary reviewer, Rufus Griswold, wrote "There are too many persons, who imagine they demonstrate their superiority to their fellows, by disregarding all the politeness and decencies of life, and, therefore, justify themselves in indulging the vilest imaginings and shamefullest license" (1971: 32). For Griswold, the most offensive aspect of Whitman's work was its allusion to "*Peccatum illud horribile, inter Christianos non Nominandum*" (that horrible sin not to be mentioned among Christians) – sodomy (p. 33). However, Michel Foucault writes that at this time the Western cultural understanding of the concept of homosexuality was undergoing a shift "characterized . . . less by a type of sexual relations than by a certain quality of sexual sensibility, a certain way of inverting the masculine and the feminine in oneself. . . . The sodomite had been a temporary aberration; the homosexual was now a species" (Foucault 1978: 43). This shift into a more permanent status accompanied other significant changes in the nineteenth century: urbanization, the industrial revolution, the rise of science, evolutionary theory, the decline of religious faith. Betsy Erkkila points out that "the term homosexual was probably introduced into English by John Addington Symonds, who referred to 'homosexual instincts' in *A Problem in Modern Ethics* (1891). It was not until the 1930s that the term received wide currency in English" (Erkkila 1989: 338, n.12). Interestingly, Symonds, an ardent admirer of *Leaves of Grass*, recognized homoerotic overtones in Whitman's verse, and wrote to him specifically about the "Calamus" poems. Whitman demurred, telling Traubel in 1888: "Symonds is right, no doubt, to ask the questions: I am just as much right if I do not answer them. . . . my first instinct about all that Symonds writes is violently reactionary – is strong and brutal for no, no, no. Then the thought intervenes that I maybe do not know all my meanings" (quoted in Whitman 2001: 85). This episode has been characterized by some biographers and critics as indicative of a defensiveness and misplaced overcautiousness on Whitman's part; however, Whitman handled Symonds's overture in a manner very much in keeping with one of the central strategies of his poetic expression: indirection. Peter Coviello notes that in his poetry Whitman "had developed an idiom of self-presentation capable of the most intimate prodding and solicitation yet whose often thrilling interpellating effects depend precisely upon the mutual anonymity of author and reader" (Coviello 2001: 86). Symonds was asking Whitman to abandon this technique. In the end, Whitman did what he thought was best for *Leaves of Grass*.

By continuing to publish his poetry over the course of four decades, Whitman contributed to a revision of attitudes toward sexuality. Michael Moon notes that "The revisionary effects which the texts of *Leaves of Grass* are designed to have on his culture's prevailing (or coming-to-be prevailing) conceptions of bodiliness manifest themselves most clearly when one follows them from edition to edition" (Moon 1991: 2). Yet sexuality as a theme and "bodiliness" as an emphasis are more prominent in the first four editions (1855, 1856, 1860, 1867) than in the last two (1871, 1881) editions. Many reasons have been offered for this gradual de-emphasis: Whitman's aging body and health problems, the emotional experience and traumatizing impact of the Civil War, the death of his mother, economic concerns. In the last decades of his life Whitman increasingly withdrew from public life and became an observer of American culture, content with daily excursions and with receiving guests and admirers.

The 1855 edition of *Leaves of Grass* contains 12 poems, the most remarkable of which is "Song of Myself," Whitman's "greatest work, perhaps his one completely realized work, and one of the great poems of modern times," as Malcolm Cowley notes in his introduction to the 1855 edition (Whitman 1959: x). It also serves, for many readers, as an introduction to Whitman's poetry and to Whitman's daring approach to sexuality and to the body:

> I believe in you my soul . . . the other I am must not abase itself to you,
> And you must not be abased to the other. . . .
> I mind how we lay in June, such a transparent summer morning;
> You settled your head athwart my hips and gently turned over upon me,
> And parted the shirt from my bosom-bone, and plunged your tongue to my barestript heart,
> And reached till you felt my beard, and reached till you held my feet.
>
> (Whitman 1959: 28–9)

Whitman affirms the body and the soul, his own and those of others, and does not see the body as divorced from the soul. Although the speaker of these lines is gendered as male, the "you" addressed here could be another male, a female, an imagined person, or the soul. This experience, whether real or imagined, induces in the speaker a quasi-mystical state of being as his consciousness opens up to the wonder of the created universe:

> Swiftly arose and spread around me the peace and joy and knowledge that pass all the art and argument of the earth;
> And I know that the hand of God is the elderhand of my own,
> And I know the spirit of God is the eldest brother of my own,
> And that all the men ever born are also my brothers . . . and the women my sisters and lovers,
> And that a kelson of the creation is love. . . .
>
> (Whitman 1959: 29)

Language cannot adequately capture this experience; the knowledge that floods the speaker both embraces and exceeds the bounds of ordinary perception. The speaker's vision widens to include all humanity and then narrows to expound upon the smallest evidence of the miraculous power of creativity. This experience also leads the speaker into a deeper understanding of the sacredness of existence as well as a feeling of connectedness to "the hand" and "the spirit" of God. The specific sexuality of the partner remains unclear, but it matters little whether the sexuality of the "you" is precisely defined; through contact with this other being the speaker is filled with a new vision charged with intimacy, love, and acceptance.

Sections 11 and 28 of "Song of Myself" share commonalities in their emphasis upon the sense of touch and by the presence in both sections of a group of males who aid in facilitating the expression of desire and the release of sexual energy. In section 11, a woman watches 28 young men bathe by the shore. She is separated from them by physical barriers but also by class distinctions ("She owns the fine house by the rise of the bank, / She hides handsome and richly drest aft the blinds of the window."). Isolated and "all so lonesome," even the "homeliest" of the young men "is beautiful to her." A voyeur, she participates in the waterplay of the young men by imagining herself among them, "Dancing and laughing," and passing her "unseen hand . . . over their bodies" (Whitman 1959: 34). The sight, the sounds, and the imagined physical contact with these glistening bodies gradually transforms her; entering the water, even if only vicariously, enables the woman to open herself to an erotic and liberating sexual moment of union and contact. The speaker/poet latches on to her desire, thus giving voice to his own homosexual impulses. This section thus at once gives expression to female heterosexual desire, autoerotic desire, and male homosexual desire, but also demonstrates the fluidity of desire and sexuality.

The group of males becomes the object of desire and appropriation by the lone woman in her house and by the homosexual speaker who recognizes and articulates her desire. Interestingly, it is the woman who seems to be allied with the dominant power structures in this scene: she owns the house and is part of the market capitalist economy. Yet she is forbidden from directly experiencing the playful sensuality of the 28 young men she watches; despite her ownership of the house and her expensive clothing, she cannot literally partake in the sexual economy that she fantasizes about. The house and her clothing are part of a larger structure of domination that encloses her and that she is part of; she does not possess the agency to take part in the scene she witnesses. The men below her (her house is on the "rise of the bank") literally and figuratively constitute her social and economic inferiors. Despite her class advantages of wealth, ownership, and privilege, the young men (because they are men) still have access to an economy of expression that she can never enter into. Her sex hems her in, just as the speaker who witnesses the scene is hemmed in by his homosexuality. Both share the fantasy of joining the young men, but it remains a fantasy because the speaker, as a homosexual male, and the woman, as a female, are nevertheless excluded from the structure of domination that the male heterosexual order maintains, an order that in the nineteenth century increasingly came to regulate sexualities through religious, medical, and later, psychological discourse. Because of this exclusion, ironically, the speaker both captures and gives voice to the otherwise censored and silenced plurality of desire inherent in the bathing scene, thus underscoring its existence.

Section 28 begins with an abrupt question: "Is this then a touch?" (Whitman 1959: 53). Touch, perhaps the most underappreciated and unrecorded of all the senses, is also the most erotic. In this section of "Song of Myself" Whitman personifies the sense of touch as a band of shameless marauders who, in contrast to the group of 28 young men playing in the water in section 11, are conscious of their desire, surround the speaker, and will not be turned away. Whitman describes them as "Behaving licentious toward me, taking no denial, / Depriving me of my best as for a purpose, / Unbuttoning my clothes and holding me by the bare waist." The interplay between the many "fellow-senses" and the single "red marauder" of touch is characterized as a playful conspiracy to seduce the initially unwilling "me" who speaks; the tone in this passage varies from disbelief and surprise to anger and a sense of betrayal ("I am given up by traitors"), to grudging acceptance of the speaker's role in this sexual interlude. The last two lines of the section can be read as affectionately corrective: "You villain touch! what are you doing? .... my breath is tight in its throat; / Unclench your floodgates! you are too much for me" (1959: 54). The speaker now welcomes touch, and invites the opening of the "floodgates" that precedes the entrance of "Blind loving wrestling touch!" in section 29, an allusion to the 29th bather of section 11.

In addition to "Song of Myself," in other poems from the first edition such as "The Sleepers" and "I Sing the Body Electric" Whitman includes sexual themes by peeling away clothing and other coverings that obscure the expression of desire and the body. In "The Sleepers," for instance, the speaker translates the dreams of naked sleepers into poetry: "The sleepers are very beautiful as they lie unclothed, / They flow hand in hand over the whole earth from east to west as they lie unclothed" (Whitman 1959: 114). Initially "confused," "lost to myself," "ill-assorted" and "contradictory," the speaker is transformed as he gains a deeper insight into the human condition. Despite the crimes, sins, and shortcomings of their daytime activities, the night embraces even those who are most wretched and most broken: "The wretched features of ennuyes, the white features of corpses, the livid faces of drunkards. . . . / The gash'd bodies on battle-fields, the insane in their strong-door'd rooms, / The sacred idiots, the new-born emerging from gates. . . . " Once the speaker stands by the "worstsuffering and restless" he sees the beauty of the night and of the earth and is now able to "sleep close with the other sleepers" and "become the other dreamers." The speaker is taken up by a "gang of blackguards with mirthshouting music and wildflapping pennants of joy" (earlier described as "nimble ghosts") who "surround me and lead me and run ahead when I walk" (1959: 106) – an action that recalls Whitman's earlier description in section 28 of "Song of Myself" of the band of marauders. When he can characterize himself as part of a crowd, preferably a rowdy and uncontrolled group of men, Whitman often portrays the release of sexual energy. As a member of the crowd, the speaker is at once anonymous yet feels singled out, seduced but also coerced into actions that he might not otherwise go along with. And out of this mélange of emotions the speaker is given license to voice the fluidity of desire, attraction, and sexual impulse.

In the context of this poem, the speaker's absorption into this "gang of blackguards" serves as a prelude to another extended female fantasy in which the speaker enters a woman's autoerotic dream sequence:

> I am she who adorned herself and folded her hair expectantly,
> My truant lover has come and it is dark.
>
> Double yourself and receive me darkness,
> Receive me and my lover too. . . . he will not let me go without him.
>
> I roll myself upon you as upon a bed. . . . I resign myself to the dusk.
>
> He whom I call answers me and takes the place of my lover,
> He rises with me silently from the bed.
>
> Darkness you are gentler than my lover. . . . his flesh was sweaty and panting,
> I feel the hot moisture yet that he left me.
>
> My hands are spread forth . . . I pass them in all directions,
> I would sound up the shadowy shore to which you are journeying.
>
> Be careful, darkness. . . . already, what was it touched me?
> I thought my lover had gone . . . else darkness and he are one.
> I hear the heart-beat. . . . I follow . . . I fade away.
>
> (Whitman 1959: 107)

Whether or not Whitman consciously crafted this section within the larger poem of "The Sleepers" as a sonnet, this part of the poem could be read as such. Five of the stanzas are comprised of two-line pairings, except for the last section, which possesses three lines, and the significant third section, which has only one line and thus marks a turn (both literally and figuratively) in the sonnet. Killingsworth writes that the female speaker of this section emerges "in a passive, female role" from the "range of possibilities" (1989: 19) in the preceding lines, yet this is not so. Of the three characters named in the poem, darkness (also referred to as the "dusk") is the most passive. The lover is asleep beside the woman, until he merges with the darkness in the last stanza. It is the woman who is active throughout, until the last line: she readies herself for her lover, rolls herself upon the darkness, calls the darkness, spreads her hands "in all directions," and gives voice to ("sound up") the place to which darkness is "journeying." The woman's voice merges with the male speaker of the poem in lines 55 and 56, just as in section 11 of "Song of Myself" when the male speaker inserts himself and his desire into the scene he is describing. These lines could be voiced by the woman or by the dream-speaker, or both, but they echo line 25: "I pass my hands soothingly to and fro a few inches from them." The speaker's desire, however, is not as obviously inserted into this scene as it is in section 11; he does not address the woman directly. Rather, the speaker merges with her desire, simultaneously capturing the duality of desire and articulating it.

The many human stories that the poem's speaker reads in the night lead him again to a larger vision of interconnectedness, healing his earlier self-division and creating in him the certainty that all are "hand in hand," – "Asiatic and African," "Europeans and American," "Learned and unlearned," "male and female." Those divided by space and ethnic background, or class and education, or sex, are ultimately united in this dream vision, prefiguring in some ways the new political order that "Calamus" and *Democratic Vistas* call for. In the poem's conclusion, the night becomes the poet's mother who gives life to the poet, and sparks his creative powers.

Before writing "I Sing the Body Electric" Whitman sketched out a plan for its composition: "A poem in which is minutely described the particulars and ensemble of a *first-rate healthy Human Body* – it looked into and through, as if it were transparent and of pure glass – and now reported in a poem" (*NUPM*, 1: 304). Whitman also jotted down some ideas for gathering material. Underneath the above passage, he wrote: "Read the latest and best anatomical works / talk with physicians / study the anatomical plates / also casts of figures in the collections of design." In the 1855 edition of *Leaves of Grass* this poem was left untitled, and simply presented as No. 5. A year later, in the 1856 edition, Whitman added the title "Poem of the Body" and the final section of the poem, the "remarkable anatomical inventory" (Whitman 1973: 92). Whitman's additions and revisions in this instance go against the more general trend in his editing and sifting of material; instead of excising passages that might be found objectionable, as in, for instance, "The Sleepers," in "I Sing the Body Electric" he adds them.

In the 1840s and 1850s Whitman increasingly turned to the language of phrenology to conceptualize and to articulate the different kinds of sexualities he wished to include in his poetry. Phrenologists believed that the brain could be mapped as the locus of certain kinds of emotion and, as Michael Lynch notes, "the stronger the particular function, the larger the particular part of the brain which produces it" (1985: 70). Friendship, for instance, could be located in a specific part of the brain. Initially skeptical about phrenology (Whitman published three reviews in the Brooklyn *Eagle* on March 5, March 7, and March 11, 1846 that were ironic in tone), Whitman's respect for the science of phrenology grew, Thomas L. Brasher points out, "sometime between March and November of 1846," so that "by 10 March 1847 Whitman was able to say with apparent sincerity, 'there can be no harm, but probably much good, in pursuing the study of phrenology. . . . Among the most persevering workers in phrenology in this country must be reckoned the two Fowlers and Mr. Wells'" (Brasher 1958: 96–7). In July 1849 Whitman had a phrenological study of his head completed by Lorenzo Fowler, the founder of *The American Phrenological Journal and Miscellany*. Whitman's highest scores were in the areas of Self-Esteem and Caution (6 out of a possible 7), followed by a 6 in "Amativeness, Adhesiveness, Philoprogenitiveness, Concentrativeness, and Combativeness" (Reynolds 1995: 247).

Whitman borrowed from phrenology two terms, "amativeness," to signal love between men and women, and "adhesiveness," to signal deep friendship. However, the meanings of these terms were shaped and revised by Whitman. Adhesiveness, a term crafted by the phrenologists, originally took its meanings from the Friendship tradition and signified the affection and emotional bonds that women felt for one other. This kind of attachment, phrenologists noted, was "especially strong in women and in criminals" (Lynch 1985: 71). This strong affection, which sometimes resulted in a lifelong bond, was concretely manifested by a telltale bump on the skull of the women, and was often thought to be indicated by the sideward movement of the women's heads toward each other, a gesture that signified a deeper attachment to each other. Although some phrenologists had also used the term to refer to male/male friendship, this meaning would be more fully developed and advanced by Whitman. Robert K. Martin points out that in *Leaves of Grass* adhesiveness "lost its phrenological associations and took on new ones; it evoked the qualities Whitman admired – loyalty, fidelity, sharing, touching" (Martin 1979: 35). Many of the "Calamus" poems unabashedly use the term to refer to same-sex male desire, affection, and commitment.

In their themes, emphasis, and setting, the "Calamus" poems, as many critics have noted, mark a turn inward in Whitman's life and work. Although in the final (1881) edition of *Leaves of Grass* Whitman placed these poems after "Children of Adam," they were composed before the "Children of Adam" cluster. In the 1855 edition of "Song of Myself" Whitman had referred to the phallic-shaped sweet flag for which he would name this cluster: "Root of washed sweet-flag, timorous pond-snipe, nest of guarded duplicate eggs" (Whitman 1959: 49). Many of these poems use a rural setting for clandestine, secretive, intimate meetings with single lovers; yet these meetings do not always result in the peaceful and connected feeling that the speaker of section 5 in "Song of Myself" utters. Rather, throughout "Calamus" the speaker captures a wide range of emotions: anger, jealousy, love, happiness, satisfaction, completeness, brokenness. These emotions signal the effects of commitments that are entered into and then set aside, reaffirmed, then dispensed with. These combustible, difficult, satisfying, and yet challenging relationships engross the speaker, whose poems record the moment-to-moment heartbreak of individual attachment. The difficulty of expressing this heartbreak is hinted at in "Calamus. 15":

> Trickle drops! my blue veins leaving!
> O drops of me! trickle, slow drops,
> Candid from me falling, drip, bleeding drops,
> From wounds made to free you whence you were prison'd,
> From my face, from my forehead and lips,
> From my breast, from within where I was conceal'd, press forth red drops, confession drops,
> Stain every page, stain every song I sing, every word I say, bloody drops,
> Let them know your scarlet heat, let them glisten,
> Saturate them with yourself all ashamed and wet,
> Glow upon all I have written or shall write, bleeding drops,
> Let it all be seen in your light, blushing drops.
>
> (Whitman 1973: 125)

Perhaps Whitman was referring to this poem when he wrote in his *Notebooks*, "*Make a poem the central theme of which should be* the *Untellable*, That which can not be put in fine words, Nor in any words or statement or essay, poem" (*NUPM*, 4: 1411). "Trickle Drops" records the untellable, the unmentionable. Nevertheless, the "drops" can be read metaphorically in many ways – as the words of the *Calamus* poems, as sweat from the brow of the writer, as blood, as tears, as semen. The words become fleshly in their linkage to the "blue veins" of the writer and signify a life force which cannot be checked or denied. The "wounds" (l. 4) signify both suffering and healing. The irony, of course, is that the poem depicts the act of revelation rather than revelation itself. Purportedly a confession, the drops spill over onto the page ("them" of l. 8, perhaps also in this instance meaning the audience as well) but remain part of a larger whole which is not revealed. As such, the "trickle drops" become metonymic, part of a larger whole.

But what is the whole? In 1884 Whitman told Edward Carpenter,

> There is something in my nature furtive like an old hen! You see a hen wandering up and down a hedgerow, looking apparently quite unconcerned, but presently she finds a concealed spot, and furtively lays an egg, and comes away as though nothing had happened! That is how I felt in writing *Leaves of Grass*. (Carpenter 1906: 43)

This method of concealment was a necessary strategy for the inclusion of radical utterances about human desire and sexuality in the poems. As Joseph Cady points out, "Whitman's chief problem in *Calamus* is to invent a way of speaking affirmatively about a subject that his popular audience considered literally unspeakable and that his general culture gave him no positive way of understanding" (Cady 1978: 6). The drops in this poem signify the anguish that the writer feels in the knowledge that the sexual desire he feels is part of human experience, but he cannot name it directly.

Public venues and occasions that tolerated the physical expression of emotion between men could be appropriated and transformed as a way of simultaneously expressing and cloaking relationships. The occasion of greeting and parting, for instance, enabled Whitman to mask homosexual expression in moments sanctioned by society during which public displays of affection between men could be expressed openly. "Calamus. 19" illustrates this dynamic of inclusion/exclusion:

> Behold this swarthy face, these gray eyes,
> This beard, the white wool unclipt upon my neck,
> My brown hands and the silent manner of me without charm;
> Yet comes one a Manhattanese and ever at parting kisses me lightly on the lips with robust love,
> And I on the crossing of the street or on the ship's deck give a kiss in return,
> We observe that salute of American comrades land and sea,
> We are those two natural and nonchalant persons.
>
> (Whitman 1973: 126)

In the first three lines of the poem the speaker identifies himself as a member of the working class, someone whose skin, beard, and attitude reflect the hard physical labor that he exchanges for wages. Despite his physical gruffness and seeming lack of "charm" (signified by the "Yet" in l. 4), a "Manhattanese" finds him attractive, and kisses him "lightly with robust love," tenderly yet with passion. The speaker returns this kiss, not only at parting but in public places like the street or the ship's deck. The poem ends by avowing that the relationship signified by their tender yet passionate kiss is not uncommon; in fact, it is shared and understood by countless "American comrades" as a "salute," a call to attention for those who can read the signal. The kiss of the two men serves as the emblem of the larger body politic, a means of communication that is understood by comrades as a signal of homoerotic love and affection. The expression of that love and affection is not only "natural" (rather than unnatural) but also "nonchalant," done without fanfare; the radical claim that the poem makes is that in the parting kiss of the lovers may be observed a larger connection, one so ingrained as perhaps to be unnoticeable.

Whitman expressed this idea again in *Democratic Vistas*, written a decade after "Calamus":

> I confidently expect a time when there will be seen, running like a half-hid warp through all the myriad audible and visible worldly interests of America, threads of manly friendship, fond and loving, pure and sweet, strong and life-long, carried to degrees hitherto unknown. . . . I say democracy infers such loving comradeship, as its most inevitable twin or counterpart, without which it will be incomplete, in vain, and incapable of perpetuating itself. (*PW*, 2: 414–15n.)

As Robert K. Martin notes in writing about this passage from *Democratic Vistas*, "Whitman's metaphor is important in that it suggests the coexistence of homosexuality with heterosexuality to an extent undreamed of by the ordinary observer" (1979: xvii). Indeed, Whitman's allusion to the naturalness of the continuum between "manly friendship" and democracy is also one of the main impulses of the "Calamus" cluster. The poems "For You O Democracy," "This Moment Yearning and Thoughtful," "I Dream'd in a Dream," and "To the East and to the West" incorporate this belief in the establishment of a society of comrades and lovers whose consciousness could be united behind political action. Yet during the time when Whitman composed the "Calamus" poems, between 1857 and 1859, the United States was on the verge of disintegration; anxiety about the stability of the political system was heightened. In these years, as many biographers note, Whitman suffered from a disturbing emotional relationship. Stephen John Mack writes, "given the fact that he had always identified himself with the specifically public, political, and cosmic content and theoretical purpose of his poetry, a psychological crisis was inevitable when an intense emotional relationship made it urgent that he utilize poetic language for the very contradictory purpose of shaping private emotion" (Mack 2002: 91). It is probably not surprising, then, that Whitman would ultimately create a continuum between his own personal situation and the wider cultural and political crisis.

In the "Enfans d'Adam" poems Whitman's attempt to incorporate a more inclusive sexuality – specifically, the procreative heterosexual couple – does not always succeed. As he thought about this project, Whitman declared in his notebooks his wish to create "A string of Poems (short etc.) embodying the amative love of women – the same as *Live Oak Leaves* [the original title for the "Calamus" poems] do the passion of friendship for man" (*NUPM*, 1: 412). Nevertheless, the very title of this poem cluster excludes Eve, who fulfills her function as procreator in the poems but does not merit equal billing with her spouse or her progeny. Vivian Pollak notes that "the title itself diminishes Eve's importance" (2000: 130). Betsy Erkkila points out that the original French title "was itself a means of defying the sensibilities of Puritan America by connecting the amative theme of the poems with the sexual freedom and libertarian traditions associated in the popular mind with France" (Erkkila 1989: 177). The title of the cluster was changed to "Children of Adam" in 1867. The critical reception of these poems over the last 150 years has undergone many variations. Initially, critics objected to their sexual explicitness, and Whitman was urged repeatedly to expurgate the more objectionable passages. After the 1860 edition was released, Emerson advised Whitman to remove "Children of Adam" from the collection and to excise other more controversial passages in order to reach a wider audience. Whitman refused. In 1877 Robert Buchanan, writing from England, asked Whitman to reconsider the "Children of Adam" section: "I shall ever regret the insertion of certain passages in your books (*Children of Adam* etc).... I think your reputation is growing here, and I am sure it deserves to grow. But your fatal obstacle to general influence is the obnoxious passages" (quoted in Whitman 2001: 83). Whitman again refused. Later critics, beginning most notoriously with D. H. Lawrence, find Whitman's treatment of women lacking in nuance. Kerry C. Larson, for instance, writes of the "Children of Adam" cluster:

> The awkward demarcation between songs of "amativeness" and those of "adhesiveness" anticipates the artificiality of Whitman's project. . . . In veering away from the richly ambiguous and often explosive blurring of sexual identity acted out in previous poems . . . Whitman monumentalizes, pairing the shrill virilism of *Children of Adam* incongruously with the tender-hearted idylls of *Calamus*. Out of this bifurcation the women of the poet's new Eden emerge, as many have noted, as little more than faceless breeders in attendance upon the egregious strutting of a poet. (Larson 1988: 154)

However, there are poems in "Children of Adam" that merit study because they allow a deeper understanding of the limitations placed on poetic discourse by cultural constraints and by dominant ideologies. The "Children of Adam" poems may be fruitfully isolated from the larger critical histories of *Leaves of Grass* and studied as an example of how sexuality, particularly women's sexuality, continues to disturb and to vex, whether because it is expressed at all or because it indicates a writer's imbrication in contemporary discourse.

The first two poems of the cluster demonstrate Whitman's attempt to incorporate the theme of amativeness into the poem cluster. "To the Garden the World" announces Whitman's intentions: to present a post-Edenic (yet no less utopian) cycle of poems that celebrate the heterosexual couple who in turn produce a new, worldly citizenry:

> To the garden the world anew ascending,
> Potent mates, daughters, sons, preluding,
> The love, the life of their bodies, meaning and being,
> Curious here behold my resurrection after slumber,
> The revolving cycles in their wide sweep having brought me again,
> Amorous, mature, all beautiful to me, all wondrous,
> My limbs and the quivering fire that ever plays through them, for reasons, most wondrous,
> Existing I peer and penetrate still,
> Content with the present, content with the past,
> By my side or back of me Eve following,
> Or in front, and I following her just the same.
>
> (Whitman 1973: 90)

Erkkila writes that "The hierarchies and polarities of the past collapse as Eve and Adam nimbly switch places – from front to back to side by side – in an egalitarian economy in which the terms female and male are just the same" (1989: 178). But the economy and the terms are not "just the same" in this poem. The word "mates" in the second line is nongendered. Just as Whitman cuts women out of the title of the cluster, he cuts their female identity out of the garden. The mate, of course, could be another male. Eve is not named until the last lines of the poem, and then, even though she is in alternate lines described as "By my side" "Or in front" her name is placed between two telling concepts: "back of me" and "following." Adam alone speaks, just as he does in the biblical narrative of Genesis 2: 21–5. Whitman uses the word "resurrection" here purposely, to connote not just an awakening but a new and different state of being. But it is also a religiously loaded term, evoking Christ's miraculous resurrection from the dead. Adam has often been seen as a precursor to Christ; Whitman thus employs a postlapsarian figure who, coming after Christ, will inhabit and populate a fallen Eden along with his "mates," surely an allusion not to Eve but to those comrades with whom Whitman envisioned creating a new democratic society.

Despite Whitman's determination to be inclusive by embracing the phrenological concept of amativeness, which connoted heterosexual impulses, many of his poems cannot escape incorporating male homoerotic desire as a subtext despite their announced intentions. This commingling is evident, for instance, in the poem "From Pent-up Aching Rivers":

> From my own voice resonant, singing the phallus,
> Singing the song of procreation,
> Singing the need of superb children and therein superb grown people,
> Singing the muscular urge and the blending,
> Singing the bedfellow's song (O resistless yearning!
> O for any and each the body correlative attracting!
> O for you whoever you are your correlative body! O it, more than all else, you delighting)!
> (Whitman 1973: 91)

The speaker wants to sing the song of procreation, but his desire for the "bedfellow" keeps slipping into the text, so much so that he must bracket this desire in parenthesis. Later in the poem, Whitman claims the "work of fatherhood" even as he leaves the "bedfellow's embrace in the night" (ll. 46–7), remembering and chronicling not the "act divine and you children prepared for" (l. 56) but rather "the one so unwilling to have me leave, and me just as unwilling to leave" (l. 52) – the "tender waiter," the male lover, not the wife or the woman.

David Cavitch notes that in this poem cluster Whitman "wanted to define an ideal of sex that reflected the personal freedoms of an expanding society in the natural abundance of the New World. He ascribed to sex a socially progressive, public utility that he often illustrated with topical imagery of westward expansion into the vast, undeveloped continent of national resources waiting to be discovered and used" (Cavitch 1985: 115). Heterosexual union becomes part of the discourse of conquest, absorption, colonization. Along with expansion of the national borders would come those who would settle the land and continue the natural cycle of birth, maturation, and death. The Adam figure in these poems speaks to Eve hyperbolically of his role as one who will "beget babes" in order to "grow fierce and athletic girls, new artists, musicians, and singers" ("A Woman Waits for Me," Whitman 1973: 103). These will be the next generation of the new Republic, the progeny who will make the new world into a new Eden. Nevertheless, in many of the "Children of Adam" poems, Whitman glosses over women and women's sexuality even as he provides testimony about women's potency and their centrality to the kind of democratic society he envisioned.

The seven years between the third (1860) and fourth (1867) editions of *Leaves of Grass* had serious implications for Whitman's work. He spent much time in Washington, DC, visiting the Civil War hospitals and tending to the wounded and the dying. In these years Whitman wrote the "Drum-Taps" poems and his "Memories of President Lincoln" poems, but the tone and the subject matter of his poetry was influenced by the bloodshed and the national tragedies he witnessed. In some ways, Whitman was traumatized by these events. Until he visited the hospitals, he had no conception of the horrors of the war and wrote the bellicose, martial poetry that opens "Drum-Taps"; this changed in 1862, when he went to Washington to try to find his brother George, wounded at the Battle of Fredericksburg. What Whitman found in Washington was a new subject for his work: the broken, wounded body of the soldiers. As a poem cluster, these poems "preserved more autonomy through the successive editions of *LG* than most of the groups," Blodgett and Bradley write. "In his final arrangement, the poet attained a concentration not before achieved" (Whitman 1973: 279). Whitman combined with the new subject matter a theme and a focus that he had developed in the "Calamus" poems: adhesiveness. The manner of its presentation, though, changed. The public venue of the battlefield and the hospital became the setting for the expression of male/male desire, affection, and love. Whitman used the occasion of the war to slip homoerotic desire into the text in such poems as "Vigil Strange I kept on the Field One Night," "A March in the Ranks Hard-Prest, and the Road Unknown," "A Sight in the Camp in the Daybreak Gray and Dim," "As Toilsome I Wander'd Virginia's Woods," "The Wound-Dresser," "Dirge for Two Veterans."

The poems that end the cluster – such as "How Solemn as One by One," "As I Lay With My Head in Your Lap Camerado," "To a Certain Civilian," "Spirit Whose Work is Done," and "Adieu to a Soldier" – include references to "pulses of rage," "currents convulsive," and the need to turn to "fiercer, weightier battles." Whitman does not explain in these poems what these references mean, but in his 1876 Preface to *Leaves of Grass* Whitman made the significance of the connection between the "Calamus" and the "Drum-Taps" poems more explicit:

> Besides, important as they are in my purpose as emotional expressions for humanity, the special meaning of the *Calamus* cluster of *Leaves of Grass*, (and more or less running through that book, and cropping out in *Drum-Taps*,) mainly resides in its Political significance. In my opinion, it is by a fervent, accepted development of Comradeship, the beautiful and sane affection of man for man, latent in all the young fellows, North and South, East and West – it is by this, I say, and by what goes directly and indirectly along with it, that the United States of the future, (I cannot too often repeat,) are to be most effectually welded together, intercalated, anneal'd into a Living Union. (as quoted in Whitman 1973: 753, 175n.)

Adhesiveness, "the beautiful and sane affection of man for man," would act as the catalyst and the unifying principle for the utopian political order that Whitman envisioned and that he believed he had witnessed, to some degree, on the battlefield and in the hospitals. The anger and rage expressed in the latter poems of "Drum-Taps" reveal Whitman's deep anxieties and uncertainties about the creation of this new order.

Increasingly in the two final editions of *Leaves of Grass* (1871 and 1881) Whitman focused less on sexual themes and more on editing and sifting through what he had already written, changing the shape of some of the clusters, reordering the poems, deleting material. The reason for this may have been physical; in 1871 Whitman suffered a stroke and this event, combined with the death of his beloved mother, levered Whitman into old age. He took on the role of the "Good Gray Poet" and became enmeshed in the process of ensuring a place for *Leaves of Grass* in literary history.

Judith Butler writes that "language is bound to founder on the question of desire, that it is forced to seek modes of indirection, and that the writings of and on desire that we might consider are ones which seek, in the end, to cancel themselves as writing in order better to approximate the desire they seek to know" (1995: 370). If this is the case for contemporary discourse, how much more so for nineteenth-century Victorian America.

It seems no less than astonishing that Whitman was able to write out and to publish the many kinds of desire evident in *Leaves of Grass*, and to challenge cultural assumptions about sexuality, heterosexuality, and sexual difference. No wonder, then, that John Addington Symonds wrote Whitman over the course of almost two decades in an effort to sort out the sexual implications Symonds saw in the verse. "At another level," Sedgwick writes, noting the class, cultural, and national differences between Whitman and Symonds, "the ravishing and peculiar eros in *Leaves of Grass* resisted translation as insistently as it demanded it" (1990: 121). Symonds understood that Whitman was pushing the boundaries of discourse; Whitman understood that the boundaries of discourse were complicated by the fluidity of the sexualities encompassed in human beings.

References and Further Reading

Brasher, Thomas L. (1958). Whitman's Conversion to Phrenology. *Walt Whitman Newsletter*, 4: 95–7.

Butler, Judith (1995). Desire. In Frank Lentricchia and Thomas McLaughlin (eds.), *Critical Terms for Literary Study*, 2nd edn. Chicago: University of Chicago Press, pp. 369–86.

Cady, Joseph (1978). Not Happy in the Capital: Homosexuality and the *Calamus* Poems. *American Studies*, 19: 5–22.

Carpenter, Edward (1906). *Days With Walt Whitman*. London: George Allen.

Cavitch, David (1985). *My Soul and I: The Inner Life of Walt Whitman*. Boston: Beacon.

Coviello, Peter (2001). Intimate Nationality: Anonymity and Attachment in Whitman. *American Literature*, 73 (1): 85–119.

Erkkila, Betsy (1989). *Whitman the Political Poet*. Oxford: Oxford University Press.

Foucault, Michel (1978). *The History of Sexuality. Volume I: An Introduction*, trans. Robert Hurley. New York: Pantheon.

Griswold, Rufus W. (1971). Unsigned review. *New York Criterion*, November 10, 1855. In

Milton Hindus (ed.), *Walt Whitman: The Critical Heritage*. New York: Barnes & Noble, pp. 31–3.

Killingsworth, M. J. (1989). *Whitman's Poetry of the Body: Sexuality, Politics, and the Text*. Chapel Hill: University of North Carolina Press.

Larson, Kerry C. (1988). *Whitman's Drama of Consensus*. Chicago: University of Chicago Press.

Lawson, Andrew (2003). "Spending for Vast Returns": Sex, Class, and Commerce in the First *Leaves of Grass*. *American Literature*, 75: 335–65.

Lynch, Michael (1985). "Here is Adhesiveness": From Friendship to Homosexuality. *Victorian Studies*, 29: 67–96.

Mack, Stephen John (2002). *The Pragmatic Whitman: Reimagining American Democracy*. Iowa City: University of Iowa Press.

Martin, Robert K. (1979). *The Homosexual Tradition in American Poetry*. Austin and London: University of Texas Press.

Moon, Michael (1991). *Disseminating Whitman: Revision and Corporeality in* Leaves of Grass. Cambridge, MA: Harvard University Press.

Pollak, Vivian R. (2000). *The Erotic Whitman*. Berkeley: University of California Press.

Reynolds, David S. (1995). *Walt Whitman's America: A Cultural Biography*. New York: Knopf.

Sedgwick, Eve Kosofsky (1983). Whitman's Transatlantic Context: Class, Gender, and Male Homosexual Style. *Delta: Revue du Centre d'Etudes et de Recherche sur les Ecrivains du Sud aux Etats-Unis*, 16: 111–24.

Sedgwick, Eve Kosofsky (1990). *Epistemology of the Closet*. Berkeley: University of California Press.

Traubel, Horace (1908). *With Walt Whitman in Camden, vol.* 2. New York: Appleton.

Traubel, Horace (1914). *With Walt Whitman in Camden, vol.* 3. New York: Mitchell Kennerley.

Whitman, Walt (1959). *Leaves of Grass: The First (1855) Edition*, ed. Malcolm Cowley. New York: Viking.

Whitman, Walt (1973). *Leaves of Grass*, ed. Sculley Bradley and Harold Blodgett. New York: Norton.

Whitman, Walt (2001). *Intimate With Walt: Selections from Whitman's Conversations with Horace Traubel, 1888–1892*, ed. Gary Schmidgall. Iowa City: University of Iowa Press.

12
Gender
Sherry Ceniza

"What is a man anyhow? what am I? what are you?" (*LG*: 47). Walt Whitman posed these questions in his 1855 "Song of Myself," a line of query that continues in various forms throughout *Leaves of Grass*. Catherine Belsey, in *Critical Practice*, provides a response I like to imagine Whitman affirming: "Unfixed, unsatisfied, the human being is not a unity, not autonomous, but a process, perpetually in construction, perpetually contradictory, perpetually open to change" (1980: 132). Though at times Whitman speaks in his poetry as if sure of his identity, as if it is stable – "Walt Whitman, a kosmos, of Manhattan the son" and "I know I am solid and sound, / To me the converging objects of the universe perpetually flow" (*LG*: 52, 47) – in his 1860 poem "Thoughts, (Of these years I sing)," he also speaks of "The vehement struggle so fierce for unity in one's self" (*LG*: 492). Years later, in 1889, he told his young friend Horace Traubel, "I am but a fragment, anyhow – Leaves of Grass is a modality of but fragments" (Traubel 1964: 399). So there is a tension. On one hand, Whitman, like Belsey, affirms change. "Do I contradict myself? / Very well then I contradict myself, / (I am large, I contain multitudes)" (*LG*: 88). On the other hand, he searches for cohesion.

In 1889 Whitman said to Traubel: "Tell me about things – don't tell me theories. I have theories of my own" (Traubel 1953: 510). In this essay, I explore what might be Whitman's theory about what we now refer to as gender but what Whitman calls in his poetry "identity." A dictionary sense of the word "gender" is that of "the societal or behavioral aspects of sexual identity." Eve Kosofsky Sedgwick says in her 1990 *Epistemology of the Closet* that in relation to the word "sex" "[g]ender . . . is the far more elaborated, more fully and rigidly dichotomized social production and reproduction of male and female identities and behaviors . . . " (pp. 27–8). Though at times Whitman's poetry names ideal individual characteristics, thereby seeming to fix identity, his poetry, at the same time, calls for fluidity.

Gender theory asks *how* identity comes to be. Feminist theory has focused on the question of gender, in the past falling into groups of those who privileged essentialism and those who felt that societal forces largely determined or shaped one's identity. Queer theory has widened the discussion of gender, making the binarism of male/female too restrictive. Marjorie Garber's essay "Spare Parts: The Surgical Construction of Gender" takes another step, theorizing that the distinction of essentialism and social construction becomes not really a distinction at all; rather, the two keep circling in on each other. Using the example of Renee Richards – originally Dick Raskind – Garber states, "The phenomenon of Transsexualism is both a confirmation of the constructedness of gender and a secondary recourse to essentialism – or, to put it a slightly different way, Transsexualism demonstrates that essentialism *is* cultural construction" (1994: 254). Garber holds that "it is to transsexuals and transvestites that we need to look if we want to understand what gender categories mean" (p. 254). Gender, then, has the body at its core and the way the person presents that body. Though reading poems like "I Sing the Body Electric" leads one to believe that, like gender critics, Whitman prioritizes the relationship between the body and identity, I find that while Whitman celebrates the body, his poetry raises other questions as well, and it is on these other questions that I will focus.

A problem in placing the templates of gender theory or queer theory onto Whitman's poetry is that it is almost impossible to speak of Whitman's poetry and of the sense of identity that it inscribes without speaking of the soul. And I don't read much talk in gender theory about the soul. Therefore, rather than take current theory and apply it to Whitman's poetry, in this essay I take Whitman at his word, looking for a theory of his own relating to the question of identity.

Whitman himself considered gender. Volume 3 of *Daybooks and Notebooks* contains a long section titled "Words." In this notebook, Whitman has written the following:

> through, a *common* gender ending in *ist* as
> lovist   both
> hatist   masc
>   &
>   fem
> –hater   m
>   &c
> hatress   f
>
> (*DBN*, 3: 666)

He includes, as well, a definition of "Kosmos," a noun, he says, "masculine or feminine, a person who[se] scope of mind or whose range in a particular science, includes all, the whole known universe" (p. 669). The distinction of *kosmos* as being either a masculine or a feminine noun suggests the fluidity of gender identity, in a way contradicting Whitman's construction of gendered suffixes which mark difference but complementing his poetry's push for a voice that at times takes on the persona of others, as in section 33 of "Song of Myself" when he speaks of many "others," among them the "mother of old, condemn'd for a witch."

Twenty pages later in the notebook, Whitman again works with gender suffixes:

masc.	orator
	oratist both masc & fem.
fem.	oratress
m	reader
	readist – both m and f
fem.	Readress (*DBN*, 3: 686)

Whitman's concerns were not idiosyncratic. In an article titled "The Woman's Rights Convention," published in the *Lily*, Paulina Wright Davis, editor of the *Una*, is referred to as "editress":

> The Rev. Mr. Dickerson was introduced to the meeting, and in a few preliminary remarks, introduced a letter from Mary R. Ramsdale, of Providence, R. I., respecting the publication of the *Una*, of which her sister, Paulina Davis, is the editress. This paper is devoted to the dissemination of the principles of Woman's Rights, but as the health of the Editress has become much impaired in consequence of her editorial labors, a few suggestions were made for the establishing of a national paper, as a central organ, devoted to the advocacy of Woman's Rights. . . . (Woman's Rights Convention 1989)

One of the many articles Whitman has tipped into his "Words" notebook is one on names. This article addresses what the writer sees as the inappropriateness of last names, how countless women's last names are words of trade (a male province at this time) and some males' last names sound distinctly "feminine" (*DBN*, 3: 695–6). Farther on in the notebook is another article tipped in discussing the misuse, in the United States, anyway, of the term "lady." Far more correct to use is the term "woman" (p. 707). Whitman says, "The woman should preserve her own name, just as much after marriage as before. Also all titles must be dropped – no Mr. or Mrs. or Miss any more" (p. 712). Here are some of the gendered forms of common nouns Whitman created that appear in *Leaves of Grass*: quakeress, translatress, oratresses, originatress, dispensatress, all-acceptress, protectress. While not the most felicitous terms, possibly Whitman felt the need to use the feminine suffix for the same reason he used both feminine and masculine pronouns, to make sure that his female readers did not feel subsumed by common nouns ending in *–or* or *–er*.

Questions/Doubts

Though in differing guises, Whitman reiterates the question opening this essay throughout *Leaves*: "What is a man anyhow? what am I? what are you?" He performs a balancing act in his poetry, on one hand *questioning* identity and on the other hand, affirming or *naming* it. Like the unseen buds in Whitman's poem of that name, the doubts Whitman expresses about the reality of the material world, his questions of an afterlife, and more so his worry about the wisdom of what he often calls the pattern that he so wants to trust – these moments of doubt lie almost unseen, closed in by the many lines of exuberance and positiveness. The moments questioning or doubting identity are sufficiently poignant to resonate long after reading them. In fact, some of Whitman's starkest images come in the lines where he *questions*. In an odd way, reading the lines that through questioning pull the stable, celebrated worldly world out from under the reader's feet gives more credibility to the lines that affirm a stabilized self, a stability that occurs through Whitman's naming, through his assertions.

Images of masks, veils, mirrors, and shadows appear with regularity in *Leaves*. Some poems have these images in their titles, such as "That Shadow My Likeness," "A Hand-Mirror," "Visor'd," and "Out from Behind This Mask." In the 1860 "That Shadow My Likeness," Whitman uses the shadow image to question and doubt his identity, but as in "Of the Terrible Doubt of Appearances," the presence of "my lovers" causes the doubt to dissipate.

> That shadow my likeness that goes to and fro seeking a livelihood, chattering, chaffering,
> How often I find myself standing and looking at it where it flits,
> How often I question and doubt whether that is really me;
> But among my lovers and caroling these songs,
> O I never doubt whether that is really me.
>
> (*LG*: 136)

The appearance and the reappearance of lines such as the above in which the poet questions his identity form a pattern.

The most upfront articulation of self-questioning comes in the 1866 "When I Read the Book":

> (. . . Why even I myself I often think know little or nothing of my real life,
> Only a few hints, a few diffused faint clews and indirections
> I seek for my own use to trace out here.)
>
> (*LG*: 8)

Reading such an unabashed admission of one's ultimate lack of complete control of one's self not only prepares the reader for a complex persona in *Leaves*, it also causes readers to question self. A more intensified articulation of self-doubt comes in Whitman's 1860 "As I Ebb'd with the Ocean of Life." Using the imagery of the sea – windrows, drifts, sand, dead leaves, voices of people shipwrecked – and using the undulating rhythm that waves suggest as well as playing on the sounds of the words, Whitman creates a persona far different from one who sends a barbaric yawp over the rooftops:

> As I wend to the shores I know not,
> As I list to the dirge, the voices of men and women wreck'd,
> As I inhale the impalpable breezes that set in upon me,

> As the ocean so mysterious rolls toward me closer and closer,
> I too but signify at the utmost a little wash'd-up drift,
> A few sands and dead leaves to gather,
> Gather, and merge myself as part of the sands and drift.

As the poem goes on and Whitman speaks of the "real Me," questioning that "Me," the reader is moved to question self as well.

> O baffled, balk'd, bent to the very earth,
> Oppress'd with myself that I have dared to open my mouth,
> Aware now that amid all that blab whose echoes recoil upon me I have not once had the least idea who or what I am,
> But that before all my arrogant poems *the real Me* stands yet untouch'd, untold, altogether unreach'd,

We then hear humility:

> I perceive I have not really understood any thing, not a single object, and that no man ever can,
> Nature here in sight of the sea taking advantage of me to dart upon me and sting me,
> Because I have dared to open my mouth to sing at all.
> (*LG*: 254, emphasis added)

The 1874 "Prayer of Columbus" has lines that sound much like the "As I Ebb'd" lines quoted above:

> What do I know of life? What of myself?
> I know not even my own work past or present,
> Dim ever-shifting guesses of it spread before me,
> Of newer better worlds, their mighty parturition,
> Mocking, perplexing me.
> (*LG*: 423)

Tellingly, this poem, coming shortly after Whitman's stroke and his mother's death, speaks much the same sentiment of the 1860 Whitman, lending substance to my point that the appearance and reappearance of Whitman's questioning the self validate the significance of such questioning in Whitman's sense of identity.

Instead of the "real Me," lines in "Of the Terrible Doubt of Appearances" question the realities of the material world and of the afterlife. It's the "real something" that "has yet to be known." Later in the essay, I address Whitman's belief in the absolute necessity of a grounding when I talk about a nation's identity, making the point that without a ground base the individual becomes null. The terror in "Terrible Doubt" addresses not only the individual's perception but also the terror of a consciousness shorn of hope, the terror that optimism is groundless:

Of the terrible doubt of appearances,
Of the uncertainty after all, that we may be deluded,
That may-be reliance and hope are but speculations after all,
That may-be identity beyond the grave is a beautiful fable only,
May-be the things I perceive, the animals, plants, men, hills, shining and flowing waters,
The skies of day and night, colors, densities, forms, may-be these are (as doubtless they are) only apparitions, and the real something has yet to be known,
(How often they dart out of themselves as if to confound me and mock me!
How often I think neither I know, nor any man knows, aught of them,)
May-be seeming to me what they are (as doubtless they indeed but seem) as from my present point of view, and might prove (as of course they would) nought of what they appear, or nought anyhow, from entirely changed points of view;
To me these and the like of these are curiously answer'd by my lovers, my dear friends,
When he whom I love travels with me or sits a long while holding me by the hand,
When the subtle air, the impalpable, the sense that words and reason hold not, surround us and pervade us,
Then I am charged with untold and untellable wisdom, I am silent, I require nothing further,
I cannot answer the question of appearances or that of identity beyond the grave,
But I walk or sit indifferent, I am satisfied,
He ahold of my hand has completely satisfied me.

(*LG*: 120)

One can read this "Calamus" poem more as a validation of male/male bonding than as a poem of doubt. The turn for this reading occurs in line 10. But as in "That Shadow My Likeness," the intensity of the poem lies in the words and lines voicing doubt. The following phrases, appearing in lines 1–9, set the tone of the poem: "terrible doubt," "uncertainty," "deluded," "may-be reliance and hope," "speculations," "may-be identity beyond the grave," "beautiful fable only," "apparitions," "real something has yet to be known," "confound me and mock me." The syntax in that amazing ninth line – with its parenthetical interruptions and its use of the negative "nought" – works organically through the form of the line itself to create its thought. We see the workings of the mind as the line (the mind) doubles back on itself and changes its point of view; the "messiness" of the line so commands my attention that I find the lines that follow a falling off.

The 1855 "There Was a Child Went Forth" begins with certitude, laying out the effects on the speaker of the home, family, town, and countryside:

There was a child went forth every day,
And the first object he look'd upon, that object he became,
And that object became part of him for the day or a certain part of the day,
Or for many years or stretching cycles of years,

The poem moves along rich with imagery, with, all in all, a sense of well-being, yet midway in the poem the mood changes as the poem questions:

> Affection that will not be gainsay'd, the sense of what is real, the thought if after all it should prove unreal,
> The doubts of day-time and the doubts of night-time, the curious whether and how,
> Whether that which appears so is so, or is it all flashes and specks?
> Men and women crowding fast in the streets, if they are not flashes and specks what are they?
>
> (*LG*: 364–5)

The poem then shifts back to naming what the child encounters: "streets themselves and the facades of houses, and goods in the windows" and on for seven more lines of naming, and then the poem ends with the last line – line 39 – declaring: "These became part of that child . . . " (pp. 365–6). "These," referring to the previous 38 lines, includes the lines that question. Oddly, it's the "or is it all flashes and specks" lines that haunt the mind, not the affirmations.

Affirmation

The poetry also questions what Whitman sometimes calls the "pattern." Whitman uses the term "pattern" in the 1855 "To Think of Time," here voicing affirmation:

> Something long preparing and formless is arrived and form'd in you,
> You are henceforth secure, whatever comes or goes,
> The threads that were spun are gather'd, the weft crosses the warp, the pattern is systematic.
>
> (*LG*: 438)

Whitman needed to believe in some form of an afterlife in order for a strong sense of identity to matter. Since ships going down at sea were not an unusual occurrence in Whitman's time, an event such as this provoked questioning of the pattern, as in his 1860 "Thought (As I sit with others)":

> Of the veil'd tableau – women gather'd together on deck, pale, heroic, waiting the moment that draws so close – O the moment!
> A huge sob – a few bubbles – the white foam spirting up – and then the women gone,
> Sinking there while the passionless wet flows on – and I now pondering,
> Are those women indeed gone?
> Are souls drown'd and destroy'd so?
> Is only matter triumphant?
>
> (*LG*: 453)

In the 1856 "Salut au Monde!," however, Whitman sees the pattern as inevitable and positive:

> Each of us inevitable,
> Each of us limitless – each of us with his or her right upon the earth,
> Each of us allow'd the eternal purports of the earth,
> Each of us here as divinely as any is here.
>
> (*LG*: 147)

In "Passage to India," he asks, rhetorically, "For what is the present after all but a growth out of the past?" (*LG*: 412) and speaks of an "inscrutable purpose, some hidden prophetic intention" (p. 414). He voices confidence in the pattern in "Song of Myself": "I believe in those wing'd purposes" (p. 40). In the 1885 "You Tides with Ceaseless Swell," though put in the form of questions, he affirms: "central heart," "pulse," "clue to all" – creating a "fluid, vast identity":

> You tides with ceaseless swell! you power that does this work!
> You unseen force, centripetal, centrifugal, through space's spread,
> [. . .]
> What central heart – and you the pulse – vivifies all? what boundless aggregate of all?
> What subtle indirection and significance in you? what clue to all in you? what fluid, vast identity,
>
> (*LG*: 514)

"To the Sun-Set Breeze" ends with a question, an ending line that like "You Tides" looks at the unknown force behind the pattern, but through the use of the negatives "no" and "not," this poem, differing from "You Tides," ends with an impatient tone, the poet frustrated, perhaps, in not being able to identify, in not being without a doubt: "Hast thou no soul? Can I not know, identify thee?" (*LG*: 546)

Sexuality

Jonathan Katz's 2001 *Love Stories: Sex Between Men Before Homosexuality* provides a solid context in talking about Whitman's sexual orientation. While not a biography of Whitman, Katz's book "does offer the most fully contextualized study we so far have of Whitman's affections for males," writes Ed Folsom in his review of Katz's book in the *Walt Whitman Quarterly Review* (2004: 179). Folsom called for "a revisionist biography of Whitman that does not assume that the poet was *heterosexual*... or that he was *asexual* or *omnisexual* or *monosexual* or passively *homoerotic*... but one that... represents a full life built on the assumption that (not built out of the suspicion that) Whitman was gay" (2004: 179). Katz's book historicizes sexuality and puts Whitman's poetry, especially the "Calamus" poems, into cultural context: "I ask that we consider sexual desire and sexual acts, along with sexual identities, as fundamentally changing and fully historical, a still-controversial, counterintuitive idea" (Katz 2001: 9). Because Katz furthers the historicizing of sexuality, he believes we can "radically remake love and lust in ways more satisfying to our souls and to our flesh" (p. 12). Katz makes the case for change: "everything about sexuality is historical and changing" (p. 331). He frequently makes the point that for much of the nineteenth century, anyway, no distinction was made between biological sex and masculine or feminine mannerisms or acts (p. 301). Whitman, Katz says, "like his society, did not yet link unorthodox sexuality with gender nonconformity" (p. 110).

Katz distinguishes between the Whitman narrator in the poetry and Whitman in practice, saying that

> for Whitman's narrator, love is various, suffocating, and empowering, lust free and lustful, sad . . . as well as joyful. His love objects are men, women, himself, nature, and God; his love is simultaneously genital-love, body-love, sensual-love, and spirit-love. His proclaimed love is often indifferent to the sex of its object, a passionate affection not yet officially divided between a same-sex or different-sex object. But, in practice, his love is often focused strongly on a particular sex: men. (Katz 2001: 104–5).

Katz sees Whitman's greatest contribution in freeing people to experience sexual acts according to their sexual orientation as lying in his language. Katz selects poems from the "Calamus" cluster and discusses both their role in creating a language for male/male love and also discusses strategies Whitman uses in his writing in order to create a new consciousness yet not alienate readers. Speaking of Whitman's strategic wordplay, he uses the term "escape clause" to name it. The escape-clause strategy works in various ways, one of which is not to specify the sex of one or both parties in the poem. The reader, then, supplies the sex and thereby the relationship of the poetry's subjects with the reader is created. Katz notes other strategies that Whitman uses to achieve ambiguity and thereby protect his poetry against charges of licentiousness, "permitting," he says, "his speech yet protecting his words" (Katz 2001: 114).

"Naming," Katz says, "became one of Whitman's most pressing tasks" (p. 116):

> The world of not-sodomy, like that of sodomy, stood separate from the world of asexual, sentimental love. The world of sodomy depicted in the appeals case reports, in a few sensationalistic newspapers, and in an occasional novel, made no reference to romantic, spiritual love – the dominant genteel ideal. And the world of pure, true love included no mention of sodomy or sodomites. Romantic lovers and sodomites inhabited separate, parallel universes, leaving a great unmapped space between. This was a site in which Walt Whitman began to explore the erotic intimacy of men and to invent a new language to express it. (Katz 2001: 90)

Katz emphasizes Whitman's role in language: "The struggles of Walt Whitman, John Addington Symonds, and other men for an affirmative language of lust between men were among the major projects of their lives – probably the major insight of this study" (p. 337). He historicizes gender: "We inhabit different social arrangements of human reproduction and gender, construct different ways of producing affection and pleasure. The social ordering of sex and affection can be made, unmade, and remade" (p. 338).

Nation/Fusion

The self and the material world often interplay and coexist, as in these lines following the long catalogue in section 15 of "Song of Myself" in which Whitman gives us a sweeping view of people going about their everyday, workaday life: "And these tend inward to me, and I tend outward to them / And such as it is to be of these more or less I am, / And of these one and all I weave the song of myself" (*LG*: 44). Identity of self and country worked in tandem, the need for identity of the latter clearly stated in his 1871 *Democratic Vistas:* "I know not a land except ours that has not, to some extent, however small, made its title clear. The Scotch have their born ballads, subtly expressing their past and present, and expressing character. The Irish have theirs. England, Italy, France, Spain, theirs. What has America?" (*PW*, 2: 413). This call for identity in 1871 is preceded by poems which proclaim identity as having already been achieved, such as in "Starting from Paumanok," begun in 1856 and making its first appearance in the 1860 edition. Here, Whitman fuses union and identity and time: "Victory, union, faith, identity, time" (*LG*: 16). The 1860 "So Long!" calls for a unified identity: "I announce that the identity of these States is a single identity only" (p. 504). "Paumanok" and "So Long!" serve to inscribe into consciousness a clear title – "union," "a single identity only."

The post-Civil-War *Democratic Vistas*, however, faces the fragmentation of interests that brought on the War and the intensified fragmentation resulting from the war. Edmund S. Morgan's essay "The Great Political Fiction," appearing in his 2004 *The Genuine Article: A Historian Looks at Early America,* furnishes a suggestive context for *Democratic Vistas*. "All government, of course," Morgan says, "rests on fictions, whether we call them that or self-evident truths; and political fictions, like other fictions, require a willing suspension of disbelief on the part of those who live under them" (p. 208). The essay continues with a rich discussion of the making of early America, focusing on the notion of "popular sovereignty." Morgan says: "At the same time doubts and uneasiness about the fiction were drowned in the emerging mystical sense of identity that we call nationalism" (p. 219). That "emerging mystical sense of identity that we call nationalism" catches the spirit of much of Whitman's poetry and prose.

In *Democratic Vistas*, Whitman also stresses the point that without a strong grounding – the Union, in this case – the individual cannot develop. In the 1865 "Drum-Taps" poem "Song of the Banner at Daybreak," the speaker – "Poet" – with his all-seeing vision, sees "the Identity formed out of thirty-eight . . . States" (*LG*: 288). Later in this poem, Banner speaks, responding to the Father's charge to his child that a war – civil war – would be too costly. Banner charges that nothing is too costly to save the Union, implying that without risking the ultimate, there would be no Union, no identity: "The Continent, devoting the whole identity without reserving an atom" (p. 289). In the 1872 "Thou Mother with Thy Equal Brood," the poem addresses the Mother, saying, "Thou varied chant of different States, yet one identity only" (p. 455).

Betsy Erkkila makes the point that after the Civil War, Whitman focused more on community than before: "Whereas in his early poems he imagined himself regenerating the republic by planting seeds of individual growth, in the preface poem to *As a Strong Bird*, "One Song, America, Before I Go" (later incorporated into "Thou Mother with Thy Equal Brood"), he imagines himself sowing seeds of 'endless Nationality' " (Erkkila 1989: 278).

Though many poems conflate the individual and the Union, others give the impression that the individual is a free agent, molding his or her self through the will, or through following the poet's admonitions. The poetry often *calls for* the ideal citizen, indicating that through the ideal citizen the country can proudly make its title clear. The 1855 "Song for Occupations" privileges the self over institutional inscriptions:

> We consider bibles and religions divine – I do not say they are not divine,
> I say they have all grown out of you, and may grow out of you still,
> It is not they who give the life, it is you who give the life,
> Leaves are not more shed from the trees, or trees from the earth, than they are shed out of you.
> [. . .]
> List close my scholars dear,
> Doctrines, politics and civilization exurge from you,
> Sculpture and monuments and any thing inscribed anywhere are tallied in you,
> The gist of histories and statistics as far back as the records reach is in you this hour, and myths and tales the same.
> If you were not breathing and walking here, where would they all be?
> The most renown'd poems would be ashes, orations and plays would be vacuums.
> All architecture is what you do to it when you look upon it,
> (Did you think it was in the white or gray stone? Or the lines of the arches and cornices?)
> [. . .]
> When the minted gold in the vault smiles like the night-watchman's daughter,
> When warrantee deeds loafe in chairs opposite and are my friendly companions,
> I intend to reach them my hand, and make as much of them as I do of men and women like you.
>
> (*LG*: 214–15, 218–19)

In the 1860 poem "Thoughts (Of these years I sing)," Whitman voices what he in turn emphasizes in the 1871 *Democratic Vistas*, his belief that the ideal United States democracy was no accomplished fact, that the United States and democracy were in process, that American citizens have yet to accomplish what Whitman saw as the third stage of his country's evolution, the stage of spiritual democracy:

> How many hold despairingly yet to the models departed, caste, myths, obedience, compulsion, and infidelity,
> How few see the arrived models, the athletes, the Western States, or see freedom as spirituality, or hold any faith in results,

> [...]
> How society waits unform'd, and is for a while between things ended and things begun.
> (*LG*: 492–3)

Whitman privileges interconnections, saying in "On the Beach at Night Alone" "A vast similitude interlocks all" (*LG*: 261). In "Years of the Modern," he asks: "Are all nations communing? is there going to be but one heart to the globe?" (p. 490). "Passage to India" cries out against fragmentation: "the earth to be spann'd, connected by networks," "the land to be welded together," "Who binds it to us," "All these separations and gaps shall be taken up and hook'd and link'd together," "Nature and Man shall be disjoin'd and diffused no more / The true son of god shall absolutely fuse them," "Europe to Asia, Africa join'd, and they to the New World" (pp. 411–21). Those in gender theory who argue that identity is not a matter of either/or – not a matter of essentialism or social construction, but, rather, a fusion of the two, the outer world and the inner interacting – find a soulmate in Whitman. The "vehement struggle so fierce for unity" exists for Whitman in terms of the individual and in terms of America:

> Singing the song of These, my ever-united lands – my body no more inevitably united, part to part, and made out of a thousand diverse contributions one identity, any more than my lands are inevitably united and made ONE IDENTITY; (*LG*: 176; capitals in original)

It was a bedrock belief in self that Whitman felt marked Lincoln's greatness and, consequently, after Bull Run, saved the Union:

> If there were nothing else of Abraham Lincoln for history to stamp him with, it is enough to send him with his wreath to the memory of all future time, that he endured that hour, that day, bitterer than gall – indeed a crucifixion day – that it did not conquer him – that he unflinchingly stemm'd it, and resolv'd to lift himself and the Union out of it. (*PW*, 1: 30)

The 1865 poem "Quicksand Years" speaks to this reliance on one's self:

> Quicksand years that whirl me I know not whither,
> Your schemes, politics, fail, lines give way, substances mock and elude me,
> Only the theme I sing, the great and strong-possess'd soul, eludes not,
> One's-self must never give way – that is the final substance – that out of all is sure,
> Out of politics, triumphs, battles, life, what at last finally remains?
> When shows break up what but One's-Self is sure? (*LG*: 448)

Whitman's 1865–6 poem "O Me! O Life!" asks the old question: what is it all about and is it worth it? The poem answers: "That you are here – that life exists and identity" (*LG*: 272). The tone of "Oh Me! O Life!" is contemplative, validating the sense of self, though not so steeped in the wisdom of lived life as "Quicksand Years": "When shows break up what but One's-Self is sure?" (p. 448).

Identity

But how does identity happen? In "Song of Myself," touch contributes: "Is this then a touch? quivering me to a new identity?" (*LG*: 57). And in "Crossing Brooklyn Ferry": "I too had receiv'd identity by my body" (p. 162). In "A Song for Occupations," the poem celebrates the fact of the body and identity: "The light and shade, the curious sense of body and identity . . . " (p. 214). In "Thoughts (Of seeds dropping into the ground)," rather than the body's participating in the creation of self, the natural and human-made world take over: "Of the temporary use of materials for identity's sake" (p. 494). In "A Song of Joys," identity and materials are again linked, and added to them is the role of other people, all of these tied in with the soul: "O the joy of my soul leaning pois'd on itself, receiving identity through materials and loving them, observing characters and absorbing them" (p. 181). Perhaps the most eloquent acknowledgment of the role that the outer world plays in the creation of the inner world of self comes in the first 24 lines of section 9 of "Crossing Brooklyn Ferry" where Whitman names elements of the world around him: rivers, waves, clouds, sunset, the tall masts of Mannahatta, the beautiful hills of Brooklyn. Then, in line 125 he addresses these objects, calling them "you dumb, beautiful ministers," going on to say: "We use you, and do not cast you aside – we plant you permanently within us" (p. 165). In "Thoughts (Of these years I sing)," identity is in process, this time identity not of self but of states – "Of what Indiana, Kentucky, Arkansas, and the rest, are to be" (p. 493).

The marriage is of body and soul: "Wisdom is of the soul, is not susceptible of proof, is its own proof," Whitman says in "Song of the Open Road" (*LG*: 152), using soul here to refer to character. Then, in "Adieu to a Soldier," Whitman addresses his soul as an argumentative companion: "Myself and this contentious soul of mine," (p. 325). In the 1888 poem "Life," the soul is in process: "Ever the undiscouraged, resolute, struggling soul of man," ending the poem: "Ever the soul dissatisfied, curious, unconvinced at last; / Struggling to-day the same – battling the same" (pp. 524–5). The soul in the "Song of the Open Road" quotation indicates stability, but in the "Life" passage just quoted, the emphasis is on process. In "Song of Myself," there is no ambiguity in the lines that claim equality of the body and soul. Body and soul, Whitman said repeatedly, cannot be separated. Memorable lines celebrate the two: "If any thing is sacred the human body is sacred" (p. 99), "And if the body does not do fully as much as the soul? / And if the body were not the soul, what is the soul?" (p. 94), "Sex contains all, bodies, souls" (p. 101), "Human bodies are words, myriads of words, / (In the best poems re-appears the body, man's or woman's, well-shaped, natural, gay, / Every part able, active, receptive, without shame or the need of shame)" (p. 219), "Be not afraid of my body" (p. 111). Body and soul merge in the following lines from "Song of Myself," creating the "one's self": "I have said that the soul is not more than the body, / And I have said that the body is not more than the soul, / And nothing, not God, is greater to one than one's self is" (p. 86).

But again, what defines one's self, or establishes identity? Lines in "To Think of Time" speak of identity in terms of the unknown: "And I have dream'd that the purpose and essence of the known life, the transient, / Is to form and decide identity of the unknown life, the permanent" (*LG*: 439). Whitman ends this poem in praise of immortality:

> I swear I think there is nothing but immortality!
> That the exquisite scheme is for it, and the nebulous float is for it, and the cohering is for it!
> And all preparation is for it – and identity is for it – and life and materials are altogether for it!
>
> (*LG*: 440)

The editors of the Comprehensive Reader's Edition of *Leaves of Grass*, Harold Blodgett and Sculley Bradley, say of the word "eidolon": "WW employs the word as a refrain to express the concept, central in *LG*, that behind all appearance is soul, the ultimate reality, eternal and changeless" (p. 5). Here is the next to last stanza of "Eidolons":

> Thy body permanent,
> The body lurking there within thy body,
> The only purport of the form thou art, the real I myself,
> An image, an eidolon.
>
> (*LG*: 8)

It's this soul, the "real I myself," that Whitman keeps coming back to. We find "the real I myself" appearing as the "real Me" in "As I Ebb'd" and echoed in "Ah Poverties, Wincings, and Sulky Retreats," when we read "real self" ("Ah think not you finally triumph, my real self has yet to come forth") (*LG*: 479). In the 1856 "A Song of the Rolling Earth," towards the end of the poem where Whitman is declaring the superiority of the "unspoken meanings of the earth," appears this line: "But the soul is also real, it too is positive and direct" (p. 224). As in the line "But that before all my arrogant poems the real Me stands yet untouch'd, untold, altogether unreach'd" in the 1860 "As I Ebb'd," we hear of "the real me" in section 4 of "Song of Myself": "People I meet, the effect upon me of my early life or the ward and city I live in, or the nation, / [. . .] These come to me days and nights and go from me again, / But they are not the Me myself. / Apart from the pulling and hauling stands what I am" (p. 32). Unlike in "As I Ebb'd," in this section from "Song of Myself" the "real me" stands almost indifferent, not doubting: "I have no mockings or arguments, I witness and wait" (p. 32).

Some poems speak of identity as a given, something within the individual that she or he has to find. In "To Think of Time," identity is spoken of in this way, and it is as if the speaker admonishes the reader: "It is not to diffuse you that you were born of your mother and father, it is to identify you" (*LG*: 438). Though Whitman acknowledges in his prose his indebtedness to his mother and to a lesser extent to his father for certain character traits and says that his national ancestry also contributes to his identity, the poetry itself often exhorts the reader herself or himself to develop personal qualities, to create identity. "And nothing endures but personal qualities," Whitman says in "Song of the Broad-Axe" (p. 188). Whitman lists some of the personal qualities he admires in his 1860 "To a Pupil": "Go, dear friend, if need be give up all else, and commence to-day to inure yourself to pluck, reality, self-esteem, definiteness, elevatedness, / Rest not till you rivet and publish yourself of your own Personality" (p. 391). Self-esteem does not so much suggest ego as it does self-respect. In his 1860 "So Long!" pride suggests self-respect: "I announce the justification of candor and the justification of pride" (p. 504). In "To a Historian," pride clearly means self-respect or self-esteem: "Pressing the pulse of the life that has seldom exhibited itself, (the great pride of man in himself)" (p. 4).

In the 1855 edition of *Leaves*, Whitman voices what becomes a theme reiterated throughout his life. He says in "Song of Myself," "Always a knit of identity, always distinction" (*LG*: 31). In the 1855 Preface, he says it this way:

> The soul has that measureless pride which consists in never acknowledging any lessons but its own. But it has sympathy as measureless as its pride and the one balances the other and neither can stretch too far while it stretches in company with the other. The inmost secrets of art sleep with the twain. The greatest poet has lain close betwixt both and they are vital in his style and thoughts. (*LG*: 716)

The "distinction" and the "measureless pride" represent Whitman's call for individuality. The "knit of identity" and "sympathy" voice Whitman's belief in community, and as 1855 jolted toward 1861, his ever-increasing concern was with Union. In his 1860 "Our Old Feuillage," we hear much the same sentiment: "Encircling all, vast-darting up and wide, the American Soul, with equal hemispheres, one Love, one Dilation or Pride" (p. 174). "Song of Prudence" articulates the two concepts this way: "Charity and personal force are the only investments worth any thing" (p. 374).

"Justice, health, self-esteem," he says in "By Blue Ontario's Shore," "clear the way with irresistible power" (*LG*: 351). Power appears in connection with self-esteem in "Song of the Open Road": "Allons! With power, liberty, the earth, the elements, / Health, defiance, gayety, self-esteem, curiosity; / Allons! From all formulas!" (p. 155). In the 1860 "Thoughts (Of public opinion)," the following line marks a turn in the poem from the enervation found in authorities (such as the "frivolous Judge," the "corrupt Congressman, Governor, Mayor") to the inner wisdom of the people, and personality and self-esteem are once more paired: "Of the rising forever taller and stronger and broader of the intuitions of men and women, and of Self-esteem and Personality" (p. 480). Personality and self-esteem will result in power, the power that is needed in order to influence change, explicitly stated in the 1860 "To a Pupil": "Is a reform needed? Is it through you? / The greater the reform needed, the greater the

Personality you need to accomplish it" (p. 390). "By Blue Ontario's Shore" declares: "He or she is greatest who contributes the greatest original practical example" (p. 351).

In "To a Historian," Whitman calls himself the "Chanter of Personality, outlining what is yet to be" (p. 4). In "Starting from Paumanok," he says: "I will effuse egotism and show it underlying all, and I will be the bard of personality" (p. 22). In "Song of the Broad-Axe," Whitman speaks of "The power of personality just or unjust" (p. 188). "To a Pupil" focuses on an ideal personality:

> You! Do you not see how it would serve to have eyes, blood, complexion, clean and sweet?
> Do you not see how it would serve to have such a body and soul that when you enter the crowd an atmosphere of desire and command enters with you, and every one is impress'd with your Personality?
> O the magnet! The flesh over and over!
> Go, dear friend, if need be give up all else, and comence to-day to inure yourself to pluck, reality, self-esteem, definiteness, elevatedness,
> Rest not till you rivet and publish yourself of your own Personality.
>
> (*LG*: 390–1)

Thirteen short poems make up a cluster Whitman titled "Old Age Echoes," first appearing as a posthumous cluster in the 1897 *Leaves*. Gay Wilson Allen says that the cluster "included some uncollected fragments of earlier years, but most of the poems were Whitman's last compositions" (Allen 1975: 159). "To Be at All" bears a close affinity to section 27 in "Song of Myself," the section that begins "To be in any form, what is that?" (*LG*: 57). The 1897 version does not theorize identity; it celebrates life: "To be at all – what is better than that?" (p. 580).

What caught my attention as I prepared to write this essay on Whitman and gender was not a focus in the poetry on maleness, femaleness, or a blending of the two when speaking of identity, but rather an attention paid to intrinsic values held regardless of gender. If indeed one of Whitman's theories was a theory of gender, then I suggest that he was reaching beyond the binaries of male/female, seeing identity as more accountable to a being's spirit than contemporary gender theorists posit. In Whitman's 1871 poem "Passage to India," Whitman calls for a reaching out. His own life was just that, a passage, and as a line towards the end of the poem says, even more so, a "Passage to more than India!" (p. 420)

References and Further Reading

Allen, Gay Wilson (1975). *The New Walt Whitman Handbook*. New York: New York University Press.

Aspiz, Harold (2004). *So Long! Walt Whitman's Poetry of Death*. Tuscaloosa: University of Alabama Press.

Belsey, Catherine (1980). *Critical Practice*. New York: Methuen.

Ceniza, Sherry (1998). *Walt Whitman and 19th-Century Women Reformers*. Tuscaloosa: University of Alabama Press.

Erkkila, Betsy (1989). *Whitman the Political Poet.* New York: Oxford University Press.

Fausto-Sterling, Anne (2000). *Sexing the Body: Gender Politics and the Construction of Sexuality.* New York: Basic Books.

Folsom, Ed (1994). *Walt Whitman's Native Representations.* Cambridge, UK: Cambridge University Press.

Folsom, Ed (2004). Review of Jonathan Ned Katz's *Love Stories. Walt Whitman Quarterly Review*, 21: 179–82.

Garber, Marjorie (1994). Spare Parts: The Surgical Construction of Gender. In Anne C. Herrmann and Abigail J. Stewart (eds.), *Theorizing Feminism: Parallel Trends in the Humanities and Social Sciences.* Boulder, CO: Westview Press, pp. 238–55.

Katz, Jonathan Ned (2001). *Love Stories: Sex Between Men Before Homosexuality.* Chicago: University of Chicago Press.

Martin, Robert K. (1994). Walt Whitman and the Politics of Identity. In Ed Folsom (ed.), *Walt Whitman: The Centennial Essays.* Iowa City: University of Iowa Press, pp. 172–81.

Morgan, Edmund S. (2004). The Great Political Fiction. In *The Genuine Article: A Historian Looks at Early America.* New York: Norton, pp. 207–24.

Ostriker, Alicia (1992). Loving Walt Whitman and the Problem of America. In Robert K. Martin (ed.), *The Continuing Presence of Walt Whitman.* Iowa City: University of Iowa Press, pp. 217–31.

Sedgwick, Eve Kosofsky (1990). *Epistemology of the Closet.* Berkeley: University of California Press.

Traubel, Horace (1953). *With Walt Whitman in Camden*, vol. 4, ed. Sculley Bradley. Philadelphia: University of Pennsylvania Press.

Traubel, Horace (1964). *With Walt Whitman in Camden*, vol. 5, ed. Gertrude Traubel. Carbondale: Southern Illinois University Press, 1964.

Wardrop, Daneen (2002). *Word, Birth, and Culture: The Poetry of Poe, Whitman, and Dickinson.* Westport, CT: Greenwood Press.

"The Woman's Rights Convention" (1989). In Patricia B. Holland and Ann D. Gordon (eds.), *Papers of Elizabeth Cady Stanton and Susan B. Anthony.* Wilmington, DE: Scholarly Resources, Microfilm, series 3, reel 8.

13
Religion and the Poet-Prophet

David Kuebrich

I too, following many, and follow'd by many, inaugurate a religion, I descend into the arena,
(It may be I am destin'd to utter the loudest cries there, the winner's pealing shouts,)
[. . .]
My comrade!
For you, to share with me, two greatnesses, and a third one rising inclusive and more resplendent.
The greatness of Love and Democracy – and the greatness of Religion.
("Starting from Paumanok," ll.102–3, 131–3, Whitman 2002: 18–20)

Whitman always insisted *Leaves of Grass* was a religious text – an effort to begin a post-Christian faith appropriate for America's emerging scientific and democratic culture; and some of his contemporaries fully agreed, even to the point of declaring him a major prophet and the *Leaves* a new Gospel. But with the demise of these early disciples, few readers, especially critics, have approached the *Leaves* as an attempt to forge a modern religion. Although Whitman has obviously failed in his prophetic intentions, yet it is still important, I would argue, to read him as a would-be religious founder. Only by doing so can we fully comprehend his poetic mission as well as the poetry itself. Accordingly, in the following essay, in an effort to explain how Whitman came to conceive of his bold religious project, I discuss various European intellectual developments that contributed to a marginal and diffuse antebellum American cultural formation that defined the highest form of poetry as religious prophecy. I then provide an introduction to Whitman's mysticism, outline how he conceived of God and the divine–human relationship, and present a brief analysis of his understanding of history and call for a religious democracy. In doing so, I hope to demonstrate the value of reading the *Leaves* as a religious text.

Poetry and Prophecy

American Romanticism's conflation of literary authorship and religious prophecy could not occur so long as the Bible enjoyed a privileged status in the Western world as a unique and final revelation. To call for a new prophet superior to Christ and a new bible more perfect than the Christian Testaments, as Emerson does in the Divinity School Address (1838), or to speak of one's poetic project as the "Great Construction of the New Bible," as Whitman does in 1857 (Whitman 1899: 57), required a major shift in Western religious thought. Christ had to be reduced to just one of a number of prophets who had arisen in the religious history of humankind, perhaps the greatest but not unique, and the Bible had to be redefined as only one of a number of religious scriptures. In the early nineteenth century, such bold new ideas were fiercely uncontested and did not gain widespread assent, but they did become intellectually respectable and take hold among a cultured minority in both Europe and America.

One major factor contributing to this new perspective was the unorthodox religious thought known as deism that emerged in seventeenth-century England. The founder of deism, Edward Herbert, proposed that Christianity be replaced by or become subordinate to a body of rational religious beliefs that were either innate or discernible by reason. Herbert constructed a theology consisting of several affirmations about God plus an ethical code stressing service to others. According to Herbert and his successors, this simple set of beliefs was the true catholic (universal) faith constituting the core of all religions. Departures from it were corruptions introduced by a superstitious and venal priesthood. An early student of world religions, Herbert argued that his investigations of other religions proved the universality of the deistic creed (Herrick 1997: 24–39).

In addition to opposing Christianity's claim to a unique and final revelation, the deists also made two criticisms of Christianity that have special relevance for our present discussion. As believers in *rational* religion, they rejected the orthodox concept of *revelation* that conceived of God as speaking through human scribes who passively recorded his message. This understanding of divine inspiration, along with the Christian belief in miracles, was considered not only irrational but also an insult to divine intelligence. The distant god of deism, perfect in his omniscience, had designed the universe to operate according to unerring laws and thus had no need to subsequently intervene in the world of nature and human affairs (Herrick 1997: 30–2, 36–8).

After achieving a degree of currency among late seventeenth- and early eighteenth-century British intellectuals, deism subsequently spread to Germany where it contributed to the scientific spirit of early nineteenth-century biblical scholarship which also problematized the orthodox view of revelation (Herrick 1997: 39–43). Using refined philological analysis and approaching the Bible as they would any other text, scholars detected differing patterns of diction, style, and viewpoint within many books of the Bible. Such discoveries suggested that canonical texts previously held to be the creation of one inspired author who composed under divine guidance were actually the products of multiple writers. In addition new historical research disclosed that the texts were not timeless documents but that they employed the literary forms and reflected the social conditions and religious conceptions of the periods in which they were written (Krentz 1975: 16–27, Rogerson 1985: 15–78). This new scholarship caused many intellectuals to forever reject the traditional notion of revelation. Even if they continued to believe the Bible was somehow inspired, they nevertheless conceived of it as a work of the human imagination. Not surprisingly, this new understanding of revelation would soon lead some unconventional religious voices to suggest that similarly "inspired" texts might be produced anew.

Enlightenment theology and the new biblical studies also contributed to a Christology that humanized the person of Jesus. To the deists, Christ was neither the son of God nor a worker of miracles but a moral exemplar and teacher of an exalted ethical code who might be compared to the Buddha, Confucius, or Socrates. The most important and controversial of the new German interpretations of Christ, a landmark in biblical studies, was David Friedrich Strauss's *Life of Jesus Critically Examined* (1835) which concluded that "Jesus can have been nothing more than a person, highly distinguished indeed, but subject to the limitations inevitable to all that is mortal" (Baird 1992: 254). Strauss argued that Jesus was simply a spiritually gifted rabbi who collected a group of loyal disciples. Following his death, under the influence of strong messianic hopes, these followers invested their leader with mythic qualities and constructed a biography in which he fulfilled the Old Testament prophecies. This and other nineteenth-century studies led some to distinguish between the "religion *of* Jesus" and the "religion *about* Jesus" (Baird 1992: 397) that implied Jesus was by nature no more divine than other men but that he possessed a heightened sense of God's presence and power.

Another significant development in religious studies that challenged the uniqueness of the Bible was the emergence of a fresh understanding of ancient mythology. The dominant attitude of the eighteenth century, shared by orthodox Christians and deists, was to depreciate ancient myths as erroneous explanations of natural phenomena, as falsified history, or as pagan idolatry. Two influential eighteenth-century British scholars, however, laid a foundation for the ensuing Romantic endorsement of myth by opposing the reductive myth criticism of their day (Richardson 1978: 25–8). In *Enquiry into the Life and Writings of Homer* (1735) and *Letters concerning Mythology* (1748), Thomas Blackwell argued that Homer's use of mythology added beauty and power to his poetry and that myth itself embodied allegorical wisdom and served important social functions. Blackwell's positive assessment of myth was extended by Robert Lowth's *Lectures on the Sacred Poetry of the Hebrews* (1753). Observing that the ancient Greeks considered poetry a gift from the gods and the poet an ambassador from heaven, Lowth argued for a similar approach to the poetry of the Old Testament. In building his case, he noted that Hebrew writers used the same word for "poet" and "prophet" and that poetry provided the best medium for the expression of religious truth. Despite his orthodoxy, Lowth thus prepared the way for subsequent writers to suggest that poetry might once again give rise to religious myth.

Also contributing to the revaluation of myth was the publication of previously inaccessible mythic materials from Northern Europe and Southern Asia. During the last three decades of the eighteenth century, translations of Norse mythology, the sacred writings of the Zoroastrian religion, and Persian and Hindu scriptures, including the *Bhagavad Gita*, became available to European readers for the first time. Among the many accomplishments of the period's most important transmitter of Indic literature and culture, Sir William Jones, was a Lowth-like study of Persian religious poetry, *Poeseos Asiaticae commentatorium libri sex* (1774) and an influential essay in comparative mythology titled "On the Gods of Greece, Italy, and India" (lecture 1785, publication 1799) in which the orthodox Jones at times puzzled over the similarities of some of these stories to biblical narratives. Further interest in Northern mythology was brought about by James Macpherson's publication of *Fingal* (1762) and *Temera* (1763); and even after Macpherson's deceptions were exposed, his Ossianic poetry continued to spur interest in "the idea that a modern poet can transmit, refashion, and even perhaps create myth" (Richardson 1978: 30).

Deism, the higher biblical scholarship, and the recuperation of myth – all of these influenced the development of late eighteenth- and early nineteenth-century German literature, giving rise to innovative views on religion and the poetic imagination that, in turn, as transmitted by Coleridge and more especially by Carlyle, had a profound effect on American literature. Carlyle energetically set about translating, summarizing, and explicating German philosophy and literature, calling attention to those writers and ideas that could best be used, on the one hand, to supplant British rational Christianity and common-sense philosophy and, on the other, to legitimate the notion that the highest task of the writer was to sanctify the contemporary world by creating a new religious vision.

In "Life and Writings of Werner" (1828), Carlyle noted that among the Germans it was a "common theory" that "every Creed, every Form of worship, is a *form* merely . . . in which the immortal and unchanging *spirit* of Religion is, with more or less completeness . . . made manifest and influential among the doings of men" (Carlyle 1904: 143). As an example of this, he commended Jean Paul Friedrich Richter's frank discussion of religion, citing an illustrative quotation in which Richter put Christianity on a level with other religions, speaking of it as simply the imperfect religious perceptions of a particular ethnic group: "[A]re all your Mosques, Episcopal Churches, Pagodas, Chapels of Ease, Tabernacles, and Pantheons, anything else but the Ethnic Forecourt of the Invisible Temple and its Holy of Holies?" (1904: 22).

Carlyle also lauded the German aesthetic that defined poetic beauty as "united to all love of virtue, to all true belief in God." Given this understanding of poetry, Carlyle observed that the "character of a Poet does, accordingly stand higher with the Germans than with most nations" (Carlyle 1904: 56); and he approvingly cited Fichte's belief that every culture gives expression to a "Divine Idea" of which the "visible universe is indeed but its symbol and sensible manifestation." For most humans, this "Divine Idea... lies hidden," but in each age writers arise as its "appointed interpreters." They constitute a "perpetual priesthood" who dispense "God's everlasting wisdom" in the "particular form" required by "their own particular times" (1904: 58). Carlyle marshaled important philosophical support for this identification of poetry and prophecy by his transmutation of Kant's notion of pure Reason from a rational faculty into the voice of God speaking from within the human soul. For Carlyle, the "grand characteristic" of Kant's philosophy was his distinction between the Understanding (*Verstand*, the faculty of ordinary reasoning) and the Reason (*Vernunft*) whose domain was "that holier region, where Poetry, and Virtue and Divinity abide" (Carlyle 1904: 81, 83). In *Sartor Resartus,* the "Pure Reason" is presented as the source of religious revelation or the true scripture "whereof all other Bibles are but Leaves." The book's protagonist, Professor Diogenes Teufelsdroeckh, who gives expression to many of the German themes, calls for an inspired poet, the "Pontiff of the World... who, Prometheus-like, can shape new Symbols and bring new Fire from Heaven" (Carlyle 1974: 155, 179).

To focus upon these particular innovations in religious thought is not to suggest that Whitman was immune to other intellectual currents coming out of Europe, such as phrenology, or that he was unresponsive to distinctive aspects of American culture such as the call for a national literature or Protestant emphases on millennialism and perfectionism. Rather my point is that these new European ideas provide an indispensable context for understanding how it became feasible for Whitman to conceive of his poetic project as an effort to found a new religion. I will now, while also calling attention to the role of Hicksite Quakerism, attempt to outline how the above-mentioned themes became a part of Whitman's intellectual and religious development. That this is the case is truly remarkable given that early nineteenth-century America was, of course, a cis-Atlantic outpost of the European community, preoccupied with practical concerns and committed to the creation of a Protestant republic. Furthermore, Whitman was reared by working-class parents with little or no formal education, and he himself dropped out of a weak public school system at age 11. Whitman's parents, however, were open to unconventional ideas and probably encouraged religious and political discussion. In addition, Whitman, always an avid reader, continued to educate himself through his employment as a school teacher and newspaperman. If Melville could assert that "a whaleship was my Yale college and my Harvard," Whitman could speak similarly, and more literally, of the educative influence of the various newspaper offices in which he worked.

Whitman's family unwittingly provided a religious culture conducive to the idea of ongoing revelation and the creation of a modern faith. His paternal grandfather and parents were admirers of the liberal Quaker leader Elias Hicks who, to the consternation of more traditional Friends, insisted the soul's inner light was a higher spiritual authority than the Bible and the source of all religious inspiration (Reynolds 1995: 37–9). In his old age, Whitman still recalled that as a 10 year old he had heard the "very mystical and radical" Hicks, whose significance was that he pointed "to the fountain of all naked theology, all religion, all worship... namely in *yourself*" (*PW*, 2:

638, 627, emphasis in original). Hicks's emphasis upon the human soul as the source of all religion clearly provided Whitman with an early foundation for later constructing himself as a religious prophet.

From his early home life Whitman also imbibed an appreciation of deistic thought. Although never a large movement, American deism could boast of such notables as Paine, Franklin, Washington, Jefferson, and Madison among its members. Whitman's father, an acquaintance of Paine, embraced deistic ideas; and as an adult, Whitman fondly recalled his father's association with the militant deist (Reynolds 1995: 36–7). As a young man, Whitman's interest in Paine was reinforced by the octogenarian Colonel John Fellows with whom he often took dinner. Fellows, a minor Democratic official and editor of a deist monthly, the *Theophilanthropist*, had known Paine; and he reprinted his deistic tract, *The Age of Reason* (Rubin 1973: 103–4). Whitman was undoubtedly familiar with Paine's radical manifesto, which retained a considerable audience throughout the nineteenth century.

Deism seems to have provided Whitman with many of his adult religious beliefs: for instance, an eschewal of miracles and conviction that God governed the world through universal laws; a view of the creation as a reflection of divine intelligence and benevolence; a distrust of priests and organized religion; a rejection of miracles; a denial of Christ's divinity. In the early 1850s, as Whitman mulled over the possibility of forging a new faith, he may have found support in two of Paine's opening claims in *The Age of Reason*: his prediction that "a Revolution in the System of [American] Government, would be followed by a revolution in the system of religion" and his assertion that a new religion must be promulgated in order to preserve an understanding "of morality, of humanity, and of the theology that is true" (Paine 1995: 666–7).

As a child Whitman also probably received some introduction to ancient mythology from his family, for one of the few books owned by Whitman's father was Volney's *Ruins* (Stovall 1974: 50) which, in arguing that organized religion was responsible for the downfall of ancient civilizations, discussed Osiris, Bacchus, and Buddha, although not in a positive manner. The Ossianic poems were also part of Whitman's youthful reading, and his notes and clippings from periodicals in the late 1840s and early 1850s indicate that as he conceived of and produced *Leaves of Grass*, he had an on-going interest in Ossian (Stovall 1974: 177–8). Perhaps Whitman read about Indian religion in various New York libraries he is believed to have frequented in the early 1850s. At this time, he could have accessed over 500 relevant books and articles, including the *Bhagavad Gita,* the translations of Sir William Jones, and the accessible short translations of Hindu scriptures by Rammohun Roy, the famous Indian convert to Unitarianism (Rajasekharaiah 1970: 126–32). It is likely that much of Whitman's early knowledge of Hindu texts was gained at least in part from magazines and reviews. For instance, he clipped a review of Jones's *Institutes of Menu* from the May, 1845 *Whig Review*, and he took notes on an article titled "Indian Epic Poetry" in the October, 1848 *Westminster Review* that discussed the *Ramayana* and the *Mahabharata* (Stovall 1974: 165). During the decade prior to publishing the

Leaves, Whitman also became familiar with the religion of ancient Egypt. He refers to a lecture by George R. Gliddon, an expert on Egypt, in a November 7, 1846, article in the Brooklyn *Daily Eagle*, and he cut and saved a January 1849 article from the *Westminster Review* that summarized the German historian von Raumer's views on Indian and Egyptian theology (Rubin 1973: 375n.). From 1853 to 1855, Whitman frequently visited the Egyptian museum of Dr Henry Abbott, and Stovall concludes that he read widely about Egypt in books, magazines, and newspapers during the 1840s and 1850s (Stovall 1974: 161–4).

Whitman acquired a rudimentary familiarity with German thought directly through Joseph Gostwick's *German Literature* (1849) from which he took notes (Stovall 1974: 195); and he also read Henry Hedge's *Prose Writers of Germany* "perhaps as early as 1847 . . . and almost certainly by 1852" (Reynolds 1995: 253). More important, however, was the influence of Carlyle and the impact of Carlyle's ideas as Americanized by Emerson. In his later years, recalling Carlyle's crucial role, Whitman stated that he "certainly introduced the German style, writers, sentimentalism, transcendentalism etc. etc. etc. from 1826 to 1840 – through the great reviews and magazines – and through his own words and example" (Whitman 1902: 123). This implies that Whitman read Carlyle's seminal essays or read about them in such periodicals as the *Westminster Review* and the *North American Review*, both of which regularly carried articles by or about Carlyle. In addition, Whitman would have learned of Carlyle's call for an inspired poet from *Sartor Resartus* and also of his admiration for religious founders in *Heroes and Hero Worship*, both of which he reviewed for the Brooklyn *Daily Eagle* in 1846 (Stovall 1974: 106). That Carlyle influenced Whitman's sense of vocation is strongly suggested by a note in which Whitman refers to Carlyle's call for "a new Poet for the world in our own time, of a new Instructor and preacher of Truth to all men" (*NUPM*, 4: 1511).

In the 1830s and 1840s Emerson was so indebted to the Scottish historian and critic that it is impossible to determine where Carlyle's influence on Whitman shades off and Emerson's begins. Emerson oversaw the American publication of both *Sartor Resartus* and a collection of Carlyle's essays, and he enthusiastically embraced Carlyle's misappropriation of Kant, making the distinction between Reason (understood as the inner divinity, soul, or poetic imagination) and the Understanding the foundation of his thought. Whitman heard Emerson lecture on "Nature and the Powers of the Poet" in 1842, and as he was composing the 1855 *Leaves* he read a revised version of the lecture, titled "The Poet," in *Essays, Second Series*, which asserts that all of "sacred history attests that the birth of a poet is the principal event in chronology" (Emerson 1983: 7) – a statement that defines Christ and other seminal religious figures as poets. Essentially a prescription for an American poet-prophet, the essay concludes with Emerson's anticipation of the advent of this "timely man, the new religion, the reconciler, whom all things await" (Emerson 1983: 21).

In sum, although not well versed in European theology, biblical criticism, non-Christian religions, or German literature, Whitman nevertheless read widely and perceptively, and by the time he began writing the *Leaves* he no longer believed that

Christ was divine or the Judeo-Christian religion unique. By virtue of having shed these beliefs, he was free to embrace the idea that a poet might be a religious prophet and the corollary conviction that America and the world were in need of a new religion. As a result Whitman could develop an intellectual framework for placing his poetic undertaking within the context of world religions. Consider the following passage from the 1855 "Song of Myself":

> Taking myself the exact dimensions of Jehovah and laying them away,
> Lithographing Kronos and Zeus his son, and Hercules his grandson,
> Buying drafts of Osiris and Isis and Belus and Brahma and Adonai,
> In my portfolio placing Manito loose, and Allah on a leaf, and the crucifix engraved,
> With Odin, and the hideous-faced Mexitli, and all idols and images,
> Honestly taking them for what they are worth, and not a cent more,
> Admitting they were alive and did the work of their day,
> Admitting they bore mites as for unfledged birds who have now to rise and fly and sing for themselves,
> Accepting the rough deific sketches to fill out better in myself. . . . bestowing them freely on each man and woman I see,
> Discovering as much or more in a framer framing a house.
>
> (ll.1028–37, Whitman 2002: 65–6)

By simply listing Jehovah and the crucifix alongside Greek, Egyptian, Hindu, Algonquin, Muslim, Norse, and Aztec deities Whitman indicates that he considers Christianity as just another of humankind's many religions. Without attempting to judge their respective merits, he asserts they all served an important function within their respective cultures: "they were alive and did the work of their day." However, there is a progressive evolution in religion as in all other aspects of life, so these faiths, while acknowledged with appreciation, are also dismissed as no longer appropriate. They nourished the human spirit in its young or infantile phase much as mother birds give "mites" to their still unfeathered chicks. Now a new era has arisen, requiring a new faith that will provide for the development of mature religious personalities (the young birds must "arise and fly and sing for themselves"). Whitman, of course, is presenting himself as the founder or first prophet of this needed new religion that will, he suggests, draw upon the imperfect spiritual insights of the earlier myths, accepting their "rough deific sketches." However, Whitman will not project new gods or saviors but instead emphasize the divinity present in the human spirit that is the source of all earlier religions.

A note, probably written by Whitman in the 1860s, for an intended lecture on religion, further clarifies the above passage. Whitman speaks of the "sublime creeds of different eras" as "each fitting its time and land" but as "giving place to the more needed one that must succeed it." All of these religions, however, are "subordinate to the eternal soul of the woman, the man . . . the decider of all." He goes on to add: "I know well enough the life is in my own soul, not in the traditions . . . I know, too, that I am the master and overseer of all religions – and you shall be – Not their slave"

(*NUPM*, 6: 2070). These are, of course, quite revolutionary religious sentiments – sentiments that reflect Whitman's awareness of recent innovations in Western religious culture that relativized Christianity and provided an opening – in fact, even a moral imperative – for aspiring poets to assume the mantle of prophecy.

Reading Whitman's Mysticism

The above transformation in religious thought provided the requisite intellectual conditions for Whitman to conceive of himself as a prophet but what prompted him to do so was his conviction that he possessed an extraordinary degree of spiritual awareness and the imaginative power to integrate his religious experience with the dominant forms of modern culture. Attempting to explicate Whitman's religious consciousness is the most problematic aspect of interpreting the *Leaves* because it requires the critic to elucidate the mysticism that forms the marrow of Whitman's verse. In the following discussion, I will try to provide a helpful entrance into Whitman's mysticism by drawing upon several phenomenological studies of key elements of religious experience.[1]

I will begin with the assertion that all "felt" religious experience (as opposed to the lifeless re-enactment of religious forms or the mere giving of intellectual assent to articles of a religious creed) has a mystical dimension. This leads to the problem of defining the essence of "lived" religion and how it differs from secular experience. To answer this query, it is helpful to turn to the minimal definition provided by Mircea Eliade, a distinguished scholar of comparative religions, whose writings emphasize that sacred or religious experience constitutes itself in the mind of the religious subject as having a special "power" or "reality":

> the *sacred* is equivalent to a *power*, and, in the last analysis, to *reality*. The sacred is saturated with *being*. Sacred power means reality and at the same time enduringness and efficacity. The polarity sacred–profane is often expressed as an opposition between *real* and *unreal* or pseudoreal. [. . .] Thus it is easy to understand that religious man deeply desires *to be*, to participate in *reality*, to be saturated with power. (Eliade 1959: 12–13, emphases in original)

Eliade explains that the religious speaker, especially in archaic societies (his principal field of investigation), may not use the philosophical terms "real" and "unreal" but that religious utterance distinguishes between degrees of reality.

Building upon Eliade's definition, the mystic may be defined as the religious subject who effectively pursues this desire to "participate in *reality*." Thus one of the most gifted students of mysticism, Evelyn Underhill, in searching for a suitably broad understanding of mysticism that "finds room at once for the visionaries and philosophers, for Walt Whitman and the saints," proposes this succinct definition: "*Mysticism is the art of union with Reality. The mystic is a person who has attained that union in greater or less degree; or who aims at and believes in such attainment*" (Underhill 1915: 3, emphasis in original). This distinguishing between levels of reality is the cornerstone of Whitman's religious vision. Again and again he indicates that his religious experience discloses the existence of a more real spiritual dimension present in his soul and the outer world – a dimension of reality that enhances this life and provides an anticipatory experience of the next.

To understand Whitman's religious epistemology, it is crucial to recognize that for him the "soul" provides the human body with a deep layer of consciousness that allows the knowing subject to intuit the spiritual essence of the objects of the natural world. Accordingly, we can say that Whitman believed humans could know the world in two ways: in a secular manner that involves the senses and intellect or in a mystical manner that involves the senses and intellect *plus the soul*. Since this latter form of knowing engages deeper levels of the psyche, Whitman speaks of the soul as providing a supersensory and more real form of knowledge:

> O the joy of my soul leaning pois'd on itself, receiving identity through materials and loving them . . .
> My soul vibrated back to me from them, from sight, hearing, touch, reason . . .
> The real life of my senses and flesh transcending my senses and flesh,
> My body done with materials, my sight done with my material eyes,
> Proved to me today beyond cavil that it is not my material eyes which finally see.
> ("A Song of Joys," ll. 98–102, Whitman 2002: 153)

This more powerful way of encountering the natural world discloses the invisible spiritual dimension of material phenomena – a dimension that Whitman speaks of in "Chanting the Square Deific" as "Santa Spirita" or the "Essence of forms, life of the real identities, permanent, positive, (namely the unseen,)" (l. 42, Whitman 2002: 373).

These more than sensory experiences develop the soul, to which Whitman ascribes a greater reality than to his human body, sometimes referring to it as the "real body": "How can the real body ever die and be buried?" ("Starting from Paumanok," l. 180, Whitman 2002: 22), "My real body doubtless left to me for other spheres" ("Song of Joys, l. 142, p. 154). After its human death, the soul will pass on to a new level of existence in which it will enjoy a still more real life, that is, a fuller participation in the divine consciousness: "The soul, its destinies, the real real" ("Thou Mother with Thy Equal Brood," l. 123, p. 386). Indeed, as will be discussed below, it is Whitman's ability to experience moments of special reality in this world that convinces him "that death is not the ending, as was thought, but rather the real beginning" (*PW*, 2: 420).

Before proceeding, however, it may be helpful to relate this mystical perception of the "real" to the reader's own experience. To understand this initial level of mystical experience, Underhill explains, does not require us to have the "great powers and sublime experiences of the mystical saints and philosophers" (Underhill 1915: 11–12). Rather we all have certain experiences, "certain happy accidents," that induct us into a "richer and more vital world." In these moments, which she describes as "a pure feeling-state," our sensory experience merges into a "wholeness of communion which feels and knows all at once." As examples of this type of "knowing," Underhill mentions special moments of loving another person or the "moment at the concert" when one's whole being merges with the spirit of the music (Underhill 1915: 18, 31). Other examples of these "onsets of involuntary contemplation" (p. 31) might be suggested: the feeling of being at one with the universe when one gazes upon the starry heavens (as Whitman does at the end of "Song of Myself") or the sense of encompassing calm that steals over one when listening to rustling ocean waves during a quiet night (as Whitman does in "Out of the Cradle").

To approach Whitman's mystical consciousness in this way is to suggest that it is not, at a fundamental level, a highly rarified order of experience, inaccessible to ordinary readers, but that it arises from experiences common to everyone. Like Whitman, we all have experiences that seem to connect us to a different order of reality. The decisive issue is how these are to be interpreted. Are they simply transitory emotional states? Or are they revelations of a supersensory level of being? A secular personality will answer "yes" to the first question; a mystic like Whitman gives assent to the second. However, whichever answer readers may give, they can draw upon their own moments of especially powerful feeling to gain an intuitive entrance into the inner world of Whitman's mysticism.

Whitman's experience of specific natural or historical facts as religious symbols is a special form of mystical knowing in which the religious subject perceives an external fact not only as sacred but also as revelatory of an attribute of divine transcendence (or of a particular spiritual truth or meaning related to this reality). In describing the dynamics of this experience, the theologian Paul Tillich explains that religious symbols "unlock" or disclose both a dimension of the soul and also of God's nature (Tillich 1958: 42). I will clarify this revelatory function of religious symbolism by discussing several examples of Whitman's symbolism.

One of Whitman's most detailed accounts of experiencing an aspect of nature as symbol occurs in a small, late poem, "To the Sun-Set Breeze" (Whitman 2002: 458–9), in which the aged and ailing poet finds that the refreshing evening breeze speaks to his soul, affecting him in an especially powerful manner: "(Thou hast, O Nature! Elements! Utterance to my heart beyond the rest – and this is of them)." The breeze, "cool-freshing, gently vitalizing," fortifies the poet's failing spirits, convincing him that it is a wind-sent breath or kiss from the soul of a deceased lover or from God: "Thou [breeze] blown from lips so loved, now gone – haply from endless store, God-sent." Thus for Whitman, the breeze, referred to as a "messenger-magical," is infinitely more than a natural fact that cools his body; as symbol, it also affects deeper levels of consciousness, soothing his inner self (or "soul") and reinforcing his belief in a loving God who cares for him in the time of his approaching death. Drawing upon Tillich's analysis, we may say that the breeze discloses or "unlocks" a dimension of Whitman's own being – awakening within him a calming sense of being cared for in his time of need – and also reveals an aspect of God, namely, the divine attributes of peace and love that Whitman's soul will enjoy after death when it advances to a fuller participation in the divine reality.

Moving from this example, I will quickly comment on the revelatory meaning of two other symbols that contribute to important themes in the *Leaves*. When Whitman speaks of the grass as "the flag of my disposition, out of hopeful green-stuff woven" or as the "beautiful uncut hair of graves" ("Song of Myself," ll. 101, 110, Whitman 2002: 30), he is suggesting that the green-colored, ubiquitous grass, growing even over graves, was created by God to address the hopeful longings latent within the human breast and to encourage the human desire to believe that death is but a transition to further life. The grass, perceived as religious symbol, reinforces Whitman's hopefulness and reveals the existence of a benevolent God who has designed the universe to speak to human needs. Or again, in "One Hour to Madness and Joy," Whitman likens his sexual excitement and desire for passional abandonment to the powerful, liberating sense he experiences in raging storms:

> One hour to madness and joy! O furious! O confine me not!
> (What is this that frees me so in storms?
> What do my shouts amid lightning and raging winds mean?)
> (ll. 1–3, Whitman 2002: 91)

In lines such as these, Whitman sanctifies human sexuality by interpreting sexual passion as giving expression to the soul's desire for freedom and power; and in such moments the soul participates in the freedom and power of God. The storm and sexual passion "mean" because God has created them as a way of revealing aspects of himself to the human soul.

I will close this discussion by suggesting how readers can use their experience of human love to approach the mystical meaning of one of the *Leaves*' most important poems, "Scented Herbage of My Breast." In this second *Calamus* poem, Whitman asserts that the special power of manly love provides him with the strongest proof of the existence of a spiritual reality that his soul will know more fully in the afterlife. Accordingly, he conflates the experience of comradeship with death: "For how calm, how solemn it grows to ascend to the atmosphere of lovers, / Death or life I am then indifferent, my soul declines to prefer" (ll. 13–14, Whitman 2002: 98). These lines show Whitman interpreting the soothing sense of well-being induced by manly love as an anticipatory experience of the afterlife. In an effort to reinterpret the word "death," to invest it with positive connotations, he uses it to name the more real spiritual realm, thus making "death" nearly a synonym of "heaven" or "God":

> For now it is convey'd to me that you [Death] are the purports essential,
> That you hide in these shifting forms of life, for reasons, and that they are mainly for you,
> That you beyond them come forth to remain, the real reality,
> That beyond the mask of materials you patiently wait, no matter how long,
> That you will one day perhaps take control of all,

> That you will perhaps dissipate this entire show of appearance,
> That maybe you are what it is all for...
>
> (ll. 31–7, Whitman 2002: 98–9)

Whitman conceives of his emotionally satisfying experiences of manly love as prophetic of the life his soul will know after death when it will encounter the "real reality," that is, the transcendent spiritual world. This spiritual reality is also immanent within "these shifting [transient] forms of life, for reasons," that is, to address and develop the human soul, preparing it for a future existence "beyond the mask of materials" (or illusory "show of appearance").

By drawing upon their personal experiences of love, readers can achieve an intuitive understanding of the mystical dimensions of Whitman's "manly" love. Regardless of whether Whitman's love arises out of homosexual experience, as most critics believe, or from homosocial friendships, as Whitman claimed in his old age, there is an important religious theme in "Scented Herbage" and throughout "Calamus": namely that the love celebrated in these poems is the highest form of spiritual love and the experiential foundation of Whitman's faith.

Religious Cosmology

"With science, the old theology of the East, long in its dotage, begins evidently to die and disappear" (1872 Preface, Whitman 2002: 650).

Whitman rejected Christianity as dated and ineffective, in part, because it reflected a prescientific understanding of the world, and he continually promoted his new religion as being consistent with modern science. In "Song of Myself" he sings out "Hurrah for positive science! Long live exact demonstration" (l. 485, Whitman 2002: 45). Yet in affirming science, Whitman always makes clear that his most important truths lie beyond the reach of empiricism. For instance, in "Song of the Universal" he calls attention to science: "Lo! Keen-eyed towering science"; but he quickly adds, "Yet again, lo! The soul, above all science" (ll. 10, 13, p. 190). Like many of the deists, Whitman believed that the discoveries of modern science were not an obstacle to faith but the basis for a more lofty understanding of God's wisdom and power. Whitman differs from the deists, however, in that his scientific understanding incorporates early nineteenth-century evolutionary theory and his epistemology insists that empirical fact is subordinate to mystical truth. Accordingly, the *Leaves* depicts a universe, carefully designed by an intelligent and loving God, that has four overlapping characteristics:

Sacrality: Consistent with a scientific perspective, Whitman rejects the traditional belief in miracles, but he declares that everything in the universe, properly perceived, is a miracle. Even a mouse is "miracle enough to stagger sextillions of infidels"; "Seeing, hearing, feeling, are miracles, and each part and tag of me is a miracle" ("Song of Myself," ll. 523, 669, Whitman 2002: 46).

Order: Every object of the universe is in its proper place: "(The moth and the fish-eggs are in their place, / The bright suns I see and the dark suns I cannot see are in their place)" ("Song of Myself," ll. 353–4, Whitman 2002: 40). Even though Whitman has the audacity to proclaim himself a religious founder, he asserts that he is not conceited but is merely assuming his proper position as a poet-prophet in a cultural context that requires a new religion: "[I] am not stuck up, and am in my place" ("Song of Myself," l. 351, p. 40).

Process: The world is not static but progressive. In one of his many acknowledgments of evolutionary theory, Whitman proclaims that even the "blossoms we wear in our hats [are] the growth of thousands of years" ("Song of Myself," l. 973, Whitman 2002: 63). Or again, he presents himself as having evolved upward from the beginning of the creation, the "huge first Nothing," to his present human existence: "All forces have been steadily employed to complete and delight me, / Now I stand on this spot with my robust soul" (ll. 1168–9, p. 71). And he affirms that his soul will continue to evolve into higher stages in the afterlife, for like the expanding heavens revealed by modern science, "All goes onward and outward, nothing collapses" ("Song of Myself," l. 129, p. 31). Looking out upon the "crowded heaven" at night, he asks his spirit if it will be "*satisfied*" when they are the "*enfolders of those orbs*," and his soul replies: "*No, we but level that lift to pass and continue beyond*" ("Song of Myself," ll. 1220–2, p. 73, emphasis in original). Whitman's eventual destination is the transcendent God beyond the creation: "My rendezvous is appointed, it is certain, / The Lord will be there and wait till I come on perfect terms" ("Song of Myself," ll. 1199–1200, p. 72).

Benevolence: To Whitman's imagination, all of the facts of the universe are evidence of a world designed to nurture the human body and soul. Evolution is not subject to chance but is guided by a loving deity. Thus Whitman speaks of his own evolution as a process in which he was "hugged close" and assisted by "friendly" arms. For his sake, the "stars kept aside in their own rings" and the "nebula cohered to an orb" ("Song of Myself," ll. 1156–64, Whitman 2002: 70–1). Convinced that the world is informed by a spirit of love ("a kelson of the creation is love") and that humans are the beneficiaries of this love, he promises, in turn, to lovingly celebrate the universe: "Prodigal! you [the earth] have given me love!. . . . therefore I to you give love!" ("Song of Myself," ll. 95, 446, pp. 30–43). Near the end of "Song of Myself," Whitman passionately sums up his sense of God's benevolent design: "Do you see O my brothers and sisters? / It is not chaos or death – it is form, union, plan – it is eternal life – it is Happiness" (ll. 1317–18, p. 76).

Whitman's theology does not smoothly fit into any of the conventional models – deism, pantheism, and theism – for defining the divinity and its relationship to the creation. Despite his many debts to the deists, he does not, like them, conceive of God as a distant creator best known through human reason. Because of his emphasis on the divine presence in nature and humans, he is sometimes placed among the pantheists who believe God to be infused throughout the natural world and coterminous with it.

Whitman's religious cosmology is best understood as a form of theism because the very structure of his worldview presupposes a God that is both immanent and transcendent. For instance, the belief that natural facts are religious symbols assumes the existence of a transcendent deity who creates the natural world as a symbolic text that addresses the human soul. Or again, Whitman's belief in the soul's immortality and ongoing development presupposes a spiritual reality above the creation that the soul will know more fully after death. Whitman's theology, not surprisingly, continues the theism of Christianity but with important differences. He is perhaps best defined as a new type of theist – a process theist who strongly emphasizes divine immanence. Influenced by evolutionary science and a belief in historical progress, Whitman imagines divine immanence, including the human soul, to be engaged in a process of progressive development. Also influenced by the deistic respect for natural law, he does not conceive of God as performing miracles or as responding to human prayer. Nor does he believe in a punishing God but instead affirms, like the recently emergent Unitarians and Universalists, a "salvation universal" ("Song of the Universal," l. 61, Whitman 2002: 191). Whitman's religious understanding of America's history and destiny shares much with contemporary Christian public theology, but he does not, in contrast to many Protestant leaders, assume the stance of an American Jeremiah who places an errant citizenry under threat of divine punishment.

Religious Democracy

Whitman's political vision is a post-Christian version of the nineteenth-century American civil religion that defined the United States as a chosen people charged with bringing history to its millennial fulfillment. Like his Christian compatriots, Whitman also conceived of the United States as a religious nation; and like them, he conceived of it as leading the historical process to its grand culmination. For instance, in the 1872 Preface, he asserts that the world is approaching "some long-prepared, most tremendous denouement" in which the United States is "unquestionably designated for the leading parts," for in America "history and humanity seem to seek to culminate" (*PW*, 2: 460).

For many antebellum American Christians, the idea of an imminent millennium was not an abstract belief based upon passages in Revelation but an interpretation of American progress: an explanation of the nation's geographical expansion, swelling population, advancing technology, and remarkable growth in political rights, church membership, and literacy. Such evidences of divine blessing were interpreted as a sign that God had chosen America for a noble mission. Reflecting upon his nation's remarkable achievements and unprecedented potential, Whitman also interprets these facts as investing the nation with a special religious purpose. The United States provided an appropriate arena for conducting a "grand experiment of development, whose end," perhaps requiring "several generations," would "be the forming of a full-grown man or woman" (*PW*, 2: 380). The United States was poised to produce such perfect individuals because it had already passed through two great stages of development: a political phase that established the "political foundation rights," presumably civil rights and the franchise, for "immense masses of people"; and a second phase consisting of "material prosperity, wealth, produce, labor-saving machines." What America needed now was a cultural revolution, that is, a movement that would bring about a psychological and spiritual emancipation of the American people. This would result in a third level of development, a fulfillment of the earlier two, that Whitman spoke of as a "sublime and serious Religious Democracy" (*PW*, 2: 409–10).

In the opening movement of the *Leaves*, Whitman establishes the above millennial understanding of human history as a process that will produce a race of fully developed men and women. After briefly sketching a portrait of this new personality or "Modern Man" in the book's first poem, he then, in the next, presents all previous history as an ongoing struggle in which humankind, impelled by its inner divinity, has striven to realize its physical, intellectual, and spiritual potential. Thus he responds to the epic muse, who chastises him for not writing about warfare, that he sings of a much more important conflict, a war "*longer and greater*... *than any*":

> ... *the field the world,*
> *For life and death, for the Body and for the eternal Soul,*
> *Lo, I too am come, chanting the chant of battles,*
> *I above all promote brave soldiers.*
> ("As I Ponder'd in Silence," ll. 13–18, Whitman 2002: 4, emphasis in original)

In succeeding introductory poems, Whitman describes history as an incessant battle for the "good old cause" ("To Thee Old Cause," l. 1, Whitman 2002: 6) defined as the "great idea, the progress and freedom of the race" ("To a Certain Cantatrice," l. 3, p. 11). And he declares that his poetry is written to promote this cause: "These chants for thee [the "Old Cause"], the eternal march of thee" ("To Thee Old Cause," l. 7, p. 6).

Of course, Whitman differed from his Christian counterparts on how this millennial era was to be achieved. They felt the proper means were more effective recruitment through revivals, home missions, Sunday schools, Bible and tract societies, and the elevation of society to godly standards through such reform movements as abolitionism and temperance. Whitman, however, like Emerson, believed that the American churches, despite their surface bustle, were devoid of inner life. In his notes on religion, he refers to the "outward & technical religious beliefs of the sects of this age" as "a mere crust crumbling everywhere under our feet" and declares that the "souls of the people" in search of "something deeper and higher – have irrevocably gone from those churches" (Whitman 1928: 42). The people were "awake" and deserved more than was being offered by the Christian ministry (*NUPM*, 6: 2076); they needed a "real athletic and fit religion" (*NUPM*, 6: 2061), that is, a challenging religion that would require its members to actively pursue their spiritual development.

A key element of this new religion would be a redefinition of the divine–human relationship. As we have seen, Whitman wanted to make the individual believer the "master and overseer" of his or her religion and not its "slave." Another of his notes on religion, titled "A Spinal Thought," outlines a revolutionary shift in religious thought: "The relative positions change. – Man comes forward, inherent superb, – the soul, the judge the common average man advances, – ascends to place. God disappears. – The whole idea of God, as hitherto, for reasons, presented in the religions of the world, for thousands of past years . . . disappears. –" (*NUPM*: 2097). In the *Leaves* Whitman gives expression to this theological reorientation by de-emphasizing divine transcendence and repeatedly bringing to the fore the divinity inherent in the human being. For instance, he tells his readers that "nothing, not God, is greater to one than one's self is" and that he sees God in "the faces of men and women . . . and in my own face in the glass" ("Song of Myself," ll. 1271, 1285, Whitman 2002: 75). Whitman waxes ecstatic over being "this incredible God I am!" ("Song at Sunset," l. 29, p. 415), and in "Laws for Creations," he asks future artists, teachers, and leaders: "What do you suppose I would intimate to you in a hundred ways, but that man or woman is as good as God?" (l. 8, p. 325). The purpose of his poetry, he asserts, is not to create "ornaments" but to "chisel with free stroke the heads and limbs of plenteous supreme Gods, that the States may realize them walking and talking" ("Myself and Mine," ll. 8–9, p. 199). On the few occasions when Whitman does depict the transcendent God, there is no suggestion of the soul's inferiority: it meets the "great Camerado, the lover true" on "perfect terms" ("Song of Myself," ll. 1199–1200, p. 72); or it is a meeting in which "the Elder Brother found, / The Younger melts in fondness in his arms" ("Passage to India," ll. 222–3, p. 352).

For Whitman, the political significance of this new emphasis upon human divinity was that it provided a solid spiritual basis for nurturing citizens with a strong sense of self. The myths and theologies of Christianity and other earlier religions were inappropriate for a democracy, Whitman believed, because they depicted God as an absolute authority and encouraged human submissiveness. A religion such as Christianity was appropriate for the subjects of a feudal society but not the citizens of a democracy, especially an emergent democracy like the United States, which required plucky and defiant citizens who would insist upon their rights. Accordingly, Whitman consistently presents a message that empowers the individual, reduces authority, and encourages revolt. For instance, he rejects the Christian view of pride as sinful and announces that he will press "the pulse of life that has seldom exhibited itself, (the great pride of man in himself,)" ("To a Historian," l. 5, Whitman 2002: 5). He advocates for "men and women whose tempers have never been master'd" ("By Blue Ontario's Shore," l. 289, p. 297); and he distinguishes himself from previous spiritual teachers who "would subordinate you" by asserting that "I only am he who places over you no master, owner, better, God beyond what waits intrinsically in yourself" ("Birds of Passage," "To You," ll. 16–17, p. 196). Whitman acknowledges the "latent right of insurrection" ("Still Though the One I Sing," l. 3, p. 13), his words "beat the gong of revolt" ("Song of Myself," l. 496, p. 45), and he proclaims himself "the sworn poet of every dauntless rebel the world over" ("To a Foil'd European Revolutionaire," l. 11, p. 311).

Given America's political freedom and material prosperity, Whitman felt that now the people could, if they acknowledged their inner divinity and insisted upon their rights, create a society that allowed for humans to completely realize God's plan for their existence. In this future America, the culmination of history, Whitman envisions a humanity that is, for the first time, fully free. Thus he projects pictures of an ideal democracy in which "the men and women think lightly of the laws" and the "children are taught to be laws to themselves" ("Song of the Broad-Axe," ll. 119, 125, Whitman 2002: 159–60). Whitman can depreciate the importance of legal systems and all forms of external authority because he anticipates a future citizenry whose souls are fully integrated with the divine will: "Land in the realms of God to be a realm unto thyself, / Under the rule of God to be a rule unto thyself" ("Thou Mother with Thy Equal Brood," ll. 99–100, p. 385).

Conclusion

As a would-be prophet of a next and, in his mind, perhaps final era, Whitman attempts to provide his readers with a vital sense of God's presence within themselves and the world as well as a belief that all of evolution and history contributes to the soul's development. *Leaves of Grass* does not possess a unified logical or narrative structure, but from 1855 onward it is informed by a coherent religious purpose and worldview. To assert this is not to argue that Whitman's poetry is free of gaps and contradictions, but it is to emphasize the importance of reading the *Leaves* as a unified text that aims to lay the basis for a new religion. If this is not done, then we inevitably overlook much of Whitman's spiritual and artistic achievement.

Note

1 My exposition of Whitman's mysticism, religious cosmology, and millennialism in this and the next two sections of my essay receive different treatment and more extensive documentation in Kuebrich (1989). For other discussions of Whitman's spirituality, see Miller (1957), Chari (1964), and Hutchinson (1986).

References and Further Reading

Baird, William (1992). *History of New Testament Research*, vol. 1. Minneapolis: Fortress Press.

Carlyle, Thomas (1904). *Critical and Miscellaneous Essays*, vol. 1. New York: Charles Scribner's Sons.

Carlyle, Thomas (1974). *Sartor-Resartus*. New York: AMS Press.

Chari, V. K. (1964). *Whitman in the Light of Vedantic Mysticism*. Lincoln: University of Nebraska Press.

Eliade, Mircea (1959). *The Sacred and the Profane*, trans. Willard R. Trask. New York: Harcourt Brace.

Emerson, Ralph Waldo (1983). *Essays, Second Series*. Cambridge, MA: Harvard University Press.

Herrick, James A. (1997). *The Radical Rhetoric of the English Deists*. Columbia: University of South Carolina Press.

Hutchinson, George B. (1986). *The Ecstatic Whitman: Literary Shamanism and the Crisis of the Union.* Columbus: Ohio State University Press.

Krentz, Edgar (1975). *The Historical-Critical Method.* Philadelphia: Fortress Press.

Kuebrich, David (1989). *Minor Prophecy: Walt Whitman's New American Religion.* Bloomington: Indiana University Press.

Miller, James E., Jr. (1957). *A Critical Guide to Leaves of Grass.* Chicago: University of Chicago Press.

Paine, Thomas (1995). *Thomas Paine: Collected Works,* ed. Eric Foner. New York: Library of America.

Rajasekharaiah, T. R. (1970). *The Roots of Whitman's Grass.* Rutherford, NJ: Fairleigh Dickinson University Press.

Reynolds, David S. (1995). *Walt Whitman's America: A Cultural Biography.* New York: Alfred A. Knopf.

Richardson, Robert D., Jr. (1978). *Myth and Literature in the American Renaissance.* Bloomington: Indiana University Press.

Rogerson, John W. (1985). *Old Testament Criticism in the Nineteenth Century: England and Germany.* Philadelphia: Fortress.

Rubin, Joseph Jay (1973). *The Historic Whitman.* University Park: Pennsylvania State University Press.

Stovall, Floyd (1974). *The Foreground of Leaves of Grass.* Charlottesville: University of Virginia Press.

Tillich, Paul (1958). *The Dynamics of Faith.* New York: Harper & Row.

Traubel, Horace L. (1908). *With Walt Whitman in Camden.* New York: Appleton.

Underhill, Evelyn (1915). *Practical Mysticism.* New York: E. P. Dutton.

Whitman, Walt (1902). *The Complete Writings of Walt Whitman,* vol. 10, ed. Richard Maurice Bucke, Thomas B. Harned, Horace Traubel, Oscar Lovell Triggs, and Walter P. Chrysler. New York: Putnam's Sons.

Whitman, Walt (1992). *Leaves of Grass.* New York: Collectors Reprints.

Whitman, Walt (1899). *Notes and Fragments,* ed. Richard Maurice Bucke. London, ONT: A. Talbot and Company.

Whitman, Walt (1928). *Walt Whitman's Workshop,* ed. Clifton Joseph Furness. Cambridge, MA: Harvard University Press.

Whitman, Walt (2002). *Leaves of Grass and Other Writings,* ed. Michael Moon. New York: Norton.

14
Science and Pseudoscience

Harold Aspiz

I

In his Preface to the 1855 *Leaves of Grass*, Whitman credits "exact science" as his "encouragement and support." "Scientists may not be poets," he says, "but they are the lawgivers of poets, and their construction underlies the structure of every perfect poem" (*LG*: 718). Calling his poetry a pioneer effort to incorporate science into literature, together with "the vast fields and expansions laid open to us in astronomy, geology, and the like," he claims that *Leaves of Grass* "is the first attempt at an expression in poetry . . . to give the wonder and the imagination a new and true field – the field opened by scientific discovery" (Burroughs [1928] 1967: 56–7). He boasted in 1874 that "a distinguished scientist, in Washington, told me not long since, that, in its tally & spirit, Whitman's was the only poetry he could mention that is thoroughly consistent with modern science & philosophy and that does not infringe upon them in a single line" (Whitman, *NUPM*, 4: 1515–16). After reading section 45 of "Song of Myself," in which the persona views the ever-expanding, ceaseless motion of the heavens, the English mathematician William Kingdon Clifford said in 1877 that Whitman should be admitted into the company of scientists because his delineation of the infinity of space produces a "poetic thrill and rhapsody in contemplating the world as a whole, its chemistry and vitality, its bounty, its beauty, its power and applicability of its laws and principles to human aesthetics and art products" (Burroughs 1924: 224). And in his 1893 biography of the poet, John Addington Symonds credited Whitman with linking creation to "the great thought of the universe" that corresponds "exactly to the Scientific Principia of the modern age; to the evolutionary hypothesis . . . to the correlation of forces and the conservation of energy, which forbid the doubt of any atom wasted, any part mismade or unaccounted for eventually" (quoted in Miller 1989: 85). But the best contemporary assessment is that of John Burroughs, the naturalist who capped a 30-year friendship by maintaining that Whitman had the kind of mind that could *absorb* the principles of science into his poetry from his limited reading, not merely as coloration but as fundamental insights. He summarized Whitman's scientific principles as follows:

> That all things are alike divine, that this earth is a star in the heavens, that the celestial laws are here underfoot, that size is only relative, that good and bad are only relative, that forces are convertible and interchangeable, that matter is indestructible, that death is the law of life, that man is of animal origin, and that the sum of forces is constant, that the universe is a complexus of powers inconceivably subtle and vital, [and] that motion is the law of all things. (Burroughs 1896: 249)

Whitman's observations of nature, Burroughs explained, were animated by his feeling of kinship with all living creatures and all inanimate creation.

Not all critics have praised Whitman's approach to science. Norman Foerster's *Nature in American Literature* (1923), which influenced a generation of Whitman's critics, belittled Whitman's pretense to science. Newton Arvin's 1938 biography devoted some 80 pages to science but concluded that Whitman used science largely for color and allusion and failed to achieve the sort of materialist attitude which is essential to objective science. Frederick William Conner's *Cosmic Optimism* credits Whitman with keen insights into some scientific currents of his time, but finds his scientific knowledge largely superficial and derived from the reading of popular sources (Conner 1949: 95–6). Joseph Beaver's painstakingly detailed study, *Walt Whitman: Poet of Science*, concludes that despite careful observations of the heavens, some familiarity with earth sciences, and good descriptions of flora and fauna, "Whitman was not a scientist. No one has ever claimed that for him" (Beaver [1951] 1974: ix). More recently, Robert J. Scholnick has deemed Whitman a serious student of science, particularly because, like Herbert Spencer and other contemporaries, he believed in the unity of all forces, that all phenomena develop subject to a unifying, overriding "law" and that there can be no loss of essential substance and energy (Scholnick 1986: 394).

Although Whitman was excited by scientific concepts, he possessed only a layman's knowledge of scientific phenomena and principles. He was, after all, an autodidact, whose knowledge of science was gleaned from direct observation and from unsystematic reading of popular materials. Although he applauds the achievements of science, he is not consistently objective, often subordinating scientific objectivity to his own intuitional-poetic insights. His observations are rarely systematic or consistent, and his conclusions are not necessarily derived from carefully coordinated data and hard evidence. A brilliant and enthusiastic observer of the world around him, he never applied the scientific method nor the patient research and data gathering that were fundamental to the researches of Karl Humboldt or Charles Darwin. Science served him as a resource of poetic ideas, insights, coloration, and language – and he sometimes invoked science to buttress ideas that were not fundamentally scientific. He esteemed the precision and reliability of science (particularly of astronomy) as poetic analogues or support for idealistic or extrascientific assumptions. For him language and intuition generally took precedence over scientific investigation – an assumption fraught with ambiguity. For, as Thomas Huxley observed, the language arts can never adequately represent scientific fact. Scientific knowledge, he said, "is dependent upon the extent to which the mind of the student is brought into immediate contact with facts" and "acquir[es] through his senses concrete images of those properties of things, which are, and always will be, but approximately expressed in language" (Huxley 1867: 138).

Whitman gleaned magazines, newspapers, and popular books, from which he improvised scrapbooks of clippings which could be used for his poems, but they reveal little interest in science. Of the more than 500 surviving clippings, mostly dating from the 1850s, Dr Maurice Bucke counted some 120 from periodicals, including such prestigious journals as *Edinburgh Review*, *Blackwoods*, and *Westminster Review*, but only four of these deal with geography and geology, and two with botany. Additionally, the *American Phrenological Journal*, the principal organ of the pseudosciences, which Whitman knew well, occasionally published reputable articles on science. Floyd Stovall's careful study of Whitman's sources concludes that

> These notes on the sciences were obviously written by a person who . . . had picked up his information from newspapers, magazines, dictionaries, and perhaps a few popular textbooks. . . . [T]hese notes prove only that he wished to include the sciences in his comprehensive plan for *Leaves of Grass*. He knew something about geology and biology, including some evolutionary theory that he could easily have found in [Robert Chambers'] *Vestiges of Creation*, or perhaps in reviews, but there is no evidence in the poems of the 1855 edition that anything more than the romance of science had interested him seriously. (Stovall 1974: 144–53)

Whitman's journalism sometimes dealt with scientific matters; and the relatively few scientific and pseudoscientific books he reviewed during his editorship of *The Brooklyn Daily Eagle* (1847–8) and *The Brooklyn Daily Times* (1857–9) included William Paley's *Natural Theology*, Elias Loomis's *Elements of Natural Philosophy*, Karl Humboldt's *A Description of the Universe*, N. F. Moore's *Account of Mineralogy*, George Combe's *Physiology*, and several pseudoscientific texts (White 1969).

The word *science* acquired its present connotations beginning only in the 1830s. Whereas modern science, taking its tone from Einstein and Heisenberg, is largely attuned to what might be called an uncertainty principle, many mid-nineteenth-century intellectuals viewed science in terms of what might be called a certainty principle – a conviction that the truths of the universe will ultimately be found to conform to an overarching "law" that governs all animate and inanimate phenomena. This is the approach generally taken by *Leaves of Grass*. In an era when scientific boundaries were fluid and permeable, the distinctions between science and pseudoscience or between fact-based and faith-based assumptions were not always clear, even to many scientists. Two conflicting standards flourished side by side: one following Francis Bacon and John Locke required precise observation, careful collation of data, generalizations drawn only from the examined evidence, and the rejection of a priori assumptions. The other approach, inspired by *Naturphilosophie* and the Romantic tradition, attracted many intellectuals who viewed scientific advance and discovery largely as confirmations of a governing set of a priori principles and assumptions (often religious in nature).

Karl Humboldt, whose *Kosmos* appeared in English in 1845, became something of an American hero because of his researches in America. Humboldt exemplifies "pure" science based on careful measurements and precise analysis of data, on generalizations derived solely from those data, and on scientific conclusions derived from the intrinsic properties of the matter being studied. He assumed that matter is amoral and does not conform to, or prove, any divine or evolutionary principle; and he rejected the dualistic idea (dear to Romantic theorists like Coleridge, Carlyle, Louis Agassiz, and Whitman) that the discoveries of science are valuable primarily because they confirm the divinity of creation or some other governing principle. He rejected, for its lack of empirical evidence, the idea that the universe and everything in it are somehow evolving (Walls 1995: 88–100). By way of contrast, Whitman often conformed his observations to a priori assumptions, using them to illustrate what he perceived to be a quasi-divine principle. He assumed that the universe and everything in it are somehow "unfolding" and developing in response to a – possibly divine – evolutionary "urge." In section 44 of "Song of Myself" he speculates playfully that he may be the culmination, so far, of that evolutionary-creative urge. "Passage to India" clearly articulates the idea of a universe governed by the steady unfolding of a cosmic purpose. Although Whitman tended to be a philosophical idealist, he nevertheless always felt firmly planted in the tangible world, relishing all material things, and excited and inspired by the tangible feel, look, heft of everything around him.

Like Emerson, who tended to relate scientific facts to a central governing principle or to the "thought of God," Whitman related virtually all phenomena to a vaguely religious universal "law" or impulse predicated on the unity of mind and matter and of spirit and matter. (The words *law* or *laws* appear – most often with this connotation – some six dozen times in the poems.) Whitman generally assumed that this (often divine) universal "law" took precedence over – or incorporated – material fact. Emerson's holistic principles imply that matter embodies, or "bodies forth," spirit and that spirit is primary, so that tangible nature is best conceived as a spiritual veil or garment; therefore the function of science in studying matter is to identify its organizing law – the spirit and moral truth that it embodies. Whereas Emerson sees physical nature in a state of flux – always "becoming" – he sees the organizing (spiritual) "law" as "a process, eternal and immutable" and views nature as essentially "polar," perennially moving upward to God (Walls 1995: 60–1). Similarly, Agassiz' *Study of Natural History* (1847) maintains that the scientists' "rationale for classification" should be directed to an understanding of the order which God has established in the universe, to enable us to view phenomena as "objects of the Creator," and so exhibit "the design of God in nature." Because we have immortal souls, he maintains, we are privileged to see facts as moral principles (Bode 1967: 122–6). This ideology, part of the popular intellectual currency of the day, although not precisely identical with Whitman's thinking, is closely related to the poet's assumption of an essential unity and sacredness in all phases of existence, whether they be physical (material) or spiritual (ideological).

Whitman's delight in natural phenomena (an attitude which Humboldt had credited to the true scientist) was one side of his philosophic dualism which sought a higher nonmaterial "cause" or "purpose" in creation. Before 1860 Whitman had commented that as "an American literat" he views science as a miracle: "did you think the demonstrable less divine than the mystical?" he demanded (Killingsworth 1989: 151–2). But in section 23 of "Song of Myself," after expressing a rather ironic "Hurrah for positive science" and "exact demonstration" and paying mock tribute to a chemist, an anthropologist, a geologist, a physician, and a mathematician, he relegates their sciences to a secondary status in his thinking:

> Gentlemen, to you the first honors always!
> Your facts are useful, yet they are not my dwelling,
> I but enter by them to an area of my dwelling.
> (*LG*: 51; see also p. 718)

That "dwelling" represents the essential selfhood of Whitman's persona or his spiritual center, which he will not subordinate to any material consideration. In a note probably dating from the same period, Whitman declares that he considers himself (as the ideal Poet) to be a "translator" of truths; which may manifest themselves in any material or spiritual form without being mutually contradictory (*NUPM*, 1: 60–1). Manuscript notes of the late 1860s or early 1870s indicate that he believed in a law of "universality" – "the conception of a divine purpose in the cosmical world & its history – the realization that knowledge and sciences however important are branches, radiations only – each one relative" to a governing truth or principle (Benton 2003: 74–5). For him science facilitates the discovery of this "governing truth" or essential mystery to which every aspect of nature conforms. Unlike the "pure" scientists for whom investigation must always be objective, the Whitman persona situates his selfhood, his imagination, and his spirit at the pivotal center of the universe, assuming that the truest insights into the unknown (and possibly unknowable) will be revealed to him in some fashion. Another undated note (possibly of secondary origin) explains this premise:

> Body and mind are one, an inexplicable paradox, yet no truth truer. The human soul stands in the centre, and all the universes minister to it, and serve it and revolve around it. They are one side of the whole, and it is the other side. It escapes utterly from all limits, *dogmatic standards and measurements,* and adjusts itself to the ideas of God, of

> space, and of eternity, and sails them at will as oceans, and fills them as beds of oceans. (*NUPM*, 6: 2011–12, italics added)

Those mocked "dogmatic standards and measurements," we may recall, were at the heart of Humboldt's scientific method; which resulted in some of the most precise measurements the world had known, and which rejected the idea of a mysterious grand plan.

As a dualist, Whitman accepts as truth what he observes or studies as well as what he feels or intuits: he interprets the material and the extramaterial worlds as complementary aspects of reality. Attempting to balance objective knowledge with what he *felt* must be true – an ambiguity that he struggled to resolve – he asked rhetorically in an 1857 note: "compared to the vast oceanic vol[ume] of spiritual facts, what is our material knowledge before the immensity of that which is to come, the spiritual, the unknown, the immensity of being and facts around us [of] which we cannot possibly take any cognizance[?]" (*NUPM*, 6: 2051–2). In "Song of the Open Road" (1856) the persona maintains that each natural or manufactured object he encounters along the mythic road of life is palpable and real but it also embodies the ruling spirit or the divine principle that shapes his world. The material road, the developments along it, and the very air he breathes, he asserts, are "latent with unseen existences" whose emanations convince him that spirit or divinity is latent in every material phenomenon:

> The earth is rude, silent, incomprehensible at first, Nature is rude and incomprehensible at first,
> Be not discouraged, keep on, there are divine things, well envelop'd,
> I swear to you; there are divine things more beautiful than words can tell.
>
> (*LG*: 154)

The Preface to the 1872 edition of *Leaves of Grass* praises science for illuminating literature "like a new sunrise," but stresses that its greatest contribution may be its inspiring of what Whitman calls a new theology (*LG*: 741–2). "Thou Mother With Thy Equal Brood" (1872) predicts a "true New World, the world of orbic science, morals, literatures to come" (*LG*: 458). But "Passage to India," which praises the exploits of inventors, scientists, and explorers as precursors to feats of spiritual discovery, clearly shows Whitman ceding the primary role of human development not to science but to the mystic impulse: "After the noble inventors, after the scientists, the chemist, the geologist, ethnologist" have laid the groundwork for the future, he proclaims, "The true son of God shall come singing his songs" – not only the "facts of modern science, / But myths and fables of eld . . . The far-darting beams of the spirit" (*LG*: 412, 415). "Song of the Universal" (1874), a hymn to the "mystic evolution" that will bring about a future-perfect America by resolving the differences between the material and the spiritual, pictures "towering science" issuing "absolute fiats" and acting as a potential obstacle to genuine faith, so that the poet reiterates: "Yet again, lo! the soul, above all science" (*LG*: 226–7).

However, the Preface to the 1876 *Leaves of Grass* (much like the 1855 Preface) appears to endorse science wholeheartedly for its positive influence on literature and, particularly, as a key component of his own poems:

> Without being a Scientist, I have thoroughly adopted the conclusions of the great Savans and Experimentalists of our time, and of the last hundred years, and they have interiorly tinged the chyle of all my verse, for purposes beyond. Following the Modern Spirit, the real Poems of the Present . . . must vocalize the vastness and splendor and reality with which Scientism has invested Man and the Universe (all that is called Creation,) and must henceforth launch Humanity into new orbits, consonant with the vastness, splendor, and reality, (unknown to the old poems,) like new systems of orbs, balanced upon themselves, revolving in limitless space, more subtle than the stars. Poetry . . . will be revivified by this tremendous innovation, the Kosmic Spirit, which must henceforth, in my opinion, be the background and underlying impetus, more or less visible, of all first-class Songs. (*LG*: 752–3)

(Whether that "kosmic spirit" is necessarily scientific remains conjectural.) For although the 1876 mystical poem "Eidòlons" (an *eidolon* is an emanation of the world spirit) includes the sciences as one aspect of "the old urge" that propels the soul to higher levels, Whitman is so attracted to the idea of a divine principle governing the world (and to the idea of universal immortality) that the poem, in effect, rejects the reality of matter and of the material world in favor of a spiritual world. In a show of philosophical Idealism, the poem maintains that only the spirit underlying the illusion of matter is pure (*LG*: 6–7).

Whitman's *Specimen Days* (1882) defines the essential unity of the material world and the world of the spirit by calling them "necessary sides and unfoldings . . . in the endless process of Creative Thought" – the eternal law governing both "the visible universe" and "the invisible side of the same" (*PW*, 1: 258–9). Insisting that science and secular knowledge are insufficient in themselves to reveal the ultimate truths of life and death, he takes a middle course. Only "tyros," he says, can be certain either way. He declares that he values science because it supports his "own feeling, conviction" of the possibility of immortality – a stand rejected by Burroughs and many other scientists. And (because he refuses to endorse any orthodoxy) he appreciates the essential skepticism of the scientists, their "not-too-damned-sure-spirit," as "the glory of our age." As a nonscientist he readily admits his inability to take a definitive stand on the nature of science:

> Beyond that, when it comes to launching into mathematics – tying philosophy into the multiplication table – I am satisfied: if they can explain let them explain: if they can explain they can do more than I can do . . . What the world calls logic is beyond me: I only go about my business taking on impressions. (Aspiz 2003: 31–2)

Ultimately, he appears to favor subjective truth, declaring that "what establishes itself in the age, the heart, is finally the only logic – can boast the only real verification" (Traubel 1982: 147).

II

Humboldt had specified that the poet must be a careful observer who avoids artificial descriptions of nature and artificial diction – one who pictures a world based on his own observation, uninhibited by "the circuit of his own mind" (Walls 1995: 91). Whitman understood that the poet should not "daguerreotype" an exact likeness of material creation but must leave much to his "image-making faculty." Therefore he chose to curtail "scientific and similar allusions" in the poems because he believed that "the theories of Geology, History, Language, &c., &c., are always changing," and that he must "put in only what *must* be appropriate centuries hence" (*PW*, 2: 419, Aspiz 1980: 155). Nevertheless, Joseph Beaver counted over one hundred allusions to science in Whitman's prose and several hundred references in the poems, where science is often cited as a touchstone of truth. The sciences with which Whitman demonstrated some knowledge included medicine, anatomy, astronomy, geology, geography, archaeology, physics, chemistry, ornithology, botany, and biology. The poems contain many scientific references and terms, among them words like acoustics, aeronautics, dynamics, meteorology, centripetal and centrifugal motion, osteology, and many medical terms (Beaver 1974: 132–3). Furthermore, his poetic catalogues, which compress large numbers of related concepts and images into such brilliant passages as sections 15 and 33 in "Song of Myself" and in "Salut au Monde!," may also owe something to Linnaeus's principle of scientific categorizing.

Whitman was fascinated by the human body, by its structure, and by medical science and practice. Devoted to the sick and hospitalized, he judged prevailing medicinal practice to be "full of nonsense" (Aspiz 1980: 38). His journalism deplored prevailing medical practices – including bleeding, mercury solutions, cupping, leeching, and scarifying. He denounced as humbugs those doctors and druggists who prescribed drugs but knew "few real *specifics*" of disease and understood "very little of physiology and anatomy." He excoriated the "drug theory" as a "poisonous viperous notion," according to which physicians, without understanding the nature of an ailment, "doctor a part of a man" (Brasher 1979: 179–87). His description of amputations without anesthesia in section 36 of "Song of Myself" evokes the horrors of primitive surgery. Advocating a sort of holistic medicine, he trusted to the *vis*, the body's vital forces, to restore health. However, he recognized the poetic possibilities of medical terminology, noting in *An American Primer* that "Medicine has hundreds of useful and characteristic words – new means of cure – new schools of doctors – the wonderful anatomy of the body." He praised the doctors whom he observed in the New York Hospital in the early 1860s, and some of their advanced surgical and medical procedures he witnessed (Aspiz 1980: 54–5, 70–4, 103–4). He reviewed books on female health and anatomy by Dr Edward H. Dixon and Mary Gove Nichols. Colbert (1997: 312–13) speculates that Whitman's description of midwifery in section 49 of "Song of Myself" may owe something to Orson S. Fowler's 1851 lectures on the subject. Whitman was an astute amateur critic of medical practice during his volunteer service in the Civil War military hospitals, where asepsis was so poor that many amputees died of gangrene, although Dr Lister had long ago established a procedure for cleansing infections. As he grew older and more appreciative of the talented physicians who attended him, Whitman's attitude toward medicine became a mixture of the scientific, the semiscientific, and the intuitive approaches to health.

Whitman was intrigued by human anatomy as an object of study and as a theme for art, carefully describing and praising all bodily attributes in the poems – for example, his own (mythic) body, the lithe bodies of the blacksmiths in section 7 and the stalwart "negro" atop his load in section 13 of "Song of Myself." "I Sing the Body Electric"(1855) describes the bodily attributes of persons from all walks of life – including slaves at auction – and stresses the poet's faith that future generations can be physically upgraded. But desirous to prepare "a poem in which is minutely described the whole particulars and ensemble of a "*first-class* healthy *Human Body*," Whitman reminded himself "to read the latest medical works, to talk with physicians," and "to study the anatomical plates" (Aspiz 1980: 67–9). The result is the poem's concluding section, appended to the poem in the 1856 edition – a 36-line anatomical catalogue listing more than one hundred real and a few fanciful bodily components, beginning with the "hair, neck, and ears" and ending with the feet and toes as it descends along the body, scanting neither "bowels sweet and clean" nor male and female genital organs. Although many "Drum-Taps" poems and the moving on-the-spot war reportage of *Memoranda during the War* (1875) reveal him to be a careful observer of wounds, sickness, the hospital milieu, medical procedures, and, particularly, the ways men faced death (Whitman was a connoisseur of death and dying), the poems written during his last quarter century show little objective interest in the body – except for the "rivulet" of old-age "poemets" describing his own ailments.

Closely related to his interest in medicine was his advocacy of pure water and pure air. Hydropathy, or water-cure, a semiscientific approach to health in an era when the Americans were an unwashed people, promoted sanitation, public and private bathing, various forms of baths and douches, the copious drinking of water, and medical gradualism. Although Whitman deplored some bizarre hydropathic practices, his concern with personal cleanliness and pure water is evident throughout the journalism and the poems, where the persona boasts of being a water drinker, of his cleanliness, and even of his swimming. He counted hydropathic physicians – who generally advocated phrenology, reformed medicine, and a range of humanitarian causes and reforms – among his friends (Wrobel 1987: 82 and passim, Stern 1975: 52). Although he showed little sympathy with the methods of the Thomsonians, or "steam doctors," he was intrigued by their democratic premise that each person could become his or her own doctor. And like many reformers, he advocated fresh open air to counteract the stifling effects of tenement life and as a form of physical therapy. In some poems, fresh air and open space become powerful metaphors for personal freedom and for the receptivity to the divine afflatus. The air cure became popular at the end of the century when it was promoted by Whitman's physician, the neurologist and man of letters Dr Silas Weir Mitchell. *Specimen Days* contains a charming account of the paralyzed poet's regimen at Timber Creek, New Jersey, where he inhaled drafts of fresh air beside a shallow stream and dipped his feet in the water and the mud (*PW*, 1: 150–2).

As an observer of his world and his universe, Whitman was interested in the earth sciences and astronomy. Beaver estimated that "the body of astronomical imagery, color, and allusion in *Leaves of Grass* is probably as large as that of all other scientific references combined," because it is in "astronomy and the related sciences that we expect the closest correlation between poetry and science" (Beaver 1974: 80). Whitman was intrigued by the structure, origin, and destiny of the universe and by such related sciences as physics, mathematics, chemistry, and the pre-Darwinian version of evolution. A poetic reflection of the evolutionary idea appears in section 44 of "Song of Myself," where the persona conjures up the sequence of life forms he may have assumed in evolving from "the first nothing" to his present fulfilled self.

Much of Whitman's knowledge of astronomy may have come from reading such texts as Ormsby McKnight Mitchell's *A Course of Six Lectures on Astronomy* (1848) and attending Mitchell's lectures. The poems indicate that he understood Mitchell's three laws of inertia, gravity (attraction of bodies to each other), and centrifugal force (the tendency of a revolving body to fly away from the center). The persona's fantasized "speeding through space" in "Song of Myself," section 33, and his other imagined flights through the universe may have been inspired by Mitchell (Allen 1975: 182, Beaver 1974: 83). In checking Whitman's references to planets, stars, constellations, and various heavenly phenomena (including his dating of astronomical events), and his use of terms like *centrifugal*, *centripetal*, *gravitate*, *rotate*, *revolve, perturbation* (deviation from its course of a heavenly body due to the pull of another body), Beaver found Whitman to be consistently accurate. In "Out from Behind This Mask," with its astronomical imagery, the description of a body "spin[ning] through space revolving sideling" refers accurately to "the inclination of the earth's axis to the plane of the ecliptic, and even the slow gyration of its axis" (*LG*: 382). The moon's rising in "A Dirge for Two Veterans" is accurate to the very hour as is the description of the voluptuous lingering Venus and the movement of constellation in the *Specimen Days* entry for May 21, 1877 (*PW* 1: 147–8, Beaver 1974). The stars in "On the Beach at Night Alone," which symbolize "a vast similitude [that] interlocks all" the secrets of the universe and the innumerable solar systems that the persona beholds in a cosmos that is "always expanding, / Outward and outward and forever outward" in "Song of Myself," section 45 (*LG*: 82), represent his concept of a purposive and developing universe in which all of creation is an interrelated continuum whose uniform laws govern the structure, movement, and development of creatures and materials great and small – rocks, motes, butterflies, and worlds. Each object, he says in "Song of Myself," can form "the hub for the wheel'd universe." That "hub" has both material and spiritual connotations. Whitman apparently accepted Paley's and Chambers' theory that the earth was formed originally of gases and evolved in gradual stages, steadily carrying forward some of its transferable advances toward the ultimate development of humankind, when, as Whitman says in "Song of Myself," "the nebula cohered into an orb," from which nebulous orb (Whitman's "float") humankind, including the poet himself, were "struck" (*LG*: 86, 81). Whitman recorded a simple atomic theory in which every form of matter is in motion:

> Every molecule of matter in the whole universe is swinging to and fro; every particle of ether which fills space is in jelly-like vibration. Light is one kind of motion, heat another, magnetism another, sound another. Every human sense is the result of motion . . . every thought is but the motion of the molecules of the brain. . . . The processes of growth, of existence, of decay, whether in worlds, or in the minutest organisms, are but motion. (Beaver 1974: 90)

Whitman demonstrated some knowledge of anthropology, geology, and geography. He visited Dr Henry Abbott's extensive collection of Egyptian antiquities in New York in 1853, and may have read books on Egypt recommended by Dr Abbott. He was interested in fossil remains and the evidences of past civilizations that have flourished and disappeared. Among the books on the earth sciences with which Paul Zweig assumes that Whitman was familiar and which could have afforded him a layman's background in the earth sciences are Charles Lyell's *Principles of Geology*, S. G. Goodrich's *A Glance at the Physical Sciences* (1844), and Richard Owen's *Key to the Geology of the Globe* (1857) (Zweig 1984: 144, 160–1). Whitman's periodical clippings included articles on Herschel's observation of the heavens, the remains at Nineveh, a physical atlas, and a physical geography (Stovall 1974: 159–60). In "Unnamed Lands" (*LG*: 372–3) he speculates on the fates of those who lived in now-disappeared civilizations. His most ambitious attempt to incorporate geography into poetry is "Salut au Monde!" (1856), in which the persona imaginatively circumnavigates the world, describing landscapes, seascapes, and peoples. But much of the poem reads as though the poet were following an atlas or geography text. The poem (influenced by Volney's *Ruins*) also includes mythic elements.

Whitman refers to the "absolute" accuracy of chemistry in the 1876 Preface and to chemistry applied to "food and its preservation" in "Song of the Exposition." He quotes Dr Dixon's assertion, in *The Brooklyn Daily Times*, that miasma (the gases given off by morbid and decaying matter) is the source of typhus and yellow fevers, although every living creature "is evolved from the gases and the earths" and is prevented from decay by a life principle (Aspiz 1980: 63–5). However, he transforms the chemical process of the decomposition and transformation of matter into inspired metaphors for personal renewal and resurrection. Reviewing Justus Liebig's *Chemistry, in Its Application to Agriculture and Physiology* in 1846, Whitman called chemistry a "noble science . . . that involves the essences of creation, and the changes, and the growths, and the formations and decays of so large a constituent part of the earth" (Aspiz 1980: 64). "What Chemistry!" the persona exclaims in "This Compost" (1856) of the earth's "kosmical antiseptic power" to ingest corpses and corrupt matter and transform them into fertile and abundant life, such as "the resurrection of the wheat"

(*LG*: 368–70). This chemical process is the basis for powerful tropes for the evolution of the human spirit and for the perpetual evolution of life out of death. Some 20 years earlier the phrenologist George Combe had articulated a similar "fundamental principle": "Death removes the old and decayed," he said, "and the organic law introduces in their place the young, the gay, and the vigorous, to tread the stage with new agility and delight" (Colbert 1997: 145). Whitman later employed this "chemical" trope effectively in the "Drum-Taps" poem "Ashes of Soldiers," in which he prays that the foul effluvia from the graves of the buried soldiers be purified by the earth's chemistry and the resulting fragrance inspire his poems (*LG*: 492). In *Democratic Vistas* he illustrates his premise that America's political and social corruption will ultimately be healed by comparing the chemical cleansing potential of American democracy to the absorptive and transformative chemical powers of the earth (*PW*, 2: 382).

One of Whitman's defining characteristics is his intimate identification with all persons, creatures, and natural phenomena. He views animate life and all elements of nature as "living companions" and finds a "cognizant lurking something" in nature to which he responds as to human companions (Briggs 1952: 79). In 1846 he commented that the study of botany was "well calculated to develop a refinement and a sense of beauty" and that by examining the simplest flower and its features one may appreciate "the wisdom and vastness of God" (Brasher 1979: 213). The birds that appear in the poems are often personified projections of the persona; the wild gander and the spotted hawk in "Song of Myself," the mocking bird in "Out of the Cradle Endlessly Rocking" and the thrush in "Lilacs" are virtually his alter egos. Although Whitman is not known to have pursued the sciences of botany and ornithology, nevertheless the ailing paralytic at his rural retreat at Timber Creek, New Jersey, was able to name some 40 land and sea birds that he could identify and occasionally characterize. He mentioned at least 30 varieties of local trees, sometimes with a sense of affection and intimacy, and over 30 local wild flowers that he recognized and could describe. He also named local rodents, small animals, and insects (*PW*, 1: 122–80, passim). He even contemplated writing a poem on insects (Zweig 1984: 289–90). The animals, such as those described in sections 13 and 14 of "Song of Myself," and the plants all appear to be intimately related to him.

III

Because the boundaries of science were ill-defined in Whitman's day, the pseudosciences, which combined the known and the hypothetical, enjoyed great popularity and were endorsed by many intellectuals. Among the identifiable pseudosciences that influenced Whitman's thinking and his writings were phrenology, physiognomy, pathognomy, "electricity," mesmerism, primitive eugenics or hereditary science, and (as we have seen) the medical semisciences. Chief among these was phrenology. The brain surgeon Johann Gaspar Spurzheim, who popularized this primitive faculty psychology, theorized that each human function – physical, sexual, moral, social, and spiritual – is regulated by an identifiable area of the brain and that its development can be measured by the degree to which the specific brain segment protrudes on the skull (hence, the vulgar appellation " head bumps"). Phrenology created a sensation when its inventor Franz Josef Gall came to America in the 1830s. By the 1840s, the Fowler brothers, phrenologists and publishers, had popularized the idea that almost every aspect of human life could be interpreted phrenologically, and phrenological jargon filtered into common speech and adorned many passages of the first three editions of *Leaves of Grass*. Whitman used phrenological terms to describe himself and others in the poems; thus "Song of the Broad-Axe" lists 16 phrenological faculties belonging to the Whitman persona and the first edition of "Crossing Brooklyn Ferry" names the brain as the "organ of the soul." The Fowlers' *American Phrenological Journal*, which Whitman read and cited in his journalism, reported on all sorts of pseudoscientific and reformist causes – and on a variety of other matters. Among their phrenological books that Whitman owned were Orson S. Fowler's *Hereditary Descent* and *Love and Parentage,* which influenced his ideas on heredity, sexuality, and nurture. In 1849 Lorenzo Fowler performed a phrenological examination of the poet, judging him to be healthy, serious, a bit sluggish, but gifted with the phrenological traits ideally suited to a newspaperman and an aspiring poet – organs of memory, language skills, a mechanical eye (Whitman was identified as a printer), and such phrenological faculties as Caution, Hope, Ideality, Amativeness, and Parental Love (Stern 1975: 99–123). He was attracted to phrenology's claim that, taken together with other sciences and related pseudosciences, it constituted "anthropology – the science of man" (Stern 1975: 212) – a concept vaguely related to Whitman's ideas of human and racial development. Phrenology's emphasis on the workings of the human brain made it relevant to the development of modern psychiatry in the days before sonograms, CAT scans, and X-rays. Whitman's descriptions in "The Sleepers" of the conscious and semiconscious mental states of the dreamer-persona and his fellow "sleepers" – of their overt and submerged thought processes – have suggested that he was something of a pioneer in the study of the subconscious.

The popularity of phrenology, physiognomy, and other pseudosciences may have convinced Whitman that his many allusions to them in the *Leaves* would be intelligible to his readers. Phrenology, physiognomy (interpreting the character through the facial features), and pathognomy (interpreting character through physical bearing and carriage) are evident in many poems, particularly in "Song of Myself" and "I Sing the Body Electric." Nor was Whitman unique in this practice. The precepts of phrenology and physiognomy governed the works of such graphic artists as Rembrandt Peale, Hiram Powers, Sidney Mount, Thomas Cole, and George Catlin. Like Whitman, they practiced the honest depiction of the body and used the facial and bodily features to reveal the essential character of their subjects (Colbert 1997 passim). Their idealization of natural beauty probably influenced Whitman's stress on "natural forms," his glorification of ideal bodies (including his own), and his frank descriptions of nudity. His many poetic references to facial features (including his own) indicate the importance to him of physiognomy as an artistic resource. He declared in "Song of Myself" that "I carry the plenum of proof [of his remarkable self] in my face" and in a later verse boasted that the self-portrait prefacing his book was his "Heart's geography's map," as readable as any astronomic chart (*LG*: 55, 382). "Faces" (1855) is a tour de force in which Whitman analyzes the characters of individuals in the crowds of urban passers-by by "reading" the relevant pseudoscientific clues he beholds in their heads, their facial features, and their physical carriage. The poem predicts that in the course of many millennia flawed humankind will breed out its physical and moral defects and evolve into superior beings.

Some of the most dazzling imagery in *Leaves of Grass* derives from the science and the pseudosciences associated with electricity, which many of Whitman's contemporaries believed could unlock the secrets of the universe and bridge the chasm between the material and the spiritual worlds. The electrical nature of the nervous system had been long established. By 1843 Whitman may have read a volume by Percy Hare Townshend, defining the human body as an "electric machine" – a concept that strongly colors the imagery throughout *Leaves of Grass*. Blood, sperm, and "brain fluid" were widely assumed to be electrical in nature. Orson S. Fowler termed electricity "the great agent and instrumentality of life, in all its forms . . . the great executive of every animal function, or mental exercise." Emerson and Tennyson referred to electricity as the creative center of life; Whitman made a similar definition in "As I Ebb'd with the Ocean of Life" (Aspiz 1980: 143–4). Phrenologists sometimes called electricity the living fire; Whitman uses the images of "electric fire" and "quivering fire" in a pair of "Calamus" poems to describe the persona's sexual drive (*LG*: 90, 136). He incorporated electrical and pseudoelectrical terminology in his discussions of sexuality and in his descriptions of the persona as an ideal breeder. Although the function of the ovarian egg had been known since 1827, embryology was not an established science in the 1850s, and Whitman was no worse informed about the nature of the birth process than many of his medical contemporaries. The persona's role in the "Children of Adam" poems in proposing to create a generation of perfect offspring by impregnating legions of eligible females with his electrically charged sperm was rooted in the pseudoscientific ideas of phrenologists and other sexual reformers. Thus Dr Dixon implied that inasmuch as no other basis of life has been discovered, the origin of life must be purely electric and that the sexes are mutually attracted because the male is positively charged and the female negatively charged. In such sexually oriented poems as "A Woman Waits for Me" and "I Sing the Body Electric" Whitman may also have toyed with the bizarre theory that the sperm of the electrically charged male contains the nucleus of the offspring – a miniature homunculus or spermatozoid – and that the pregnant female only "shapes" and nurtures it (Aspiz 1980: 145–8, Reynolds 1995: 207). Even the poems' heroic copulations (such as the "bridegroom night of love" in "I Sing the Body Electric") relate to the notion of sexual reformers that a prolonged sexual interaction of male and female electricity was essential to successful reproduction.

The electrical "mental science" of mesmerism – incorporating hypnotism (which had a brief vogue as an anesthetic before the discovery of chloroform and ether), mental thought control, thought transference, and clairvoyance – was based on Franz

Mesmer's hypothesis of an electrical brain fluid through which one's mental force could be projected by an act of the will. Mesmerism claimed to be an optimistic practice that harnessed hitherto unexploited forces for human good, one American mesmerist boasting that mesmerism had "climbed aboard that 'glorious chariot of science with its ever increasing power, magnificence, and glory...ever obeying the command of God: ONWARD'." Mesmer called it the link between mind and spirit, the great science of man, and Whitman called it "omnient" (Wrobel 1987: 216–17, 229–30). It was heralded as a means of transmitting impulses from the brain of the dominant mesmerizer to the passive subject and as a way to delve into the (as yet undefined) subconsciousness of individuals. Emerson was so impressed by mesmerism's exploration of the subcurrents of thought that he credited it with affirming "the unity and connection between remote points, and as such was excellent on the narrow and dead classification that passed for science" (quoted in Wrobel 1987: 6). The mesmerizing process involved the magnetizer passing his hands from the top of the patient's head down the patient's face and arms, and shaking them at each pass to get rid of the "diseased magnetism." This procedure is apparently followed in Whitman's "Salut au Monde!" in which an operator mesmerizes the persona and renders him clairvoyant, so that he can visualize and describe in great detail his imaginary voyage around the world. In section 40 of "Song of Myself" the persona applies his electrical therapeutics by blowing "grit" into a weak, loose-kneed subject to revive him and "dilates" an apparently dying man "with tremendous breath" to ward off death and decay (*LG*: 74). In "The Sleepers" the persona passes his hands "soothingly to and fro" near the bodies of the restless sleepers to soothe them and, through his clairvoyant-electrical powers, enters into – and is able to *share* – their deepest dreams. In *Memoranda During the War* and *Specimen Days* Whitman credits himself with possessing something akin to a mesmeric-magnetic touch with which he was able to revive the desire to live, to repel the fear of dying, and to expedite the healing of many invalided soldiers during the War. (When combined with the stimulation of the appropriate phrenological organ to evoke the desired response, mesmerism was called phreno-magnetism.)

A possible "electrical" or phrenological offshoot of phrenology was "Adhesiveness," originally identified by phrenologists as the mental "faculty" governing personal attraction and the desire to bond socially with others. In *Democratic Vistas* Whitman defines adhesiveness as "love that fuses, ties, and aggregates, making the races comrades, and fraternizing all" (*PW*, 2: 381). But "Song of the Broad-Axe," "Song of the Open Road," several "Calamus" poems, and Whitman's self-description as an empathetic healer in *Specimen Days* frequently endow the term with a homoerotic nuance, so that it has been widely interpreted as a code word for Whitman's presumed homosexuality. The concept of adhesiveness may have originated in Karl Ludwig Reichenbach's notion that the human body emits attractive quasi-electrical odylic emanations that mysteriously attract and bond others to oneself (Aspiz 2003: 103).

Whitman assumed that the sciences and the pseudosciences would facilitate the process of social and individual betterment. In outlining a program of physical, moral, and social upgrading of human beings, Orson S. Fowler's 12-part series, "Progression a Law of Nature: Its Application to Human Improvement" (1843), anticipated Whitman's appeals to his readers to avail themselves and their progeny of opportunities for physical and spiritual upgrading. The Lamarckian premise that humanity is steadily evolving, rejected by Darwin and Huxley, was a mainstay of Whitman's belief system. He assumed that the human race is "surely going somewhere" and "bettering itself" through space and time (*LG*: 525, 740). He assured his readers in "To You" that in democratic America, "Through birth, life, death, burial, the measures are provided, nothing is scanted . . . whatever you are picks its way" (p. 235). Poems like "Song of the Broad-Axe" and "So Long!" imply (while articulating few specific reforms) that the individual's will and effort, combined with the operation of natural evolutionary forces, will facilitate the development of splendid individuals and advanced races and promote a genuine democracy. Like most of his generation, who were inspired by national expansion and the idea of Manifest Destiny, his ideal person was modeled on the Anglo-European. In a version of evolution that he called "Ethnological Science" or "natural selection," he noted that "certain races" must disappear "by the slow, sure progress of laws, through sufficient periods of time" (Aspiz 2003: 218). Small wonder that "Song of the Redwood-Tree" implies that the presumably inferior native Americans will happily die off to make room for the supposedly ethnically superior (white) races.

In *Democratic Vistas*, where the word *science* and its variants appear 18 times, Whitman further develops his evolutionary premise by assuming (like many social critics of the day) that the body politic is subject to the same laws of development as the body personal. Posing as a physician, or "moral diagnostician," he examines the "osseous structure," the "scrofulous wealth," the "cankerous imperfection," and the tubercular "hectic glow" of Gilded Age America. Any cure of her social ailments, he observes, will "come down to one single, solitary soul," to the "You and Me," who form the spiritual center of the universe. "In addition to the established sciences," he declares, "we suggest a science as it were of healthy personalism, on original-universal grounds, the subject of which should be to raise up and supply through the states a copious race of superb American men and women, cheerful, religious, ahead of any yet known." "Will the time come," he wonders, "when motherhood and fatherhood shall become a science – and the noblest science?" (*PW*, 2: 393–7). He reiterates his belief that science will elevate literature and help to inspire great poets and "literatuses" – like himself – who will then inspire and guide the nation's personal and social advancement. Whether in matters of the social sciences or the natural sciences, the individual remains at the center of Whitman's thinking.

References and Further Reading

Allen, Gay Wilson (1975). *The New Walt Whitman Handbook*. New York: New York University Press.

Aspiz, Harold (1980). *Walt Whitman and the Body Beautiful*. Urbana: University of Illinois Press.

Aspiz, Harold (2003). *So Long! Walt Whitman's Poetry of Death*. Tuscaloosa: University of Alabama Press.

Beaver, Joseph ([1951] 1974). *Walt Whitman: Poet of Science*. New York: Octagon Books.

Benton, Paul (2003). Elbert Hubbard's Manuscript Muddle: Restoring Walt Whitman's "Sunday Evening Lectures" Manuscripts. *Walt Whitman Quarterly Review*, 21: 65–79.

Bode, Carl (ed.) (1967). *American Life in the 1840s*. Garden City, NY: Anchor Books.

Brasher, Thomas (1979). *Walt Whitman as Editor of the Brooklyn Daily Eagle*. Detroit: Wayne State University Press.

Briggs, Arthur E. (1952). *Walt Whitman: Thinker and Artist*. New York: Philosophical Library.

Burroughs, John (1896). *Whitman, a Study*. Boston and New York: Houghton, Mifflin

Burroughs, John (1924). *Birds and Poets, With Other Papers*. New York: Wm Wise.

Burroughs, John ([1928] 1967). *The Heart of Burroughs's Journals*, ed. Clara Barrus. Port Washington, NY: Kennikat.

Colbert, Charles (1997). *A Measure of Perfection: Phrenology and the Fine Arts in America*. Chapel Hill: University of North Carolina Press.

Conner, Frederick William (1949). *Cosmic Optimism: A Study of the Interpretation of Evolution by American Poets from Emerson to Robinson*. Gainesville: University of Florida Press.

Huxley, Thomas H. (1867). On the Study of Geology. In Edward Livingston Youmans (ed.), *The Culture Demanded by Modern Life*. New York: Appleton and Co.

Killingsworth, M. Jimmie (1989). *Whitman's Poetry of the Body: Sexuality, Politics, and the Text*. Chapel Hill: University of North Carolina Press.

Miller, Edwin Haviland (ed.) (1989). *Walt Whitman's "Song of Myself": A Mosaic of Interpretations*. Iowa City: University of Iowa Press.

Reynolds, David (1995). *Walt Whitman's America: A Cultural Biography*. New York: Knopf.

Scholnick, Robert J. (1986). "The Password Primeval": Whitman's Use of Science in "Song of Myself." In Joel Myerson (ed.), *Studies in the American Renaissance, 1986*. Charlottesville: University Press of Virginia, pp. 385–435.

Stern, Madeleine B. (1975). *Heads & Headlines: The Phrenological Fowlers*. Norman: University of Oklahoma Press.

Stovall, Floyd (1974). *The Foreground of Leaves of Grass*. Charlottesville: University of Virginia Press.

Traubel, Horace (1982). *With Walt Whitman in Camden*, vol. 6., ed. Gertrude Traubel and William White. Carbondale and Edwardsville: Southern Illinois University Press.

White, William (1969). *Walt Whitman's Journalism – a Bibliography*. Detroit: Wayne State University Press.

Walls, Laura Dassow (1995). *Seeing New Worlds: Henry Thoreau and Nineteenth-Century Natural Science*. Madison: University of Wisconsin Press.

Wrobel, Arthur (ed.) (1987). *Pseudo-Science and Society in 19th-Century America*. Lexington: University Press of Kentucky.

Zweig, Paul (1984). *Walt Whitman: The Making of a Poet*. New York: Basic Books.

15
Nineteenth-century Popular Culture

Brett Barney

It has been said that although "Whitman never used the term 'popular culture'... he came to personify it" (Fishwick 1999: 10), and a substantial body of recent criticism has been devoted to proving the truth of that statement. The most prominent examples of this trend are David S. Reynolds's acclaimed books, *Beneath the American Renaissance* and *Walt Whitman's America*. In the first, Reynolds discusses Whitman as one of seven "responsive authors" who created "the major literature" of the antebellum era by transforming the "language and value systems [...] of popular culture," into "dense literary texts" (Reynolds 1988: 3). In *Walt Whitman's America*, Reynolds develops this argument further to show that Whitman drew from such discursive fields as sentimental fiction, theatrical performance, pornography, and charismatic religious movements, in each case "transforming them through his powerful personality into art" (Reynolds 1995: 590). Reynolds's approach typifies the way "popular culture" has been employed in Whitman criticism: to define, implicitly, a category of products and practices as artistically and/or intellectually inferior to the productions of "high culture" or "elite culture" (Reynolds's "dense literary texts" and "art").

Scholarship that traces connections between Whitman and so-called "subliterary" forms is valuable, as it makes us more competent readers, better equipped to navigate the allusive terrain of Whitman's writing and to assess Whitman's achievements in historical context. This essay will, in part, contribute to the growing "inventory" of Whitman's affinities with currently devalued literary and social forms. In addition, though, I will attempt to redress the problem of anachronism that exists in current scholarship on Whitman and popular culture, exploring his literary career in the context of contemporaneous nineteenth-century understandings of culture. Lawrence Levine has pointed out that to define popular culture "aesthetically rather than literally," as has become customary, is to "obscure the dynamic complexity of American culture in the nineteenth century" (Levine 1988: 31). He and others have demonstrated that rigid boundaries between elite and nonelite entertainment simply did not exist until around the turn of the twentieth century. Furthermore, when applied in the realm of human activity prior to the mid-nineteenth century, "culture" almost always denoted nurturance – a metaphorical extension of its original reference to agricultural husbandry. Only later was it commonly used to mean either "aesthetic sophistication" or "a way of life," its most usual senses today (Williams 1976: 80). Richard Teichgraeber has observed that the word was ambiguous and unstable in nineteenth-century America, but that at least until after the Civil War, "culture for most Americans" meant "individual self-development or self-construction," and thus "remained roughly synonymous with 'self-culture' . . . " (Teichgraeber 1999: 11, 13).

Self-culture and Rational Amusement

For antebellum writers, especially Unitarians and Transcendentalists, self-culture was a common theme. Rev. William Ellery Channing's influential 1838 sermon on the topic was apparently important to Whitman, though its influence has received little attention. Whitman recommended the text to readers of the *Brooklyn Eagle* in 1847, saying, "No terms are too high for speaking in favor of this little work – [. . .] vaster than many great libraries in the objects which it involves, and the large purpose it so clearly elucidates . . . " (*Brooklyn Daily Eagle Online*, June 28, 1847: 2). It is easy to understand Whitman's enthusiasm; the sermon reads like an introduction to the poet's thinking on many topics. For instance, Channing declares that "every man, in every condition, is great" (Channing [1838] 1969: 6); identifies with and honors manual laborers (pp. 5–6); sees America as a unique field of opportunity for average persons (p. 11); and treats the soul as an authority higher than custom or the opinions of others (pp. 43–5). He defines self-culture broadly, as "the care which every man owes to himself to the unfolding and perfecting of his nature" (p. 11), and recommends a balanced approach, believing that "all the principles of our nature grow at once by joint harmonious action [. . .]" (p. 15). A program of self-culture involves, therefore, "a regard to the rights and happiness of other beings" (p. 16); attention to one's spiritual self (p. 17); the strengthening of instinctive affections "which bind together" family members, neighbors, and humanity (p. 23); and an effort to become "efficient in whatever we undertake" (p. 23). Channing further observes that although intellectual cultivation is important, "we are in no danger of overlooking" it, as "it draws more attention than any" other principle. He therefore warns against a course of "exclusively intellectual training" that emphasizes "accumulating information," instead recommending the "building up a force of thought which may be turned at will on any subjects . . . " (pp. 18, 20–1).

Besides agreeing with the tenets of *Self-Culture*, Whitman must have drawn personal inspiration from Channing's message that "[s]elf-culture is something possible. It is not a dream" (Channing 1969: 12). Ed Folsom has characterized Whitman's education as "the original relativistic training," drawing attention to the contrast between his self-directed study (plus six years of public schooling) and the norm of "classical, structured educations" for literary artists (Folsom 1990: 139). In

Specimen Days Whitman recalls receiving, at the age of about 11, a subscription to "a big circulating library" – an act he terms "the signal event of my life up to that time." Later, during the years immediately before and after the first edition of *Leaves of Grass*, he poured considerable energy into studying newspapers, periodicals, and reference books. In his account of the "leading sources and formative stamps to [his] character," Whitman emphasizes the educational importance of a wide range of experiences: boyhood explorations of Long Island, training in newspaper publishing, membership in debating societies, observing life from the ferries and omnibuses of Brooklyn and New York, and "experiences afterward in the secession outbreak" (*PW*, 1: 10–23). Education is one of the most frequent topics of Whitman's early editorial writing, where he explicitly endorses Channing's brand of self-culture. Several times, he advocates a broad informal education for people in whatever circumstance. For example, in an 1846 article Whitman argues that, whether "old or young, mechanic, man of business, or man of leisure [. . .] [e]very one owes it to himself to cultivate those powers which God has given him . . . " (*Brooklyn Daily Eagle Online*, Nov. 6, 1846: 2). The same year, Whitman advised the "young men of Brooklyn, instead of spending so many hours, idling in bar-rooms, and places of vapid, irrational un-amusement," to "occupy that time in improving themselves in knowledge . . . " (ibid., Dec. 17, 1846: 2). The phrase "irrational un-amusement" is worth noting as a humorous negation of "rational amusement," a term commonly understood in Whitman's time as shorthand for the widely held belief, most famously articulated by Rousseau, that the pleasures of entertainment could and should be made to serve intellectual and moral development. As we will see, "rational amusement" was an elastic term that could accommodate a surprising assortment of enterprises.

The belief that the laboring classes could improve themselves through a program of self-culture informed the ways Whitman thought about his own writing. From the beginning of his quest to become the American bard, Whitman conceived his project as an effort to cultivate the masses. The 1855 Preface announces that "the genius of the United States" is not in its political and religious leaders, "but always most in the common people" (Whitman 1855: iii). Even more forceful is his statement, in an essay from about the same time, that "the great mass of mechanics, farmers, men following the water, and all laboring persons" are "to all intents and purposes, the American nation, the people" (*NUPM*, 6: 2120). As their model representative, "commensurate with a people," the American bard invites them to see themselves clearly, as he does: "You shall stand by my side and look in the mirror with me" (Whitman 1855: iv, vii). The poems themselves continue the theme of poet-as-teacher. In what later became "Song of Myself" Whitman proclaims, "I am the teacher of athletes / [. . .] He most honors my style who learns under it to destroy the teacher." Another poem indicates that the words of the poet are "no lesson," but they "[let] down the bars to a good lesson," so that the poet is able to "remind you, and you can think [his thoughts] and know them to be true . . . " (Whitman 1855: 52, 53, 92).

In announcing himself the "teacher of athletes," Whitman introduced what proved to be a key concept of his writing philosophy: in the "classroom" of literary study, readers become fit through exertion. Whitman expresses this idea in the introductory poem of the 1860 edition of *Leaves of Grass*, later titled "Starting from Paumanok," when he writes, "I have arrived, / To be wrestled with as I pass, for the solid prizes of the universe, / For such I afford whoever can persevere to win them" (Whitman 1860: 20). The image also appears in *Democratic Vistas*, which asserts that "the process of reading is not a half-sleep, but, in highest sense, an exercise, a gymnast's struggle." Because of this, literature has the potential to "make a nation of supple and athletic minds, well-train'd, intuitive, used to depend on themselves, and not on a few coteries of writers" (*PW*, 2: 424–5). Statements of this kind recur frequently in Whitman's writings; figuring personal growth through reading as athletic development gave Whitman a way to think about his readers and his relationship to them, and this conception of the relationship became habitual.

Besides its value as metaphor, physical training also has a literal value in the program of self-culture that Whitman recommends. Interestingly, when advocating physical activity he often treats intellectual cultivation as an oppositional rather than a complementary process. In *Democratic Vistas* he writes, "[A] clear-blooded, strong-fibred physique, is indispensable; the questions of food, drink, air, exercise, assimilation, digestion, can never be intermitted." The "enlargement of intellect," on the other hand, "especially in America, is so overweening [. . .] that, important as it is, it really needs nothing of us here – except, indeed, a phrase of warning and restraint" (*PW*, 2: 397). While pronouncements like this have led some to talk of Whitman's turn toward anti-intellectualism, he had long held this view. It should be noted that Whitman's sentiments closely echo Channing's, and Whitman had expressed the same reservations in his 1840s editorials for the *Eagle*. In one, he had denounced a too-exclusive "'devotion to learning' – to the forgetfulness of every thing else, of the laws of physical health, and the claims which the ordinary things of life have upon a man . . . " (*Brooklyn Daily Eagle Online*, Aug. 21, 1846: 2). In another, on "Fostering Precocity in Children," he takes "the liberty of deprecating *too much mental exercise*" and suggesting "plenty of *out-door* exercise – active physical recreation and employment" (ibid., Jan. 4, 1847: 2). Whitman was committed, early and late, to the idea that the populace should cultivate both mind and body.

Gymnastics and the Circus

The combination of physical and mental cultivation that Whitman recommended is strongly reminiscent of the ideas about "gymnastics" or physical training developed by Friedrich GutsMuths and spread in America through "Turner societies" established by German immigrants. According to GutsMuths, "orthodox education methods neglect the body and practise an excessive 'refinement' which leads to debility." Because "body and mind interact intimately and continuously upon one another," proper education "seek[s] to promote harmony between them" (Dixon 1981: 117). New York City's Turner society was, in 1848, one of the first of scores that were established before the Civil War. Their mission, according to Emmett Rice, was "to promote physical education, intellectual enlightenment and sociability among the members." To that end, their buildings included libraries and facilities for lectures and debates, as well as gymnasia that accommodated men, women, and children. Rice observes that "[a]n atmosphere of brotherhood and friendship pervaded all the activities of the society" (Rice 1929: 162). Turner societies implemented many of the ideas and practices in Whitman's vision of "a perfect school": "gymnastic, moral, mental and sentimental, – in which magnificent men are formed. – old persons come just as much as youth – gymnastics, physiology, music, swimming bath, – conversation, – declamation – – large saloons adorned with pictures and sculpture – great ideas not taught in sermons but imbibed as health is imbibed –" ("Poem – A Perfect School," Folsom and Price 1995–). Whitman may have encountered "German" gymnastics philosophy in Phokion Heinrich (a.k.a. Peter Henry) Clias's *Elementary Course of Gymnastics*, a manual also based on the work of GutsMuths and translated into English in 1823; a citation for the often reprinted book appears in one of Whitman's early notebooks (*NUPM*, 1: 248). Regardless of his level of familiarity with any particular school of gymnastics, Whitman showed a strong interest in physical fitness. In 1842 he wrote a short notice, favorable though unenthusiastic, of "Hudson & Ottignon's gymnasium," where he claims to have spent "an hour's lounge," first taking "a few shots in the pistol gallery" and then "observ[ing] the feats of those who were practising on the various gymnastic apparatus . . . " (*Jour*, 1: 84). Furthermore, he clipped and summarized articles on fitness and even apparently planned to publish an original series of articles on the topic of "Manly Health and Training," draft advertisements for which are partially extant (*NUPM*, 6: 2257–8).

Whitman's comments about Hudson & Ottignon's make it clear that a visit to the gymnasium was part education, part entertainment. During the poet's early adult life, Brooklyn and New York offered a multitude of amusements described (and thereby justified) as "rational," many of which are no longer familiar – at least not as educational. One example is the circus, which, in 1854 New York was "still the most popular of public amusements . . . " (Places of Public Amusement 1854: 152). Like gymnastics generally, the circus benefited from a historical association with the military. Circus performers demonstrated physical feats of all kinds, including horseback performances by former cavalrymen or their imitators. By most accounts, the modern circus came into being when "hippodrama," the exhibition of equestrian stunts, merged with the traveling menagerie in the 1830s. Typically, the circus also featured acrobatic gymnasts, sometimes on apparatus, and by midcentury these gymnastic performances had assumed an increasingly visible role (Flint 1983: 212). At the same time, circus acrobats were often criticized for endangering public morality, either because they encouraged dangerous behavior or because their bodies were too conspicuously displayed (Flint 1979: 187–8, Lewis 2003: 108–9).

In the summer of 1856, Whitman attended one of the most renowned circuses and wrote a review that reflects upon the value of circus as a type of physical education, as well as upon two other of his characteristic preoccupations: crowd behavior and

American nationalism. Observing that the circus is for many "the only public amusement which breaks the monotony of the year," Whitman also maintains that it is no mere entertainment, but "a national institution" that "has here reached a perfection attained nowhere else" (Whitman 1936: 193). To judge by the space devoted to different aspects of the event, the crowd of spectators was as meaningful to Whitman as anything else. In 1855, Whitman had claimed the ability to participate fully in events and at the same time to record them objectively, to be "[b]oth in and out of the game, and watching and wondering at it" (Whitman 1855: 15). He displays this kind of dual enjoyment in his account of the circus, where he is "one of a compressed mass of human beings melting under the tent. . . . " The "[s]even thousand persons [. . .] seated in great ascending circles around the ring" are "a stilled whirlpool of human faces" and constitute "a moral lesson" of orderly and respectful behavior, "admirable to witness" (Whitman 1936: 195). Besides this "moral lesson," Whitman finds the circus also commendable as athletic instruction. He pronounces the various human performers "all perfect in their several ways," especially appreciating them as "evidence of what practice will enable men to do." He specifically sanctions children's attendance, using language that recalls his arguments against narrow intellectualism. He maintains that "[i]t can do no harm to boys to see a set of limbs display all their agility," and "although [i]t is a pity [. . .] that the education of any man should be confined to his legs," it is equally "a pity [. . .] that the education of any man should be confined to his brain." And since children are allowed to be taught at school by "men who have no other than a brain development," we should "not refuse occasionally to let them attend the evening school of these wonderfully leg-developed individuals" (Whitman 1936: 195–6). In the circus, Whitman saw a double-duty classroom: a place to observe proper social behavior and to learn lessons in human anatomy and locomotion.

The few faults Whitman finds with the circus have to do with the performance of its "star," Dan Rice. As steward of an institution "which amuses a million persons a year," the circus manager, Whitman asserts, "should regard himself somewhat in the light of a public instructor." Whitman professes to have been "entertained exceedingly," but he expresses some qualms over Rice's occasional "approach to a *double entendre*" (Whitman 1936: 193–4). In addition, Whitman finds Rice's idiosyncratic pronunciation irritating and judges the famous clown "not equal to his reputation" (p. 195). That Whitman mentions Rice's reputation is interesting; from it he very possibly gained another memorable and practical lesson – the value of publicity. Like newspaper editor James Gordon Bennett and novelist George Lippard, whom David Reynolds has discussed as pioneers in the "commercialization of controversy" (Reynolds 1995: 355), Rice welcomed notoriety, counting denunciations from the pulpit and arrests for vagrancy as particularly effective and inexpensive advertising (Toll 1976: 61). Whitman may or may not have consciously followed Rice's model for turning negative publicity to his advantage, but he was certainly familiar with the showman's reputation, and it is reasonable to think that the circus formed part of Whitman's schooling in the art of cultivating celebrity.

Commercial Museums

Although Rice's fame has faded, that of another nineteenth-century circus manager has endured; even today the name P. T. Barnum epitomizes self-promotion through controversy. That well-deserved reputation was established, in fact, decades before 1871, when Barnum began his association with the circus company that his name still calls to mind. To Whitman and his contemporaries in the 1840s and 1850s, Barnum was the famous operator of New York's American Museum, located at the intersection of Broadway and Ann Street, an area to which Whitman made frequent visits and in which he lived and worked for a time. After buying the museum in 1841, Barnum transformed it into a business venture so successful that by 1850 it had become "the premier attraction of New York City" (Bogdan 1988: 33), hosting during its 23-year existence 38 million customers – a number, in proportion to the national population, unmatched by Disneyland (Saxon 1989: 107–8). Even before buying the museum, Barnum was well-known as the owner/exhibitor of Joice Heth, a slave billed as George Washington's 165-year-old nursemaid. The public's curiosity in her was heightened by denunciations that Barnum sent – anonymously – to newspapers. Barnum frequently employed such methods, the logic of which his ticket seller spelled out: "First he humbugs them, and then they pay to hear him tell how he did it" (Washburn 1990: 201). In words that Whitman might have penned to describe the marketing of *Leaves of Grass*, Barnum explained: "I thoroughly understood the art of advertising, not merely by means of printer's ink, [. . .] but by turning every possible circumstance to my account. It was my monomania to make the Museum the town wonder and talk" (Toll 1976: 31). Barnum's tireless pursuit (and creation) of the bizarre ensured that the town always had plenty to discuss.

From the distance of a century and a half it may be difficult to comprehend, but mid-nineteenth-century America could view Barnum's collection of unusual animals, human curiosities, waxworks, art, and miscellany as the stuff not just of respectable entertainment but even of intellectual and morally uplifting instruction. This is true in part because, while he certainly pushed the boundaries of sensationalism in some of his exhibits, Barnum worked within an established museum tradition in which paintings by famous artists commonly appeared alongside two-headed calves, cases of rocks, and wax depictions of notorious crimes. Charles Willson Peale, most of whose collections Barnum eventually purchased, is generally credited with establishing the museum tradition in the United States. To emphasize its educational value, above the door of his pioneering Philadelphia Museum Peale posted the motto "Whoso would learn Wisdom, let him enter here!" and on the first admission tickets printed an open book with the words "The Birds and Beasts will teach thee!" (Dennett 1997: 13, Porter 1999: 2). Peale promoted his museum as "a fund of rational and agreeable amusement to all" (Peale 1991: 422) – a fund that included an 80-pound turnip, wood from the English coronation chair, a chicken with two sets of wings and feet, and the preserved finger of a murderer (Hudson 1975: 35). A few people did express doubts about the educational and moral value of such museum exhibits, and Whitman himself disapproved of a particularly gruesome collection of waxworks that visited Brooklyn in 1847 (*Brooklyn Daily Eagle Online*, May 8, 1847: 2). But museums like Peale's were generally thought to serve an important patriotic and educational function. Barnum carefully nurtured this reputation, proclaiming his to be "the focal point of attraction, to the lovers of rational amusement, from every section of the union" (Lewis 2003: 30). Cast in this light, museums like Barnum's seemed an almost ideal tool for fostering the wide-ranging curiosity that Whitman believed in. In *Democratic Vistas*, he looks forward to a day when "in the cities of These States" there will be "immense Museums, [. . .] containing samples and illustrations from all places and peoples of the earth." In them, "[h]istory itself [. . .] will become a friend, a venerable teacher . . . " (*PW*, 2: 755).

Upon his return from Europe in 1846, Barnum was interviewed by Whitman, who approvingly relates the assessment that there "every thing is frozen – kings and *things* –" whereas "here it is *life*. Here it is freedom, and here are *men*" (*Brooklyn Daily Eagle Online*, May 25, 1846: 2). We know that Whitman also went to the museum at least twice because he recorded those visits in newspaper pieces. In one of these, written in March 1842, Whitman terms his visit the renewal of "an old custom [. . .] long since disused." Once at the museum, he immediately positions a chair in front of a window, where he can watch the passing traffic, "the busiest spectacle this busy city can present." He divides the scene into three groups: omnibuses and their drivers, fashionable women, and imitators of European aristocracy. Notably missing is any description – or even mention – of a single museum attraction (*Jour.*, 1: 66–7). As with his visit to the circus, Whitman's "old custom" of going to the museum is an occasion for cultivating an understanding and appreciation of humans, who make a more educational and entertaining display than the deliberately constructed exhibits. It is odd that in this editorial Whitman betrays no hint of interest in the museum's "curiosities," but other of his writings do suggest that museum displays influenced his thinking in important ways. Most obviously, they served as resources of factual information. The best-documented example of Whitman's use of a museum for this purpose involves Henry Abbott's Egyptian Museum, which he frequented around the time of the first edition of *Leaves of Grass*. In an article for *Life Illustrated* entitled "One of the Lessons Bordering Broadway" Whitman announces that "there is probably nothing in New York more deeply interesting" than the museum and recommends it as "a place to go when one would ponder and evolve great thoughts" (Whitman 1936: 40). The memory of Abbott's museum as an important educational site remained with the poet. In *Specimen Days*, he recalls visiting Abbott's museum "many many times," having liberal access to "the formidable catalogue" of artifacts, and benefiting from the "invaluable personal talk, correction, illustration and guidance of Dr. A. himself" (*PW*, 1: 696). Images of Egypt are prominent in several Whitman poems, especially "Song of Myself" and "Salut au Monde!," and the ideas they express about Egyptian philosophy and everyday life owe much to Abbott's museum, as well as to popular texts and lectures, some of which Abbott may have recommended. Critics have seen

Osiris – figures of which abounded at the museum – as an important model for Whitman's immortal and transpersonal persona, and they have pointed out other echoes in *Leaves of Grass* of museums' representations of Egypt (see Tapscott 1978, Gates 1987). Perhaps Whitman was willing to credit the Egyptian Museum openly because no one could mistake it for the American Museum. For one thing, in contrast to the many hoaxes that had generated controversy (and revenue) at Barnum's, the artifacts at Abbott's museum, Whitman assures readers, are absolutely authentic: "[A]mong antiquaries there has never been any question of the collection being bona fide." Even the collection's lack of economic success is evidence of its worthiness as a place of study: "It is not the kind of an exhibition that would attract crowds. Only. . . a thoughtful and inquiring person" is likely to find it interesting (Whitman 1936: 40). But despite Whitman's apparent pains to distinguish between "serious" museums and what would later be known as "dime museums," in the 1850s no clear boundaries divided the two. As a historian of dime museums has explained, even the most reputable museums, lacking governmental support, featured sensational items in hopes of attracting customers, so that "[b]y mid-century they had become venues for all sorts of popular entertainments and their education agenda virtually had vanished" (Dennett 1997: 22). We know that Whitman patronized and enjoyed proprietary museums, at least occasionally, and his writing bears the direct or indirect impressions that they made.

In an 1862 newspaper article Whitman remembered an eighteenth-century steam-driven fire engine as "almost as great a curiosity as anything in Barnum's Museum" (Whitman 1921, 2: 279). Museum attractions furnished a rich stock of metaphors, perhaps the most pervasive of which is the poet's custom of seeing things, people, and events as "specimens." Comparisons to fossils also abound, almost always as a signal of disapproval. The word is used, for example, to describe various kinds of stagnation: in language (*PW*, 2: 577), in religion (*NUPM*, 5: 1723, 6: 2091, *PW*, 2: 409), and in society generally (*PW*, 2: 383, 389, 423, 519). Displays of insects also piqued Whitman's imagination; twice he jotted memos to get a complete list of insects from "Mr. Arkhurst," a taxidermist who probably operated a small "cabinet of curiosity." It was Whitman's intention to write a "little poem" that would "simply enumerate them with their sizes, colors, habits, lives, shortness or length of life – what they feed upon" (*NUPM*, 1: 287, 4: 1349). He never published such a poem, but the image of museum cases filled with insects does appear in the 1860 poem "Unnamed Lands," where the poet envisions the earth's dead inhabitants standing in a variety of poses, "[s]ome naked and savage – some like huge collections of insects" (Whitman 1860: 413). One of the most striking museum-inspired descriptions comes, appropriately, from *Specimen Days*, where Whitman tells of seeing a group of Union soldiers who had been released from Confederate prisons. Alluding to several kinds of museum exhibits at once, he asks, "Can those be *men* – those little livid brown, ash-streak'd, monkey-looking dwarfs? – are they really not mummied, dwindled corpses?" (*PW*, 1: 100).

Dwarfs were a cornerstone of museums' human exhibitions, the most famous being Charles Stratton ("Tom Thumb"), one of Barnum's first and most lucrative museum attractions. In the draft of an apparently unpublished essay, Whitman calls Stratton "my little friend Tom Thumb" (*NUPM*, 1: 244). Whether the two ever met – let alone became friends – is uncertain, but such was Stratton's fame that 20 million people are said to have paid to see him during his lifetime (Wallace 1967: 112). During the years Whitman was formulating his distinctive poetry, Stratton's celebrity made him unavoidable. Nor could Whitman easily have avoided acquaintance with another of the century's famous human curiosities, Chang and Eng Bunker, the "Siamese" conjoined twins. Beginning in 1829 the two exhibited themselves around the country, and by the time of their highly lucrative engagement at Barnum's in 1860, "Siamese Twins" had entered the vernacular in various ways; it was a popular play, a boat, and a figure of speech for any pair of objects or ideas thought to be "inseparably joined," as the Bunkers were almost invariably characterized. Later in the decade, the museum featured "the Two Headed Nightingale," conjoined twins "Millie-Christine," who had been born into Southern slavery. The question of whether conjoined twins could be surgically separated fascinated the public and conjured up an image strongly suggestive of the country's sectional strife. During the Bunkers' 1865 tour, a reporter remarked, "As long as they go in for Union, they will do," but "the moment they attempt to separate they will perish as the Confederates perished" (Kunhardt, Kunhardt, and Kunhardt 1995: 147). In a similar vein, Whitman alluded to the dilemma of conjoined twins when he wrote in 1867 that "Democracy" and its "twin-sister," "the indissoluble Union of These States" are "so ligatured [. . .] that either's death, if not the other's also, would make that other live out life, dragging a corpse [. . .]," (Whitman 1867: 927).

Nineteenth-century museum displays furnished Whitman with more than vivid images; they also offered models for some of his most characteristic rhetorical strategies. One that he assiduously cultivated and that drew frequent comment in early reviews (his own anonymously written ones included) was the candid and unabashed exhibition of the self. A vivid example is found in the second poem of the 1855 edition, where the poetic persona entreats the reader:

> Come closer to me,
> Push close my lovers and take the best I possess,
> [. . .]
> I pass so poorly with paper and types . . . I must pass with the contact of bodies and souls.
>
> (Whitman 1855: 57)

The combination of attraction and discomfort evoked by this solicitation was familiar to visitors at the American Museum. One way Barnum encouraged interactions between spectators and human exhibits was by posting explicit invitations. Next to the bearded lady, for example, a sign read, "Visitors are allowed to touch the beard" (Fern 1854: 373). As another commentator has pointed out, such interactions created an unusual dynamic, in which "part of the fascination was [. . .] identifying with [. . .]

these perplexing, bewildering, mysterious creations of God's universe" (Lewis 2003: 53). The reviewer of *Leaves of Grass* for the *London Weekly Dispatch* betrayed just this sort of fascination, declaring it "one of the most extraordinary specimens of Yankee intelligence and American eccentricity in authorship," possessing "an air at once so novel, so audacious, and so strange as to verge upon absurdity . . . " (Price 1996: 41).

More remarkable than the direct address of the narrative voice was Whitman's frank and explicit treatments of the body. The 1855 edition's opening poem insists, "Welcome is every organ and attribute of me [. . .] / Not an inch nor a particle of an inch is vile, and none shall be less familiar than the rest" (Whitman 1855: 14) – a pledge made good by the addition, in 1856, of a long section to the poem that would become "I Sing the Body Electric." This famous list is, by turns, unflinchingly mundane (e.g., "roof of the mouth," "freckles," "digestion") and routinely indecorous (e.g., "man-balls," "bowels sweet and clean," "teats"). As others have pointed out, precedent for both the content and tone in Whitman's treatment of the body is found in nineteenth-century anatomical texts written for general audiences. Some of these were published by the same firm and at the same time as Whitman's first edition. Museums were an important source as well. In a manuscript note that appears to be the germ for the catalogue in "I Sing the Body Electric," Whitman plans "[a] poem in which is minutely described the whole particulars and ensemble of a first-rate healthy Human Body." Besides reading and talking with doctors, Whitman plans to study printed illustrations and "casts of figures in the collections of design" (*NUPM*, 1: 304). This last reference is probably to exhibits like the "Pathological Museum" of "Dr. J. J. Hull," a description of which Whitman wrote in 1862 for the New York *Leader*. Hull's museum contained "marked illustrations of disease, deformity" as well as "interesting normal specimens of anatomy, &c.," all displayed "for surgical, medical, and scientific enlightenment" (Whitman 1933: 32). An 1850 advertisement for another of the area's "anatomical museums" similarly justifies its exhibits as instructional, even while it highlights their voyeuristic appeal. A visitor, we are told, will gain a "perfect idea of the organs and functions of his own body" by examining "two life-like figures, capable of being dissected, so as to show all the muscles, and viscera in their natural positions." Also on display are a cadaver "divested of the skin"; life-size models of "exquisite venuses" with "the fetus in utero in sight"; and "more than two hundred" body parts illustrating "[d]isease in all its forms, [. . .] upon the skin, the scalp, the limbs, the eyes, nose, lips, and organs of reproduction, etc." (*Brooklyn Daily Eagle Online* 1850). An echo of New York's anatomical museums' combination of clinical detachment and titillation can be heard in Whitman's poems.

Furthermore, like the range of other exhibitionary forms that critics have more commonly treated, commercial museums of various kinds were important nonliterary analogues for the catalogue itself, one of the most characteristic features of *Leaves of Grass*. Whitman's listing technique, described by Miles Orvell as an apparently "loose, free-flowing, disorganized encyclopedia" (Orvell 1989: 28), has been linked to art gallery exhibitions, daguerreotype studios, and world's fairs, each of which displayed objects in such large numbers and variety that they could be thought to collectively represent the entire world. Whitman's interest in paintings, photography, and international expositions is well documented, and each undeniably left a lasting impression on him and his poetry. As aggregations of diverse and abundant materials, however, these forms were building on a framework that was already well established in the institution of the museum. By Whitman's time, the museum was an emblem of the encyclopedic and educational – as attested by the emergence of several popular journals that incorporated "Museum" into their titles. *Merry's Museum*, for example, began publication in the late 1830s in New York to educate children in "the most abstruse subjects [. . .] in a manner intelligible to all . . . " (*Brooklyn Daily Eagle Online*, June 7, 1842: 2). Likewise, *The Philadelphia Saturday Museum* was begun as "a newspaper for all classes" and "devoted to the useful Arts, Education, Morals, Health and Amusement" (ibid., May 15, 1843). Charles Willson Peale had opened his museum in 1784 as "a collection of everything useful or curious – A world in miniature!" (Peale 1988: 274). Barnum similarly advertised his museum as an "encyclopedic synopsis of everything worth seeing in this curious world" (Dennett 1997: 27), an idea also communicated visually by the assortment of international flags lining the roof and by the "Cosmographic Department," where visitors gazed through peepholes at detailed representations of 194 faraway locales (Kunhardt et al. 1995:140). Whitman's famous boast, "I am large . . . I contain multitudes" (Whitman 1855: 55), would have made an apt marketing slogan for the American Museum.

In Whitman's poems, particularly the early ones, the seemingly exhaustive lists enact Whitman's commitment to be "the arbiter of the diverse and [. . .] the key" (Whitman 1855: iv). We are repeatedly told that, like a museum, the poet represents the entire world. He is "a kosmos" (1855: 29); "an acme of things accomplished, and [. . .] an encloser of things to be" (p. 50). His words, "[i]f they do not enclose everything [. . .] are next to nothing (p. 24). The 1855 passage that eventually became section 31 of "Song of Myself" resembles, in fact, nothing so much as a museum guidebook description:

> I find I incorporate gneiss and coal and long-threaded moss and fruits and grains and esculent roots,
> And am stucco'd with quadrupeds and birds all over,
> [. . .]
> In vain the plutonic rocks send their old heat against my approach,
> In vain the mastadon retreats beneath its own powdered bones,
> In vain objects stand leagues off and assume manifold shapes,
> In vain the ocean settling in hollows and the great monsters lying low,
> In vain the buzzard houses herself with the sky,
> In vain the snake slides through the creepers and logs,
> In vain the elk takes to the inner passes of the woods,
> In vain the razorbilled auk sails far north to Labrador [. . .]
>
> (Whitman 1855: 34).

The mention of "the mastadon" [sic] is telling. Peale's museum had had its first "hit" with the 1801 exhibition of a mastodon skeleton, which Barnum acquired at auction in 1849. By the time Whitman's lines appeared six years later, other skeletons were being unearthed and exhibited with some frequency and the mastodon was becoming a defining symbol of museums. The lines also contain what is likely an intentional and rather direct comparison between the poet and Barnum's museum. The claim to be "stucco'd with quadrupeds and birds all over" has been called "presurrealistic" and linked to the "distortions and odd juxtapositions" sometimes seen in human exhibits and in the visual arts of the day (Reynolds 1995: 304–5). But Whitman's readers in the 1850s would more probably have seen in this line a reference to the striking and famous facade of the American Museum building itself, which Barnum decorated with several dozen large color images of exotic animals (see Plate 15.1).

Among the most striking of Whitman's gestures of inclusiveness are his ethnographic sketches, and it is perhaps in these, more than anywhere else, that he relies on museum discourse. In the late eighteenth century, Peale had presented a group of wax figures depicting natives from Africa, Kamchatka, China, Hawai'i, and North and South America to "make a group of contrasting races of mankind" (Sellers 1980: 92), and around 1850 Barnum made plans to exhibit, under the title "Congress of

Plate 15.1 Engraving of Barnum's American Museum from *Gleason's Pictorial Drawing Room Companion* (1853). Gleason's pictorial. PS 501.G43, Clifton Waller Barrett Library of American Literature, Special Collections, University of Virginia Library.

Nations," live male and female specimens of "every accessible people, civilized and barbarous, on the face of the globe." Although he abandoned this project, "living curiosities" always figured prominently in his museum, and he very often created names for them based on ethnic designations – usually pure fabrications – which were reinforced by simple visual cues such as "exotic" hairstyles, clothing, or props to imply stereotypical, often primitive identities. Thus mentally retarded men and women that Barnum brought from around the United States were transformed into "Wild Men of Borneo," "Wild Australian Children," "Aztec Children," and "The What Is It?" or "Man-Monkey." As an institution of popular education, the museum conveyed the message that ethnic others were "our" developmental precursors, adequately represented by the caricature-like "specimens" on display. The portrayal of human variety was expansive, but also inculcated in patrons a comforting sense that clear boundaries separated them from the ethnically alien.

Leaves of Grass evinces a similar strategy of affirmation and denial. The third poem of 1855 (later titled "To Think of Time") declares that "[t]he barbarians of Africa and Asia are not nothing," and neither are "the American aborigines," or "[a] zambo or a foreheadless Crowfoot or Camanche." The awkward and dismissive wording in this expression of willingness to ignore race in defining humanity holds the "included" groups clearly apart and subordinate. Acknowledged to count in the totality of humanity – but just barely – they are grouped with such others as "[t]he interminable hordes of the ignorant and wicked," lower-class Europeans, diseased immigrants, murderers, and prostitutes. These, too, are "not nothing" (Whitman 1855: 68). In the 1856 "Poem of Salutation" (later "Salut au Monde!"), the ethnic cataloguing is more extravagant, but similarly ambivalent. Those peoples considered most remote from White America are largely segregated into separate sections, most strikingly in a list near the end, where the poet addresses, among others, a "Hottentot with clicking palate," a "dwarf'd Kamtschatkan," a "haggard, uncouth, untutored Bedowee," and a "benighted roamer of Amazonia" (Whitman 1856: 119–20). Whitman's poems and popular museums shared an understanding of the value of ethnographic displays, which were used to promote knowledge of and curiosity toward the larger world in a way that upheld American assumptions of racial superiority.

Of course, the most frequently exhibited "savages" at Barnum's and other museums were American Indians. In Whitman's own portrayal of Indians, there is evidence that he not only shared with museums an established racial ideology, but that he also drew directly on their exhibitions, especially the traveling "Indian Gallery" (1837–39) of George Catlin, whom he remembered as "a wise, informed, vital character" (Traubel 1908: 354). During his tour of the Eastern United States, Catlin gave lectures and exhibited not only the paintings for which he is famous, but also Native American artifacts such as clothing, weapons, and an entire teepee. On some occasions he dressed as a Blackfoot medicine man in full regalia, and on others he presented members of Indian delegations. Beginning in 1843 the American Museum, too, put Indians on display. The precise nature of Whitman's acquaintance with Catlin is uncertain, but on the wall of his house in Camden hung a print of the artist's portrait of Osceola

(Traubel 1908: 348, 354), and he told Horace Traubel that his 1890 poem about the Seminole chief was "given almost word for word out of conversations [he had] had with Catlin" (Traubel 1982: 400). Martin Murray has argued that Whitman could not have met Catlin until the early 1870s (Murray 1999), and Whitman's own statements are contradictory. He said in 1888 that they had met when the painter was "already old" but "before the war, maybe as many as forty years ago" (Traubel 1908: 348, 354). All in all, however, it seems most likely that Whitman received the portrait during a visit to Catlin's show in the summer of 1839, not long after the prints were produced as promotional items. In any case, Whitman's American Indians often bear traces of having been drawn from a museum exhibit, whether Catlin's or another. A manuscript fragment apparently drafted for the unpublished pre-1855 poem "Pictures" reads:

> And here a tent and domestic utensils of the primitive Chippewa, the red-faced aborigines,
> See you, the tann'd buffalo hides, the wooden dish, the drinking vessels of horn [. . .]
>
> (*LG*: 649)

As Paul Reddin points out, "the 'domestic implements'" in Catlin's exhibit were unusual in "reveal[ing] a home life usually obscured" (Reddin 1999: 23). The initial poem of *Leaves of Grass* 1855 contains at least two references to Indian women. In the first, Whitman depicts the marriage of a "red girl" to a trapper (Whitman 1855: 18–19) – a section that others have shown to be based on the work of artist Jacob Miller. The other is a single line: "The squaw wrapt in her yellow-hemmed cloth is offering moccasins and beadbags for sale." The context in which this line appears is significant. In a structure that recalls the combination of chaos and order of Barnum's museum, Whitman presents a series of brief snapshots showing people engaged in sundry tasks. Images are piled up and juxtaposed as the reader moves through the poem, unable to predict what relation the next line will bear to the current one. Some consecutive lines seem wholly unrelated; some are clearly linked together logically and grammatically; others have an ambiguous connection. Intentionally or not, the line that follows the description of the woman selling handicrafts appears to reflect the extent to which Whitman's Indians were drawn from exhibits: "The connoisseur peers along the exhibition-gallery with halfshut eyes bent sideways . . . " (Whitman 1855: 22).

Images of the museum-made Indian persisted in Whitman's writing, even after his work in the Indian Bureau in 1865 gave him unusual opportunities for personal interaction. In his account of those months, "An Indian Bureau Reminiscence," Whitman employs a steady stream of language derived from museum exhibits, representing Indians as specimens, either of nature or of nature revealed through art. The first published version of the piece refers to meetings with Indian delegations as "exhibitions" (later revised to "conference collections"); the visitors themselves are "the most wonderful proofs of what Nature can produce," other "frailer samples" having been eliminated through evolutionary processes. "Every head and face is impressive, even artistic," and while the older men have a "unique picturesqueness," some of the younger ones are "magnificent and beautiful animals." From these meetings Whitman has formed "one very definite conviction." This turns out to be a version of the idea that we've already observed as characteristic of museum-style encounters with alien others: Indians, "in their highest characteristic representations, essential traits, and the ensemble of their physique and physiognomy," possess "something very remote, very lofty. . . . " The Indians, profoundly incommensurable, even if tantalizingly near, remain "great aboriginal specimens" (*PW*, 2: 577–80). Thus personal encounters, rather than modifying Whitman's simplistic notions of Indians, instead were themselves modified to fit the museum logic of his earlier poems.

Moving Panoramas

In another of his published reminiscences, Whitman writes of his "debt" to "the stage in New York [. . .] and to plays and operas generally" (*PW*, 2: 693–4). Decades of critics have demonstrated his indebtedness to opera and other forms of drama. However, considerable work remains to be done regarding Whitman's ties to stage entertainments, especially those now considered unsophisticated. At the beginning of Whitman's career, drama of all sorts, including opera, was tainted by associations with prostitution and other practices that disqualified them as rational entertainment, and as a journalist Whitman wrote several pieces calling for theater reform. He tended, however, to view the problems of the theater in patriotic rather than simplistic moral terms, calling for "some great revolution [. . .], modernizing and Americanizing the drama," that would allow it to attain "the first rank of intellectual entertainments" and become "one of those agents of refining public manners and doing good" (*Jour.*, 2: 251). Society at large did not share Whitman's perspective on the problem. Instead, as Richard Butsch explains, theaters were disreputable because "they endangered the reputation of a middle-class woman." Certain stage entertainments successfully overcame antitheatrical bias simply by avoiding theatrical terminology and appealing to a respectable female clientele, museums being "the first to systematically seek women, particularly mothers," to fill their "[t]heaters disguised as 'lecture rooms'" (Butsch 2000: 67, 71).

One of the prominent features of the American Museum was such a hall, in which Barnum presented entertainments free "of the dissipation, debaucheries, profanity, vulgarity, and other abominations" of regular theater (Toll 1976: 30). Performances in Barnum's "Moral Lecture Room" benefited from the respectability of lectures and museums. After renovating the hall in 1850 to accommodate 3,000 persons, Barnum told the audience that he had been motivated by a community need for a "place of public amusement, where we might take our children, and secure much rational enjoyment, as well as valuable instruction, without the risk of imbibing moral poisons . . . " (Barnum's Museum 1850). Not surprisingly, performances incorporated a variety of elements calculated to give the medicine of moral improvement an enticing flavor. For example, in "The Drunkard," which depicted the decline and redemption of the title character in a run of over 100 performances, no fewer than four of the museum's human curiosities appeared: a fat boy, two dwarfs, and a "nigger chap that is turning himself white" (*Brooklyn Daily Eagle Online*, Sept. 11, 1850). Performances of *Uncle Tom's Cabin* a few years later "featured a beautiful panoramic view of a Mississippi River sunrise and a riverboat that smoked grandly as it moved across the stage" (Toll 1976: 153).

This use of elaborate scenery and mechanical contrivances to produce startlingly realistic effects was by no means unique. In fact, various techniques formed the basis of several "panoramic" forms that were staged as rational entertainments in their own right. Any discussion of the nineteenth-century panorama must acknowledge the ambiguity of the term, which was widely adopted to denote two rather different commercial public entertainments. The first was a circular hall with interior walls painted to offer an accurate 360° scenic view to spectators standing on a central platform. It was for this 1789 invention that the word "panorama" was coined, from Greek words meaning "view all." Panorama was also the name given to a kind of enormous painting executed on sheets of canvas and scrolled from one large spool to another (see Plate 15. 2). Yet another related form, sometimes also called "panorama" but more generally known as "diorama," was distinguished by the use of various lighting effects to create the impression of movement or change. The situation is further complicated by the fact that both "true" panorama forms sometimes went by other names and by the existence of hybrid forms, such as the "moving diorama."

Recent critics have pointed out correspondences between nineteenth-century panoramas and Whitman's poetry, most often in terms of what might be called the

Plate 15.2 Engraving of Banvard's moving panorama from *Scientific American* Vol. 4, No. 13, 1848, p.100. Love Library at University of Nebraska-Lincoln.

"panoramic mode," a way of apprehending and representing the world as expansive that was manifested in a broad range of pictorial (and literary) forms (see Bergman 1985, Orvell 1989). These studies, by demonstrating that Whitman's own expansive mode paralleled the development in the visual arts of techniques to "view all," have begun to restore an important aspect of the social context in which Whitman's poetry emerged, but a number of clarifications are warranted and will perhaps foster further scholarship. One thing to note is that no definite proof exists of Whitman's ever having visited a panorama of any kind. The first that he might have seen were the circular variety, for which at least three exhibition rotundas were built in New York during the first four decades of the century. The last and most successful of these belonged to Frederick Catherwood, who opened it in 1838. Before it burned in 1842, Catherwood's Panorama displayed depictions of Jerusalem, Niagara Falls, Lima, Thebes, and Mayan ruins in Central America to enthusiastic crowds (Oettermann 1997: 320–3). By the late 1840s, however, "moving panoramas," first introduced in about 1830, had become the form clearly preferred in the United States.

Given their popularity and Whitman's love of crowds, stagecraft, and the visual arts – not to mention his thirst for the historical and geographical information that many of the panoramas touted – it is hard to believe that Whitman saw none of the scores of moving panoramas that New York hosted in the 1840s and 1850s. In fact, what appears to be a manuscript fragment from Whitman's review of a moving panorama from this period is preserved at Amherst College. In any case, the moving panorama's phenomenal success during the very years when *Leaves of Grass* was taking form affected the development of Whitman's masterpiece in profound ways. As Oettermann argues, panoramas (of whatever kind) "became a medium of instruction on how to see," their lessons specifically fitted to people's need to cope with the expanding horizons of the nineteenth century: the development of "'[p]anoramic' vision [was] a way of getting a grip on things . . . " (Oettermann 1997: 22). Moving panoramas had particular appeal for Americans, who were "dealing with dimensions in their own country that could not be grasped or conquered [through the simulated experience of] climbing to an elevated point and surveying the horizon." For them, "[t]he circular painting was visually inadequate to the situation in which they found themselves." In contrast, the method of the moving panorama, in which the painted canvases moved across the stage in front of the audience, could accommodate a subject of potentially limitless scope. The most celebrated moving panoramas illustrate a stunning exploitation of that advantage. Advertisements for Samuel Hudson's 1848 "Mammoth Panorama of the Ohio and Mississippi Rivers," for example, claim that it covered "over 20,000 feet of canvass," making it "by far the largest painting ever before executed." During its year-long tour, half a million people paid 25 cents each to watch the "over 1400 miles of River Scenery, bordering on nine different States," pass before them while a lecturer provided instructive commentary (*Brooklyn Daily Eagle Online*, June 15, 1848: 2, Oettermann 1997: 326).

Moving panoramas were especially well suited to depict long journeys, so it is not surprising that river scenery was the most common subject; at the peak of their popularity in the late 1840s and early 1850s, residents of large cities could sometimes choose among competing panoramas of the Mississippi. However, the format of the continuous, moveable canvas was also highly adaptable, and, contrary to the assumptions of some commentators, a number of moving panoramas were rendered and presented not as single continuous landscapes but as series of related scenes or as a combination of static and moving scenes. For example, "Evers' Grand Original, Gigantic Series of Moving Panoramas" – proclaimed, as usual, "the largest painting in the world" – comprised depictions of "New York city, city of Brooklyn, Williamsburgh, East River, Hudson River, and the Atlantic Ocean" (*Brooklyn Daily Eagle Online*, Nov. 19, 1849: 3). Moreover, to renew audiences' interest or to respond to the work of competitors, a panorama artist could add additional scenes. Like the world itself, panoramas were conceptually infinite. Another popular moving panorama depicted scenes from *Pilgrim's Progress*, advertisements declaring that "while it fascinates and charms with its loveliness, it instructs and teaches lessons never to be forgotten" (ibid., May 8, 1850: 2). Still other moving panoramas taught viewers about the life of Napoleon, famous battles, the New Testament, Mormon history, Mammoth Cave, a whaling voyage, and Indian history and archeology (Oettermann 1997: 314, 337–40, *Brooklyn Daily Eagle Online*, May 8, 1855: 2).

In *Specimen Days*, Whitman writes of his life in New York and Brooklyn during the period from about 1840 to 1860 as "curiously identified with Fulton ferry," which he rode frequently, "often" ascending to the pilot house to "get a full sweep, absorbing shows, accompaniments, surroundings." From there, he enjoyed sights of "great tides of humanity," "river and bay scenery," and "the changing panorama of steamers, all sizes . . . " (*PW*, 2: 16). Both Charles Zarobila and Eugene McNamara have commented on a striking three-way similarity among this passage, "Crossing Brooklyn Ferry," and panoramic entertainments. Zarobila, who found "a dozen or so instances" of the word "panorama" in all of Whitman's writings, sees the passage as evidence that the panorama gave the poet a way "to organize that famous poem which seeks to describe the unity of all men" (McNamara 1984, Zarobila 1979: 58). James Dougherty has also developed this idea, although he sees the circular panorama and the diorama as the pertinent models, and has argued that two of Whitman's other poetic mentions of "panorama" allude to the circular form as well. One of these is in the 1855 version of the poem that eventually became "Song of Myself":

> My words are words of a questioning, and to indicate reality:
> [. . .]
> The panorama of the sea. . . . but the sea itself?
> The well-taken photographs. . . . but your wife or friend close and solid in your arms?
> (Whitman 1855: 47)

As Dougherty perceptively notes, this passage treats the panorama as an "artifact" that "delivers us into the presence of the reality," one that, like the photograph, "open[s] a new path by making sight self-conscious" (Dougherty 1993: 165). The other passage in which Dougherty detects a reference to circular panoramas comes near the end of "When Lilacs Last in the Dooryard Bloom'd," where the poet records scenes of war that appear in "long panoramas of visions."

While much of the critical commentary on the importance of panoramic techniques to Whitman's poetry is provocative and compelling, insufficient emphasis has been placed on the moving panorama as a particular form. By the time *Leaves of Grass* debuted, the moving panorama had become so successful and dominant in America that the word "panorama" alone, without the modifier, would almost inevitably have brought to mind the image of a long, horizontally moving canvas. More to the point, as far as I've been able to determine, although Whitman frequently used the word in ways that unambiguously refer to the moving panorama, none of his uses can be certainly identified with either the circular panorama or the diorama. As Dougherty acknowledges, the passages Zarobila identified "suggest that most often Whitman was thinking of the moving panorama that unreeled before its viewers . . . " (Dougherty 1993: 165). Many of the over one dozen additional occurrences I've been able to locate are even more strongly suggestive, and several of them use the specific term "moving panorama."

Like the museum, the moving panorama was a richly suggestive analogue for Whitman's own poetic project, a device capable of teaching the American people to see the greatness of their country and themselves. One of the most successful panoramas was John Banvard's "Panorama of the Mississippi River, Painted on Three Miles of Canvas," first shown in 1846 and "promoted in Barnum-like fashion [. . .] as family entertainment," with special free showings for school groups (Oettermann 1997: 328, Hanners 1993: 45). In a statement reminiscent of Whitman's comment about the American bard, Banvard said that he had been motivated by the thought that "America has not the artists commensurate with the grandeur and extent of her scenery" (Hanners 1993: 38). Banvard claimed to have displayed his panorama for 400,000 persons in the United States (Oettermann 1997: 330), and despite the detractions of reviewers and modern critics (see, for example, Dougherty 1993: 166), a number of contemporary anecdotes suggest that for average audience members Banvard's and other river panoramas possessed a powerful verisimilitude (Hanners 1993: 44, Orvell 1989: 22, Oettermann 1997: 335).

Whitman must have been impressed, for he came to see much of the world – and more importantly his own work – in terms of a moving panorama. Because of the large number of moving panoramas devoted to water voyages, it is not surprising that the poet's own descriptions of river and ocean scenery often betray an indebtedness to the scrolling format. Two journalistic descriptions of New York's river and bay scenery during the mid-1840s make reference to moving panoramas, and similar images reappear in newspaper pieces and letters written between 1849 and 1880. Seen from the middle of the East River, a "moving panorama is upon all parts of the waters" (Whitman 1973: 350); on one trip up the Hudson, the poet remarks "the constantly changing but ever beautiful panorama on both sides of the river" (*PW*, 1: 167); on another trip the Hudson's "panorama [. . .] seems inimitable, increases in interest and variety" (*PW*, 1: 191). Likewise, Whitman developed the habit of describing another of his favorite subjects – crowds of people – as a river panorama. Very often after about 1862, panoramas and rivers and bustling crowds merge in an image that is at once chaotic and beautiful, thrilling and overwhelming. A prime example is the letter Whitman wrote to his friend Peter Doyle, detailing a scene much like the one he had witnessed 20 years earlier, while seated at a window in the American Museum. In a very long sentence with periodic syntax, Whitman breathlessly describes the "never-ending amusement & study & recreation" of riding a stage up and down Broadway. There, "[y]ou see everything as you pass, a sort of living, endless panorama" of storefronts, "crowds of women [. . .] continually passing [. . .] – in fact a perfect stream of people, men too dressed in high style, & plenty of foreigners," the street jammed with "carriages, stages, carts, hotel & private coaches, [. . .] mile after mile," impressive buildings, "& the gayety & motion on every side. . . . " Whitman concludes by reminding Doyle "how much attraction" such a sight must be to him, "who enjoys so much seeing the busy world move by him, & exhibiting itself for his amusement . . . " (*Corr.*, 2: 56–7).

The moving panorama also gave Whitman a way of thinking about and indicating his sense of the enormity of the Civil War. The passage from "When Lilacs Last in the Dooryard Bloom'd," noted above, recalls a letter Whitman wrote to his mother in 1865, in which he mentions a parade of Civil War soldiers, saying that "it was very grand – it was too much & too impressive, to be described. . . . " After a description even longer than the one of Broadway, he writes, "well, dear mother, that is a brief sketch, give you some idea of the great panorama of the Armies that have been passing . . . " (*Corr.*, 1: 260–1). But the importance of the panorama to Whitman's conception of the war is most vividly expressed in the Preface to the "Centennial Edition" of his works, published in 1876. In what is also his clearest allusion to the specific method of the moving panorama, he says that he has included "passing and rapid but actual glimpses of" the Civil War, "as the fierce and bloody panorama of that contest unroll'd itself. . . . " He adds that "the whole Book, indeed, revolves around that Four Years' War, which [. . .] becomes [. . .] pivotal to the rest entire . . . " (*PW*, 2: 469). A few years before, in the poem "To Thee Old Cause," he had characterized *Leaves of Grass* and its relation to the war in similar terms. Although the poem doesn't mention the moving panorama by name, its movement and magnitude are invoked. Whitman writes of "the strange sad war revolving" around the "old cause," which he defines elsewhere as "the progress and freedom of the race" (Whitman 1871: 12, 369). He continues,

> [. . .] my Book and the War are one,
> Merged in spirit I and mine – as the contest hinged on thee,
> As a wheel on its axis turns, this Book, unwitting to itself,
> Around the Idea of thee.
>
> (Whitman 1871: 12)

By the time these lines appeared, the moving panorama was no longer a lucrative commercial entertainment, but it had been deeply assimilated into Whitman's poetry as a fixed referent, a trope used to structure the most fundamental meanings of *Leaves of Grass* itself. In the moving panorama Whitman recognized a medium with the simultaneously encompassing and expansive qualities he desired for his poetry, a form that demonstrated the possibility of both providing a frame and transgressing it.

In fact, by the 1870s all of the commercial entertainments that I have discussed had undergone important changes. The American Museum had burned, reopened, and burned again; Barnum had begun applying his transformative entrepreneurial skills to the circus; moving panoramas had become passé. What's more, the very notion of "culture" had begun to shift. Whitman continued to believe in the ideas that he had found inspirational in Channing's sermon decades earlier – in culture as a comprehensive program of self-improvement for the masses – but he could no longer assume his readers shared his understanding. In *Democratic Vistas*, he remarks that "[t]he word of the modern [. . .] is the word Culture," which he now calls "the enemy" because of "what it has come to represent": superficial refinement. But he reaffirms his dedication to the principles it had traditionally expressed. He calls for a "programme of culture [. . .] not for a single class alone, or for the parlors or lecture-rooms, but with an eye to practical life . . . " and with "a scope generous enough to include the widest human area" (*PW*, 2: 395–6). A few years later, in "A Thought of Culture," he wrote that in America "there is one field, and the grandest of all, that is left open for our cultus [i.e., cultivation]": "to fashion on a free scale for the average masses [. . .] a splendid and perfect Personality," "specimens" of "masses of free men and women [. . .] in their physical, moral, mental, and emotional elements, and filling all the departments of farming and working life." As part of that cultivation, he advises a study of "the past and the foreign in the best books, relics, museums, pictures" – as well as firsthand experience closer to home (Whitman 1921, 2: 55).

Whitman also continued to present *Leaves of Grass* as his own contribution to the cause of self-culture. He told a visitor to his home in Camden in 1884, "I don't value the poetry in what I have written so much as the teaching; the poetry is only a horse for the other to ride" (Thayer 1919: 678). In a similar vein, his Centennial Edition introduction had declared that he "meant 'Leaves of Grass,' as publish'd, to be the Poem of average Identity," an illustration of the idea that "man is most acceptable in living well the practical life . . . " in which "he preserves his physique, ascends, developing, radiating himself in other regions [. . .]," and "fully realizes the conscience, the spiritual, the divine faculty, cultivated well . . . " (*PW*, 2: 470–1). Whitman had fashioned himself in these terms partly through recourse to the institutions of "rational amusement," and his work he fashioned as a projection of himself – both the result and the means of popular culture.

References and Further Reading

Barnum's Museum (1850). *New York Tribune*, June 19. Available at <http://chnm.gmu.edu/ lost-museum/lm/ 22/ >.

Bergman, H. (1985). Panoramas of New York, 1845–1860. *Prospects*, 10: 119–37.

Bogdan, R. (1988). *Freak Show: Presenting Human Oddities for Amusement and Profit*. Chicago: University of Chicago Press.

Brooklyn Daily Eagle Online (1841–1902). <http://www.brooklynpubliclibrary.org/eagle/>.

Butsch, R. (2000). *The Making of American Audiences: From Stage to Television, 1750–1990*. Cambridge, UK: Cambridge University Press.

Channing, W. E. ([1838] 1969). *Self-Culture*. New York: Arno.

Dennett, A. S. (1997). *Weird and Wonderful: The Dime Museum in America*. New York: New York University Press.

Dixon, J. G. (1981). Prussia, Politics, and Physical Education. In P. C. McIntosh, J. G. Dixon, A. D. Munrow, and R. F. Willetts. *Landmarks in the History of Physical Education*. London: Routledge, pp. 112–55.

Dougherty, J. (1993). *Walt Whitman and the Citizen's Eye*. Baton Rouge: Louisiana State University Press.

Fern, F. (1854). *Fern Leaves from Fanny's Port-Folio*, 2nd Series. Auburn and Buffalo, NY: Miller, Orton & Mulligan.

Fishwick, M. W. (1999). *Popular Culture: Cavespace to Cyberspace*. New York: Haworth.

Flint, R. W. (1979). The Evolution of the Circus in Nineteenth-century America. In M. Matlaw (ed.), *American Popular Entertainment: Papers and Proceedings of the Conference on the History of American Popular Entertainment*. Westport, CT: Greenwood, pp. 188–95.

Flint, R. W. (1983). The Circus in America: The World's Largest, Grandest, Best Amusement Institution. *The Quarterly Journal of the Library of Congress*, 40: 202–33.

Folsom, E. (1990). "Scattering it freely forever": Whitman in a Seminar on Nineteenth-century American Culture. In D. Kummings (ed.), *Approaches to Teaching Whitman's* Leaves of Grass. New York: Modern Language Association of America, pp. 139–45.

Folsom, E. (1994). *Walt Whitman's Native Representations*. Cambridge, UK: Cambridge University Press.

Folsom, Ed, and Price, Kenneth M. (1995–). *The Walt Whitman Archive*. <www.whitmanarchive.org>.

Gates, R. L. (1987). Egyptian Myth and Whitman's "Lilacs." *Walt Whitman Quarterly Review*, 5: 21–31.

Hanners, J. (1993). *"It Was Play or Starve": Acting in the Nineteenth-Century American Popular Theatre*. Bowling Green, OH: Bowling Green State University Popular Press.

Hudson, K. (1975). *A Social History of Museums: What the Visitors Saw*. London: Macmillan.

Kunhardt, P. B., Jr., Kunhardt, P. B., III, and Kunhardt, P. W. (1995). *P. T. Barnum: America's Greatest Showman*. New York: Knopf.

Levine, L. (1988). *Highbrow/Lowbrow: The Emergence of Cultural Hierarchy in America*. Cambridge, MA: Harvard University Press.

Lewis, R. M. (ed.) (2003). *From Traveling Show to Vaudeville: Theatrical Spectacle in America, 1830–1910*. Baltimore: Johns Hopkins University Press.

McNamara, E. (1984). "Crossing Brooklyn Ferry": The Shaping Imagination. *Walt Whitman Quarterly Review*, 2: 32–5.

Murray, M. (1999). The Poet-Chief Greets the Sioux. *Walt Whitman Quarterly Review*, 17: 25–37.

Oettermann, S. (1997). *The Panorama: History of a Mass Medium*, trans. D. L. Schneider. New York: Zone Books.

Orvell, M. (1989). *The Real Thing: Imitation and Authenticity in American Culture, 1880–1940*. Chapel Hill: University of North Carolina Press.

Peale, C. W. (1988). *Charles Willson Peale: The Artist as Museum Keeper, 1791–1810*, vol. 2 of *The Selected Papers of Charles Willson Peale and His Family*, ed. L. B. Miller, Sidney Hart, and David C. Ward. New Haven, CT: Yale University Press.

Peale, C. W. (1991). *The Bedfield Farm Years, 1810–1820*, vol. 3 of *The Selected Papers of Charles Willson Peale and His Family*, ed. L. B. Miller, Sidney Hart, and David C. Ward. New Haven, CT: Yale University Press.

Places of Public Amusement (1854). *Putnam's Monthly*, 3: 141–52.

Porter, C. M. (1999). The Natural History Museum. In M. S. Shapiro (ed.), *The Museum: A Reference Guide*. New York: Greenwood, pp. 1–30.

Price, K. M. (ed.) (1996). *Walt Whitman: The Contemporary Reviews*. New York: Cambridge University Press.

Reddin, P. (1999). *Wild West Shows*. Urbana, IL: University of Illinois Press.

Reynolds, D. S. (1988). *Beneath the American Renaissance: The Subversive Imagination in the Age of Emerson and Melville*. New York: Knopf.

Reynolds, D. S. (1995). *Walt Whitman's America: A Cultural Biography*. New York: Knopf.

Rice, E. A. (1929). *A Brief History of Physical Education*, revised and enlarged. New York: A. S. Barnes.

Saxon, A. H. (1989). *P. T. Barnum: The Legend and the Man*. New York: Columbia University Press.

Sellers, C. C. (1980). *Mr. Peale's Museum: Charles Willson Peale and the First Popular Museum of Natural Science and Art*. New York: Norton.

Stovall, F. (1974). *The Foreground of* Leaves of Grass. Charlottesville: University of Virginia Press.

Tapscott, S. J. (1978). Leaves of Myself: Whitman's Egypt in "Song of Myself." *American Literature*, 50: 49–73.

Teichgraeber, R. F., III. (1999). "Culture" in Industrializing America. *Intellectual History Newsletter*, 21: 11–23.

.Thayer, W. R. (1919). Personal Recollections of Walt Whitman. *Scribner's Magazine*, 65: 674–87.

Toll, R. C. (1976). *On with the Show!: The First Century of Show Business in America*. New York: Oxford University Press.

Traubel, Horace (1908). *With Walt Whitman in Camden*, vol. 2. New York: Appleton.

Traubel, Horace (1982). *With Walt Whitman in Camden*, vol. 6, ed. Gertrude Traubel and William White. Carbondale: University of Southern Illinois Press.

Wallace, I. (1967). *The Fabulous Showman: The Life and Times of P. T. Barnum*. New York: Knopf.

Washburn, W. E. (1990). Museum Exhibition. In M. S. Shapiro (ed.), *The Museum: A Reference Guide*. New York: Greenwood, pp. 199–230.

Whitman, Walt (1867). Democracy. *Galaxy*, 4: 919–33. Available at <http:/ / cdl.library.cornell.edu/cgi-bin/moa/sgml/moa-idx?notisid= ACB87 27-0004-118>.

Whitman, Walt (1921). *Uncollected Poetry and Prose*, ed. Emory Holloway, 2 vols. Garden City: Doubleday.

Whitman, Walt (1933). City Photographs. In *Walt Whitman and the Civil War: A Collection of Original Articles and Manuscripts*, ed. Charles I. Glicksberg. Philadelphia: University of Pennsylvania Press.

Whitman, Walt (1936). *New York Dissected, by Walt Whitman; A Sheaf of Recently Discovered Newspaper Articles by the Author of Leaves of* Grass, ed. Emory Holloway and Ralph Adimari. New York: R. R. Wilson.

Whitman, Walt (1973). Letters from a Travelling Bachelor. In J. J. Rubin, *The Historic Whitman*. University Park: Pennsylvania State University Press, pp. 311–54.

Williams, R. (1976). *Keywords: A Vocabulary of Culture and Society*. London: Croom Helm.

Zarobila, C. (1979). Walt Whitman and the Panorama. *Walt Whitman Review*, 25: 51–9.

16
Opera and Other Kinds of Music

Kathy Rugoff

Music is a central metaphor in the art of Walt Whitman. References to it abound in his poems, and sound plays a major role in their structures, from the sequence of words in a line to the development and recapitulation of image motifs. Equally important, Whitman's poetry, in many respects, approximates the characteristics of music and shares its appeal. His art resembles the response to the human condition in music and similar to it, his poetry may engage an audience emotionally, psychically, and spiritually.

In the Preface to the 1855 *Leaves of Grass* and in his poetry, Whitman passionately advocates a holistic approach to living, thinking, and writing: this perspective rejects conventional hierarchies pertaining to the mind/body dichotomy and to their multifold cultural expressions, the manifestations of Western intellectual tradition and Victorian societal mores. Whitman relates the mind/body unity to the soul. Rejecting a limited view of the relationship between sound and meaning in poetry, he proclaims in the Preface that "[t]he poetic quality is not marshalled in rhyme or uniformity or abstract addresses to things nor in melancholy complaints or good precepts, but is the life of these and much else and is in the soul. . . . All beauty comes from beautiful blood and a beautiful brain" (Whitman 1982: 11).

In "Song of Myself" (1855) and in other poems, including "Out of the Cradle Endlessly Rocking" (1859) and "When Lilacs Last in the Dooryard Bloom'd" (1865–6), images of music have a central organizational and thematic role. These poems treat such crucial areas as the genesis of Whitman – the poet – and the cosmic meaning of life and death. "Proud Music of the Storm" (1868) and "The Mystic Trumpeter" (1872) are rife with references to music and associate it with the ineffable and nature and with the great joys and sorrows in love and war. "That Music Always Round Me" (1860) unabashedly celebrates music and identifies it with profound emotion and "exquisite meanings" (Whitman 1982: 564). The significance of music in Whitman's aesthetic is further acknowledged by his admission in "The Mystic Trumpeter," "O trumpeter, methinks I am myself the instrument thou playest, /Thou melt'st my heart, my brain – thou movest, drawest, changest them at will" (Whitman 1982: 582). Finally, Whitman's poetry includes close to two hundred different musical terms (Faner 1951: 123–6).

The bonds between Whitman's poetry and music as both melody in his prosody and as a metaphor for his worldview have been recognized by musicians and composers. In the twentieth century, with the exception of passages from the Bible and possibly Shakespeare, no other poetry has received as much treatment by composers as has Whitman's. Over a thousand settings, representing a vast spectrum of musical styles, have been rendered by American and European composers.

The subject of Whitman and music has received considerable attention in the scholarship of literary studies and musicology. Several areas of discussion have emerged. They pertain to the relationship between the history of nineteenth-century American culture and Whitman's biography; they also pertain to Whitman's view of the mind and body, to the role of music in his poetry, and to the treatment of his poetry by American and European composers. Points of focus include the following: the expanded interest and performance of music from the early 1840s forward in New York; the opinions of Whitman regarding American music and opera expressed in his prose; the views on music held by nineteenth-century writers Whitman read; the role of music in the Civil War; the prosody and musical imagery in Whitman's poetry; and the treatment of his poetry by composers, whose work emerged in various cultural contexts apart from the poet's.

Whitman's move to Manhattan in May of 1841 and his return to nearby Brooklyn in 1845 gave him the opportunity to attend many musical performances. New York from this period forward provided venues for American and European performers of popular song, orchestral repertoire, and opera. For example, the Park Theatre, the Astor Place Opera House, the Castle Garden Theatre, the New York Academy of Music, Niblo's Garden Theatre, and the Olympic Theatre promoted opera performance in the 1840s and 1850s. Although Whitman was not knowledgeable about the technicalities of music, he was reputed to have a good ear and singing voice, and as people did in the nineteenth century, he often sang popular songs and melodies from operas to himself (Reynolds 1995: 186). He owned a guitar, piano, and a melodeon, a portable reed organ (Rubin 1973: 112, 280). Whitman's earliest interest was in the popular repertoire of American family singers, primarily, and minstrel groups, secondarily. He was particularly fond of Stephen Foster's songs. Whitman was a strong advocate for uniquely American musical expression; this preference is presented in articles published between 1843 and 1847 in the *Plebeian*, the *Star*, the *Brooklyn Daily Eagle*, the New York *Evening Post*, and elsewhere.

The Hutchinsons and the Cheneys, from New England, were family group singers, both of which were quartet ensembles of three brothers and a sister. The songs of the Hutchinsons were patriotic and many supported various causes, including the abolition of slavery, the rights of women, and the movement for temperance. The voices of the group meshed so well that individual parts were difficult to distinguish, but each voice was also featured in solos. David Reynolds contends that it is possible that

"Whitman's alternate singing of himself and of the masses throughout *Leaves of Grass* reflected this popular device" (Reynolds 1995: 184).

Whitman was interested in another popular mode of entertainment, the minstrel show. Its early form employed one entertainer but soon minstrel troupes, of whites (the Harmoneons and others) and a few black groups (the Georgia Minstrels and others) performed song, dance, and comedy routines in blackface. Although by twenty-first-century values any form of minstrelsy is a grotesque, perverted imitation of African Americans, Whitman praised some of the songs of the early groups, believing that the lyrics contributed to American musical expression. However, by the end of the 1850s, he felt the songs were far removed from Southern African-American sources and the antics of the groups were crude and indecent (Rubin 1973: 278–9).

Whitman's commitment to the music of the American nation was fierce. Although European family singers toured America, it was such American troupes as the Cheneys and the Hutchinsons that captured his imagination. In fact, at first, he celebrated American music and criticized music from Europe. For example, in the article "Music for the 'natural ear,' " which appeared in *The Brooklyn Daily Eagle* in April 1846, he mocks opera:

> After all – after hearing the trills, the agonized squalls . . . the painful leaps from the fearfullest eminences to a depth so profound that we for a while hardly expect the tongue to scramble up again – after sitting in the full blaze of the pit of the Italian opera . . . we turn . . . to that kind of music which seems intended for "the natural man" – (*Brooklyn Daily Eagle Online*, April 1846: 2)

Whitman terms this "heart-song" and concludes by praising American performers.

In an article published in the following December (a revision of an essay published in Poe's *Broadway Journal* in late November of 1845), he continues to argue for the legitimacy of American music:

> With all honor and glory to the land of the olive and the vine, fair-skied Italy . . . we humbly demand whether we have not run after their beauties long enough. For . . . hardly any thing which comes to us in the music and songs of the Old World, is strictly good and fitting to our nation. (*Brooklyn Daily Eagle Online*, December 1846: 2)

In addition, Whitman makes a distinction between the "heart" music of the American family groups and the "art" of the Europeans, and he maintains that "whatever touches the heart is better than what is merely addressed to the ear." He praises the simplicity and closeness to nature of American performers. "The sight of them" he writes, "puts one in mind of health and fresh air in the country, at sunrise – the dewy, earthy fragrance that comes up then in the moisture, and touches the nostrils more gratefully than all the perfumes of the most ingenious chemist." This anticipates the poet's celebration of the unadorned physical body in "Song of Myself" (1855), "I Sing the Body Electric" (1855), "Scented Herbage of My Breast" (1860), and elsewhere.

Without mentioning specific American or European performers, in an article published the following year, Whitman speaks more generally about the significance of American music, associating it with the core of American identity and the democratic values of its people. He writes: "The subtlest spirit of a nation is expressed through its music – and the music acts reciprocally upon the nation's very soul. – Its effects may not be seen in a day, or a year, and yet these effects are potent visibly. They enter into religious feelings . . . " (*Brooklyn Daily Eagle Online*, September 1847: 2). He continues that although laws and policies may reflect a particular government, "no human power can thoroughly suppress the spirit which lives in national lyrics, and sounds in the favorite melodies sung by high and low." For Whitman, music, a reflection of the spirit of democracy, is to be an expression of all peoples with no hierarchical distinction in so-called high art and low art or in the fine arts and folk arts. He claimed, in the crude terms of his era, that Southern African American pronunciation of vowels was well suited for the language of song (Faner 1951: 40). He also recommended the inclusion of banjos in orchestras to accompany vocalists (Reynolds 1995: 178).

Whitman's views, from this period, inform his vision of himself as a poet and his predisposition in poetics, addressed in the Preface to *Leaves of Grass* (1855). The essay is nothing less than a paean to the United States, to its peoples, lands, and cities and to its ideals of political liberty and social democracy. Whitman writes "[t]he United States themselves are essentially the greatest poem," the poet "incarnates its geography and natural life and rivers and lakes," and "a bard is to be commensurate with a people" (Whitman 1982: 5, 7).

Robert Faner in *Walt Whitman and Opera* (1951), a seminal book on the relations between Whitman's poetry and music, briefly discusses the impact of popular music on the poet as he argues it is overshadowed by the significance of Italian opera. In fact, this study suggests that Whitman's passion for opera was pivotal in his career, helping to determine the direction of his life's work. In detail, Faner discusses the musical climate of Whitman's day – including the venues of concert halls and theatres – and the poet's reviews, letters, and other works that address music. The second part of Faner's study presents parallels to opera in Whitman's poems' themes, prosodic phrasing, and organizational principles. Faner carefully considers the chronology of the transformation of Whitman's attitude regarding European opera and artists. A vital correlation exists in the transformation of the poet's initial criticism of opera to his passion for it and his emergence as the remarkable author of *Leaves of Grass*.

The significance of music to Whitman's development has been mentioned in most biographies since Faner's book and has been the subject of several dozen articles, a few of which preceded it. Two book-length studies devote considerable space to the music of the period, *The Historic Whitman* (1973) by Joseph Jay Rubin and *Walt Whitman's America: A Cultural Study* (1995) by David Reynolds. In a book he edited, *A Historical Guide to Walt Whitman* (2000), Reynolds comments on the transformation of Whitman as a writer in 1855 when the first edition of *Leaves of Grass* appeared: "The early 1850s witnessed his transformation from a derivative, conventional writer into a marvelously innovative poet. . . . The reasons for his poetic maturation, although impossible to pin down exactly, are nonetheless partly explainable if we explore the historical context" (Reynolds 2000: 25). From Robert Faner's perspective, Whitman's immersion in the growing opera world of New York, particularly in the early 1850s, is the most important part of that context.

Whitman's burgeoning interest in opera also has roots in the nineteenth-century construct of music as an ideal; this is evinced in texts reflecting both American and European Romantic and transcendental views. Two important voices, of this period, are those of Thomas Carlyle and Ralph Waldo Emerson. Reynolds maintains that they "provided precedent for Whitman's organic rhythms, aesthetic sensibility, and belief in the saving power of poetry" (Reynolds 1995: 317).

Whitman published a review of Carlyle's *Heroes and Hero Worship* in 1846 in the *Brooklyn Daily Eagle*. Although little is said of it, Carlyle's five lectures share many of Whitman's predilections as it celebrates the life force and describes the insights of visionaries, who are heroes, the guides for humanity. The section "The Hero as Poet" is a powerful affirmation of the vision of the poet and the all-encompassing importance of the poet's chant or song. Carlyle maintains that poetry is "*musical Thought*" and the "Poet is he who *thinks* in that manner." This relates to meter in poetry but also to nature. "See deep enough, and you see musically; the heart of Nature *being* everywhere music. . . . " Carlyle believes that the mind of the poet channeled through music corresponds to nature as "[a] *musical* thought is one spoken by a mind that has penetrated into the inmost heart of the thing." He continues: "[a]ll inmost things, we may say, are melodious; [and] naturally utter themselves in Song (Carlyle 1901: 94, 95). Carlyle identifies music with nature, with the metaphysics of the world, and with the manner of thinking of humanity. The poet's song is thereby a true simulacrum of nature.

This concept of musical thought is not far removed from Emerson's famous description, in the mid 1830s, of language and nature that opens the section "Language" of *Nature*. Emerson writes "[w]ords are signs of natural facts," "[p]articular natural facts are symbols of particular spiritual facts" and "[n]ature is a symbol of spirit" (Emerson 1981: 14). He makes reference to music in his essays and his poetry, but his statement in "The Poet" (1844), like Carlyle's depiction, places music at the heart of the poet's mentality: "For poetry was all written before time was, and whenever we are so finely organized that we can penetrate into that region where the air is music, we hear those primal warblings and attempt to write them down . . . " (Emerson 1981: 306).

While the concept is lofty, the reference to primal warblings is grounded, suggesting the actual sound of birdsong. The song of the bird, for Whitman, expresses nothing less than the meaning of life and death itself in "When Lilacs Last in the Dooryard Bloom'd," in "Out of the Cradle Endlessly Rocking," and elsewhere. "Song" in "Song of Myself" celebrates the voices of all peoples and the beauty of singers' voices, and as in Carlyle's discussion, it intimates the poet's knowledge of the self, the world of humanity, and the mysteries of the cosmos.

George Sand's novel *Conseulo*, translated into English in the early 1840s, reflects similar nineteenth-century romanticized views of music. Whitman was very much moved by the story of a beautiful female singer. The novel presents the unbounded beauty of the protagonist's voice and being. So affected by her singing, at one point her lover says that music "expresses all that the mind dreams and foresees of mystery and grandeur. . . . It is the revelation of the infinite" (quoted in Faner 1951: 47).

As early as the mid 1830s Whitman had been attending performances by European composers and by the mid 1840s he heard symphonic and choral music by Beethoven and Mozart and operas by composers such as Rossini, Bellini, and Donizetti (Rubin 1973: 112). In addition, Whitman responded to religious music. In the 1840s sacred music was performed by church choirs and given considerable further exposure through the New York Sacred Music society and, a few years later, through the New York Harmonic Society. Oratorios were performed with some frequency, including Mendelssohn's *St. Paul* and *Elijah*, Beethoven's *The Mount of Olives*, Handel's *The Messiah*, Rossini's *Stabat Mater*, and Haydn's *The Creation*. In the second half of the nineteenth century, organ builders were improving the tonal depth and richness of the pipe organ and considerable progress was made shortly after the Civil War. The organ as opposed to the piano captured the poet's imagination, and Whitman refers to its magnificent range to celebrate worldly and cosmic harmony in poems such as "I Heard you Solemn-Sweet Pipes of the Organ" (1861) and "Proud Music of the Storm" (1868).

The range and emotiveness of the operatic voice made an even greater impression on Whitman. He not only wrote about it in reviews, clustered in the 1850s, but also in his later writing. In the late 1840s Havana, the great Italian company, toured in New York. Famous singers of the 1840s and 1850s performed, including contraltos Marietta Alboni and Rosina Pico; sopranos Giulia Grisi, Balbina Steffanone, Henrietta Sontag, Jenny Lind, and Anna De La Grange; tenors Alessandro Bettini and Pasquale Brignole; and baritone Cesare Badiali. Operas by Bellini, Donizetti, Gounod, Meyerbeer, Mozart, Verdi, Rossini, and Weber among others were performed (Faner 1951: 14–15).

Between 1846 and 1847 Whitman's statements on opera begin to change. In February of 1847, he published an article praising Italian opera, but it is still within the context of its relationship to American music. He writes, "[m]ore as tending, by comparison and familiarity, to elevate the standard of music in this country – than as anything to bow down to, or servilely imitate – the *Italian opera* deserves a good deal of encouragement among us." Whitman's lavish praise for Rosina Pico, the Italian contralto, unveils his response to the operatic voice. He comments on her "rich and liquid style" and observes that some of her songs "were exquisite in quality and execution" (*Brooklyn Daily Eagle Online*, February 1847: 2). The impact of the operatic mode of song on the poet is also revealed in "Letter from Paumanok" which appeared in August 1851. Whitman confesses that the voice of the tenor Alessandro Bettini "has often affected me to tears." He continues,

> Its clear, firm, wonderfully exalting notes, filling and expanding away; dwelling like a poised lark up in heaven; have made my very soul tremble. . . . Never before did I realize

> what an indescribable volume of delight the recesses of the soul can bear from the sound of the honied perfection of the human voice. (Whitman 1921, 1: 257)

Whitman also argues that the value critics place on "perfectly artistical" in the voice rather than on what is vitally expressed is badly misguided.

Whitman's description of the tenor's voice also foreshadows the bird imagery in "Out of the Cradle Endlessly Rocking" (1859) and "When Lilacs Last in the Dooryard Bloom'd" (1865–6), although the imagery in the poetry is highly evocative whereas the reference to the lark is a stock image. The prose description, however, is vibrant and intimates the intensity of sexuality. This mystical overlapping of matters of the body and the spirit, of the voice and the soul, is also treated in one of Whitman's manuscript notebooks written sometime before 1855. In a somewhat disjointed meditation on the soul and critique of organized religion, music is the primary image for cosmic beauty and harmony, and the imagery is also highly sexually suggestive. At one point, Whitman writes,

> I want that tenor, large and fresh as the creation, the orbed parting of whose mouth shall lift over my head the sluices of all the delight yet discovered for our race. – I want the soprano that lithely overlaps the stars, and convulses me like the love-grips of her in whose arms I lay last night. – I want an infinite chorus and orchestrium, wide as the orbit of Uranus, true as the hours of the day, and filling my capacities to receive. . . . I want the chanted Hymn whose tremendous sentiment shall uncage in my breast . . . terrible ecstasies – putting me through the flights of all the passions . . . [and] lulling me drowsily . . . and awakening me again to know by that comparison, the most positive wonder in the world, and that's what we call life. (Whitman 1921, 2: 85)

Many of these phrases are altered slightly and are included in the last part of section 26 of the 1855 edition of "Song of Myself." Whitman writes,

> A tenor large and fresh as the creation fills me,
> The orbic flex of his mouth is pouring and filling me full.
> I hear the trained soprano. . . . she convulses me like the climax of my love-grip;
> The orchestra whirls me wider than Uranus flies,
> It wrenches unnamable ardors from my breast
>
> (Whitman 1982: 54)

The images in Whitman's notebook also anticipate "Proud Music of the Storm," published well over a decade later in 1868. Although some of its images are sexually charged, references to music are more concretely focused on the connections between the ineffable and the realm of humankind. The poet catalogues the musical sounds of nature, "Nature's rhythmus," and the music from various nations, "the tongues of nations." They are fused in his individual dream and in the great "celestial dream" of humanity (Whitman 1982: 525, 530).

Part of this dream is a duet between a bride and bridegroom, intimating the union between the earth and heaven. Whitman uses musical terms for the union and exclaims, "Tutti! / for earth and heaven" and speaks of the "earth's own diapason" (Whitman 1982: 526). "Diapason" is rich in meaning: it is several stops on the organ, it is the whole scale or all the notes, and it implies total harmony. Music, the central metaphor of "Proud Music of the Storm," is elaborated upon through the naming of composers, musical compositions, and singers. Marietta Alboni, the contralto, is identified as "Venus contralto, the blooming mother, /Sister of loftiest gods . . . " (p. 528). The music imagery is metaphoric and metonymic, and there is no division between tenor and vehicle in the poem.

The voice of Alboni made a strong and lasting impression on Whitman. She sang in New York in the 1852–53 season when opera was flourishing with a plethora of performances of several dozen operas. She starred in 12 concerts and 10 operas. The poet claimed he saw all her performances (*PW*, 1: 20). Thirty years later, Whitman wrote a note in his manuscript of *Specimen Days*: "I wonder if the lady will ever know that her singing, her method, gave the foundation, the start, thirty years ago, to all my poetic literary effort since?" (*PW*, 1: 235). Her remarkably expressive mode of singing resonated with him emotionally, and her tremendous popularity among New Yorkers from various walks of life appealed to his democratic vision (Reynolds 1995: 191).

Alboni was known for her bel canto (beautiful song) style of singing, which is typified by both high flute-like tones and low rich tones that require great vocal facility. It is characterized by "the flowing, simple line interrupted by vocal scroll-work that has an unearthly, almost orgasmic quality" (Reynolds 1995: 190). The moving quality of Alboni's voice combined with the contralto low pitch was anything but mundane tonally. The eerie low-pitched voice of a woman appealed to Whitman. The unusual tone and pitch suggested both the disembodied mystical soul and the sensual body.

In the 1860s Whitman became acquainted with a very different kind of music, music not of the opera divas or family quartets but of soldiers in battlefields. He visited his wounded brother in an army camp in Virginia in December of 1862 and for the next three years comforted and nursed soldiers in Washington war hospitals and in field hospitals in Virginia. In approximately six hundred visits to dozens of hospitals, Whitman saw thousands of soldiers (Reynolds 2000: 35). He wrote at length about the dead and suffering in a major section of *Specimen Days*, in other prose such as *Memoranda During the War*, and in poetry in *Drum-Taps* such as "The Wound Dresser" (1865) and "Vigil Strange I Kept on the Field One Night" (1865).

During the Civil War, music held an important place in the daily lives of the soldiers. Buglers sounded calls several times a day, martial music was used to rally troops, and funeral music accompanied the dead to their graves. Bands participated in parades, reviews, concerts, and various ceremonies for troops. Bands marched soldiers off to battle and performed while they fought. Musicians also performed in hospitals to raise the spirits of the wounded. When they were not playing, musicians had medical duties in field hospitals and assisted the surgeons in such tasks as amputations. There were hundreds of militia bands in the Union and Confederate armies.

Whitman was moved by the human tragedy of warfare and struck by the omnipresence of music, which inspired poems in his collection *Drum-Taps* published in 1865. John Picker maintains that Whitman "captures martial music's abilities both to rouse and to soothe, to energize and to calm, in the title of his text as well as individual poems . . . " (Picker 2000: 3). References to music are plentiful in the volume, and appear early in the collection in "First O Songs for a Prelude" (1865), which welcomes the inexorable course of the nation's war. It begins "First O songs for a prelude, /Lightly strike on the stretch'd tympanum pride and joy in my city" (Whitman 1982: 416). The image of the drum or membrane of the drum is concrete, picturing the actual drums used for battle, but it also emblematizes the psychological, sociological, and political commitment to the War in New York. The literal and spiritual call for war strikes the drum membrane and the ear membrane. Another reference to drums initiates a catalogue of various preparations for war.

"Eighteen Sixty-One" (1861) also treats the approach of war, and Whitman characterizes the spirit of manly resolve and bravery through images of music. Employing simile and personification, he writes "ARM'D year – year of the struggle, /No dainty rhymes or sentimental love verses for you terrible year, /Not you as some pale poetling seated at a desk lisping cadenzas piano, / But as a strong man erect . . . " (Whitman 1982: 418). The syntax is ambiguous. Piano may be a noun or adjective. In any event, the soft music or the music of the piano is mentioned to illuminate, through contrast, the vitality of the personified "masculine voice" of the year. Whitman closes the poem personifying the major weapon of war: "Year that suddenly sang by the mouths of the round-lipp'd cannon, /I repeat you, hurrying, crashing, sad, distracted year" (p. 419). The cannon graphically evokes the male voice of men at war.

"Beat! Beat! Drums!" (1861) is possibly the most widely known poem in *Drum-Taps* and is often read simply as a rallying cry for war, but it is thematically more complex. The strong sequence of one-syllable stressed words of the first line, "Beat! beat! drums! – blow! bugles! blow!," appears three times (Whitman 1982: 419–20). The words are onomatopoetic and are echoed through the poem through alliteration and assonance. However, there is some tension between the sound of the poem and its semantics. While the first line is reinforced through similar sounds and the military music advances, the poet does not describe soldiers preparing for battle or in battle; instead, the ferocity of the music of war is portrayed as omnipresent and omnipotent. With a kind of "ruthless force" it intrudes into "the solemn church," and upon "the bridegroom" and "the peaceful farmer." Whitman personifies war music and, using the imperative verb form, invokes it to "Mind not the timid /[. . .] nor the mother's entreaties" (pp. 419–20). However, the poet is simply describing the force of war rather than calling for the course of its potency and direction. "Beat! Beat! Drums!" concludes, "So strong you thump O terrible drums – so loud you bugles blow." War takes on a life of its own and overwhelms its creators. To describe its music creates a tension in syntax, sound, and semantics. Whitman suggests the language of music and the characteristics of war break the bounds of order in expository writing and daily living.

"Dirge for Two Veterans" (1865–6), however, is thematically straightforward. Of Whitman's body of work, it is one of few poems that is conventionally structured. It comprises nine four-line stanzas. Whitman abandons his typical long line, and although there is no consistent rhyme scheme or meter, lines one and four are shorter than lines two and three. Whitman wrote more than a dozen poems with "song" in the title, but this is one of the few that identifies a particular musical form. A dirge is a funeral song or hymn usually sung by a chorus without instrumental accompaniment. "Dirge for Two Veterans" is written in the first person singular, but is unadorned with relatively spare imagery. Ironically, as Whitman appears to be, on one level, imitating the musical form, the musical imagery is less compelling than elsewhere.

"To a Certain Civilian" (1865), written during the same year, is also relatively spare in imagery, but it is highly ambiguous. Music imagery functions as an extended metaphor that intimates Whitman's view of prosody, his view of war, and perhaps his perspective on sexuality. Paradoxically, the poem is addressed to a generic civilian yet a specific person, a "Certain Civilian," someone who is outside, not one of the brotherhood of soldiers. "Certain" may also mean someone who has no doubt. A chasm divides the speaker and addressee in their predilections relating to poetics and music, and in their experience or lack of experience in war. The poem begins, "Did you ask dulcet rhymes from me? /Did you seek the civilian's peaceful and languishing rhymes? / Did you find what I sang erewhile so hard to follow?" (Whitman 1982: 455). The speaker identifies with the passion of warfare and the sorrow of death in emblems of music: "(I have been born of the same as the war was born, /The drum-corps' rattle is ever to me sweet music, I love well the martial dirge [. . .])." The speaker urges his addressee to no longer read his poetry, concluding, "And go lull yourself with what you can understand, and with piano-tunes, /For I lull nobody, and you will never understand me." Whitman's vision extends far beyond the range of the domesticated parlor piano. The void between poet and the civilian is great. "Understand" is neither clarified nor qualified, so that it may apply to the poet's writing and his perspective on the world after being among the dying and wounded. This is something the civilian has not experienced and includes the poet's empathy and other feelings for these men.

"When Lilacs Last in the Dooryard Bloom'd" (1865–6), Whitman's great elegy for Lincoln and for the soldiers lost, is a meditation on death and the renewal of life. Its consolation is not one of heavenly salvation but of the poet's knowledge of death as a "deliveress" and of the ongoing cycle of life and death. This is conveyed through the intermeshing, in various combinations, of three image motifs: the lilac, star, and thrush. The poem begins in the voice of the poet, shifts to italics to the song of the bird, and returns to the poet's voice.

Calvin Brown argued, over half a century ago, that the presentation of the motifs and their variation and recapitulation is related to the sonata form (Brown 1948: 193). About 10 years later, Sydney Krause stressed the differences between language as a medium and music as a medium to argue, instead, that "the influence of music on

Whitman's poetry is actually more potential than real, more fluid and emotional than definite and formal..." (Krause 1957: 707). Forty years later, William F. Mayhan maintained that Whitman's perspective on "music as a kind of universal language of ultimate reality and deepest subjectivity becomes a force behind the meaning of the poems as well as behind their structure" (Mayhan 1996: 115). While any discussion of the relation among the arts raises thorny issues as it relies on imprecise analogies, Whitman's concept of music informed his view of poetry, and the song of the bird in "When Lilacs Last in the Dooryard Bloom'd" is presented as the source of the poet's insight.

"Out of the Cradle Endlessly Rocking" (1859) also presents Whitman's earlier but similar reflection upon his knowledge as a poet. A poet is a translator articulating, putting into words, intimations on love and death. Through sequences of synesthetic images of the ocean, the moon, and a song bird, Whitman suggests that inchoate glimmerings of the experience of love and death are at the core of his poetry. Again, two voices constitute the poem, one of the poet, who is recollecting an experience and another of a song bird, who has lost its mate. The poet looks back on a childhood experience in which he encountered love and death. Upon hearing the song bird's mournful carol over the loss of his mate, Whitman writes:

> Now in a moment I know what I am for, I awake,
> And already a thousand singers, a thousand songs, clearer, louder and more sorrowful than yours,
> A thousand warbling echoes have started to life within me, never to die.
> O you singer solitary, singing by yourself, projecting me
>
> (Whitman 1982: 392–3)

This important passage, which describes the nascent poet, is filled with references to song and singer; elsewhere the bird's song is referred to as an aria.

Through a discussion of the line phrasing and organization of this poem, Faner agues that it, like "When Lilacs Last in the Dooryard Bloom'd," follows a "recitative-aria structure..." (Faner 1951: 174). He claims that the carols of the bird – one a song of love and the other a song of mourning – are arias which are highlighted, through contrast, by recitatives (song intimating the phrasing of speech), passages spoken in the poet's voice. In addition, the symbolism is also significant in that in "Out of the Cradle Endlessly Rocking," the poet defers to the song bird's authority, its musical language.

Finally, decades later, in "The Dead Tenor" (1884), a tribute to Pasquale Brignoli, the musical language of the human voice is celebrated as a form of revelation. Whitman writes, "The perfect singing voice – deepest of all to me the lesson – trial and test of all" (Whitman 1982: 625). Thus the bond between the melodic voice and various forms of knowledge is strong throughout every period of Whitman's poetry. His images of music suggest not only the metaphysical correspondences of the transcendental writers of his era but many other correspondences.

Whitman's appeal to composers, perhaps then, is no surprise. But the number of composers and the extent of their admiration for Whitman are striking. They respond to any one or combination of various characteristics of his poetry: its mystic vision; its democratic spirit; its humanity; its homosexuality; and its passion for song – its sound, and references to performers, composers, and instruments. A poem chosen and its particular musical interpretation by a composer are the result of and revelation of not only the individual predilections of a musician but also of the social, political, and aesthetic climate of the culture out of which the composition emerged. The appeal of Whitman's prosody is a complicated subject. Whereas conventional poetry in regular metered and rhymed quatrains, for example, might lend itself or be easily translatable into various musical formulae, Whitman's long line is less rigid and thereby for some composers, evocative and fertile ground for their own rhythmic and tonal perceptions of a poem.

Ned Rorem, the pre-eminent contemporary American composer of art song (typically a setting of a poem for one voice and piano), covers much ground when he said that Whitman's work "spoke to my condition" (Rorem 1992: 214). In addition Whitman's poetics and prosody speak to his aesthetic. Rorem maintains that Whitman's style is a kind of "lack of style: an unprecedented freedom that, with its built-in void of formal versified variety, offers unlimited potential for musical variety." He continues, "Whitman is content. A poet's content is a musician's form; any other way a song is merely redundant. . . . " Rorem's views are borne out in that Whitman's poetry is the basis for his art songs and larger compositions, which include the following: *Five Songs to Poems by Walt Whitman* (1957) for voice and piano; *War Scenes* (1969), a setting of texts from *Specimen Days* for baritone and piano, written in response to the Vietnam War; and the large-scale works, *The Whitman Cantata* (1983) and *Goodbye My Fancy* (1988).

Since over a thousand musical compositions, representing a vast array of techniques and styles, respond to Whitman's words, something about his content and open form captivates composers. Some of the compositions are orchestral or instrumental interpretations, but most of them are the transformation of the poetry into song. Composers differ considerably in their faithfulness to the text. Word by word renditions are fairly common but many composers take varying degrees of liberty with the text; some repeat words or phrases and in a few cases, others render only portions of a poem or selected passages from several poems in combination with others.

Several settings of his poems were written during his lifetime such as American composer Frederic Louis Ritter's "Dirge for Two Veterans" for piano and recitation (1880). Another early composition is Irish composer Charles Villiers Stanford's treatment of "When Lilacs Last in the Dooryard Bloom'd" in his *Elegiac Ode* (1884). For the most part, at the beginning of the twentieth century, Whitman's poetry captured the imagination of British composers and from the middle of the century onward, that of Americans. German composers such as Karl Amadeus Hartmann and Hans-Werner Henze were drawn to Whitman's work as were the expatriates, Paul Hindemith and Kurt Weill.

Major and minor British composers were inspired by his poetry. "On a fundamental level," argues Jack Sullivan, "Whitman represented to the British . . . liberation from inhibition and convention. British composers," he continues, "were similar to British writers, who were entranced with the wildness and originality of nineteenth-century American literature" (Sullivan 1999: 99). Frederick Delius cherished Whitman's *Leaves of Grass* and was struck by the poet's celebration of the art of all peoples and his reverence for nature. Delius composed *Sea Drift*, a setting of part of "Out of the Cradle Endlessly Rocking" for orchestra, baritone, and chorus in 1903. Musically, through the lack of tonal closure, the composition suggests Whitman's cyclical view of life and death. About 30 years later, Delius wrote two other pieces based on Whitman's poetry and took considerable liberties with the texts. *Idyll* (1932), a song cycle drawing from passages of various poems, is scored for baritone, soprano, and orchestra. *Songs of Farewell* (1929–30) is written for double chorus and orchestra and incorporates several poems, lines from "Passage to India," and selected lines from other poems.

Another well-known British composer, Ralph Vaughan Williams, was also attracted to both the mysticism and the spirit of democracy in Whitman's poetry, and he carried a pocket edition of *Leaves of Grass*. Through much of his career, Vaughan Williams wrote compositions based on the poetry. They include *Toward the Unknown Region* (1907) for chorus and orchestra, which treats "Darest Thou Now, O Soul," and *A Sea Symphony* (1910), which is based on "A Song for All Seas, All, Ships," "On the Beach at Night Alone," and selections from *Passage to India* and "Song of the Exposition". This large-scale four-movement piece, for soprano, baritone, and orchestra, incorporates very slow passages of contemplation and rapid passages of exhilaration. Vaughan Williams also composed "Dirge for Two Veterans" in 1908, which was later incorporated into his 1936 cantata *Dona Nobis Pacem*. His *Three Poems by Walt Whitman* (1925) is based on "Whispers of Heavenly Death" and passages from "From Noon to Starry Night" and "Songs of Parting". *Dona Nobis Pacem* is scored for soprano, baritone, chorus, and orchestra; this setting of Whitman's "Beat! Beat! Drums!," "Reconciliation," and "Dirge for Two Veterans" also includes material from the Bible and from a speech denouncing the Crimean War by John Bright, a Quaker Member of Parliament.

Gustav Holst was inspired by Whitman's vatic voice and references to Eastern thought. In 1904 he published a setting of "The Mystic Trumpeter" for soprano and orchestra; in 1914, "Dirge for Two Veterans" for male chorus, brass, and percussion; and in 1919, "Ode to Death," a setting of a portion of "When Lilacs Last in the Dooryard Bloom'd" for chorus and orchestra. It is an innovative composition that mourns the death of those lost in World War I. Among other British composers, Samuel Coleridge-Taylor, Frank Bridge, Arthur Bliss, and Oliver Knussen wrote settings of Whitman's poetry.

The American composers Paul Hindemith, Kurt Weill, and Lukas Foss (émigrés from Germany), Charles Ives, Roger Sessions, Virgil Thompson, Paul Creston, Elliott Carter, Charles Naginski, David Diamond, Vincent Persichetti, Robert Strassburg, Lou Harrison, Leonard Bernstein, George Walker, George Crumb, William Bolcom, Philip Glass, and Michael Tilson Thomas, among others, wrote music based on

Whitman's poetry. Despite Whitman's passion for opera, his work has inspired few operas, perhaps because most opera librettos are plot-driven. Robert Strassburg, however, wrote the opera *Congo Square*, performed in 1998, which treats the young Whitman in New Orleans. Strassburg also composed *Leaves of Grass: A Choral Symphony* (1992) and other settings.

Paul Hindemith and Roger Sessions wrote settings for "When Lilacs Last in the Dooryard Bloom'd" for soloists, chorus, and orchestra. Both composers chose the Whitman text to commemorate the deaths of national figures for whom they had immense respect. Not long after his arrival in the United States, Paul Hindemith composed, in 1946, *When Lilacs Last in the Dooryard Bloom'd: "A Requiem For Those We Love."* He thought of it as an elegy for Roosevelt and for those lost in World War II. As a young man he had written several art songs based on Whitman texts. Roger Sessions' *When Lilacs Last in the Dooryard Bloom'd*, subtitled *Cantata for Soprano, Contralto, Baritone, Mixed Chorus and Orchestra*, which premiered in 1971, is dedicated "to the memory of Martin Luther King Jr. and to Robert Kennedy"; both were assassinated during the period of the cantata's composition. Whitman's poem yet again captured the imagination of a composer more than two decades later. George Walker's *Lilacs*, for voice and orchestra, received the Pulitzer Prize in 1996. He is the first African American composer to receive this recognition.

Whitman's disdain for hierarchy and political power and praise for all Americans inspired Kurt Weill, a Jewish refugee from Germany. After the Japanese attack on Pearl Harbor, he composed settings for poems, including "Dirge for Two Veterans," "O Captain! My Captain!," and "Come Up from the Fields." Weill's merging of classical with more popular musical forms parallels Whitman's breaking down of the divisions between high and low art. Weill scholar Kim Kowalke observes that "[l]ike virtually every one of his works for the stage, the *Whitman Songs* are hybrids, negotiating ill-defined boundaries between "serious" and "popular," "high" and "low," "cultivated" and "vernacular..." (Kowalke: 2000: 119).

Whitman's legacy in music endures into the late twentieth century and into the next one. John Adams, born shortly after World War II, is a Minimalist composer with interests in popular music such as jazz and rock, in addition to what is termed serious music. His response to Whitman's empathy for the wounded and dying is evident in *The Wound Dresser* (1989) for baritone and chamber orchestra. Gerd Kühr, born in Austria in 1952, composed *Walt Whitman for President* for soprano, flute, clarinet, guitar, viola, cello, piano, and percussion, in 1984. Lowell Liebermann, a notable American composer born in 1961, composed settings of "On the Beach at Night" for voice and piano and "Out of the Cradle Endlessly Rocking" for voice and string quartet. In addition, his second symphony includes choral settings of Whitman's poetry. Finally, American jazz pianist Fred Hersch treats Whitman's poetry in his composition *Leaves of Grass* for two voices and an instrumental octet. The piece, which premiered in 2003, incorporates elements of classical chamber music, jazz, and blues. Along with other dimensions of Whitman's poetry, Hersch, like several other composers and performers, is engaged by its sexuality.

The composers mentioned here and others respond to one or more of the multifold dimensions of Whitman's poetry. Its structural fluidity and its assertion of the mind/body unity present many avenues for interpretation and expression. The poet's celebration of knowing the world through the body and the heart as much as the mind is seductive to musicians whose art can be emotionally evocative and physically felt as it makes the foot tap or breath quicken. The experience of reading Whitman's poetry or listening to evocative music calls attention to the rhythms of the body and to the dream-like visions of the mind.

References and Further Reading

Brasher, Thomas L. (1970). *Whitman as Editor of the Brooklyn Daily Eagle.* Detroit: Wayne State University Press.

Brooklyn Daily Eagle Online (1841–1902). <http://www.brooklynpubliclibrary.org/ eagle/>.

Brown, Calvin S. (1948). *Music and Literature: A Comparison of the Arts.* Athens: University of Georgia Press.

Carlyle, Thomas (1901). *On Heroes, Hero-Worship, and the Heroic in History*, ed. Archibald MacMechan. Boston: Ginn.

Emerson, Ralph Waldo (1981). *Selected Writings of Emerson*, ed. Donald McQuade. New York: Modern Library.

Faner, Robert D. (1951). *Walt Whitman and Opera.* Carbondale: Southern Illinois University Press.

Hampson, Thomas (1997). *To the Soul: Thomas Hampson Sings the Poetry of Walt Whitman.* EMI Classics 55028-CD.

Hovland, Michael A. (1986). *Musical Settings of American Poetry: A Bibliography.* Westport, CT: Greenwood Press.

Loving, Jerome (1999). *Walt Whitman: The Song of Himself.* Berkeley: University of California Press.

Kowalke, Kim (2000). "I'm an American!" Whitman, Weill, and Cultural Identity. In Lawrence Kramer (ed.), *Walt Whitman and Modern Music: War, Desire, and the Trials of Nationhood.* New York: Garland, pp. 109–132.

Kramer, Lawrence (ed.) (2000). *Walt Whitman and Modern Music: War, Desire, and the Trials of Nationhood.* New York: Garland.

Krause, Sydney J. (1957). Whitman, Music, and "Proud Music of the Storm." *PMLA*, 72 (4): 705–21.

Mayhan, William F. (1996). The Idea of Music in "Out of the Cradle Endlessly Rocking." *Walt Whitman Quarterly Review*, 13 (3): 113–28.

Picker, John M. (2000). "Red War Is My Song": Whitman, Higginson, and Civil War Music. In Lawrence Kramer (ed.), *Walt Whitman and Modern Music: War, Desire, and the Trials of Nationhood.* New York: Garland, pp. 1–24.

Reynolds, David S. (ed.) (2000). *A Historical Guide to Walt Whitman.* New York: Oxford University Press.

Reynolds, David S. (1995). *Walt Whitman's America: A Cultural Biography.* New York: Knopf.

Rorem, Ned (1992). A Postscript on Whitman. In Robert K. Martin (ed.), *The Continuing Presence of Walt Whitman: The Life After the Life.* Iowa City: University of Iowa Press, pp. 213–15.

Rugoff, Kathy (2000). Three American Requiems: Contemplating "When Lilacs Last in the Dooryard Bloom'd." In Lawrence Kramer (ed.), *Walt Whitman and Modern Music: War, Desire, and the Trials of Nationhood.* New York: Garland, pp. 133–50.

Rubin, Joseph Jay (1973). *The Historic Whitman.* University Park: Pennsylvania State University Press.

Sullivan, Jack (1999). *New World Symphonies: How American Culture Changed European Music.* New Haven, CT: Yale University Press.

Whitman, Walt (1921). *Uncollected Poetry and Prose*, ed. Emory Holloway, 2 vols. Garden City: Doubleday.

Whitman, Walt (1982). *Complete Poetry and Collected Prose.* New York: Library of America.

17
Nineteenth-century Visual Culture

Ed Folsom

Walt Whitman grew up in a vastly different visual culture than the one we experience today. There is immeasurably more visual representation in today's world than in the first half of the nineteenth century: we now live in a world saturated with visual images – on television sets, on billboards, in newspapers, magazines, and books, on computer screens, in movie theaters. Many people in this culture spend more time looking at visual representations of people, events, and places than looking directly at the people, events, and places themselves, and recent virtual-reality technologies are dedicated to erasing the experiential line between mediated and direct visual encounters, holding out the unnerving possibility of living in an entirely represented world. In virtual reality, the visual field does not so much *represent* as *become* experience.

Whitman lived at the time that the first stirrings of this visual revolution were taking place. As he was approaching adulthood, visual representation was basically limited to painting, engraving, drawing, and sculpture. In order to recreate the world in a visual image, artists had to learn one or more of these techniques, and people could acquire permanent visual representations of other people, places, and events only through these means. Paintings could not be reproduced, though the wealthy would sometimes pay artists to paint copies of famous works for their own private pleasure; for most Americans, however, the viewing of a painting was a special one-time event, and it was common for painters to take their paintings on tour, displaying them from town to town, where people would pay to look at the traveling visual representation of famous people or exotic locales or historic events. Whitman on several occasions recalled sitting for hours in front of single paintings, taking in the visual experience, contemplating the visual field, absorbing. The technological advances in reproducing lithographs in mid-nineteenth-century America, notably those of the firm of Currier and Ives, provided cheap wall art for the masses, though these illustrations were seldom done by established artists and tended to be generic and often nostalgic images of American life.

When Whitman was around 20 years old, however, a shocking new technological development took place, one that would forever transform visual culture. What we now call photography got its start in 1839 in France, where Louis Daguerre, a stage designer and master of visual illusion, displayed images that he had taken with a lens and, through a trick of chemistry, preserved on a plate – visual images that were more detailed and "real" than any painting or piece of sculpture could be. They were the beginnings of "virtual reality" – images that appeared so real that they struck many viewers as magic, and many early commentators called them "sun paintings" or "miraculous mirrors," because suddenly the sun itself seemed to be the artist, preserving an actual visual experience, as if a fleeting glance in the mirror could be captured and kept forever. Since the sixteenth century, artists had used camera obscuras as an aid to their drawing and painting, but these devices used a lens only to project an image onto a wall or screen; there was no way to preserve the image except to trace it with a pen or pencil. Camera obscuras were a tool to aid painters in their attempts to represent the world accurately, but they were not a tool of actual representation. Daguerre's process, however, allowed the projected images to be preserved in all of their remarkable detail.

These new images were called daguerreotypes, and when the technology came to the United States in 1840, it took hold as in no other nation. Daguerreotype studios, many of them exhibiting large numbers of the new magic mirrors, quickly cropped up in most American cities and towns. Whitman in the 1840s visited John Plumbe's gallery and captured the haunting sense of actual presence that these new representations created in the viewer: he was entranced by what he called the "strange fascination of looking at the eyes of a portrait," a fascination so intense, he said, that it "sometimes goes beyond what comes from the real orbs themselves." Here was representation almost more real than reality itself. Wandering through Plumbe's gallery in 1846, struck by the "great legion of human faces – human eyes gazing silently but fixedly upon you," he mused: "We love to dwell long upon them – to infer many things, from the text they preach – to pursue the current of thoughts running riot about them" (*Jour.*, 1: 448–50). Whitman immediately saw that this new representational technology was a kind of perfection of visual art: he wrote that it was "hardly possible to conceive any higher perfection of art, in the way of transferring the representation of that subtle thing, *human expression*, to the tenacious grip of a picture which is never to fade!" (quoted in Brasher 1970: 215).

So, as Whitman began his adult writing career, his development as a writer coincided with the development of photography, and over his lifetime photographic ways of seeing the world transformed the notion of and the possibilities for visual representation: much of his poetry is what he "infers" from the stunningly realistic "texts" photographs "preached." Almost every year during Whitman's adult life, new discoveries and developments in photographic processes kept accelerating the revolution in visual representation. Daguerreotypes were actual glass plates and so were not duplicable, but within a few years processes were invented that allowed photographs to be printed from negatives on paper in endless copies; the process also became cheaper, making photographic representation widely accessible. By the end of Whitman's life, photographs could be printed on pages in books and magazines, and the first small portable cameras were taking photography out of professional hands and allowing anyone to take photos. The second half of the nineteenth century was a period of endlessly proliferating visual representation, and by the end of the century Americans' visual fields were vastly expanded from what they had been only a few decades before; now people could *see*, in photographic detail, places and faces and events that they had never actually experienced or encountered directly. Humans now experienced the world as an endless series of visual representations that surrounded them, as never before, in pervasive ways.

Some of those newly experienced visual representations, oddly, were the viewers' own younger faces. By the time he died in 1892, Whitman had accumulated well over a hundred photographs of himself, taken from the time he was in his twenties up until just months before his death, and in his final years he loved to leaf through that array of images and think about the changes they recorded. He was, after all, of the first generation of human beings to be able to look back on their lives in a series of photographs, to track their own aging in detail, to see how they looked 50 years earlier. Whitman joked about the strangeness he felt when he would come upon photos of himself he had forgotten had been taken: "I meet new Walt Whitmans every day. There are a dozen of me afloat. I don't know which Walt Whitman I am" (Traubel 1906: 108). The multiplicity of photos sometimes created for him a bewildering fragmentation of self: "It is hard to extract a man's real self – any man – from such a chaotic mass – from such historic debris" (Traubel 1906: 108). He examined each photo of himself for the way it captured a unique individual – a Walt Whitman in a particular place and time – but he also looked at them all as a kind of montage or flow, seeking the ways the single images added up to a totality, how the "elements" formed a "compound": "I guess they all hint at the man" (Traubel 1982: 395, 1908: 156). Most of the photos, he believed, were "one of many, only – not many in one," each picture an image that was "useful in totaling a man but not a total in itself" (Traubel 1914: 72). He was unsure whether the photos finally demonstrated that life was "evolutional or episodical," a unified sweep of a single identity or a jarring series of new identities: "Taking them in their periods is there a visible bridge from one to the other or is there a break?" (Traubel 1963: 425).

Seeing his life photographically, then, underscored for Whitman many of his key poetic concerns. It sharpened his sense of the relationship between the self and society (the "simple separate person" and the "En-Masse," *LG*: 1), intensified by the growing perception that any one self was in fact many selves, that our identity is always multiple. Photographs taken over a lifetime verified the ceaseless evolution and composting of identity as it keeps merging into and emerging from a float of continual change. Photography suggested for him the possibility of a poetry that could open itself to the world the way a photographic plate opened itself to everything and anything that stood in its visual field, and it taught him the power of nondiscrimination. In some essential way, the revolution in visual culture that Whitman experienced during his lifetime furnished him with the very tools for thinking about the function and purpose of his poetry:

> As in every show & every concrete object & every experience of life the serious question is, What does it stamp – what will it leave daguerreotyped for the future for weal or woe – upon the mind? These physical realities, we call the world are doubtless only essentially real in the impressions they leave & perpetuate upon the rational mind – the immortal soul. (*NUPM*, 6: 2214)

It is useful to think of Whitman's poetry in the terms of photography, because Whitman associated photography and poetry as key elements of an emerging democratic art, an art that would level experience, break down hierarchies, undermine discrimination, and foster equality. What he loved about photographs was their quality of nondiscrimination; whatever presented itself in the scope of the lens was *re*presented in the photograph itself. In photography, Whitman believed, no mediating consciousness stands between the fullness of the visual field and the representation of that field, unlike in oil paintings where the artist is always selecting what to include and what to exclude: "I find I like the photographs better than the oils – they are perhaps mechanical, but they are honest. The artists add and deduct: the artists fool with nature – reform it, revise it, to make it fit their preconceived notion of what it should be" (Traubel 1906: 131). Photographs, on the other hand, allow all the details to remain and present us with a cluttered and full image of the world, with nothing deducted.

Photography was therefore for Whitman the perfect tool of democratic art. If Americans widened their acceptance, stopped discriminating, they would find themselves more at home in a cluttered world, where everything demands recognition, where nothing can be left out. While others complained that photography was a flawed representational art because it was indiscriminate and included everything that appeared in a visual field, producing a cluttered image, Whitman embraced it for exactly that quality: beauty would no longer be defined as that which was selected out and placed above, but rather as that which included all. Whitman once said the real power of photography was that "it lets nature have its way" (unlike painters, who "want to make nature let them have their way") (Traubel 1953: 125). *Fullness of diversity* became Whitman's idea of democratic beauty, and the photograph, with its sensitive plate that absorbed the impression of every detail that formed a scene, became the model for Whitman's absorptive lines, his flowing catalogues that sought to accumulate details toward a diverse unity, excluding nothing, gathering up a grand democratic clutter. Photographs were originally known as "sun-paintings" because the sun as a painter did not discriminate and choose what it would illuminate but instead shone on everything and brought previously overlooked details to light. Whitman is our sun-poet, creating an art out of a desire to be as still, as patient, and as absorptive as a prepared and waiting photographic plate, welcoming the impress of the infinitely varied world. "In these *Leaves*," Whitman wrote, "everything is literally photographed" (*NUPM*, 4: 1523).

The challenge for Whitman, then, was to create a poetry as open and nondiscriminating as a photographic plate, ready to absorb and give representation to whatever appeared. When he designed his first edition of *Leaves of Grass*, he chose large folio pages that would give breadth to the extraordinarily long lines of his poetry. The impression those pages give is of clutter and fullness, very much unlike the conventional verse of the day, with its short, uniform lines floating in blank space; in *Leaves*, the words seem to be competing for space, crowding in, demanding their place, each a part of a vast clutter of words, images, print. Whitman was well aware that books themselves are very much a part of our visual culture, and throughout his life he was always concerned with the *look* of a book. Unless we are blind, we read primarily through the eyes, though of course the other senses contribute to the experience as well, as Whitman well knew. The smell of fresh ink or of old paper can affect our reading experience, as can the "feel" of a book – its heft and the quality and weight of the paper, or, in Whitman's day when many books were set in type that was letterpressed, the actual indentation of the letters on a page – as well as the sound of the words, especially in the nineteenth century when most readers still read aloud or mouthed the words as they read. So, when we "read" a book, we hear and touch and smell it as well as view it, but the visual experience predominates, and Whitman spent a great deal of time creating his books as a kind of visual feast, using the latest technological developments to create a more intimate and memorable encounter between his book and his reader. This involved many elements – representing himself visually in most of his books with frontispiece portraits and often multiple other portraits, creating a cover that visually indicated the significance of the book, choosing typefaces that kept readers' eyes jumping, creating poetic lines that made the eye sweep across the page far longer than conventional poetry demanded. The very muscles controlling eye movement would know the difference between conventional verse and Whitman's new open forms: the reader would experience the difference not only in the mind but in the muscles. Whitman wrote a poetry that exercised the eyes.

Whitman, in fact, always thought of reading as a physical act every bit as much as a mental one:

> Books are to be call'd for, and supplied, on the assumption that the process of reading is not a half-sleep, but, in highest sense, an exercise, a gymnast's struggle; that the reader is to do something for himself, must be on the alert, must himself or herself construct indeed the poem, argument, history, metaphysical essay – the text furnishing the hints, the clue, the start or frame-work. Not the book needs so much to be the complete thing, but the reader of the book does. That were to make a nation of supple and athletic minds, well-train'd, intuitive, used to depend on themselves, and not on a few coteries of writers. (*PW*, 2: 425)

And so his books were constructed to make the reader physically interact with them, to stare back at the portraits that looked out to the reader, to exercise more than the intellect.

Whitman develops a poetry that emerges from a physical encounter with the world. When he wrote in "Song of Myself," "My head slues round on my neck," he offered the physiological process of his poetic technique. He would simply turn his head on his neck and take in through his wide-awake senses the sweep of the world. His legs would move his body through the world, and continually reposition his eyes to take in ever-changing new scenes. When the "head slues round," it keeps *refacing* the world. The head is fronted by the face, which is the site of sensory access to the brain. The face is that part of the head that contains the organs of sight, smell, taste, and hearing: it stretches from ear to ear, from above the eyes to below the mouth. The rest of the body is subject to touch, but the face, masking the brain, is where the self primarily accesses the world through the holes in the skull that allow for sounds, tastes, odors, and sights to enter in. "Writing and talk do not prove me," Whitman writes in "Song of Myself"; "I carry the plenum of proof and every thing else in my face" (*LG*: 55). "Plenum" is the opposite of "vacuum": it is fullness, unregulated ingress of sensation, entering the skull's openings, sensing. The face provides us with the endless flow of experience that confirms for us the world's existence. Without the entry ports the face provides, we would live in a vacuum instead of a plenum. One way to think of Whitman's poetry is as an attempt to put into words the plenum that enters into us when we *face* the world. Whitman's "Crossing Brooklyn Ferry" begins with an insistence on coming "face to face" with the world, the self, and the reader:

> Flood-tide below me! I see you face to face!
> Clouds of the west – sun there half an hour high – I see you also face to face.
> [. . .]
> And you that shall cross from shore to shore years hence are more to me, and more in my meditations, than you might suppose.
>
> (*LG*: 158–9)

Whitman's poetry, then, is full of sensory imagery, but the eyesight dominates. In the Preface to his first edition of *Leaves*, Whitman defines the American poet, and the key attribute is that this new poet "hardly knows pettiness or triviality" precisely because he has learned to accept the vast gifts his eyesight lavishes on him and to represent those gifts in words:

> If he breathes into any thing that was before thought small it dilates with the grandeur and life of the universe. He is a seer. . . . he is individual . . . he is complete in himself. . . . the others are as good as he, only he sees it and they do not. [. . .] What the eyesight does to the rest he does to the rest. Who knows the curious mystery of the eyesight? The other senses corroborate themselves, but this is removed from any proof but its own and foreruns the identities of the spiritual world. A single glance of it mocks all the investigations of man and all the instruments and books of the earth and all reasoning. What is marvelous? what is unlikely? what is impossible or baseless or vague? After you have once just opened the space of a peachpit and given audience to far and near and to the sunset and had all things enter with electric swiftness softly and duly without confusion or jostling or jam. (*LG*: 713–14)

This extraordinary passage indicates the power Whitman ascribed to the visual. The poet is defined, finally, as "the seer," but in Whitman's hands this term does not have its customary prophetic connotation: for Whitman, to be a "seer" is very much to *see*, to open the eyes to the world. What the poet needs to do is precisely "what the eyesight does."

Ralph Waldo Emerson famously wrote in his essay "Nature" that, standing alone in the woods, he could become nothing but pure disembodied sight: "I become a transparent eyeball; I am nothing; I see all . . . " (Emerson 1965: 189). Whitman was indebted to Emerson, but he would stop short of imagining himself as *only* the eye; his seeing was always *embodied*, and his perceptions were synaesthetic, one sense inevitably reinforcing or stimulating another. But sight was his central trope for the poet. In the above passage from the Preface, he becomes not a "transparent eyeball" but instead forces the reader to confront the very physical fact of the eyeballs set in the skull, those organs the size of a "peachpit" that, when we unlid them, simply absorb . . . and continue to absorb. Contrariety, variation, contradiction, clutter: the eyes allow it all to enter "swiftly" and do so "without confusion or jostling or jam." The eyes, Whitman suggests, never grow tired of looking or become confused with too much detail: we don't experience a sight-jam, with visual impressions backed up like cars on a clogged freeway. Other senses are more discriminating: our hearing tends to focus on a few sounds, and too many sounds create noise and cacophony, but sight can deal with a vast multiplicity of sensations. The eyes for Whitman are exactly like the newly invented camera, open to whatever the sun illuminates, democratic in the inclusiveness of what they represent. "Not till the sun excludes you do I exclude you," writes Whitman in "To a Common Prostitute" (*LG*: 387) defining the central value of the indiscriminate democratic poet, a value endorsed by the eye itself and by the new visual technology of the camera.

Developments in visual culture, then, helped Whitman create his democratic poetry, a poetry that turned traditional artistic values on their head. Instead of celebrating discriminating tastes that sorted out the beautiful from the ugly, the meaningless from the significant, the important from the useless, the permanent from the ephemeral, Whitman developed a new democratic aesthetic that celebrated indiscriminate embrace, that defined beauty as completeness and fullness instead of selectiveness and partiality, that saw meaning in what others had dismissed as insignificant, that saw the permanent as precisely the ephemeral, since all things were composted into everything else through the ongoing processes of life: "All goes onward and outward, nothing collapses, / And to die is different from what any one supposed, and luckier" (*LG*: 35). Nothing lasts, and yet everything lasts; nothing is important, and yet everything is important; what is meaningful is always a function of the power of the observer to discover meaning where others had missed it. As, over the course of Whitman's life, a photographic and democratic aesthetic gradually eroded a more painterly and hierarchical one, his poetry came to seem to more and more readers less shocking and more essentially "American," though he would always remain anathema to the defenders of "high culture" and orthodox ideas. It is not coincidental that the growing appreciation of Whitman's inclusive poetics corresponded to the increasing acceptance of photography as "art": by the end of Whitman's life, thanks to photography, endless thousands of people and places and events had been captured and preserved in visual representations that otherwise would have been lost to our visual memory, and photographs were just beginning to enter collections of art, finally starting to gain the stature of paintings. This was a battle that had been initiated a half century earlier by Whitman's friend Gabriel Harrison, an accomplished daguerreotypist who took the daguerreotype on which the famous 1855 frontispiece engraving of Whitman was based; Harrison formed the American Daguerre Association, fought for making it a democratically open association of artisans, and pushed hard for the recognition of the new craft as art.

But in the early years of photography, few could have predicted its eventual triumph as the main vehicle of visual representation, and so Whitman was immersed in other, more traditional aspects of visual culture as well, fascinated especially with painters and the growing realistic nature of American painting. But even with painting, he was looking for ways to challenge the old conventions, and he celebrated those artists who rethought the medium. He especially admired painters who used their canvases as a kind of protocamera, turning their eyes to the world around them and representing things that often had been overlooked by artists of the past. He wrote about art frequently in his journalism in the 1840s and early 1850s, and he encouraged artists to open their eyes more fully to the world around them, to be guided by the new democratic aesthetic that photography confirmed. He was involved in the attempts to start a Brooklyn Academy of Art, and he wrote passionately about the need for a new aesthetic. He was good friends with Walter Libbey, a painter who emphasized the everyday aspects of life, and with Henry Kirke Brown, who became a well-known sculptor. Whitman loved the paintings of Long Island artist William Sidney Mount, especially his portraits of African Americans, some of the most striking early representations of blacks in the United States. Whitman may well have known Mount, and he certainly saw Mount's paintings frequently, admiring the artist's focus on working-class people and their everyday activities, images that resonated with Whitman's own poetic catalogues. David Reynolds has demonstrated how Whitman's affectionate word-portraits of Negroes in "Song of Myself" may well derive from Mount's paintings (Reynolds 1995: 292–3).

Whitman also knew the great painter of American Indians, George Catlin, and was a strong proponent of the proposal for the United States government to purchase Catlin's paintings as a national resource. Raised in Pennsylvania, Catlin was always fascinated with Indians, and, after seeing a delegation of tribal leaders from the Far West, he dedicated himself to creating an "Indian Gallery" by journeying to every remaining tribe in North America and painting the people and their activities. In the early 1830s, he traveled thousands of miles through the West, carrying rolled up canvases on his back and painting what he saw while he was directly facing it, unlike most landscape painters of the time, who still worked in their studios from sketches. Whitman got to know Catlin before the Civil War, and Catlin gave Whitman lithographs of a couple of his paintings; one was of the Seminole chief Osceola, a portrait Whitman carefully preserved and proudly displayed in his Camden home during the last years of his life. Two years before he died, inspired by Catlin's painting, Whitman wrote a poem about Osceola's tragic death after the chief had been tricked into surrender by US forces. Whitman liked Catlin's paintings for their spontaneous, direct qualities; they had an energy and lack of finish that Whitman aspired to in his poetry. He admired Catlin's "wise, informed, vital character," his devotion to capturing a key part of American experience that had not been visually represented before, and even though Whitman did not find Catlin's paintings "interesting from the art side," he celebrated them "from the human side: the side of experience, emotion, life" (Traubel 1908: 354). Like photography, Catlin's work taught Whitman to value spontaneity over too-careful planning, energy over finish, direct encounter over recollection.

Whitman admired other painters of American Indians, too, notably Alfred Jacob Miller, whose painting *The Trapper's Bride* (done in several versions during the 1840s) was the source for Whitman's famous passage in "Song of Myself" about the marriage of a trapper and an Indian woman: "I saw the marriage of the trapper in the open air in the far west, the bride was a red girl" (*LG*: 37). Kenneth Price (2004: 22–7) has recently written about the ways that Whitman's poetic portrait differs in suggestive ways from Miller's painting, but it is important to note that Miller, who traveled West in 1837 and witnessed the event he painted, is the source of Whitman's seeing: the narrator of "Song" "saw" the marriage only through the extended vision that Miller's visual representation gave him. Miller's painting suggested to Whitman the crossing and intermingling of experience that would produce the hybridization that would become "America." In the 1880s, Whitman sat for an hour before a giant painting of *Custer's Last Rally* by John Mulvany (see Plate 17.1) that, in its tensed images of a life–death confrontation between whites and Indians, condensed for Whitman his lifelong ambivalence about America's natives. "I could look on such a work at brief intervals all my life without tiring," he wrote, viewing the "grim and sublime" gigantic canvas as a kind of lens not only giving him access to Western spaces he had never actually seen, but also giving him a visual construction of American history and an image of the very workings of the American psyche (*PW*, 1: 275–6).

Whitman used certain artists and photographers, then, as extenders of his optical field, giving him visual encounters with people, places, and events he otherwise would not have seen. Later in the century, his friend Alexander Gardner became the official photographer for the Union and Pacific railroad, taking images of the creation of the transcontinental railroad; his photos served Whitman as source images for many of the Western scenes in his poetry. And earlier, Gardner, Mathew Brady, Timothy O'Sullivan, and their assistants offered Whitman another visual experience that altered his poetry, as they became the first war photographers, capturing on photographic plates many aspects of the Civil War, our first photographed war. Photography as a technology grew up with the emerging military technologies of

Plate 17.1 John Mulvany, *Custer's Last Rally*. Kansas State Historical Society, Topeka.

mass death, and it's no coincidence that photography from the beginning shares the diction of weaponry: a camera is *aimed* and *shots* are taken, and from the beginning of the art in the late 1840s, many Americans (and not just American Indians) found it threatening and intrusive and worried that each photograph somehow uncannily stole a little bit of their life or identity. Susan Sontag and others have demonstrated just how enmeshed photography and war have been ever since the Civil War was shot.

Because of the state of camera and film technology at the time, photography could not absorb actual battle (exposure times blurred quick action, cameras were large and bulky and had to be placed on tripods, plates had to be prepared and quickly developed, requiring darkroom carts to be dragged along with the photographer, and so on), and so we have come to know the Civil War visually through the things that mid-nineteenth-century photography *could* capture: the preparations and after-effects of battles. One of the most familiar Civil War photographs, taken by O'Sullivan, was named by Gardner (who included the image in his *Photographic Sketch Book of the War*) *Harvest of Death*, since it showed the Gettysburg battlefield, also a farm field, strewn with bloated corpses (see Plate 17. 2). "Here are the dreadful details!," Gardner wrote in his notes accompanying the image (Gardner [1866] 1959: notes facing Plate 36). In *Memoranda During the War*, Whitman wrote one of the great long prose sentences in American literature, offering us a literal image of the "harvest of death" by portraying all of America's farm fields now composting the blood and bone and decomposed flesh of its young soldiers back into corn and grain:

> The dead in this war – there they lie, strewing the fields and woods and valleys and battle-fields of the south – . . . the infinite dead – (the land entire saturated, perfumed with their impalpable ashes' exhalation in Nature's chemistry distill'd, and shall be so

> forever, in every future grain of wheat and ear of corn, and every flower that grows, and every breath we draw).... (*PW*, 1: 115)

Photography at this time recorded the world only in black and white, of course, and the dark exposures create an almost moonlit cast in many Civil War shots. Whitman, who knew Brady and was a good friend of Brady's assistant Alexander Gardner, who took many of the war shots, wrote a powerful little poem that seems to put into words the dim-lit black and white battlefield and the multitude of corpses lying upon what was also a farm field: a place of harvest.

> Look down fair moon and bathe this scene,
> Pour softly down night's nimbus floods on faces ghastly, swollen, purple,
> On the dead on their backs with arms toss'd wide,
> Pour down your unstinted nimbus sacred moon.
>
> (*LG*: 320–1)

Whitman does not flinch from looking at the swollen ghastly faces, but he uses the light to create a kind of halo over the scene. It is a photographic way of seeing: Whitman's mass dead are still in motion as nature's chemistry casts a nimbus around

Plate 17.2 Timothy O'Sullivan, *Harvest of Death*. Library of Congress, Prints & Photographs Division, LC-B8184-7964A.

them, then transforms them into our bloody nutriment, our future, just as the chemistry of photography takes present moments and transforms them into a vision available to the future, but a vision of a moment forever dead, as Roland Barthes (1982) has so eloquently argued, the instant that it is captured. In that sense, photography suggested to Whitman one of the great achievements of his poetry – his casting of the "Walt Whitman" of *Leaves of Grass* as a presence forever accessible to readers of the future, readers who would live long after he died, able still to confront him, interact with him, even though death and time and space separated them. Anyone who has cherished photographs of dead friends or children or partners or grandparents knows the haunted and haunting sense of presence that these images bring, in part because they are confirmations of a physical existence that has disappeared except in these photographic traces, presences confirmed because the sun illuminated them and the camera recorded that moment of illumination. Keeping this influence in mind, Whitman's various confirmations of the mystery of identity take on a new edge, as when he writes in "Starting from Paumanok":

> This then is life,
> Here is what has come to the surface after so many throes and convulsions.
> How curious! how real!
> Underfoot the divine soil, overhead the sun.
>
> (*LG*: 16)

Our identity, emerging from the "throes and convulsions" of eons of composting time, comes to the "surface," like a developing image on a photographic plate, its existence on earth ("the divine soil") confirmed by the sun that reveals its singular curiousness and its reality. When Whitman describes the African-American drayman in "Song of Myself," again it is the sun that brings his features to the surface, that allows him to emerge as a "picture" in the poem, that makes Whitman feel affection toward him:

> The sun falls on his crispy hair and mustache, falls on the black of his polish'd and perfect limbs.
> I behold the picturesque giant and love him. . . .
>
> (*LG*: 40)

To recap, then: the developments in visual culture that most excited Whitman were photography and the developing photographic realism of painting, both tools for making visual catalogues of the world more diverse and full and multitudinous than any before. Whitman joined his own poetry to this endeavor, and for him democratic art required a loosening of discrimination, a withdrawal of aesthetic and moral and class-based filters that constricted a sense of democratic beauty. We have seen how Whitman used photography and painting to literally extend his eyesight, and we have seen examples of how that extension worked for places and events. But his main fascination with photography and painting, especially after the Civil War, had to do with the revolutions in portraiture that the new art was ushering in. Whitman became the most photographed writer who died before the advent of truly portable and amateur photography in the 1890s. He sat for many of the century's best-known photographers, including Brady, Gardner, James Wallace Black, William Kurtz, Jeremiah Gurney, George C. Cox, Frederic Gutekunst, and Napoleon Sarony.

Sarony's gallery was the most famous of the 300 photographic studios in New York City in the 1870s. He was a flamboyant character, himself a celebrity who photographed other celebrities, especially actresses and actors (40,000 of them by a *New York Times* estimate). His cabinet card portraits became immensely popular, the nineteenth-century equivalent to baseball cards or fan magazines. He was one of the photographers who helped create the modern concept of celebrity, in effect marketing the faces of famous people so that others could see them in such detail that they felt they knew them personally. Before mass-produced photographs, celebrities had to be pointed out by people who knew them, but by the 1870s and 1880s, most admirers of a well-known personage would have seen or even owned multiple photographs of the celebrity and thus would be able to identify that person on the street, even if it was the first time they had seen the object of their admiration. Celebrities thus became people instantly recognizable to large numbers of people who had never seen them in person before. Sarony made this phenomenon possible; he paid some of his celebrity sitters royalties for sale of their portraits, but less well-known sitters would pay him for the publicity they received when they were added to his catalogue. Whitman, who made Sarony's catalogue in the late 1870s, was, in some ways and for many people, more recognizable for his striking bearded visage, now familiar to thousands through the sales of cabinet-card images, than he was for his poetry (see Plate 17. 3). He was one of our first celebrity writers, made easily recognizable by his photographs.

Whitman loved the idea of celebrity, of individual selves becoming representative of the people. He concluded his Preface to his first edition of *Leaves* with the injunction that "The proof of a poet is that his country absorbs him as affectionately as he has absorbed it" (*LG*: 452). The poet would openly absorb and celebrate his country, and in turn the country would absorb and celebrate its poet. It may seem odd to suggest that Whitman, a poet who did not even put his name on the title pages of the first five editions of *Leaves*, sought celebrity, but it's important to think about the implications of his decision to place, opposite his title page, images of his face and body confronting the reader. The *face*, more than the name, carries one's identity, and Whitman's books underscore the bodily and physical nature of identity. A name was just a group of letters associated with a person, but a face was identity itself, the very physiognomy of one's absorbing, sensate being. *This* is who wrote this book, Whitman's portraits seem to be saying, wordlessly, while the name remains absent from its accustomed place following the title.

It is astonishing how many of the key visual artists of his time Whitman encountered and even became friendly with: we've mentioned Gabriel Harrison, George Catlin, Mathew Brady, Alexander Gardner, and others. As his fame increased, Whitman's portrait was painted or sketched by numerous artists, including Charles Hine in 1860 (a painting that was the basis for the frontispiece engraving in the 1860

Plate 17.3 Napoleon Sarony, photograph of Walt Whitman. Library of Congress, Charles E. Feinberg Collection.

edition of *Leaves of Grass*), and, later, John W. Alexander, Herbert Gilchrist, Percy Ives, Jacques Reich, Dora Wheeler, and G. W. Waters; in the last years of his life, he was sculpted by Sidney Morse.

But one of the most productive relationships that Whitman had was with one of the most significant American artists of the century, Thomas Eakins. A Philadelphian, Eakins was a major figure in American art circles, and he was nearly as scandalous as Whitman himself. In Philadelphia newspapers in the 1880s, Eakins's name was often tied to Whitman, sometimes in terms of their celebration of "nakedness." Eakins, in fact, was dismissed from his teaching job at the Pennsylvania Academy of the Fine Arts, in part because of his insistence that his classes of male and female students work with *naked* instead of nude models ("nude" at the time indicated that the genitals remained covered). Whitman loved Eakins's scandalous behavior: he once talked about how "a girl model . . . had appeared before [Eakins's] class, nude, with a bracelet on – Eakins, thereupon, in anger, seizing the bracelet and throwing it on the floor," an act, Whitman said, that made "a great point" (Traubel 1964: 499). Eakins also photographed his students unclothed as part of his project to develop a catalogue of body types, each posed in a sequence of different stances, and each photographed from the front, side, and rear. Whitman, who often celebrated "the free exhilarating extasy of nakedness" (*PW*, 1: 150), may have been photographed naked by Eakins as part of this project (see Folsom 1996).

In 1875 Eakins completed his famous "Portrait of Professor Gross (The Gross Clinic)," which portrayed a surgical operation and shocked contemporary viewers with its stark realism, but has since come to be regarded as one of the most influential American realistic paintings. Then, sometime in the early 1880s, Eakins met Whitman, was fascinated with him, and wanted to capture his image in as many ways as possible. In 1887–88, Eakins completed a portrait of Whitman, one that remained Whitman's favorite painted image of himself (see Plate 17.4). Whitman was unhappy with most of his painted portraits, for the same reason we've already seen: he did not like the way the artists "fool[ed] with nature – reform[ed] it, revise[d] it"; he thus preferred his photographic portraits, which at least captured a momentary look accurately. But Whitman liked the way Eakins "sets me down in correct style, without feathers." Even though many of his friends disliked the portrait, Whitman maintained his affection for it, admiring its realism, the way Eakins made his canvas like a photographic plate, seeing "not what he wanted to but what he did see," creating a "strong, rugged, even daring" portrait (quoted in Folsom 1986–87: 70).

Eakins often employed his photographs as documentation for his painting and sculpture, but recently these images have been viewed as significant contributions to photographic art and to the development of photography *as* an art. He began photographing in the late 1870s, and in the 1880s he worked with Eadweard Muybridge on his photographic studies of motion, using very short exposures to capture animals and humans in motion. He brought his camera to Whitman's home in 1891 and, with his student Samuel Murray, made some of the last and most memorable images of the poet. Whitman felt a real affinity for Eakins: "Oh! there is no doubt Eakins is our man!" (quoted in Folsom 1986–87: 70). Murray accompanied the New York sculptor William O'Donovan to Whitman's home when O'Donovan was working on a bust of Whitman, and O'Donovan may well have used Murray's photographs

Plate 17.4 Thomas Eakins, *Walt Whitman*. Pennsylvania Academy of Fine Arts.

of Whitman as an aid in his work. Eakins and his team, then, used photography, painting, and sculpture to capture the visual image of Whitman in lasting media. Their work, along with that of the earlier photographers and painters, has resulted in our continuing to this day to be able to look at Whitman with our own eyes and keep him an active part of our visual culture. We have more visual images of him than of any other writer who died in the nineteenth century, and, because of his active engagement with the visual culture of his time, Whitman has remained the most familiar face in nineteenth-century American writing.

Whitman's impact on American visual culture has extended to our present time. Countless artists have painted and sculpted him over the past century, and his influence on modern and contemporary artists like John Sloan, Alfred Stieglitz, Charles Sheeler, Berenice Abbott, Joseph Stella, Ben Shahn, Mahonri Young, David Hockney, and the Dadaists, has been traced by scholars like Ruth Bohan, James Dougherty, Robert K. Martin, Kenneth Price, and Roberta K. Tarbell. His influence on other visual forms, like dance (Isadora Duncan) and architecture (Louis Sullivan and Frank Lloyd Wright) has been examined by scholars like Bohan, Kevin Murphy, and John Roche. Whitman's influence on and presence in films, from early movies by D. W. Griffith on up to contemporary films directed by Jim Jarmusch and Maria Maggenti, has recently been chronicled by Price. It is fair to say that no other nineteenth-century writer thought so much about visual culture, knew so many visual artists of his time, influenced so many visual artists both in his own era and in the century following his death, and has remained so vital a visual presence in our own time. When Whitman wrote in "Crossing Brooklyn Ferry" that "I am with you, you men and women of a generation, or ever so many generations hence" (*LG*: 160) he was right, not only in terms of his ongoing poetic voice but also in terms of his continuing visual impact.

References and Further Reading

Allen, Gay Wilson (1970). The Iconography of Walt Whitman. In Edwin Haviland Miller (ed.), *The Artistic Legacy of Walt Whitman*. New York: New York University Press, pp. 103–52.

Barthes, Roland (1982). *Camera Lucida: Reflections on Photography*, trans. Richard Howard. New York: Hill and Wang.

Bohan, Ruth L. (2003). Whitman's "Barbaric Yawp" and the Culture of New York Dada. In Martin Ignatius Gaughan (ed.), *Dada New York: New World for Old*. New Haven, CT: G. K. Hall, pp. 35–57.

Brasher, Thomas L. (1970). *Whitman as Editor of The Brooklyn Daily Eagle*. Detroit: Wayne State University Press.

Clarke, Graham (1991). *Walt Whitman: The Poem as Private History*. New York: St Martin's.

Dougherty, James (1993). *Walt Whitman and the Citizen's Eye*. Baton Rouge: Louisiana State University Press.

Emerson, Ralph Waldo (1965). *Selected Writings of Ralph Waldo Emerson*, ed. William H. Gilman. New York: Signet.

Folsom, Ed (1986–87). "This Heart's Geography's Map": The Photographs of Walt Whitman. *Walt Whitman Quarterly Review*, 4: 1–76.

Folsom, Ed (1994). *Walt Whitman's Native Representations*. Cambridge: Cambridge University Press.

Folsom, Ed (1995). Appearing in Print: Illustrations of the Self. In Ezra Greenspan (ed.), *The Cambridge Companion to Walt Whitman*. Cambridge, UK: Cambridge University Press, pp. 135–65.

Folsom, Ed (1996). Whitman's Calamus Photographs. In Betsy Erkkila and Jay Grossman (eds.), *Breaking Bounds: Whitman & American Cultural Studies*. New York: Oxford University Press, pp. 193–219.

Gardner, Alexander ([1866] 1959). *Gardner's Photographic Sketch Book of the Civil War*. New York: Dover.

Martin, Robert K. (1992). Fetishizing America: David Hockney and Thom Gunn. In Robert K. Martin (ed.), *The Continuing Presence of Walt Whitman*. Iowa City: University of Iowa Press, pp. 114–26.

Murphy, Kevin (1988). Walt Whitman and Louis Sullivan: The Aesthetics of Egalitarianism. *Walt Whitman Quarterly Review*, 6: 1–15.

Orvell, Miles (1989). *The Real Thing: Imitation and Authenticity in American Culture, 1880–1940*. Chapel Hill: University of North Carolina Press.

Price, Kenneth M. (2004). *To Walt Whitman, America*. Chapel Hill: University of North Carolina Press.

Reisch, Marc S. (1981). Poetry and Portraiture in Whitman's *Leaves of Grass*. *Walt Whitman Review*, 27: 113–25.

Reynolds, David S. (1995). *Walt Whitman's America: A Cultural Biography*. New York: Knopf.

Roche, John F. (1988). Democratic Space: The Ecstatic Geography of Walt Whitman and Frank Lloyd Wright. *Walt Whitman Quarterly Review*, 6: 16–32.

Sill, Geoffrey M., and Tarbell, Roberta K. (eds.) (1992). *Walt Whitman and the Visual Arts*. New Brunswick, NJ: Rutgers University Press.

Sontag, Susan (1977). *On Photography*. New York: Farrar, Straus & Giroux.

Sontag, Susan (2003). *Regarding the Pain of Others*. New York: Farrar, Straus & Giroux.

Trachtenberg, Alan (1989). *Reading American Photographs: Images as History, Mathew Brady to Walker Evans*. New York: Hill and Wang.

Traubel, Horace (1906). *With Walt Whitman in Camden*, vol. 1. Boston: Small, Maynard.

Traubel, Horace (1908). *With Walt Whitman in Camden*, vol. 2. New York: Appleton.

Traubel, Horace (1914). *With Walt Whitman in Camden*, vol. 3. New York: Mitchell Kennerley.

Traubel, Horace (1953). *With Walt Whitman in Camden*, vol. 4, ed. Sculley Bradley. Philadelphia: University of Pennsylvania Press.

Traubel, Horace (1964). *With Walt Whitman in Camden*, vol. 5, ed. Gertrude Traubel. Carbondale: University of Southern Illinois Press.

Traubel, Horace (1982). *With Walt Whitman in Camden*, vol. 6, ed. Gertrude Traubel and William White. Carbondale: University of Southern Illinois Press.

18
Civil War
Luke Mancuso

Prelude: "Proud Music of the Storm"

On April 13, 1861, the day the first secessionists fired on Fort Sumter, Walt Whitman attended Verdi's *A Masked Ball* in New York City. A passionate opera buff, Whitman had attended at least 25 operas up until that pivotal night. Between 1840 and 1860, the opera became a medium for the poet-journalist that enabled him to bridge the boundaries between binary oppositions on many fronts, the showcase for the human voice as "combiner, nothing more spiritual, nothing more sensuous, a god, yet completely human" (*PW*, 2: 367). So his recognition of the inaugural event of the Civil War broke through his postperformance reverie, as he made his way to the Brooklyn ferry. The operatic voice for Whitman is retrospectively cast back over this fateful 1861 evening, in the exuberance of his 1869 poem "Proud Music of the Storm," which exults in the role of music as "combiner," blurring rigid borders through images of aesthetic and material fusion, such as: "The journey done, the journeyman come home, / And man and art with Nature fused again" (*LG*: 405). Note the nostalgic longing for home and for transparent fusion of differing categories.

David Reynolds argues that in "antebellum America, boundaries between different performance genres and cultural levels were permeable" (Reynolds 1995: 193). This dream of unitary fusion between human, aesthetic, and natural identities had been nursed long and hard in Whitman's career. The unmooring of rigid boundaries between these separate orders of identity seems to have been active in his attendance at the opera, a public space where differing classes and aesthetic tastes met in the embodiment of the virtuosity of the human voice. As Reynolds suggests, Whitman's poetry "enacted this permeability of modes. In one passage he could sound like an actor, in another like an orator, in another like a singer. The same was true in his daily life: he would by turns declaim, orate, sing" (Reynolds 1995: 193). This endowment of heteroglossia, speaking in multiple voices and diverse tongues, had been a motif in Whitman's work from the beginning, and his dowry of "throbbings" creates a text which inhales the whole catalogue of musical literature past and present. Thus, by 1869, this Whitmanesque language of combining, fusion, and the merging between human identity, the natural world, and writing seems strained beyond recognition. Yet, eight years earlier, the desire for such a fusion drove many of the Civil War reveries of Walt Whitman, and became the platform for his journalism, poetry, and prose. Rather than accommodating differing voices in his work, Whitman silences the differences between identity, nature, and writing, in favor of the fusion of these three differing categories. After Appomattox, as he nostalgically glanced back in unease over the 1861–65 carnage, his desire for undifferentiated Union glazed over any lingering doubts about the vast human cost, yet his work becomes inhabited by ghosts which will preclude any such totalized personal, social, or cultural memory. The traces of ghostliness linger in his Civil War journalism and poetry to give witness to his antebellum heteroglossia, while the fusion of previously differing voices makes his nationalism dominate these wartime texts.

The critical literature on Walt Whitman's response to the Civil War is vast and variegated, ranging from biographical sources (his journalism and letters), to close textual studies of *Drum-Taps*, *Sequel to Drum-Taps*, and *Memoranda During the War* (the poetry and prose he produced during and after the War). The critical pedigree is astoundingly diverse, reading Whitman's texts as an ideologically conservative apology for the patriotic cause of war, as well as a platform in which to revise such a closed political response to the war, in favor of a more progressive critique of the material cost of the conflict on his identity as well as the nation. I want to argue that Whitman's response to the Civil War only slightly moves across this ideological spectrum from conservative to liberal, since the dominant tone is conservative nostalgia for antebellum cultural stability. This conservative tone in Whitman's prose and poetry will allow me to analyze the poet's framing of the American national legacy from the Founders to the doorstep of Fort Sumter. Furthermore, I engage in a discussion of the cultural uses of nineteenth-century representations of nationalism, nostalgia, history, and memory; as well as further exploration of the implications of Whitman's texts in the formation of national identity and subject formation on the cultural canvas of the 1860s. Whitman draws out the traces of the patriotic memory of the war in domesticated versions of nostalgic history, in Revolutionary War history, and in the traces of the uncanny intrusion of social fragmentation. By rewriting history through the discourses of local sense memory (Brooklyn neighborhoods and hospitals), domestic sentimentalism (the images of civic home and family), and patriotic mourning (the battlefields and cemeteries), Whitman moves from a libertarian antebellum confidence in confederate harmony among the states, to a more conservative recognition of the ghostly wounds that will always haunt the Union victory. The Union cemented at Appomattox is not as cohesive as the harmonic fusion of opera, and the divided allegiances to home and nation are the border territories that are traversed throughout his postwar work. Nevertheless, Whitman's practice of memorialization idealizes the social memory of heroic enlistments in home and nation, and largely ignores the excesses of patriotic nationalism. The democratic readers of Whitman's Civil War journalism and poems, then, are reoriented to the nation, home, and memory; but the conservative function of such representations is not capable of producing *total* social stability, since nostalgia produces a haunted national homestead. Contrary to his 1869 declaration, in "Proud Music of the Storm," human identity, nature, and art are not identical with each other, but caught in an uneasy embrace.

On the night of 13 April, 1865, the sublime reverie broke as the newsboys came "yelling and tearing up the street, rushing from side to side more furiously than usual," and "a small crowd of others, who gathered impromptu, read the news, which was evidently authentic" (*PW*, 1: 24). This anecdote embodies the nostalgic desire in Whitman's dream of organic fusion, for even as the operatic evening performance fades in his ears, he confronts the rebirth of Union nationalism in the face of fratricidal war. In addition, Benedict Anderson has persuasively suggested that the circulation of newspapers was one of the pivots on which turned the eighteenth-century "birth of the imagined community of the nation," namely the idea of "simultaneity," for the newspaper "provided the technical means for 're-presenting' the imagined community that is the nation" (Anderson 1983: 24–5). This evidence of authentic news about Fort Sumter, in Whitman's terms, turns on the imaginary relations that these nocturnal lamp-lit readers on Broadway have in their lateral relation to all other citizens; that is, they share an imaginary relation simultaneously broadcast across the news network, a moment frozen in what Anderson calls a "fictive" or "imagined linkage" through two conventions: "the date at the top of the newspaper, the single most important emblem on it," the mass market consumer value of the paper as a text of "ephemeral popularity" as "one-day best-sellers" (1983: 34–5). While each reader is engaged in a "mass ceremony" of "silent privacy, in the lair of the skull," it is the social imaginary that fills in the millions of other readers who create the "remarkable confidence of community in anonymity which is the hallmark of modern nations" (p. 36). Note that Whitman's anecdote underlines the anonymity, as well as the communal relation, that binds each newspaper reader to this cataclysmic event, since they read "silently" yet aloud for those who have no material print to hold on to. They are caught in their own private musings, yet are assembled together in front of the Metropolitan Hotel. In musical terms, the "authentic" cadence consists of the resolution or closure of the chord pattern, but ironically, this "authentic" news would open the greatest source of cultural instability in Whitman's life.

Thus, the "opening of the secession war," as Whitman later labels this entry, animates the renewed vigor of nationalistic fervor that would quickly sweep across the metropolitan and rural landscape of the North. In the 1875 *Memoranda During the War*, Whitman creates a textual link between his version of nationalism, and this national relation so imaginatively invoked in this local anecdote:

> What ran through the land, as if by electric nerves, and show'd itself in stupendous and practical action, immediately after the firing on the Flag at Fort Sumter . . . – the arm'd volunteers instantaneously springing up everywhere – the tumultuous processions of

> the regiments – Was it not grand to have lived in such scenes and days, and be absorb'd by them, and unloos'd to them? (Whitman 1962: 60)

Whitman's private recollection of reading of the attack on Sumter had been absorbed in the patriotic flood of renewed nationalism, when the stunned silence of the spectators had been unloosed in "pulsing and pounding" violence of the ensuing Civil War. In their collective anonymity, the news gatherers (in Whitman's memorial to the opening of the war) have risen up to respond en-masse to the reinforcement of the Union cause. Whitman's patriotic nationalism seems at fever pitch in this entry, but this entry was published in 1875 after 10 years of nostalgia, and the conservative impulse in these lines orients Union readers toward obedient patriotic enlistment. Likewise, when the Civil War convulsed the nation from June 1861 to November 1862, Whitman's nostalgia similarly consisted in a traditionalist look back at the historical settlement of Long Island and omitted any reference to the Civil War at all.

1861–62: The Role of Nostalgia and "Brooklyniana"

Rather than representing the initial violence of the war after the firing on Fort Sumter, Whitman wrote 25 nostalgic history sketches in the Brooklyn *Standard* from June 1861 to November 1862. These historical essays seek to anchor the emotions and memory of the readers to a heavily nostalgic series of past events, catalogues, and musings about New York and Long Island, stretching back to the original Dutch settlers and moving through the 120-mile trek to the other side of Long Island. There is an undiluted conservative impulse in these sketches which valorizes the social stability of "the recording and preserving of what traditions we have of the American past," as an antidote to the shifting mobility of the population (Christman 1963: 3). With an arresting set of blinders on, Whitman does not catalogue the Civil War in these occasional pieces, but mobilizes the "large mass of American readers" to look proleptically forward to a future point "here in Brooklyn, and all over America, when nothing will be of more interest than authentic reminiscences of the past" (Christman 1963: 3). Whitman's amnesia for the spreading Civil War battles may signal his expectation that the war would resolve into a speedy Union victory, but the cultural work of these "Brooklyniana" sketches regulates the consent of Brooklyn residents to favor the national Union cause, through images of an organic link to the original Dutch settlers, the spectral memory of Native American tribes, the Revolutionary past, the local sites of civic Brooklyn memory, and the memory of a leisurely holiday in the most unsettled part of the island, a natural landscape of release from social anxiety.

Svetlana Boym has coined the useful critical term "restorative nostalgia" to denote the kinds of cultural work that conservative nostalgia performs for the relationship readers have to the past, or "how we view our relationship to a collective home" (Boym 2001: 41). The restorationist impulse seeks to "rebuild the lost home and patch up the memory gaps" through "national symbols and myths" which attempt "total reconstructions of monuments of the past" (ibid.). Whitman is engaged in such a nostalgic enterprise in "Brooklyniana," on three thematic fronts: the chronological history of Brooklyn, the legacy of the Revolutionary War, and the stability of the historical landscape in the midst of social anxiety.

Whitman devotes much of his rhetorical energy in these local history sketches in his attempt to repair the gaps and holes in the collective memory of the local residents of Brooklyn. He opens with the declaration that the original Dutch settlers were "superior in physical, moral and mental qualities," and chides contemporary Brooklynites for not having "any definite or fixed dates in their minds of the settlement and growth of our great city" (Christman 1963: 11). As Boym suggests, Whitman fills in these "deficiencies" in order to rebuild a notion of the "lost home" found in antebellum America, the empirical catalogue of dates and events forming a "reconstructive" chain to draw New Yorkers to enlist in the Union cause. Long Island contained a superior natural landscape, "fertile, beautiful, well-watered, and . . . plenty of timbers," whereas Manhattan contained "rocks, bare, bleak, and without anything to recommend it except its situation for commercial purposes, which is without rival in the world" (Christman 1963: 12).

By asserting the human and natural superiority of the original settlers, Whitman longs to transcend the rending of the social fabric by the war, as well as its underpinnings in the economic structures of slave labor. The impulse to historicize the origins of North American European settlement gives his readers a sense of recovering a continuous tradition that, in the terms of Eric Hobsbawm, in his essay "Inventing Traditions," conjures up "a set of practices . . . which seeks to inculcate certain values and norms of behavior by repetition which automatically implies continuity with the past" (quoted in Boym 2001: 42).

Aside from Whitman's ritual invocation of a transcendent European origin, complete with dozens of local civic dates, reminiscences, and historical data, the spectral entrance of Native American tribes, in No. 4 of the series, signals a brief break in his nationalistic reverie. The Kanarsie tribe greeted the first Dutch settlers, and he hastens to add that "we have never seen any of these Kanarsie remnants. The last one, we have heard old Brooklynites say, became extinct between forty or fifty years ago" (Christman 1963: 23). Whitman records the "peaceful and prudent method" of European purchase of the land from the natives in these terms: "And in 1670, under the English, the authorities of Brooklyn purchased from the Indians, the large tract comprising Bedford, and a large stretch towards Flatbush and Jamaica, for the following price: '100 guilders, seawant [native money], half a tun of strong beer, three long-barrelled guns . . . , and four coats" (Christman 1963: 26). It is hard to decipher this summary of Native American removal on Whitman's part: he romanticizes Indian naïveté, but his flat, reportorial tone simply recounts the events as pieces of data without any historical reflection. Such a traditional method suggests that the removal of native peoples has been sanitized through his own devotion to European hegemony, thus marginalizing the long series of cultural tensions between Indians and Europeans.

The ghostly trace of native peoples is preserved only in Whitman's suggestion, in No. 13, that changing the name of Long Island back to Paumanok could "be a kind of poetic justice to the departed tribes," and during the national emergency of war in 1861, "it seems as if their shades deserve at least the poor recompense of the compliment connected in preserving the old name by which they themselves designated and knew this territory" (Christman 1963: 104). There does not seem to be any irony in the author's voice here, and this restorative gesture seems to betray a scent of the nationalist fervor unleashed as it was written in the first months of the war: as Boym points out, the loss of social cohesion, in times like national wars, creates a need for turning "fatality into continuity, contingency into meaning" (Boym 2001: 42). The longing for continuity here takes the form of a nostalgic return to origins, as though "poetic justice" would offer an uncanny trace of a "poor recompense," in order to remind the readers that their own "imagined community" in the Union cause had been built out of two and a half centuries of successful domination over and against native peoples. This trace of strangeness and longing therefore is lodged in Whitman's cheerful journalistic tone, which shores up social "cohesion and offers a comforting collective script for individual longing" (Boym 2001: 42); in this context, it offers a speedy end to the secession war. Nevertheless, in the end, Boym reminds us that restorative nostalgia relies on "national memory," and one of its narratives is "the restoration of origins" (p. 43).

In another restorative strand of nostalgia in the "Brooklyniana" series, Whitman makes repeated use of the Revolutionary War as a kind of recovery of the social solidarity in the nation's founding moment. In No. 5 of the series, Whitman offers an extended American viewpoint on the atrocities suffered by American soldiers, producing a patriotic tone that would easily translate into the support for the current mobilization for the Union cause in 1861–62. At every turn in his description of the ill treatment of Revolutionary prisoners by the British, Whitman's language is exceptionally fervent. The American prisoners of war faced inhuman conditions:

> The food was often the refuse of the English soldiery and of the ships of war in commission. There was the most frightful suffering from want of water. The air was fetid, in warm weather, to suffocation. Still with all these facts, these thousands of men, any of whom might have had his liberty by agreeing to join the British ranks, sternly abided by their fate and adhered to the cause of their country to the bitter end. (Christman 1963: 32)

Such martyr-like images remind us that, in Dominick LaCapra's terms, even in traditionalist histories (like Whitman's here) language cannot be relieved of its traces of "exceptional, contestatory, or even uncanny uses of language in history" (LaCapra 1985: 119). The thousands of Revolutionary heroes are being enlisted here for a re-enlistment in Whitman's desire to create a Union victory against the Confederacy – indeed, their long-suffering is illustrated again and again in this article, such as their defiant celebration of the Fourth of July in 1782 aboard the *Jersey*, when British troops killed many of the prisoners in the struggle to repress their independence. Readers engaged in the (unnamed) current Civil War as volunteers, or families back home, are being schooled in the discipline of patriotism for the Cause, through these images of individual and collective heroism. Reid Mitchell places the "discipline" of the populace on both soldiers and on the homefront: "Part of the soldiers' transformation was learning to endure – and value – discipline. That was not the only discipline they thought war required. The soldiers began to ask that those who stayed at home be disciplined as well" (Mitchell 1988: 82). Whitman is disciplining the will of these current readers to support Unionism with the lives of their husbands and brothers, by looking back in anger at the British cruelty to revolutionary patriots of 1782.

Whitman's language becomes even more memorializing toward the Revolutionary heroes after he tallies the 12 thousand casualties aboard the prison ships, and chides his contemporaries: "Few think as they cross the City Park, or pass along Flushing Avenue, of the scenes here witnessed in the early part of our national history" (Christman 1963: 34). The remainder of his piece concerns the haphazard construction of a monument for these revolutionaries, built in 1807–08 with great communal pomp, but now in "a ruinous and sluttish condition" (Christman 1963: 42), and in need of civic restoration. As Reid Mitchell has stated, both northern and southern soldiers "were reminded of their Revolutionary heritage, the heroism and purity of their forefathers, and their duty to emulate them" (Mitchell 1988: 20). Whitman's recollection without tranquility invents a tradition, in Boym's terms, through "practices of national commemoration with the aim of reestablishing social cohesion, a sense of security and an obedient relation to authority" (Boym 2001: 42).

Whitman's sense of security is threatened by the War of Secession, and he chooses to emphasize the embodiment of living local memory as the fast-diminishing sign of social cohesiveness. Michael Hertzfeld (quoted in Boym 2001: 42) relates such a conservative mentality as a concrete example of "cultural intimacy" which can undergird nationalism, but which cannot be reduced to national memory, since it is far more concerned with the embodied networks of familiar communication, what Boym calls "the glue of everyday life." For instance, in No. 6, Whitman relies on the living memory of William Hartshorne to recall details of the first newspaper published in Brooklyn in 1729: "Mr. Hartshorne had a very good memory, with an intellect bright, even in his old age, and was willing, to an appreciative listener, to give copious reminiscences of the personages, things, and occurrences, of 70, 60, or 50 years ago, and so on downwards to later times" (Christman 1963: 47). Among the restorative gestures of this article is Whitman's embodied memory of Hartshorne relating to him "the personal appearance and demeanor of Washington, Jefferson, and other of the great historical names of our early national days" (ibid.). Such a nostalgic statement recalls the war-ridden public to the origins of the common circulation of news-in-print, as well as its embodiment in a deferential relation to the Founders as they looked and sounded.

Perhaps the high point of this reliance on "cultural intimacy" comes in No. 10, which is devoted to the cemeteries: "The old graveyards of Brooklyn! What a history is contained in them!" (Christman 1963: 77). Whitman makes a distinction between segments of his reading audience, the 275,000 recent arrivals in Brooklyn versus the "old stock." It is the "old-timers" that Whitman favors in his restorationist history here – for they will embody in "the memory of those who are left of every Brooklyn born and Brooklyn raised man and woman, thoughts of other days – of the days of youth, the pleasures, the friends, scenes and persons long faded away – the appearance of Brooklyn when it was a scattered, rural village of a few hundred people" (Christman 1963: 77). Whitman describes in vivid detail the cemeteries in Civil War era Brooklyn, on a walking tour of the particularities of those who remember the illustrious families of Brooklyn: "The old graveyards would tell it all, from the beginning" (Christman 1963: 80). Whitman even creates one of his early catalogues here, by rattling off the names of the major family trees of the founders and descendants of Brooklyn: "By blood, by marriage, by some or another tie, thousands are yet connected there in those old graveyards," but he adds solemnly, "soon every trace of them, however, to be utterly rubbed out, and strangers busy buying and selling on the location of those memorial grounds" (Christman 1963: 81).

These musings are presented in a flat journalistic language, so that the living can create multiple memorial contexts to connect them to these persons and sites. The fear here rests on the rupture that has already occurred in the firing on Fort Sumter and the first months of the war. These lines from Whitman combine what Boym calls the two main "plots" of restorative nostalgia, "the restoration of origins and conspiracy theory," the latter exemplified by " 'home' . . . forever under siege, requiring defense against the plotting enemy," in this case the public amnesia of collective attachment to the past (Boym 2001: 41). As an intervention, "Brooklyniana" impedes the "enemy" of social memory, since the loss of remembrance of living ties with the dead will make it easier for citizens to step away from their martial duty in supporting the Union cause.

On the doorstep of a house divided, Whitman's desire to restore origins is also manifested in his focus in a curious essay (No. 19) which sketched out the domestic harmony of early settlers in Brooklyn, including a lengthy excerpt from Mary L. Booth's *History of the City of New York*. In this lengthy interlude the rhetoric reminds the readers of the nostalgia for a more stable domestic life, in such images as the following: "The children and negroes grouped in the spacious chimney corners, cracking nuts and telling stories by the light of the blazing pine knots, while the 'vrouws' turned the spinning wheel, and the burghers smoked their long pipes" (Christman 1963: 154–5). The typification of such a sanitized Dutch family provides a kind of rhetorical anchor in the social anxiety of the 1860s, and Whitman concludes with the chortle, "For the comparison of merit between the inhabitants here during the last century . . . with the present time, and all its vaunted educational and fashionable advantages, is not a whit in favor of our own day" (Christman 1963: 157). The writer enlists the domestic front in the war effort, providing the readers with the accent on the social simplicity and harmony of bygone times, as much-needed ballast to their own divided families.

Finally, the embryonic images of hospitals in Whitman's 1862 journalism offer a counterpoint to his later images of Civil War hospitals in his prose and poetry. After the war, in both "Drum-Taps" and *Memoranda*, Whitman's images become distressed representations of a loosening of the familiar marks of social and hierarchical stability. By contrast, in "Brooklyniana" No. 16 (1862), Whitman's verbal portrait of Brooklyn Hospital traces a conventional historical lineage from its origins in 1844, to the current "free institution," that allows patients from all social and economic classes. His presentation of a walking tour of the premises presents the orderly progression from administration to the private rooms for "lady and gentlemen patients," as well as an apartment for "the house physician" (Christman 1963: 133). The fourth floor contains two larger wards, and the north and south wings are divided into wards, with a segregated section for "colored persons" (ibid.). Whitman then presents a catalogue of statistics for the operating year 1861, without any context, as though underlining their atomistic solidity through sheer volume of social benefit.

Likewise, in the *New York Leader* in 1862, Whitman published a series of "City Photographs," four of which delineate "The Broadway Hospital," and once again extend Whitman into a nostalgic reverie. The first section of the first article is called "In Old Memories," and connects the readers with their extended families through the universal reach of the patient list of this "venerable" institution: "Then come up, too, all the tragic and thrilling associations, full of the romance of reality that is ten-fold deeper than anything born of the litterateurs" (Glicksberg 1963: 24). The romance with the hospital is truncated, however, by his hierarchical tour through the buildings, much like the one mentioned in "Brooklyniana." Hierarchically, he begins with the looming portraits of the "Governors' Room" containing paintings of "well-known physicians and surgeons" (Glicksberg 1963: 26). Then, the administrators' offices, and finally the wards, which contain the rows of patients: "What a volume of meaning, what a tragic poem is in every one of those sick wards! Yes, in every individual cot, with its little card-rack nailed at the head" (Glicksberg 1963: 29).

As Morris Vogel points out in his history of the American hospital, "Paternalism and authoritarianism greeted the hospital patient. The humane feeling of the social elite who supported and managed the hospital, and the medical elite who served it, were diminished by the cultural and social distance that divided hospital patient from patron and practitioner" (Vogel 1979: 108). Whitman attempts to mitigate the institutionalized anonymity of the hospital by naming a few of the officers, doctors, and patients ("Charles Green – fracture of leg. Beefsteak"). But, the clinical anonymity of the "photographs" illustrates what Vogel suggests was the common resistance of antebellum citizens to hospital care: "There were strong cultural biases against hospitalization. In case of illness most Americans did not seek the advice of a physician but relied on self-dosing and other home remedies or on a greater tolerance for and acceptance of affliction" (Vogel 1979: 105). Therefore, Whitman's first journalistic sketches of hospital care in 1862 provide a pedagogical function to readers, in schooling them as to how to find the interior of the hospital a more intimately familiar place.

1865–66: *Drum-Taps* and its *Sequel* as Sites of Nationalist and Uncanny Memory

When Whitman published *Drum-Taps* and *Sequel to Drum-Taps*, he had already begun to reshape the uses of cultural memory, in order to accommodate his anxiety over the loss of a cohesive national memory, ongoing sectional hatred, and the dissolution of fraternal ties that bound him to the bedside visits of up to 100,000 wounded soldiers in the Washington hospitals. While he would not publish his notebooks chronicling these experiences until 1875, in *Memoranda During the War*, his personal letters from 1863–65 confirm that his family experience was continually threatened with an array of mental and physical illnesses (rheumatism, mental incapacity, vagrancy, alcoholism, tuberculosis). Such forms of domestic dissolution provided an autobiographical soil for his nostalgic representations of homefront, nation, and the loyalist heart, in poems and prose from 1865–75, texts that will attempt to sustain cultural ideals in the national memory. The triggering event for Whitman's movement from New York to Washington, and from journalist to more direct participant in the war, consisted of his brother George's name appearing in the list of Fredericksburg casualties in the *New York Tribune*. On December 16, 1862, on reading this news, Whitman went to Washington to find George, and finding that the wound was not at all serious, he began a 10-year sojourn in Washington, which provided a cultural backdrop to his poetry and prose of the Civil War years.

The conflictual energies of *Drum-Taps* dominate the poetic collection, as though its appearance in 1865 still bears the incision marks of the immediate cultural confusion after four years of violence. In this poetic chronicle, the literary images oscillate between patriotic conformity to dominant norms (in lines about mobilization, nature, flags, sympathetic connections), and the continual disruption of those norms (in lines featuring wounds, spectral presences, doubling, defeat). Like Bakhtin's concept of the carnivalesque, *Drum-Taps* and its *Sequel* provide us with documents that enact the postwar landscape as a site of conflicting memories, where multiple voices, values, and boundaries of memory represent the "quicksand years" in competition for historical significance. Robert Leigh Davis has convincingly argued that Whitman's response to the war is best encapsulated in the image that opens the book, the "tympanum" in the text "Drum-Taps": "First, O songs, for a prelude, / Lightly strike on the stretch'd tympanum, pride and joy in my city" (Whitman [1865] 1959: 5). Davis suggests that this figure of the tympanum is "[a]t once private and public, intimate and anonymous, hidden and displayed, a sign of the body (the inner ear) and a sign of the state (the military drum)" (Davis 1997: 63).

I would like to build on this crucial foundation by suggesting that the two dominant voices in opposition in *Drum-Taps* are the voice of nationalism, a compliant voice which mobilizes consent to the Union cause, and the voice of the uncanny, which unsettles, but only intermittently, an unreflective conformity to dominant norms of Union nationalism. Further along in the title poem, "Drum-Taps," such a conflict is held at bay, as the poet sings exclamatory praises for the unanimity of Manhattan in the mobilization of the War ("How you sprang! How you threw off the costumes of peace with indifferent hand"). By inscribing a lack of difference ("indifferent"), the voice in the poem suppresses the fact that not all New Yorkers were in favor of the mobilization in equal measure. Indeed, the initial euphoria of the volunteers responding to the call from Washington to fight for Unionism roused New York to mobilize hundreds of soldiers, but such mobilization did not sustain the weight of the carnage and violence of the War, and throughout the Civil War poems Whitman shores up nostalgic voices and revisionist memorialization to justify the Union cause.

The texts that respond most unproblematically to the call for Union nationalism are the poems that repeatedly invoke, through their elegiac language, a nostalgic memorial to transcendent sites of memory, as ballast to balance both personal and historical identity in times of rapid cultural upheaval. In Whitman's Civil War poetry, the identities of personae, human subjects, and historical events are difficult to decipher in their singularity, because the poetry aims for an abstract philosophical reach that transcends such material events. Pierre Nora argues that this memorial impulse serves as an ideological tool for modern societies, as they attempt to cope with the social anxiety produced by the rupture of contemporary societies away from the stable bedrock traditional historical continuity. Whitman's *Drum-Taps* collections continually attempt to locate the value of the war, and its human toll, in terms that use specific memory traces and images to transcend the judgments of history. Nora coins the term "lieux de memoire" (sites of memory) to account for the cultural divide that separates us from a collective sense of traditional identity and social values:

> Our interest in *lieux de memoire* where memory crystallizes and secretes itself has occurred at a particular historical moment, a turning point where consciousness of a break with the past is bound up with the sense that memory has been torn – but torn in such a way as to pose the problem of the embodiment of memory in certain sites where a sense of historical continuity persists. (Nora 1989: 7)

Whitman's poems use such images as natural landscapes, flags, representative snapshots of soldiers, and political abstractions (like liberty and democracy), in order that such images can stretch the readers' identification with what Nora calls "environments of memory," as an antidote to concrete sites of postwar fragmentation: "There are *lieux de memoire*, sites of memory, because there are no longer *mileux de memoire*, real environments of memory" (Nora 1989: 7).

Whitman's mobilization poems multiply the images of collective consent to the Union cause, in such texts as "1861," which apostrophizes the year in the embodiment of "a strong man, erect, clothed in blue clothes, advancing, carrying a rifle on your shoulder, / With well-gristled body and sunburnt face and hands," and locates the "masculine voice" of this representative figure spanning the continent: "Saw I your gait and saw I your sinewy limbs, clothed in blue, bearing / Weapons, robust year; / Heard your determin'd voice, launch'd forth again and again" (Whitman [1865] 1959: 17). Whitman here is "repeating," in the etymological sense of "seeking again," a historical environment of memory that transcends the local divisions of competing political positions on the Union cause. By reciting from memory the universal embodiment of consent to war, the postwar Whitman continues to evade the "secretion" of local forms of resistance to the excessive cost of the conflict. Likewise, in other mobilization poems, such as "Drum-Taps" and "Beat! Beat! Drums," the texts focus on the anonymity of the individual participants, through identifying them as "mechanics" or "new recruits," and on their civic identity subsumed under "Mannahatta a-march! – and it's O to sing well! / It's O for the manly life in the camp!" (Whitman [1865] 1959: 6–7). Elsewhere, the drums and bugles rousing the earliest volunteers float above "the traffic of cities – over the rumble of wheels in the cities," and "Make even the trestles to shake the dead, where they lie awaiting their hearses" (p. 38). Once again, the postwar Whitman attempts to universalize a "real environment of memory," in Nora's terms, one that bridges the antebellum culture with the reconstruction social imaginary.

The most significant mobilization texts, however, are "Song of the Banner at Daybreak," an allegorical apology for masculine consent to participation in the War, and "The Centenarian's Story," a nostalgic bridge-poem to the Revolutionary War Battle of Brooklyn. These two poems confront Whitman's nostalgic desire to create a "total monument to the past," in Boym's terms, but neither delivers such a promise; rather, the anxiety over restorative nostalgia seeps into the documents, and renders them uncanny in their representation of the past: "What drives restorative nostalgia is not the sentiment of distance and longing but rather the anxiety about those who draw attention to historical incongruities between past and present and thus question the wholeness and continuity of the restored tradition" (Boym 2001: 41). The anxiety in "Song of the Banner at Daybreak" drives the Poet's voice as the key voice in the oratorio between the Poet, the Banner and Pennant, the Father and the Child. The Poet's reliance on language fails to connect ("twine") "Man's desire and babe's desire" with the "banner and pennant a-flapping," since he has to rely on words, an inadequate embodiment of historical congruity with antebellum America: "Words! book-words! what are you?" (Whitman [1865] 1959: 9). As Davis points out, Whitman's favoring of the "living immediacy of speech" over the "death-like absence of the written page" can be figured as a semantic struggle that is irresolvable in his Civil War work: "The resonant immediacy of its songs, chants, drum-beats, and hymns may also seem to cross out the deathliness of writing . . . But what we find in fact is that the hymns and songs of *Drum-Taps* are as implicated in death as everything else" (Davis 1997: 68–9). So, in "Song of the Banner at Daybreak," it is the nationalizing voice of the Poet who unsuccessfully tries to give the Union ideology its transcendent identity in images of nature and manifest destiny.

At the insistence of the Pennant and Banner, the Poet melds the natural landscape with the nationalism afoot in the war effort: "But I am of that which unseen comes and sings, sings, sings, / Which babbles in brooks and scoots in showers on the land"

(Whitman [1865] 1959: 11). The Poet also applauds the Banner "discarding peace over all sea and land," and laying claim to the pastoral landscape: "But these, and all, and the brown and spreading land, and the mines below, are ours; / And the shores of the sea are ours, and the rivers great and small; / And the fields they moisten are ours, and the crops and fruits are ours" (p. 13). Timothy Sweet has persuasively argued that the pastoral mode is one of the primary means of reinforcing nationalist ideology in the face of the violence of war: "The pastoral, as a literary mode and an American ideology, contained the means to restore itself. While death has always lurked in the margins of the pastoral . . . , the modally prescribed response to the thought of death, even one's own death, is to take consolation from nature" (Sweet 1990: 8–9). I would suggest that the incitement of the Poet's voice here is enlisting the consent of the nation to the Union cause in just such pastoral terms.

The rhetorical struggle between the Child and the Father about whether to enlist in the Union cause preoccupies most of the energy of this pivotal poem in *Drum-Taps*, with the child's desire to merge with the "banner and pennant" contradicting the father's desire to protect his son from the violence of the war. The Child exclaims that the Banner "is alive – it is full of people – it has children!" despite the Father's terror that the Child's enlistment would "gain nothing, but risk and defy everything": "Forward to stand in front of wars – and O, such wars! / what have you to do with them? / with passions of demons, slaughter, premature death" (Whitman [1865] 1959: 14). It is the Poet who resorts to the totalizing language of continental expansion to naturalize the war effort: "The CONTINENT – devoting the whole identity, without reserving an atom, / Pour in! whelm that which asks, which sings, with all, and the yield of all" (p. 15). The linking of the Union war with continental expansion explains why such a cultural narrative is apostrophized with such hysteria, for example, in the last song of the Poet: the continental spread of the United States is still "Out of reach – an idea only – yet furiously fought for, risking bloody death – loved by me!" (p. 16).

If the South can sever its continental ties with the Union at will, then such fragmentation of the ongoing territorial expansion of the US can threaten the spread of the complete absorption of North American land, as Whitman writes in "From Paumanok Starting I Fly Like a Bird," singing "the idea of all," including the desire to "absorb Kanada in myself," as well as "To Texas, and so along up toward California, to roam accepted everywhere; / To sing first, (to the tap of the war-drum, if need be,) / The idea of all – of the western world, one and inseparable" (Whitman [1865] 1959: 18). In Nora's terms, Whitman's lack of attention to local memory seeks to will into being an environment of memory, to connect the United States in this text to its antebellum mission to conquer the continent. In contrast, Reid Mitchell points out that local sites of memory were equally important to the successful enlistment and retention of soldiers for the duration of the war. The ties to local home communities were constantly informing the consent and resistance of the individual soldier to military service: "The closeness of the soldier to his community both undercut the traditional arrangements that armies make for discipline and provided a powerful impetus for military service and patriotic tenacity" (Mitchell 1993: 21). It is only in his role as hospital companion in *Memoranda During the War* (1875) that Whitman repeatedly seeks to reconnect soldiers with home through conversation and letter-writing. This tympanum-like doubleness, in Davis's terms, reminds us of the wobbly hold that continental visions had on local recruits who longed for ties to home more than to devouring territories at will.

The other major recruitment poem, "The Centenarian's Story," explicitly invokes the uncanny doubleness of competing values in its structure (the prelude by the "Volunteer of 1861," the nostalgic reverie by "The Centenarian") and in its message to patriotic readers releasing sons and husbands into service. The Brooklyn setting serves as a training camp in 1861 for new local recruits, while the Centenarian recalls the site as a decisive Revolutionary battle 85 years earlier. The Volunteer grounds his confident patriotism in the natural landscape, and chides the Centenarian for trembling and convulsive hand-clasping "While splendid and warm the afternoon sun shines down; / Green the midsummer verdure, and fresh blows the dallying breeze" (Whitman [1865] 1959: 19–20). The recruit naturalizes the mobilization efforts for the Civil War, and uses the pastoral mode to attempt to calm the reminders of the carnage of the Revolutionary War battle, in which colonist soldiers died en masse.

After the reading of the Declaration of Independence, Washington's 2,000 soldiers faced off against 20,000 well-armed British soldiers, and were mowed down in great numbers by the British ("It sickens me yet, that slaughter!"). Nevertheless, the ghostly determination of the defeated Washington refuses to capitulate, or draw up the "chapters" or terms of surrender to the enemy. These "chapters," in the etymological sense, are not divisible in historical time, and thus the "Terminus" of the poem: "The two, the past and present, have interchanged; / I myself, as connecter, as chansonnier of a great future, am now speaking" (Whitman [1865] 1959: 23). More asserted than demonstrated, the anxiety of the survivor Centenarian seems to spill over the edges of the forced closure of the text, but illustrates Boym's axiom that "[e]ven in its less extreme form, restorative nostalgia has no use for the signs of historical time – patina, ruins, cracks, imperfections" (Boym 2001: 45). As "the phantoms return" annually on the anniversary of the Battle of Brooklyn, the flag is rebaptized "in many a young man's bloody wounds, / In death, defeat, and sisters', mothers' tears" (Whitman [1865] 1959: 24). The memorialization of the "dead brigade" provides a historical example of Nora's axiom that memory is no longer fully embodied "in the concrete, in spaces, gestures, images, and objects;" but rather, historical memory "binds itself strictly to temporal continuities, to progressions, and relations between things" (Nora 1989: 9). Whitman's text does not allow either war memorial to be self-contained, because such an autonomous division would break the historical continuity that bound the Revolutionary War to the Civil War. As Reid Mitchell notes, the volunteer recruits of 1861, represented in the voice in Whitman's text, comprised the majority of the soldiers throughout the war, and while the Union ideology provided the "principal incentive" for volunteering, "[t]hey also felt that the Union was a precious legacy, handed down to them by the Revolutionary fathers.

Defending it was in many ways a familial duty, something that a son owed the generations before him" (Mitchell 1993: 154). Thus Whitman's poem performs the cultural function of mobilizing consent to the continuing enlistment in the war cause, in continuity with patriotic patrimony.

The pastoral mode crops up repeatedly in *Drum-Taps*, as mentioned earlier in the "green verdure" image in "The Centenarian's Story," and as Timothy Sweet points out, the pastoral ideology in nineteenth-century American texts served the cultural function of "a microcosm – a sociopolitical configuration that could typify American life. The American pastoral ideology entailed the representation of small-farm, free-labor agriculture as a paradigm of identity" (Sweet 1990: 8). With the interruption of the massive violence of 1861–65, the pastoral mode was picked up again in the postwar imagination, and entailed "the drawing of a recuperative pastoral frame around the violence at the end of the war" (ibid.). Thus this consoling voice in *Drum-Taps* manifests itself in such texts as "A Farm Picture," which idealizes the antebellum farm: "Through the ample open door of the peaceful country barn, / A sun-lit pasture field, with cattle and horses feeding" (Whitman [1865] 1959: 46). Again, in "Others May Praise What They Like," the short lyric connects the reader to the antebellum pastoral mode of westward expansion: "Others may praise what they like; / But I, from the banks of the running Missouri, praise nothing, in art, or aught else, / Till it has breathed well the atmosphere of this river – / also the western prairie-scent, / And fully exudes it again" (Whitman [1865] 1959: 68). Again, the recuperative voice of pastoral comfort takes up the first part of "Give Me the Splendid Silent Sun," which catalogues the facets of "a rural domestic life" in such images as "Give me solitude – give me Nature – give me again, O Nature, your primal sanities! / – These, demanding to have them, (tired with ceaseless excitement, and rack'd by the war-strife;)" (p. 47). Even in the widely known "When I Heard the Learn'd Astronomer," the taxonomy of the scientific lecture alienates the speaker, guiding him out of the lecture hall: "Till rising and gliding out, I wander'd off by myself, / In the mystical moist night-air, and from time to time, / Look'd up in perfect silence at the stars" (p. 34). The consolation of the natural "silence" steps away from the pedagogy of the academic presentation, in a way that mirrors Bill Readings' statement in his work *The University in Ruins*: "the transgressive force of teaching does not lie so much in matters of content as in the way pedagogy can hold open the temporality of questioning so as to resist being characterized as a transaction that can be concluded" (Readings 1996: 19). In these terms, the holding open of questioning can be characterized in the uncertainty of cognitive speculation in the astronomical lecture, while the speaker returns to the bedrock of the silent sky, solid and unquestioning, as a source of solace. This poem has always puzzled critics due to its inclusion in a Civil War cluster, but its comforting function, I would suggest, lies in its resistance to the unsettled nature of speculative thought, whereas the natural landscape in its pastoral mode can reassure war-torn citizens.

But Whitman's cultural work in *Drum-Taps* and its *Sequel* cannot shut out the antagonistic voices of defeat and doubt about the excessive cost to human lives for the Union cause. The uncanny presence of spectral figures, death, bodies, ghosts, and doubleness remind us of the strangeness that settles on the vocal cords of the poet, rendering a totalized celebration of the war effort impossible. The corpses, wounds, and ghosts must be written into the Union narrative, and thus these intrusions make a transparent Union ideology incommensurable, much as a self-identical human personality is undermined through desire, power, and other faculties. Even in a "snapshot" poem like "By the Bivouac's Fitful Flame," the first phantom appears in the darkness around an army encampment: "The darkness, lit by spots of kindled fire – the silence; / Like a phantom far or near an occasional figure moving; / The shrubs and trees, (as I left my eyes they seem to be stealthily watching me;)" (Whitman [1865] 1959: 16). As Nicholas Royle points out, the uncanny renders certainties uncertain: "It is a crisis of the natural, touching upon everything that one might have thought was 'part of nature': one's own nature, human nature, the nature of reality and the world" (Royle 2003: 1). The naturalized landscape that in other poems, as we have seen, undergirds popular consent to the war mobilization here turns strange and foreboding, opening up a denaturalized longing that cannot be comfortably found in the campfire or slumbering soldiers.

The transitional text in *Drum-Taps* that begins to link the cultural work of the pastoral voice and the onslaught of war death is "Come Up from the Fields Father," a dramatic poem re-enacting the notification of a family of their son's death. After the parents mistakenly respond to the messenger by thinking that the letter is from "Pete," their son, the text launches into a full-blown pastoral interlude: "Lo, where the trees, deeper green, yellower and redder, / Cool and sweeten Ohio's villages, with leaves fluttering in the moderate wind; / Where apples ripe in the orchards hang, and grapes on the trellis'd vines" (Whitman [1865] 1959: 39). Timothy Sweet argues that "the American will always be a part of the pastoral landscape, cultivating it in life and fertilizing it in death," because in the context of the Civil War, "death is part of the natural process and, simultaneously, part of the nationalist process of transforming all America into a pastoral landscape" (Sweet 1990: 9). The letter in the poem announces in "Sentences broken – *gun-shot wound in the breast, cavalry skirmish, taken to hospital, / At present low, but will soon be better*" (Whitman [1865] 1959: 40, italics in original). The mother's grief then becomes the dominant focus of the text, supplementing the fecund Ohio landscape, and thus the fecundity of her grief can fertilize the heroic sacrifice her son made by dying in the service of the Union cause: "Ah, now the single figure to me, / Amid all teeming and wealthy Ohio, with all its cities and farms, / Sickly white in the face and dull in the head, very faint, / By the jamb of a door leans" (p. 40). The process of grief is arrested in the poem, with the mother occluded at the stage of wanting "To follow, to seek, to be with her dead son"; nevertheless, I would argue that the process of grief eventually concludes in acceptance of loss; and thus, this text leaves the cultural work of readers to hasten the recuperation of loss in the "natural" course of grieving a loved one. The spectral doubleness of the mother's desire to meld with her son, even in death, swells the emotional rapport of Union readers with the appropriateness of such excessive maternal desire.

Of course, the dominant text which naturalizes death in a consoling manner is "When Lilacs Last in the Dooryard Bloom'd," which frames the death of Lincoln and all the war dead in a maximized natural landscape. As Sweet argues, "[d]rawing such a pastoral frame around death in war, however, usually implies that death resulting from war is somehow as natural as any other death" (Sweet 1990: 9). The cultural work of grief here is embedded in a fecund natural landscape, and therefore is clearly naturalizing the enormous human toll which won the war: "Passing the yellow-spear'd wheat, every grain from its shroud in the dark-brown fields uprising; / Passing the apple-tree blows of white and pink in the orchards; / Carrying a corpse to where it shall rest in the grave, / Night and day journeys a coffin" (Whitman [1865–66] 1959: 4). The unnatural violence of the assassination of Lincoln is reduced in scope through its diffusion in the pastoral mode, as an allegorical text for representing all the war dead in the composite figure of "sane and sacred death": "O death! I cover you over with roses and early lilies; / But mostly and now the lilac that blooms the first, / Copious, I break, I break the sprigs from the bushes: / With loaded arms I come, pouring for you, / For you and the coffins all of you, O death.)" (Whitman [1865–66] 1959: 5). The sanity of death in the cause of the Union is apostrophized with an opening up to the naturalization of such war violence.

Sweet further elaborates his case that the naturalization of death in war creates a textual apology for war itself: "If death in war is natural, then war itself, and the politics of war, may be regarded as natural; in such a case the ideology or politics that demand death in war cannot be effectively criticized as cultural structures which it is possible to modify or dismantle" (Sweet 1990: 9). In "Lilacs," for example, rather than critique the war deaths, the poem places them in a transcendent space where they are granted surcease from the nightmare of history:

I saw battle corpses, myriads of them,
And the white skeletons of young men – I saw them;
I saw the debris and debris of all the dead soldiers;
But I saw they were not as was thought;
They themselves were fully at rest – they suffer'd not;
The living remained and suffer'd.
(Whitman [1865–66] 1959: 11)

Whitman's idealization of the beatific memory of the thousands of war dead mobilizes the text as an apology for the work of war's wheels, as these heroic citizens replace their own bodies for the survival of the nation. The "rest" nullifies any desire in readers to rethink the political assumptions that pursued such a cataclysmic conflict, to reflect on any social measures that might have prevented such a conflict from reappearing in the social order. Also, in "Look Down Fair Moon," the lunar light on the battlefield pacifies the excessive cost to the slain soldiers without burial: "Look down fair moon, and bathe this scene; / Pour softly down night's nimbus floods, on faces ghastly, swollen, purple; / On the dead on their backs, with their arms toss'd wide, / Pour down your unstinted nimbus, sacred moon" (Whitman [1865] 1959: 66). The moon here does not raise unsettling questions about the display of human carnage, but rather provides the radiance associated with the saints or gods when they are incarnated on earth, pacifying the horror of loss.

Whitman's critical distance from the unreflective nostalgia of the mobilization poems, and the earlier journalism at the opening of the war, leaves many traces in *Drum-Taps* and the *Sequel*, every site where the fragments of traumatic memory complicate any patriotic dream of national Unionist triumph. As Michael Moon suggests, Whitman's texts multiply representations of vigils near recently deceased soldiers, near "bodies that have until very recently been alive and consequently on a border-line between being alive and being dead in the eyes of the observer" (Moon 1991: 176). For example, in "A Sight in Camp in the Day-Break Gray and Dim," the text narrates the emergence of the speaker from an encampment tent, and encountering "Three forms . . . on stretchers lying," and goes on to inspect the three bodies covered over with shroud-blankets, an elderly "dear comrade," a "child and darling" and "sweet boy, with cheeks yet blooming," and finally the third young casualty: "Young man, I think I know you – I think this face of yours is the face of the Christ himself; / Dead and divine, and brother of all, and here again he lies" (Whitman [1865] 1959: 46). The sight of these casualties at "day-break" denotes the temporal push toward the future, and indeed, despite the uncanny blurring of the borderline between life and death, it is the sacred memory of these war heroes that will furnish their parts to constructing a democratic future for the United States. As Nicholas Royle notes, "To be haunted, to be in the company of ghosts . . . is something to affirm: it is the very condition of thinking and feeling. There is no teaching without memory (however unconscious or cryptic) of the dead, without the logic of mourning that haunts . . . , without an encounter with questions of inheritance" (Royle 2003: 53). The "divinity" of the heroic sacrifice of these three figures on the ground is obviously predicated on their premature death, and they instruct the reader, in their spectral appearance, about the appropriate rituals of mourning for fallen heroes, in order to serve the rhythm of nationalism. It is only by building on this "divine and dead" patrimony that the reader can construct the future United States worthy of their lives' investment.

The democratic future for the Union is contingent on the memorializing of the private and public trauma suffered by the soldiers during the conflict. In "Hymns of Dead Soldiers," the speaker opens his social network to "Phantoms, welcome, divine and tender!" with their "silent eyes." The memorial of these dead soldiers is founded on the "love" pledge of the speaker, in response to the "perfume" of the battlefields: "Give me to bathe the memories of all dead soldiers. // Perfume all! Make all wholesome! / O love! O chant! Solve all with the last chemistry" (Whitman [1865] 1959: 60). Royle points out the crucial role that the specter can play in constructing the future: "To affirm the uncanny 'presence' and power of ghosts is not to give oneself up to some gothic fantasy or lugubrious nostalgia: it is the very basis of trying to think about the future" (Royle 2003: 53–4). It is only through the desire to make "wholesome" the cost of the war dead, rather than decrying such a human catastrophe, that the political future of the restored Union can go forward. The most extended treatment of the uncanny, as a platform for constructing a heroic memorial on which to build America's future, is in "Pensive on Her Dead Gazing, I Heard the Mother Of All," an extended naturalization of the sacrifice of the war dead for justifying Union ideology. The speaker urges the earth not to differentiate itself from the bodies of the fallen soldiers, but rather admonishes, "My dead absorb – my young men's beautiful bodies absorb – and their precious, precious, precious blood; / Which holding in trust for me, faithfully back again give me, many a year hence, / In unseen essence and odor of surface and grass, centuries hence" (Whitman [1865] 1959: 71). As Judith Butler has suggested, "[t]o the extent that nature (pleusis) is what moves us and contributes motion to desire, it seems that nature cannot be separated from norm-enforcing language" (Butler 1995: 378). The totalized absorption of the "immortal heroes" by the natural process of decay will naturalize the violence that cost these thousands of lives, and therefore, the text disciplines the reader to adopt a patriotic posture in compliance with the dominant norms of justifying the war.

In "The Dresser," the persona once again is located in a nostalgic frame, asked by "children" to recall the "unsurpass'd heroes" as to "What stays with you latest and deepest? Of curious panics, / Of hard-fought engagements, or sieges tremendous, what deepest remains?" (Whitman [1865] 1959: 31). The stability of the restorative nostalgia of several texts gives way "In silence, in dream's projections," as the persona dresses multiple wounds for the remainder of the poem. The boundary between the familiar and unfamiliar blurs in an uncanny trance-like state: "I dress the perforated shoulder, the foot with the bullet wound, / Cleanse the one with a gnawing and putrid gangrene, so sickening, so offensive, / While the attendant stands behind aside me, holding the tray and pail" (p. 33). These are the most graphic images in *Drum-Taps* of the wounds on soldiers' bodies, and rather than call into question the bodily fragmentation brought about by the battlefield, the nostalgic frame is producing the transparent contact with their martial heroism that Whitman uses in so many of the Unionist poems. Further along in "The Dresser," Whitman's vigil has a ghost-like border quality that uses the uncanny trance state to situate the reader squarely in Union ideology: "Thus in silence, in dream's projections, / Returning, resuming, I thread my way through the hospitals; / The hurt and the wounded I pacify with soothing hand" (pp. 33–4). As an observer-witness, Whitman's persona here recuperates the heroic stature of these soldiers, through his own agency, to pacify the nagging doubts about the excess of their nationalist sacrifice. Likewise, another recuperative poem such as "The Veteran's Vision," performs such an apology for the experience of heroic combat, while preserving the uncanny frame of the narrator's nostalgia:

> While my wife at my side lies slumbering, and the wars are over long,
> And my head on the pillow rests at home, and the mystic midnight passes,
> And through the stillness, through the dark, I hear, just hear, the breath of my infant,
> There in the room, as I wake from sleep, this vision presses upon me:
> The engagement opens there and then, in my busy brain unreal.
>
> (Whitman [1865] 1959: 55)

The chaotic fragments of the poem recreate the splintered experience of battle in the theater of combat, but these, in Boym's terms, work to "patch up the memory gaps" (Boym 2001: 41), and deny the human toll any chance to overcome the soldier's heroic endurance: "(The falling, dying, I heed not – the wounded, dripping and red, I heed not – some to the rear are hobbling;)" (Whitman [1865] 1959: 56). Furthermore, as Reid Mitchell suggests, the images of domestic relationships bolstered the courage of many soldiers during the chaos of battle, since

> the men of the Civil War era quite sincerely regarded their participation in the war as an extension of their duty to protect their family. It was appropriate that when the defense reached its moment of greatest stress, in battle, men should remember their sweethearts, wives, and children. Of course the duty for which these remembrances steadied men was that of killing. (Mitchell 1988: 77)

This congruity between combat aggression and family nostalgia is mirrored in the structure of "The Veteran's Vision," with the framing device of the "wife" and the "infant" in close proximity, anchoring the "unreal" vision of the battle memory in the concrete stability of the postwar domestic space.

References and Further Reading

Anderson, Benedict (1983). *Imagined Communities*. London: Verso.

Boym, Svetlana (2001). *The Future of Nostalgia*. New York: Basic Books.

Butler, Judith (1995). Desire. In Frank Lentricchia and Thomas McLaughlin (eds.), *Critical Terms for Literary Study*. Chicago: University of Chicago Press, pp. 369–86.

Christman, Henry M. (ed.) (1963). *Walt Whitman's New York: From Manhattan to Montauk*. New York: Macmillan.

Davis, Robert Leigh (1997). *Whitman and the Romance of Medicine*. Berkeley: University of California Press.

Glicksberg, Charles I. (ed.) (1963). *Walt Whitman and the Civil War: A Collection of Original Articles and Manuscripts*. New York: A. S. Barnes.

LaCapra, Dominick (1985). *History and Criticism*. Ithaca, NY: Cornell University Press.

Lindermann, Gerald F. (1987). *Embattled Courage: The Experience of Combat in the Civil War*. New York: Free Press.

Loving, Jerome (1999). *Walt Whitman: The Song of Himself*. Berkeley: University of California Press.

Lowenfels, Walter (1978). *Walt Whitman's Civil War*. New York: Knopf.

Mancuso, Luke (1997). *The Strange Sad War Revolving: Walt Whitman, Reconstruction, and the Emergence of Black Citizenship*. Columbia, SC: Camden House.

Mitchell, Reid (1988). *Civil War Soldiers: Their Expectations and Experiences*. New York: Touchstone.

Mitchell, Reid (1993). *The Vacant Chair: The Northern Soldier Leaves Home*. Oxford: Oxford University Press.

Moon, Michael (1991). *Disseminating Whitman*. Cambridge, MA: Harvard University Press.

Nora, Pierre (1989). Between Memory and History: Les Lieux de Memorie. *Representations*, 6: 7–25.

Readings, Bill (1996). *The University in Ruins*. Cambridge, MA: Harvard University Press.

Reynolds, David S. (1995). *Walt Whitman's America: A Cultural Biography*. New York: Knopf.

Royle, Nicholas (2003). *The Uncanny*. New York: Routledge.

Sweet, Timothy (1990). *Traces of War: Poetry, Photography, and the Crisis of the Union*. Baltimore: Johns Hopkins University Press.

Vogel, Morris J. (1979). The Transformation of the American Hospital, 1850–1920. In Susan Reverby and David Rosner (eds.), *Health Care in America*. Philadelphia: Temple University Press, pp. 105–16.

Whitman, Walt (1962). *Memoranda During the War and Death of Abraham Lincoln*, ed. Roy P. Basler. Bloomington: Indiana University Press.

Whitman, Walt ([1865–66] 1959). *Walt Whitman's Drum-Taps (1865) and Sequel to Drum-Taps (1865–66)*, ed. F. DeWolfe Miller. Gainesville, FL: Scholars' Facsimiles and Reprints.

19
Nature
M. Jimmie Killingsworth

Whitman's representation of nature, a topic that fascinated his earliest readers, has attracted renewed attention with the historical prominence of the environmental protection movement in the late twentieth century and the consequent development of new strains of critical inquiry, usually grouped under the heading of ecocriticism. This chapter considers a central tension in recent studies of human ecology and geography – the representation of nature as space and as place – as it plays out in Whitman's writing. The concept of space favors an abstract treatment of nature in terms of form and function, allowing for the development of a powerful analogical imagination within a largely formalist and modernist poetics: the poem as environment. The concept of place, especially as developed in bioregionalist and reinhabitational thinking, offers an alternative to the spatial imagination. Places are full of history, both human and natural, that resist their treatment as "wide open" spaces submissive to the imposition of modernist (or imperial) values and that also resist replacement by mental and poetic constructs. Approaching the sacred, they demand the respect and tribute of the poet.

Whitman made room for both concepts in his vision of American landscape. His view of nature as space suggests his connection with a burgeoning modernism in life and letters while his often-repeated identification with special places – notably the New York islands and eastern wetlands of North America – demonstrate the power of close connections with character-forming and culture-defining sacred sites. The tension between the two outlooks anticipates many of the concerns of contemporary environmental thought.

Ecocriticism and Whitman

Beginning as a thematic focus in the literary scholarship of the early 1990s, roughly comparable to the interest in race, class, and gender in the New Historicism of the

1970s and 1980s, ecocriticism has evolved from a study of the literary manifestations of environmentalist discontent into a widely varied meditation on the capabilities of human language users to represent and understand their physical surroundings and their relation to the nonhuman world (see Bate 2000, Buell 2001, Coupe 2000, Glotfelty and Fromm 1996, Kerridge and Samuells 1998, Levin 2002). Ecocritical studies of Whitman appear rather late on the scene largely because his best-known and most powerful poetry does not necessarily embrace or foretell the political agenda favored by early ecocriticism – the resistance to technological development and the emphasis on protection of nature adopted by political environmentalism in the twentieth century and anticipated by high Romanticism in the nineteenth. It was Emerson, Thoreau, and John Muir in America, Wordsworth and Shelley in England, and later writers in the Transcendentalist and Romantic mold who played best in the first round of ecocritical studies (see, for example, Bate 1991, Buell 1995, Kroeber 1994, Slovic 1992). When Whitman does get mentioned, as in Buell's influential work, he is usually pressed into the service of an argument aligning environmentalist ideals with pastoral genres and the history of Romanticism. To fit Whitman into the scheme of "environmental literature" as defined by both Buell (1995) and Murphy (2000) – a literature stressing human separation from the natural world (or an understanding of the differences between an "anthropocentric" and an "ecocentric" worldview), a rhetorical or political plea for "getting back to Nature" in one form or another, and a Romantic sense of conflict and loss in the face of modernization – the few ecocritics who do venture into Whitman studies turn as frequently to the prose as to the poetry for support. They delight in Whitman's late work *Specimen Days*, for instance, with its back-to-nature themes and strong contrast of urban and rural experience (Philippon 1998). In arguing that Whitman's New York poems share a "Romantic urbanism" with the celebrated landscape architecture of Frederick Law Olmstead, Buell (2001) draws heavily upon the poet's early journalism with its treatment of the environment as a set of political and social problems (such as water treatment and sanitation).

Such readings require underselling strong conflicts within Whitman's work that have long been recognized by scholars, not least the palpable differences between the poetry in *Leaves of Grass* and the rhetoric of his journalism and prose works, as well as the differences among the writings of his youth (such as the early journalism), his middle age (notably the first three editions of *Leaves of Grass*), and his old age (both poetry and prose written after the Civil War). Taking these tensions into account, Cummings (1992) argues compellingly that *Specimen Days* differs distinctly from the earlier poetry in viewing nature as a spectacle rather than attempting to "merge" with it poetically as a source of "original energy" (Whitman 1891–92: 29). Along the same lines, Doudna (1998) suggests that Whitman's treatment of the nonhuman world undergoes a shift at midcareer. In the two periods, the poet labored under rather different definitions of nature: "as the material world of objects and phenomena (*natura naturata*)" and "as the force – usually personified as feminine – that pervades and controls that material world (*natura naturans*)." "In Whitman's pre-Civil War poetry," writes Doudna, "the *naturata* aspect . . . tends to predominate . . . In such later [prose] works as *Democratic Vistas* (1871) or his last major poem, 'Passage to India' (1871), the *naturans* aspect predominates and nature becomes largely an abstraction" (Doudna 1998: 451). From the perspective of environmental protection, some of the later poems, above all "Song of the Redwood-Tree," come off rather poorly, as Gay Wilson Allen (1980) pointed out years ago, while poems from the middle period, such as "This Compost," must be counted among the most profound of all nineteenth-century literary ventures into ecology (Killingsworth 2002).

Another discontinuity to be considered concerns Whitman's relation to Romanticism. In the first book ever written about Whitman, *Notes on Walt Whitman as Poet and Person* – an excerpt of which appears in Mazel's (2001) collection of important forerunners to ecocriticism – John Burroughs, who was to become himself one of the most famous nature writers in American literary history, contends that Whitman is not a nature poet in the manner of his Romantic forebears: "no modern book of poems says so little about Nature, or contains so few compliments to her" (Burroughs [1867] 1971: 41). According to Burroughs, Whitman "is not merely an observer of Nature, but is immersed in her." In the work of poets like Wordsworth and Shelley, "Nature [is] talked of and discussed," but Whitman's poems "approximate to a direct utterance of Nature herself." "The poet, like Nature," he concludes, "seems best pleased when his meaning is well folded up, put away, and surrounded by a curious array of diverting attributes and objects . . . . But the word or phrase is always an electric one. He never stops to elaborate, never explains" (pp. 41, 43–4; see also Warren 2001). Burroughs no doubt overstates his "never." Whitman's writing, especially after the Civil War, does occasionally fit the picture of nature poetry as it was known in his day, though when it does, it sometimes conforms to high Romantic forms and values (as in "When I Heard the Learn'd Astronomer," whose critique of science echoes Wordsworth's "The Tables Turned" and even Poe's "Sonnet – to Science") but may also suggest something closer to the modified metaphysical strain found in his contemporaries William Cullen Bryant and Oliver Wendell Holmes. A poem like "A Noiseless Patient Spider," for example, with its observation of nature followed by an application to human life, roughly follows patterns developed in such popular poems as Bryant's "To a Waterfowl" and Holmes's "The Chambered Nautilus," which in turn hearken back to the English seventeenth century and such poems as Henry Vaughan's "The Waterfall" (see Killingsworth 2004). Other parallels have also been explored. To account for the anti-Platonic strain of meaty materialism in Whitman, which distinguishes his work from that of Wordsworth and Emerson, Wilson (2000) traces a lineage from the ancient Lucretius through the gnostic quasi-science of Whitman to chaos theory and use of the rhizome metaphor in the work of the post-structuralists Deleuze and Guattari. Angus Fletcher (2004) explores the connection of *Leaves of Grass* to the descriptive poetry of eighteenth-century England, best exemplified in the work of James Thomson.

More than merely revising the line of descent for *Leaves of Grass*, these identifications of new sources and affinities raise wide-reaching ecopoetical questions for the interpretation of Whitman's work. Pursuing the descriptive heritage leads to a fresh appreciation for Whitman's treatment of space in Angus Fletcher's (2004) *A New Theory for American Poetry*. Following the metaphysical strain, I offer a new reading of Whitman's emplacement of human beings and embodiment of nature in *Walt Whitman and the Earth* (Killingsworth 2004). Both of these recent books take us beyond the hero-seeking practices of early ecocriticism and model a form of ecological critique that might well apply to any writer even in the absence of ecopolitical intention and aim. My goal in the remainder of this essay is to advance this agenda by further delineating the relationship of space and place in Whitman's work. As I see it, instead of anticipating environmentalist values in the manner of Wordsworth, Emerson, and Thoreau, all of whom took an ironic and at times elitist attitude toward working people and their seeming disregard for nature, Whitman's poetry enacts and dramatizes the conflicts of common experience in the modern world, the sense of loss and sometimes alienation that accompany material success for the American middle classes.

Whitman's Poetic Spaces

At first blush, Angus Fletcher's (2004) approach to Whitman seems to reiterate Burroughs' point that Whitman embodies rather than writes about nature. The poems in *Leaves of Grass* "are not *about* the environment, whether natural or social," Fletcher argues, "They *are* environments" (2004: 103). But unlike Burroughs, who implies strongly that Whitman outromanticizes the Romantics by writing from the perspective of a deeper and closer communion with nature, an organic connection that he manages to convey in poetic language, Fletcher arrives at a special version of formalism that suggests a radical separation of poetic environments from the natural and social world. Though he does not make the connection himself, Fletcher's treatment of the "environment-poem" in a line of descent running from John Clare to Whitman and finally to John Ashbery seems to foretell not the ecological crises of modern times so much as the concern with virtual reality and cyberspace in artificial intelligence, computer engineering, and science fiction. In short, Fletcher's "new theory for American poetry" is more about space than about place and is particularly interested in the creation of poetic spaces.

No doubt, Fletcher's approach opens new vistas on Whitman's work in many ways. First, by placing works such as "Song of Myself" in relation to the descriptive poetry of the British eighteenth century, Fletcher offers insights into Whitman's enumerative style as well as the principles of movement and observation shared particularly among urban poets, whether on the street or rambling out into the countryside (see also Buell 2001 on the *flâneur* theme). From this perspective, we can see Whitman's famous catalogues not merely as one example after another of some general principle, such as the glory of the working class or the beauty of bodies – for many readers, far too many examples to prove a simple point – but rather as an attempt to create a virtual city of characters, objects, and actions in which the reader is invited to dwell and ramble with the poet. The poem, in this sense, is an analogue for the city; and the poetic imagination appears primarily as architectonic and self-sufficient. The poet's interest in close observation, the problem of scale, and descriptive writing connects his work not only with journalism but also with science and natural history – a connection similarly pursued by the descriptive poets of the eighteenth century (in Thomson's poem on Isaac Newton, for example). Once inside his writing, the poet – and with him the reader – tends to abandon the material world in much the same way that science tends to progress from the field observations of natural history to laboratory work with collected specimens to the simulated world studied by the experimentalists and modelers that dominate twentieth-century science (see Killingsworth and Palmer 1992, chapter 3).

Second, by referring to Whitman's lifelong geographical relationship to the ocean, Fletcher locates the origins of the persistent wave-like motion of the poems and the formation of what Fletcher calls "the Whitman phrase," the paramount syntactical unit in Whitman's compositions. The prominent figure of anaphora, for example, in which the beginning of a line is repeated and the end altered (a rhetorical technique all but perfected in the speeches of Martin Luther King, Jr.), suggests the landing of waves on the shore. The arrival of every wave is predictable, but each wave brings something new.

Third, by recalling Whitman's background in journalism, Fletcher explains the openness of the structure of *Leaves of Grass*, its unfolding over the years in newly expanded editions, as well as the resistance to closure we find in the best poems, the tendency of the poetic topic or even the figure of the poet to solidify before our eyes and then dissolve back into the fabric of life. While we can see traces of the journalist in *Leaves of Grass*, however, it was the poet in Whitman, says Fletcher, "that caused his troubles and his final break with the news business that he knew so well, from print shop and pressroom all the way up to the publisher's office. The poet in him had to slow up the pace of his perceptions, placing them at the service of diurnal knowledge, instead of yesterday's news" (Fletcher 2004: 84–5). "Clare, Whitman, and Ashbery," in Fletcher's view, "all write poetry as if it were a revelatory or metaphysical journalism" (p. 76).

What's missing in Fletcher's description-centered theory, however, is any way of accounting for the "revelatory or metaphysical" content in this poetically transformed journalism. His approach might well yield a good reading of the catalogues in "Song of Myself," the prosody of "Out of the Cradle Endlessly Rocking," and such later works of observation on the street as "Sparkles from the Wheel," but what about "This Compost," arguably the most powerful ecological poem in American literature, the drama of which seems to resist the tag of "descriptive"; or "Song of the Rolling Earth," which takes on directly (if mysteriously) the problem of how to bring nature and the body into language, suggesting that Whitman considered carefully the problems entailed in poetic representation and did not find the poetic world a satisfactory substitution for nature; or "Song of the Redwood-Tree," a rhetorical tour de force that replaces the descriptive power of the witness with the abstraction of allegory at a distance and exchanges the democratic leveling of hierarchies for a reissue of the Great Chain of Being?

Fletcher argues that thinking about poetics in relation to Jacksonian reforms in American democracy sheds light on the leveling of hierarchies involving not only people but also objects observed and organized into poetic descriptions. The poetic space in the "environment poem" supposedly receives each person and object in turn without judging its superiority or inferiority; but in fact in such poems as "This Compost," "Song of the Rolling Earth," "Song of the Redwood-Tree," and "Passage to India," Whitman pursues at length the separation and hierarchical relationship of nature and humankind. His aim is to reconcile the separation and put the wayward human race on an equal footing with nature, but the drama of the poems depends upon acknowledging the painfulness of this process; and the result of the reconciliation rarely seems entirely satisfactory. Thus the poet mourns the spirits of the redwood trees as they depart before the axes of the "superber race" of human settlers (Whitman 1891–92: 167), but a sense of tragic loss lingers at the end of the poem, a tone that has led biographically inclined readers to suggest that Whitman, who had recently suffered a stroke when he wrote the poem and felt left behind by events in the life of the nation, identified more with the mighty redwoods than with the wood-clearing pioneers of the poem despite his ostensible celebration of manifest destiny and the ideology of progress (see Loving 1999).

Moreover, from the perspective of ecocriticism, the idea of "leveling" in the Jacksonian sense invokes "leveling" in the sense of clearing the land, opening the space for development. Another possible substitution, suggested by the mention of "race" in "Song of the Redwood-Tree," hints at the dark side of the Jacksonian legacy – the substitution of "red" people for redwoods. If Andrew Jackson was the author of the form of democracy to which Whitman subscribed and dedicated his poetic form, Jackson was also the architect of the Indian removal policy that led to the infamous Trail of Tears and a long string of Indian wars. What appeared to be wide-open spaces ready for the architectonic imagination for Jackson and his followers was – for the displaced natives and the indigenous flora and fauna of the West – home. And more than any other concept of place, it is home that resists the designation of the land as space. "There is no place like home" (Tuan 1977: 3).

Poetic Space and Geographical Place as an Alternating Gestalt

"Place is security, space is freedom," writes the geographer Yi-Fu Tuan (1977), "we are attached to the one and long for the other." "Geographers study places," he goes on to explain; "Planners would like to evoke a 'sense of space' " (p. 3). Writing in the Jacksonian mode (with Jackson as an ancestor of the modern planner and the developmental view of landscape), Whitman evokes the feeling of freedom associated with that sense of space, not only in the boosterism of poems like "Pioneers! O Pioneers!," "Passage to India," and "Song of the Redwood-Tree," but even in what appears to be the simplest of nature poems, the much-loved anthology piece "A Noiseless Patient Spider":

> A noiseless patient spider,
> I mark'd where on a little promontory it stood isolated,
> Mark'd how to explore the vacant vast surrounding,
> It launched forth filament, filament, filament, out of itself,
> Ever unreeling them, ever tirelessly speeding them.
> And you O my soul where you stand,
> Surrounded, detached, in measureless oceans of space,
> Ceaselessly musing, venturing, throwing, seeking the spheres to connect them,
> Till the bridge you will need be form'd, till the ductile anchor hold,
> Till the gossamer thread you fling catch somewhere, O my soul.
>
> (Whitman 1891–92: 343)

The first stanza works in the descriptive mode, offering an observation of a spider in a place. The place is schematic but definable – "a little promontory" – and the activity described is natural, the poetry working to capture the repetitive yet tireless work of the spider through wave-like repetitions of various kinds (the mini-anaphora of "mark'd," the alliteration and whole-word repetition of "little . . . launch," "vacant vast," and "forth filament, filament, filament," the assonance of "unreeling" and "speeding"). In the second stanza, the spider becomes a metaphor for the poetic soul, and the place (promontory) becomes "measureless oceans of space"; the spider's natural environment (literally "surrounding"), though "vacant" and "vast," is emptied entirely of substance, suggesting a mental or imaginary space: "musing, venturing, throwing, seeking the spheres to connect them" – the "spheres" with their hint of geometric regularity inclining toward the purely mental, the world of the Platonic forms, the dwelling of the soul.

This movement from place to space, from natural object to mental metaphor, from body to soul, no doubt suggests a sense of release, of freedom (foretelling the longing of science fiction author William Gibson's cyberpunk "cowboys" to pull free of the "meat world" and live entirely in the matrix of cyberspace). But it also entails a sort of wistful sadness at the inability of the spider-soul to connect the spheres and make the ductile anchor hold. The sadness gains weight when we consider the publication history of the poem (discussed in detail in Killingsworth 2004). The spider image originated in a manuscript poem about a soldier whom the poet encounters in passing, whose eyes suggest a longing for contact. The filament does not catch, however, and the loving connection goes unrealized. Instead of the published version's "measureless oceans of space," the manuscript poem laments "fathomless oceans of love" that remain thus unexplored (Whitman [1921] 1972, 2: 93). So it is that the trace of sadness remaining in the published version has roots in what Whitman scholars often refer to as the "Calamus emotion," the homoeroticism of *Leaves of Grass*, the often unfulfilled longing typical of poems from the early 1860s. Space is all about longing, as Tuan suggests, and as the old Kris Kristofferson song says, "Freedom's just another word for nothing left to lose."

The feeling of freedom implied in the soul set free from its moorings also ties in dangerously with the imperialist mood. The best example appears at the end of "Passage to India," a poem from the same period as "A Noiseless Patient Spider" – written after the Civil War but before the collapse of the poet's health in the early 1870s, a time when Westward expansion was the order of the day:

> O sun and moon and all you stars! Sirius and Jupiter!
> Passage to you!
> Passage, immediate passage! the blood burns in my veins!
> Away O soul! hoist instantly the anchor!
> Cut the hawsers – haul out – shake out every sail!
> Have we not stood here like trees in the ground long enough?
> Have we not grovel'd here long enough, eating and drinking like mere brutes?
>
> (Whitman 1891–92: 322–3)

The command "hoist instantly the anchor" recalls the spider poem in the longing to break free from the hold of place and anticipates "Song of the Redwood-Tree" in its grappling with hierarchical relationships, but the wistfulness in the tone of the one and the world-weariness of the other are missing. Now the imperial drive to encompass one frontier after another predominates. Reaching above the level of "trees" and "brutes," now mere objects without value, like used and discarded resources, the soul wants more. The hunger for new spaces to discover and claim foreshadows the words of the notorious British imperialist Cecil Rhodes, who once said, "To think of the stars that you see overhead at night, these vast worlds which we can never reach. I would annex the planets if I could" (quoted in Killingsworth 2004: 81).

In other poems, neither space nor place dominates the conceptual frame. What emerges instead is an alternating gestalt. If we can read the following passage from "Crossing Brooklyn Ferry" according to Fletcher's method, for example, and see the images of the poem as pieces of a poetic environment rather than the representation of an actual place and moment in history from which the poet is addressing us, then Whitman's claim that time and place and distance don't matter is literally true. We see the words and occupy the poetic space as readers more or less the same way he did himself once the poem was committed to the page:

> It avails not, time nor place – distance avails not,
> I am with you, you men and women of a generation, or ever so many generations hence,
> Just as you feel when you look on the river and sky, so I felt,
> Just as any of you is one of a living crowd, I was one of a crowd,
> Just as you are refresh'd by the gladness of the river and the bright flow, I was refresh'd,
> Just as you stand and lean on the rail, yet hurry with the swift current, I stood yet was hurried,
> Just as you look on the numberless masts of ships and the thick-stemm'd pipes of steamboats, I look'd.
>
> (Whitman 1891–92: 130)

The river, the ferry, and the dock are not real things, after all, but only images in poetic space. They are virtual.

Seen in another way, however, the poem suggests a near-tragic environmental loss. When contemporary readers think of the referents of these signs, the places actually named in Whitman's poem and the passage from Manhattan to Brooklyn, they can only be struck by the discontinuity between modern experience and that of Whitman's day. Instead of rubbing shoulders with fellow citizens on the ferry, each individual is enclosed within the automobile's glass and steel, denied direct contact with other people, the engines spewing fumes that change the very color and quality of the sunset as Whitman knew it, careening across the river on asphalt and steel high above the water, unable to tell whether it is flood tide or ebb tide below. More than the communal merge with Whitman, we are likely to feel an environmentalist irony when the poet asserts, after a long catalogue of waterfront images – the high-masted ships with white sails, sailors scrambling in the riggings, even the ferry itself which came to be replaced by the Brooklyn Bridge – "These and all else were to me the same as they are to you" (Whitman 1891–92: 131). We can treasure Whitman's preservation of the images, we can see what we have lost, but we will never be able to enjoy the poem as a reflection of a living natural environment as Whitman himself presumably could – at least for a fleeting moment.

In the view of Arthur Geffen (1984), the vision of communion with future readers and citizens that informs "Crossing Brooklyn Ferry" may have been spoiled for Whitman himself by the building of the Brooklyn Bridge. In his boosterizing mode, Whitman had nothing but praise for the engineering achievement of the Mississippi River bridge in St Louis, but he remained curiously silent about the building of the great bridge in his own hometown. Here we have one of the best examples of Whitman's ecological double-mindedness, his ideological commitment to technological progress and human achievement at odds with his realization that the bridge of bridges rendered the Fulton Ferry obsolete and destroyed the neighborhood upon which it depended, a site that Whitman considered "almost a holy place" (Geffen 1984: 2). If Geffen is right, Whitman is an early exemplar of what environmentalists call the "Not in My Backyard," or NIMBY, phenomenon. Again, there's no place like home.

Embodiment, Emplacement, and Relocation in Whitman

The transformation of place into space, both imperial and poetic, and the invocation of an alternating gestalt between space and place, however, remain only two possibilities for reading among the complex set of relationships between humankind and nature that Whitman explores in *Leaves of Grass*. The effect of place on character formation is suggested in any number of meditations on identity with nature. Such passages are likely the very ones that gave Burroughs the feeling that Whitman embodies nature rather than merely discussing or praising it.

Embodiment gets worked out through personification, metaphor, and a variety of other tropes of identity in *Leaves of Grass*. A sort of resonating interaction is set up within the tropes, the body and its environment alternately substituting for one another in a rush of poetic energy. In sections 21 and 22 of "Song of Myself," for example, the earth is personified as smiling, "voluptuous," and "elbowed"; the sea beckons with "crooked fingers" and "amorous wet" (Whitman 1891–92: 46). In section 5, the body becomes virtually indistinguishable from the landscape, the earth offering plentiful analogues for the masculine genitalia and the skin with its pores and hair: "leaves stiff or drooping in the fields," the "little wells" of the ants, and "mossy scabs of worm fence, heap'd stones, elder, mullein and poke-weed" (Whitman 1891–92: 32–3).

Whitman's figurative language thus again suggests an alternating gestalt, this time between literal and figurative terms, or between the foreground and background of images. An excellent example appears in the notorious poem of the body, "Spontaneous Me," which originated in the 1856 edition when it was called "Bunch Poem" after the odd image of semen as a bunch of seed tossed to fall where it may. In contrast to the figure of a shame-filled lad struggling to master his sexual impulses, the poem celebrates the heroic masturbatory figure of the poet at home with his body and at one with nature. The experience of identity with the earth begins with the enjoyment of the body, particularly the penis, metaphorically conceived as the "poem" that "all men carry" in a scene of autoerotic fantasy:

> Beautiful dripping fragments – the negligent list of one after another, as I happen to call them to me, or think of them,
> The real poems, (what we call poems being merely pictures,)
> The poems of the privacy of night, and of men like me,
> This poem, drooping shy and unseen, that I always carry, and that all men carry,
> (Know, once for all, avowed on purpose, wherever are men like me, are our lusty, lurking, masculine poems,)
> Love-thoughts, love-juice, love-odor, love-yielding, love-climbers, and the climbing sap,
> Arms and hands of love – lips of love – phallic thumb of love – breasts of love – bellies pressed and glued together with love,
> Earth of chaste love – life that is only life after love,
> The body of my love – the body of the woman I love – the body of the man – the body of the earth,
> Soft forenoon airs that blow from the south-west,
> The hairy wild-bee that murmurs and hankers up and down – that gripes the full-grown lady-flower, curves upon her with amorous firm legs, takes his will of her, and holds himself tremulous and tight upon her till he is satisfied.
>
> (Whitman 1891–92: 89–90)

From the image of the bee upon the flower, the catalogue of images continues through a number of earthy scenes, arriving finally back where it began, at the poet's contemplation of his own genitals ("The sensitive, orbic, underlapped brothers, that only privileged feelers may be intimate where they are") (Whitman 1891–92: 90). Swearing the "oath of procreation," the poet links himself to Nature, which can be conceived as the Other only in the sense of the Other within, the Spontaneous Me, the identity of the self with something like instinct, the "greed that eats me day and night with hungry gnaw," the erotic impulse to connect and reproduce.

Whitman scholars will be familiar with this line of interpreting the famous "poetry of the body" (see Killingsworth 1989). What is not as commonly recognized is that the poem celebrates the emplacement of the body as surely as it insists on the naturalness of physical life and the embodiment of nature. The poet's erotic imagination drifts from the hillside whitened with the spring blossoms of mountain ash – an earthy analogue for his own body littered with his "seed," the semen, "this bunch pluck'd at random from myself" – to the old home ground of the ocean shore, with "the souse upon me of my lover the sea, as I lie willing and naked" (Whitman 1891–92: 90–1). The particularity of the images – "The smell of apples, aromas from crush'd sage-plant, mint, birch-bark" (p. 90), much like the "elder, mullein and poke-weed" in "Song of Myself" (p. 33) – bespeak place as surely as the names of the cities in "Crossing Brooklyn Ferry." The flora, the fauna, and the landscape features suggest that the setting of the poem, as with so many of the erotic passages in *Leaves of Grass* (whether homo-, hetero-, or autoerotic), is the northeastern American shoreline. Everything points to Whitman's Long Island home.

In "This Compost," another 1856 poem, a similar metaphorical linking of place and body occurs, but only after the poet has dramatized the initial state of alienation from the earth that suggests the need for the poetic reunion. Disgusted by something he happens upon while walking in the woods and fields, the poet's imagination turns with near-gothic revulsion to thoughts of all the dead and diseased matter that returns to the earth, but a turn of the plow and further reflection shows the power of the earth's chemistry to absorb, replenish, and renew life in a miracle of resurrection. Reunited with the earth, the poet slides into another of his rhapsodic meditations on oneness with the earth, the body again emplaced, the earth embodied:

What chemistry!
That the winds are really not infectious,
That this is no cheat, this transparent green-wash of the sea which is so amorous after me,
That it is safe to allow it to lick my naked body all over with its tongues,
That it will not endanger me with the fevers that have deposited themselves in it,
That all is clean forever and forever,
That the cool drink from the well tastes so good,
That blackberries are so flavorous and juicy,
That the fruits of the apple-orchard and the orange-orchard, that melons, grapes, peaches, plums, will none of them poison me,
That when I recline on the grass I do not catch any disease,
Though probably every spear of grass rises out of what was once catching disease.
(Whitman 1891–92: 286)

And once again, the emplacement of this reunion is specific and particular, the images consistent with the landscape of Whitman's homeland, from the sea that "licks" the human body to the fruit that the poet puts in his own mouth.

The idea of reunion suggested in "This Compost" hints toward a number of other "re-" words that apply significantly to Whitman's treatment of place. Place is something to which the poems always seem to be returned, as if poetic space for the modern poet ultimately requires renewal by a return to the body (in many ways, the place of places, the self's own site) and the home or other "almost sacred sites," to repeat the felicitous phrase of Geffen (1984: 2). The "almost" suggests the reality that Whitman is primarily a modern writer – if not fully urban in his leanings, then certainly caught up in the urbanization of his times; if not always fully committed to technological achievement and the ideal of progress, then certainly aware of the benefits for working people and society as a whole and occasionally given to over-the-top celebrations of technology and development; if not a fully secularized denizen of the modern world – with rather frequent recourse to the language of soul and spirit – still mainly the enemy of organized religion and oppressive priestcraft. Even so, he retains a view of the land that suggests older tribal models, an attachment that resists the free-ranging mobility of modern times. His best poems, if they do not stay close to home, return to the shoreline or the wetlands for the purpose of spiritual renewal. In addition to the passages from "Song of Myself," "Spontaneous Me," and "This Compost" already mentioned, think of the "Sea-Drift" pair of "As I Ebb'd with the Ocean of Life" and "Out of the Cradle Endlessly Rocking," in which the grown poet confronts a moment of self-doubt and recalls the child-poet's first deep experience of the pains and joys of life, the realization of the power of love and death, represented in his encounter with the mockingbird mourning the loss of its mate at the edge of the sea, the ocean itself figured as the ancient mother lisping the "low and delicious" word "death"; or "Crossing Brooklyn Ferry" with its images of returning to home from the great city at the water's edge, its flood-tide joy standing in contrast to the depressed spirits of "As I Ebb'd with the Ocean of Life"; and "When Lilacs Last in the Dooryard Bloom'd," in which the poet retreats to the swamp to mourn the death of the beloved president to the strains of the solitary hermit thrush singing in the dark pines. In such poems the sacred places resonate with the mood of the poet, they offer renewal and revived inspiration, they return him to the rhythms of the earth with tides replacing the clock time and seasons replacing the calendar time of life in the modern industrial world. Whitman kept renewing his writing on the old places to the end, in such works as *Specimen Days* and "Sands at Seventy." It is on these grounds that I follow Loving's (1999) designation of Whitman as "essentially an island poet" (p. 26). Even the cities whose poet he claimed to be – Brooklyn and Manhattan – were island cities. The smell of salt air and the sound of the wave upon the shore are never far away in *Leaves of Grass*.

In this sense, at least one more alternating reading is necessary to make sense of Whitman's representation of nature. We need to see him as simultaneously a regional and a universal poet. He is an island poet in the same way that Faulkner and O'Connor are southern writers. While modern criticism tends to value the universal and catholic over the regional and provincial, the global over the local, ecocriticism attempts to restore the value to the local with concepts like reinhabitation and bioregionalism (for summary discussions of which, see Buell 1995, 2001). An ecocritical reading suggests that Whitman's best poems tend to stay close to home, and in doing so, paradoxically extend their reach.

References and Further Reading

Allen, Gay Wilson (1980). How Emerson, Thoreau, and Whitman Viewed the Frontier. In Louis J. Budd, Edwin H. Cady, and Carl L. Anderson (eds.), *Toward a New American Literary History: Essays in Honor of Arlin Turner*. Durham, NC: Duke University Press, pp. 111–28.

Bate, Jonathan (1991). *Romantic Ecology: Wordsworth and the Environmental Tradition*. London: Routledge.

Bate, Jonathan (2000). *The Song of the Earth*. Cambridge, MA: Harvard University Press.

Buell, Lawrence (1995). *The Environmental Imagination: Thoreau, Nature Writing, and the Formation of American Culture*. Cambridge, MA: Harvard University Press.

Buell, Lawrence (2001). *Writing for an Endangered World: Literature, Culture, and Environment in the U.S. and Beyond*. Cambridge, MA: Harvard University Press.

Burroughs, John ([1867] 1971). *Notes on Walt Whitman as Poet and Person*. New York: Haskell House.

Coupe, Laurence (ed.) (2000). *The Green Studies Reader: From Romanticism to Ecocriticism*. London: Routledge.

Cummings, Glenn N. (1992). Whitman's *Specimen Days* and the Theatricality of "Semirenewal." *American Transcendental Quarterly*, 6 (3): 177–87.

Doudna, Martin K. (1998). Nature. In J. R. LeMaster and Donald D. Kummings (eds.), *Walt Whitman: An Encyclopedia*. New York: Garland, pp. 451–4.

Fletcher, Angus (2004). *A New Theory for American Poetry: Democracy, the Environment, and the Future of the Imagination*. Cambridge, MA: Harvard University Press.

Geffen, Arthur (1984). Silence and Denial: Walt Whitman and the Brooklyn Bridge. *Walt Whitman Quarterly Review*, 1: 1–11.

Glotfelty, Cheryll and Fromm, Harold (eds.) (1996). *The Ecocriticism Reader: Landmarks in Literary Ecology*. Athens: University of Georgia Press.

Kerridge, Richard and Samuells, Neil (eds.) (1998). *Writing the Environment: Ecocriticism and Literature*. London: Zed.

Killingsworth, M. Jimmie (1989). *Whitman's Poetry of the Body: Sexuality, Politics, and the Text*. Chapel Hill: University of North Carolina Press.

Killingsworth, M. Jimmie (2002). The Voluptuous Earth and the Fall of the Redwood Tree: Whitman's Personifications of Nature. In Ed Folsom (ed.), *Whitman East and West: New Contexts for Reading Walt Whitman*. Iowa City: University of Iowa Press, pp. 14–25.

Killingsworth, M. Jimmie (2004). *Walt Whitman and the Earth: A Study in Ecopoetics*. Iowa City: University of Iowa Press.

Killingsworth, M. Jimmie and Palmer, Jacqueline S. (1992). *Ecospeak: Rhetoric and Environmental Politics in America*. Carbondale: Southern Illinois University Press.

Kroeber, Karl (1994). *Ecological Literary Criticism: Romantic Imagining and the Biology of Mind*. New York: Columbia University Press.

Levin, Jonathan (2002). Beyond Nature? Recent Work in Ecocriticism. *Contemporary Literature*, 43: 171–86.

Loving, Jerome (1999). *Walt Whitman: The Song of Himself*. Berkeley: University of California Press.

Mazel, David (ed.) (2001). *A Century of Early Ecocriticism*. Athens: University of Georgia Press.

Murphy, Patrick D. (2000). *Farther Afield in the Study of Nature-Oriented Literature*. Charlottesville: University of Virginia Press.

Philippon, Daniel J. (1998). "I Only Seek to Put You in Rapport": Message and Method in Walt Whitman's *Specimen Days*. In Michael P. Branch, Rochelle Johnson, Daniel Patterson, and Scott Slovic (eds.), *Reading the Earth: New Directions in the Study of Literature and the Environment*. Moscow, ID: University of Idaho Press, pp. 179–93.

Slovic, Scott (1992). *Seeking Awareness in American Nature Writing: Henry Thoreau, Annie Dillard, Edward Abbey, Wendell Berry, Barry Lopez*. Salt Lake City: University of Utah Press.

Tuan, Yi-Fu (1977). *Space and Place: The Perspective of Experience*. Minneapolis: University of Minnesota Press.

Warren, James Perrin (2001). Whitman Land: John Burroughs's Pastoral Criticism. *Interdisciplinary Studies in Literature and the Environment*, 8: 83–96.

Wilson, Eric (2000). *Romantic Turbulence: Chaos, Ecology, and American Space*. New York: St Martin's.

Whitman, Walt (1891–92). *Leaves of Grass*. In Kenneth M. Price and Ed Folsom (eds.), *The Walt Whitman Archive*. <http://jefferson.village.Virginia.EDU/whitman/>.

Whitman, Walt ([1921] 1972). *Uncollected Poetry and Prose of Walt Whitman*, 2 vols., ed. Emory Holloway. Gloucester, MA: Peter Smith.

20
Death and the Afterlife

William J. Scheick

During the nineteenth century it must have seemed that death rarely took a holiday. A high mortality rate, especially among children and victims of epidemic diseases, made death particularly prominent during the first half of the century. Nor could death be kept under wraps as a private family matter. It announced itself through tolling church bells, elaborate funeral processions, prescriptive mourning dress, conspicuously wreathed doors, heavily curtained windows, prominent wall photos or paintings of closed-eyed deceased children, pale death masks displayed inside homes, among other communal rituals and domestic memorials (Jalland 1996: 284–99, Laderman 1996: 27–38). In many regions of the United States, as well, there were public executions by hanging, invariably detailed in newspapers which also routinely printed sensational reports of loss of life due to fires, natural disasters and other tragic occasions. Graveyards, positioned beside churches or near the center of towns, were often traversed daily in the course of usual human activity. At such times the increasingly elaborate cemetery masonry, wrought with emblems of death, could hardly be overlooked.

This was Walt Whitman's milieu. Whitman's personal encounters with death commenced with the loss of an infant sister when he was six years old. Besides his own periodic episodes of life-threatening illness, he lost his father, mother, brother, sister-in-law, and other cherished relatives, including children. With the rest of the nation, Whitman shared President Abraham Lincoln's grief over the sudden demise of his 12-year-old son, who seemed at first to have simply contracted a minor illness. The entire nation, as well, knew of Mary Todd Lincoln's inconsolable anguish. As a newspaper man, in fact, Whitman contemplated human mortality far beyond average for most people, and such news accounts sometimes informed his poetry. So, for example, section 33 of "Song of Myself" features violent ends, including graphic images of an ambulance "trailing its red drip" and a "mash'd fireman with breast-bone broken" (Whitman 2002: 58–9).

During the 1850s Whitman, who claimed to have nursed injured stage drivers, frequently visited hospitals in Brooklyn and New York. But nothing surpassed the agonies he witnessed while serving as a nurse tending wounded and dying Civil War soldiers. The immense carnage of the Civil War, with its unfathomable toll in human lives, was death's most dramatic performance in nineteenth-century America. Whitman's direct experience with this bloodbath, explicitly reflected in such poems as "A March in the Ranks Hard-Prest," eroded his personal support for the war. Indeed, stark images of human destruction, conveyed in widely distributed news stories and photographs, stunned the reading public in general. Then in 1865, an already traumatized poet and nation were further shocked by the assassination of President Lincoln, the occasion for Whitman's "When Lilacs Last in the Dooryard Bloom'd." Composed like a musical composition, this consummate elegy was indeed designed as "an instrument of healing for the nation and for himself" (Zweig 1984: 129).

Whitman's milieu evinced still other symptoms of a preoccupation with dying. Cultural anxieties were evident in the elaborate rituals associated with the human corpse. The three-day vigil, most important at night, represented unacknowledged superstitious apprehensions about the deceased's vulnerability to sinister forces. These vigils also indicated fears concerning premature burial, a genuine, if exaggerated, possibility before the post-Civil War practice of embalming. Besides bizarre news accounts of people reviving in their coffins, such popular fictional works as Edgar Allan Poe's "The Premature Burial" (1844) and Wilkie Collins's *The Moonstone* (1868) contributed to a societal fixation on dying. It was during this time that funereal entrepreneurs marketed pickaxes or shovels to be placed beside the dead in a casket designed with an escape hatch. Available, too, was Bateson's Revival Device, a bell-rope tied to the deceased's hand.

In a less obvious manner, particularly before the Civil War and its aftermath, related societal anxieties were expressed in sentimental representations of dying. Typical of this tradition was Henry Peach Robinson's *Fading Away* (1858), a painting of enormous popularity on both sides of the Atlantic. In fact, a full-page engraving of this picture appeared in the November, 1858, issue of *Harper's Magazine*. Robinson's painting depicts a dying tubercular young woman, almost angelic in her light-saturated white gown, as she serenely passes away in a darkened room with heavily curtained windows. Her grieving sister and parents ritualistically participate in a deathbed watch. Such melodramatic scenes of dying young girls became a staple of nineteenth-century literature. Most dramatic, perhaps, was the slow demise of Little Nell Trent in Charles Dickens's *The Old Curiosity Shop* (1841), which was widely read in serial format in England and America. So popular was this story that as a London ship carrying the latest chapters of this Dickens novel approached a New York pier, a crowd of avid readers assembled to await word from the crew about whether Nell had died.

Harriet Beecher Stowe's *Uncle Tom's Cabin* (1852), another widely read serial, later published as a book selling 300,000 copies in its first year, featured the sentimental death of Little Eva as a result of her delicate constitution. Such romance fantasies promoted the fashionable nineteenth-century ideal of a "good" or "beautiful" death, a latter-day version of centuries-old Christian expectations concerning the final deathbed struggle of the soul. Whatever the authorial intention or the cultural impetus behind the sentimentalizing of the final moments of life, such widely encountered pictorial and literary deathbed scenes effectively served as communal *memento mori* devices maintaining death's disconcerting visibility during the nineteenth century.

With such a cultural emphasis on death, it is not surprising that by the middle of the century spiritualism attracted public interest. During the 1850s the Rochester ghost knockings reported by teenagers Catherine and Margaretta Fox seized American attention. With the authoritative endorsements of such social figures as *New York Tribune* editor Horace Greeley and judge John W. Edwards, author of *Spiritualism* (1853), the Fox sisters became a successful touring attraction. Instead of dying virginal girls sentimentally radiating angelic rapture, spiritualism tended to offer vibrant young girls serving as mediums connecting the living to the dead. Revising the pietism of the "good" or "beautiful" death of earlier melodramatic representations of dying, sensationalistic spiritualists unveiled an otherworldly community still in touch with the earthly community. While spiritualism seemed to weaken death's grip insofar as it promoted a sense of eternal selfhood free from the threat of the Christian notion of hell, it was nonetheless as thoroughly infused with the same pervasive death-consciousness evident in so many other cultural features of nineteenth-century America.

Whitman, who appreciated the endorsement of spiritualists while he explicitly rejected the fraudulent elements of their sensationalistic exhibitions (Aspiz 2004: 126–7), spoke of himself as a medium and "true spiritualist" (Hindus 1972: 39). A spiritualist sensibility toward death permeates his poetry, and so it is not surprising that he has been described as a "very great post mortem poet" whose best writings "are really huge fat tomb-plants, great rank graveyard growths" (Lawrence 1962: 13, 17). Whitman's abiding interest in – some would say his peculiar preoccupation with – death has in fact puzzled, even annoyed, many later readers. Some detect slight inconsistencies in Whitman's attitude toward dying, but on the whole they find a coherent concept of humanity's passage from this world to somewhere unknown which somehow completes or fulfills the present version of our life (Carlisle 1973: 144–51). Others reach for more exotic explanations of Whitman's alleged "perverse attraction to death," including the claim that he wished for "a heroic death that [would] liberate him from the death-in-life which he associate[d] with erotic bereavement and with sexual repression" (Pollak 1994: 185, 189). There are those, as well, who simply deny the poet's affirmation of death. For them, Whitman's "shouted pronouncements on immortality bespeak not the exultation of the man assured that he will never die, but the anxiety of the man terrified that he will" (Mark 1976: 124). The fullest and best discussion of Whitman's attitude on this matter traces the development of his representation of death through each edition of *Leaves of Grass* and concludes: "The fear that had surfaced in earlier poems – that death may be only [an] eternal nothingness – has [in the later poems] become sublimated into a faith in an afterlife during which the elements of conscious (mortal) identity are somehow preserved" (Aspiz 2004: 209).

Whitman's poems not only reflect his century's acute awareness of death and his own negotiation of apprehensions relating to mortality, they also reveal the poet's deliberate effort to revise his culture's attitude toward dying. This effort is apparent in the unconventional deathbed and funeral scenes in "To Think of Time," which unsentimentally and enigmatically urges that the "living look[ing] upon the corpse with their eyesight" become "a different living [who] looks curiously on the corpse" (Whitman 2002: 365). Revision especially characterizes his verse addressing the death of Lincoln. This elegiac poetry is designed to supersede the standard *Memoria* tradition – the short-term memorial intended to console the living and finally disconnect them from the dead. "When Lilacs Last in the Dooryard Bloom'd," for example, transforms the death of Lincoln into a wondrously affirmative "eternal drama of the motive-forces of the universe" (Miller 1957: 119).

If Whitman's poetry is often a form of consolation literature, it is a specifically Transcendentalist recasting of *ars moriendi*, art-of-dying writings devoted to a right understanding of death. This is why ritualistic and liturgical elements inform his Civil War poems (Thomas 1995: 36). Like Christians, albeit with very significant differences, Whitman insisted that the deceased was not sentenced to a grave of unfulfilled earthly desires (Kuebrich 1989). Unlike the evangelical Christian understanding of a "good" death, however, Whitman insisted that the soul's destiny is neither hell nor heaven. Earthly life is not a stage where the forces of good and evil contest for each individual soul, and mortality is not a punishment for any primal transgression against God. For Whitman, death is a good in itself. It is simply a productive stage in the infinite and progressive development of each individual consciousness. "Nothing can happen more beautiful than death," he thus boldly pronounced in "Starting from Paumanok" (Whitman 2002: 23). "*Praise! praise! praise!*" he similarly wrote in "When Lilacs Last in the Dooryard Bloom'd," "*For the sure-enwinding arms of cool-enfolding death*" (Whitman 2002: 281, italics in original). Such a radical claim was provocative in its day, just as the poet intended it to be.

For insight into such a thought-provoking claim, it is helpful to closely consider a handful of Whitman's poems. Although many of these works are rarely identified as verse about death, read as a sequence they yield an appreciation of the poet's essentially Transcendentalist convictions about dying and the afterlife.

Resurrection After Slumber: "To the Garden the World" and "By the Bivouac's Fitful Flame"

"To the Garden the World," a well-wrought if syntactically difficult meditation on the physical realm, is not generally read as a poem about death. Yet it offers an excellent introduction to Whitman's belief in the immortality of human consciousness. Narrated by humanity's essential Adamic spirit, the poem ebulliently celebrates the perennial re-emergence of a fundamental collective human identity – often referred to as "soul" in Whitman's writings. Personal identity is "The Soul, / Forever and forever" ("Starting from Paumanok," Whitman 2002: 17). This deathless spirit, it is important to note, always remains located *within* creation. At once "linear and cyclic" (Schwiebert 1998: 730), every human self successively and infinitely undergoes progressive transitions and translations specifically within the Eden-like garden of nature.

In the poem this collective soul-identity is imaged as "the quivering fire that ever plays" in each individual human body (Whitman 2002: 78). While the participle form of "quiver" indicates "a state of process" (Greenspan 1995: 104) and while the word "ever" is especially notable for its stress on the self's immortality, a fuller appreciation of their allied implication is provided by related imagery in "By the Bivouac's Fitful Flame" (Whitman 2002: 253). In this slightly later and far more pensive poem detailing a night scene at a Civil War camp, human lives are likened to "spots of kindled fire." The flames of this fire are twice described as "fitful," suggesting the restless nature and changing configurations of the collective life-spark in its various individual human manifestations. For the poem's meditating observer sitting in the dark, the fitfulness of the flickering campfires corresponds to a "procession" of "occasional" shadowy figures appearing like restless silent "phantom[s]" in the nocturnal gloom of the camp edge. Are these "phantom" figures only barely visible sleepless soldiers? Are they uncanny projections of presently sleeping men who are fated to die in some future battle? Or are they dead soldiers whose restless souls have returned to the camp? All of these possibilities coalesce in the narrator's gloomy or "solemn" thoughts, as if in a dream (Hutchinson 1986: 144) of vague definition (Dougherty 1993: 110–11). It is especially significant, however, that these spectral figures appear beyond the "tents of the sleeping army," a spatial positioning also suggestive of temporal distancing (past, present, future) similar to loved ones "far away." In the observer's "tender and wondrous" thoughts about "life and death," both present sleeping soldiers and past or future posthumous spirits appear to form a "winding" procession. These glimpsed (or imagined) figures could be "far or near." Like the dead, they appear distant from our specific space and time, but also like the living, their immortal "fitful flame[s]" somehow continue to proceed forward within creation. Ghost-like figures indeed seem to populate the camp's shadowy margins.

Such a view of the afterlife was hardly consonant with the Christian concept of eternity typical of Whitman's time. A Transcendentalist understanding informs the camp observer's image of a "procession winding" in "By the Bivouac's Fitful Flame" and the Adamic narrator's reference in "To the Garden the World" to the "revolving cycles in their wide sweep" that have "brought [him] again" into creation. Such perennial garden-like cycles, which we will explore more fully in Whitman's "Sparkles from the Wheel," keep "the world anew ascending." These "wondrous" miracle-like generative cycles unify all temporal antitheses, including life and death: "behold my resurrection after slumber," proclaims the Adamic collective self.

The non-Christian suggestion that the human self exhibits a natural protean capacity for perennial resurrections *within* the material world was provocative in Whitman's time. Such a view implies that there is no need for a redeemer of the kind celebrated in the New Testament. Always at once Old Adam (nature) and Second Adam (divine), the human self, collectively and individually, endlessly remains "the same" in its deathless essence. This point is also made in "As Adam Early in the Morning," also printed in the "Children of Adam" sequence of *Leaves of Grass* (Whitman 2002: 96). In this poem the Adamic narrator likewise associates early-morning awakening from sleep with resurrection after death. When he says, "touch the palm of your hand to my body," he speaks like the risen Christ addressing his apostles (Luke 24: 39), especially skeptical Thomas (John 20: 27). Touching any new body or other perennial manifestation of nature's regenerative power within creation, the narrator insists, instills faith in each identity's afterlife.

That there is no death is likewise indicated in the narrator's revision of Genesis 3: 8: "They heard the voice of the Lord God walking in the garden." In this biblical scene mortally fated Adam and Eve, who are about to be punished for their disobedience, hide themselves out of fear and shame. In "As Adam Early in the Morning," however, humanity is invited to "approach," "touch," and "be not afraid." "To the Garden the World" similarly contests the Old Testament account of Adam and Eve's loss of paradise and subsequent condemnation to mortality. In this poem the garden of Eden (perfect nature) never was lost, nor can it be. From the dawn of humanity – "Potent mates, daughters, sons, preluding" – the essential idea of Eden has steadily become more realized through and in time. So, too, the equally essential human self, represented in the account of Adam and Eve, never fell from its perfection and was never punitively exiled in time. Through the ages this Adamic self remains "just the same," both divine and immortal in the ever-burgeoning garden of creation.

This understanding informs the poet's startling claim in "Scented Herbage of My Breast": to "[d]eath or life I am then indifferent, my soul declines to prefer" (Whitman 2002: 97–8). Given the perennial character of the collective soul in each individual in the eternal garden of creation, no emotional weight should be assigned to either life or death. Both finally are only two features of the same wondrous immortality. Nor is the poet concerned with the afterlife in any conventional religious sense. Neither heaven nor hell exists in this scheme. "To the Garden the World" Transcendentally posits that creation is already a heavenly place where each soul undergoes an *ad infinitum* and asymptotic succession of developmental stages. Death, then, is simply a passage to another "preluding" stage. Relying on an age-old metaphor, Whitman pertinently proclaims that "the soul" is an "immortal ship" forever "voyaging, voyaging, voyaging" ("Aboard at a Ship's Helm," Whitman 2002: 216). Or as he represented this idea in "Pioneers! O Pioneers!" (2002: 192–5), the human soul collectively and individually undertakes "the task eternal" of progressively "debouch[ing] upon a newer mightier world" always *within* the heavenly garden of creation.

In "To the Garden the World," then, the corporeal stage of human life as we know it is just one wonderful phase in an endless sequence of "world[s] anew ascending," a point also made by the "chanter of Adamic songs" in the aptly titled "Ages and Ages Returning at Intervals" (Whitman 2002: 92). In "To the Garden the World" each experience of this spring-like resurrection is represented as a pleasant surprise to the newly awakened soul: "Curious here behold my resurrection after slumber." After death, which is little more than a sleep akin to the passage of winter in the garden, we spring-like arise anew with a fresh appreciation of "here," the always burgeoning present moment. With each such revival, the resurrected consciousness finds itself emotionally and instructively "curious" about itself, somehow essentially "just the same" yet also in a "world anew" that imparts increasingly advanced ("ascended") insights into the divine mystery of nature.

The Lesson Done: "A Clear Midnight"

A late poem first printed in the 1881 edition of *Leaves of Grass*, "A Clear Midnight" (Whitman 2002: 408) develops further the idea of human immortality celebrated in "To the Garden the World." While this four-line poem focuses on the individual experience of time more than on the collective human self, it shares the earlier poem's emphasis on the binaries typical of everyday life – specifically, in this instance, day and night, sound and silence, experience and thought, rising and reclining. Such commonplace antitheses are a characteristic feature of Whitman's verse, early and late, and as we saw in "To the Garden the World" they figure importantly in the poet's response to death.

This four-line poem addresses the soul, which is said to relish its imaginative free flight when the body sleeps. Then, the poem discloses, the soul is liberated from worldly duties and pleasures alike, freer now to appreciate better the mysterious noumenon, the spiritual core of being. The soul relates to this deep mystery in a "wordless" manner. In a Platonic or Kantian sense, it will then participate in a way of knowing (belief) not quite available yet by way of sensory perception.

It is easy to misunderstand Whitman's binary on this and other occasions. The Platonist element of the poem's imagery might seem to imply some disaffection toward the body. Whether or not, as some have argued (notably Aspiz 2004: 85–6), Whitman harbored an ambivalence toward the body, in this poem and elsewhere his intended point appears to stress the unitary relationship, rather than the antagonism between the binaries experienced in life. The oppositions imaged in "A Clear Midnight" actually comprise mutually constitutive elements of a unifying dynamic, just as the numerous contrary motions in "The Dalliance of Eagles" paradoxically form "the twain yet one" (Whitman 2002: 229).

In "A Clear Midnight," as in "To the Garden the World," the body wondrously expresses the inherent divinity of nature. But as we individually experience it, the body is also only a phase to be surpassed in the spiritual progression of each personal identity (soul). So in "A Clear Midnight" the physical world is imaged as a "lesson," something contributively important (rather than antagonistically resistant) to the soul's spiritual development. Each such life-as-lesson, we already heard the poet explain in "Pioneers! O Pioneers!," participates in the larger "eternal task" of our "debouch[ing] upon a newer mightier world," a collective errand that the poet assigns both to future generations on earth and also to souls departing the physical world (Whitman 2002: 192–5). Here Whitman insists on an integrative relationship between the seeming opposites of life and death. And so, as the poet similarly indicates in "Gliding O'er All," he contemplates and sings about the "voyage of the soul – not life alone, / Death, many deaths" (p. 232).

This is the exact point of "Youth, Day, Old Age and Night," a four-line extract from an earlier 1855 poem excluded from the 1881 *Leaves of Grass* (Whitman 2002: 189). In this extract Whitman juxtaposes youth and old age, both equally presented as fascinating and graceful. Just as the days of youth are brightened by "the immense sun," life after death will witness "millions of suns," like the stars imaged at the end of "A Clear Midnight." Just as refreshing sleep follows the activities of youth, death is only a "restoring darkness" after the passing of a life. In short, youth leads to old age, which in turn leads to a youth-like new-world beginning. Such is the "*unseen mystery*," the soul's participation in the "*endless motion*" of "*ebb* [from one life] *and flow* [into another life]" ("In Cabin'd Ships at Sea" Whitman 2002: 4, italics in original).

"Stars," the final image in "A Clear Midnight," significantly locates the soul's imaginative free flight *within* the created Cosmos. Its intimated release from the corporeal phase of its own earthly tutelage – "Night, sleep, death and the stars" – is not (as in Platonic or Gnostic thought) a release from creation. The temporary bodily version of its life, not the divine creation itself, will be transcended through death. Each of the self's various relationships with creation, in contrast to the intrinsic divinity of nature (noumenon), will change with every successive stage of the soul's voyaging. Sequential metamorphoses characterize the way each individual identity experiences the perenniality celebrated in "To the Garden the World." The soul in "A Clear Midnight" is said to be reverently "silent" – comparable to the mute "mystical" appreciation of the star-gazing narrator at the end of "When I Heard the Learn'd Astronomer." The soul is silent because its experience of each new stage in its developmental progression is astonishing, as if it were an amazed pioneer among distant suns. Moreover, the soul's evolutionary process itself is as limitless as the universal expanse of stars, still another implication of the aptly positioned final image of the poem.

This poem's emphasis on transformation includes its title. Midnight, commonly understood as the division point between day and night, has long symbolized transition. Known in past ages as the witching hour, midnight was often said to be the moment when certain powers were optimal, for either good or evil (depending on the tradition). Long before the nineteenth century, people were thought to be particularly vulnerable to sinister forces at midnight. On the other hand, this hour also enjoyed positive associations, such as observed in the biblical psalmist's resolve: "At midnight I will rise to give thanks" (Psalm 119: 62). Truth was thought to be revealed at midnight, an understanding that likely figured in the image of the midnight angel announcing the birth of Jesus to shepherds. It is possible, in fact, that "A Clear Midnight" alludes to and revises the celebration of this angelic visitation in "It Came Upon a Midnight Clear," a Christmas hymn based on Edmund Hamilton Sears's "The Angel's Song" (1850). If so, the prophecy of "the ever circling years" that "come round the age of gold" in Sears's popular hymn would, for Whitman, refer to more than the Christian millennial fulfillment of the Messiah's birth and his second coming. For Whitman, these words from the Sears song would suggest the Christmas-like nativity of *every* soul – reverently referenced as "thy," "thee," and "thou" – forever self-redemptively transitioning from the present moment toward a future of new lives.

The poem itself goes through a structural transition that amounts to an instructive translation. Ostensibly the poem is about sleep, when the work of the day is left behind and another part of the mind ranges more freely in dreams. It is only in the last line – "Night, sleep, death and the stars" – that an ancient association between sleep and death becomes as evident as do stars on a clear night. At this clarifying transitional point in the poem – a point anticipated by its title – the reader can better comprehend the lines already read. The significance of these lines, like the significance of our past experiences generally, occurs only when understood retrospectively. The deeper implication of these lines, specifically their insight concerning death, depends on the reader leaving them behind (the past) and encountering the next lines (the future) of the poem. Past and future, however, are not antithetical. As with body and soul in the poem, past and future are paradoxically "the twain yet one." "A Clear Midnight" closes with an insight-imparting translation that enacts the very theme of the poem: that a related progressive clarifying process of translation awaits each of us after the transition of death.

Thematically and structurally, then, the poem imparts a "lesson": that death is merely the "hour" of transition when the individual soul starts over at a more advanced level of its progressive development. Then the soul not only leaves behind its body but also the particular corporeally determined constructions of reality, such as are registered in the temporally bound thoughts and words recorded in books and art. But this migrating individual identity, which is part of the collective Adamic identity defined in "To the Garden the World," always undergoes its ongoing transitions and translations distinctly within the garden of creation.

In "A Clear Midnight" the perennial soul remembers and relishes "the themes" it has always "loved best," the immutable themes underlying all the stages of its fitful voyaging. Especially cherished is the theme of immortality that informs the cyclic (unified) binary of sleep and awakening, death and resurrection. This point is made, as well, in "As I Ponder'd in Silence" when the "*one theme for ever-enduring bards*" is declared: "*life and death*," "*the Body and . . . the eternal Soul*" (Whitman 2002: 3–4, italics in original). These themes, particularly the integrative interaction of opposites, are lessons learned from sleep and dreams, among other insubstantial features of our physical lives. But just as the body will be shed, so too will the husks of verbal and artistic representation, such as the earth-bound language of the very poem we are reading. Born again through death into a new phase of existence, the soul will become "wordless." "Gazing" anew with childlike wonder, the poem implies, will be followed by a mystical thought-free "pondering," which in turn will eventually be followed by a succession of progressively clarifying otherworldly translations of the essential beloved themes of creation's "*unseen mystery*" – imaged at the end of "A Clear Midnight" in the infinite wonder of stars.

Lines Give Way: "Quicksand Years"

"Quicksand Years" (Whitman 2002: 376) embellishes Whitman's observations about the afterlife. This is especially so in its final placement in *Leaves of Grass*, where its original Civil War nuances are muted (Killingsworth 1989: 134). On first encounter the title is likely to be unsettling. Quicksand, referring to treacherous loose and wet patches that swallow anything of weight, initially suggests that the poem will be another maudlin nineteenth-century lament concerning the passage of years, like the quick sands of time in an hour glass. But in Whitman's characteristic bait-and-switch manner, the poem actually embraces death. As in "A Clear Midnight" and "To the Garden the World," the poet defines death in terms of an underlying unitary life-force that integrates all perceived opposites. So by the end of "Quicksand Years" the word "quick" paradoxically includes contrary meanings that become mutually constitutive. "Quick" refers to dying, as in the expression "quick sands of time," and to the living, as in the expression "the quick and the dead" found in the King James translation of the Bible (Acts 10: 42). In this poem, then, the experience of time as fatal quicksand is balanced by its seeming opposite meaning, life itself. In the poem life and death are reciprocal interactive agents of the progressive quickening or enlivening of "One's-Self." It is in this sense that Whitman speaks elsewhere of being "part of the sands and drift" of nature ("As I Ebb'd with the Ocean of Life," p. 213).

One's "real life," for the poet, supersedes one's temporal achievements ("When I Read the Book," Whitman 2002: 9). Each "real life" is far more mysterious than its time-bound incarnation. It is in this sense that Whitman similarly claims that one's "real body... will elude the hands of the corpse-cleaners" ("Starting from Paumanok," 2002: 22). Our temporal self is always grounded on this deeper mysterious reality but tends to get distracted by nonenduring "schemes, politics" and other "substances" as superficial as a theatre performance. How else could it be, as Whitman suggests in "Visor'd," when the corporeal world is a "perpetual natural disguiser" and each of us is effectively "mask[ed]" (p. 231)?

"When shows break up," when our theatre-like masked dramas end, "lines give way," referring to the stage-like script everyone briefly performs in his or her version of physical life. In this sense, any particular temporally staged life is "maya, illusion" ("Are You the New Person Drawn to Me?," Whitman 2002: 106). That is, corporeal being is not a substantive end in itself. Bodily existence is but a "show of appearance" ("Scented Herbage of My Breast," p. 99; cf. "Of the Terrible Doubt of Appearances"); a temporary exhibition of the "forms and shows" of a life; "varied pageants" ("Pioneers! O Pioneers!," p. 194). Life, in short, is like a "powerful play," Whitman declares in

"O Me! O Life!" (p. 228). We "play... the part," the "same old role," which finally "is what we make of it" ("Crossing Brooklyn Ferry," p. 138).

So, too, when his own role ends in this world, Whitman forecasts, the politics and the schemes of his drama-like lines – literally his poetry – will likewise give way or not survive. This point is made more directly in "Shut Not Your Doors": "The words of my book [are] nothing, the drift of it everything" (Whitman 2002: 13). Only the theme of his work will endure – the theme, as we saw in "A Clear Midnight," "To the Garden the World," and "As I Ponder'd in Silence," emphasizing the progressively clarifying "drift," the fitful process of the life–death translation into other modes of being that awaits everyone. "Only the theme I sing," the poet writes in "Quicksand Years," the theme of "the great and strong-possess'd soul." Like the soul after the body perishes, this theme of the soul's endurance beyond temporality survives the perishing of the poet's time-bound language-performance. This theme celebrates the soul as "the final substance" – the "real life" – that can "never give way."

There is, then, no need to be frightened by the seeming quicksand nature of time. "Be not afraid of [the] body," the poet councils in "As Adam Early in the Morning" (Whitman 2002: 96) because (as "Quicksand Years" also promises) mortal lives are not ultimately founded on the insubstantial sands of time. Nor do lives treacherously sink into quicksand oblivion. What is most needed when caught in quicksand is always already available to the self-redeeming Adamic spirit or soul. Most needed is the fact that One's-Self "is sure," meaning that it is not subject to the temporal laws governing the body. One's-Self is eternal, and being *sure* in this sense provides the soul (from within itself) a solid *shore* in response to time's quicksand. Being sure/shore, the soul is effectively self-redemptive (as also claimed in "A Clear Midnight"). Here, in contrast to "On Christ, the solid rock, I stand; / All other ground is sinking sand" (in Edward Mote's Baptist hymn "The Solid Rock," 1832; set to music, 1863, and based on Matthew 7: 24–27), the soul is said to provide itself with all the shore-like hope it needs while seeming to sink into the time's sands in a world that "break[s] up."

The enabling pun on sure/shore at the end of "Quicksand Years," like the introduction of the word "death" at the end of "A Clear Midnight," recasts the meaning of several earlier images. We now understand better the double sense of "quick" and "sand," both (as we have seen) simultaneously conveying negative and positive implications. "Lines give way," too, refers not only to the passing of Whitman's drama-like poetry but also (in an opposite sense) to the disappearance of old-age skin wrinkles after One's Self commences a new beginning in another mode of being. In retrospect, as well, a similar reversal occurs in the opening line: "Quicksand years that whirl me I know not wither." What at first seems an anxious expression of uncertainty in outcome for a whirled-about soul can now be read more positively as an image of time whirling nonbinding ropes of sand incapable of effecting permanent withering. Moreover, "whirl" loses its initial implication of human powerlessness, suggested by sand roping downward in an hourglass. The hourglass, a prominent *memento mori* device engraved on nineteenth-century tombstones, can be turned over after the coiling sand has emptied into the bottom chamber. Then, to apply a pertinent image from "By the Bivouac's

Fitful Flame," souls and thoughts continue to "wind in procession" (Whitman 2002: 253). Empty and full, ebb and flow, death and life – once again Whitman celebrates the paradoxical "twain yet one." In "Quicksand Years" the divergent meanings of "quick," "lines," "sand," and "whirl" are likewise turned upside-down; they are emptied of their early fearful implications (human powerlessness) and refilled with reassurances about the eternal life of the self-redemptive (sure/shore) soul within creation.

Showers of Gold: "Sparkles from the Wheel"

"Sparkles from the Wheel," a poem that first appeared in *Leaves of Grass* in 1871, is arguably Whitman's most explicit representation of the afterlife. Critics, however, have not found this frequently anthologized poem easy to interpret. Their commentary has primarily emphasized the knife-grinder, who has variously been said to represent a Jehovah figure, the creative artist, or the poet himself (Nelson 1998: 677–8). It is significant, however, that the title and the refrain of the poem highlight the treadle wheel and its sparkles rather than any particular individual in the scene. This primary emphasis, as we will see, determines the rationale for the presence of the knife-grinder and others in the poem.

The knife-grinder is described as an "old man" (Whitman 2002: 328). He marks the end of the human life cycle. Others in various stages of aging also appear in the poem. Most obvious are "the attentive, quiet children." Least obvious are their parents and other adults who, in specific contrast to the settled watching children, comprise the "city's ceaseless crowd." These adults "move on the livelong day" – that is, they engage in the welter of life-transactions, and in the process they advance along all the phases comprising the transit of lived time between childhood and old age. "The livelong day" alludes, in part, to the triadic pattern of morning, noon, and night – traditional symbols for representing the cycle of a human life through childhood, adulthood, and old age.

But in "Sparkles from the Wheel" there is, as well, another figure who does not belong to any of these three stages. It is the speaker of the poem who describes himself as "a phantom curiously floating." We should take him at his word, something critics have been reluctant to do, when he says he is a phantom, a ghost. Note that he floats, that he is "effusing and fluid." He is noncorporeal, an experience so new to him that he describes his response as *curious*. This reaction corresponds to the response of the Adamic spirit in "To the Garden the World": "Curious here behold my resurrection after slumber" (Whitman 2002: 78). It is also suggested by the look of curiosity on a corpse in "To Think of Time" (p. 365), and by another ghost narrator's reflection on those he has left behind – "how curious you are to me!" – in "Crossing Brooklyn Ferry" (p. 135). In each instance the reporter is bemused, not alarmed. In "Sparkles from the Wheel" Whitman tells a ghost story in which he imagines himself as a postmortem specter who finds himself surprisingly and fascinatingly still within creation.

Instead of feeling like a displaced, solitary, and marginalized person, as some have described him (Thomas 1987: 173), he enjoys the situation, which he associates with the experiences of children pleasantly passing time. He specifically "joins a group of children watching." He has not returned to their youthful stage exactly, but he identifies with them and their watchfulness because he is at present in the childhood stage of his new postmortem existence. If the narrator is unobtrusive, not inclined "to assume the centrality of his ego" (Pascal 1982: 23), one reason is his alignment with these quiet children. As the insights of the very poem narrated by this ethereal advanced-child indicate, the ghost remembers all that he experienced as a youth, an adult, and an old man in his previous life-phases. This point is explicitly made in the final version of "Starting from Paumanok," where the poet states that when our "real body" passes on "to fitting spheres" it "Carr[ies] what has accrued to it from the moment of birth to the moment of death" (Whitman 2002: 22). Equipped with this knowledge and also with a related deeper appreciation of the meaning of "livelong day," the resurrected narrator commences a life-adventure as if he were a child in a different version of the world he once knew.

He now understands why children in his previous life and he at this youthful stage of his present life are mutually fascinated by the seemingly insignificant sparks from a grinder's wheel. The children do not know why such glints of light draw and hold their attention; and when they become adults caught up in the whirl of life's business, they will either forget or devalue such juvenile curiosity. The more insightful phantom, however, now better appreciates the significance of the wheel and its sparkles. He returns to "this scene and all its belongings" (its implications), and like the children beside him he is "seize[d] and affect[ed]." There is something in particular about the nature of time that his reborn self now understands with delight.

The focal site of this knowledge is the "whirling" wheel, one of the two central images in this ghost-narrated poem. The wheel is a significant image elsewhere in Whitman's verse, with perhaps "The Dalliance of Eagles" providing the best indication of its meaning for the poet. In this poem two mating eagles form "a living, fierce, gyrating wheel" (Whitman 2002: 229–30). This generative wheel (the "twain yet one" we observed earlier) strikes the poet as a dramatic example of the originating cosmic spiral force that unifies everything throughout creation. He has in mind the spiral pattern Transcendentalists learned about from Plato, Giambattista Vico, Georg Hegel, and Alexander von Humboldt, among others. It is the spiral pattern replicated in the mandala structural design of *Walden* (1854), in which Henry David Thoreau insisted that all life is circle-sailing.

There is also an even more conventional iconographic pattern behind "the whirling stone" as the determiner of life. In Shakespeare's *King Lear*, for instance, a character implores Fortune to "smile once more; turn thy wheel" (II, ii, 180), and later in this play we learn that the "wheel has come full circle" (V, iii, 174). Behind Shakespeare's imagery in this instance is a very long tradition, still proverbially available in Whitman's time, of representing fate as a revolving wheel of fortune. As numerous still earlier medieval pictorial representations and fire-wheel ceremonies indicated, humans were thought to ascend this wheel of life at birth and to fall from it at the time of their death.

This long-lived tradition, replete with mystical associations, informs Whitman's depiction of copulating birds in "The Dalliance of Eagles" to suggest the generative binary-uniting wheel of the life-force. This wheel-of-fortune tradition likewise underlies his image of a treadle wheel throwing off glints of light, as if to suggest a "creative act" (Miller 1957: 153). The distinct description of the "sharp-chinn'd old man" invites us to ask: What is it about the "measur'd tread" of the time he keeps at the wheel that correlates the chin-sharpening effects of aging on him and his activity of "sharpening a great knife"? It is as if the wheel of time, like the treadle wheel in relation of blades, has honed the grinder, readied him for his next life-application.

The glints, also imaged as "Sparkles hot, seed ethereal down in the dirt dropping" in "So Long!" (Whitman 2002: 423), represent the mysterious "copious" generation of human identities from the "whirling" cosmic spiral force. These sparks are as important as the wheel to the phantom narrator. In the traditional iconography of the wheel of fortune a person rises and falls, whereas in Whitman's Transcendentalist revision every sparkle-self drops and (the poet carefully adds) darts sideways. Specifically, each person is a precious (golden) divine spark whirled off the wheel of life and thrust outwardly into expanding orbital motion around its generative origin.

After its brief arc off the stone, each sparkle from the wheel may seem to expire because it is no longer visible to the corporeal eye. But, as the reborn phantom now understands about his own unextinguished soul-flame, each spark endures beyond the temporal realm. Each life-spark is a "fitful flame" ("By the Bivouac's Fitful Flame"), a "quivering fire that *ever* plays" ("To the Garden the World," my italics). It spirals outwardly and asymptotically *ad infinitum* as one completed orbit (lifetime) expands into another, more enlightened circuit around the "living, fierce, gyrating wheel" generating all life. "There is really no death," Whitman writes, because "all goes onward and outward," (Whitman 2002: 34–5) along a "whirling current . . . with curves" ("After the Sea-Ship," p. 221). Pertinent here, too, is the poet's spiral image of "years that whirl" him ("Quicksand Years," p. 448), corresponding to Thoreau's image of life as an ever-expansive circle-sailing like rings rippling outward from a stone dropped into a pond. Similarly pertinent is Whitman's image of his poetry as a wheel turning on a single ideational axis ("To Thee Old Cause"), as if his verse whirled around the one eternal theme we saw celebrated in "A Clear Midnight," "As I Ponder'd in Silence," and "Quicksand Years."

The starward flight in "A Clear Midnight," the progressive passage "to fitting spheres" in "Starting from Paumanok" (Whitman 2002: 22), the "world anew ascending" in "To the Garden the World" (p. 78), and the bubbling up of souls and the postmortem "phantom looking down" in "As I Ebb'd with the Ocean of Life" (p. 214) each indicate that sometimes Whitman resorted to the imagery of ascent to suggest the soul's outward migration in successive orbits around the wheel-like generative life-force. Instead of the typical nineteenth-century Christian belief in an ascent to heaven, Whitman expresses a thoroughly Transcendentalist understanding of the afterlife derived from various adapted and modified sources, including Asian and Swedenborgian thought. Especially influential on Transcendentalist thought was Emanuel Swedenborg's notion of the migration of human spirit through heavenly spheres, a view expounded in such books as Andrew Jackson Davis's *The Principles of Nature* (1847), *Great Harmonia* (1850), and *Death and the After-Life* (1874).

In "The American Scholar" (1837) Ralph Waldo Emerson described this process as a never-ending ascent toward higher things. In *A Week on the Concord and Merrimack Rivers* (1849) Thoreau images this progression as a succession of door openings. For Thoreau, death is like leaving our home to go outdoors, where nature in turn becomes a new home with a doorway to still another mansion-like exterior. The soul, that is, ceaselessly passes from a previous to a new and better home, or as Thoreau wrote in *Cape Cod* (1865), our spirit leaves the dead body and emigrates to a world unknown to science. In Whitman's similar description of this perennial transition within creation, "the dead advance as much as the living advance" ("Song of the Broad-Axe," Whitman 2002: 159). Again, as he similarly wrote in "So Long!," we all undergo "many translations, from [our] avataras ascending" to an "unknown sphere more real than [we] dream'd" (2002: 424). Throughout his poetry, Whitman's explicit and implied imagery of ascent conveys a Transcendentalist belief in the soul's ongoing and endless progression along successive orbits expanding infinitely from a wheel-like generational life-force.

This is the narrator's absorbing insight about his own curious spectral situation in "Sparkles from the Wheel." Having returned to the world as a phantom who mentally retains everything he has learned in his previous life, the narrator also now understands better why children in the corporeal world are so intensely fascinated by seemingly insignificant glints from a knife-grinder's wheel. These children unconsciously sense the wonder represented in this act of "golden" generation; they intuit the marvel of their own sparkle-like births. Hence they sit "attentive, quiet," in distinct contrast to the noisy bustle of the city around them. What they deeply sense without understanding, the new-born phantom appreciates more fully, though he is as yet only in the childhood stage of his new life-circuit. He now possesses an expanded understanding about the soul as a "fitful flame" – how each person is a precious sparkle spun spirally and asymptotically outwardly through successive expanding orbits or celestial spheres (lifetimes), as if ever ascending starward (the emphasized final image in "A Clear Midnight").

"Sparkles from the Wheel," then, images each individual life as a ceaseless movement, a circuiting whirl of significant motion. It features children, adults, and an old man – the triadic temporal span of the reader's world – but it particularly features the advanced point of view of a neophyte ghost as he begins a new orbit of experience. This phantom confirms that life is an ongoing sequence of centripetal spirals – Ezekielian wheels within wheels (Ezekiel 10: 10), as it were – transforming every ending into a novel and enhanced beginning.

But to what end? Transcendentalists do not say what purpose informs the soul's spiral progression within creation. Time and again Whitman confesses his own inability to explain this mystery. Moving steadily inward in search of the "real," the heart of his own life's concentric layering in "When I Read the Book," he confesses to have identified "Only a few hints, a few diffused faint clews and indirections" (Whitman 2002: 9). He is even more candid in "As I Ebb'd with the Ocean of Life": "I have not once had the least idea who or what I am" (2002: 213). Whitman's faith in an abiding divine spiral power remained at heart an intuitive conviction, itself a little mystery circuiting within the larger mystery of creation.

References and Further Reading

Aspiz, Harold (2004). *So Long! Walt Whitman's Poetry of Death*. Tuscaloosa: University of Alabama Press.

Carlisle, E. Fred (1973). *The Uncertain Self: Whitman's Drama of Identity*. East Lansing: Michigan State University Press.

Dougherty, John (1993). *Walt Whitman and the Citizen's Eye*. Baton Rouge: Louisiana State University Press.

Greenspan, Ezra (1995). The Poetics of "Participle-Loving Whitman." In Ezra Greenspan (ed.), *The Cambridge Companion to Walt Whitman*. Cambridge, UK: Cambridge University Press, pp. 92–109.

Hindus, Milton (ed.) (1972). *Walt Whitman: The Critical Heritage*. New York: Barnes and Noble.

Hutchinson, George B. (1986). *The Ecstatic Whitman: Literary Shamanism and the Crisis of the Union*. Columbus: Ohio State University Press.

Jalland, Pat (1996). *Death in the Victorian Family*. New York: Oxford University Press.

Killingsworth, M. Jimmie (1989). *Whitman's Poetry of the Body: Sexuality, Politics, and the Text*. Chapel Hill: University of North Carolina Press.

Kuebrich, David (1989). *Minor Prophecy: Walt Whitman's New American Religion*. Bloomington: Indiana University Press.

Laderman, Gary (1996). *The Sacred Remains: American Attitudes toward Death, 1799–1883*. New Haven, CT: Yale University Press.

Lawrence, D. H. (1962). Whitman. In Roy Harvey Pearce (ed.), *Whitman: A Collection of Critical Essays*. Englewood Cliffs, NJ: Prentice-Hall, pp. 11–23.

Mark, Ivan (1976). *The Trial of the Poet: An Interpretation of the First Edition of Leaves of Grass*. New York: Columbia University Press.

Miller, James E., Jr. (1957). *A Critical Guide to Leaves of Grass*. Chicago: University of Chicago Press.

Nelson, Howard (1998). Sparkles from the Wheel (1871). In J. R. LeMaster and Donald D. Kummings (eds.), *Walt Whitman: An Encyclopedia*. New York: Garland, pp. 677–8.

Pascal, Richard (1982). Whitman's "Sparkles from the Wheel." *Walt Whitman Review*, 28: 20–4.

Pollak, Vivian R. (1994). Death as Repression, Repression as Death: A Reading of Whitman's "Calamus" Poems. In Geoffrey M. Sill (ed.), *Walt Whitman of Mickle Street: A Centennial Collection*. Knoxville: University of Tennessee Press, pp. 179–93.

Schwiebert, John E. (1998). To the Garden the World (1860). In J. R. LeMaster and Donald D. Kummings (eds.), *Walt Whitman: An Encyclopedia*. New York: Garland, p. 730.

Thomas, M. Wynn (1987). *The Lunar Light of Whitman's Poetry*. Cambridge, MA: Harvard University Press.

Thomas, M. Wynn (1995). Fratricide and Brotherly Love: Whitman and the Civil War. In Ezra Greenspan (ed.), *The Cambridge Companion to Walt Whitman*. Cambridge, UK: Cambridge University Press, pp. 27–44.

Whitman, Walt (2002). *Leaves of Grass and Other Writings*, ed. Michael Moon. New York: W. W. Norton.

Zweig, Paul (1984). *Walt Whitman: The Making of a Poet*. New York: Basic Books.

21

Twentieth-century Mass Media Appearances

Andrew Jewell and Kenneth M. Price

Readers of the May 2004 issue of *O: The Oprah Magazine* could hardly miss two bold fuchsia-colored pages made from especially firm stock. These pages are perforated and feature quotations that readers could tear out and make into postcard-sized objects. All the quotations concern the body, and readers are instructed to "post these cards on a mirror to remind yourself to rejoice – daily and non-fault-findingly – in the power, glory, and potential of your beautiful physical self." The quotations come from Aimee Mullins, Naomi Shihab Nye, and, finally, Walt Whitman – "If anything is sacred the human body is sacred." Ironically, the fuchsia pages are lodged between an advertisement to wake up to Atkins and join "the low-carb revolution" and another advertisement for Zelnorm, a medicine for treating "abdominal pain, bloating, and constipation." (Celebration of the body exists here in uneasy relationship to anxieties about the body, worries deepened by advertising and by the desire to sell products.) When we find Whitman in *O: The Oprah Magazine*, we know that he has been appropriated by the media that support our consumer-oriented society.

Mass media, the various means of communication designed to reach a large portion of the public, include but are not limited to film, radio, television, advertising, popular music, the internet, newspapers, and magazines. Whitman's appearances in mass media have not been studied much, though they deserve attention because the evolving uses of his image and words can illuminate important aspects of his cultural afterlife. Until the 1960s, Whitman was invoked with surprising frequency as an icon of high literary stature. Advertisers in particular relied on his fame – not on his challenges to orthodox thinking and ordinary social arrangements – to sell a host of products that used him, paradoxically, to bolster the respectability of everything from containers to insurance to whiskey. As the twentieth century progressed, however, the use of Whitman's image began to change. Writers of teleplays, magazines, and music began to evoke Whitman with more complexity, ambiguity, and playfulness. No longer was he simply a symbol of cultural authority; instead, he often signaled irreverence and daring, and he became an iconic presence in widespread efforts to push mass media beyond traditional limits of decorum. The change over the last half-century is underscored by the difference between the confident stride and dignified look of Whitman as depicted in an advertisement for the John Hancock Insurance Company in 1952 and the animated television character Homer Simpson bellowing "Leaves of Grass, my ass!" in 1995.

In discussing the evolution of Whitman's image in the mass media from his lifetime to the present, we analyze a representative sampling of his varied popular culture appearances. Certain emphases are worth noting: we have chosen not to focus on Whitman's appearances in film so as to avoid duplicating Kenneth M. Price's recent chapter "Whitman at the Movies" in *To Walt Whitman, America* (2004), and we have also not analyzed Whitman's impact on classical and jazz music (which is discussed elsewhere in this volume) but have instead focused on forms of music that have more consistently reached a wide popular audience. Our selective treatment of Whitman images in mass media highlights the recent proliferation of images that are often ironic, funny, and rich with sexual overtones.

Starting from Camden: The Walt Whitman Hotel and the Whitman Stamp

During the first half-century after his death Whitman's image and words were frequently used as a way to lend credibility to institutions and products, whether or not there was any real relationship with the writer. A good example of an authentic connection to the poet (and his community) can be found in the Walt Whitman Hotel in Camden, New Jersey. The hotel, which opened in 1925 and remained in business for approximately 50 years (it was demolished in the 1980s), was in fact built and owned by the community. According to an article in the *Camden Courier-Post* of July 5, 1926, even the name was based on a "majority of letters received after suggestions for a name were asked through the columns of the Courier" (*Camden Courier-Post* 1926). The hotel was a project of the Greater Camden Movement, a civic group that had been effective in raising funds to support American soldiers during World War I. Following the war, the group's plan was to boost the local economy by building a bridge between Camden and Philadelphia (eventually named the Walt Whitman Bridge). The article cited above explains that the hotel aimed to become a center for Whitman art. "Paintings of the poet, portraits and murals depicting his varied interests in life have been installed in various of the public rooms, and more are being added." The hotel generated ephemera such as postcards and matchbooks to spread its name while also promoting itself on towels, plates, and other matter along with placing advertisements in mass media outlets, especially newspapers.

In 1940, Whitman's connection to his final home in New Jersey was also fittingly stressed when the United States Postal Service unveiled first in Camden a Whitman postage stamp as part of its series of stamps called "Famous Americans." The Postal Service selected five individuals for each of its seven categories: "Authors," "Poets,"

"Educators," "Scientists," "Composers," "Artists," and "Inventors." Whitman, along with Henry Wadsworth Longfellow, John Greenleaf Whittier, James Russell Lowell, and James Whitcomb Riley, was selected as one of five famous American poets. Whitman's inclusion in this group may be surprising to modern readers since he is seldom grouped with the popular "Fireside Poets" or with the dialect poetry of Riley. But it is consistent with other representations of Whitman in the mass media of the 1940s – he was included precisely because of what the series highlights, his fame. His revolutionary poetic agenda is barely suggested; instead, he, like the more conservative "Famous American" poets in this series, is presented on the stamp with a traditional head and shoulders portrait. The only distinction is that unlike all the other portraits of writers in the series, Whitman is wearing a hat. A wide variety of first-day covers exist, postmarked "Camden, New Jersey, February 20, 1940." The idea of a Whitman stamp emanating from Camden is especially appropriate because Whitman often served as a one-man distribution center, mailing out copies of the 1876 *Leaves of Grass*, for example, one at a time, as the orders came in.

Advertising

Early in the twentieth century, the Camden Grocers Exchange apparently offered an assortment of Walt Whitman products. Kenneth Price owns a Walt Whitman coffee tin that bears an advertisement urging brand name loyalty: "Ask your grocer for Walt Whitman products." Whitman's image and name were also invoked elsewhere in the US and UK to peddle cigarettes, cigars, pencils, ice cream, and drug treatments for medical ailments in the early twentieth century and to sell coffee in both the early and late twentieth century. Whitman's image was reproduced commercially to persuade consumers to associate products with his work and legacy. Occasionally this was fitting: one company advertised a printing press using Whitman's name and likeness. Given the poet's notoriety (both in his own time and in continuing controversies about his work and its meaning in the twentieth century), it is intriguing that advertisers blithely used Whitman as an innocuous famous figure. The Whitman represented is the writer who will unsettle the fewest possible people in the marketplace. For example, an Old Crow whiskey advertisement, distributed in 1962, used a gift to the poet in 1891 to claim Whitman as one of its "famous customers" and to depict a life wildly at odds with Whitman's actual circumstances. The ad offered a stylized, well-groomed but still recognizable image of Whitman seated at his desk in a neat, orderly room filled with books and portraits of himself. With him is an attractive maid who serves him from the complimentary bottle of Old Crow whiskey he received in the mail. The ad presents Whitman's life as filled with the adornments of the wealthy elite. To dignify its product, Old Crow depicts a Whitman who never existed, constructing the poet as refined, orderly, and discriminating in his taste for spirits. Old Crow projects conventional signs of the culturally elite onto a poet who had fashioned himself in opposition to ordinary affluence. In truth, Whitman lived in his final years in a modest house awash in an extraordinary chaos of papers. (Ironically, Whitman wrote a temperance novel, *Franklin Evans*, early in his career, and several of his early writings deplore the "livid faces of drunkards." Not an excessive drinker himself at any time of his life, Whitman favored beer during his bohemian days at Pfaff's in the late 1850s, and Burgundy and champagne in his final years.) Here advertising severs Whitman's name and image from his life and poetic agenda in order to reduce him to a generic famous dead poet.

In the 1990s, Borders Bookshop Espresso Bar in Minnetonka, Minnesota, cleverly altered the famous photograph of Whitman with a cardboard butterfly perched on his fingertip in such a way as to substitute a cup of coffee for the butterfly, thus creating an image that shows Whitman holding up and deeply contemplating what can only be a satisfying cup of coffee. The wit of the image depends of course on our being aware of the advertiser's sleight-of-hand. As in representations of Whitman earlier in the century, he has currency here as a "famous poet," he lends a certain high culture appeal to a business, and his image gratifies those sufficiently in the know to appreciate the joke. At the same time, coffee houses in the late twentieth and early twenty-first centuries have taken pains to give themselves the air of bohemia and the veneer of literary sophistication. Whitman, who is increasingly understood as a poet of love and freethinking, helps in creating this atmosphere. The positive feelings generally directed toward Whitman in American culture no doubt encouraged Starbucks, too, to include, on one of their coffee cards (to be used in lieu of cash), a Whitman quotation about America being "not merely a nation, but a teeming nation of nations." Presumably Starbucks hoped that would help teeming nations line up to order more venti lattes.

Humor

At the same time as the Old Crow whiskey advertisement appeared, Whitman was beginning to be represented in other forms of media in ways that were less reverential. In January 1962, *Mad Magazine* published "Inspirational Poems by, for and about the Nation's Building Men," one of which spoofs the lamentations of "O Captain! My Captain!":

> O Builder! My Builder! Our dreadful house is done,
> There's devastation in your wake, it looks just like Bull Run;
> The toilets leak, the closets creak, the basement's filled with water,
> We're killing termites by the score, come back and watch the slaughter;
> But O heart! Heart! Heart!
> O the bleeding drops of red,
> My dreams of joy and pleasure lie
> Fallen cold and dead. (*Mad Magazine* 1962: 20)

This parody exemplifies a new attitude toward Whitman that begins to emerge in mass media. Rather than using the image of the poet to give cultural legitimacy, the references highlight the oddity, irony, and asymmetry caused by the distance between mid-nineteenth-century and mid-twentieth-century American culture. The "O Captain" parody distances itself from Whitman by locating humor in the incongruity between the poet's heroic vision of Abraham Lincoln and mundane details of mid-twentieth-century life. Whitman's expression of sorrow at the loss of Lincoln becomes part of the humor when the focus changes to leaking toilets and termite problems, and when the Civil War – Bull Run in particular – becomes a metaphor for sloppy contractors. *Mad Magazine*, consistently irreverent about virtually every topic since its inception in 1952, would parody "O Captain! My Captain!" several times (see *Mad* issues for April 1959, September 1967, and March 1983). The recognizable rhythms and elevated emotionalism of the poem apparently provided an irresistible target.

Music

In contrast to *Mad*'s lampooning of Whitman, Joan Baez invoked Whitman for political uplift. One of the foremost folk musicians of the 1960s, Baez included a reading from Whitman on her 1967 concept album *Baptism*. The album, which the liner notes explain "was conceived as a means of 'saying something' through a synthesis of poetry and music," joins a section of Whitman's "When Lilacs Last in the Dooryard Bloom'd" (titled "I Saw the Vision of Armies" on the album) with works by James Joyce, William Blake, John Donne, Arthur Rimbaud, e. e. cummings, and Countee Cullen, among others. Baez, a peace activist, evokes Whitman in much the way he was evoked by socialists and communists earlier in the century (Michael Gold, for example, claimed that Whitman "rose from the grave to march with us"). Baez sees Whitman as the "most uniquely American of great poets" who possessed "visions of world human brotherhood" (Baez [1967] 2003).

These two different versions of Whitman in the mass media of the 1960s – ironic and playful on the one hand, idealistic and reverent on the other – foretell the media's continuing complex relationship with Whitman throughout the last decades of the twentieth century. Treatments of Whitman provide a way to gauge the type of stories popular culture was telling about US history in this time period. In popular music, for example, Whitman's name and work continued to be evoked in multiple ways. Irish singer and songwriter Van Morrison's 1983 album *Inarticulate Speech of the Heart* contains a track entitled "Rave On, John Donne." The song, in which Morrison sings about the persistence and influence of literature ("Rave on words on printed page"), mentions Whitman along with John Donne, William Butler Yeats, Omar Khayam, and Kahlil Gibran, and specifically envisions Whitman as "nose down in wet grass," filling his senses with "nature's bright green shady path." Morrison's lyric pays homage to *Leaves of Grass* when he mentions Whitman in a catalogue of famous writers. Morrison chooses to invoke him specifically as a nature poet and includes him with a group that "raves on" "through the industrial revolution, Impericism [sic], atomic and nuclear age" (Morrison 1983). The poet's ability to find spirit in nature is for Morrison a sign that Whitman speaks across time periods. Morrison's evocation of Whitman is reminiscent of Baez in attitude if not in the details. Both songwriters venerate Whitman as a truth-teller. Perhaps less directly than Baez, Morrison, too, turns Whitman to political purposes, portraying his poetry as an implicit condemnation of the destructive tendencies of contemporary life.

In 1992 Lindsey Buckingham, a member of the popular band Fleetwood Mac, directly connected his own artistic growth with Whitman's by titling a solo album *Out of the Cradle*. In addition to using a title virtually identical to one of Whitman's, Buckingham fills his album art with, among other things, old photographs of himself as a young boy with guitars and a "collage poem" taken directly from Whitman's "Out of the Cradle Endlessly Rocking." The "collage poem" consists of nine handwritten lines from the first line group in Whitman's poem. The poem, combined with pictures of Buckingham learning to play the guitar, works to connect the musician's own artistic "awakening" to Whitman's. Though Buckingham's album employs Whitman to underscore his serious artistic aims, there is also a playfulness present. The handwritten poem, which begins with Whitman's first line, "Out of the cradle endlessly rocking," is flanked by two large photographs: on the left is a young boy playing a guitar and singing, on the right is the adult Buckingham playing a guitar and singing. In other words, Buckingham puns, he has been "endlessly rocking" throughout his life. As painful as that pun is – at least he didn't title the album "Endlessly Rocking" – it is made subtly, and demonstrates the more complex relationship songwriters are beginning to have with Whitman. Rather than just venerating him as a great poet, Buckingham uses humor in his Whitman references.

Perhaps the best known (and most enigmatic) use of Whitman in popular music in the last decade is the song "Walt Whitman's Niece" on the 1998 album *Mermaid Avenue*. The album has several major musical contributors: the lyrics were all written by Woody Guthrie in 1946, and the music was composed and performed by Billy Bragg and Wilco. As the opening track on the album, "Walt Whitman's Niece" is raucous, irreverent, and sexually charged in a way that other evocations of Whitman have not been. The lyrics tell a story about two men, one of them a "seaman," who walk up to a "big old building" and meet "two girls," go into their "big long room" with a "deep blue rug," where one girl "took down a book of poems" and reads as the narrator lays his head down in her lap. After that, the "seaman buddy and girl moved off" and "there I was, / All night long, laying and listening and forgetting the poems." "My girl had told us that she was a niece of Walt Whitman," the narrator says, "but not which niece, / And it takes a night and a girl and book of this kind / A long long time to find its way back" (Bragg and Wilco 1998).

The use of Whitman in "Walt Whitman's Niece," then, is quite different than the political and spiritual uses made by Baez and Morrison. There is an air of gleeful nonsense about the entire song. Bryan K. Garman, who focuses on the leftist politics that connects the poet to Guthrie and others in the folk-singing tradition, calls the song "unremarkable" (Garman 2000: 191), but it is significant when seen as part of the broader pattern of Whitman references in mass media. In most forms of popular culture up until the time Guthrie wrote his lyrics, "Whitman" had been associated with profundity and spiritual truth; here, however, the reference adds to the depth and complexity of the sexually suggestive content. Whitman has meant so many different things to people as a poet of love and eroticism that a cryptic invocation of his name in an amorous context raises a host of possibilities. In sharp contrast to "Walt Whitman's Niece" is another song on *Mermaid Avenue* called "Ingrid Bergman." It is another fantasy involving a more directly expressed tryst with a celebrity. By writing a song about Whitman's niece, Guthrie, famous for his heterosexual appetites, can imagine a Whitman-mediated sexual encounter while remaining within a heterosexual frame.

"Walt Whitman's Niece," released in 1998, evoked an eroticized image of Whitman that was increasingly common in the mass media of the late twentieth century. In *To Walt Whitman, America*, Price has documented the way Whitman's poetry, image, and name have often been used as love currency. He notes that after 1980 Whitman has the most cultural resonance in cinema as the poet of love, and references to him and his work are often used by filmmakers to tell a story of desire and romance. Whitman is used by characters who are trying to woo a partner, by lovers affirming their relationship, by characters exploring same-sex love and so on. The Billy Bragg and Wilco performance of "Walt Whitman's Niece" is part of this mass media conception of Whitman as a poet of love and desire.

One other pop music reference to Whitman from the late 1990s relies on a similar understanding of Whitman. Ben Lee's song, "Portable Walt Whitman," released on the soundtrack to the Australian film, *Blackrock*, features amusing lyrics about the narrator's unrequited desire for an anonymous woman who is "so damn pretty she should be against the law." The song's narrator claims "I'd give my left lung to be hers for one night" and "she breaks my heart every time that she smiles," but the only mention of Whitman is in the title. The precise relevance of the title is unclear: does it refer to the Viking Press's *Portable Walt Whitman*? Is it a personal, intentionally obscure reference? Is "Walt Whitman" meant to be symbolic of the narrator's fickle, or "portable," emotional and sexual desire (the woman he longs for he has just seen "walking down the street")? Whatever the title's meaning may be, Ben Lee clearly understands that Whitman resonates in the culture as a poet of love.

Television

Regrettably, Whitman's first television performance, like his first adaptation in film, *The Carpenter*, appears to be lost. Fred Ziv, a pioneer in television syndication, once planned to use Arthur Fitz-Richard's adaptation of the Whitman story "One Wicked Impulse" for his series "Favorite Story TV." Kenneth Price has in his collection a copy of script number 72B, the final master script dated May 17, 1954, of "One Wicked Impulse." (Records concerning "Favorite Story TV" are spotty, and it is unclear if the

Whitman episode actually ran.) This story may have come to Ziv's attention not because he was studying Whitman's lesser-known texts, but because *Ellery Queen Mystery Magazine* had published "One Wicked Impulse!" as #122 in January 1954. The TV script borrows Whitman's title and gives the name Mr Covert to a major character, but in other respects the stories differ markedly from one another. This seems to be an example of invoking Whitman just to gain the power of his name. There is, however, a rough similarity in the premises of the two stories: a man causes the death of another, and both in effect ask the question: what can redeem him?

Like "Favorite Story TV," Fox's *The Simpsons* invoked Whitman primarily for the power of his name. In the "Mother Simpson" episode (first aired November 19, 1995), Homer goes to the Springfield Hall of Records to straighten out one of his son Bart's pranks, which has convinced the record keepers that Homer is dead. In his confrontation with the bureaucrat, Homer becomes involved in a debate over whether Homer's mother is dead. He believes that she is because he can point to her grave marker at the top of the cemetery hill. However, Homer takes the bureaucrat's suggestion and decides to inspect more closely. When he moves the foliage to reveal not his mother's name but that of Walt Whitman, he cries out: "Walt Whitman?! Aargh! Damn you, Walt Whitman! [kicking grave] I! Hate! You! Walt! Freaking! Whitman! 'Leaves of Grass,' my ass!" Frivolous, light-hearted, earthy, crass – it is hard to know exactly how to characterize Homer's declaration. What does seem clear, though, is that American culture has developed an easy familiarity with Whitman. Alvaro Cardona-Hine once remarked of Whitman, "He has the careless and forgiving odor of someone who will let you live" (Cardona-Hine 1998: 371). Poets, artists, advertisers, and others speak about Whitman with little of the reserve and formality that characterizes the treatment of other revered figures in our cultural past. To borrow Gary Schmidgall's description of Horace Traubel's relationship to Whitman, American culture is "intimate with Walt."

Like *The Simpsons*, other television programs, including *ER*, *Six Feet Under*, *Twilight Zone*, and *Law & Order*, turned to Whitman when treating death. The *ER* episode "Sleepless in Chicago" (NBC, first aired February 23, 1995) features a scene in which John Carter, Chief Resident, brings several books to a dying patient, a former high school English teacher, Mr Klein, who brusquely rejects an unspecified book by Melville and one other unnamed text before grabbing the Whitman book. Later, Carter reads to him from "Passage to India":

> O soul thou pleasest me, I thee,
> Sailing these seas or on the hills, or waking in the night,
> Thoughts, silent thoughts, of Time and Space and Death, like waters flowing,
> Bear me indeed as through the regions infinite,
> Whose air I breathe, whose ripples hear, lave me all over,
> Bathe me O God in thee, mounting to thee,
> I and my soul to range in range of thee.
> O Thou transcendent,
> Nameless, the fibre and the breath.

The show implies that Whitman (famous for his own work in the Civil War hospitals), knew better than other writers everything from hospital settings to eternity.

One episode of the HBO series *Six Feet Under*, "The Plan" (first aired March 17, 2002), features a plot involving the death of Michael John Pipher, whose wife is psychic. At a service for her husband, the wife asks that a man read from "Michael's favorite poet, Walt Whitman." The passage is from section 6 of the final version of "Song of Myself":

> What do you think has become of the young and old men?
> And what do you think has become of the women and children?
> They are alive and well somewhere,
> The smallest sprout shows there is really no death.

The facial expression of the bereaved wife indicates that she is pleased and consoled by these lines. She also takes them quite literally because she believes she is still able to communicate with her husband. Indeed psychic connection with the dead is an ongoing motif here, since both funeral director brothers communicate with their dead father during the episode.

One of the earliest uses of Whitman in television also touched on the theme of death in an adaptation of Ray Bradbury's story "I Sing the Body Electric." This episode of CBS's *Twilight Zone* (first aired May 18, 1962) features some unhappy children whose mother has apparently died. The boy in the story, however, reads from a magazine called *Modern Science* something called "I Sing the Body Electric," an advertisement for an electronic data-processing system in the shape of a woman. In a touch that seems reminiscent of Whitman's catalogue of body parts in his poem "I Sing the Body Electric," clients are able to select eyes, ears, arms, hair, and so on. The beleaguered family is able to select bits and pieces, put them down a chute, and compile as needed a grandmother. Whitman's poem is also directly quoted once: "The armies of those I love engirth me and I engirth them." This grandmother-robot, who possesses more-than-human powers and can fly a kite when the kids don't have string, appears to die when she throws herself in front of a van to push Anne, one of the children, out of harm's way. Anne, who had remained aloof, now embraces the grandmother-robot tearfully. It turns out, however, that Anne need not have worried because, as the grandmother-robot explains, it is her job to live (and love) forever. In this episode, Whitman's poem celebrating the natural body is ironically used in a narrative about machines replacing humans in order to provide more permanent love. Our only hope, this version of "I Sing the Body Electric" suggests, is to program love and generosity into robots that do not have the weaknesses – chief among them mortality – that plague humankind.

Whitman appears in a more grim context in an episode of NBC's *Law & Order: Special Victims Unit*, "A Single Life" (first aired September 27, 1999). In this episode, a young woman, Susan Sodarsky, has died from a fall from a highrise. The case ultimately involves her psychiatrist, a television anchorman, and her own father who had sexually abused her. At the beginning of the show, when Detective Benson and the regular New York City police start to squabble over whether or not this is a routine case (and thus over who has jurisdiction), Benson says sarcastically about the imagined suspect, "Oh yeah, he read her a little Walt Whitman; they made hot passionate love; and, right before he fell asleep, he threw her out the window – excuse me – *through* the window." We later find out that the victim was in fact a suicide, who has been driven to it by abuse from her father. She is hard to track, with few friends or relatives. The key to unlocking the case is finding a Sylvia Plath book, 20 years overdue, from Paterson High School that shows that she has changed her name and identity to flee her father. The invocation of Whitman raises the possibility of a tender and compassionate love in contrast to the abuse that destroyed the victim's life. The Whitmanian life-affirmation is also sharply at odds with the suicidal Plath and the victim at the heart of this story.

Whitman's connection to love and eroticism is pursued in many other television programs as well. In some cases, as in an episode of NBC's situation comedy *Friends* entitled "The One at the Fertility Clinic" (first aired May 1, 2003), Whitman serves both as famous icon and poet of love. In this episode, Joey, the dimwitted but lovable friend, is dating a woman named Charlie, who is a professor at New York University. Charlie suggests that they enjoy some highbrow entertainment – listening to a string quartet, going to the Met (Joey mistakenly thinks she means seeing the Mets play baseball), or seeing an exhibit of Walt Whitman letters at the New York Public Library. This brief mention of Whitman relies on him as a symbol of refinement and sophistication, and, because the reference occurs in the context of planning a date, he also is the poet of eros.

Controversies over Whitman's sexual proclivities appear not only in critical writing but on television as well. The episode of CBS's *Dr. Quinn, Medicine Woman* entitled "The Body Electric" (first aired April 5, 1997) is a treatment of Whitman and gay issues. This series, though set in the nineteenth century, regularly addressed late twentieth-century issues. In this particular episode, Whitman has traveled to Colorado Springs where he is initially greeted as a poet and a minor celebrity. Only gradually through euphemisms is it intimated that Whitman "prefers the company of men." Even Dr Quinn panics when her young adopted son, Brian, goes off alone with the poet to interview him for the town newspaper. Eventually Dr Quinn's moral crisis is resolved when, contrary to her worst fears, she discovers Whitman innocently having a discussion with her boy. The story closes with calm restored to the community but with the poet looking on saddened at the intolerance he has seen. This episode has been called the prime-time outing of Walt Whitman (Henderson 1999: 69).

Television references to Whitman have increased significantly since the early 1990s. Consistent with references to Whitman in popular music, television has treated Whitman as an iconic famous writer, as a person who embodies controversial sexuality, or as the poet of love and eroticism. An episode of CBS's *Northern Exposure*, "Brains, Know-How and Native Intelligence" (first aired on July 19, 1990) opens with the philosophical disc jockey, Chris, reading Walt Whitman over the airwaves and reflecting on the book that "completely and irrevocably changed my life." He had come upon the book while stealing a car with another 15 year old in West Virginia. (A similar account is given in the December 14, 1992 episode entitled "Crime and Punishment.") When he spends time in jail, the jailer tells him that Whitman's homoerotic impulses were not acceptable in a place of correction. Chris's further reflections on Whitman indicate that he is now remorseful about the "queers I had previously kicked around." In his role as disc jockey, he reads lines first from "When Lilacs Last in the Dooryard Bloom'd" and then "Out of the Cradle Endlessly Rocking." Maurice Minnifield (who owns the radio station) pulls him from the mike by his hair and throws him through a plate glass window. The controversy over Whitman's sexuality piques the public interest. The small library in Cicely, Alaska now has a three-month waiting list for its only Whitman book.

Another *Northern Exposure* episode emphasizes an additional familiar aspect of Whitman's reputation – the poet as democratic bard. In "Democracy In America" (first aired on February 24, 1992), the long-time mayor, Holling Van Coeur, is surprised to learn that he faces a significant challenge from his friend Edna Hancock, who is angered that he has forgotten to act on her request to install a stop sign near her house. The election prompts Chris's patriotic reflections on the radio, and he quotes Whitman several times to assert that the genius of the United States is to be found in the common people. "I feel at one with Whitman, shepherd of the great unwashed, O 'Democracy! Near at hand to you a throat is now inflating itself and joyfully singing.' " Whacky and entertaining, the program drops references to Thoreau, Jefferson, Lincoln, and de Tocqueville along with Whitman, yet does so with a light touch that avoids being ponderous or pedantic. The Whitman who emerges is the democratic bard, the sexual iconoclast, the godfather of freethinking.

Mass-distributed Paperbacks

If television sometimes reduced Whitman to a one-dimensional message, another form, the mass-distributed paperback edition, lent itself readily to more complex depictions of Whitman. The many commercial paperback editions of Whitman's writings produced from the time of the first paperback printing in his lifetime of the so-called Deathbed edition (preceding the hardback first issue) to the innumerable modern commercial Whitman editions are too numerous to detail and analyze here. Two notable cases in free or nearly free distribution of Whitman materials should be recorded, however, both because they are important experiments in book publishing and because they anticipate the internet in their capacity to distribute very widely free or nearly free content. We have in mind the Little Blue Book series of Emanuel Haldeman-Julius, based in Girard, Kansas, and the World War II Armed Services Editions (ASEs), overseen by the Library Section, a division of the Morale Branch in the US War Department.

Haldeman-Julius sold a huge number of books: his series ran to almost 2,000 numbered items and sold at least 300 million copies, perhaps as many as 500 million. Flourishing primarily in the inter-war years, Haldeman-Julius managed to make money selling books at 10 cents apiece, later 5 cents apiece, and, occasionally, at his rock bottom price of 2.5 cents apiece (a limited time offer made in 1942). Harry Golden recognized the singular accomplishment of Haldeman-Julius: "No other publisher will ever create so wide a reading audience" (Golden 1960: 7). The Haldeman-Julius books were a fascinating mix of types: literary classics, self-help books, atheist and socialist polemics, and what he called "sexology." The audience for the Little Blue Books was primarily working class. These books were especially popular in small towns and rural areas in the US, but they were read in the entire English-speaking world.

The Little Blue Books include quite a variety of Whitman items. There are three different versions of #73: *Walt Whitman's Poems*, *Poems of Walt Whitman*, and *Best Poems of Walt Whitman*. Other Whitman volumes include # 299 *Prose Nature Notes* and #351 *Memories of President Lincoln*. There was also a critical volume: #529 Emily Hamblen's *Walt Whitman: Bard of the West*. For the purposes of this essay, we will focus most of our remarks on two states of Little Blue Book #73. In the first version of #73, Whitman is presented as a writer of short lyrics. This is a volume that favors very short Whitman poems, often of three lines or less. Although the Little Blue Book is only 3.5 by 5 inches, a single page (40) has five poems on it: "Hast Never Come to Thee an Hour," "Thought" [of Equality], "To Old Age," "Locations and Times," and "Offerings." The longest poem included in the book is "I Sing the Body Electric." *Walt Whitman's Poems* lacks a copyright notice, date of publication, table of contents, and introduction.

Poems of Walt Whitman (a new version of #73) is a different type of volume. It advertises itself as "Edited, with Introduction and Notes, by Nelson Antrim Crawford" and is copyrighted 1924 by the Haldeman-Julius company (though probably the only thing they could legitimately copyright was Crawford's contributions). It has features that the first version of #73 lacks: a table of contents, introduction, and extended excerpts from Whitman's longer poems. Without noting the fact, this volume of Whitman's poetry relies on the rarely reprinted 1872 version of *Leaves* (possibly because of copyright reasons). Thus we get assorted sections of the poem "Walt Whitman" rather than, as it was later called, "Song of Myself." This book presents the full range of Whitman's work and offers a fairly routine sampling. In addition to the "Walt Whitman" poem, Crawford offers "Out of the Cradle Endlessly Rocking," "Come up from the Fields Father," and many short lyrics including a variety of "Calamus" poems. He mentions in his introduction "comradeship between persons of the same sex," but he veers away from any serious consideration of the issue: "The erotic implications of the latter form a problem for the psychologist more than for the literary critic" (p. 19).

In his conversations with Horace Traubel, Whitman once entertained an idea that seems eerily to predict the Little Blue Books. Traubel says:

> We discussed the point – why not some time issue an edition of L. of G. in small vols, for pocket wear and tear? Song of Myself, Children of Adam, &c. &c., in separate books? W. believed in it. "It has long been my ambition to bring out an edition of Leaves of Grass with margins cut close, paper cover: some book rid of the usual cumbersome features. . . . It is a theory to be seriously considered: now it is perhaps too late: but others may one day think of it–act on it." (Traubel 1914: 258–9)

The Armed Services Editions, narrower in scope and more confined in duration than the Little Blue Books, was also an eye-opening venture and has rightly been called the largest book give away in history (Bruccoli 1984: 26). This publishing experiment paved the way, after the war, for the mass-market paperback movement. For the Armed Services Edition, the audience was US soldiers stationed overseas. Many of these soldiers had not been enticed by reading before, but now they found themselves with time on their hands and little entertainment. The Armed Services Editions came about when the Library Section decided by 1942 that American soldiers needed a new type of book to replace hardbacks. They needed books light in weight, compact enough for a GI's pocket, appealing to varied readers, and cheap to produce. Fortunately, the rotary presses used for large circulation magazines were available between issues. This fact made possible the Armed Services Editions, produced as softcover books in landscape rather than the usual portrait format (i.e., the books are wider than they are tall).

The Council on Books in Wartime wanted the full support of the publishing community. So the Council insisted – even to those who volunteered to forego royalties – that one cent would be paid to the author and publisher of each book. Given that press runs were of over 100,000 copies or more, this had significance. These were huge press runs for writers and publishers used to much smaller circulation figures. Some publishers worried that these volumes would flood the market after the war, but these paperbacks were designed, if not exactly to self-destruct, at least not to last. The series published classics, contemporary literature, biographies, humor, and mysteries. Despite wartime circumstances, few ASE books were censored. Reaction to them by the soldiers was extremely favorable. They tended to be read primarily behind the front lines, though just before the Normandy invasion there was mass distribution to the troops, with one copy of an Armed Services Edition handed to each soldier upon boarding the invasion barge (Cole 1984: 9).

A Wartime Whitman was edited by Major William A. Aiken. In Aiken's introduction, Whitman is presented as a poet who champions the American way of life, the very thing being defended in the war, according to the introduction. Interestingly, the introduction goes to some pains to make Whitman's comradely love safe for the troops. In fact, Whitman becomes, in some ways, a suggestive heterosexual poet through strategic quoting of the poem ultimately entitled "Faces." Aiken writes, "Many will respond to the instant urge of Whitman's woman as she stands by the picket fence and calls to her 'limber-hipped' man." The introduction raises – in order to dismiss – the question of homosexuality: "The gulf between a man's love of woman and the love he bears his fellow man is clearer to most Americans than it may sometimes seem in Whitman's works; yet the soldier whose buddy lies dying in a foxhole at his side will understand this identification in the mind of the poet more readily than will the literary critic, with his passion for pathology, by the fireside at home" (p. 9).

Compared to the Haldeman-Julius Little Blue Books, *A Wartime Whitman* is marked by a more obvious editorial intrusiveness. In *A Wartime Whitman*, the poet's work is categorized into seven sections. The groupings are: "America Singing," "A Poet's World," "A Poet's Love," "Pioneers," "War," "Aftermath," and "Toward the Future." Not surprisingly, there is a whole section on war, generally emphasizing the common soldier, and including the sea battle from "Song of Myself." *A Wartime Whitman* asserts that its text is taken from Emory Holloway's Inclusive Edition of *Leaves of Grass* copyrighted by Doubleday, Doran, and Co., but then proceeds to reconfigure the poetry, providing names for groups of poems that have no authority in anything Whitman wrote or that Holloway edited. For example, Aiken retitled sections of "Song of Myself" as if they were separate poems.

There was even a wartime biography of Whitman issued through the Armed Services Editions – Henry Seidel Canby's *Walt Whitman an American: A Study in Biography*. As the front cover proclaimed, "This Is The Complete Book – Not A Digest." The back cover indicates why the Council thought the book might appeal to men at war:

> Rubicund and tumultuously bearded, egotistical, publicity-mad, idolized by his friends, slandered or ignored by his contemporaries, Walt Whitman, the man who put sex back on to the printed page, was the problem child of American literature. But he was also the prophet and seer of democracy; a poet who made articulate the American dream and the American faith, and who created a new literary style to express himself and his country in poetry.

The Little Blue Books and the Armed Services Editions, two publishing efforts that yielded pocket Whitmans, were series with contrasting purposes that were driven by different political ideologies. Yet they shared a fundamental desire to expand the reading audience and underscored the value of education. And both experiments spread word of Whitman to large new audiences.

Whitman Online and in the Academy

Walt Whitman's presence in this newest form of mass media is rich and varied. Like the creators of other media representations that we've discussed, website designers employ Whitman's image and work toward a variety of ends, some startling and some unsurprising. The worldwide web, featuring interlinking and intralinking information, offers a deluge of content to users, often sinking Whitman's presence in a sea of details about other topics. "I too am but a trail of drift and debris," as Whitman wrote in "As I Ebb'd with the Ocean of Life," and the web gives the line new resonance. With a few major exceptions, Whitman's web presence can be sorted into a handful of categories: sites that provide interpretations of Whitman's life and work, sites that provide brief, encyclopedia-like entries on Whitman and other major cultural figures (these often include transcriptions of selected poems), sites that use Whitman's fame to draw in tourists, and sites that narrowly define Whitman's identity (the "spiritual" Whitman, the "gay" Whitman, the "democratic" Whitman) in order to promote an explicit agenda.

Like other mass media representations of Whitman, web representations range from celebratory to audaciously irreverent. In the first category are sites like the creation of Mitchell Santine Gould (2004a). Gould's site, dedicated to the 150th anniversary of the first publication of *Leaves of Grass* in 1855, offers a visually rich interpretation of Whitman's book, focusing on Quakers, homosexual love, sailors, women, and spiritualism. Gould's presentation, though whimsical, borders on the worshipful, as he presents several artist's renderings of Whitman: as a muscular, patriotic superhero; as a cap-wearing, smiling, trim old ballplayer in the main banner; and as a determined, shouting voice of the people in the logo for the sponsoring company, "General Picture."

Among the more irreverent Whitman sites is the animated "video" for the techno-pop song, "Walt Whitman." This animation, part of a site created by performance artist My Robot Friend, features moving text; pulsating, flying images of Whitman; old photographs of nude boys; and suggestive lyrics about Whitman's sexual experiences (including a sexually charged reading of Whitman's line from "Salut au Monde!" "What widens within you, Walt Whitman?"). The song (and its accompanying visualizations by Adam Shecter) demonstrates that Whitman's representation in movies, television, and music – as poet of love and sex – is also on the internet where it comes to users, for better and worse, with few if any of the filtering devices that commonly tame other forms of mass media. In fact, the song and animation by My Robot Friend is among the most explicit sexual readings of Whitman in all of early-twenty-first century mass media. The animation begins with a cartoon of a nude Whitman, and the big nostrils, foolish grin, and deformed-looking genitals convey the tone of the entire piece: My Robot Friend understands Whitman as a playful cultural figure, one whose image is deeply intertwined with sexuality and can gleefully accommodate irony and humor.

With the advent of the web, scholars, too, are making use of mass media to spread Whitman's work and are experiencing for the first time the power of having direct access to mass media. The *Walt Whitman Archive* (Folsom and Price 1995-) is a case in point. The *Whitman Archive* serves as a vast teaching and scholarly resource that sets out to make all of Whitman's writings freely accessible to scholars, students, and general readers. It meets the same needs addressed in the familiar multivolume scholarly edition, while also addressing needs that go well beyond the capacity of a print edition. And unlike scholarly print editions of the past, the *Whitman Archive* can have more than a specialized audience, can approach the ideal of bringing together popular and scholarly audiences in a way that seems fitting for Whitman who once said (at the end of the Preface to the 1855 edition of *Leaves of Grass*) that the "proof of a poet is that his country absorbs him as affectionately as he has absorbed it." The *Whitman Archive* currently includes teaching materials, a substantial biography of the poet, all 130 photographs of Whitman (with full annotations), searchable finding guides to manuscripts, a regularly updated annotated bibliography of scholarship since 1975, a growing body of critical work, and a great deal of contextual material, both encyclopedia entries about various topics relating to Whitman and selected writings by Whitman's associates. After 10 years of work by a fairly extensive team, the *Archive* has accomplished about one-fourth of the total work it has outlined, an indication of how prolific Whitman was and how extensive are the materials relevant to scholarship about him.

The *Whitman Archive* delivers digital images of the original source material to its users so that they can witness Whitman's process of composition, and so that they can do their own transcriptions of manuscripts, if they wish, and challenge the editors' interpretations of hard-to-decipher passages. Making the source material available enables teachers to demonstrate that a poet like Whitman achieved his often majestic phrasing not through a magical process that led to the perfectly etched final products appearing, say, in an anthology. Instead his most memorable phrasing emerged only after multiple drafts, innumerable false starts and bungled lines. His pasted over, heavily deleted and interlineated manuscripts bear witness that, for all his praise of spontaneity, his best writing was achieved through laborious and often brilliant revision. There is a democratization at work as the *Archive* opens locked rare book rooms to students and the interested public. Whitman was trained as a printer and was fascinated by book design. The *Archive* provides high quality images not only of his manuscripts but also of his printed pages, allowing users to examine his choices as to typeface, layout, margins, and ornamentation and to consider how these textual features contributed to his meanings.

This essay has moved from advertising and television to scholarly treatments of Whitman and finds both popular and scholarly approaches very common now in mass media representations of Whitman. In addition to the web, there is one further form that we don't usually think of as a mass medium: the college and university. As Gerald Graff has written, "Though academic humanists have too often been reluctant to recognize the fact, the university's growth into an institution servicing great masses of people necessarily turns it into an agency of cultural popularization. It is even fair to call today's university a form of popular culture, in competition with journalism and other media as an alternative interpretation of experience" (Graff 1992: 352). There isn't space to attempt to delineate and categorize the great range of Whitman-related work that has occurred in university and college classrooms, and in the scholarship emerging from the academy as a whole. Suffice it to say that we have witnessed the growth of a vast amount of critical, biographical, historical, and bibliographical information. Since 1990, over 120 books and well over 1,100 articles have been published about Whitman, his work, and his relationship to American history,

American culture, and cultures around the world. That explosion of work in the academy has underwritten, in a rough and ready way at least, the flowering of interest in Whitman in recent film, television, music, and other forms of popular expression.

Meanwhile references to Whitman and his work continue to multiply both in the academy and seemingly everywhere else: in celebrity interviews (Julia Roberts's claim that Whitman was her crucial reading in high school), in odd bids for associated fame and profundity (the explanation of the creator of Gumby that he made Gumby green because that was the color of *Leaves of Grass*), in the assertion that *Leaves* is one of the hippest books of all time (Leland 2004), and in a private gift that gained mass publicity (President Clinton's present to Monica Lewinsky of a copy of *Leaves*). Both the scholarly and the popular culture interest in Whitman may have at its base the appeal that undergirded a recent PBS advertisement (November 2004). The very brief ad celebrates a guy who built a baseball park for kids with cancer after hearing Walt Whitman (perhaps on Ken Burns's baseball series) say that it is a great game and that it will "repair our losses." PBS concludes the ad with the tag line, "Be more inspired."

References and Further Reading

Baez, Joan ([1967] 2003). *Baptism, A Journey Through Our Time*. Vanguard Records, CD-79240, LP-79275.

Bragg, Billy and Wilco (1998). *Mermaid Avenue*. Elektra, 7559 62204 2.

Bruccoli, Matthew J. (1984). Recollections of an ASE Collector. In John Y. Cole (ed.), *Books in Action: The Armed Services Editions*. Washington: Library of Congress, pp. 23–8.

Buckingham, Lindsey (1992). *Out of the Cradle*. Warner Brothers CD, 26182; ASIN: B000002LL9.

Camden Courier-Post (1926). Built and Owned by the Community. July 5. Accessed from <http://www.dvrbs.com/CamdenNJ-WaltWhitmanHotel.htm>.

Canby, Henry Seidel (nd). *Walt Whitman, an American: A Study in Biography*. New York: Editions for the Armed Services.

Cardona-Hine, Alvaro (1998). I Teach Straying from Me – Yet Who Can Stray from Me? In Jim Perlman, Ed Folsom, and Dan Campion (eds.), *Walt Whitman: The Measure of His Song*, rev. edn. Duluth, MN: Holy Cow! Press, pp. 279–83.

Cole, John Y. (1984). Introduction. *Books in Action: The Armed Services Editions*. Washington: Library of Congress, pp. 1–12.

Folsom, Ed, and Price, Kenneth M. (1995-). *The Walt Whitman Archive*. <www.whitmanarchive.org>.

Garman, Bryan K. (2000). *A Race of Singers: Whitman's Working-Class Hero from Guthrie to Springsteen*. Chapel Hill: The University of North Carolina Press.

Gold, Michael (1998). Ode to Walt Whitman. In Jim Perlman, Ed Folsom, and Dan Campion (eds.), *Walt Whitman: The Measure of His* Song. Duluth, MN: Holy Cow! Press, pp. 168–71.

Golden, Harry (1960). Foreword. In Emanuel Haldeman-Julius, *The World of Haldeman-Julius*, compiled by Albert Mordell. New York: Twayne.

Gould, Mitchell Santine (2004). Celebrate Yourself: 150 Years of *Leaves of Grass*. <www.leavesofgrass.org>.

Graff, Gerald (1992). The Scholar in Society. In Joseph Gibaldi (ed.), *Introduction to Scholarship in Modern Languages and Literature*, 2nd edn. New York: Modern Language Association, pp. 341–62.

Henderson, Desirée (1999). Dr. Quinn, Medicine Woman and the Prime-Time 'Outing' of Walt Whitman. *Walt Whitman Quarterly Review*, 17: 69–76.

Mad Magazine (1962). Inspirational Poems by, for and about the Nation's Building Men. *Mad Magazine*, 68: 20.

Lee, Ben (1997). Portable Walt Whitman. *Blackrock Soundtrack*. Mercury Australia, CD 5535392.

Leland, John. (2004). *Hip: The History*. New York: HarperCollins.

Morrison, Van (1983). *Inarticulate Speech of the Heart*. Polydor Incorporated, LP 839 604–1.

My Robot Friend (2004). Walt Whitman. <www.myrobotfriend.com/waltwhitman.html>.

Palmer, Carole (2004). Thematic Research Collections. In Susan Schreibman, Ray Siemens, and John Unsworth (eds.), *Companion to Digital Humanities*. Oxford: Blackwell, pp. 348–65.

Price, Kenneth M. (2004). *To Walt Whitman, America*. Chapel Hill: The University of North Carolina Press.

Traubel, Horace (1914). *With Walt Whitman in Camden*, vol. 3. New York: Mitchell Kennerley.

Whitman, Walt (1924). *Poems of Walt Whitman*, ed. Nelson Antrim Crawford. Little Blue Book No. 73. Girard, Kansas: Haldeman-Julius.

Whitman, Walt (nd). *Walt Whitman's Poems*, ed. E. Haldeman-Julius. Ten Cent Pocket Series No. 73. Girard, Kansas: Haldeman-Julius.

Whitman, Walt (nd). *A Wartime Whitman*, ed. Major William A. Aiken. New York: Editions for the Armed Services.

PART III
The Literary Context

Inspired by a photograph taken by Napoleon Sarony (1878). Tonal graphite drawing by Doug DeVinny.

22
Language
Tyler Hoffman

In his final years in Camden, New Jersey, Whitman told his devoted friend Horace Traubel that "The subject of language interests me – interests me: I never quite get it out of my mind. I sometimes think the Leaves is only a language experiment." He goes on to say to him that "The new world, the new times, the new peoples" demand a new speech that will be able to express their modernity and highest ideals (Traubel [1904] 1987: viii–ix). This statement has provoked much critical discussion. What does it mean to call *Leaves of Grass* a "language experiment"? What aspect of language did it experiment with? How do the poems in the book revolutionize the word, if, in fact, they do? How does the experiment relate to the intellectual temper of the time? How does the language of *Leaves* compare to the language showcased in other poems of Whitman's day? What is the social, political, and cultural effect of his linguistic innovation?

In his Preface to the first edition of *Leaves* in 1855 Whitman broadcasts his interest in language and begins what would become a lifelong effort to mythologize it – to imagine the relationship that exists between the vitality of English and the character of the new nation:

> The English language befriends the grand American expression – it is brawny enough and limber and full enough. On the tough stock of a race who through all change of circumstance was never without the idea of political liberty, which is the animus of all liberty, it has attracted the terms of daintier and gayer and subtler and more elegant tongues. It is the powerful language of resistance – it is the dialect of common sense. It is the speech of the proud and melancholy races and of all who aspire. It is the chosen tongue to express growth faith self-esteem freedom justice equality friendliness amplitude prudence decision and courage. It is the medium that shall wellnigh express the inexpressible. (*PW*, 2: 456–7)

Notably, English does not appeal to Whitman merely on the basis of its phonetic quality – it is not just the sounds that the words make, but the ideological principles that are embodied by the words, which are stamped by the native traits of the user of them. This fiction of language is a powerful one, and Whitman repeatedly reads American English through a political lens, as a sign of the heartiness of the American people, their fierce independence, rugged individualism, and democratic impulses. He announces the advent of a "language-shaper" in his 1855 Preface, forecasting a poet who will emerge in the land to give expression to the grandeur of American vernacular in verse. *Leaves* was meant to be the first shining example.

Recognized as revolutionary in its use of language at the time of its publication, *Leaves* prompted both pleasure and dismay. Some critics and fellow writers disapproved of Whitman's use of words unable to be found in the dictionary, his license with English. Emerson, though, praised the mélange of language in the book, hailing its "remarkable mixture of the *Bhagvat-Geeta* and the *New York Herald*." The tension between these two linguistic poles – abstract philosophical discourse on the one hand, a journalistic pungency and directness of speech on the other – captures the multifariousness of Whitman's linguistic forays, his deep-seated and evolving philological sense. While some have felt that *Leaves* does not go far enough in the direction of one or the other pole, it is in the shuttle between these linguistic registers that much of the poetic power of *Leaves* resides.

Whitman thought about language extensively, and wrote notes to himself about the subject beginning early in his career. But his sense of words as an artist attempting to connect with an audience was ambivalent. Whitman sometimes fretted over the need to rely on the printed word to make such connections, and at other times celebrated the seemingly limitless potential of the English tongue in America. On the one hand, he once told Traubel of his antipathy to language, exclaiming that he undergoes "such emotional revolts: against you all, against myself: against words – God damn them, words: even the words I myself utter: wondering if anything was ever done worth while except in the final silences" (Teller 1973: 203). His fear of the failure of words to communicate fully would haunt him throughout his life, and he occasionally lamented the unbridgeable gap between signifier and signified. On the other hand, Whitman recognized the exquisite range of the English language in all its forms, saying (again to Traubel) that "I should not wonder but the English tongue is the richest in possibilities of expression – potential for the most varied combinations, beauties, wonders, of speech!" (Teller 1973: 202).

For Whitman language is not just a system of signs we humans have at hand to express ourselves; rather, it stands as a cultural complex, one that registers our deepest beliefs as a people and as a nation. To understand the workings of language in *Leaves* is to come to terms with America and the promise of America, as Whitman understood them; it is to see how deeply connected language is to the democratic literary enterprise in which he was engaged, how his appreciation of America and the life of its average citizens is reflected at the most basic level of his art.

Whitman's Language Studies: The Foreground of *Leaves*

Whitman's interest in the study of language grew to intensity between 1854 and 1856, as the first edition of *Leaves* was underway. He read Christian C. J. Bunsen's *Outlines of the Philosophy of Universal History, Applied to Language and Religion* and Maximilian Schele de Vere's *Outlines of Comparative Philology* during this time, and he kept two linguistic notebooks, *Words* and *The Primer of Words*, the latter of which was edited and published by Traubel as *An American Primer* in 1904. In addition to these early prose jottings, Whitman wrote parts of the book *Rambles among Words*, even though it does not bear his name. C. Carroll Hollis first conjectured that Whitman was tutored by William Swinton in French and historical linguistics and collaborated with him on *Rambles*, which was published in 1859 (Hollis 1959). James Perrin Warren argues that Whitman served as ghostwriter of *Rambles*, and he points to conceptual and stylistic evidence that indicates that Whitman wrote the final two chapters, "The Growth of Words" and "English in America" (Warren 1984).

In the penultimate chapter of *Rambles*, Whitman acknowledges his debt to a specific tradition of language theorists. In the epigraph to that chapter, Whitman quotes the comparative philologist Wilhelm von Humboldt: "An idiom is an organism subject, like every organism, to the laws of development. One must not consider a language as a product dead and formed but once: it is an animate being and ever creative"; as Warren explains, Humboldt is a principal figure in the tradition of "organic," or transcendental, language theory, and Whitman's understanding of Humboldt is informed by his readings in Bunsen and Schele de Vere (Warren 1990: 11–12). During the nineteenth century the Transcendentalists countered the empiricist theory that language was "an arbitrary set of conventional signs designed by human beings to further communication," proposing rather that "language is essentially an activity of the spirit, functioning to unify sense-data and concepts" (Warren 1990: 12). Humboldt posits that the development of language reveals the development of the human spirit and, as Whitman speculates under the inspiration of Humboldt, "the spirit or individuality of a nation" (*DBN*, 3: 721). Whitman's theory of linguistic evolution is, then, at heart a theory of spiritual evolution, with the animate nature of language – its evolving presence – a sign of our own spiritual growth as a people.

Whitman's views of language were also substantially shaped by practicing artists, including British Romantic poets and American Transcendentalists, in particular Emerson. In his essay "Slang in America," published in November 1885, Whitman says of English that "The scope of its etymologies is the scope not only of man and civilization, but the history of Nature in all its departments, and of the organic Universe, brought up to date; for all are comprehended in words, and their backgrounds. This is when words become vitaliz'd, and stand for things" (*PW*, 2: 572). Whitman's sense of language as thing – as a vehicle for concrete facts – is one that he inherits from the Romantic poets through Emerson, who in his journal in 1831 notes that "in good writing, words become one with things"; in the same passage Emerson reflects on Coleridge, who observes similarly, "I would endeavor to destroy the old antithesis of Words and Things: elevating, as it were, Words into Things and living things too" (quoted in Matthiessen 1941: 30). What the critic F. O. Matthiessen acknowledges as Emerson's hyperbole was a motivating force for writers of Emerson's day, especially Whitman.

Emerson laid out his language theory in essays and speeches, one of which, "The Poet," Whitman heard Emerson perform in New York in 1842 and reported on for the *New York Aurora*. The concept that all words are rooted in physical reality and have embedded in them human history is articulated clearly in that oration: "The etymologist finds the deadest word to have been once a brilliant picture. Language is fossil poetry" (quoted in Matthiessen 1941: 33). Emerson first asserted that words symbolize natural things in his essay *Nature* (1831), and Whitman similarly sees that language is hieroglyphic, that it contains within it "the farthest history" (Whitman 1936: 55).

It is the creative writer, Whitman believes, who can liberate us from an inert diction by reattaching word to thing. In his opinion, a "perfect writer" is one who "would make words sing, dance, kiss, do the male and female act, bear children, weep, bleed, rage, stab, steal, fire cannon, steer ships, sack cities, charge with cavalry or infantry, or do any thing, that man or woman or the natural powers can do" (Traubel [1901] 1987: 16). This sense of the need of language to be generative and vital – to be an active agent in the world – responds to a prevailing cultural attitude: that language had been uprooted from its sources in the concrete and lost its verve. Whitman is after words that "are alive and sinewy," that "walk, look, step with an air of command" (Traubel [1901] 1987: 11), and here, too, Emerson's presence is felt; as Emerson observes of Montaigne, in praise of his vivacious diction and style: "Cut these words and they would bleed; they are vascular and alive; they walk and run" (quoted in Matthiessen 1941: 35). In *Rambles* Whitman sends out the call for a poet possessed of a "large knowledge of the philosophy of speech" and "rich aesthetic instincts" to resuscitate literary expression, which, he contends, has become a "watery affair," by channeling the multiethnic idioms that inform American English (*NUPM*, 5: 1661).

Language and Nation

In "America's Mightiest Inheritance," published in April 1856 in Fowler and Wells's magazine *Life Illustrated*, Whitman articulates a philosophy of American exceptionalism in his discourse on the English language. He imagines English as that language appropriate to all spheres – public and domestic, literary and commercial – one that exudes "common sense": "It is a language for great individuals as well as great nations" (Whitman 1936: 55). "Character," he observes, "makes words," and the American character – independent, individualist, antiauthoritarian – underwrites the nation's language, being "grandly lawless like the race who use it" (Traubel [1901] 1987: 6).

Americans refuse to submit to external restraints, Whitman contends, and American English is likewise free-form: it is "a language fann'd by the breath of Nature, which leaps overhead, cares mostly for impetus and effects, and for what it plants and invigorates to grow – tallies life and character, and seldomer tells a thing than suggests or necessitates it" (*PW*, 2: 424). As with Emerson, who found strict adherence to grammatical rules and regulations an impertinence, Whitman insists that the rough and roiled English actually spoken by Americans – the way in which words are put together in common speech – defies systematization: "[T]he forms of grammar are never persistently obeyed, and cannot be" (Traubel [1901] 1987: 6).

Whitman realized that new words were being called into being by a vast network of emergent technologies across America, and he intended to sing the praises of all of those technologies in their own vocabularies, to ordain these new words and expressions in the idiomatic structures of his verse. His notebook listings of the range of industries around which terms are shaped resemble the exhaustive catalogues that we encounter in his poetry:

> Geography, shipping, steam, the mint, the electric telegraph, railroads, and so forth, have many strong and beautiful words. Mines – iron works – the sugar plantations of Louisiana – the cotton crop and the rice crop – Illinois wheat – Ohio corn and pork – Maine lumber – all these sprout in hundreds and hundreds of words, and tangible and clean-lived, all having texture and beauty. (Traubel [1901] 1987: 3)

One such word is "Tender-Foot," which he defines as "a new comer at Leadville, (or in the mines of Colorado any how)" (*NUPM*, 5: 1706).

As Whitman held, the reality of democracy in the US, apart from its commercial interests, also demanded new coinage: "In America an immense number of new words are needed, to embody the new political facts," from "the compact of the Declaration of Independence, and of the Constitution – the union of the States – the new States – the Congress" to "the modern, rapidly spreading faith of the equality of women with men" (Traubel [1901] 1987: 9). The political conditions of liberty, equality, and fraternity will evoke the words to express them, and Whitman can but wonder at the "elasticity" of American English, its absorptive quality: "Whatever we want, wherever we want any addition, we seize upon the terms that fit the want, and appropriate them to our use" (Whitman 1936: 56–7).

Whitman was fond of reading language through the prism of his own nationalism. In "America's Mightiest Inheritance" he finds that "the history of language . . . is the history of movements and developments of men and women over the entire earth. In its doings every thing appears to move from east to west as the light does" (Whitman 1936: 57). Here he reads westward expansion in terms of manifest destiny, with America as the culmination of linguistic progress. In a notebook entry he makes the connection between American English and the cohesion of the country particularly clear: "without a uniform spoken and written dialect, elastic, tough and eligible to all, and fluid and enfolding as air – , – the Liberty and Union of these Thirty Eight or

Forty States, representing so many diverse origins and breeds would not be practicable" (*NUPM*, 5: 1682). In this rumination Whitman reveals that, to his mind, the United States of America could not exist at all without a lingo to prove the motto *e pluribus unum*.

In *Rambles* Whitman's sketch of the historical development of a composite English also entails his ideological perspective. In "The Growth of Words" he expresses the need for a dictionary of the English language, a language that descends from "the grand Germanic stock – a stock in which the instinct of personal and political independence has always been powerfully present"; he goes on to argue, though, that the glory of English lies in the grafting onto it of the French tongue through "that great political and social revolution, the Norman Conquest," which infused into the vocabulary "terms indicative of the new political and social relations" unknown to Saxon life before conquest, and of Latin and Greek words (*NUPM*, 5: 1654). Whitman concludes in an imperialist tone that there is "scarce a tongue on the planet which the all-absorbing Saxon genius has not laid under contribution to enrich the exchequer of its conquering speech" (*NUPM*, 5: 1657).

As these statements suggest, Whitman's linguistic views are not without prejudice. While it is true that Whitman's "theory of language is but an extension of his vision of natural democracy," it is also the case that it lapses into jingoism (Mack 2002: 3). As Ed Folsom notes, "In some of his more nationalistic later writings, Whitman even termed his hoped-for language 'imperial' "; he goes on to quote Whitman: "America is become already a huge world of peoples . . . forty-four Nations curiously and irresistibly blent and aggregated in ONE NATION, with one imperial language" (Folsom 1994: 25). Whitman's ethnocentrism flows directly from the Transcendental theory of language that he picks up in Bunsen and Schele de Vere (Warren 1990). Somewhat ironically, in light of his linguistic nationalism, Whitman points to the glory of American Indian words that have persisted and will persist in language long after their cultures fade away: "Nantucket, Montauk, Omaha, Natchez, Sauk, Walla-Walla, Chattahoochee, Anahuac, Mexico, Nicaragua, Peru, Orinoco, Ohio, Saginaw, and the like" (Whitman 1936: 58). It is a recuperative gesture on Whitman's part, as he sees in language the residue and "resistance" of native peoples to the process of westward expansion – an expansion that he celebrates. When Whitman reports that the English language, which "is the accretion and growth of every dialect, race, and range of time," "is indeed a sort of universal absorber, combiner, and conqueror," we see just how thoroughly his sense of his Americanism is tied up in his sense of linguistic Americanisms.

In "America's Mightiest Inheritance" Whitman invariably turns to the use to which artists put words, insisting that many American writers and speakers arrange words "for mere show," but that the best use language that is throbbing with the life of the nation (Whitman 1936: 58). He laments the present state of journalism, finding that "[e]very newspaper in America, the best as well as the worst, is full of diffuse and artificial writing – writing that has no precision, no ease, no blood, no vibration of the living voice in the living ear"; along with Emerson, Whitman advocates a more hearty language, one in touch with the masses, p. 59). Indeed, he sees that language grows out of customs, the rituals of daily life, that it "is not an abstract construction of the learn'd," but rather "something arising out of the work, needs, ties, joys, affections, tastes, of long generations of humanity, and has its bases broad and low, close to the ground" (*PW*, 2: 573). It is the poet's job to break away from "stale phrases" and speak the truth of his or her historical situation, to defer no longer to precedent but rather to inaugurate an American literature out of the linguistic resources at hand.

Whitman celebrates his inheritance of the English tongue and its immense possibilities not only in his prose, but also in the poetry of *Leaves*, where it occasionally becomes a theme. In the 1856 version of "By Blue Ontario's Shore" Whitman artfully exclaims (through the pattern of anaphora) his belief in the capacity of English to radiate commendable traits and values:

> Language-using controls the rest;
> Wonderful is language!
> Wondrous the English language, language of live men,
> Language of ensemble, powerful language of resistance,
> Language of a proud and melancholy stock, and of all who aspire,
> Language of growth, faith, self-esteem, rudeness, justice, friendliness, amplitude, prudence, decision, exactitude, courage,
> Language to well-nigh express the inexpressible,
> Language for the modern, language for America.
>
> (*LG Var.*, 1: 200)

In what would become Section 23 of "Song of Myself," Whitman singles out "the lexicographer" and the comparative philologist in his praise of modern science, and often in his notebooks he predicts that a comprehensive dictionary of American English will some day be compiled to encode in it the nation's noble heritage. In "Great Are the Myths," language is characterized as "the mightiest of the sciences":

> Great is the English speech – what speech is so great as the English?
> Great is the English brood – what brood has so vast a destiny as the English?
> It is the mother of the brood that must rule the earth with the new rule;
> The new rule shall rule as the Soul rules, and as the love, justice, equality in the Soul rule.
>
> (*LG Var.*, 1: 157)

In this poem English and its speakers are imagined as one day presiding over the entire world, shedding upon it the light of democracy.

In Whitman's poem "Song of the Answerer," the figure of the poet (the "answerer") proves to be "the arbiter of the diverse" and "the equalizer of his age and land" as prophesied in the 1855 Preface: he is able to interpret local idioms and make them accessible to the universe of men and women, binding people together into a cohesive social unit:

Every existence has its idiom, every thing has an idiom and tongue,
He resolves all tongues into his own, and bestows it upon men, and any man translates, and any man translates himself also,
One part does not counteract another part, he is the joiner, he sees how they join.
He says indifferently and alike, *How are you my friend?* to the President at his levee,
And he says *Good-day my brother*, to Cudge that hoes in the sugarfield;
And both understand him and know that his speech is right.
(*LG Var.*, 1: 139–40, italics in original)

Here the poet is seen as interpreting the language of nature for others in his role as linguistic exchange; he is a person who makes all intelligible to all. As Whitman describes the process elsewhere: "Great writers penetrate the idioms of their races, and use them with simplicity and power" (Whitman 1936: 56).

Slang Speech

Whitman's poetic resolution of tongues draws on a knowledge of "native idiomatic words," what he refers to as words "of the national blood," and in his poems he enlists popular terms and phrases from a range of fields – astronomy, opera, phrenology, to name just a few – as a sign of his eclecticism and democratic inclusiveness (Traubel [1901] 1987: 35). In "Song of the Banner at Daybreak" the figure of the poet expresses his distance from literary language, embracing "a new song" that flows freely through the land, untempered by literary turnings:

Words! book-words! what are you?
Words no more, for hearken and see,
My song is there in the open air, and I must sing,
With the banner and pennant a-flapping.
(*LG Var.*, 2: 458)

As Whitman insists, "the words continually used among the people are, in numberless cases, not the words used in writing, or recorded in the dictionaries by authority" (Traubel [1901] 1987: 5). His stated interest in importing language into his poetry from daily life – his desire to get away from "book-words" and come closer to the actual speech of men and women in passionate talk – points to Emerson, who in his journal for 1840 hails "the language of the street": "I confess to some pleasure from the stinging rhetoric of a rattling oath in the mouth of truckmen and teamsters. How laconic and brisk it is by the side of a page of *North American Review*." Emerson even cites Whitman as "our American master" in his "command of the language of the common people" (quoted in Matthiessen 1941: 35).

This colloquial urge also hearkens to Wordsworth, who has much to say about language in his Preface to *Lyrical Ballads* (1800). Believing that words are "emanations of reality and truth," he advocates that writers adopt "language really used by men" and eschew conventional poetic diction (quoted in Matthiessen 1941: 31). Humble people, Wordsworth argues, speak in "simple and unelaborated expressions," using a more beautiful and even "far more philosophical language" than that of the poets who indulge in "arbitrary and capricious habits of expression." Whitman shared this view, and similarly sought to renew poetic expression on that basis.

Whitman's alertness to the vernacular is on display in his notebooks. In *Words* he tucked clippings from newspapers, magazines, and books on the subject of language, and he recorded fragments of conversation and striking idiomatic phrases heard on the street, such phrases as "Did he do it a purpose?"; "That's so, easy enough. – "; "That's a sick ticket" (*DBN*, 3: 668). Of another popular turn of phrase he writes: "the common people say of nourishing food that 'it stays with a man' " (*DBN*, 3: 713). It is, he insists, through the vocabularies and intonations of the American working class – "the wit – the rich flashes of humor and genius and poetry – darting out often from a gang of laborers, railroad-men, miners, drivers or boatmen!" – that American English, and American literature with it, will be enlivened, as slang is "the start of fancy, imagination and humor" (*PW*, 2: 576–7).

Whitman was impressed by current regionalisms as well. In one notebook entry he cites a couple of "Virginia idioms": "How's all"? [sic] and "Where you been at?" (*DBN* 3: 675). "So long," he notes, is "a delicious American – New York – idiomatic phrase at parting equivalent to 'good bye' " (*DBN*, 3: 669). Again in the role of ethnographer, Whitman records the full-bodied exclamation of the "New York Bowery boy": "Sa-a-y!" (*DBN*, 3: 669). He also had his ear turned to the expressions of African Americans that had seeped into and tinged the speech of an entire region: "In the South, words that have spouted up from the dialect and peculiarities of the slaves. – the Negroes. – The South is full of negro-words. – Their idioms and pronunciation are heard every where" (*DBN*, 3: 695). Whitman considers all of these local expressions fit to enter into literature, and recognizes the inherent "poetical" quality of colloquial English, which represents "an attempt of common humanity to escape from bald literalism, and express itself illimitably" (*PW*, 2: 573, 574). In this, he paves the way to Robert Frost.

Whitman's thoughts on slang carry with them a distinct gender and class politics. He scorns those "castrated persons, impotent persons, shaved persons," who "cry down the use of strong, cutting, beautiful, rude words," believing that "to the manly instincts of the People they will forever be welcome" (Traubel [1901] 1987: 22). His sense of his own masculinity is further pointed up when he maintains that "the muscular classes, where the real quality of friendship is always freely to be found" stand in need of a language to characterize their "passionate" attachments (p. 15). Opposed to "delicate lady-words" and "gloved gentleman-words," the effete talk and mannerisms of the upper class, Whitman seeks to forge instead a linguistic register of adhesiveness in *Calamus* (p. 22).

Throughout his early poetry, Whitman's attraction to technical terms, colloquial and dialectical phrases, and slang is strong. As Matthiessen observes, some of the most "easy and relaxed" of these in *Leaves* include:

I reckon I am their boss, and they make me a pet besides.

And will go gallivant with the light and air myself.

Shoulder your duds, my son, and I will mine.

Earth! you seem to look for something at my hands,
Say, old top-knot, what do you want?
(quoted in Matthiessen 1941: 527)

His "barbaric yawp" (*LG Var.*, 1: 82) sounded near the end of "Song of Myself" (what would become Section 52) sets the tone. The word *yawp* signifies a loud or coarse utterance, and is not typically a term used in poetry or applied to poetry; it helps to picture the elemental force behind Whitman's lyric voice. At another place in the poem Whitman uses the Americanism *carlacue* (p. 26), meaning a caper or boyish trick, a form known in New York. The word "foofoo," a slang term for dandy which was in current usage on the New York stage in 1855, also appears in "Song of Myself," with Whitman celebrating his own robust manliness while he expresses his contempt for the affected class: "Washes and razors for foofoos. . . . for me freckles and a bristling beard" (p. 31). Conjuring forth the sensual chaos of the city in sound-symbolic slang, "Walt Whitman, an American, one of the roughs," also spends a moment taking in "The blab of the pave, tires of cars, sluff of boot-soles, talk of the promenaders" (p. 9).

Place names were especially dear to Whitman, and he spent much time talking and writing about his thoughts on the matter; indeed, his poetry is filled with these names, in and out of catalogue form. He told Traubel he loved the "beautiful names" of Germantown outside of Philadelphia, names such as "Wingohocking" and "Tulpehocken," and he lamented the change of the name Longacoming, a town south of Camden, to Berlin (Teller 1973: 200). As he attests: "Of races, places, countries much of the essence of their History, often the subtlest part, is in their Names" (*NUPM*, 5: 1693). He also appreciated the richness and spiritual resonance of American Indian names, and used such native words as Paumanok and Mannahatta in his verse. In the poem "Mannahatta," he exalts: "I was asking for something specific and perfect for my city, / Whereupon lo! upsprang the aboriginal name // Now I see what there is in a name, a word, liquid, sane, unruly, musical, self-sufficient" (*LG Var.*, 2: 419). As Whitman believed, "The whole osseous muscular and fleshy structure of language is its Names, (nouns) and the Verbs are its blood and circulation" (*NUPM*, 5: 1697). Proper names should follow from "[t]he best women, the freest leading men, the proudest national character" (Traubel [1901] 1987: 33). Indeed, it is seen as a political struggle ("Names are the turning point of who shall be master"), and Whitman bristled at European names unbefitting a democracy, feeling that names should be changed if they are not indigenous (p. 34). At stake was nothing short of the formation of a national literature and culture: "Nothing is more important than names. . . . No country can have its own poems without it have its own names" (pp. 31–2).

Whitman finds fascinating American nicknames current during the Civil War, both the names soldiers had for generals (for example, "Stonewall" Jackson) and the slang names for soldiers based on their home states: "Those from Maine were called Foxes; New Hampshire, Granite Boys; Massachusetts, Bay Staters; . . . " (*PW*, 2: 574–5). Names emanating from the Western states ("special areas of slang, not only in conversation, but in names of localities, towns, rivers, etc"), he remarks, are particularly catchy, including such "amusing" and "characteristic" nicknames as "Gophers" for Iowans, "Buckeyes" for Ohioans, and "Hoosiers" for Indianians (*DBN*, 3: 813–14). He further notes the vivid imagination behind geographical names in the West such as "Shirttail Bend," "Loafer's Ravine," and "Toenail Lake" (*PW* 2: 576). Whitman heaps praise on place names that are figuratively rich and original to the locales they seek to describe, and concludes that "Indian words" are "often perfect," as in the case of the proposed name for one of the new territories, "Oklahoma" (*PW*, 2: 576).

Neologisms and Borrowings

Even as Whitman expressed an interest in vibrant idiomatic speech, he sometimes resorted to coining words to fit present cultural circumstances if no word yet had been minted. Whitman was particularly proud of his coinage of the word "Presidentiad," which appears in *Leaves*. Of it, Whitman had this to say to Traubel: "my word 'Presidentiad.' Oh! That is eminently a word to be cherished – adopted. Its allusion, the four years of the Presidency: its origin that of the Olympiad – but as I flatter myself, bravely appropriate, where not another one word, signifying the same thing, exists!" (Teller 1973: 201). The term appears in "Year of Meteors," where he writes of 1859–60 in the wake of John Brown's execution and in anticipation of the coming election: "Year of meteors! brooding year! / I would bind in words retrospective some of your deeds and signs, / I would sing your contest for the 19th Presidentiad" (*LG Var.*, 2: 501).

Whitman did not coin many words and, as Matthiessen observes, "Probably the largest group is composed of his agent-nouns, which is not surprising for a poet who was so occupied with types and classes of men and women" (Matthiessen 1941: 528–9). Some of these are common forms designating well-established occupations, such as hunter, trapper, plougher, and swimmer. Other deverbal nouns (that is, nouns formed from a verbal base) are more unusual, and are designed to emphasize "the dynamic aspect of personal identity" (Warren 1990: 54). In "Song of Myself" we get such constructions as thruster, howler, scooper, partaker, extoller, stander, provoker, reacher, hummer, buzzer, vexer, winder, moper, enfolder, and latherer (1990: 56). The 1855–56 editions brim with such nouns, including some that are formed by the conversion of a verb to a noun (as with the substantives rise, fall, click, knock). Most important is the present participle, which can be both verb and noun and is used often by Whitman in his early poetry to "create the impression of dynamic, ongoing activity" (Warren 1990: 65, see also Greenspan 1995). All of these words, by retaining their "inherently active, verbal quality," allow Whitman to highlight the equivalence between identity and activity, and his "dynamic deverbal style becomes a formal equivalent to his theory of linguistic and spiritual evolution" (Warren 1990: 56, 58).

In addition to forming new words, Whitman looked to other nations for words appropriate to the American condition. Although Whitman admittedly "never knew any other language but the English," he borrowed words from other languages freely, most notably from the French, to which he was exposed when he lived for a time in New Orleans (Teller 1973: 202). Matthiessen credits Whitman's working-class orientation with his borrowing of words from non-English tongues: "His belief in the need to speak not merely for Americans but for the workers of all lands seems to have given the impetus for his odd habit of introducing random words from other languages, to the point of talking about 'the ouvrier class'!" (Matthiessen 1941: 529). The 1855–56 editions of *Leaves* include many instances of such borrowings, and Warren makes a list of words from the 1855 version of "Song of Myself" that illustrates this range: omnibus, promenaders, experient, savans, embouchures, vivas, venerealee, amies, foofoos, en masse, cartouches, kosmos, recitative, chef-d'oeuvre, amie, sierras, savannas, ambulanza, eleves, naivete, admirant, promulges, rendezvous, accoucheur, and debouch (Warren 1990: 48). In some of these cases Whitman takes an English word and attaches a foreign ending to it; in others, he alters the foreign base to create an original word.

The most interesting cases are those where Whitman uses foreign borrowings "for expressive effect, to mark a poetic difference in the subject he treats," not at all a random procedure (Warren 1990: 48). The word *amie* is one such instance, and it appears twice in the 1855 "Song of Myself": "Extoller of amies and those that sleep in each other's arms"; "Picking out here one that shall be my amie, / Choosing to go with him on brotherly terms." Whitman opts for a "sexually ambivalent" term in these lines, employing the feminine form of the French word for friend but applying it to male companions; he borrows from the French in an attempt to "spiritualize the [English] language and its users," to designate a relationship for which the English has no term in an effort "to project a new social relation between men" and to help bring it about (Warren 1990: 49). Whitman's use of other French terms – *eleves*, *en masse*, and *ensemble*, for example – adds to his "vocabulary of spiritual progress" (Warren 1990: 50), as does his employment of the Spanish "camerado," which he invokes in lieu of "comrade" to "communicate a kind of personal closeness and intimacy" among men (Stein 1967: 124).

After 1860, Whitman began to scale back on his use of Americanisms, neologisms, and technical terms. Warren, who explicates Whitman's theory of language as he developed it from around 1854 to 1856, shows how the theory applies to the diction and syntax of the first two editions of *Leaves*; he also reveals that Whitman changed the focus of his theory of language between 1856 and 1892, with the diction and syntax of the last four editions reflecting Whitman's changed theoretical concerns (Warren 1990). Hollis (1983) notes a similar shift in Whitman's poetics, presenting a statistical analysis that indicates dramatic decreases after 1860 in Whitman's use of finite verb elements and dramatic increases after 1860 in his use of Romance-Latin based words, a change that constitutes a retreat from concrete language.

Matthiessen claims that the "two diverging strains in his use of language [that is, the abstract and the concrete] were with him to the end," and yet Whitman seems not to have noticed "the contrast between the clumsy stilted opening and the simple close" of a line like "I concentrate toward them that are nigh, I wait on the door slab"; as he contends, in the late"Sands at Seventy" such sweeping orotund expressions as "Of ye, O God, Life, Nature, Freedom, Poetry" further dilute the linguistic freshness and potency of *Leaves* (Matthiessen 1941: 530). Matthiessen concludes that despite Whitman's railings against "book-words," his "language is deeply ingrained with the habits of a middle-class people," his diction "clearly not that of a countryman but of what he called himself, 'a jour printer' " (pp. 532, 531).

Language and Performance

In his *American Primer* Whitman "promulges" (to use one of his famous French borrowings) that "Pronunciation is the stamina of language, – it is language. – The noblest pronunciation, in a city or race, marks the noblest city or race, or descendants thereof" (Traubel [1901] 1987: 12). He takes up this thread again at the close of "America's Mightiest Inheritance": "*Pronunciation.* – What vocalism most needs in these States, not only in the few choicer words and phrases, but in our whole talk, is ease, sonorous strength, breadth, and openness" (Whitman 1936: 60). It is not surprising, in light of these remarks, that the art of oratory was immensely attractive to Whitman. He saw himself as some day "founding a *new school* of Declamation/ Composition far more direct, close, animated and fuller of live tissue and muscle than any hitherto" (Whitman 1928: 34). In a notebook entry entitled "The Perfect Human Voice," Whitman records his admiration for the oracular power of the spoken word: "Beyond all other power and beauty, there is something in the quality and power of the right voice (*timbre* the schools call it) that touches the soul, the abysms" (*PW*, 2: 674). His love of the launched voice grows out of his anxiety about the ability to communicate through inert signs and symbols, about the intermediation of the printed page.

Whitman goes so far as to distance himself from the material conditions of print in some of his poems, ironically naming these devices as obstacles to be surmounted. The 1855 version of "A Song for Occupations" expresses his desire to bypass the printed word even as he must succumb to it: "I was chilled with the cold types and cylinder and wet paper between us" (*LG Var.*, 1: 84). In "Now Precedent Songs, Farewell" he finds that some of the best of himself is left unrevealed on the printed page: "The personal urge and form for me – not merely paper, automatic type and ink" (*LG Var.*, 3: 728). Indeed, Whitman favored terms such as "song," "chant," and "utterance" to describe his performances, and often referred to himself, and the figure of the poet generally, as "bard."

In "A Song of the Rolling Earth" (originally called "Poem of the Sayers of the Word of the Earth" and later "Carol of Words"), Whitman expresses his anxiety when he insists on seeing words as things, and things as words: "Earth, round, rolling, compact – suns, moons, animals – all these are words, / Watery, vegetable, sauroid advances – beings, premonitions, lispings of the future – these are vast words." Departing from the notion that language can "well-nigh express the inexpressible," he takes a much bleaker view here, even of the spoken word:

> I swear I begin to see little or nothing in audible words,
> All merges toward the presentation of the unspoken meanings of the earth,
> Toward him who sings the songs of the body and of the truths of the earth,
> Toward him who makes the dictionaries of words that print cannot touch.
>
> I swear I see what is better than to tell the best,
> It is always to leave the best untold.
>
> (*LG Var.*, 1: 265)

As Tenney Nathanson explains, in this poem Whitman rejects the social use of language, or what the linguist J. L. Austin terms "constative" language; instead he exalts in the poet's "shamanistic power," his ability to work magic with words: "Given the poet's apparent power to act on the world directly by speaking, language that limits itself to a mere discursive or representational function, making reports about conditions it has not itself caused and does not change, has flagrantly relinquished its true calling" (Nathanson 1992: 177).

Hollis has shown the extent to which the style of the early editions of *Leaves* relies on oral features for their rhetorical effect by analyzing the range of style markers in these poems, including the *cursus* (a rhetorical feature that shapes oratorical cadence), negation, journalistic language, and the figure of metonymy (Hollis 1983). He also has examined the "rhetorical dots" of the first edition of *Leaves*, convincingly concluding that these dots signal rhetorical pauses meant to score our oral performance of the passage (Hollis 1984). As Hollis claims, there are more illocutionary acts in Whitman than in any other American or English poet: "It is, indeed, *the* stylistic feature of *Leaves* up to and including the 1860 edition" (Hollis 1983: 74). As opposed to "constative utterances," performative utterances (or illocutionary speech acts) are not true or false and actually perform the utterance to which they refer; they perform the action they designate. A few examples from "Song of Myself" serve to illustrate the range of illocutionary acts that structure discourse there:

> This hour I tell things in confidence,
> I might not tell everybody, but I will tell you.
>
> I swear I will never mention love or death inside a house,
> And I swear I will never translate myself at all, only to him or her who privately stays with me in open air.
>
> Have you felt so proud to get at the meaning of poems?
> Stop this day and night with me and you shall possess the origin of all poems.

I speak the pass-word primeval, I give the sign of democracy,
By God! I will accept nothing which all cannot have their counterpart of on the same terms.

Camerado, this is no book,
Who touches this touches a man.

(quoted in Hollis 1983: 69–74 passim)

The illocutionary act involves direct personal interchange, a feat achieved through the use of the present tense and direct address (Hollis 1983: 88). In Whitman's verse the act is frequently marked by the pronouns "I" and "you," and rhetorical questions directed to "you," which proliferate in *Leaves* through the 1860 edition. Although Mark Bauerlein (1986) has challenged the illocutionary force behind Whitman's writings, arguing that such force evaporates when a word is committed to the printed page, Hollis has defended his position ably, noting that even though there is a diminution of illocutionary force in writing, it remains to a degree and constitutes a compelling poetic fiction, especially for Whitman (Hollis 1986). As with slang, instances of illocutionary verb forms drop dramatically in later editions of *Leaves*, as Whitman moves away from his "vocative technique" and toward a more conventional poetics (Greenspan 1995).

Whitman's revisions of the poems in *Leaves* highlight his ambivalence toward language – his desire both to find a fit language in which to sing America's praises and to resist the pressure of words to define him and his relationship with his audience once and for all. To a great extent, the performance of language in *Leaves* makes possible his articulation of a dynamic American cultural identity and reveals his understanding of the performative nature of selfhood. Whitman's retrospective view of *Leaves* as "an attempt to give the spirit, the body, the man, new words, new potentialities of speech" is a bold one that yields some of the most successful patternings of his poetry, but it is also one that looks to the linguistic adventures of future poets for continuance; as Whitman attests, "[T]here is no finality to a Language! The English has vast vista in it – vast vista in America" (Traubel [1901] 1987: viii–ix; *NUPM*, 5: 1660).

References and Further Reading

Asselineau, Roger (1962). *The Evolution of Walt Whitman: The Creation of a Book*, trans. Roger Asselineau and Burton L. Cooper. Cambridge, MA: Belknap Press.

Bauerlein, Mark (1986). The Written Orator of "Song of Myself": A Recent Trend in Whitman Criticism. *Walt Whitman Quarterly Review*, 3: 1–14.

Bauerlein, Mark (1991). *Whitman and the American Idiom*. Baton Rouge: Louisiana State University Press.

Folsom, Ed (1994). *Walt Whitman's Native Representations*. Cambridge, UK: Cambridge University Press.

Greenspan, Ezra (1995). Some Remarks on the Poetics of "Participle-loving" Whitman. In Ezra Greenspan (ed.), *Cambridge Companion to Walt Whitman*. Cambridge, UK: Cambridge University Press, pp. 92–109.

Hollis, C. Carroll (1957). Whitman and the American Idiom. *Quarterly Journal of Speech*, 43: 408–20.

Hollis, C. Carroll (1959). Whitman and William Swinton: A Co-operative Friendship. *American Literature*, 30: 425–49.

Hollis, C. Carroll (1983). *Language and Style in* Leaves of Grass. Baton Rouge: Louisiana State University Press.

Hollis, C. Carroll (1984). Rhetoric, Elocution, and Voice in *Leaves of Grass*: A Study in Affiliation. *Walt Whitman Quarterly Review*, 2: 1–21.

Hollis, C. Carroll (1986). Is There a Text in this Grass? *Walt Whitman Quarterly Review*, 3: 15–22.

Mack, Stephen John (2002). *The Pragmatic Whitman: Reimagining American Democracy*. Iowa City: University of Iowa Press.

Matthiessen, F. O. (1941). *American Renaissance: Art and Expression in the Age of Emerson and Whitman*. London: Oxford University Press.

Nathanson, Tenney (1992). *Whitman's Presence: Body, Voice, and Writing in Leaves of Grass*. New York: New York University Press.

Railton, Stephen (1995). "As if I were with you" – the Performance of Whitman's Poetry. In Ezra Greenspan (ed.), *Cambridge Companion to Walt Whitman*. Cambridge, UK: Cambridge University Press, pp. 7–26.

Stein, Marian (1967). "Comrade" or "camerado" in *Leaves of Grass*. *Walt Whitman Review*, 13: 123–5.

Teller, Walter (1973). *Walt Whitman's Camden Conversations*. New Brunswick, NJ: Rutgers University Press.

Traubel Horace ([1904] 1987). *An American Primer by Walt Whitman*. Stevens Point, WI: Holy Cow! Press.

Warren, James Perrin (1984). Whitman as Ghostwriter: The Case of *Rambles Among Words*. *Walt Whitman Quarterly Review*, 2: 22–30.

Warren, James Perrin (1990). *Walt Whitman's Language Experiment*. University Park: Pennsylvania State University Press.

Whitman, Walt (1928). *Walt Whitman's Workshop: A Collection of Unpublished Manuscripts*, ed. Clifton J. Furness. Cambridge, MA: Harvard University Press.

Whitman, Walt (1936). America's Mightiest Inheritance. In *New York Dissected: A Sheaf of Recently Discovered Newspaper Articles by the Author of Leaves of Grass*, ed. Emory Holloway and Ralph Adimari. New York: Rufus Rockwell Wilson, pp. 51–65.

23
Style
James Perrin Warren

Pictures of Innovation

Whitman's style is most remarkable for its perpetual innovation. The newness of the poetry was apparent from the beginning, when the Rome Brothers printed the slim folio edition of *Leaves of Grass* in July 1855. It persists to the present, as new generations of readers discover a style unlike any they have read before. Many readers prefer the first edition of *Leaves of Grass*, with its 12 untitled poems, long lines, and strange ellipses, but the key to Whitman's style is the persistence with which it changes. No single edition of *Leaves of Grass* registers that quality, for it is a characteristic of Whitman's entire career, spanning the years before he discovered the style of the 1855 *Leaves* and including even the prose and poetry of his old age.

As a stylistic innovator, Whitman is unlike the prevailing models of writing available to him in antebellum American culture. The works of his early career as a journalist, fiction writer, and poet reveal almost no sense of innovation at all. Instead, they show the style of an uninspired imitator. In the extensive journalism of the late 1830s and 1840s, Whitman writes in an unremarkable editorial prose. There are elements of sensationalism and of hyperbolic political rhetoric, but no one would claim that the prose is at all new in style. Similarly, short stories such as "Death in the School-Room" (1841) and "Wild Frank's Return" (1841) are supercharged with melodramatic action and moralistic sensationalism, as is the temperance novel *Franklin Evans* (1842). The early prose work does show, however, that Whitman could write for a popular audience, using a style that would be sure to appeal to popular tastes. In the two dozen short stories, the novel, and the countless newspaper articles, he was experimenting constantly with popular genres of writing.

The early poetry is perhaps even more conventional than the prose. Whitman certainly knew the poetry of Ralph Waldo Emerson, whose *Poems* (1847) include many experiments in free verse, but in his own poems from the same period Whitman does not imitate Emerson's accentual versification, free rhyming, or varied line lengths. Instead, he often writes in tetrameter quatrains with alternate rhymes, surely the most predictable stanza form in English verse. A good example is the nature poem "The Mississippi at Midnight." Stemming from Whitman's trip to New Orleans in 1848, it features some of the same sensationalistic and didactic imagery that marks the early prose. After the Compromise of 1850 was passed, Whitman expressed his outrage at the Fugitive Slave Act in a series of newspaper poems. "Dough-Face Song" is written in extended ballad stanzas, while "Blood-Money" and "Wounded in the House of Friends" are free-verse experiments, driven more by the speaker's anger than by any formal techniques.

The earliest indication of Whitman's new style comes in the poem "Pictures," a notebook manuscript that was unpublished in his lifetime. The poem operates on the conceit of images as pictures that are hung in the poet's head, a "little house" that still has room for "hundreds and thousands" of pictures (*LG*: 642). The poem is written in Whitman's long lines, and each line tends to present a new, self-contained image. The lines vary in length from a dozen to over 50 words, and the length is determined by the idea or image conveyed rather than by a formal device. In order to create the effect of rhythm, Whitman employs syntactic parallelism and anaphora (repetition of initial elements from one line to the next). In a description of a Greek philosophical "master," for instance, he begins three lines with the formula "He places . . . / He shows . . . / He shows . . . " (*LG*: 644). In other parts of the poem, he repeats the conjunction "And" as the anaphoric repetend, along with the adverb "here" or "there" to indicate that he is presenting a new picture. Together with his use of direct address to the reader ("see you" and "you see" occur frequently), the speaker's deictic language gives the sense of performative gesture, as if he were actually holding up pictures and commanding the reader to look at them. The poem abounds in geographical place names, both American and international, and it also features a mixture of modern and historical scenes.

Twice during "Pictures" the speaker asserts, "I name every thing as it comes" (*LG*: 642, 648), and the cataloguing style surely does create an effect of randomness. Still, there are clear tendencies to Whitman's naming. First, he focuses on particular scenes and individuals, delighting in the surprising juxtaposition of opposites. So, for example, he imagines Marie Antoinette's execution and then shifts to "But this opposite, (abruptly changing,) is a picture from the prison-ships of my own old city – Brooklyn city" (*LG*: 644). The prison ships refer to the Revolutionary War prisoners kept in ships at Wallabout Bay at the mouth of the East River, an image Whitman returned to in the old-age poem, "The Wallabout Martyrs." There is some temporal proximity between the French Revolution and the American Revolution, but the two lines create the effect of opposing monarchy and democracy, the single symbolic death of the French queen (herself an Austrian) and the multiple deaths of the martyrs for America. Such effects of antithesis occur in several other places, suggesting that Whitman is experimenting with the technique.

Several other stylistic traits stem from this first one. For instance, Whitman's second tendency is to focus on American scenes and characters. Plenty of historical and exotic figures occur, but they usually are subsidiary to the images of nineteenth-century America. Third, Whitman tends to celebrate the pictures he presents, even when they feature suffering and death. The tone is always laudatory, the pictures "inimitable" (*LG*: 649), though some of the images are quite grim. Fourth, the American characters tend to be working-class men, figures of Emersonian self-reliance, though Whitman also includes a line describing Emerson himself "at the lecturer's desk lecturing" (p. 647). Fifth, Whitman clearly holds up the individual self as an ideal, comparing the self favorably with the ancient wonders of the world, which he calls "the Wonders of eld, the famed Seven" (p. 646): "(But for all that, nigh at hand, see a wonder beyond any of them, / Namely yourself – the form and thoughts of a man, / A man! because all the world, and all the inventions of the world are but the food of the body and the soul of one man;)" (pp. 646–7).

These remarks suggest why Emory Holloway called the poem an "embryo" of Whitman's verse. Most of the innovative stylistic techniques of the 1855 *Leaves of Grass* appear in "Pictures," but they are employed at random and without the kind of sustained power one finds in Whitman's best poems. Similarly, most of the themes Whitman develops over the next 35 years are present in the experimental poem: liberty and slavery, feudalism and democracy, the many and the one, history and the present, sexuality and spirituality, "divine friendship" (*LG*: 644), "the phallic choice of America" (p. 648), the frontier life. None is developed in enough detail to become thematically significant, and because of this the poem itself suffers from the absence of a thematic center.

Though the style of "Pictures" can be dispersed and telegraphic, it effectively forecasts Whitman's career of innovation. The sheer number of stylistic and thematic experiments suggests that future career. Even the style of the poem itself is a microcosm of innovation. The pictures are often vivid and dynamic, both in themselves and in the swift movement from one image to another, one line to the next. Several times the speaker creates an illusion of physical presence, and that illusion functions in concert with a clearly original poetic voice. The language is unadorned and direct, both on the level of diction and on the level of syntax. Each line is a new beginning; there is no rule of predictability. Because the next line may change everything the reader has come to expect, Whitman's style of innovation effectively becomes the content of the poem.

The merging of style and content in a career of innovation is the hallmark of major American writers. The two best models from Whitman's own day are Nathaniel Hawthorne and Herman Melville. Hawthorne wrote three major novels in rapid succession, and each is a new experiment in novelistic form. *The Scarlet Letter* (1850) is, among many things, an historical romance, a psychological and moral analysis, a conservative undercutting of Emersonian self-reliance, and an advance in the use of symbolic literary language. Having found a fertile ground for his imagination, Hawthorne could easily have written more novels of colonial New England, just as the Southern novelist William Gilmore Simms was writing novel after novel set in colonial South Carolina. But Hawthorne's next novel, *The House of the Seven*

Gables (1851) deliberately moves to the nineteenth century and to the very question of the past and its burdens. It features two interpolated tales that call into question the nature of storytelling itself. Indeed, the novel seems so self-conscious that Hawthorne's gestures at symbolic language appear ironic, if not parodic. The third novel, *The Blithedale Romance* (1852), is even more self-consciously a romance of artists and writers. It investigates some of the hottest social issues of the day: utopian communism, feminism, prison reform, and mesmerism. At the same time, it tells its tale through a series of fragmentary scenes and interpolated stories, none of which adds up to a completely coherent, unified narrative. The narrator, Miles Coverdale, is perhaps the only innocent bystander in the novel, and yet he may also be the guiltiest character of all. On the level of sentences, Hawthorne's style varies very little, and it is a model of clarity and mellifluous beauty, recalling the earlier style of Washington Irving. On the level of narrative, however, each novel is an exploration of a new path toward the finished artwork. Hawthorne is not content to exploit a tried and true form; he must refashion the form of the novel anew.

Melville's career is similarly instructive but uniquely disastrous. After writing the first two "South Sea" novels and establishing himself as a popular writer of adventure narratives, he begins to experiment in *Mardi* (1849), returns to safe adventure narratives in *Redburn* (1849) and *White-Jacket* (1850), and then finds his most successful innovations in his one real masterpiece, *Moby Dick* (1851), which he rewrote after having met Hawthorne. The finished novel, dedicated to Hawthorne "in token of my admiration for his genius," is truly encyclopedic in theme and style, mixing the revenge plot of Ahab with the cetological meditations of Ishmael and performing its own innovations, as if it were refashioning the form of the novel with each chapter. The effect is not cumulative but transformative. In *Pierre* (1852), Melville's persistently innovative style meets with disaster. The book begins as a domestic idyll, becomes a sensationalistic "dark lady" romance, a philosophical meditation on time and truth, a Dickensian urban novel, and finally a self-conscious portrait of the artist as *poète maudit*. Better, it is all of these things – yet none of them wholly enough. The novel is continually revising itself, reforming itself, and then beginning anew. This tendency can also be detected in "Bartleby the Scrivener," in *Benito Cereno*, in *The Confidence Man* (1857), and even in the posthumously published *Billy Budd, Sailor*, for in all of these texts the narrative is told and retold in more than one way, ultimately calling into question the very nature of storytelling as a means of telling the truth.

The pattern of these two exemplary careers is as risky as it is innovative. It involves the writer in a continual process of reinvention and investigation, both thematic and stylistic. In the case of both Hawthorne and Melville, it appears to play into an extreme form of self-conscious artistry, one that brings the writer dangerously close to self-parody and, ultimately, silence. The career pattern does not lend itself to longevity. Yet the pattern is also a telling measure of greatness. The persistently innovative writer makes a career of innovation by fashioning a style in order to investigate particular themes, then refashioning a style – even fashioning a new style altogether – in order to investigate new themes and tell new truths.

The pattern of persistent innovation, marked by constant reinvention and refashioning, clearly applies to Walt Whitman's career from 1855 to 1892. The six editions and other printings of *Leaves of Grass* form a narrative of stylistic experiments, ending only with Whitman's death. Whitman does not create the narrative by following some master plan for his poetic career. Instead, he devotes himself to exploring the possibilities of poetic language because he assumes that each poem is a new experiment in language. As he told Horace Traubel in his last years, "I sometimes think the *Leaves* is only a language experiment" (*DBN*, 3: 729). The experimentation occurs, moreover, on several linguistic levels – diction, figuration, syntax, rhythm, poetic line, stanza, and section. The result is a complex web of innovative writing.

The First and Second Editions of *Leaves of Grass*

Whitman wrote the 32 poems that appeared in the first and second editions of *Leaves of Grass* in a rush of inspiration and reaction. He was surely responding to the political and social upheaval of the 1850s, especially the controversies surrounding African American slavery and the extension of slavery to the new western territories. If Whitman's experiences in party politics led him to become disenchanted with American democracy, he restored his faith by focusing on American democratic culture. One of the principal influences on the first two editions was oratory. Nineteenth-century America was alive with excellent speakers. Political orators like Daniel Webster and Henry Clay were legendary, and pulpit preachers like Henry Ward Beecher and Elias Hicks packed their churches. In addition, the lyceum circuit expanded greatly in the decade of the 1850s, affording audiences the addresses and lectures of such luminaries as Emerson, Frederick Douglass, Bayard Taylor, and Wendell Phillips. Whitman, too, dreamed of a career on the lecture circuit.

The main evidence for Whitman's interest in public speaking comes in the form of manuscripts. Both "The Primer of Words" and "The Eighteenth Presidency!" date from late 1855 and early 1856, and in both Whitman theorizes and practices the role of the orator. Whitman told Horace Traubel that the *Primer* notebook was "first intended for a lecture" (*DBN*, 3: 729) but eventually it became a book-length meditation on the power of language to bring about social change. *The Eighteenth Presidency!* is a printed, unpublished pamphlet, but it is supposed to function as the published version of a delivered speech. It is subtitled "Voice of Walt Whitman to each Young Man in the Nation, North, South, East and West." Thus the *Primer* becomes a theoretical background for the practical performance suggested by the *Eighteenth Presidency!* pamphlet. The style of the pamphlet is direct – even coarse at times – and it is most direct in addressing the "listener." Whitman employs question and answer, direct address, legal argumentation, invective, and personal testament, creating a complex weave of rhetorical performance. The performance is a fiction, as is the pamphlet itself. Whitman never delivered the speech, nor did he manage to have the pamphlet reproduced and distributed. Likewise, he never managed to become the "wander-speaker" he wished to be. Instead, his oratorical impulse found an outlet in the poems of 1855 and 1856.

In fact, the innovative style of the 1855 poems is already clearly at work in the Preface to the 1855 edition. In the 1856 edition, Whitman would use parts of the 1855 Preface in "Poem of Many in One," later titled "By Blue Ontario's Shore." The particular passages in the two texts are fascinating to compare, but the larger point is that the distinction between prose and poetry is questionable. The 1855 Preface is marked by repetition, syntactic parallelism, cataloguing, and direct address, the very techniques that Whitman uses in the poems of 1855 and 1856. In the Preface, Whitman remarks that

> the greatest poet has less a marked style and is more the channel of thoughts and things without increase or diminution, and is the free channel of himself. He swears to his art, I will not be meddlesome, I will not have in my writing any elegance or effect or originality to hang in the way between me and the rest like curtains. (*LG*: 717)

In some ways this is an accurate representation of Whitman's art, for the writing in the 1855 Preface is marked less by any dominant stylistic trait than by the cumulative effect of the style, delivering the sense of a specific, vivid voice.

The 12 poems of the 1855 *Leaves of Grass* appear without titles or section numbers, and they feature the same dots of ellipsis that Whitman uses prominently in the 1855 Preface. The dividing line between poems is slight, as is that between the Preface and the poems that follow. Likewise, the style of the poetry seeks to render the boundary between writer and reader as transparent as possible. One of Whitman's main techniques for accomplishing that task is direct address, as in the following lines from "Song of Myself": "Have you reckoned a thousand acres much? Have you reckoned the earth much? / Have you practiced so long to learn to read? / Have you felt so proud to get at the meaning of poems?" (*LG*: 30). The address to the reader is colloquial and informal, especially in the word "reckoned" and the phrase "get at." It is also insistent in its questioning, an effect created by the repetition of the syntactic formula "Have you" four times in three lines. The syntactic framework is also quite supple, allowing Whitman to vary the line length and move the figuration from the ownership of land to the understanding of poetry.

The colloquial address suggests a second stylistic innovation in the 1855 and 1856 editions. Whitman's poetic diction is a rich amalgam of neologisms (especially new words created by suffixes and by compounding), foreign borrowings, geographical place names, slang, Americanisms, and grammatical conversions. The result is a wealth of familiar and exotic words to describe the new reality of nineteenth-century America as Whitman perceives it. Moreover, the diction creates the figure of a speaker who will say anything in order to say the right thing, as in this line deleted from "Song of Myself" after 1871: "Washes and razors for foofoos. . . . for me freckles and a bristling beard" (Whitman 2002: 679). The tone of bravado is disarming in its sincerity, but tone and meaning are also constantly shifting. So, a few lines later, the speaker exclaims, "Endless unfolding of words of ages! / And mine a word of the modern . . . a word en masse" (*LG*: 51). Although "en masse" was already an accepted foreign borrowing in the 1847 *Webster's Dictionary*, Whitman uses it to suggest a new, incipient mass movement in American democratic culture. The diction shifts, as do tone and meaning, and these shifts clearly gesture toward larger shifts in nineteenth-century America.

Whitman wrote in the 1867 version of "Song of Myself," "I know perfectly well my own egotism, / Know my omnivorous lines and cannot write any less" (*LG*: 77). The long poetic line is a clear stylistic innovation of 1855 and 1856. In the latter edition, in fact, the format of the printing was intended to make the book fit easily into a coat pocket, so the long lines often look like blocks of prose. The prevailing poetic conventions dictated an accentual-syllabic versification, but Whitman instead used the English Bible as a source for his prosody. The long line captures the expansive freedom of Whitman's poetic style and evokes his vision of an expansive American culture, but it is nonetheless an orderly poetic practice.

The three most important techniques in Whitman's long lines of free verse are syntactic parallelism, repetition, and cataloguing. Whitman tends to write in sequences of coordinate clauses, from two to four lines long, based on the parallels between syntactic units within the lines. Repetition is a related technique. Whitman uses *anaphora*, the repetition of the same word or phrase at the beginning of lines; *epistrophe*, the repetition of the same word or phrase at the end of lines; or *symploce*, the repetition of both initial and terminal words or phrases. Cataloguing is the expansion of syntactic parallelism and repetition. The catalogue expands beyond the frame of two to four coordinate clauses, and it employs parallelism and repetition to build a rhythm. In the first two editions of *Leaves*, Whitman experiments constantly with these three techniques of free verse, creating the sense of an oracular, visionary speaker in many instances. Long poems are especially given to these free-verse techniques, and readers should note such poems as "Song of Myself" (especially the catalogue sections 15 and 33), "The Sleepers," "Song for Occupations," "Crossing Brooklyn Ferry," "Song of the Open Road," "By Blue Ontario's Shore," and "Song of the Broad-Axe."

Whitman's attempts to advertise and understand his own new type of poetry are a fascinating adjunct to the question of style. Writing anonymously in the *United States Review*, for instance, he used the language of the 1855 Preface to describe the effects of the first edition and its poet:

> The style of the bard that is waited for is to be transcendent and new. It is to be indirect and not direct or descriptive or epic. Its quality is to go through these to much more. Let the age and wars (he says) of other nations be chanted, and their eras and characters be illustrated, and that finish the verse. Not so (he continues) the great psalm of the republic. Here the theme is creative and has vista. Here comes one among the well-beloved stonecutters, and announces himself, and plans with decision and science, and sees the solid and beautiful forms of the future where there are now no solid forms. The

> style of these poems, therefore, is simply their own style, new-born and red. Nature may have given the hint to the author of the Leaves of Grass, but there exists no book or fragment of a book, which can have given the hint to them. All beauty, he says, comes from beautiful blood and a beautiful brain. His rhythm and uniformity he will conceal in the roots of his verses, not to be seen of themselves, but to break forth loosely as lilacs on a bush, and take shapes compact as the shapes of melons, or chestnuts, or pears. (Walt Whitman and His Poems 1855)

Whitman's pronouncement on his own style merges innovative literary writing with the perpetual newness of the United States. That is the sense of the ever-creative "vista" that Whitman sees both for his verse and for the republic. In addition, Whitman claims that his style owes a debt to the dynamic forms of nature, which provide the only appropriate models for his verse. Thus the anonymous review raises questions for readers concerning the potential political effect of poetry and the problem of "organic" or "natural" form.

In raising these questions, Whitman's poetry seeks to leap beyond the confines of the printed page. That is clearly the sense of this paradoxical stanza from Section 42 of "Song of Myself":

> Not words of routine this song of mine,
> But abruptly to question, to leap beyond yet nearer bring;
> This printed and bound book – but the printer and the printing-office boy?
> The well-taken photographs – but your wife or friend close and solid in your arms?
> The black ship mail'd with iron, her mighty guns in her turrets – but the pluck of the captain and engineers?
> In the houses the dishes and fare and furniture – but the host and hostess, and the look out of their eyes?
> The sky up there – yet here or next door, or across the way?
> The saints and sages in history – but you yourself?
> Sermons, creeds, theology – but the fathomless human brain,
> And what is reason? and what is love? and what is life?
>
> (*LG*: 77–8)

Until the very last line of this remarkable stanza, Whitman omits any verb at all, and even then he uses the weakest verb in the language for the telling questions of the final line. Still, the style is dynamic and vivid, mainly because the poet uses a pattern of antithesis to balance the lines, yet he also varies the length and syntax of each line by varying the number of syntactic elements he is balancing. There is no way for a critic to say exactly how this kind of writing could have "vista" and affect the future of the United States. Nor could one give an accurate picture of how this stanza resembles a melon or a lilac blossom. Instead, Whitman uses the resources of language to gesture beyond the printed word, even though he does so within the very format of the printed page. This is to argue that Whitman's style exists, in part, in the reader's imaginative movement beyond the page. That would seem to be the strategy behind the 1856 poem "Poem of the Sayers of the Words of the Earth," later titled "A Song of the Rolling Earth." It may also account for the strangely incantatory quality of great poems such as "The Sleepers" (1855) and "Crossing Brooklyn Ferry" (1856).

In the 1856 "Letter" to Emerson which served as a preface to the second edition of *Leaves of Grass*, Whitman is less sanguine about the potential effects of poetic style. The essay is a jeremiad, lamenting the absence of a native literature and culture in America. Thus Whitman finds that "those things most listened for, certainly those are the things least said," and he relentlessly asks the United States, "Where are any mental expressions from you, beyond what you have copied or stolen? Where the born throngs of poets, literats, orators, you promised? Will you but tag after other nations?" (Whitman 2002: 641–2). Whitman answers his own criticisms in the poems and prose of the first two editions of *Leaves of Grass*. But he also answers the questions he raises by proposing that the real answers lie in the future. Thus he finds the present conditions of the United States perfect "for wording the future with undissuadable words . . . Always America will be agitated and turbulent. This day it is taking shape, not to be less so, but to be more so, stormily, capriciously, on native principles, with such vast proportions of parts! As for me, I love screaming, wrestling, boiling-hot days" (Whitman 2002: 645). Whitman's style enacts the undissuadable, for it insistently refuses to be confined within conventional literary models. In that rhetorical sense, at the very least, his style helps to create "that newer America" that he calls for in the 1856 "Letter" (p. 646).

The Civil War Poetry and Prose

Immediately after the publication of the second edition of *Leaves of Grass*, Whitman began contemplating a larger sense of his poetic style. In a June 1857 note, for instance, he wrote the following advice to himself: "The Great Construction of the New Bible. Not to be diverted from the principle [sic] object – the main life work – the three hundred and sixty-five. – It ought to be ready in 1859" (*NUPM*, 1: 353). The "New Bible" figures Whitman's sense of messianic mission, and the number of poems seems to suggest a correspondence between the poetry and the days of the year. But that is only one of many "organic" models Whitman produces. In a letter from the same period, he imagines an edition of a hundred poems as "the *true* Leaves of Grass" with "the new character given to the mass." By the time Whitman brought out the third edition in 1860–61, *Leaves of Grass* included 146 new poems, but the "new character" was an effect of quality rather than quantity or "mass" (*Corr.*, 1: 44).

The most striking stylistic innovation in the third edition is the new arrangement of poems into groups that Whitman called "clusters." This technique of gathering poems into thematic, figurative, or topical groups would persist through the three remaining editions of *Leaves of Grass*. In addition, Whitman would fashion a second grouping, called an "annex," to designate poems not included in the organizational scheme of *Leaves*. But even in the annexes Whitman would refer to the poems as a cluster, so that the real distinction between a definitive, "complete" *Leaves of Grass* and the annexes that appeared after 1881 is suspect. The continuity between the editions and printings of Whitman's poetry rests, in fact, in the constant experimentation with style and meaning.

Several stylistic traits of the prewar poems persist in the third and fourth editions of *Leaves of Grass*. The poet continues to employ a host of foreign borrowings, neologisms, place names, and slang. The characteristics of Whitman's oracular free verse also persist. In addition to these stylistic traits, however, Whitman's use of clusters causes him to write many short lyric poems for the third edition. Most important are the clusters "Enfans d'Adam" (later titled "Children of Adam") and "Calamus." The poems of these two clusters are short, both in the poetic line and in the total number of lines. They gather power as a group, rather than singly, and in some cases they create narrative effects that Whitman does not develop in the earlier editions. The poems of "Calamus," for instance, stem from a prewar sequence of 12 poems called "Live Oak, with Moss," which tells the story of a same-sex love relationship. That narrative is submerged and dispersed in the "Calamus" cluster, but its narrative effects persist none the less.

The cluster style has an important effect on other poems written during and immediately after the Civil War. Whitman published a separate volume of poems in 1865, *Drum-Taps*, and at one point he wrote to William D. O'Connor that the new book was to be "superior to *Leaves of Grass*," partly because of its "proportions, & its passions," but partly because it expressed "this *Time & Land we swim in*" (*Corr.*, 1: 246). The letter suggests that Whitman was attempting to escape the confines of his own poetic project, fashioning a new style and a new format in the 1865 *Drum-Taps*. Likewise, the poems of *Sequel to Drum-Taps* (1865–66), including "When Lilacs Last in the Dooryard Bloom'd," were initially kept separate from *Leaves of Grass*. In the fourth edition of *Leaves*, published in 1867, Whitman added only six new poems, but he changed the clusters, titles, and typography in several ways. He also appended *Drum-Taps*, *Sequel to Drum-Taps*, and *Songs Before Parting* as annexes to the volume.

This pattern of completion and escape to a new project continues after the 1867 edition. In 1871, Whitman incorporated most of the poems of the 1867 annexes into *Leaves of Grass*, renaming them as clusters. "Drum-Taps" becomes a permanent title, as do "Children of Adam," "Calamus," and "Songs of Parting." But other war poems are distributed in three new clusters which eventually disappear in the 1881 edition of *Leaves of Grass*. Other separate publications, such as *Passage to India* (1871), *After All, Not to Create Only* (1871), and *As a Strong Bird on Pinions Free* (1872), show Whitman's impulse to make a new start at his experimenting, but these works are eventually included in the final arrangement of the clusters in the 1881 edition.

Whitman's search for a new experimental writing project extended, during the Civil War years, to his work in prose. In 1863, he wrote to the Boston publisher James Redpath that he wished to write "a book of the time," a prose narrative he imagined as "Memoranda of a Year." The book would collect Whitman's notes and sketches written while he worked in the military hospitals of Washington, DC. Only after the War, however, was Whitman able to publish the hospital sketches. Six articles titled "'Tis Ten Years Since" appeared in the New York *Weekly Graphic* in 1874, and Whitman republished the articles as a book in 1875 and in the second volume of *Two Rivulets* in 1876. They eventually appeared in *Specimen Days & Collect* (1882), Whitman's best single collection of prose works. The style of the Civil War prose is direct, reportorial, and vivid. Whitman sketches a variety of scenes, some from firsthand experience and some from secondhand report, and he renders all of them in graphic, concrete terms. Many of the sketches focus on individual bravery and the everyday heroism of rank and file soldiers. Whitman does not tell the stories of officers and glorious victories; instead, he narrates the "interior history" of the War by fastening upon the "latent personal character and eligibilities of these States, in the two or three millions of American young and middle-aged men, North and South, embodied in those armies – and especially the one-third or one-fourth of their number, stricken by wounds or disease at some time in the course of the contest" (*PW*, 1: 116–17). Even though Whitman's Civil War sketches are few in number, they deliver some of the most powerful portraits of everyday soldiers in Civil War literature.

Postwar Poetry and Prose

In both poetry and prose, Whitman's style becomes more ornate and florid after the Civil War. For many readers, these changes in style are marks of declining health and lost artistry. But it is also possible to interpret the postbellum career as continuing the persistent experimentation and innovation of Whitman's best years. One could hardly argue that Whitman's artistic energy flagged significantly immediately after the end of the war. In 1871, he published the fifth edition of *Leaves of Grass*, with 14 new poems; *Passage to India*, with 23 new poems; *After All, Not to Create Only*, with 11 new poems; and the pamphlet *Democratic Vistas*, a major statement on American democracy and literature.

After the war, it is true, Whitman's experiments with the long poem are not as frequent or as fruitful as they were between 1855 and 1865. The one exception to that generalization may be "Passage to India." In notebook drafts of the poem, Whitman admonished himself to write "strong florid poetry," and the term "florid" may (according to the *Oxford English Dictionary*) carry the musical meaning of "running in rapid figures, divisions, or passages." In nine sections, the poem shifts focus rapidly among several themes: material progress, evolution, spiritual transcendence, time in its guises of past, present, and future. The poet celebrates the scientific materialism of the nineteenth century, but he clearly recognizes that this is not enough for the soul. At times the archaic direct addresses to the soul ("Lo soul for thee of tableaus twain," *LG*: 413) may be florid in an unmusical sense, but at the same time Whitman can summon enough imaginative and stylistic power to create a tableau of the American landscape of the West. This may not equal the great catalogues of "Song of Myself," but that is not the purpose of the passage. The poetic diction is different from the early style, but that is part of Whitman's innovative experimentation in the poem – to combine the archaic and the modern. In some ways, then, Whitman's style is at its most complex in 1871, for he is attempting to create a new combinatory style of writing, one that is more evolutionary than revolutionary.

Whitman's experiments with short lyrics occupy much more of his attention than critics tend to recognize, both before and after the war, and many of the short poems of 1871 are remarkably successful as stylistic experiments. "Sparkles from the Wheel" is first printed in *Passage to India*, but Whitman drafted the poem as early as 1858. In three stanzas, the poem presents an urban scene and suggests the metaphor by which the "curiously floating" speaker can understand mortality. "A Noiseless Patient Spider" is a clear experiment in analytic form, balancing two five-line stanzas in a web of description and analogy. In "On the Beach at Night," the archaic syntactic inversion "Something there is" may bother some readers, but it clearly did not bother Robert Frost, who uses it in "Mending Wall." The strophic "Warble for Lilac-Time" is nowhere near the elegiac majesty of "When Lilacs Last in the Dooryard Bloom'd," but it effectively escapes the confines of elegy in joyously celebrating the return of spring and the perpetual reawakening of the soul.

Poetic techniques play a large role in the postwar prose, especially in *Democratic Vistas*. The style of the essay combines, among other things, history and idealism, a backward-looking vision and a forward-looking vision, the literary and the political. Whitman's purpose is no less grandiose than to reconstruct American politics, religion, and culture, and the purpose requires a certain grandeur of style. The grand style appears in the long, sinuous sentences, with their numerous qualifying phrases and subordinate clauses. It comes out in the numerous new compound words that Whitman creates. It comes out clearly in panoramic catalogues of New York City and its prosperous postwar crowds. It comes forth in the curiously floating "I," which functions as a speaker rather than a writer, making the style seem oratorical in its eloquence. The style of *Democratic Vistas* shows that Whitman unmistakably employs many of the techniques of the early poetry, but in doing so he creates a new form of prose essay.

After the publication of "Thou Mother with Thy Equal Brood" in the supplement *As a Strong Bird on Pinions Free* (1872), Whitman nearly abandons the long poem as a formal experiment. The 1876 poem "Prayer of Columbus" employs some of the oracular style of repetition and syntactic parallelism, but it is an experiment in reduction rather than expansion, evoking Columbus as a figure for Whitman himself, "a batter'd, wreck'd old man" (*LG*: 421). In "Song of the Redwood-Tree," Whitman returns to the use of dual speakers that was so successful in "Out of the Cradle Endlessly Rocking" and "When Lilacs Last in the Dooryard Bloom'd," but ultimately the "true America" the poet envisions depends on the unlamented devastation of the coastal redwoods. Modern readers would find it difficult to see that as a "grander future."

Whitman is much more successful in continuing to experiment with short lyric poems. In the 1881 edition of *Leaves of Grass*, he includes new poems like "The Dalliance of the Eagles," "Spirit That Form'd This Scene," and "Patroling Barnegat." The last of these three poems is a *tour de force*, for it builds its rhythm with 14 lines of epistrophe. The terminal present participle functions to create a scene of constant, ongoing action, and that is also the case in "The Dalliance of the Eagles," one of Whitman's most erotic poems. In "Spirit That Form'd This Scene," Whitman revisits his earliest attachment to nature and the "savage spirit" underlying his own poetry. The annexes "Sands at Seventy" and "Good-Bye My Fancy," joined to the Deathbed Edition of 1891–92, include a host of short lyrics, some only two lines long. But many of these poems are particularly interesting as stylistic innovations. It is as if Whitman were determining how little material can constitute a poem. The group of eight poems forming *Fancies at Navesink*, for instance, returns to the great themes of Whitman's seashore poems, but each poem is a new attempt to capture the "mystic human meaning" of the sea.

The sense of perpetual renewal is pervasive in Whitman's poetry, no less so at the end of his career than at the beginning. Even when the poet is bidding farewell to his imagination in "Good-Bye My Fancy," he turns the poem around, imagining that he will not be separated from his poetic self in death: "May-be it is you the mortal knob really undoing, turning – so now finally, / Good-bye – and hail! my Fancy" (*LG*: 558). For Whitman, there seems to be no style appropriate for a final valediction. Thus we find 13 poems in the posthumous annex *Old Age Echoes*, edited by Horace Traubel. Not all of the poems are new, but the last is remarkable for being Whitman's last poem, completed just days before he died. This is "A Thought of Columbus," which recurs to the figure in "Passage to India" and "Prayer of Columbus." The style is recognizably that of Whitman's old age, for it seems to summarize or "resume" some of his favorite themes. The "thought" or idea becomes the occasion of the poem, and then Whitman transfers his thought of Columbus to the thought Columbus himself must have had – the "phantom of the moment, mystic, stalking, sudden, / Only a silent thought, yet toppling down of more than walls of brass or stone" (*LG*: 582). The thought becomes that of America itself, the modern world. Then Whitman turns the poem one more time. In the final stanza, he adds yet one more word to the song, directly addressing Columbus as "far Discoverer" and sending him the "one manifold, huge memory" the modern world has of him (p. 582). The mental gymnastics of the poem are especially remarkable since they are the thoughts of a man who might die at any moment.

The complicated sense of retrospect that Whitman creates in the postwar prose and poetry is evident in "A Backward Glance O'er Travel'd Roads," the essay that functions as an afterword for *Leaves of Grass*. The essay was originally the introduction to *November Boughs* (1888), a book that combined the "Sands at Seventy" cluster and such essays as "Slang in America," "Elias Hicks," and "The Bible as Poetry," later collected in *Prose Works 1892*. In "A Backward Glance," Whitman avows his idea that *Leaves of Grass* is "experimental – as, in the deepest sense, I consider our American republic itself to be." As he surveys his poetic accomplishment, however, Whitman turns to the future:

> There are, I know, certain controlling themes that seem endlessly appropriated to the poets – as war, in the past – in the Bible, religious rapture and adoration – always love, beauty, some fine plot, or pensive or other emotion. But, strange as it may sound at first, I will say there is something striking far deeper and towering far higher than those themes for the best elements of modern song. (*LG*: 565)

And even though Whitman admits that other works from the past doubtless surpass his in "verbal melody" and "the approved style," he insists that "it still remains to be said that there is even towards all those a subjective and contemporary point of view appropriate to ourselves alone, and to our new genius and environments, different from anything hitherto." Thus Whitman recurs, in his final assessment of his poetic achievement, to the perpetual renewal of poetry, for "the strongest and sweetest songs yet remain to be sung" (*LG*: 574).

In the "Sea-shore Fancies" section of *Specimen Days* (1882), Whitman recalls how he realized that his poems should evoke the seashore, "that suggesting, dividing line, contact, junction, the solid marrying the liquid – that curious, lurking something" (*PW*, 1: 139). Afterward, he decided that "the seashore should be an invisible *influence*, a pervading gauge and tally for me, in my composition." In the seashore Whitman finds an image for his sense of an elusive, pervading "something" that draws him perpetually to further reflection and further imaginings. That is a fitting image for his style, which insists on constantly reinventing itself and thereby eluding the form it has already taken. Each wave is unique; each is merely a fragment of the whole.

References and Further Reading

Bauerlein, Mark (1991). *Whitman and the American Idiom*. Baton Rouge: Louisiana State University Press.

Erkkila, Betsy (1989). *Whitman the Political Poet*. New York: Oxford University Press.

Goodblatt, Chanita (1990). Whitman's Catalogs as Literary Gestalts: Illustrative and Meditative Functions. *Style*, 24: 45–58.

Hollis, C. Carroll (1983). *Language and Style in "Leaves of Grass."* Baton Rouge: Louisiana State University Press.

Kirby-Smith, H. T. (1996). Bards and Prophets. In *The Origins of Free Verse*. Ann Arbor: University of Michigan Press, pp. 135–77.

Miller, Cristanne (1982). The Iambic Pentameter Norm of Whitman's Free Verse. *Language and Style: An International Journal*, 15: 289–324.

Nathanson, Tenney (1992). *Whitman's Presence: Body, Voice, and Writing in "Leaves of Grass."* New York: New York University Press.

Scholnick, Robert J. (1996). "Culture" or Democracy: Whitman, Eugene Benson, and *The Galaxy*. *Walt Whitman Quarterly Review*, 13: 189–98.

Schwiebert, John E. (1992). *The Frailest Leaves: Whitman's Poetic Technique and Style in the Short Poem*. New York: Peter Lang.

Sedgwick, Eve Kosofsky (1983). Whitman's Transatlantic Context: Class, Gender, and Male Homosexual Style. *Delta*, 16: 111–24.

Simpson, David (1990). Destiny Made Manifest: The Styles of Whitman's Poetry. In Homi K. Bhabha (ed.), *Nation and Narration*. London: Routledge, pp. 177–95.

Smith, Gayle L. (1992). Reading "Song of Myself": Assuming What Whitman Assumes. *American Transcendental Quarterly*, 6 (3): 151–61.

Southard, Sherry G. (1984). Whitman and Language: An Annotated Bibliography. *Walt Whitman Quarterly Review*, 2: 31–49.

Thomas, M. Wynn. (1983). Whitman's Achievements in the Personal Style in *Calamus. Walt Whitman Quarterly Review*, 1: 36–47.

Walt Whitman and His Poems (1855). *United States Review* 5 (September), 205–12. In Ed Folsom and Kenneth M. Price (eds.), *The Walt Whitman Archive*. <http://www.whitmanarchive.org/criticism>.

Warren, James Perrin (1990). *Walt Whitman's Language Experiment*. University Park: Pennsylvania State University Press.

Warren, James Perrin (1995). Reading Whitman's Post-War Poetry. In Ezra Greenspan (ed.), *The Cambridge Companion to Walt Whitman*. Cambridge, UK: Cambridge University Press, pp. 45–65.

Warren, James Perrin (1999). Whitman's Agonistic Arena. In *Culture of Eloquence: Oratory and Reform in Antebellum America*. University Park: Pennsylvania State University Press, pp. 169–95.

Whitman, Walt (2002). *Leaves of Grass and Other Writings*, ed. Michael Moon. New York: Norton.

Ziff, Larzer (1981). Public Son, Private Native: Theory, Style, and Content in Whitman's Poetry. In *Literary Democracy: The Declaration of Cultural Independence in America*. New York: Viking Press, pp. 230–43.

24
Literary Contemporaries

Joann P. Krieg

Walter Whitman, Jr. entered a literary scene that throbbed with a sense of an imperative need for a national literary identity that would state the case for democracy and equal the prodigious feats already accomplished in other areas of American life, such engineering marvels as the Erie Canal and the Fulton steamboat. The very youthfulness of the nation gave rise to a literary movement that took its name from this attribute, and Young America energetically set about the business of creating a literary establishment. Fueled by a wide literacy and a thirst for popular entertainment via the burgeoning print industry, eastern cities, especially New York, offered writers opportunities that usually amounted to catering to a buying public that was far from discriminating. Whitman found his way into this world of opportunity as quickly as possible, even though he often had to take on less desirable (to his mind) work in order to maintain himself and contribute to his needy family.

The print culture of New York followed the political tides and Whitman flowed in their currents, writing first for penny newspapers and later editing the more prestigious Brooklyn *Eagle* until he could no longer follow the politics of that paper and was dismissed. In between these writing stints he managed to break into the pages of the *United States Magazine and Democratic Review*, a monthly magazine that garnered the more respectable writers of the New England region, men who had college degrees and most often (excepting Nathaniel Hawthorne) came before the public with the three-name byline indicating pride of place and family. Whitman's early pieces of short fiction and his somewhat flat, conventional poems bore his full name, but did little or nothing to enhance his reputation. The New England writers, however, were bringing something to the American literary scene that would, strangely, both calm and stir the roiling waters of New York's popular literature and call forth Walt Whitman.

As early as 1823 New England's William Ellery Channing had been voicing the need for a national literature, and a decade later Ralph Waldo Emerson took up Channing's call and urged the creation of a network of American scholars who would actively fulfill the role of "Man Thinking" in American society. Emerson saw in the political developments of his time a new importance vested to the individual and envisioned a literature that would do the same. When he contemplated the poetic needs of the nation he combined this vision with one that saw the poet as not only an individual, but a representative of other individuals in America, speaking to and of them and their daily doings. This, perhaps more than his Transcendentalist philosophy, reached the heart of Walter Whitman so that the New Yorker ceased his restless quest for literary acceptance within the confines of the conventional and released to the world the persona bearing his "nearest name," Walt Whitman. With the first edition of *Leaves of Grass* in 1855, Whitman thrust himself into the field of contemporary literature, there to remain until death. Many already prominent in the field were uncomfortable with his presence, however, and Whitman found himself drawing support mainly from lesser lights, writers who gladly turned their abilities in his direction and kept his name and cause before the public. Eventually, that public reached beyond national boundaries and Whitman found admirers and adherents among the European literati who, though excited by his genius, did not always understand fully the circumstances of his American environment and at times viewed his work through a somewhat skewed lens. To take the long view of Whitman among his literary contemporaries is to see him surrounded by the great and small, the consequential and the less significant of his time; ridiculed or dismissed by some, he was, to those who had learned well his lessons of democracy, the first among equals.

Whitman's earliest literary contacts, in the 1840s and 1850s, were with those engaged, as he was, in the world of New York newspapers and magazines. Among these Edgar Allan Poe and William Cullen Bryant loom largest, though at the time of their acquaintance with Whitman their positions in the literary world were quite different. Poe was editor of the *Broadway Journal* where in 1842 Whitman published an early essay on American music. Poe's first tale of detection, "The Murders in the Rue Morgue," appeared that same year and was well received but he had not yet established himself as a poet. This brief contact and the one in-person meeting it produced was the extent of the relationship, but Whitman found something fascinating about the man and, later, his writings, to the extent that he would eventually (in 1875) offer testimony to Poe's place in literary history. This was something he had declined to do, however, earlier in the same year when he was the sole literary figure to attend the reburial of Poe's remains in Baltimore. At that event, to which he made his way despite the physical difficulties caused by a major stroke two years before, he sat on the dais but did not join in the accolades. The relationship between Whitman and Bryant, editor of the *Evening Post* and already a widely respected poet, was greater and involved the older (Bryant) and younger man in long walks about the city while Bryant spoke of his European travels and of poetic theory.

A perusal of the poetry of all three – Bryant, Whitman, and Poe – reveals the presence of but one common topic, death. Each sought ways to deal with the subject of death in a nation and in a time when the subject no longer carried the weight of Puritanism's emphasis and just prior to the national obsession with mourning so comically assailed by Mark Twain in *The Adventures of Huckleberry Finn*. On this topic Whitman found a greater affinity to Bryant, and the influence of Bryant's naturalistic philosophy of death, articulated in "Thanatopsis," can be found in Whitman's thought as well, though from 1855 and the first *Leaves of Grass* their prosody took sharply differing directions. Bryant remained, for the most part, within the confines of poetic convention while Whitman sought to range as far beyond those conventions as was possible.

While New York was important for its newspapers and magazines, the hub of American literature in the 1840s and 1850s was clearly New England, with the headiness of Transcendentalism and the fervor of an almost unrelenting drive toward social reform to fuel its energies. With all the area had to offer culturally, it is more than a little surprising that so much notice should have been taken there of an obscure Manhattan journalist who had produced a small book of poems unlike anything that had appeared in its precincts. This may not have been the case, however, had the brash young New Yorker not sent a copy of his book to the premier Transcendentalist, Ralph Waldo Emerson, seeking his approval. The ploy succeeded, perhaps beyond the poet's greatest expectations. Not only did he receive approval, in the form of a highly laudatory missive in which Whitman was hailed "at the beginning of a great career," but Emerson himself came to visit the *Leaves* author in his Brooklyn home in December of the year of its first edition, 1855. By that time Whitman had published, without asking Emerson's permission, the full text of his endorsement. Emerson appears not to have taken issue with this brashness, which by then he no doubt knew to be one with Whitman's self-congratulatory, though unsigned, reviews of the book in New York newspapers.

While the 1855 meeting – when Emerson took Whitman to dinner at a hotel after which Whitman took him to visit a social club for New York firemen – was their first face-to-face meeting, Whitman was well aware of Emerson's writings and in 1842 had heard him lecture on "Nature and the Powers of the Poet." At the time the young New Yorker was greatly impressed, indicating this in his review in the *Aurora*, and it is not difficult to imagine the degree to which he then took to heart Emerson's call for an American poet, and the effect of the subsequent essay, "The Poet" (1844), where the ideas begun in the lecture were more fully expanded. Admonitions such as those Emerson addressed to any who would further the cause of American poetry, that America itself was already a poem that would not wait to be fit into meters, and that the everyday life of Americans engaged in the work that sustained them and sustained a democracy was worthy of the highest poetic use, clearly fueled Whitman's ardor and, as he later acknowledged, brought him "to a boil." While the acknowledgment was nicely phrased, Whitman is known to have credited a number of sources as catalysts for his poetry. At another time – perhaps while experiencing a fit of anxiety of influence – he allowed a published report denying he had read anything of Emerson's prior to the 1855 *Leaves*, a claim that would be hard to credit even if his later actions and words had not indicated otherwise. But the influence was all in the way of inspiration, even empowerment, for there is little to be found of the one in the other's poems. Whitman is verbose, colloquial, effusive, while Emerson, despite a willingness to break with convention, remains, for the most part, constrained and restricted in expression and more exact in diction. Though he is not dependent on rhyme and willingly varies stanzas, his still apparent regularity shows little of Whitman's loose constructions. Happily, however, Emerson's tendency toward the epigram, evident so often in his prose, finds its way into the poetry as well. At its best the tendency can lead to constructions that surpass many of Whitman's lengthy convolutions, as in "Ode, Inscribed to W. H. Channing," where Emerson masterfully condemns the materialism of his time with the dismissive, "Things are in the saddle, / And ride mankind" (Emerson 1994: 374). It is fascinating, however, to find Emerson, in the 1846 "Hamatreya," opening with a roll call of names of New England families followed by a brief (especially by Whitmanian standards) catalogue of produce from the farms belonging to these families, "Hay, corn, roots, hemp, flax, apples, wool and wood" (1994: 367), and to find him mimicking the colloquial expressions of his neighbors referring to their ownership of the land. All of this technique finds its way into Whitman's poems as well, though they are widely expanded.

Though it is true that Emerson had written encouragements similar to that addressed to Whitman to other Americans who aspired to the ranks of poet, by his own admission he had "looked in vain" for the poet he described (thereby humbly confessing his own inability to meet the test), and thus can be said to have genuinely hailed Whitman as the fulfillment of his hopes. When the 1856 edition of *Leaves of Grass* appeared with Emerson's words of greeting emblazoned on the spine and the entire letter reproduced within (still without permission), Emerson seems to have had some doubts about the young poet's sense of propriety but issued no word of condemnation – perhaps because Whitman had also included a response to the letter in which he addressed Emerson as "dear Friend and Master."

The second edition of *Leaves* brought from New England two more Transcendentalists, Amos Bronson Alcott and Henry David Thoreau, who, perhaps at Emerson's urging because of their admiration for the book, journeyed to Brooklyn as Emerson had the year before to visit this wild young man. One cannot imagine, however, Thoreau arriving as Emerson had, with what Whitman later described as a gentle knock and sweet voice asking to "see Mr. Whitman" (Traubel [1908] 1961: 130). Thoreau would have displayed his customary brusqueness, with the result that he and Whitman – possessed of an equally strong will – failed to make true contact. Thoreau and Whitman both had taught at earlier times and neither had found it a rewarding experience, but other than this and their shared literary aspirations the two had little in common. More the naturalist than was the city-dwelling Whitman, Thoreau may have related to the latter as to a wild creature, later commenting that in Whitman's sex poems it was "as if the beasts spoke" (quoted in Kaplan 1980: 222). For his part, Whitman – perhaps at a loss to attribute the lack of empathy to anything else – later claimed Thoreau was disdainful of the working class. It may be that their conversations tended too much in the direction of social reform with too little exploration of Transcendental ideas to which both had been exposed via Emerson. Textual evidence of an affinity they seem not to have recognized can be seen in at least one instance. In the splendidly evocative description of returning "Spring" in chapter 17 of Thoreau's *Walden*, he speaks of the grass flaming on the hillsides like fire and suggests Whitman's still to come reference (in section 6 of "Song of Myself") to the grass as the color of his own hopeful disposition, "of green stuff woven," when he tells us "not yellow but green is the color of its flame; – the symbol of perpetual youth. . . . "

Alcott, the philosopher and schoolteacher, was more congenial and more receptive of the Whitman pose. Because Alcott was as caught up in social and individual reform as any man might be, it was precisely Whitman's carefully projected persona of working-class reformer that caught his admiration. Whitman, in his "man-Bloomer" (a unisex style of pants invented by women's rights advocate Amelia Bloomer), his rough flannel undershirt, boots, and air of the "loafer," a manner of indifference affected by some young, male Manhattanites of the time, seemed to Alcott to suggest Bacchus-and-satyr-like qualities of a type he had probably never encountered in the regions of Boston. Before the two men left the city they took Whitman on a visit to Samuel Longfellow, brother of the eminent poet Henry Wadsworth Longfellow; Whitman wore his Bloomer and was on his best behavior but, as Alcott later wrote, was clearly "not at home" in a parlor (Alcott 1966: 286). At the time probably neither Alcott nor Whitman could have imagined that in a few years a further connection would be forged between them when Alcott's daughter, Louisa May, would join the nursing ranks in a Washington, DC, war hospital in the same year, 1862, that Whitman became a hospital visitor there.

In these early years of his new status as poet, Whitman, though not in awe of the New England literary establishment, was obviously trying to make an impression when on his own "turf," among the familiar New York throng of firemen, omnibus drivers, and the general working class of the city. There he could play the "rough" for his college-educated, gentlemanly visitors who could either accept him as he was (with plainly visible chamber pot under the bed, as Alcott noted) or reject him. In either case he would sound his "barbaric yawp" over the rooftops of the city. It was a different matter, however, when he found himself on their turf and surrounded by the kinds of political and social turmoil he had all but put behind him when he turned from journalist to poet.

In 1860 Whitman was offered what seemed to him the chance of a lifetime when a Boston publishing firm proposed a new edition of *Leaves of Grass*. To this point the volume had been virtually self-published, with Whitman employing a New York printing house to produce the first two editions. Now the firm of Thayer and Eldridge was eager to add the work to its growing list of offerings. Whitman was to have a free hand in the production, and to that purpose he settled into a Boston boarding house so that he could spend every day overseeing the publication process. Emerson lost no time in coming to visit, and in Boston, where he felt more comfortable to do so, he advised against including the sex poems of the "Enfans d' Adam" section in the new edition. In warning that they might prove objectionable to some, Emerson was not being prescient, for these poems had already raised some strenuous objections both in

New York and in Boston. (Interestingly, though Bronson Alcott was impressed by *Leaves*, his daughter, the prolific writer Louisa May Alcott, claimed she had not been allowed to read the book as a girl and avoided doing so later in life.) Emerson may have been thinking of his own reputation, given Whitman's exploitation of his endorsement, but he surely had the younger man's interests at heart as well. Whitman firmly refused on the conviction that to do so would indicate that there was something morally wrong in the subject matter. Unknown is whether he explained that the new edition would have a counterbalancing section, "Calamus," poems that spoke of same-sex love and comradeship, and that to eliminate the heterosexual poems of "Enfans" would destroy a planned structure within the book. To Emerson's credit the refusal seems never to have made him regret his early enthusiasm, though it may have been a factor in his exclusion of Whitman from *Parnassus*, his 1875 anthology of great American poems. As for Whitman, his affection and admiration for Emerson remained unaltered.

As is so often the case, there was one "hitch" to the Thayer and Eldridge offer. William Thayer and Charles Eldridge were deeply involved in New England's abolitionism and most of their publishing was to further this cause. They had been led to believe, because of certain political pieces Whitman had published in New York and sections of *Leaves* that indicated a sympathy with the abolitionist cause, that their interests were his, and that his work belonged on the same list of offerings as James Redpath's hagiography of the "martyr" John Brown, and *Harrington: A Story of True Love*, a novel of an escaped slave written by a man who would later play a large role in Whitman's life, William Douglas O'Connor. While sympathetic to the plight of slaves, Whitman was not an abolitionist, having taken as his stance the less radical Free Soil position, which hoped to stop the spread of slavery into newly established states in the American West. Earlier in his life, before the first edition of *Leaves of Grass*, Whitman had been deeply involved in the politics of New York City and, through that involvement, in partisan politics. Bitterly disappointed by the in-fighting and betrayal of democratic principles that he encountered in these activities, he had turned away from such involvement and in his new role as spokesperson to and for the nation determined to speak not with a partisan voice, but to all sides and all sections. For this reason he was reluctant to be drawn into the abolitionist fervor that drove his new publishers, and when one of their associates in the cause, Franklin B. Sanborn, was on trial for his part in the conspiracy to support John Brown, Whitman attended but kept a very low profile. While he is eloquent and deeply moving in his expressed sentiments for the slave, and displays a most biting sarcasm toward the Fugitive Slave law in "A Boston Ballad," not for Whitman was the role embraced by John Greenleaf Whittier, the Quaker poet who devoted his talent to the abolitionist cause.

Whittier was one of the "Fireside Poets" in nineteenth-century America, so called because their poems, beloved by the people, were read in homes across the nation by the light of fireside hearths. Others of this group were Bryant, Longfellow, and Oliver Wendell Holmes, all, like Whittier, very respectable and, except for Bryant, unable to find anything of merit in Whitman's poetry. Nor was there much in Whitman's poetry to recommend him to the typical fireside reader who took pleasure in committing to memory poems that rhymed. Only Whitman's 1866 "O Captain! My Captain!" afforded that kind of pleasure and thus became the most popular of his works. There were other factors, too, that distinguished their poems from his, one of which was the use the Fireside Poets so often made of natural objects to teach a moral lesson. The practice can be traced back to the Puritans where one finds it in such works as Anne Bradstreet's "Contemplations" and Edward Taylor's Preface to "God's Determinations." The Young America movement of the 1830s and 1840s not only sought to foster a peculiarly American literature, but believed one of the marks of that literature should be its moral cast. The two ideas, nature and morality, combined and figured most prominently in the poems of William Cullen Bryant, most notably in "To a Waterfowl" (1818), where the poetic persona bluntly speaks of "the lesson" the flight of the bird has engraved on his heart and, in what amounts to a stunning five-word summation of both Miltonic epics, *Paradise Lost* and *Paradise Regained*, describes the human condition as "Lone wandering but not lost" because of the "Power" that directs both bird and man (McMichael 2004: 719). Emerson echoes the thought in his 1834 "The Rhodora" when he resolves his questioning of the reason for the existence of an all but unseen flowering bush with the platitudinous, "The self-same Power that brought me there brought you" (Emerson 1990: 364). Later, Oliver Wendell Holmes would write of "The Chambered Nautilus" (1858) as an object lesson, in its natural growth contours, of the need for the individual to steadily enlarge his spirit. This is "the heavenly message" for which thanks are offered in the poem. Nineteenth-century America's unproclaimed "poet laureate," the much-beloved Longfellow, set the brevity of human life against the eternal tides in "The Tide Rises, the Tide Falls" (1879), also designed to teach a moral. Of course, such moralizing did not permeate all of the century's poetic output. There were also evident such uses of nature as Emerson's self-reflexive "The Snow-Storm" where the "myriad-handed" north wind teaches a Whitmanesque lesson in poetic invention – "nought cares he / For number or proportion" (Emerson 1990: 369) – and when a natural object, "Snow-Flakes," allows the grieving Longfellow (at the death of his wife) to effectively image "the secret of despair." Overall, so much poetic use was made of nature as a didactic tool that Poe denounced it, claiming it made poetry the handmaiden of morality.

Whitman, for all his love of nature, often was inclined to skepticism and questioned it for the "appearances" it presented, appearances that he included in his questioning of all phenomena (as in the "Calamus 7" of the 1860 *Leaves*), or wondered at it (as in the 1856 "Poem of Wonder at the Resurrection of the Wheat," later "This Compost") for its ability to absorb into itself all the dead of the earth and send forth new and healthful growth. In a brief meditation on a natural object, "A Noiseless Patient Spider," which bears some similarity to those of his contemporaries, the intention was not to draw from nature a moral lesson but rather a lesson in survival. Equating his poetic faculty, his soul, with the spider that creates out of its own being the web on which its sustenance depends, the poetic persona urges himself to similar action via the creation of poems and, in so doing, to ensure his own survival "in measureless oceans of space" (*LG*: 450). Here is no moral dictum or lesson intended for the edification of reader and/or poet, but rather a command, self-directed and born of the greatest necessity, the survival of the poetic soul in a "vacant, vast surrounding. . . . "

One of the truly outstanding Transcendentalists who may well have joined Emerson in appreciating Whitman, had she lived to see the publication of *Leaves of Grass*, was Margaret Fuller. Fearless in her championship of women's rights, and a first-rate literary critic, Fuller might have joined another woman journalist, Sara Payson Parton (Fanny Fern), in praising the poet's forthrightness and candor as well as his embrace of gender equality. What is certain is that Whitman found Fuller's comments on the future of American literature impressive enough to have saved them from the time of their 1846 publication (when he reviewed favorably her *Papers on Literature and Art*) until his death. Fuller's thoughts seem to have joined with those of Emerson in his mind and her essay on literature and her reviews of American authors were often the basis of his own ideas and comments.

Two other, but less likely, Whitman contemporaries were Herman Melville and Emily Dickinson, less likely in the sense that neither can be seen to have had an influence on Whitman or to have been influenced by him. Nonetheless, it is interesting to tease out the connecting links, however tenuous, among American writers in this most fruitful and exciting era of literary inventiveness. Whitman became aware of Herman Melville in 1846 when he reviewed *Typee* in the *Brooklyn Eagle*, finding it "a strange, graceful, most readable book" (*Jour.*, 1: 330), and again the following year when *Omoo* appeared. Melville no doubt knew of Whitman, but the two did not cross paths in life or in work except that the conclusion of the Civil War saw each producing a book of poems on the war. Whitman's *Drum-Taps* preceded, making its appearance in 1865, followed the next year by Melville's *Battle-Pieces*. At the time Melville's was the more remarkable, for to that point he was known solely as a writer of fiction. It had been almost a decade, however, since his last such effort, *The Confidence Man* (1857), and the impulse to memorialize the war poetically did not strike until the conflict had almost ended. Whitman, of course, had begun his war poems in 1861, with his rallying cry, "Beat! Beat! Drums!," and he continued their composition throughout the remaining years of the conflict and beyond. The biggest difference between the two books is in their perspective: Melville writes as an "outsider" to the events of those years while Whitman had the advantage of his first-hand experiences as hospital visitor, or, as he presents himself in the poems, as "wound-dresser" to the ill and injured battle participants. It is in this chosen role that Whitman touches the heart of the reader and the nation, seeming to offer a binding-up of national wounds such as that Lincoln spoke of before being deprived, by the assassin's bullet, of the opportunity to do so. It is not to denigrate Melville to point out the problems in *Battle-Pieces*, chiefly those of an inconsistency of voice and point of view, which reflect his own inner conflict created by his belief that slavery was wrong coupled with his dire outlook on the consequences of a northern victory. Given the frame of reference for the two books there are, inevitably, coincidental poems, such as Melville's "The Martyr," which focuses on the emotions of an entire people at the death of Abraham Lincoln, and Whitman's Lincoln poems which, even in the now oft-neglected "O Captain! My Captain!," succeed by narrowing the scale of emotion to the grief of one individual whose pain reflects that of the nation. At every point it is this note of personal involvement that makes the Whitman pieces so affective and its absence from Melville's so distancing – and, incidentally, so contradictory of the young Henry James who in deploring Whitman's recounting of the war's tragedy in *Drum-Taps* unwisely claimed that such events could only properly be told by one "who views them from a height" (Woodress 1983: 59–63).

Battle-Pieces concludes with a "Meditation" on the need for forbearance on the part of the victor north; *Drum-Taps*' "Reconciliation," on the same topic, images the scriptural accomplishment of divine love, "Justice and Mercy have kissed each other" (LG: 321), as the poetic persona recognizes the divinity of his fallen enemy to be as great as his own and bends to kiss the dead lips. As many have commented, however, Melville was just feeling his way poetically, while Whitman was at the peak of his powers, evidenced by *Drum-Taps*' "When Lilacs Last in the Dooryard Bloom'd," so that it is perhaps no more fair to compare the two, other than for the purpose of noting here their proximate publication, than it would be to compare *Franklin Evans* with *Moby-Dick*.

In the case of Whitman and Dickinson the lines of connection are so slight as to be hardly even tenuous, with the former remaining (so far as is known) unaware of the latter's existence. On April 25, 1862 Dickinson wrote her literary mentor Thomas Wentworth Higginson that though she had heard of "Mr. Whitman" she had never read his book, adding "but was told that he was disgraceful –" (Dickinson 1958: 404–5). Higginson, a clergyman who was once a leading radical in the abolitionist movement and later a colonel in the northern army, was a minor luminary in the New England literary establishment when Dickinson sent him a sampling of her poems and asked his advice. Higginson recognized the poetic talent demonstrated in the offerings but advised against publication. He did agree to remain in touch with the poet and offered continued mentoring, which may in part have contributed to her further experimentation in matters of prosody but may have also served to strengthen her resolve to resist publication for the rest of her life. It is somewhat strange that Higginson asked Dickinson about her knowledge of Whitman, unless he thought her indebted to the Brooklyn poet for her inventiveness and daring. Higginson had been among the most vociferous in his condemnation of Whitman's poetry and carried it into personal attacks on the poet's moral character, accusing him of having shirked his duty during the Civil War by choosing the role of hospital visitor over that of soldier. Her preceptor's relentless criticism of Whitman (which actually followed the poet to his grave because of a scathing rehash of Whitman's supposedly debauched life Higginson published two weeks after Whitman's death) may have reinforced Dickinson's belief that it was better to remain "a Nobody" than to risk attracting public attention.

The contrasting poetic styles of Dickinson and Whitman so lend themselves to facile comparisons that one is tempted to stop after simply looking at examples of their work on a page. As a budding critic in a freshman college course once pointed out, one looks like poetry because of all the blank space around it, while the other looks like prose. Yes, indeed; and beyond that there is the matter of precision and compression of diction in those short lines with all the blank space around them, as opposed to the inexactness and expansiveness of the other, seemingly prosodic, lines. For the most part, there is little to be gained from such oversimplifications since the poems defy them in their distinctiveness. What links these two are the breathtaking chances each was ready to take in the creation of poems that pulse with their own lifeblood and connect to the lives of others.

The same sense of pulsing lifeblood that energizes Whitman's poetry flowed also into his friendships, whether with literary people or with railway workers and ferry operators. So alive was he to the electric currents zigzagging between and among humans in their daily contacts, that the effects of these contacts found their way into his poems as readily as into the warm relationships he enjoyed with others. The instantaneous attraction he felt to William Douglas O'Connor at their meeting in Boston in 1860 developed into a lifelong friendship that not even a decade-long estrangement could destroy. A similar, if not so intense, connection occurred linking him to John Burroughs, and later to Richard Maurice Bucke. All three of these were writers of prose who gladly used their talents for Whitman's benefit in one way or another, as did numerous of his friends and acquaintances, among them editors, publishers, and literary critics who did what lay within their powers to advance the Whitman "cause," as the poet proclaimed it.

William Douglas O'Connor was a writer of short fiction, poetry, and of the earlier mentioned novel, *Harrington*, when he met Whitman. The Civil War brought the two together again when Whitman took up residence in Washington, DC, and went to work in a government office to subsidize his hospital visits. O'Connor was living in the same city with his wife, Ellen, and was similarly engaged in government work. The three established a close relationship that saw Whitman living with the O'Connors for a time and later spending many evenings and weekends at their home. When Whitman was dismissed from his clerkship in the Office of the Department of Interior, in part for writing what Secretary of the Interior James Harlan considered indecent poems, O'Connor came instantly to his defense. His *The Good Gray Poet: A Vindication* (1866) was a spirited and laudatory polemic condemning not only Harlan but any others who failed to see the genius of Whitman. He continued this defense of the poet throughout the 1860s and 1870s in letters to newspapers, and in 1862 produced a short story called "The Carpenter" that portrayed Whitman as a Christ-like figure emanating love for humankind. In 1882 the Boston, Massachusetts, district attorney declared the sixth edition of *Leaves of Grass,* published the year before in that city, to be "obscene literature," and it was O'Connor who rushed once again to Whitman's defense despite a 10-year period in which they had not spoken. The reasons for the estrangement, probably a mix of personal and political, centered on their disagreement over the proposed Fifteenth Amendment to the Constitution (giving black males the right to vote), supported by O'Connor and opposed by Whitman, and the fact that in the bitter argument that ensued Ellen O'Connor took Whitman's side against her husband, a choice that seems to have followed from her deep personal attachment to the poet. The friendship renewed, O'Connor did not cease to use his writing talent in support of Whitman until his own death, in 1889.

His sojourn in Washington, DC, in the Civil War years also brought Whitman the friendship of another budding author, John Burroughs, who later made his mark as a naturalist writer with a special interest, encouraged by Whitman, in writing observations of birds. Like William O'Connor, Burroughs wrote of Whitman's genius, first in *Notes on Walt Whitman* (1867) and in 1896, *Whitman, A Study*. The first of these was, in truth, a collaboration with Whitman and O'Connor which presented a nicely constructed picture of Whitman designed to confirm O'Connor's designation of him as "the good gray poet" and to offset any bad impressions created by the Harlan incident. The book was published in the same year as the fourth edition of *Leaves of Grass*, an edition that also seemed to offer a corrective of Whitman's earlier, more sexually open, persona, and the two works can be seen as complementary. Burroughs's second Whitman book, written in the years immediately after the poet's death, belongs to that period of discipleship when praise exceeded candor and literary portraits of Whitman were too brightly lit by the glow of the halo with which he was surrounded to produce a true likeness.

A similar attempt to create the image of a saintly Whitman while he was yet living was thwarted by the poet. *Walt Whitman*, a biographical study published in 1883, was another collaborative effort between Whitman and yet another writer friend, Richard Maurice Bucke. Bucke was a Canadian, a physician and alienist (psychiatrist) who was director of an asylum for the mentally ill. His first encounter with Whitman's poetry was through the 1867 edition of *Leaves*, the one in which Whitman seems to have made a conscious effort to improve his image. If that was his motive, he certainly succeeded in convincing the Canadian doctor of his moral superiority. Bucke's belief was intensified by meeting Whitman in 1877, and two years later, in his wide-ranging exploration of *Man's Moral Nature* (by which Bucke meant emotional development), Whitman is offered as the perfect example of a human in whom the emotive has reached the highest evolutionary level. When the doctor undertook to write a full biographical study Whitman exercised the same degree of oversight, correction, and revision as he had with Burroughs. Bucke's interest lay in presenting Whitman as the epitome of the emotional in human development and in so doing to make extravagant claims for him, but Whitman wanted a picture of robust physical health to emerge. Almost a decade had passed since his first severe stroke, and the poet was eager to convey the idea that he had made an almost full recovery. He also was eager to capitalize on his victory over forces powerful enough to have halted temporarily the dissemination of the latest edition of *Leaves*, in 1881, but not powerful enough to halt its progress. The banning of the book by the Massachusetts attorney general had brought William Douglas O'Connor back into the Whitman fold, and now to his defense offered on the poet's behalf could be added this new study written by a doctor and attesting to his mental, physical, and moral health. Thanks in part to O'Connor, Whitman's finances were also healthier than usual, the temporary ban and the controversy that ensued having created the usual curiosity and the closest thing to a commercially successful edition of *Leaves of Grass* that the poet would see. Richard M. Bucke later produced a final work, *Cosmic Consciousness* (1901), in which Whitman again figured prominently as a prime example of advanced human consciousness. This, and his functioning as one of three executors of Whitman's literary estate, were his final tributes to the man he admired above all others.

While Whitman had many admirers among his literary contemporaries he also had his detractors, though some of these lived to change their opinions of him. Probably the most notable change of heart was that of Henry James. James was just 22 in 1865 when he reviewed *Drum-Taps* and claimed reading it was "a melancholy task" and writing about it "still more melancholy." But it was not the subject matter, the war, that caused his emotion, rather it was the writing, for "Mr. Whitman" (as he is referred to throughout) is said to be neither a writer of verse nor of good prose. Deeming the volume "an offence against art," James castigates the author for the lack of "a single idea" and for having offered instead "nothing but flashy imitations of ideas." The review concludes with a brief lecture on writing for and about the American people and – striking Whitman where it must have hurt the most – strongly implying that the poet was far from being "a national poet" (Woodress 1983: 59–63). Between this and Thomas Wentworth Higginson's attack on his manhood, James's thrust must have been the more palpable hit though we have no record of Whitman's reaction. But where James saw a lack of artistry in Whitman's poetic style, another *Drum-Taps* reviewer, William Dean Howells, who, like James, would gain fame as a fiction writer, saw in it too much evidence of the poetic mills grinding. Howells (who had met Whitman once, in 1860) complained the work was all process and no result, that it was in fact, "unspeakably inartistic." Not satisfied with savaging the work under review, Howells took the opportunity to raise the already familiar question of indecency in *Leaves of Grass*. Claiming that Whitman had heeded the rejection by readers of his indecent poems and, in *Drum-Taps*, "cleansed the old channels of their filth" (Woodress 1958: 56–8), Howells nonetheless saw Whitman as having once again raised the question of his worth as a poet. The review left little doubt of Howells's judgment on the question, nor of how he felt the American public should decide.

Howells later changed his mind about Whitman and used a review of *November Boughs* as an opportunity to offer a retrospective on the poet's achievement. To his mind, the desired emancipation of poetry from rhyme and meter had not been achieved, but, Howells averred, Whitman had succeeded in introducing something with a "formless beauty of its own" (Price 1996: 318–21).

James, too, came to see things differently though not until after Whitman's death. In 1898 he reviewed *Calamus*, a collection of letters that passed between Whitman and Peter Doyle, the poet's working-class companion of some eight years. James saw in the mundaneness of the everyday life reflected in the letters "an illustration of democratic social conditions," and in the letters themselves a manifestation of "the beauty of the particular nature" that was Whitman's (Hindus 1971: 259–60). That he also came to appreciate the poems as well as the man we know from two sources, the first being the quotations from and references to various Whitman poems that can be found scattered among his notes and letters. And from Edith Wharton (1934: 186) we learn of an evening at her home in Lenox, Massachusetts, when she and James sat reading together from *Leaves of Grass*, with James's voice filling the room "like an organ adagio" as he read from "Song of Myself," "Out of the Cradle" and "When Lilacs Last in the Dooryard Bloom'd." The choice of reading matter could have been Wharton's as well as her guest's, for Wharton was a great admirer of Whitman's artistry and at some point had prepared notes for an essay of appreciation, which was never written.

When Howells saw too much of the poet-at-work in Whitman, and James (at least in his early days) saw no poet at all, the fault lay in the inability of either to see and hear in *Leaves of Grass* a new kind of poetry. Whitman's poetry is deliberately self-conscious, and many of his poetic devices – the chanted catalogues, the repetitions at the beginning of lines, the intimacy created between poet and reader, and so forth, are similar to the stage effects wrought by sets and lighting even in the somewhat primitive kinds of operatic and theatrical productions of Whitman's time, and which we know he enjoyed immensely. The poems are also highly musical, a quality noted by another of Whitman's poetic contemporaries, Sidney Lanier, who could not accept Whitman's lack of artistic form but nonetheless recognized in the content a musical beauty that was to Lanier the mark of true poetic genius.

It is often claimed that Whitman, disappointed at not having gained the audience he had hoped for in his own country, turned elsewhere, directing his attention overseas to gain recognition there. While this is true (and given a somewhat exaggerated importance by the poet), it must also be remembered that the initiative came from foreign sources and was not created by Whitman, the point being that it was really they who turned to him as a result of reading *Leaves of Grass*. Naturally enough, the first attention came from English-speaking European contemporaries, some of whom deplored his efforts, while others could not help but respond to him, almost despite themselves. But when William Michael Rossetti (brother of artist Dante Gabriel Rossetti) edited *Poems by Walt Whitman* (1868), an audience began to develop in the British Isles, an audience attracted variously by the joyfulness and vigor of the poems, their democratic impulse, their sincerely expressed love for all humanity, and their revolutionary style. Rossetti was encouraged to the editing by both Whitman and the American Moncure Conway, then living in London. With a facsimile of the 1867 *Leaves* in hand, supplied by Whitman, Rossetti proceeded to choose those poems he considered his personal favorites and that would not scandalize English readers. Though Whitman initially put up a fight against what he perceived as an expurgation, he acquiesced on learning that the edition was already at the printers. It was through this abbreviated (some would say bowdlerized) edition that *Leaves* first reached most of its readers in the British Isles. Happily, some of those readers were led to the complete *Leaves* and on this basis became strong adherents. Among them were such literary figures as the poet Algernon Charles Swinburne and the literary critic John Addington Symonds, as well as a woman who had distinguished herself as a critic of great merit, Anne Gilchrist. Swinburne extolled Whitman in both prose and poetry, but later had a change of heart publicly registered in an 1887 essay titled "Whitmania," where he not so much attacked the poet as he did the enthusiasts who avidly proclaimed what Swinburne saw as an uncritical and unhealthy adulation of the poet. Symonds remained loyal throughout Whitman's remaining life, but exasperated him by repeatedly seeking an explanation of the "Calamus" poems, which seemed to him to indicate Whitman's homosexuality, or, at the very least, his support for same-sex romantic love. It was in response to one such urging that Whitman wrote a letter in which he claimed, disingenuously, to have fathered six illegitimate children. Anne Gilchrist became so enamored of the poet that she came to America, three grown children in tow, firmly believing that she and Whitman were destined to marry. Though they neither married nor became lovers, they did form a friendship that was treasured by both until Gilchrist's death in 1885. While not what one could call an adherent, Alfred Tennyson, England's poet laureate, also admired Whitman's poetry and the two corresponded infrequently over a period of years.

From Ireland came another important voice, that of Edward Dowden, literary scholar and professor of English literature at Trinity College, Dublin. He, too, had come to Whitman first through the Rossetti edition of *Leaves of Grass*, which led him to the full work. So impressed was he (by 1875 he would place Whitman in the same company with Wordsworth, Shelley, and Browning as the leading modern poets) that in 1871 he wrote a lengthy appreciation for London's pre-eminent literary periodical, the *Westminster Review*. That piece has retained its importance for the way in which Dowden identified Whitman not just with America, but with democracy as a political principle, seeing in him much that Alexis de Tocqueville had described so approvingly in his *Democracy in America* (1835–40). Because of its highly political tone and content, the article figured in many of the discussions and differences that resulted from the Irish literary revival of the succeeding two decades. Dowden himself was a political conservative, a unionist who never supported the revival and remained at odds with William Butler Yeats over the question of what should constitute a national literature. As for that, Dowden feared that if Irish literature veered from both earlier aristocratic and present democratic models (America being the sole example in the latter category), it would devolve into narrowness, and lack the broad vision found in Whitman, encompassing all of human experience.

Though never as effusive in his affection as were many of Whitman's admirers, Edward Dowden had a streak of evangelism about him that brought into the Irish fold many whose names figure prominently in Irish culture at the end of the nineteenth century. Among these were poet John Todhunter; artist John Butler Yeats, father of the poet William and the painter Jack; Bram Stoker, later famed for his novel *Dracula*; T. W. H. Rolleston, who received Whitman's eagerly granted permission to translate

Leaves of Grass into German but who never completed the task; and Standish James O'Grady, a literary personage who gained the accolade, "father of the Irish Literary Revival." In fact, Dowden introduced so many of his students and friends to Whitman's work that the poet could not fail to note with great satisfaction the high number of book orders that arrived from Ireland.

For a time it appeared that Whitman's Irish coterie would include William Butler Yeats. Initially Yeats shared Dowden's enthusiasm for the poet of democracy, but eventually he rejected him, perhaps partially due to his disagreement with Dowden over the direction of Irish literature. Dowden refused to promote Irish writers over English, and remained apart from the goal taken up by Yeats of producing a national literature that would look back to Irish roots in legendry and folklore. Ultimately, Yeats rejected Whitman as a model for Irish poets, offering as a rationale Whitman's failure to capture the hearts of his own people. This, of course, was the source of Whitman's deepest disappointment, that he was not accepted in the United States as its poetic spokesman, neither by the country's literary establishment nor by its populace. Always divided within his own mind as to which of these groups he wished the more to win to his great "cause," Whitman found himself, late in his life, with a growing acceptance among the literati of Europe, and, to his surprise, a group of obscure provincial English admirers, some of whom had literary aspirations though none became distinguished.

They were, in truth, not the kinds of workers Whitman had visualized in his early days, rough and ready urbanites who would carry copies of *Leaves of Grass* in their back pockets to be read on hurried lunch breaks. Instead they were lower middle class, clerks and apprentices, many not college educated, who met weekly in the Lancashire town of Bolton to read and discuss politics and literature. Socialist in their ideology, they found in Whitman a voice that seemed to them to herald a future classless world of working brothers. The group was headed by two men who were the best of friends, J. W. Wallace and Dr John Johnston. Not content with the almost daily missives that passed between them and the Camden, New Jersey, poet, these two made their way there on what can only be termed a pilgrimage. Though Bolton remained the heartland of this band of brothers, their reach came to include such luminaries as Edward Carpenter and John Addington Symonds, who were drawn to this particular circle of Whitmanites not only by a shared love of the poet but by the political and sexual liberalism that shaped their views and practices. More out of devotion than genius, J. W. Wallace produced some poetry in the style of Whitman, as did Horace Traubel in America, with whom Wallace formed a deep friendship that extended well beyond Whitman's death. Traubel, a Camden resident who recorded his daily visits with Whitman in the poet's final years, was also a socialist who had much in common with the Boltonites.

Oscar Wilde was not part of the Bolton circle but like them he embraced Whitmanian ideals and, like Carpenter and Symonds, was no doubt drawn to the poetry by its profession of what Whitman termed "adhesiveness," or the love of men for men. When his career as playwright brought him to America in 1882, Wilde eagerly sought the Camden residence and presented himself there on two occasions before leaving on a lecture tour that took him as far as the regions of the Western frontier. Just 26 years old, the young aesthete was a socialist of a different stripe. His concern for the working class led him to the belief that in the face of increasing industrialization workers should, for the sake of their souls, develop an appreciation for beauty and surround themselves with objects of art. It was this he had come to preach to Americans, but when he attempted to convey his ideas to Whitman, the older man was unimpressed. He was impressed by Wilde, however, and proclaimed him "a fine large handsome youngster" (*Corr*, 3: 264). The two talked of poetry, drank some elderberry wine, and were quickly on close terms. Wilde expressed his admiration for Whitman in a gift of his own poems and later sent a large photo of himself. The young Irishman claimed that they parted with a kiss, a gesture that was habitual with Whitman, but however much he may have admired the young beauty his admiration did not extend to Wilde's poetry, which he saw as exquisite but lacking in substance. Whitman did not live to see Wilde's disgrace and imprisonment which, it is safe to conjecture, would have pained him deeply.

By the end of his life Whitman had no outstanding poetic contemporaries in his own country. Emerson and Longfellow had died in 1882, the other New England poets were no longer writing (Lowell died in 1891, Whittier in 1892, Holmes in 1894). Despite the disdain, and at times outright hostility, shown earlier by some of these New England Brahmins, in their twilight years they offered Whitman some modicum of respect or sympathy, age – or in the case of Longfellow, face-to-face meetings – having mellowed them. Sidney Lanier, the southern poet whose poems had extolled both music and nature, had died young, leaving the field to imitators of Bayard Taylor and the poets of the weekly magazines. Realistic fiction held sway in America, and Howells, James, and Mark Twain were first among its writers. Literature did not flourish in the Gilded Age of commerce and affluence, and Whitman's death caused but small ripples on the national tide. Whitman clearly knew from a very early point, as early as 1860, that his true contemporaries would not be those of his own time but rather, as he wrote, "Poets to Come."

References and Further Reading

Alcott, Amos Bronson (1966). *The Journals of Bronson Alcott, 1799–1888*, ed. Odell Shepherd. Port Washington, NY: Kennikat Press.

Blodgett, Harold (1934). *Walt Whitman in England*. Ithaca, NY: Cornell University Press.

Burroughs, John ([1896] 1969). *Whitman, A Study*. New York: AMS Press.

Dickinson, Emily (1958). *The Letters of Emily Dickinson*, vol. II, eds. Thomas H. Johnson and Theodora Ward. Cambridge, UK: Cambridge University Press.

Emerson, Ralph Waldo (1990). *Selected Essays, Lectures & Poems*, ed. Robert D. Richardson, Jr. New York: Bantam Books.

Emerson, Ralph Waldo (1994). *Collected Poems and Translations*, ed. Paul Kane and Harold Bloom. New York: Library of America.

Hindus, Milton (1971). *Walt Whitman: The Critical Heritage*. New York: Barnes and Noble.

Kaplan, Justin (1980). *Walt Whitman: A Life*. New York: Simon and Schuster.

Krieg, Joann P. (2000). *Whitman and the Irish*. Iowa City: University of Iowa Press.

Loving, Jerome (1982). *Emerson, Whitman and the American Muse*. Chapel Hill: University of North Carolina Press.

McMichael, George (ed.) (2004). *Anthology of American Literature*, vol. I, 8th edn. Upper Saddle River, NJ: Prentice Hall.

Myerson, Joel (ed.) (1991). *Whitman in His Own Time*. Columbia, SC: Omnigraphics.

Price, Kenneth M. (ed.) (1996). *Walt Whitman: The Contemporary Reviews*. Cambridge, UK: Cambridge University Press.

Price, Kenneth M. (1990). *Whitman and Tradition: The Poet in His Century*. New Haven, CT, and London: Yale University Press.

Spengemann, William C. and Roberts, Jessica F. (eds.) (1996). *Nineteenth-Century American Poetry*. New York: Penguin Books.

Traubel, Horace ([1908] 1961). *With Walt Whitman in Camden*, vol. 2. New York: Rowman and Littlefield.

Wharton, Edith (1934). *A Backward Glance*. New York: Charles Scribner's Sons.

Woodress, James (1983). *Critical Essays on Walt Whitman*. Boston: G. K. Hall.

25
The Publishing History of *Leaves of Grass*

Amanda Gailey

Leaves of Grass, the centerpiece of Whitman's writing, and one of the most important books in US literary history, is also one of the most difficult texts in literary history to define. Whitman envisioned his magnum opus as a living, growing, organic creation, and he saw the book through six significantly different editions in his lifetime, most of which contained many variant issues. Today we are accustomed to a relative homogeneity among copies of a particular edition: modern printing and marketing ensure that, provided we both own either the hardback or paperback issue of a particular volume, the differences between your copy and mine will be almost imperceptible. But Whitman and his readers worked within a technologically different publishing economy, and most editions of *Leaves of Grass* would have been available in often strikingly different forms. Not only were alternate bindings available, but – because Whitman was such a tireless reviser and was so involved in the physical production of his own books – there were also significant textual variations among particular copies.[1]

Since Whitman's death, most publishers and readers have come to think of *Leaves of Grass* as synonymous with the "deathbed edition," the expanded reissue of the 1881 edition that Whitman released in 1892. Indeed, Whitman asked that the deathbed edition be considered authoritative, and many – though not all – publishers and scholars complied, perhaps spurred by the ease and lower costs associated with studying and printing one book, and surely inspired by scholarly notions of final intentions and authoritative texts that dominated much of twentieth-century editing. But this practice has come at the cost of neglecting the rich, fluid, and complex historical presence that *Leaves of Grass*, in all of its instantiations, had in American culture from its first edition in 1855 to its last authorized issue in 1892. While it may be convenient to think of *Leaves of Grass* as the deathbed edition, it is neither as historically accurate nor as textually rewarding as is a more careful consideration of this evolving and often elusive book.

Scholarship concerning the publication history of *Leaves of Grass* has often disagreed about even such factual matters as how many editions of the book existed in

Whitman's lifetime. Some scholars have erroneously claimed there were up to nine editions, arriving at inflated numbers by counting impressions (separate printings of an edition) and varying states of editions as editions in their own rights. Whitman himself contributed to the confusion by referring (as was common in the nineteenth century) to impressions as editions, as in his request that the 1892 "edition" be considered authoritative. The standard definition of "edition" among bibliographers today, though, is "all copies of a book that are printed from one setting of type, whether directly from the type or indirectly through plates made from it" (Williams and Abbott 1989: 22). Most textual scholars now agree that in order to qualify as a new edition, type resetting should be substantial and should not simply be a matter of correcting isolated errors (Greetham 1992: 167). Using current bibliographic standards, we find that Whitman released six editions of *Leaves of Grass*: in 1855, 1856, 1860, 1867, 1871–72, and 1881–82. Each of these editions encompassed considerable variations, and each enjoyed its own reign – whether for only one year in the case of the 1855 edition, or now over 120 in the case of the 1881 – as the most recent, authoritative edition that the American public would have known as *Leaves of Grass*. After the first, each edition bore many similarities to its predecessor, but each contained significant changes: the addition of new poems, subtractions and revisions of old poems, shifting and recombining poems, and differing bindings and layouts.

The 1855 Edition

The first edition of *Leaves of Grass* appeared in bookstores in Brooklyn and Boston in July of 1855. Whitman was virtually unknown as a poet at the time, and though many scholars have viewed the 1855 edition as a miraculous birth of sorts, Whitman had, in fact, been laboring for some time before his apparent 1855 debut as a radically new experimental poet (Folsom 2001). In addition to publishing his maudlin (but successful) temperance novel, *Franklin Evans*, and working as a journalist, he had published four poems in periodicals five years earlier, most of which bore little resemblance to the signature style of flowing free verse evident in the 1855 edition, but one of which, "Resurgemus," did appear untitled in the book.[2]

In the 150 years since the appearance of the first *Leaves of Grass*, scholars have suggested various theories for what may have prompted the poet to produce such a revolutionary work. Emerson even wondered in 1855 about the "long foreground" of Whitman's "great career" in his letter to the poet. Whitman contributed to the apparent spontaneity of *Leaves of Grass* by reinventing himself as Walt – not Walter – and by responding somewhat coyly to questions about the germination of the book: he told a friend later that the copy left with his publishers was later used "to kindle the fire or feed the rag man," implying that most or all evidence of the creation of *Leaves of Grass* had been destroyed (Traubel 1906: 92). However, some very important drafts that contributed to the first *Leaves of Grass* still exist today: the "Talbot Wilson" notebook, now housed at the Library of Congress (Notebook #80), which dates back at least a year before the appearance of the 1855 edition, as well as scattered drafts at the University of Texas, the University of Virginia, the University of Tulsa, and Duke University. The Talbot Wilson notebook, with its workings and reworkings of key ideas and expressions, demonstrates that Whitman's first edition was anything but spontaneous: it was a project he labored at with great intensity.

Individual manuscript drafts shed light on Whitman's early planning for the book. One manuscript, held at the University of Texas, has long been valued for the early draft contributing to what would eventually be titled "Song of Myself" on its verso, but which was, like the other 11 poems in the 1855 edition, untitled in the book's debut. On the verso of the manuscript are some seemingly cryptic scribbles that had long been overlooked in favor of the more overtly relevant writing on the recto. But as Ed Folsom has recently shown, the jottings on the back, which include many mathematical calculations, are actually evidence of Whitman's meticulous planning for the 1855 edition. Perhaps the most striking aspect of this planning is his listing, previous to 1855, of the 12 first *Leaves of Grass* poems by title, even though he would withhold those titles from the book. Most of the poems he lists are called simply by their first lines (some of these would retain those names in later editions of the book, such as "Great Are the Myths"). But Whitman gives unique titles to some of the poems in the 1855 edition, most notably one he calls in this manuscript "Slaves," but which would later go by "I Sing the Body Electric." The calculations on the page, apparently irrelevant at first glance, are Whitman's efforts to figure out how long his book would be. He also counts the number of letters in one of his poems and compares it to how many letters fit per page in a Shakespeare volume. His math was, incidentally, fairly far off, and he overestimated the book's length by more than 20 pages (Folsom 2001).

The odd book that a relatively few readers found on shelves that summer was quite unlike anything the journalist had publicly produced before, and, in fact, was very much unlike what most book buyers would have been accustomed to at the time. Its size was strange – a large, thin quarto; and the copies most shoppers would have seen had solid dark green covers sprouting unruly, viny gold letters spelling *Leaves of Grass* across the center of the front. No author's name appeared on the cover, and, in fact, none was on the title page. Curious readers could attribute the book to the anonymous man in the now famous frontispiece, who met them confidently, in his work clothes, head cocked, hand on hip. Whitman's name appears twice: on the copyright notice, and on page 29, when, in the middle of the first poem (ultimately titled "Song of Myself"), he offers the verbal counterpart of his frontispiece portrait: "Walt Whitman, an American, one of the roughs, a kosmos,/ Disorderly fleshy and sensual . . . eating drinking and breeding,/ No sentimentalist . . . no stander above men and women or apart from them . . . no more modest than immodest."

Whitman himself paid for the publication of the 1855 edition. This practice was fairly common in the nineteenth century, especially among fledgling authors, and did not carry the same stigma that vanity publications do today. The book was printed by Andrew and James Rome of Brooklyn, and was published by Fowler and Wells, a phrenological firm, who distributed and promoted the work. Whitman's association with the phrenologists went back several years. In 1849 he visited their Phrenological Cabinet, where he had his skull analyzed (Stern 1998). The analysis was very flattering to Whitman, and seems to have bolstered his faith in the pseudoscience, as he reprinted the phrenologists' findings several times and sought out their firm as publishers for his book.

There were 795 copies of the 1855 edition printed, and copies ranged in price from 75 cents for cheaper ones in paper wrappers to two dollars for the more famous green cloth binding (Myerson 1993: 17). In a letter to Emerson that Whitman would write the next year, he claims to have "printed a thousand copies, and they readily sold" which by all other accounts is hardly accurate (Whitman 1856: 346). In fact, Whitman's mathematical estimates, even as early as his page-count projections in the Texas manuscript, should usually be approached with skepticism: in the same letter to Emerson, he predicts, "A few years, and the average annual call for my Poems is ten or twenty thousand copies – more, quite likely," a highly inflated claim.

Scholars have long suggested that the 1855 edition laid out the key themes and concerns that future editions would expand upon. Many critics believe that "Song of Myself," as the first poem of the 1855 edition would eventually be called, consistently held an axial position in each edition of *Leaves of Grass*, and indeed that the poem itself serves as a miniature for the book as a whole even as it morphed over the years. In the 1855 edition, that single poem took up over half of the book's pages. In *The Structure of Leaves of Grass*, Thomas Crawley (1970) argues that with the 1855 edition Whitman established a trajectory in his poems that did not significantly change – except to expand – over the next editions. Crawley believes that in this early edition Whitman establishes his recurring dichotomy of body and soul, the material and the spiritual, that would pattern all future editions. This much seems right, and indeed poems such as "Song of Myself," recurrent in every edition, suggest such a dichotomy overtly to the reader. Later, Whitman would even experiment with separating these two strains into separate books, *Leaves of Grass* and *Passage to India*. However, contrary to the claims of critics such as Crawley, Whitman could not have foreseen the many developments in the various versions of *Leaves of Grass* in 1855, especially since such events as the Civil War would be so formative to his project, and since on a few occasions he aborted other plans for his poems, such as separating them into different volumes. While it may not be evident that in 1855 Whitman had a decided strategy for developing *Leaves of Grass* over the coming decades, it is clear that the timbre he struck with his first 12 poems was one to which he felt committed for the rest of his life. In fact, of the 12 poems he included in the 1855 edition, only the final one, which was later titled "Great Are the Myths," was not retained through to the 1881 edition, though even lines from that one were salvaged in "Youth, Day, Old Age, and Night," which did survive to the end. Even Whitman's long prose preface, which functions as both a poetic and political manifesto, would be partially reworked later into the poem "By Blue Ontario's Shores."

One of the most striking aspects of *Leaves of Grass* is how it became so widely synonymous with its creator. Certainly many extratextual aspects of the book lend itself to this: Whitman, resisting the nineteenth-century divisions of labor in industrialized book production, did not view his poet's role as ending at the publisher's door. He was involved in every aspect of the book's production – its physical design, its type, its printing and binding. Both the semantic content and the physical features of the volume were Whitman's creations, and the few buyers of the first edition brought home something that was as much the product of an artisan as a mechanized process. Whitman himself explained, "My theory is that the author might be the maker even of the body of his book – set the type, print the book on a press, put a cover on it, all with his own hands" (*Corr.*, 2: 480). Furthermore, the striking frontispiece portrait asked readers to associate the words with a physical being and not just a name. The repeated use of "I" throughout the book accentuated the metonymy, and the book was met at once with such an interpretation. An anonymous reviewer for the *Brooklyn Daily Eagle* wrote on September 15, 1855, a mere two months after the book's release: "Its author is Walter Whitman, and the book is a reproduction of the author. His name is not on the frontispiece, but his portrait, half length, is. The contents of the book form a daguerreotype of his inner being, and the title page bears a representation of its physical tabernacle" (Leaves of Grass – an Extraordinary Book 1855). This view of the book's relationship to Whitman would only strengthen as the book developed with its author over the following 26 years.

That critic for the *Brooklyn Daily Eagle* ended his review of the 1855 edition on a lukewarm note: "We have said that the work defies criticism; we pronounce no judgment upon it; it is a work that will satisfy few upon a first perusal; it must be read again and again, and then it will be to many unaccountable." Such a reception seemed favorable, though, compared to many other reviews the book first received. The same month that the *Eagle* review appeared, Charles Eliot Norton, writing for *Putnam's Monthly*, reported:

> words usually banished from polite society are here employed without reserve and with perfect indifference to their effect on the reader's mind; and not only is the book one not to be read aloud to a mixed audience, but the introduction of terms, never before heard or seen, and of slang expressions, often renders an otherwise striking passage altogether laughable. (Norton 1855)

A less courteous reviewer, Rufus Griswold, wrote in November for *Criterion*:

> . . . it is impossible to imagine how any man's fancy could have conceived such a mass of stupid filth, unless he were possessed of the soul of a sentimental donkey that had died of disappointed love. This poet (?) without wit, but with a certain vagrant wildness, just serves to show the energy which natural imbecility is occasionally capable of under strong excitement. (Griswold 1855)

The book did, though, receive some praise. One review stated:

> An American bard at last! One of the roughs, large, proud, affectionate, eating, drinking, and breeding, his costume manly and free, his face sunburnt and bearded,

> his posture strong and erect, his voice bringing hope and prophecy to the generous races of young and old. We shall cease shamming and be what we really are. We shall start an athletic and defiant literature. (Walt Whitman and His Poems 1855)

If the tone of this glowing praise seems familiar, it is because Whitman himself wrote this review. He published it anonymously in the *United States Review*, and others in the Brooklyn *Daily Times* and the *American Phrenological Journal*. Luckily for American literature, Whitman was persistent in developing his poetic vision, and embarked on an aggressive campaign to strengthen his readership. The anonymous reviews are only one illustration of his public relations savvy.

The 1856 Edition

After the 1855 debut, Whitman promptly began work on a second edition, and the resulting product seems as motivated by marketing strategy as by artistic development. The phrenologists Fowler and Wells, who had published the first edition, were leery of associating themselves with the book after the condemnatory reviews, and published the second edition secretly, withholding their imprint (Allen 1975: 81). The new edition had Whitman's name on it – either because the cat was out of the bag after the year's reviews, or because Whitman now had a defiant pride in his work, or because he no longer found anonymity necessary to his poetic purpose. The edition was physically quite different from its predecessor: unlike the thin, tall quarto, the 1856 edition was a fat, portable volume that Whitman hoped could fit in the pockets of his readers.

The 1856 edition included several strategically incorporated addenda that Whitman viewed as necessary to counter the first edition's reception. Most notably, Whitman printed on the spine of the book an excerpt from a letter from Emerson that he had received after sending him a copy of the 1855 edition. Under "Leaves of Grass" was printed in gold letters: "I Greet You at the/ Beginning of A/ Great Career / R. W. Emerson." Inside, Whitman published the flattering letter in its entirety, though he did not pay Emerson the courtesy of asking his permission to print either the blurb or the letter itself. In fact, Whitman had already reprinted the letter in the *New York Tribune* in October of 1855, and had tipped it into copies of the first edition that were still waiting to be bound (Aspiz 1998). Emerson's prominent endorsement lent prestige to *Leaves of Grass*, and Whitman's scandalous use of it was his most effective public relations maneuver in his early career. The *Christian Examiner*, which condemned the book in 1856, made particular note of Whitman's offense at the end of a barrage of insults directed at *Leaves of Grass* and its author:

> There is one feature connected with the second edition of this foul work to which we cannot feel that we do otherwise than right in making a marked reference, because it involves the grossest violation of literary comity and courtesy that ever passed under our notice. Mr. Emerson had written a letter of greeting to the author on the perusal of the

> first edition, the warmth and eulogium of which amaze us. But 'Walt Whitman' has taken the most emphatic sentence of praise from this letter, and had it stamped in gold, signed 'R. W. Emerson,' upon the back of his second edition. This second edition contains some additional pieces, which in their loathsomeness exceed any of the contents of the first. Thus the honored name of Emerson, which has never before been associated with anything save refinement and delicacy in speech and writing, is made to indorse a work that teems with abominations. (*Christian Examiner* 1856)

Readers may have doubted the tact of including Emerson's letter, but the weight of the venerable poet's praise was clear. He asserted: "I am not blind to the worth of the wonderful gift of 'LEAVES OF GRASS.' I find it the most extraordinary piece of wit and wisdom that America has yet contributed" (Whitman 1856: 345). In addition to his exchange with Emerson, Whitman included nine reviews of the book, including two of his own anonymous ones, as well as a few whose condemnations Whitman seemingly viewed as attracting healthy controversy to his book.

The 1856 edition, like its predecessor, opened with the poem that would eventually be titled "Song of Myself." In this edition it was titled "Poem of Walt Whitman, an American" – not only did the 1856 edition display Whitman's name on the cover, it also placed his name prominently in the first poem's title. The second edition included 19 new poems, 18 of which survived to the final edition, though almost always under different titles (see Table 25.1).

Many readers have held that the 1856 edition is less clearly organized and less balanced than the 1855, likely the result of growing pains as the book began its series of expansions and mutations, which is not surprising considering Whitman released the second edition after only one year. In this edition, Whitman widens his focus from the individual to the national. In the 1855 edition of *Leaves of Grass*, the word "America" or some form of it appears 23 times; in the 1856 volume, it appears 107 times. Many of the new poems are concerned with the development of the United States, and Whitman's letter to Emerson at the end of the book makes clear Whitman's poetic intent as it has coalesced in the new volume:

> America is not finished, perhaps never will be; now America is a divine true sketch. There are Thirty-Two States sketched – the population thirty millions. In a few years there will be Fifty States. Again in a few years there will be A Hundred States, the population hundreds of millions, the freshest and freest of men. Of course such men stand to nothing less than the freshest and freest expression. (Whitman 1856: 354)

Many of the political ideas in the 1855 preface move to poems in the 1856 edition: the most notable example of this movement is "A Poem of Many in One" (later "By Blue Ontario's Shore"), which would persist as one of Whitman's most notable political poems throughout the evolution of the book.

Amid the controversy surrounding this edition, sales suffered. Whitman, in usual hyperbolic style, claimed to have printed thousands of copies, but his friend John Burroughs later claimed that only a thousand had been printed (Myerson 1993: 25).

Whatever the precise number printed, the second edition (which sold for a dollar) did not significantly outsell the first. Whitman blamed the reluctant publishers, Fowler and Wells, and decided to switch agents for his next edition.

The 1860 Edition

The third edition of *Leaves of Grass* was published by a much more enthusiastic (even if less business-savvy) company. In February of 1860, the Boston publishing firm of Thayer and Eldridge sent Whitman a letter asking him to allow them to publish his next edition. Whitman consented, and he contracted with the company to receive 10 percent of retail sales of the book (Myerson 1993: 33). The publishers agreed to give Whitman creative control over the printing process, even though they consequently paid more to print Whitman's book than they had for any other (Donlon 1998). The result was at least five different bound forms, some of which showcase Whitman's extraordinary talents as a designer. One version includes pictures of a cloudy globe and a sunrise on the covers. Another version displays on its spine a hand with a butterfly perched on a finger, which would become a recurring image with Whitman – years later he would even pose for a portrait in which he fashioned a cardboard butterfly to perch on his hand.

Probably over 2,000 copies of the 1860 edition were sold, and some estimates push the number closer to 5,000. Readers quickly bought up the first issue, which was printed in the spring, and a second issue had sold out in the summer (Myerson 1993: 34–6). Whitman was excitedly making plans with the publishers for a third issue, as well as for another book, when the firm went bankrupt. The publishers sold their plates to Horace Wentworth, who eventually sold them to Richard Worthington, which resulted in several unauthorized reprintings of the 1860 edition through the 1880s (Donlon 1998, Eiselein 1998). The 1860 edition was consequently one of the most widely read versions of *Leaves of Grass* in the years before the deathbed edition gained wide currency.

With the 1860 edition, Whitman fully developed his practice of organizing most of the poems into clusters.[3] Unlike the previous editions, the 1860 opens with "Proto-Leaf," later titled "Starting from Paumanok." In the four years since the previous edition, Whitman was hard at work, and the 1860 bears the fruits of his efforts, with 121 new poems (see Table 25.1).[4]

Three of the poems new to the 1860 edition would not have been new to close followers of Whitman's career. "A Word Out of the Sea," later "Out of the Cradle Endlessly Rocking," was published as "A Child's Reminiscence" in the *Saturday Press* in December of 1859. "You and Me To-Day" appeared in the same newspaper in January of 1860, and would re-emerge as number 7 of "Chants Democratic" in the new edition of *Leaves of Grass*. Finally, "Bardic Symbols," which appeared in the April 1860 edition of the *Atlantic Monthly*, reappeared as the first poem in the "Leaves of Grass" cluster. Whitman probably had several reasons for spreading his *Leaves* into periodicals. First, and most practically, it allowed him to bring in additional income between editions. Second, by publishing poems between editions, he could keep himself in the public eye and bolster his public image. The *Atlantic Monthly* publication of "Bardic Symbols" is a good example of this: it was a prestigious publication, and gave Whitman positive publicity only a couple of months before the appearance of his new edition. William Dean Howells, writing for the *Daily Ohio State Journal* in March, drew readers' attention to the *Atlantic*:

> Walt Whitman has higher claims upon our consideration than mere magazine contributorship. He is the author of a book of poetry called "Leaves of Grass," which, whatever else you may think, is wonderful . . . It drew the attention of critics, but found no favor with the public, for the people suspect and dislike those who nullify venerable laws, and trample upon old forms and usages. Since the publication of his book, Walt Whitman has driven hack in New York, and employed the hours of his literary retiracy in hard work. Some months ago he suddenly flashed upon us in the New York *Saturday Press*, and created eager dissension among the "crickets." Now he is in the *Atlantic*, with a poem more lawless, measureless, rhymeless and inscrutable than ever. (Howells 1860)

Whitman received such publicity only because he stayed active in periodicals. The *Atlantic* publication also reveals how strategic Whitman was with both his various publication venues and his revisions. "Bardic Symbols" was titled in the *Atlantic* in March, but was simply numbered within a cluster in the book months later. Whitman must have made a deliberate choice to present the poem differently according to publication medium, or he significantly shifted his view of the work from a standalone poem (when it was published in the *Atlantic*) to a contributing part of a larger whole within a matter of weeks, when he prepared copy for *Leaves*.

Whitman's publication of poetry in periodicals fit squarely within the same attitudes toward publishing that he demonstrated throughout his six editions of his book. For Whitman, *Leaves* was not a fixed text, but, like his persona, was a sprawling, omnivorous, dynamic thing, which throughout its lifetime gathered into itself as much as possible. Whitman's periodical poems usually were outcroppings of *Leaves of Grass*. In "Song of Myself," he wrote, "My ties and ballasts leave me . . . I travel . . . I sail [. . .] my palms cover continents, I am afoot with my vision" (Whitman 1855: 35). Periodicals gave *Leaves of Grass* legs. They moved the poet into the busy streets of the democracy he sought to articulate and celebrate. With the 1860 edition he began his ongoing project of extending *Leaves of Grass* into these public venues, and he would further develop the policy with each edition.

Some of the most significant poetic developments within the 1860 edition are the "Chants Democratic," "Calamus," and "Enfans d'Adam" clusters. With "Chants Democratic and Native American" Whitman began to cull his poems that most explicitly dealt with politics. One of the striking developments from the previous edition, "Poem of Many in One" (ultimately "By Blue Ontario's Shores") found a place here. The cluster included an introduction plus 21 poems about various aspects of American politics and society. The introductory poem, "Apostroph," offers an overview of many of the subjects Whitman addresses in the numbered poems that follow it. He would cut "Apostroph" in the following edition, likely because while the introduction is functional, its three and a half pages of exclamations become somewhat tedious, as the first few lines may illustrate:

> O mater! O fils!
> O brood continental!
> O flowers of the prairies!
> O space boundless! O hum of mighty products!
> O you teeming cities! O so invincible, turbulent, proud!
> O race of the future! O women!
> O fathers! O you men of passion and the storm!
> O native power only! O beauty!
> O yourself! O God! O divine average!
>
> (Whitman 1860: 105)

"Calamus," long prized as one of Whitman's greatest poetic achievements, arose in this edition. In 1860 "Calamus" was a cluster of 45 numbered poems; by 1881 Whitman had retooled it to a cluster of 39 titled ones. It is in this cluster in 1860 that Whitman developed his well-known use of the term "comrade" to refer to a range of male–male relationships that are perhaps, due to the passage of time and dramatic changes in cultural context, not altogether recoverable by us today. Whitman chose the word carefully for its ambiguity: sometimes it refers to male–male sexual love and other times to more platonic, intense friendship between men. Kenneth Price has argued that Whitman's terms for male–male relationships "retain an insistent mystery, a feature Whitman prized highly in his love poetry" (Price 2001). While "comrade" often suggests carnality in Whitman's poetry, he always stops short of describing an unambiguous sexual relationship. In fact, manuscript drafts of the poem show Whitman considering using "lover" in place of "comrade," ultimately opting for the nuance of the latter. "Calamus," while not as explicitly sexual as other poems in the 1860 edition, is historically significant precisely because of its relative elusiveness, which contributed to the development of a sexual vocabulary that has proven influential to readers and writers since.

"Enfans d'Adam," later "Children of Adam," helped solidify Whitman's reputation as a risqué or – in many readers' eyes – obscene poet. The "Enfans d'Adam" poems were meant to act as a counterpart to the "Calamus" cluster by focusing on love between men and women. Whitman was aesthetically committed to them even when they strained his relationship with his "master," Emerson, after he refused Emerson's advice to excise the most controversial poems (Miller 1998). A writer for the *Westminster Review* that year specifically invoked Emerson, in fact, in his moral condemnation of Whitman:

> Mr. Emerson has much to answer for, and will in reputation dearly pay for the fervid encomium with which he introduced the Author to the American public. That to the

> public defence of polygamy and slavery, should now be added that of the emancipation of the flesh, is an indication of a moral disorganization in the States, which is of every evil promise. That a drunken Helot should display himself without shame in the market place, speaks sad reproach to the public that does not scourge him back to his cellar. (*Westminster Review* 1860)

Poems like the ones in "Enfans d'Adam" helped spread Whitman's notoriety: even as his books were selling, the press buzzed with striking condemnations. As far away as London reviewers lashed out at Whitman. In July a writer for the *Literary Gazette* began his review: "Not the least surprising thing about this book is its title. Had it been called 'Stenches from the Sewer,' 'Garbage from the Gutter,' or 'Squeals from the Sty,' we could have discerned the application." He argued that "throughout the work there is a tone of consistent impurity which reaches its climax in some compositions entitled 'Enfans d'Adam,' " and concluded: "We say . . . that of all the writers we have ever perused, Mr. Walt Whitman is the most silly, the most blasphemous, and the most disgusting; if we can think of any stronger epithets, we will print them in a second edition" (Leaves of Grass 1860).

Indignation blazed on both sides: critics seized the opportunity to defend public virtue, and Whitman found the outcry evidence of the slack and wan in the culture he hoped to invigorate. A reviewer for the *Saturday Press*, who was possibly Whitman himself or at least a crony, wrote in May of that year, "Walt Whitman, who presents himself as the Poet of the American Republic in the Present Age . . . refuses to confine and cripple himself within the laws of what to him is inefficient art" (Walt Whitman: *Leaves of Grass* 1860). And, "The intellectual attitude expressed in these Leaves of Grass, is grand with the grandeur of independent strength, and beautiful with the beauty of serene repose. It is the attitude of a proud, noble, vigorous life" – even if he did, perhaps, say so himself.

The 1867 Edition

Seven years passed until Whitman issued another edition of *Leaves*. Though dated 1867, the edition first appeared in the fall of 1866, sold for three dollars, and was published by William E. Chapin, who would reissue it twice in 1868. It is not clear exactly how many copies were printed, but the fourth edition was not as successful as the third (Myerson 1993: 45–6).

The intervening years were transformational for both Whitman and *Leaves of Grass*: the nation fought the Civil War in the interim, and it left an indelible mark on the poet and his evolving artistry. Though no new edition of *Leaves of Grass* had emerged during the war, these years were not devoid of poetic production. Since the appearance of the 1860 edition, Whitman had published five poems in periodicals: "Errand-Bearers (16th, 6th Month, Year 84 of The States)" in June 1860 in the *New York Times*; "Beat! Beat! Drums!" in September 1861 in the *Boston Daily Evening Transcript*; "Little

Bells Last Night" in October 1861 in the *New York Leader*; and "Old Ireland" in November 1861 in the same newspaper. He published no poetry during the rest of the war; then in November of 1865 "O Captain! My Captain!" appeared in the *Saturday Press*. Each of these poems was overtly political. All but "Old Ireland," which addresses immigration, were explicitly about the war (though it was only looming at the time of publication of most of them), and all were folded into the 1867 edition of *Leaves of Grass* ("Little Bells Last Night" as "I Heard You, Solemn Sweet Pipes of the Organ"), though their route was indirect. All of them came to *Leaves of Grass* via *Drum-Taps*, which Whitman published in 1865 and annexed into *Leaves of Grass* in 1867.

The publication history of one of these poems, "O Captain! My Captain," demonstrates Whitman's understanding of the mid-nineteenth-century literary marketplace, and his ability to use that understanding in the service of *Leaves of Grass*. "O Captain!" is a curiosity, in that it is a very un-Whitmanlike poem: saccharine, allegorical, rhyming, and metrically strict. In 1865, when it first appeared, this poem seemed to dismiss the poetics that Whitman had been cultivating for over a decade. Indeed, when read within *Leaves of Grass*, where he eventually incorporated it, it is to many contemporary readers a blemish on the aesthetic of the rest of the book. Whitman published "O Captain" in the *Saturday Press* just as he was releasing *Drum-Taps and Sequel to Drum-Taps*, which contained the poem. In keeping with Whitman's history of clever public relations maneuvers, the poem essentially functioned as a "teaser," however misleading, for *Drum-Taps*.

Whitman published the poem in a Northern newspaper only a few months after both the end of the War and the assassination of Lincoln. The editor of the *Saturday Press*, the bohemian Henry Clapp, Jr., had been a great promoter of Whitman for years, and had already published "A Child's Reminiscence" and "You and Me To-Day." The readers of this "Northern slang-whanging organ," as a Southern editor called it,[5] were likely reeling from recent events much as "O Captain"'s narrator was, and were primed for the poem. Whitman probably concluded that a traditional, formal poem like "O Captain" would be very effective with a Northern audience mourning Lincoln's death, and that it might, in fact, attract a wider, traditionalist audience to his poetry.

Earlier in 1865, Whitman had begun publishing his collection of war verse, *Drum-Taps*, but had postponed publication after Lincoln's assassination until he had time to incorporate a sequel honoring the president. Two months later, in June of 1865, Whitman was fired from his job with the Indian Bureau when his boss, James Harlan, snooped through Whitman's desk and found his marked-up copy of the 1860 edition, which Harlan deemed obscene. Whitman's reputation took a blow, and prompted, among other things, the publication of William Douglas O'Connor's vindication, *The Good Gray Poet*. By this point, Whitman's notoriety exceeded his readership. So, when, a few months later, Whitman published "O Captain" in the *Saturday Press*, it was likely his savvy more than his poetics that inspired him to give a Northern, mourning audience – perhaps skeptical of him but eager to make sense of the tumult around them – a poem that they would find ideologically and aesthetically satisfactory.

Ed Folsom (2000: 54) has noted that Whitman sometimes turned to conventional poetics during times of political upheaval, as in his "Ethiopia Saluting the Colors," but it seems that this shifting was not at all automatic, but instead was Whitman's deliberate making of a salve for his ailing country.

This view is corroborated by an early manuscript of "O Captain!" held in the Library of Congress. This early draft, written sometime between Lincoln's assassination in April and the publication of "O Captain!" in the fall, shows Whitman's earlier intent to write the poem in free verse. Before its appearance in *Drum-Taps* and the *Saturday Press*, though, something changed his mind, and the manuscript shows Whitman's alterations of the free verse into rhyme. Sometime soon after his first conception of the poem, then, Whitman thought a conventional rhyme-scheme would better serve his purposes than his more controversial style.

If it was, in fact, Whitman's intention to redeem his reputation and build a wider audience for his poetry through the publication of the conventional "O Captain," his plan worked. Three months after its appearance in the *Saturday Press*, a reviewer for the Boston *Commonwealth* wrote, "this displaced and slighted poet has written the most touching dirge for Abraham Lincoln of all that have appeared," before quoting it in its entirety. "O Captain! My Captain!" soon became Whitman's most anthologized poem and perhaps his most famous poem, to Whitman's eventual chagrin. In 1889, he told his friend, Horace Traubel, "It's My Captain again: always My Captain: the school readers have got along as far as that! My God! When will they listen to me for whole and good?" (Traubel 1953: 392). Whitman had created a monster.

But the poem had, as he apparently hoped, attracted readers to *Leaves of Grass*. Before the publication of "O Captain" in 1865, a few anthologies of Civil War verse were printed, and none included any of Whitman's poems, even though he had published two war poems in 1861. Whitman was not included in these collections until "O Captain" earned him a wide audience, buttressed his reputation, and retroactively called attention to his earlier war poems. In fact, in the decade preceding the publication of "O Captain," Whitman was excerpted in only one book, three lines from "Song of Myself" being published as the preface to a novel titled *Abbie Nott and Other Knots*. In the decade following "O Captain," he was included in 11 collections. No Whitman war poems were apparently anthologized before the publication of "O Captain," and "O Captain" is by far the most anthologized of his war poems, usually present in any early anthology that holds any other of the war poems. This suggests that specifically this poem reeled readers in, even if it kept them from listening to Whitman "for whole and good." The strategy was so successful that for the rest of his career Whitman would continue to publish poems of popular interest in periodicals between editions.

The 1867 edition raises further problems for defining *Leaves of Grass*, since only six new poems were incorporated into this edition of *Leaves of Grass* proper, and the rest of the new poems were from *Songs Before Parting*, *Drum-Taps* and *Sequel to Drum Taps*, which were sewn wholesale into the book. The 1867 *Leaves* was actually four publications with four different paginations sewn into one cover.

Even counting the books that comprise the 1867 is problematic. One of these books, *Songs Before Parting*, was a short "coda" – only 36 pages long – of poems that spoke to nationhood, cannibalized from the 1860 *Leaves of Grass* (Mancuso 1998). To call *Songs Before Parting* a separate book is accurate insofar as it is titled as such and follows its own pagination; yet since the poems are lifted and revised from the previous edition of *Leaves*, and since the "book" only exists within *Leaves of Grass*, it does not, in another view, seem to be a book any more than other clusters that mutate from edition to edition. To further complicate matters, the subsequent reissues in 1868 did not include all four of these books: the first reissue included only *Leaves of Grass* and *Songs Before Parting*, and the second reissue only included *Leaves of Grass*.

As a book, the 1867 edition is confused and wildly varied. It is chaotically organized, and scholars have argued that its chaos – its varied fonts, its containment of different texts thrust together – mimic the social and political disorganization of the United States at the time (Folsom and Price 1997). The instability present in the 1867 edition would never quite leave *Leaves of Grass*, and for the next several years at least, Whitman would seem much less comfortable in his plans for the book.

The 1871–72 Edition

Whitman finished the fifth edition of *Leaves of Grass* in late 1870 (which is when it is copyrighted), but the first issue is dated 1871. He published the volume through the New York firm of J. S. Redfield, and it quickly went through a second issue in the summer of 1871. In 1872, the edition was reprinted with a new title page dated 1872; this edition included tipped-in annexes bound into the volume (Myerson 1993: 53–9). As Gay Wilson Allen has argued, the fifth edition of *Leaves of Grass* is more significant for the shifts in Whitman's thinking that it evidences than for the new poetry it contains (1975: 132–9).

The 1871–72 edition was put out in significantly different forms: one contained only *Leaves of Grass* (1871), one added *Passage to India* (1871), and a third (1872) added to the second the pamphlet "After All, Not to Create Only" (later known as "Song of the Exposition"). Most significant to Whitman scholarship, though, is *Passage to India*. In 1871, when the fifth edition was first issued, Whitman had moved almost one-third of the poems from the previous edition of *Leaves of Grass* to *Passage to India*, which contained a total of 75 poems, 50 of which were recycled.

Also of significance to the 1871–72 edition, most of the poems that had been annexed in the previous edition, *Drum-Taps* and *Sequel to Drum-Taps* and "Songs Before Parting," were fully integrated into either *Leaves of Grass* proper or the *Passage to India* annex in 1871. The Civil War had altered the cluster structure of the new edition: Whitman added three clusters, *Drum-Taps* "Marches Now the War Is Over," and "Bathed in War's Perfume," to address the Civil War and hold the integrated *Drum-Taps* poems.[6]

Although the fifth edition did not receive much critical attention, Whitman had, within its pages, fundamentally altered the plan for *Leaves of Grass*: he conceived of the two books, *Leaves of Grass* and *Passage to India*, as complementary texts that would sever the material and spiritual strands of his work. With the fifth edition, Whitman viewed *Leaves of Grass* as essentially complete, and saw himself as embarking on a new, more mystical project. Allen writes that in the fifth edition, "*Leaves of Grass* comes to a great climax, and probably what Walt Whitman intended to be the end of this book and the beginning of a new one . . . " (1975: 132). It is important to note that this new project was not entirely new – it involved, first and foremost, a reshaping of *Leaves* by culling 50 poems from its pages. Whitman himself notes his plan in his introduction to the 1876 reissue of the fifth edition:

> It was originally my intention, after chanting in "Leaves of Grass" the songs of the body and existence, to then compose a further, equally needed volume, based on those convictions of perpetuity and conservation which, enveloping all precedents, make the unseen soul govern absolutely at last . . . But the full construction of such a work is beyond my powers, and must remain for some bard in the future. (Whitman 1981: 531)

By the time Whitman was tipping *Passage to India* into the 1871–72 edition, he had already scrapped this scenario, and had returned to his original practice of incorporating almost all of his poetry into *Leaves of Grass*. Yet his temporary plan to separate the volumes shows that Whitman's vision for his work was not static.

Whitman reissued the 1871–72 edition in 1876, and called the reissue the Centennial Edition, which he viewed "partly as my contribution and outpouring to celebrate, in some sort, the feature of the time, the first centennial of our New World nationality – and then as chyle and nutriment to that moral, indissoluble union . . . " (1981: 530). This volume contained *Leaves of Grass* and some new intercalated poems, "As in a Swoon," "The Beauty of the Ship," "When the Full-Grown Poet Came," and "After an Interval." It was issued in different forms, the most striking of which was sold with *Two Rivulets*, where he had moved "Passage to India" and some prose work. The set was sold as "Walt Whitman's Complete Works" for $10 (Myerson 1993: 72). Clearly, even at this point, Whitman was still tinkering with how and if he should divide up *Leaves*.

Since the 1867 edition, Whitman had again been sending poems out to periodicals and folding them back into the pages of *Leaves of Grass*, though this batch took rather circuitous routes. "A Carol of Harvest for 1867" appeared in the *Galaxy* in September of 1867, and was brought into *Passage to India* – and therefore some copies of *Leaves of Grass* – in 1871. "Proud Music of the Sea Storm" was published in the February, 1869 issue of the *Atlantic Monthly*, after Emerson pulled some strings with the editor (*LG*: 402). The *Atlantic* published poems anonymously, and Whitman himself stated anonymously in the *Washington Star* in January, "The Atlantic for February contains a long poem from his sturdy pen, and one of the very best, to our notion, that he has yet written" (ibid.). Whitman was, it seems, using anonymity to claim credit for his prestigious publication. It, too, would appear in *Passage to India*.

Later that year, in December, Whitman published one of his less successful poems, "The Singer in the Prison," in the *Saturday Evening Visitor*. In January of 1870, "Brother of All With Generous Hand," later "Outlines for a Tomb," appeared in the *Galaxy*. Both of these poems were occasional, the first commemorating the concert of a singer in Sing Sing Prison, and the second the death of a philanthropist. Publishing these poems in periodicals allowed them to be read at an appropriate time by a wide audience before they were subsumed into the pages of his more enduring project. That year, Whitman published one more poem in the *Galaxy*, "Warble for Lilac-Time," which would join the other periodical publications from this time period in *Passage to India*.

The 1881–82 Edition

In the 10 years between the 1871–72 and 1881–82 editions, Whitman dramatically increased his rate of publishing poems in periodicals. Twenty-six appeared in the decade since the fifth edition. Several of these poems were occasional: "The Fair of the American Institute" (*New York Evening Post*, September 1871); "As A Strong Bird on Pinions Free" (*New York Herald*, June 1872, incorporated into the 1876 reissue); "Nay, Tell Me Not To-day the Publish'd Shame: Winter of 1873, Congress in Session" (*New York Daily Graphic*, March 1873); "Spain 1873–74" (*New York Daily Graphic*, March 1873); "A Kiss to the Bride: Marriage of Nelly Grant" (*New York Daily Graphic*, May 1874); "A Death Sonnet for Custer" (*New York Daily Tribune*, June 1876); "What Best I See in Thee" (*Philadelphia Press*, December 1879); and "The Sobbing of the Bells" (*Boston Daily Globe,* September 1881). By this point in his career, Whitman was deftly and frequently using periodicals as a way to give his poetry and himself an ongoing public relevance beyond the pages of *Leaves of Grass*.

In April of 1881, Whitman was notified that the Boston publisher James R. Osgood was interested in publishing *Leaves of Grass* (Myerson 1993: 86). This offer was fairly prestigious: Osgood was the publisher of authors such as William Dean Howells and Mark Twain (Renner 1998). Whitman pushed a hard bargain, and negotiated to receive 25 cents on every two-dollar copy sold. Whitman went to Boston to oversee the printing of his book, and it hit the shelves in October of 1881. The book did well, and while Whitman characteristically exaggerated the numbers – claiming 3,000 were published when 1,600 were – he was experiencing reasonable financial success with this edition, and received a check for over four hundred dollars in April of 1882 as payment for the first issues. Meanwhile, the edition was also selling well in Britain (Myerson 1993: 86–7).

In March of that year, the Boston district attorney deemed the edition obscene, and demanded that it be withdrawn. Initially, Whitman agreed to modify the book in order to keep it in print, but he was not willing to excise entire poems, which is what the district attorney would have found satisfactory. The publisher balked at publishing the book, but they did, fortunately, hand over all the plates and leftover unbound copies to Whitman, along with a hundred dollars' compensation (Renner 1998, Myerson 1993: 96).

Whitman was not long in need of a publisher. David McKay, who worked for the Philadelphia company Rees Welsh, wrote Whitman three weeks after Osgood handed over the plates. Whitman asked for even higher royalties than Osgood had given him, since Rees Welsh would be using plates that were now his: the firm agreed to pay Whitman 35 cents a copy and to give him space to work in their store (Myerson 1993: 98).

According to Whitman, Rees Welsh was careful at first, printing a conservative 1,000 copies, since the firm did not know how consumers would respond to a book deemed obscene. Perhaps unsurprisingly, consumers reacted by buying out all 1,000 copies in only two days. The book quickly went through several printings, and by December had sold almost 5,000 copies (Myerson 1993: 98–103).

Late in 1882, David McKay bought out many of the Rees Welsh titles, including *Leaves of Grass*. McKay was committed to the continued publication of *Leaves*, and reprinted it several times before the significant reissue of 1891–92. In fact, in the decade after Osgood relinquished the book, Rees Welsh and later McKay sold over 6,000 copies of *Leaves of Grass*, and paid Whitman $2,244.90 (Myerson 1993: 112). Whitman's book had not become less controversial in the years since its 1855 debut, but it certainly had become more lucrative since that first edition that Whitman paid for himself.

The 1881–82 edition did not contain a strikingly large number of new poems, but it did significantly reorder older poems, and, importantly, it definitively brought back together the *Leaves of Grass* and *Passage to India* poems that Whitman separated, then, on second thought, physically yoked a decade before. This edition enlarged older clusters, especially "Inscriptions" and "Drum-Taps," and added four new ones: "By the Roadside," "Autumn Rivulets," "Birds of Passage," and "From Noon to Starry Night."[7] Many of the new poems in the final edition were short and added little to the overall scope of the project. As Allen has noted, and as Whitman's periodical poetry evidences, as Whitman got older he turned increasingly to poems based on "borrowed observations, journalistic articles, and events in the day's news" (1975: 148). The poems new to this edition are largely such poems.

Whitman significantly shifted the poems in this final edition, and critics have posited various and often contradictory theories trying to make sense of the rearrangement. Allen, who offers a detailed description of the ordering of the book, notes persuasively that the final edition of *Leaves* does not have a consistent, overarching organizational structure, but that individual clusters and orderings have their own internal logic, even if they at times fail (1975: 147–53). Whitman himself wrote in 1886, "... 'Leaves of Grass' is, or seeks to be, simply a faithful and doubtless self-will'd record. In the midst of all, it gives one man's – the author's – identity, ardors, observations, faiths, and thoughts ... " (Whitman 1981: 433). Starting from Whitman's own description, critics have looked for ways in which the final ordering of *Leaves* is autobiographical, and Allen ultimately concludes that "this is a poetic record, not objective history or prosaic autobiography" (Allen 1975: 152).

Indeed, while resisting chronological schemas, the 1881 ordering of *Leaves of Grass* was the one that the poet was most content with. When the book was reprinted in 1891, he made no major changes, except to add annexes. Whitman's health was rapidly failing, and he was aware, as he had been for some time, that he had limited opportunity to complete his project. He had published dozens of poems in periodicals during the last 10 years, helping him to shape the annexes that he would add to the 1881 edition: "November Boughs" (1888), including its famous prose preface, "A Backward Glance O'er Travel'd Roads," and "Good-Bye My Fancy" (1891). But he chose to fully integrate none of these into the edition that he had reordered conclusively 10 years before.

After the copyright notices in the 1891 edition, Whitman made his wishes regarding *Leaves of Grass* clear: "As there are now several editions of L. of G., different texts and dates, I wish to say that I prefer and recommend this present one, complete, for future printing, if there should be any; a copy and fac-simile, indeed, of the text of these 438 pages" (Whitman 1891: 2). Whitman, a consummate printer to the end, was still giving instructions for the publication of his work. As previously noted, publishers have largely honored his request that the deathbed edition be considered authoritative. But if we are to take to heart Whitman's life project, and believe his claim in "So Long!" that "This is no book,/ Who touches this, touches a man," we can not so readily dismiss the five earlier editions and countless permutations of this master work: surely the many younger Whitmans that the book has recorded – the anonymous Whitman of 1855, the Whitman reeling from the Civil War hospitals – are of no less interest than the sagacious Whitman at the end of his life.

Leaves of Grass Titles

In Table 25.1, for each edition, each new poem is listed on the left by the title of its debut in *Leaves of Grass*. On the right is the title it ultimately received. Unless a date is otherwise noted in brackets, the titles on the right are from the 1881–82 edition. In several cases, the beginning of the poem is given in brackets after the title to distinguish it from other poems with the same title.[8]

Table 25.1 *Leaves of Grass* Titles

1855 Title	Final Title
Leaves of Grass [I celebrate myself]	Song of Myself
Leaves of Grass [Come closer to me]	A Song for Occupations
Leaves of Grass [To think of time]	To Think of Time
Leaves of Grass [I wander all night in my vision]	The Sleepers

Leaves of Grass [The bodies of men and women engirth me]	I Sing the Body Electric
Leaves of Grass [Sauntering the pavement or riding the country byroad here then are faces]	Faces
[A young man came to me with a message from his brother]	Song of the Answerer; Now List to My Morning's Romanza [71]; The Indications [71]
[Suddenly out of its stale and drowsy lair]	Europe, the 72d and 73d Years of These States
[Clear the air there Jonathan]	A Boston Ballad (1854)
[There was a child went forth every day]	There Was a Child Went Forth
[Who learns my lesson complete]	Who Learns My Lesson Complete?
[Great are the myths]	Great Are the Myths [71]; Youth, Day, Old Age and Night

1856 Title	Final Title
Broad-Axe Poem	Song of the Broad-Axe
Bunch Poem	Spontaneous Me
Clef Poem	On the Beach at Night Alone
Faith Poem	Assurances
Liberty Poem for Asia, Africa, Europe, America, Australia, Cuba, and The Archipelagoes of the Sea	To a Foil'd European Revolutionaire
Poem of the Heart of the Son of Manhattan Island	Excelsior
Poem of the Last Explanation of Prudence	Song of Prudence
A Poem of Many in One	By Blue Ontario's Shore
Poem of Perfect Miracles	Miracles
Poem of Procreation	A Woman Waits for Me
Poem of the Propositions of Nakedness	Respondez! [71]; Reversals; Transpositions
A Poem of Remembrances for a Girl or a Boy of These States	Chants Democratic 6 [60]; Think of the Soul
Poem of the Road	Song of the Open Road
Poem of the Sayers of the Words of the Earth	Song of the Answerer; Song of the Rolling Earth
Poem of Salutation	Salut Au Monde!
Poem of Wonder at the Resurrection of the Wheat	This Compost
Poem of Women	Unfolded Out of the Folds
Poem of You, Whoever You Are	To You [Whoever you are]
Sun-Down Poem	Crossing Brooklyn Ferry

1860 Title	Final Title
Apostroph	Leaves of Grass 1 [67]; O Sun of Real Peace [71]
Beginners	Beginners
Calamus 1	In Paths Untrodden
Calamus 2	Scented Herbage of My Breast
Calamus 3	Whoever You Are Holding Me Now in Hand
Calamus 4	These I Singing in Spring

Calamus 5	Over the Carnage Rose Prophetic a Voice; For You O Democracy
Calamus 6	Not Heaving from My Ribb'd Breast Only
Calamus 7	Of the Terrible Doubt of Appearances
Calamus 8	[Not continued]
Calamus 9	[Not continued]
Calamus 10	Recorders Ages Hence
Calamus 11	When I Heard at the Close of Day
Calamus 12	Are You the New Person Drawn Toward Me?
Calamus 13	Roots and Leaves Themselves Alone
Calamus 14	Not Heat Flames Up and Consumes
Calamus 15	Trickle Drops
Calamus 16	[Not continued]
Calamus 17	Of Him I Love Day and Night
Calamus 18	City of Orgies
Calamus 19	Behold This Swarthy Face
Calamus 20	I Saw in Louisiana a Live-Oak Growing
Calamus 21	That Music Always Round Me
Calamus 22	To a Stranger
Calamus 23	This Moment Yearning and Thoughtful
Calamus 24	I Hear it Was Charged Against Me
Calamus 25	The Prairie-Grass Dividing
Calamus 26	We Two Boys Together Clinging
Calamus 27	O Living Always, Always Dying
Calamus 28	When I Peruse the Conquer'd Fame
Calamus 29	A Glimpse
Calamus 30	A Promise to California
Calamus 31	What Ship Puzzled at Sea; What Place Is Besieged?
Calamus 32	What Think You I Take My Pen in Hand?
Calamus 33	No Labor-Saving Machine
Calamus 34	I Dream'd in a Dream
Calamus 35	To the East and to the West
Calamus 36	Earth, My Likeness
Calamus 37	A Leaf for Hand in Hand
Calamus 38	Fast-Anchor'd Eternal O Love!
Calamus 39	Sometimes with One I Love
Calamus 40	That Shadow My Likeness
Calamus 41	Among the Multitude
Calamus 42	To a Western Boy
Calamus 43	O You Whom I Often and Silently Come
Calamus 44	Here the Frailest Leaves of Me
Calamus 45	Full of Life Now
Chants Democratic and Native American 4	Our Old Feuillage
Chants Democratic and Native American 7	With Antecedents
Chants Democratic and Native American 8	Song at Sunset
Chants Democratic and Native American 9	Thoughts [Of these years I sing]
Chants Democratic and Native American 10	To a Historian

Chants Democratic and Native American 11	Thoughts [Of these years I sing]
Chants Democratic and Native American 12	Vocalism
Chants Democratic and Native American 13	Laws for Creations
Chants Democratic and Native American 14	Poets to Come
Chants Democratic and Native American 16	Mediums
Chants Democratic and Native American 17	On Journeys through the States
Chants Democratic and Native American 18	Me Imperturbe
Chants Democratic and Native American 19	I Was Looking a Long While
Chants Democratic and Native American 20	I Hear America Singing
Chants Democratic and Native American 21	As I Walk These Broad Majestic Days
Enfans D'Adam 1	To the Garden the World
Enfans D'Adam 2	From Pent-Up Aching Rivers
Enfans D'Adam 6	One Hour to Madness and Joy
Enfans D'Adam 7	We Two, How Long We Were Fool'd
Enfans D'Adam 8	Native Moments
Enfans D'Adam 9	Once I Pass'd through a Populous City
Enfans D'Adam 10	Facing West from California's Shores
Enfans D'Adam 11	[Not continued]
Enfans D'Adam 12	Ages and Ages Returning at Intervals
Enfans D'Adam 13	O Hymen! O Hymenee!
Enfans D'Adam 14	I Am He that Aches with Love
Enfans D'Adam 15	As Adam Early in the Morning
France, the 18th Year of These States	France, the 18th Year of These States
A Hand-Mirror	A Hand-Mirror
Kosmos	Kosmos
Leaves of Grass 1	As I Ebb'd with the Ocean of Life
Leaves of Grass 10	Myself and Mine
Leaves of Grass 13	You Felons on Trial in Courts
Leaves of Grass 15	Night on the Prairies
Leaves of Grass 16	The World Below the Brine
Leaves of Grass 17	I Sit and Look Out
Leaves of Grass 18	All Is Truth
Leaves of Grass 19	Germs
Leaves of Grass 20	[Not continued]
Leaves of Grass 22	What Am I After All
Leaves of Grass 23	Locations and Times
Leaves of Grass 24	To the Reader at Parting [71]
Longings for Home	O Magnet-South
Mannahatta	Mannahatta
Perfections	Perfections
Poem of Joys	A Song of Joys
Proto-Leaf	Starting from Paumanok
Savantism	Savantism
Says	Suggestions [71]
So Long!	So Long!
Tests	Tests
Thought [Of public opinion]	Thoughts [Of public opinion]
Thoughts 1	Thoughts 1 [Of the visages of things][67]

Thoughts 2	Thoughts [Of ownership]
Thoughts 3	Thought [Of persons arrived at high positions]
Thoughts 4	Thoughts [Of Justice–]; Thoughts [Of Ownership–]; Thought [Of Equality–]
Thoughts 5	Thought [As I sit with others at a great feast]
Thoughts 6	Thought [Of what I write from myself] [71]
Thoughts 7	Thought [Of obedience, faith, adhesiveness]
To a Cantatrice	To a Certain Cantatrice
To a Common Prostitute	To a Common Prostitute
To a President	To a President
To a Pupil	To a Pupil
To Him That Was Crucified	To Him That Was Crucified
To My Soul	As the Time Draws Nigh
To Old Age	To Old Age
To One Shortly to Die	To One Shortly to Die
To Other Lands	To Foreign Lands
To Rich Givers	To Rich Givers
To the States, To Identify the 16th, 17th, or 18th Presidentiad	To the States, To Identify the 16th, 17th, or 18th Presidentiad
Unnamed Lands	Unnamed Lands
Walt Whitman's Caution	To the States
A Word Out of the Sea	Out of the Cradle Endlessly Rocking
Debris	Stronger Lessons; Yet, Yet Ye Downcast Hours; Offerings; Visor'd; Beautiful Women; Not the Pilot; As if a Phantom Caress'd Me; Debris [He is wisest who has the most caution] [67]; Debris [Any thing is as good as established] [67]; Leaflets [67]

1867 Title	Final Title
Inscription	Small the Theme of My Chant; One's-Self I Sing
The Runner	The Runner
Leaves of Grass 2	Tears
Leaves of Grass 3	Aboard at a Ship's Helm
When I Read the Book	When I Read the Book
The City Dead-House	The City Dead-House
(*Drum-Taps*)	
Drum-Taps	First O Songs for a Prelude
Shut Not Your Doors to Me Proud Libraries	Shut Not Your Doors; As They Draw to a Close
Cavalry Crossing a Ford	Cavalry Crossing a Ford
Song of the Banner at Day-Break	Song of the Banner at Daybreak
By the Bivouac's Fitful Flame	By the Bivouac's Fitful Flame
1861	Eighteen Sixty-One
From Paumanok Starting I Fly Like a Bird	From Paumanok Starting I Fly Like a Bird
Beginning My Studies	Beginning My Studies
The Centenarian's Story	The Centenarian's Story
Pioneers! O Pioneers!	Pioneers! O Pioneers!
Quicksand Years that Whirl Me I Know Not Whither	Quicksand Years

The Dresser	The Wound-Dresser
When I Heard the Learn'd Astronomer	When I Heard the Learn'd Astronomer
Rise O Days from Your Fathomless Deeps	Rise O Days from Your Fathomless Deeps
A Child's Amaze	A Child's Amaze
Beat! Beat! Drums	Beat! Beat! Drums!
Come Up From the Fields Father	Come Up from the Fields Father
City of Ships	City of Ships
Mother and Babe	Mother and Babe
Vigil Strange I Kept on the Field One Night	Vigil Strange I Kept on the Field One Night
Bathed in War's perfume	Bathed in War's Perfume
A March in the Ranks Hard-Prest, and the Road Unknown	A March in the Ranks Hard-Prest, and the Road Unknown
Long, Too Long, O Land	Long, Too Long America
A Sight in Camp in the Day-Break Grey and Dim	A Sight in Camp in the Daybreak Gray and Dim
A Farm Picture	A Farm Picture
Give Me the Splendid Silent Sun	Give Me the Splendid Silent Sun
Did You Ask Dulcet Rhymes from Me	To a Certain Civilian
Year of Meteors	Year of Meteors
The Torch	The Torch
Years of the Unperform'd	Years of the Modern
Year that Trembled and Reel'd Beneath Me	Year that Trembled and Reel'd Beneath Me
The Veteran's Vision	The Artilleryman's Vision
O Tan-Faced Prairie-Boy	O Tan-Faced Prairie-Boy
Camps of Green	Camps of Green
As Toilsome I Wander'd Virginia's Woods	As Toilsome I Wander'd Virginia's Woods
Hymn of Dead Soldiers	Ashes of Soldiers
The Ship	The Ship Starting
A Broadway Pageant	A Broadway Pageant
Flag of Stars, Thick-Sprinkled Bunting	Thick-Sprinkled Bunting
Old Ireland	Old Ireland
Look Down Fair Moon	Look Down Fair Moon
Out of the Rolling Ocean, the Crowd	Out of the Rolling Ocean the Crowd
World, Take Good Notice	World Take Good Notice
I Saw Old General at Bay	I Saw Old General at Bay
Others May Praise What They Like	Others May Praise What They Like
Solid, Ironical, Rolling Orb	Solid, Ironical, Rolling Orb [71]
Hush'd Be the Camps To-Day	Hush'd be the Camps To-day
Weave in, Weave in, My Hardy Soul	Weave in, My Hardy Life
Turn, O Libertad	Turn O Libertad
Bivouac on a Mountain Side	Bivouac on a Mountain Side
Pensive on Her Dead Gazing, I Heard the Mother of All	Pensive on Her Dead Gazing
Not Youth Pertains to Me	Not Youth Pertains to Me
(Sequel to Drum-Taps)	
When Lilacs Last in the Door-Yard Bloom'd	When Lilacs Last in the Door-Yard Bloom'd
Race of Veterans	Race of Veterans
O Captain! My Captain	O Captain! My Captain!

Spirit Whose Work Is Done	Spirit Whose Work Is Done
Chanting the Square Deific	Chanting the Square Deific
I Heard You, Solemn Sweet Pipes of the Organ	I Heard You Solemn Sweet Pipes of the Organ
Not My Enemies Ever Invade Me	Not My Enemies Ever Invade Me
O Me! O Life	O Me! O Life!
Ah Poverties, Wincings, and Sulky Retreats	Ah Poverties, Wincings, and Sulky Retreats
As I Lay with My Head in Your Lap, Camerado	As I Lay with My Head in Your Lap Camerado
This Day, O Soul	This Day, O Soul
In Clouds Descending, in Midnight Sleep	Old War-Dreams
An Army on the March	An Army Corps on the March
Dirge for Two Veterans	Dirge for Two Veterans
How Solemn, as One by One	How Solemn, as One by One
Lo! Victress on the Peaks	Lo, Victress on the Peaks
Reconciliation	Reconciliation
To the Leaven'd Soil They Trod	To the Leaven'd Soil They Trod

"Over the Carnage Rose Prophetic a Voice," not listed here, is a reworking of the 1860 Calamus 5. It is the only *Drum-Taps* poem to be included in *LG* before 1867.

1871 Title	Final Title
As I Ponder'd in Silence	As I Ponder'd in Silence
In Cabin'd Ships at Sea	In Cabin'd Ships at Sea
For Him I Sing	For Him I Sing
To Thee, Old Cause!	To Thee Old Cause
The Base of All Metaphysics	The Base of All Metaphysics
Drum-Taps [Aroused and angry]	[Not continued]
Adieu to a Soldier	Adieu to a Soldier
Delicate Cluster	Delicate Cluster
Ethiopia Saluting the Colors	Ethiopia Saluting the Colors
Still Though the One I Sing	Still Though the One I Sing
(*After All, Not to Create Only*)	
After All, Not to Create Only	Song of the Exposition
(*As a Strong Bird on Pinions Free*)	
One Song, America, Before I Go	Thou Mother with Thy Equal Brood
Souvenirs of Democracy	My Legacy
As a Strong Bird on Pinions Free	Thou Mother with Thy Equal Brood
The Mystic Trumpeter	The Mystic Trumpeter
O Star of France	O Star of France
Virginia—The West	Virginia—The West
By Broad Potomac's Shore	By Broad Potomac's Shore
(*Passage to India*)	
[Epigraph]	Gliding o'er All
Passage to India	Passage to India
Proud Music of the Storm	Proud Music of the Storm
[Ashes of Soldiers: Epigraph]	[Not continued]
This Dust was Once the Man	This Dust was Once the Man
Whispers of Heavenly Death	Whispers of Heavenly Death
Darest Thou Now, O Soul	Darest Thou Now O Soul

A Noiseless, Patient Spider	A Noiseless Patient Spider
The Last Invocation	The Last Invocation
As I Watch'd the Ploughman Ploughing	As I Watch'd the Ploughman Ploughing
Pensive and Faltering	Pensive and Faltering
On the Beach, at Night	On the Beach at Night
A Carol of Harvest, for 1867	The Return of the Heroes
The Singer in the Prison	The Singer in the Prison
Warble for Lilac Time	Warble for Lilac-Time
Sparkles from the Wheel	Sparkles from the Wheel
Brother of All, with Generous Hand	Outlines for a Tomb
Gods	Gods
Lessons	[Not continued]*
Now Finale to the Shore	Now Finale to the Shore
Thought	As They Draw to a Close
The Untold Want	The Untold Want
Portals	Portals
These Carols	These Carols
Joy, Shipmate, Joy!	Joy, Shipmate, Joy!
(1876 Intercalations)	
[Come, said my soul]	[Not continued]
[As in a Swoon]	[Not continued in *LG*; included in 1891 *Good-Bye My Fancy*]
The Beauty of the Ship	[Not continued]
When the Full-Grown Poet Came	When the Full-Grown Poet Came
After an Interval	[Not continued]
To the Man-of-War Bird	To the Man-of-War Bird
A Death Sonnet for Custer	From Far Dakota's Cañons
(*Two Rivulets*)	
Two Rivulets	[Not continued]
Or from that Sea of Time	[Not continued]
Eidólons	Eidólons
Spain, 1873-'74	Spain, 1873-74
Prayer of Columbus	Prayer of Columbus
Out from Behind this Mask	Out from Behind this Mask
To a Locomotive in Winter	To a Locomotive in Winter
The Ox-Tamer	The Ox-Tamer
Wandering at Morn	Wandering at Morn
An Old Man's Thought of School	An Old Man's Thought of School
With All Thy Gifts, &c.	With All Thy Gifts
From My Last Years	[Not continued]
In Former Songs	[Not continued]
After the Sea-Ship	After the Sea-Ship
(*Centennial Songs*)	
Song of the Redwood-Tree	Song of the Redwood-Tree
Song of the Universal	Song of the Universal
Song for All Seas, All Ships	Song for All Seas, All Ships

*"Lessons," new to *Passage to India*, was not included in copies bound with the 1872 *LG*.

1881 Title
Thou Reader
Patroling Barnegat
The Dalliance of the Eagles
Roaming in Thought
Hast Never Come to Thee an Hour
As Consequent, Etc.
Italian Music in Dakota
My Picture-Gallery
The Prairie States
A Paumanok Picture
Thou Orb Aloft Full-Dazzling
A Riddle Song
What Best I See in Thee
Spirit That Form'd This Scene
A Clear Midnight
As at Thy Portals Also Death
The Sobbing of the Bells

Post-1881 annexes included in Deathbed Edition
(*Sands at Seventy*)
Mannahatta {My city's fit and noble name resumed}
Paumanok
From Montauk Point
To Those Who've Fail'd
A Carol Closing Sixty-Nine
The Bravest Soldiers
A Font of Type
As I Sit Writing Here
My Canary Bird
Queries to My Seventieth Year
The Wallabout Martyrs
The First Dandelion
America
Memories
To-day and Thee
After the Dazzle of Day
Abraham Lincoln, Born Feb. 12, 1809
Out of May's Shows Selected
Halcyon Days
(Fancies at Navesink)
The Pilot in the Mist
Had I the Choice
You Tides With Ceaseless Swell
Last of Ebb, and Daylight Waning

And Yet Not You Alone
Proudly the Flood Comes In
By That Long Scan of Waves
Then Last of All
Election Day, November, 1884
With Husky-Haughty Lips, O Sea
The Death of General Grant
Red Jacket (from Aloft)
Washington's Monument, February, 1885
Of That Blithe Throat of Thine
Broadway
To Get the Final Lilt of Songs
Old Salt Kossabone
The Dead Tenor
Continuities
Yonnondio
Life
"Going Somewhere"
True Conquerors
The United States to Old World Critics
The Calming Thought of All
Thanks in Old Age
Life and Death
The Voice of the Rain
Soon Shall the Winter's Foil Be Here
While Not the Past Forgetting
The Dying Veteran
A Prairie Sunset
Twenty Years
Orange Buds by Mail From Florida
Twilight
You Lingering Sparse Leaves of Me
Not Meagre, Latent Boughs Alone
The Dead Emperor
As the Greek's Signal Flame
The Dismantled Ship
Now Precedent Songs, Farewell
An Evening Lull
Old Age's Lambent Peaks
After the Supper and Talk
(*Good-Bye My Fancy*)
[Last droplets of and after spontaneous rain]*
Sail Out for Good, Eidòlon Yacht
Lingering Last Drops
Good-Bye My Fancy
On, on the Same, Ye Jocund Twain

My 71st Year
Apparitions
The Pallid Wreath
An Ended Day
Old Age's Ship & Crafty Death's
To the Pending Year
Shakspere-Bacon's Cipher
Long, Long Hence
Bravo, Paris Exposition!
Interpolation Sounds
To the Sunset Breeze
Old Chants
A Christmas Greeting
Sounds of the Winter
A Twilight Song
Osceola
A Voice from Death
A Persian Lesson
The Commonplace
"The Rounded Catalogue Divine Complete"
Mirages
L. of G.'s Purport
The Unexpress'd
Grand is the Seen
Unseen Buds
Good-Bye My Fancy!

*This brief, untitled poem is included within the prose preface.

Notes

1 Often Whitman decided to incorporate additional works into an edition after the type had already been set, and so would tip in any number of additional pages at different points in an edition's lifetime. So, while some copies of the 1871–72 edition contain only the text of *Leaves of Grass* proper, others have tipped in pages of other Whitman publications: some with *Passage to India* and others with both *Passage to India* and *After All, Not to Create Only*. To further complicate matters, multiple editions of *Leaves of Grass* would often occupy the market simultaneously. The 1860 edition, for example, was pirated through the 1880s, so while some consumers were buying the 1881 edition, others were still finding the 1860 available.

2 "Blood Money," "The House of Friends," and "Resurgemus" were published in *The New York Tribune* in 1850, and "Song for Certain Congressmen" was published in *The New York Post* the same year.

3 Ed Folsom, Ken Price, and Brett Barney, in their work on the *Walt Whitman Archive*, have argued convincingly that the page titling pattern in the 1855 edition results in a cluster of the final seven poems under the title "Leaves of Grass."

4 Bibliographers have arrived at conflicting numbers regarding the 1860 edition: Crawley (1970) counts 123 and Allen (1975) finds 146, for example. The discrepancies result partially from error (Crawley seems to confuse a couple

of poems) and partially from different ways that they can be counted. Counting the strophes of "Says" raises the number, and scholars will arrive at higher numbers if they count both the new poems to this edition and the poems that were eventually born of them – in some cases, more than one poem emerged.

5 The "Editor's Table" of the July, 1860, *Southern Literary Messenger* referred to the *Saturday Press* as it described how to understand Whitman: "Take a pair of frog-legs, put a tongue to every toe of both legs, and place the legs under a galvanic battery—and you have the utterings of Whitman."

6 Another cluster, "Songs of Insurrection," also arose in this edition. Some critics have held that this cluster contained those war poems that were not about the Civil War: Allen writes, "The title ... may possibly have been suggested by the war, but its contents are ... early poems ... This new grouping is merely an attempt to give these poems a context in the aftermath of the national struggle" (1975: 133–4). Allen is not entirely correct. More than the title frames these poems and gives them a Civil War context. The first poem in the cluster, "Still Though the One I Sing," is new to this edition, and certainly could be interpreted as a Civil War poem:

> Still, though the one I sing,
> (One, yet of contradictions made,)
> I dedicate to Nationality,
> I leave in him Revolt, (O latent right of insurrection! O quenchless, indispensable fire!)

7 Some critics have called "Sea-Drift" a new cluster, but it seems more accurate to think of it as an enlargement of the 1871 "Sea-Shore Memories" cluster, as it incorporated it in its entirety.

8 The Bradley et al. *Textual Variorum of the Printed Poems* is an excellent resource for tracking these changes; I have begun these tables with their research but have differed from their findings in several cases.

References and Further Reading

Allen, Gay Wilson (1975). *The New Walt Whitman Handbook*. New York: New York University Press.

Aspiz, Harold (1998). *Leaves of Grass*, 1856 Edition. In J. R. LeMaster and Donald D. Kummings (eds.), *Walt Whitman: An Encyclopedia*. New York: Garland Publishing. Online at Ed Folsom and Kenneth M. Price (eds.), *The Walt Whitman Archive*. <http://www.whitmanarchive.org/archivephp/criticism/encyclopedia/indexframeset.php>.

Christian Examiner (1856). November, 60 (also numbered as 4th series, 26, no. 3), 471–3. In Ed Folsom and Kenneth M. Price (eds.), *The Walt Whitman Archive*. <http://www.whitmanarchive.org/criticism>.

Crawley, Thomas Edward (1970). *The Structure of Leaves of Grass*. Austin: University of Texas Press.

Donlon, David Breckinridge (1998). Thayer, William Wilde [1829–1896] and Charles W. Eldridge [1837–1903]. In J. R. LeMaster and Donald D. Kummings (eds.), *Walt Whitman: An Encyclopedia*. New York: Garland Publishing. Online at Ed Folsom and Kenneth M. Price (eds.), *The Walt Whitman Archive*. <http://www.whitmanarchive.org/archivephp/criticism/encyclopedia/indexframeset.php>.

Eiselein, Gregory (1998). *Leaves of Grass*, 1860 Edition. In J. R. LeMaster and Donald D. Kummings (eds.), *Walt Whitman: An Encyclopedia*. New York: Garland Publishing. Online at Ed Folsom and Kenneth M. Price (eds.), *The Walt Whitman Archive*. <http://www.whitmanarchive.org/archivephp/criticism/encyclopedia/indexframeset.php>.

Folsom, Ed (2000). Lucifer and Ethiopia: Whitman, Race, and Poetics before the Civil War and After. In David S. Reynolds (ed.), *A Historical Guide to Walt Whitman*. New York: Oxford University Press, pp. 45–95.

Folsom, Ed (2001). Whitman's Manuscript Drafts of "Song of Myself." In *The Classroom Electric: Dickinson, Whitman, and American Culture*. <http://bailiwick.lib.uiowa.edu/whitman/>.

Folsom, Ed and Price, Kenneth M. (eds) (1997). Introduction. *Major Authors on CD-ROM: Walt Whitman*. CD-ROM. Primary Source Media.

Greetham, D. C. (1992). *Textual Scholarship: An Introduction*. New York: Garland Publishing.

Griswold, Rufus (1855). Untitled review. *Criterion*, 1, 24. In Ed Folsom and Kenneth M. Price (eds.), *The Walt Whitman Archive*. <http://www.whitmanarchive.org /criticism>.

Howells, William Dean (1860). Bardic Symbols. *Daily Ohio State Journal*, 28 March, 2. In Ed Folsom and Kenneth M. Price (eds.), *The Walt Whitman Archive*. <http://www.whitmanarchive.org/criticism>.

Leaves of Grass – an Extraordinary Book (1855). *Brooklyn Daily Eagle*, September 15, 2. In Ed Folsom and Kenneth M. Price (eds.), *The Walt Whitman Archive*. <http://www.whitmanarchive.org/criticism>.

Leaves of Grass (1860). *Literary Gazette* 4, July 7, 798–9. In Ed Folsom and Kenneth M. Price (eds.), *The Walt Whitman Archive*. <http://www.whitmanarchive.org/criticism>.

Mancuso, Luke (1998). *Leaves of Grass*, 1867 Edition. In J. R. LeMaster and Donald D. Kummings (eds.), *Walt Whitman: An Encyclopedia*. New York: Garland Publishing. Online at Ed Folsom and Kenneth M. Price (eds.), *The Walt Whitman Archive*. <http://www.whitmanarchive.org/archivephp/criticism/encyclopedia/indexframeset.php>.

Miller, James E (1998). "Calamus [1860]." In J. R. LeMaster and Donald D. Kummings (eds.), *Walt Whitman: An Encyclopedia*. New York: Garland Publishing. Online at Ed Folsom and Kenneth M. Price (eds.), *The Walt Whitman Archive*. <http://www.whitmanarchive.org/archivephp/criticism/encyclopedia/indexframeset.php>.

Myerson, Joel (1993). *Walt Whitman: A Descriptive Bibliography*. Pittsburgh, PA: University of Pittsburgh Press.

Price, Kenneth M. (2001). Sex, Politics, and "Live Oak with Moss." *The Classroom Electric: Dickinson, Whitman, and American Culture. The Walt Whitman Archive*. <http://jefferson.village.virginia.edu/fdw/volume3/price/>.

Norton, Charles Eliot (1855). Whitman's Leaves of Grass. *Putnam's Monthly: A Magazine of Literature, Science, and Art*, 6, 321–23. In Ed Folsom and Kenneth M. Price (eds.), *The Walt Whitman Archive*. <http://www.whitmanarchive.org/criticism>.

Renner, Dennis K. (1998). *Leaves of Grass*, 1881–82 Edition. In J. R. LeMaster and Donald D. Kummings (eds.), *Walt Whitman: An Encyclopedia*. New York: Garland Publishing. Online at Ed Folsom and Kenneth M. Price (eds.), *The Walt Whitman Archive*. <http://www.whitmanarchive.org/archivephp/criticism/encyclopedia/indexframeset.php>.

Stern, Madeleine B. (1998). Fowler, Lorenzo Niles (1811–1896) and Orson Squire (1809–1887). In J. R. LeMaster and Donald D. Kummings (eds.), *Walt Whitman: An Encyclopedia*. New York: Garland Publishing. Online at Ed Folsom and Kenneth M. Price (eds.), *The Walt Whitman Archive*. <http://www.whitmanarchive.org/archivephp/criticism/encyclopedia/indexframeset.php>.

Traubel, Horace (1906). *With Walt Whitman in Camden*, vol. 1. Boston: Small, Maynard.

Traubel, Horace (1953). *With Walt Whitman in Camden*, vol. 4, ed. Sculley Bradley. Philadelphia: University of Pennsylvania Press.

Walt Whitman and His Poems (1855). *United States Review* 5 (September), 205–12. In Ed Folsom and Kenneth M. Price (eds.), *The Walt Whitman Archive*. http://www.whitmanarchive.org/criticism>.

Walt Whitman: *Leaves of Grass* (1860). New York *Saturday Press*, May 19, 2. In Ed Folsom and Kenneth M. Price (eds.), *The Walt Whitman Archive*. <http://www.whitmanarchive.org/criticism>.

Westminster Review (1860). 74, n.s. 18 (1 October), 590. In Ed Folsom and Kenneth M. Price (eds.), *The Walt Whitman Archive*. <http://www.whitmanarchive.org/criticism>.

Whitman, Walt (1973). *Leaves of Grass*, ed. Sculley Bradley and Harold W. Blodgett. New York: Norton.

Whitman, Walt (1981). *Leaves of Grass and Selected Prose*, ed. Lawrence Buell. New York: Random House.

Whitman, Walt (1855, 1856, 1860, 1867, 1871, 1891). *Leaves of Grass*, facsimiles and transcriptions of 1855, 1856, 1860, 1867, 1871–72, 1891–92 editions. In Ed Folsom and Kenneth M. Price (eds.), *The Walt Whitman Archive*. <http://www.whitmanarchive.org>.

Williams, William P. and Abbott, Craig S. (1989). *An Introduction to Bibliographical and Textual Studies*, 2nd edn. New York: Modern Language Association of America.

26
The Poet's Reception and Legacy

Andrew C. Higgins

In 1897, five years after Walt Whitman's death, E. A. Robinson wrote a poem titled "Walt Whitman." It wasn't the first poem with this title. At least two other poets had used the title already, and several others had already addressed Whitman in verse (see Ed Folsom's 1998 exploration of poets addressing Whitman). In the poem, Robinson sings, "The master-songs are ended, and the man / That sang them is a name" (Perlman, Folsom, and Campion: 93).[1] This passage from body of flesh and blood to body of works meant that the words "Walt Whitman" were now more complex than ever. Robinson mourned "we do not hear him very much to-day" because his songs are "too pure for us – too powerfully pure." But he consoled himself with the thought that "there are some that hear him, and they know / That he shall sing to-morrow for all men" (ibid.). Robinson's poem re-enacts a rhetorical move that Whitman himself made over and over in *Leaves of Grass*: overcoming present division by envisioning union in the future. Only in this poem, the present division is primarily about Whitman himself. I start with this observation because it underscores one of the major facets of the way future readers have come to terms with Walt Whitman (and "Walt Whitman"). The man – the human being who strolled through New York City, nursed stricken soldiers, and loved Peter Doyle, among a myriad other things – is dead. That person is the only phenomenon who could justly lay claim to being the unitary "Walt Whitman." Upon his death, Walt Whitman, like Auden's William Butler Yeats, "became his admirers," and Whitman's admirers have been many. This essay will look at Walt Whitman's legacy as the dramatic actions of his admirers, as dramatizations of the written record left by the flesh and blood Walt Whitman, in which "Walt Whitman" becomes a marker, a signifier, used by his admirers, each claiming, to greater or lesser degrees, understanding of a real or an ideal Walt Whitman. This means that when I speak of Whitman's "influence" or "legacy," terms I will use frequently in this essay, I am not referring to a positive cause and effect, but rather to the way the works and life of Walt Whitman have intersected the concerns and ambitions of his readers, and how those readers have construed and made use of the poet as a symbol or example. Most of these attempts have been made in fierce earnestness, others somewhat tongue in cheek, but all lay claim to what is perhaps the most contested ground in American literature: Walt Whitman.

We can parse the multitudes of "Walt Whitman" in several ways. At the most general level, Whitman's work is shot through with a tension between Romantic individualism and the modern social self. The first two lines of *Leaves of Grass* (from 1871 on) declare this struggle:

> One's-Self I sing, a simple separate person,
> Yet utter the word Democratic, the word En-Masse
> (*LG*: 1)

This is the major fault line in Whitman's legacy. There are those, such as D. H. Lawrence and Federico Garcia Lorca, who take him as an elemental self. And those, such as Pablo Neruda and June Jordan, for whom he is the spokesperson of The People, en masse. And then there are those, such as Randall Jarrell, for whom Whitman remains simply a very good, very skilled poet.

At a more specific level, the reception of his own varied carols gives us a great many other Walt Whitmans. While he was alive, of course, *Leaves of Grass* kept changing, and most of the commentary written during his life refers to editions few contemporary readers have read. But this mutation did not end with his death. Different groups of readers have turned to different poems over the years. He has been at various times the poet of "O Captain! My Captain!," "Song of the Open Road," "Song of Myself," "When Lilacs Last in the Dooryard Bloom'd," "Passage to India," and, more recently, "Live Oak, with Moss." This shifting canon of Whitman's poetry means that the Whitmans that writers such as Charles Swinburne, Ezra Pound, Langston Hughes, Allen Ginsberg, and Alicia Ostriker talk about are different people – and occasionally people who wouldn't recognize each other.

Despite these complexities, it is possible to identify, in broad terms, some of the ways Whitman's example has shaped poetry in the last 150 years. Whatever the mechanisms and metaphysics of influence, since the first publication of *Leaves of Grass* in 1855, poetry in America, and increasingly the world over, has generally changed in these four ways, all of which have their first great modern example in *Leaves of Grass*. First, nonmetrical verse – free verse – has become the dominant prosody of American poetry. Though Whitman was not the first poet to write in free verse, he was the first major poet to base his major works on it. Second, though largely a Romantic, Whitman created a realist poetics focused on the precise, everyday image. Third, Whitman made sex and the body possible, if not fundamental, topics to the poet. Fourth, Whitman created the example of the American poet as prophet, existing both at the center and the margins of the culture. Prior to Whitman, the American poet was largely an establishment figure. After Whitman, the American poet increasingly became a figure of the counterculture. Finally, with "Song of Myself," Whitman created the model for the modern long poem as a lyric exploration of self and culture, as distinct from the long poem as narrative.

Early Responses

From the very beginning Whitman's work elicited both high praise and condemnation. While Ralph Waldo Emerson famously recognized the first edition of *Leaves of Grass* as "the most extraordinary piece of wit and wisdom that America has yet contributed" (Perlman et al. 1998: 79), other writers were far less charitable. Rufus W. Griswold called it "a mass of stupid filth" (Loving 1999: 184). Charles Eliot Norton expressed more general confusion towards the book, calling it "this gross yet elevated, this superficial yet profound, this preposterous yet somehow fascinating book" (Miller 1969: 3). Some critics weren't even sure if it should be called poetry.

Thirty years later, as Whitman approached death, people still weren't sure what to make of *Leaves of Grass*. But though he liked to play up the idea that he was neglected, Whitman had already become well known in America. In 1886, when Whitman's English admirers, led by William Michael Rossetti, raised nearly a thousand dollars for him because they believed that America had left its great poet living in squalor, none other than Andrew Carnegie thundered, "I felt triumphant democracy disgraced. Whitman is the greatest poet of America so far" (quoted in Reynolds 1995: 557). Carnegie soon followed with his own donations. And Whitman's 1887 lecture on Abraham Lincoln attracted many famous Americans, including Mark Twain, John Hay, the author Edward Eggleston, and sculptor Augustus Saint-Gaudens (Loving 1999: 450–1).

Despite his general fame, though, Whitman's reputation rested largely in the hands of a passionate group of disciples in America, including John Burroughs and William Douglas O'Connor. Burroughs's *Notes on Walt Whitman* (1867) was the first book-length study of the poet (though Whitman revised and rewrote large sections of it), while O'Connor wrote *The Good Gray Poet: A Vindication* (1866), a defense of Whitman after Secretary James W. Harlan fired Whitman from his job at the Department of the Interior because he found *Leaves of Grass* immoral. O'Connor's pamphlet emphasized Whitman's morality and moderation. With the phrase "the good gray poet," O'Connor had struck upon a formula to make Whitman acceptable to middle-class Victorian culture, at least much more so than the poet's own image of himself as "hankering, gross, mystical, nude" (*LG*: 47). O'Connor's later writings on Whitman, though, would portray Whitman in Christ-like terms, and link his poetry firmly to progressive politics (this despite the fact that the two men's friendship eventually broke up over Whitman's refusal to support the Fifteenth Amendment, which gave black men the right to vote). In doing so, O'Connor established an approach to Whitman that would dominate Whitman's reception for the next 40 years, until the arrival of the modernists.

When he moved to Camden in 1873, Whitman's group of disciples expanded, as he met Horace Traubel, Thomas Harned, and Richard Maurice Bucke. These last three Whitman named his literary executors, and perhaps no writer has ever been more energetically served by his or her executors. Traubel, Harned, and Bucke worked tirelessly to get Whitman's own writings into print, but even more so they published their own memoirs. Most famous is Traubel's nine-volume *With Walt Whitman in Camden*, in which he records his almost nightly conversations with the poet from 1888 to 1892. But these "hot little prophets," as Bliss Perry called them (Perry 1906: 286), didn't simply promote Whitman; they promoted a vision of Whitman that would become one of the most vibrant strands of his legacy. Traubel especially, but also Bucke and, to a lesser degree, Harned, presented Whitman as a semidivine prophet of socialism. Though during his life Whitman somewhat resisted both the effort to enlist him in socialism and to beatify him, after the poet's death Traubel worked nearly full-time to recast Whitman as an unambiguous political radical, while Bucke, in his book *Cosmic Consciousness* (1901), portrayed Whitman as the ultimate example of humanity's moral and spiritual evolution.

The work of these writers securely established Whitman as the prophet – and at times, the messiah – of the American left. Figures as prominent as American socialist leader Eugene Debs and anarchist and labor activist Emma Goldman read Whitman avidly. Goldman joined Traubel in helping promote Whitman by regularly delivering lectures on the poet, and Debs pronounced Whitman's idea of fraternity as "the quintessence of human kinship: Born of freedom, consecrated in brotherhood and expressed in love" (quoted in Garman 2000: 56–7).

As in the United States, Whitman came to be seen by many British writers as a prophet of liberal democracy. In 1868, William M. Rossetti published an expurgated edition of *Leaves of Grass*, the first edition published in England. There soon arose a group of writers and intellectuals whose Whitmania rivaled that of Burroughs, O'Connor, and Whitman's Camden associates. In 1871, Algernon Charles Swinburne published an effusive poem, "To Walt Whitman in America." A number of respected writers and critics, such as George Saintsbury, the Shakespearian scholar Edward Dowden, and the writer Robert Louis Stevenson became admirers of Whitman. But Whitman also drew the attention of an emerging community of homosexual writers, which included Edward Carpenter, Oscar Wilde, and John Addington Symonds. Carpenter and Wilde both visited Whitman in Camden, with Wilde writing Whitman that "there is no one in this wide great world of America whom I love and honor so much" (quoted in Loving 1999: 412). But it was Symonds who took the bull by the horns, so to speak, and asked Whitman directly in a letter whether the "adhesive" relationships between men celebrated in the Calamus poems included sex. Whitman's panicked denial probably reveals more about the differences between the British and American homosexual communities than about Whitman's own sexual preferences. But by the turn of the century, in both Great Britain and the United States, Whitman was well known as a radical prophet of socialism and sexual liberation.

As well known as Whitman was, though, few poets, other than imitators such as Traubel, took Whitman seriously as a poet. One curious feature of Whitman's early reception is that in the English-speaking world he was praised for his ideas more than his art. It was in France, where he had to appear in translation, that Whitman's poetics first had a major influence on a group of poets: the Symbolists.

Though the first French commentaries on Whitman were negative, they included enough lines in translation to give readers a taste of Whitman's poetry. In 1886, though, symbolist poet Jules Laforgue published translations of several poems. It was over the next few years that writers such as Laforgue, Arthur Rimbaud, Edouard Dujardin, and Francis Vielé-Griffin developed *vers libre* as a clear, intentional prosody. And Vielé-Griffin, who Dujardin credits with writing the first book of *vers libre*, *Joies*, in 1889, was born in America and able to read Whitman in English (see Erkkila 1980: 91–2). The writing of these French poets would, in turn, have a major influence on the English-language high modernist poets, including Ezra Pound, T. S. Eliot, and Wallace Stevens, though Eliot and others would strongly deny Whitman's role in the development of *vers libre* (Erkkila 1980: 231–7).

But Whitman did not long remain an artistic inspiration in France. As the influence of the Symbolists waned in the opening decade of the twentieth century, the French version of Whitman came to resemble that in America and Great Britain and elsewhere in Europe: Whitman the social reformer. In 1908, Léon Bazalgette transformed Whitman from the object of intellectual interest to a widely popular phenomenon in France by publishing the first complete French translation of *Leaves of Grass* and a biography of the poet. However, Bazalgette's Whitman was, like that of Bucke, a mystical figure and a prophet (see Allen and Folsom 1995: 237). Thus by 1910, in the United States, England, and France, Walt Whitman had become a figure of considerable importance in the iconography of left-wing politics, but as a poetic innovator, he was largely ignored. Perhaps at no other point in the history of Whitman's reception was there such a sharp divergence between Whitman's sociopolitical and his poetic influence.

Whitman in the Modernist Era

By the beginning of the twentieth century, Walt Whitman had begun to exert a profound influence on a wide variety of arts. In 1888, Vincent van Gogh proclaimed in a letter, "He sees in the future, and even in the present, a world of healthy, carnal love, strong and frank – of friendship – of work – under the great starlit vault of heaven a something which after all one can only call God – and eternity in its place above this world" (quoted in Miller 1969: 95). Thomas Eakins, perhaps the most important American realist painter, was a great admirer of Whitman, and Eakins' own interest in celebrating the human body through detailed, realistic portrayals was, if not influenced by *Leaves of Grass*, in great sympathy with it. In 1887, Eakins painted Whitman's portrait (which now hangs in the National Portrait Gallery in Washington, DC), and may have photographed Whitman in the nude as part of his photographic study of the human body. Through Eakins, Whitman's influence spread through a number of American painters, including Robert Henri, who met Whitman when he studied in Philadelphia in the late 1880s, and who would later go on to teach such notable American artists as Edward Hopper, Rockwell Kent, and George

Bellows. And composers such as Gustav Holst, Frederick Delius, and Ralph Vaughan Williams had already begun the rich tradition of setting Whitman's poetry to music, a tradition that would go on to include Charles Ives, Paul Hindemith, and Kurt Weill. But one of the most explicit examples of Whitman influencing an artist in another medium is that of Isadora Duncan, the creator of modern dance, who called Whitman one of her "dance masters" (quoted in Bohan 1995: 166). Like other modernists, Duncan found in Whitman freedom from the formal constraints of classical art (in her case, ballet), the possibility of finding inspiration in all aspects of life, and perhaps most importantly, a celebration of the body and sexuality. As Ruth L. Bohan explains, "like Whitman's poetic tribute to the body, Duncan's dance celebrated the beauty, physicality, and mystery of the human form while forcefully rejecting prurient Victorian attitudes toward morality and sexuality" (1995: 176).

Fiction writers of late realism and early modernism responded enthusiastically to Whitman. This was especially true of American women writers, including Willa Cather, who borrowed the title of her novel *O Pioneers!* from a Whitman poem; Kate Chopin, whose portrait of the sexual and artistic awakening and subsequent suicide of a young New Orleans housewife in *The Awakening* is heavily indebted to the novelist's reading of Whitman; and Edith Wharton, whose own life featured many of the tensions Chopin wrote about, and which Wharton would explore in her fiction, particularly in the character of Lily in *The House of Mirth* (see Price 2004: 37–55). In Europe, fiction writers such as E. M. Forster (who, like Cather, named a novel – *A Passage to India* – after one of Whitman's poems), D. H. Lawrence, André Gide, and Thomas Mann read Whitman attentively, seeing him, as Duncan had, as an example of an artist who had glimpsed a new relationship between the self, the body, and the world.

Up through the first decade of the twentieth century, though Whitman's ideas had had an effect, few poets had been shaped by his poetics. Then in 1913, Ezra Pound published a short but audacious poem that mentioned Walt Whitman. "A Pact" consists of only nine lines, which hardly compares to the hundreds of pages to which his *Cantos* would stretch. But arguably, this poem is of equal importance in American literary history, since it marked a new development in Whitman's influence on American literature. When Ezra Pound declared, in "A Pact," "It was you that broke the new wood" (Perlman et al. 1998: 111), he became the first major American poet to acknowledge Whitman's aesthetic importance.

The early high modernists represent a vital moment in the history of American poetry and Whitman's place in it. Every major poet of this generation was shaped by Whitman, whether overtly, as in the cases of Pound, Hart Crane, and William Carlos Williams, or covertly, as in the case of Eliot (Miller 1979). Though it may not have been clear at the time, the variety of responses by these major poets firmly established Walt Whitman as the central figure in American poetry.

Whitman, however, made many of the high modernists anxious. Whitman's progressive politics – and the early twentieth-century Whitman seemed much more solidly socialist than he does today, thanks largely to the efforts of Traubel – made him seem dangerous to writers on the political right such as Pound, T. S. Eliot, D. H. Lawrence, and Amy Lowell. And so they tried mightily to drive a wedge between the poet's aesthetic and his content. Eliot, for example, makes a distinction between Whitman the artist and Whitman the thinker, making clear he favors the former: "When Whitman speaks of lilacs or of the mockingbird, his theories and beliefs drop away like a needless pretext" (Perlman et al. 1998: 153). And his "barbaric yawp" vexed these poets who were frustrated by America's lack of high culture. Further, none of the American early high modernists – Pound, Eliot, Lowell, Crane, or Williams – would acknowledge Whitman's sexuality or the importance of sex in any large measure in their poetry. And so Pound's poem both acknowledges and limits Whitman's influence. He describes Whitman as a destructive force, not a creative one; his Whitman didn't grow or season the new wood, he just broke it. So Pound declares, "Now is a time for carving" (Perlman et al. 1998: 111), and sees himself as just the poet to do the carving, the craftsmanship. Though the poem acknowledges Whitman's importance, in effect Pound is declaring himself to be, as Eliot would call him, the better craftsman.

Few poets in American literature seem more antithetical to Whitman than T. S. Eliot. Where hope in humanity underlies Whitman's poetry and poetics, despair of humanity underlies Eliot's. After all, Eliot's favorite mid-nineteenth-century book of poems was *Les Fleurs du mal*, not *Leaves of Grass*. And the impersonalism of *The Waste Land*, with its horror of sexuality, seems like the anti-"Song of Myself." Not surprisingly, in his few comments on Whitman, Eliot worked hard to distance himself from the poet, declaring him "a great representative of America, but emphatically of an America which no longer exists" (Perlman et al. 1998: 153). But as James E. Miller, Jr has shown, Eliot's often implausible denials of Whitman's influence on himself and other high modernists may stem from Eliot's own anxiety about influence, from his desire to hide from the fact that *The Waste Land*, underneath its impersonal exterior, is a very personal poem of companionship, love, and loss. Miller observes that many of the passages Eliot cut from the original draft – on Pound's advice – reveal the poem to be a poem of personal crisis: "a poem much closer in form to such poems of Whitman's *Leaves of Grass* as 'Out of the Cradle Endlessly Rocking' or 'When Lilacs Last in the Dooryard Bloom'd,' poems in which biography had been transfigured into poetic drama" (Miller 1979: 122).

Two American high modernists, however, did openly embrace Whitman. Whitman's example was central to the work of both Hart Crane and William Carlos Williams, though in most ways these two poets couldn't be more different. Crane is largely a formalist, writing in the meters of the British Romantics, while Williams is one of the most original innovators in free verse. And both came to Whitman for different things. While both valued Whitman's attachment to the local, to the American scene, for Crane, Whitman was the visionary mystic, uniting the multitudes, while for Williams, he was the poetic rebel with a journalist's eye.

Crane's long poem *The Bridge* was written out of a number of concerns, one of which was the desire to respond to *The Waste Land* with something more affirming.

Though Crane was interested in Whitman for reasons of content, he differed starkly from the left's political interest in Whitman. Crane's Whitman was akin to the semidivine Whitman of Richard Bucke. The goal of *The Bridge* is to figure out a way to reattach the new world to the archetypal patterns of the old, from which modern society had seemingly broken. Whitman figures significantly in Crane's imagination as a someone who was able to link these diverse elements together.

William Carlos Williams's conception of the poet as "just another dog / among a lot of dogs" in *Paterson* is a long way from Crane's visionary protagonist in *The Bridge*. Like Crane, Williams wrote much of his mature verse as an American response to the Europeanized poetry of Eliot and Pound. But unlike Crane, Williams drew from Whitman a love of the local and the particular, which he combined with an openness to Whitman's aesthetic innovations. He saw in Whitman's new line the authentic, original American aesthetic, grounded in the American soil, an idea that would be central to Williams's poetics and his own identity as a poet.

By reconnecting Whitman's attention to specific, local details to his abandonment of traditional metrics, Williams inaugurated what may be the most prevalent way that Whitman influenced American poets in the second half of the twentieth century. Between the 1950s and today, poets such as Galway Kinnell, A. R. Ammons, and Gary Snyder produced a body of poetry that combined the Whitmanian line with a close attention to the natural world, indeed that saw that line as a product of that world.

The modernist suspicions of Pound, Eliot, Lowell, Allen Tate, and Yvor Winters, however, seem to have been largely an American phenomenon. European modernists, such as Fernando Pessoa of Portugal, Federico Garcia Lorca of Spain, André Gide of France, and D. H. Lawrence of England read Whitman enthusiastically and closely. More interestingly, though the American modernists tended to downplay Whitman's focus on sexuality and the body, many European modernists found this one of the most energizing aspects of Whitman.

D. H. Lawrence may be the only major English writer whose work clearly bears the marks of Whitman's influence. The long lines of his poetry and the emphasis on sexuality in his writings are only the two most obvious signs of Whitman's influence. Lawrence exulted in Whitman because he provided "a great new doctrine. A doctrine of life. A new great morality. A morality of actual living, not of salvation" (Lawrence [1923] 2003: 157). For Lawrence, Whitman was great because he rejected the superiority of the soul over the body, and celebrated the body and life. But Lawrence could accept this version of Whitman only by jettisoning the sympathy and empathy for others in Whitman's poetry.

One of the most fascinating responses to the work of Walt Whitman is that of Fernando Pessoa, the great Portuguese modernist, who wrote poetry in different "heteronyms" or voices. Pessoa literally enacts Whitman's claim to "contain multitudes," creating over 70 heteronyms who were distinct identities with not just names, but lives. For Pessoa, the various voices were a way around the stifling subjectivity of the late Victorian world, just as T. S. Eliot's monologues were for him. And this body of work, one of the high points of literary modernism, originated in Pessoa's encounters with Whitman and *Leaves of Grass* (see Allen and Folsom 1995: 147–59).

The modernist anxieties about Whitman would have a large impact on his scholarly reception through much of the twentieth century. Though the high modernists absorbed Whitman's formal innovations, they strongly rejected his faith in democracy and his belief in the mass, and, in the case of the Americans, ignored his sexuality and his focus on the body. As such, they were able to cut him off from his subject matter, to depoliticize his poetry. It wasn't until historical scholarship of the 1980s that Whitman's sexual and political themes became a major, if not primary, concern of Whitman scholars.

The high modernist and scholarly neglect of Whitman's political and sexual themes, however, did not prevent Whitman from figuring largely in American literature and culture during the first half of the twentieth century. Though conservative writers held Whitman at arm's length, the political and cultural left embraced him. The enthusiasm of leftists such as Eugene Debs and Emma Goldman was carried on through the 1930s. During the Depression, Whitman's profile on the political left was raised even higher as Communist writers such as Mike Gold, Granville Hicks, and Clifford Odets celebrated him as an example of the working-class hero (Garman 2000: 61–2). Gold's work in particular is interesting in the way its playful frustration anticipates Allen Ginsberg's voice in "Howl."

Whitman as "Father Walt," the spirit of the American worker, was not confined to poets. Painters also regularly invoked Whitman's image during these years. Perhaps most famous is the 1938 Bronx General Post Office mural of Ben Shahn and Bernarda Bryson Shahn, which features a bearded Whitman, before a crowd of workers, pointing to lines from his 1860 poem "Chants Democratic" (see Price 2004: 77–85).

Lewis C. Daniel's illustrations for the Doubleday, Doran & Company's 1940 edition of *Leaves of Grass*, however, which features singing, muscular workers engaged in all sorts of labors, including building the Hoover Dam, though it shares many stylistic features with the Shahns's mural, was hardly part of the radical left. Beautifully bound in rough green cloth and packaged in a green slip case, this was a book manufactured to be displayed in the bookshelf in a comfortable family home. As such, this widely popular edition illustrates Whitman's prominence and popularity among the American middle class. But this Whitman was not the radical Whitman of Mike Gold or the sensualist of D. H. Lawrence. Rather, this was the nationalist Whitman, the Whitman of the populist poets – Carl Sandburg, Edgar Lee Masters, and Stephen Vincent Benét – who wrote what is possibly the last burst of widely popular poetry in America.

Of all Whitman's poetic descendants, Carl Sandburg wrote poetry that most clearly looked like Whitman's. When his poem "Chicago" was published in *Poetry* in 1914, it seemed that Whitman had been resurrected in the Midwest. The poetry contained many of the formal features of Whitman's poetry: the long lines, the rhetorical addresses, the expansive voice, the focus on work, the ability to find beauty in the gritty corners of life. In addition to these formal similarities, Sandburg's life often paralleled Whitman's. Like Whitman, Sandburg worked at a variety of jobs, finally settling on journalism, before he reached maturity as a poet, which happened, as with Whitman, in his mid-thirties. But like many of the American writers of this era, Sandburg's poetry overlooked the importance of the body and sexuality. And Sandburg's close imitation of Whitman's style surely goes against Whitman's own injunction in "Song of Myself," "He most honors my style who learns under it to destroy the teacher" (*LG*: 84). Though Sandburg's poetry reflects the profound influence of Walt Whitman, his vision ultimately stems more from Midwestern populism than from Whitman.

Stephen Vincent Benét, perhaps the most popular American poet between the wars, occupies an odd position in the pantheon of Whitman's poetic heirs. Though not a strict populist, he is often included with the populists because of his nationalism and his popularity. Though his early poetry was formally conservative, his later, overtly political works, poems such as "Litany for Dictatorships," "Ode to Austrian Socialists," and "Ode to Walt Whitman," employ the long line and oratorical parallelisms of *Leaves of Grass*. Even his early formalist work, though, reflects some of the themes and content of Whitman's poetry. What Benét shared most with Whitman is a vision of the nation as a sacred union, forged in the melding of rugged individuals (usually men) and American landscape and history, a Whitman-derived vision that would make Benét the unofficial poet laureate of the New Deal. The central topic of Benét's poetry was, of course, the central event of Walt Whitman's life: the Civil War. And Benét's attitude toward the war in his epic poem *John Brown's Body* strongly resembles Whitman's in his post-Civil War literature, especially *Memoranda During the War*.

In some respects, this populist tradition is a poetic dead end. Few American poets today have extended the tradition of Sandburg, Masters, and Benét. In part this is due to aesthetic reasons, but it also reflects the inability or unwillingness of American poets today to speak for middle-class American culture. Sandburg and Lindsay embodied the idea of the poet as singer, as Whitman suggests in many of his poems. Sandburg, especially, helped launch the folk-song revival of the 1950s and 1960s, a tradition in which, as Bryan K. Garman argues in *A Race of Singers*, Whitman's vision of the working-class hero lives on through the music of Woody Guthrie, Pete Seeger, Bob Dylan, and Bruce Springsteen. And though Benét's poetry has had little impact on American poets, his blend of lyricism, American history and folk culture, and the American landscape, lives on especially in American film, most notably in the work of Ken Burns, who features Whitman in many of his films, including *The Civil War*, *Baseball*, and *The Brooklyn Bridge*.

Post-World War II Era: 1940–2004

In the years just after World War II, the world's sense of Whitman began to change once more. In the later half of the twentieth century, Whitman would become still more an international poet, at the same time that he became more firmly the

American poet. The world, of course, had changed dramatically between the late 1930s and the mid-1940s. Whitman's America had gone from the throes of depression to the heights of world supremacy. But that new status proved a poor counterfeit of Whitman's dreams of America as "the greatest poem" (*LG*: 709). Over and over during the postwar years, poets would remark on the failure of America to live up to Whitman's vision. Allen Ginsberg, in "A Supermarket in California," would lament an America that now wandered the grocery store aisles instead of the open road, and Louis Simpson would complain, "The Open Road goes to the used-car lot" (Perlman et al. 1998: 272).

But Whitman himself had changed too. A series of biographies, beginning with Newton Arvin's *Walt Whitman* (1938) and ending with Henry Seidel Canby's *Walt Whitman: An American* (1943), along with the Whitman scholarship that accompanied the first flowering of American studies in the 1930s and 1940s, including F. O. Matthiessen's *The American Renaissance* (1941), began to solidify the image of the man Walt Whitman. This image would become even more solid with the appearance of two excellent scholarly biographies in the 1950s, Roger Asselineau's *L'Évolution de Walt Whitman* (1954, published in English in 1960 and 1962), and Gay Wilson Allen's *The Solitary Singer: A Critical Biography of Walt Whitman* (1955), Allen's having been inspired by a Danish biography of Whitman written by Frederik Schyberg.

These factors illuminate two productive tensions that would shape Whitman's legacy in the second half of the 1900s. The first is between a nationalist and a global Whitman, and the second between the historic Whitman of the scholars and the imaginative Whitman of the artist and the reader. Whitman had always had a vibrant international readership, and this readership mushroomed in the post-World War II era, to the point that by 1995, Whitman's poetry had been translated into at least 32 languages (Allen and Folsom 1995: 437–66). At the same time, the tendency of Cold War American Studies to view America as an exceptional nation invested heavily in the idea of Whitman as a nationalist poet. R. W. B. Lewis, for example, in his book *The American Adam*, declares, "The fullest portrayal of the new world's representative man as a new, American Adam was given by Walt Whitman in *Leaves of Grass*" (Lewis 1955: 28). Chilean poet Pablo Neruda would confront this tension by proclaiming, in his "Ode to Walt Whitman," "you taught me / to be an American" (Perlman et al. 1998: 225), defining "America" in hemispheric terms rather than national ones. Neruda imagined Whitman as a truly global figure, one whose people

> walk among the peoples with your love
> caressing
> the pure development
> of brotherhood on earth.
> (Perlman et al. 1998: 229)

Neruda's conception of Whitman, though, was in many senses a throwback to earlier leftist visions of Whitman. Neruda, a Communist, shared the vision of Mike Gold and Ben Shahn of Whitman as leader who would inspire and lead the people to revolution. These Whitmans may lead or represent the people, but they are not intimate with people. Other writers, however, began to see Whitman more in terms of a transforming spirit, one that enters directly into an intimate relationship with the reader. Three writers working in the late 1940s – Langston Hughes, Jorge Luis Borges, and Muriel Rukeyser – present early versions of this new Whitman.

Walt Whitman's poetry had been fundamentally involved in the development of African American literature since shortly after his death. As George B. Hutchinson has shown, writers such as Alain Locke, James Weldon Johnson, and Jean Toomer, as well as Langston Hughes, all cite Whitman as a major influence on their own writing. Locke's connection was direct; he lived his high school years (1898–1900) just a block from Whitman's house in Camden, and his mother was involved in many of the same political groups as Horace Traubel (Hutchinson 1994: 202). More so than any other group writing during the modernist era, these Harlem Renaissance writers were able to digest Whitman's attitude toward politics, the body, and sexuality, as well as his aesthetic. Aesthetically, Whitman's use of the American vernacular provided them with an alternative to Paul Laurence Dunbar's dialect poetry, and both Johnson and Hughes wrote early poetry in the Whitmanian style, including Hughes's famous poem "The Negro Speaks of Rivers," before they turned to African American culture for their sources. So we can see Whitman's legacy in Johnson's use of the African American sermon in *God's Trombones: Seven Negro Sermons in Verse* (1927) and Hughes's use of jazz and the blues in *Weary Blues* (1926) and *Fine Clothes for the Jew* (1927).

Throughout his career, Hughes promoted Whitman's work, editing three collections of his poetry and including some of Whitman's poems in his anthology *The Poetry of the Negro*. And in 1953, writing in *The Chicago Defender*, he called Whitman "the Lincoln of our Letters," and consistently urged African Americans to read his poetry (Hutchinson 1992: 17). Because Hughes did not partition off the political from the physical or the aesthetic in Whitman, it's not surprising to find him offering a version of Whitman that differed markedly from that of the other modernist poets. In his 1946 essay "The Ceaseless Rings of Walt Whitman," Hughes praised Whitman as a spiritual shape shifter, able to transcend his own physical and historical limitations in order to sympathize with all oppressed people. Hughes locates the germ of this in Whitman's friendship with young black children in his own childhood:

> There had been a half-dozen or so slaves on the ancestral Whitman farm, and young Walt had played with them as a child. Perhaps that is where he acquired his sympathy for the Negro people, and his early belief that all men should be free – a belief that grew to embrace the peoples of the whole world, expressed over and over throughout his poems, encompassing not only America but the colonial peoples, the serfs of tsarist Russia, the suppressed classes everywhere. His spiritual self roamed the earth wherever the winds of freedom blow however faintly, keeping company with the foiled revolutionaries of Europe or the suppressed coolies of Asia. (Perlman et al. 1998: 186)

Where Hughes's Whitman differs from earlier radical invocations is that Whitman here transcends his own body. He doesn't simply exist as an example or teacher for the oppressed; he becomes their animating spirit: "Whitman's 'I' is not the 'I' of the introspective versifiers who write always and only about themselves. Rather it is the cosmic 'I' of all peoples who seek freedom, decency, and dignity, friendship and equality between individuals and races all over the world" (Perlman et al. 1998: 187). If Crane, Lorca, and Benét imagined the spirit of Whitman as a kind of Christ figure, redeeming what is lost, Hughes here imagines him as the Holy Ghost. Jorge Luis Borges, writing from Buenos Aires in 1947, conceives Whitman similarly when he argues that the poet is important because he created Whitman the character, who Borges describes as "the semidivine hero of *Leaves of Grass*, as Don Quixote is the hero of the *Quixote*" (Perlman et al. 1998: 236). This character Whitman is "the eternal Whitman," who "derives a personal relationship with each future reader" (p. 239).

In 1949, Muriel Rukeyser published a remarkable essay on Whitman: "Whitman and the Problem of the Good," in which, like Hughes and Borges, she rejects any attempt to create a unitary Whitman, and grounds her approach to Whitman in the poet's own multitudinous sense of self. She found, in the report of Whitman's autopsy, physical evidence of the poet's sexual ambiguity, which she believed resulted in the inclusive persona of *Leaves of Grass* (Perlman et al. 1998: 194). Whatever the factual implications of Whitman's autopsy, Rukeyser not only highlighted the difference between the physical person Walt Whitman and his identities, in a sense setting Whitman free from the confines of himself, she also grounded that multiplicity in Whitman's sexuality. Rukeyser here signals one of the most important differences between early and late twentieth-century views of Whitman: as the twentieth century progressed, there would be an increasing recognition that Whitman's sexuality was central to his vision of unity and his sympathy with others.

The first group of writers to embody this new Whitman in their poetry was the Beats, and they did so in a way that would permanently alter American poetry. The Beat poets' celebration of individualism, direct democracy, literary experimentalism, and sexual freedom has direct roots in Walt Whitman. Like the Harlem Renaissance writers, the Beats, including Allen Ginsberg, Gregory Corso, LeRoi Jones/Amiri Baraka, Gary Snyder, and others, did not attempt to divide Whitman's politics, sexuality, and aesthetics. When "Howl" first appeared in 1955, the parallels between Ginsberg and Whitman were unmistakable. The poem's long lines, use of parallelisms and catalogues, the speaker's prophetic authority, his compassion for the oppressed, his frank sexuality, all these marked the poet as one deeply shaped by *Leaves of Grass*. And as with Whitman, the writings of Ginsberg and the other Beats elicited disdain and confusion from the majority of establishment critics. Their impact on contemporary poetry, however, was unmistakable. Robert Lowell, for instance, credited Ginsberg's "Howl" for the dramatic changes in his own poetry between *Mills of the Kavanaughs* and *Life Studies*. One of the shocking elements of Ginsberg's poetry was its personalism. Poems such as "Howl" and "Kaddish" are songs of himself, and like Whitman, Ginsberg understood that sexuality was fundamental to the self. This personalism would become a fundamental feature of late twentieth-century poetry. In reacting to the impersonalism of high modernism, poets such as John Berryman, Galway Kinnell, Frank O'Hara, Adrienne Rich, Audre Lorde, and many, many others, invested themselves in their writing in a way that is unmistakably Whitmanian.

The Beats and other advocates of open form continued to gain currency through the 1960s, especially as the anger over the Vietnam War and the civil rights movements burgeoned, and American poets found it increasingly difficult to remain silent in the face of what many saw as injustice done in the name of America. For many of the poet activists of the 1960s, including Robert Bly, Ted Berrigan, Adrienne Rich, Whitman's vision of America as "the race of races" (*LG*: 711) rather than the nation-state inspired their opposition to the war. And over the last decades of the twentieth century, Whitman would continue to serve as an inspiration to the civil rights movements that grew, in part, out of the 1960s, including movements for women's rights, multiculturalism, homosexual rights, and the environment.

By the 1970s, it seems safe to say, Walt Whitman was fully integrated into American poetry. While there may still be important poets who don't display a deep engagement with Whitman – poets such as Elizabeth Bishop, Richard Wilbur, or Timothy Steele, for example – no poet would seriously reject Whitman as a major force, in the way Eliot and Amy Lowell did. Of course, by this time Whitman's poetic and cultural genes had become widespread, turning up both in places expected and unexpected.

In addition to politically oriented poets such as Rich, Bly, and Ginsberg, Whitman continued to exert a profound influence on more aesthetic American poets. In his book *Discovering Ourselves in Whitman*, Thomas Gardner (1989) extends James E. Miller, Jr.'s exploration of Whitman's influence on the twentieth-century long poem (see Miller 1979) to the works of such diverse poets as John Berryman, Galway Kinnell, Theodore Roethke, Robert Duncan, John Ashbery, and James Merrill. And while June Jordan and others continue to explore "the word Democratic, the word En-Masse" (*LG*: 1), other poets carry on Whitman's investigation of "the Me myself" (*LG*: 32), as Jorie Graham does in her 1993 book *Materialism*.

The 1980s and 1990s saw an explosion of excellent scholarship on Whitman, as the academy caught up with the poets in recognizing Whitman's centrality to American literature and culture. At the same time, Whitman continued to maintain a vibrant, rambunctious existence in American culture at large. He appeared to the American public at large at uncomfortable moments. Susan Sarandon reads "I Sing the Body Electric" to an almost naked, tied-up Tim Robbins in the 1988 movie *Bull Durham*. And in the 1989 movie *Dead Poet's Society*, Whitman inspires a schoolboy's awakening and suicide in a way reminiscent of Edna Pontellier in Kate Chopin's *The Awakening*. (Kenneth M. Price discusses the long history of Whitman in film in *To Walt Whitman, America*, 2004: 108–38.) And the appearance of an openly gay Whitman on NBC's popular drama *Dr. Quinn, Medicine Woman* (1998) sparked outrage from many viewers. More seriously, perhaps, Whitman played a role in the Clinton/Lewinsky scandal, as a copy of *Leaves of Grass* was one of the gifts President Clinton gave to Monica Lewinsky (whose critical comments on the book are preserved in Ken Starr's report). George W. Bush's administration also ran afoul of Whitman when First Lady Laura Bush's attempt to host a White House celebration of American poetry, featuring Whitman, became an occasion for many American poets to signal their opposition to the war in Iraq. War, sex, love, beauty, race, the body, America. The People. The individual. These were Whitman's themes, and complexities, ambivalences, and urgencies that surround his attitude towards them often still inspire and worry us today, which would probably please him immensely. As he said himself:

> I teach straying from me, yet who can stray from me?
> I follow you whoever you are from the present hour,
> My words itch at your ears till you understand them.
> (*LG*: 85)

Note

1 Whenever possible, I have quoted from anthologies about Whitman – including *Walt Whitman: The Measure of His Song,* edited by Jim Perlman, Ed Folsom, and Dan Campion – rather than the standard scholarly editions of the works of individual writers.

References and Further Reading

Allen, Gay Wilson and Folsom, Ed (eds.) (1995). *Walt Whitman & the World.* Iowa City: University of Iowa Press.

Bohan, Ruth L. (1995). "I Sing the Body Electric": Isadora Duncan, Whitman, and the Dance. In Ezra Greenspan (ed.), *The Cambridge Companion to Walt Whitman.* New York: Cambridge University Press, pp. 166–93.

Cherkovski, Neeli (1999). *Whitman's Wild Children: Portraits of Twelve Poets.* Royalton, VT: Steerforth Press.

Coghill, Sheila and Tammaro, Thom (eds.) (2003). *Visiting Walt: Poems Inspired by the Life and Work of Walt Whitman.* Iowa City: University of Iowa Press.

Erkkila, Betsy (1980). *Walt Whitman Among the French: Poet and Myth.* Princeton, NJ: Princeton University Press.

Erkkila, Betsy and Grossman, Jay (eds.) (1996). *Breaking Bounds: Whitman & American Cultural Studies.* New York: Oxford University Press.

Folsom, Ed (1998). Talking Back to Walt Whitman: An Introduction. In Jim Perlman, Ed Folsom, and Dan Campion (eds.), *Walt Whitman: The Measure of His Song.* Duluth, MN: Holy Cow! Press, pp. 21–74.

Gardner, Thomas (1989). *Discovering Ourselves in Whitman: The Contemporary American Long Poem.* Urbana: University of Illinois Press.

Garman, Bryan K. (2000). *A Race of Singers: Whitman's Working-Class Hero from Guthrie to Springsteen.* Chapel Hill: University of North Carolina Press.

Grünzweig, Walter (1995). *Constructing the German Walt Whitman.* Iowa City: University of Iowa Press.

Hutchinson, George B. (1992). Langston Hughes and the "Other" Whitman. In Robert K. Martin (ed.), *The Continuing Presence of Walt Whitman: The Life After the Life.* Iowa City: University of Iowa Press, pp. 16–27.

Hutchinson, George B. (1994). The Whitman Legacy and the Harlem Renaissance. In Ed Folsom (ed.), *Walt Whitman: The Centennial Essays.* Iowa City: University of Iowa Press, pp. 201–16.

Katz, Wendy R. (2004). Untying the Immigrant Tongue: Whitman and the "Americanization" of Anzia Yezierska. *Walt Whitman Quarterly Review*, 21 (3–4): 155–65.

Lawrence, D. H. ([1923] 2003). *Studies in Classic American Literature*, ed. Ezra Greenspan, Lindeth Vasey, and John Worthen. New York: Cambridge University Press.

LeMaster, J. R. and Kummings, Donald D. (eds.) (1998). *Walt Whitman: An Encyclopedia*. New York: Garland.

Lewis, R. W. B. (1955). *The American Adam: Innocence, Tragedy, and Tradition in the Nineteenth Century*. Chicago: University of Chicago Press.

Loving, Jerome (1999). *Walt Whitman: The Song of Himself*. Berkeley: University of California Press.

Lowell, Amy (1927). Walt Whitman and the New Poetry. *Yale Review*, 16: 502–19.

Martin, Robert K. (ed.) (1992). *The Continuing Presence of Walt Whitman: The Life After the Life*. Iowa City: University of Iowa Press.

Martin, Robert K. (1979). *The Homosexual Tradition in American Poetry*. Austin: University of Texas Press.

Miller, Edwin Haviland (ed.) (1969). *A Century of Whitman Criticism*. Bloomington: Indiana University Press.

Miller, James E., Jr. (1979). *The American Quest for a Supreme Fiction: Whitman's Legacy in the Personal Epic*. Chicago: University of Chicago Press.

Miller, James E., Jr., Shapiro, Karl, and Slote, Bernice (1960). *Start with the Sun: Studies in the Whitman Tradition*. Lincoln: University of Nebraska Press.

Perlman, Jim, Folsom, Ed, and Campion, Dan (eds.) (1998). *Walt Whitman: The Measure of His Song*. Duluth, MN: Holy Cow! Press.

Perry, Bliss (1906). *Walt Whitman*. Boston: Houghton Mifflin.

Price, Kenneth M. (1990). *Whitman and Tradition: The Poet in His Century*. New Haven: Yale University Press.

Price, Kenneth M. (2004). *To Walt Whitman, America*. Chapel Hill: University of North Carolina Press.

Reynolds, David S. (1995). *Walt Whitman's America: A Cultural Biography*. New York: Alfred A. Knopf.

Trachtenberg, Alan (1995). Walt Whitman: Precipitant of the Modern. In Ezra Greenspan (ed.), *The Cambridge Companion to Walt Whitman*. New York: Cambridge University Press, pp. 194–207.

Witemeyer, Hugh (1985). Clothing the American Adam: Pound's Tailoring of Walt Whitman. In George Bornstein (ed.), *Ezra Pound Among the Poets*. Chicago: University of Chicago Press, pp. 81–105.

PART IV
Texts

Works of Poetry

Inspired by a Samuel Hollyer engraving of a daguerreotype by Gabriel Harrison (1854). Tonal graphite drawing by Doug DeVinny.

27
The First (1855) Edition of *Leaves of Grass*

Edward Whitley

Throughout his nearly half-century career as a poet, Walt Whitman published numerous books of poetry, including such volumes as *Drum-Taps*, *Passage to India*, *As a Strong Bird on Pinions Free*, and *Leaves of Grass*. Today, readers associate Whitman almost exclusively with the last title in this list, largely because he eventually incorporated his other published works into the book of poems that has now become all but synonymous with his name. Before he died in 1892, Whitman compiled a comprehensive "deathbed" edition of *Leaves of Grass* that included his other various collections of poetry, indicating that this final edition of *Leaves of Grass* was the version of his life's work that he wanted preserved for posterity. Around the same time, however, Whitman wrote in a note to himself, "I do not suppose that I shall ever again have the *afflatus* I had in writing the first *Leaves of Grass*" (quoted in Bradley and Blodgett 1965: xxix, italics in original).

The original edition of *Leaves of Grass* published in 1855 differs in many ways from the 1892 edition that Whitman established as his poetic legacy. The deathbed version of *Leaves of Grass*, with its nearly four hundred poems meticulously parceled into discrete clusters, feels like a retrospective compilation designed to preserve every utterance that the poet ever made. (The reality, however, is quite different from the appearance: Whitman omitted numerous poems and sections of poems from the final edition of *Leaves of Grass* and left unpublished even more.) In contrast to the feeling of deliberate and labored attention that attends the deathbed *Leaves of Grass*, the 12 poems of the 1855 edition give an impression of spontaneity. The strong creative impulse that Whitman calls the "afflatus" he had when writing the first *Leaves of Grass* is evident in both the flow of the poetry and the appearance of the book itself.

The text of the 1855 *Leaves of Grass* is set in an unadorned typeface that David Reynolds calls a typographical "primitivism" (Reynolds 1995: 313). Similarly, the sentences are punctuated with irregular periods of ellipses, the poems are untitled, and there is no table of contents. As Justin Kaplan says, "[F]or a book so momentous, there was something casual, *ad hoc*, even accidental, about its first publication" (Kaplan 1980: 198). Taken together, however, these odd typographic features contribute to the feeling that the book's seemingly hasty production was done in an attempt to keep pace with the overwhelming force of the poet's inspiration. It is a paradox of the first edition of *Leaves of Grass* that the austere interior of the book gives the appearance of a rushed printing job while the elaborate and decorative exterior expresses exactly the opposite. The primary issue of the 1855 edition features an olive-green cloth cover stamped with images of leaves and vines that frame the gold-leaf lettering of the words in the title, "Leaves of Grass." The hand-designed font of the title itself is ornate and intricate as leaves grow out of the letters' ascenders and roots grow out of their descenders.

Despite the disparate interior and exterior designs of the 1855 *Leaves of Grass*, the idea of organic growth unites both elements of the book: the unrefined typeface of the text testifies to the spontaneous energy of Whitman's "afflatus" just as the nature imagery on the cover similarly represents the unfettered expression of his creativity. The same organicism that links the ornamental design of the cover with the intentionally unembellished design of the text also informs a principal message of the book, namely, that there is something unique and wonderful inside every human being that deserves to flourish and grow. The poems in the first edition of *Leaves of Grass* collectively make the argument that the essence of an individual's identity – what Whitman calls the "Me myself" (Whitman [1855] 1959: 28) – is a living organism whose growth and development should never be restricted. The value of this individual essence, Whitman audaciously claims, rivals anything else in existence: "And nothing," he writes, "not God, is greater to one than one's self is" (p. 82).

To a greater or lesser degree, each of the 12 poems of the collection reinforces this belief in the importance of the individual, whether it be the individual who wrote *Leaves of Grass*, the individual who reads it, or the individuals who make up the nation and world around it. The first poem of the collection, which would eventually be titled "Song of Myself," begins with the now-famous declaration, "I celebrate myself," and subsequently sings the praises of both the poet and those who share the world with him: "In the faces of men and women I see God, and in my own face in the glass" (Whitman [1855] 1959: 25, 83). The following 11 poems further develop the theme of the individual's absolute worth. In "A Song for Occupations" (the title, as for all the poems mentioned herein, comes from the final edition of *Leaves of Grass*), Whitman addresses as vast a readership as he can imagine and expresses his confidence in their infinite worth, writing, "The sum of all known value and respect I add up in you whoever you are" (p. 91).

Similarly, in "To Think of Time" Whitman encourages his reader to join him in the self-celebration that begins in "Song of Myself" – "Yourself! Yourself!," he cheers, "Yourself forever and ever!" (Whitman [1855] 1959: 102) – and in "The Sleepers" he finds beauty in a nighttime vision of the world at rest: "I swear they are all beautiful, / Every one that sleeps is beautiful. . . . every thing in the dim night is beautiful" (p. 113). "I Sing the Body Electric" and "Faces" also reveal a poet with a profound respect for both the physical and spiritual beauty of humanity. He says in "I Sing the Body

Electric" that "the human body is sacred," and in "Faces" he demonstrates a universal respect for human life, writing, "I except not one.... red white or black, all are deific" (pp. 122, 126). In "Song of the Answerer" Whitman says that there is more to a person than what appears on the surface ("A man is a summons and challenge," he writes, p. 130), just as in "There Was a Child Went Forth" he shows how the psychic imprint of a person's life experiences is only visible to those who fully appreciate the complexity of human life. The two poems of the collection that are most explicitly political, "Europe: The 72d and 73d Years of These States" and "A Boston Ballad," focus on individuals whose determination and resolve Whitman deems praiseworthy, whether it be the European revolutionaries of 1848 or the Boston abolitionists who opposed the Fugitive Slave Law in 1854. The final poems of the collection, "Who Learns My Lesson Complete" and "Great Are the Myths," reinforce the overall message of the book: "everyone is immortal," he writes in the former, and "Great are yourself and myself" in the latter (pp. 141, 142).

Whitman's desire to celebrate the infinite value of individuals is the source of one of the most distinctive elements of his poetry: the lengthy catalogues of people that fill the pages of *Leaves of Grass*. (Ivan Marki says that the poems of the 1855 edition are "dominated by catalogues," Marki 1982: 231.) In one section from "Song of Myself," for example, Whitman makes a list of close to 50 different people from various walks of life, all of whom he values for their distinctiveness and individuality:

> The pure contralto sings in the organloft,
> The carpenter dresses his plank.... the tongue of his foreplane whistles its wild ascending lisp,
> The married and unmarried children ride home to their thanksgiving dinner,
> The pilot seizes the king-pin, he heaves down with a strong arm,
> The mate stands braced in the whale-boat, lance and harpoon are ready,
> The duck-shooter walks by silent and cautions stretchers,
> The deacons are ordained with crossed hands at the altar,
> The spinning-girl retreats and advances to the hum of the big wheel.
> (Whitman [1855] 1959: 37)

In the Preface to the 1855 *Leaves of Grass* – the 10-page, manifesto-style document wherein Whitman situates his book in the history of American poetry and claims for himself the title of American bard – he says that it is "not consistent with the reality of the soul to admit that there is anything in the known universe more divine than men and women" (p. 15). He puts this theory into practice by focusing every line of his catalogues on a separate individual who comes within his purview, each of whom, he says in "Song of Myself," is "immortal and fathomless" (p. 31).

Towards the end of this long list of people from "Song of Myself," Whitman buries an important detail about the relationship between the publication history of the first *Leaves of Grass* and the book's emphasis on individual human worth. As he celebrates a group of common laborers who form part of his processional of "immortal and fathomless" individuals, he writes, "In single file each shouldering his hod pass onward the laborers; / Seasons pursuing each other the indescribable crowd is gathered . . . it is the Fourth of July . . . what salutes of cannon and small arms!" (Whitman [1855] 1959: 39). Up until this point in "Song of Myself," Whitman has not identified any specific setting for his poem. The individuals he praises seem to float freely through the world, unmoored from any concrete sense of time or space. In this passage, however, he turns an abstract mass of individuals into an actual crowd that has gathered together for an Independence Day celebration. Donald Pease has noted that "Whitman's poetry seems to take place against the backdrop of a national celebration" (Pease 1987: 113), but here Whitman's poem takes on more than just the appearance of a national celebration; instead, it specifically conjures up the scene of an American Fourth of July, complete with an assortment of national citizens who have come together to participate in the festivities of the day.

Whitman put the first edition of *Leaves of Grass* up for sale around July 4, 1855. By invoking the scene of an Independence Day celebration in "Song of Myself," Whitman succeeds in connecting the internal events of his poetry with the external circumstances of his book's publication. While there is some debate over whether the 1855 *Leaves of Grass* actually went on sale around the Fourth of July – Marki, for example, attributes the July Fourth publishing date to "pious tradition" (Marki 1976: ix) – there is substantial evidence to indicate that the book was on the market soon after the Fourth. Whitman registered *Leaves of Grass* for copyright as early as May 15, 1855, but the first advertisement for the book did not appear until July 6, 1855 (Allen 1956, White 1957). Bookstores would not have been open for business on the Fourth of July in 1855, which would have made it all but impossible for Whitman to make the symbolic gesture of releasing his self-proclaimed collection of American poetry on Independence Day. Nevertheless, going on sale in the days immediately following July Fourth insured that *Leaves of Grass* would share bookshelf space with other Independence Day-related material.

It was common practice in the antebellum United States for publishers to compile the speeches, toasts, poems, and songs from Fourth of July celebrations into books, pamphlets, and broadsides that were then sold as commemorative records of the year's festivities. Whitman, it appears, timed the release of his book to correspond with these other Independence Day publications. The fragmentary phrases and densely packed lines of the first *Leaves of Grass* would have resembled these piecemeal compilations of orations and occasional poetry. In particular, the unbound, paper-wrapped copies of *Leaves of Grass* that were sold for 75 cents each – as opposed to the two-dollar cloth-bound copies – would have blended in with these inexpensive Fourth of July commemorative publications.

The most common type of July Fourth publication was a brief pamphlet that featured the complete text of a speech by a prominent orator, followed by a list of the toasts that were offered after the oration itself. (The same kind of material also appeared in newspapers and single-issue broadsides.) The long line and celebratory tone of Whitman's poetic catalogues would have found good company with these published lists of Independence Day toasts, such as the following from this early nineteenth-century broadside:

> 1st. *THE DAY WE CELEBRATE*—May this, and every revolving fourth of July, inspire us with the spirit of 76.
> 2d. *THE UNITED STATES*—May those who administer our Government, learn wisdom, and fidelity, from the example of their predecessors.
> 3d. *THE MEMORY OF WASHINGTON*—The historic page, proud of its treasure, shall convey his name to latest times, while the affections of a grateful country, shall guard, and immortalize the trust.
> [...]
> 9th. *THE JUDICIARY OF THE UNITED STATES*—May they never sacrifice their independence to Virginia's usurpation.
> 10th. *THE NAVY OF THE UNITED STATES*—The guardian of commerce, may it flourish in its true element, and the honor of this establishment be bestowed where due.
> 11th. *AGRICULTURE, COMMERCE,* and *MANUFACTURES*—Dependent on each other, may neither branch be ever destroyed by the visionary wanderings of a meer [sic] speculatist.
> [...]
> 15th. *THE PRESS*—Free as air, in disseminating truth, and only shackled from lies, and scandal.
> 16th. *One more AMENDMENT to the NATIONAL CONSTITUTION*—More *free* votes, and less slavish ones.
>
> (quoted in Waldstreicher 1997: 220, italics in original)

This list of toasts is representative of the toasts offered on antebellum Independence Day celebrations in a number of ways. The first people to raise their glasses call upon the history of the American Revolution to unite the celebrants in a common "spirit of 76." As the toasts progress, however, this spirit of national unity is challenged by a specter of disunion: the laudable Judiciary of the United States, the ninth toast suggests, is in danger of succumbing to the sectional authority of the slaveholding South ("Virginia's usurpation"). Similarly, the 16th toast calls for an amendment to the Constitution that will not only free the slaves and grant them voting rights ("More *free* votes"), but will also free Northern politicians from their obligation to compromise with the South ("and less slavish ones"). But slavery is not the only internal dispute mentioned here: the freedom of the press is questioned in the 15th toast, the stability of American commerce is doubted in the 11th, and the honor of the armed forces is suspected in the 10th.

These lists of toasts were designed to create an image of a united nation; that is, they proposed that each toastmaker could add his or her individual voice to the unified voice of the national celebration. At the same time, however, the fragility of this union was evident in such toasts as those that emphasize national rifts over national unity. The multiple participants of Independence Day toasts – each of whom had a different take on the nation's past, present, and future – recall the heterogeneous mix of figures in Whitman's poetic catalogues. When Whitman puts opera singers and day laborers in the same list as slaves, prostitutes, and immigrants, he creates a scene similar to that of a Fourth of July celebration, with the characters of his poem taking their turns to raise their glasses and say what America means to them. In its similarities to the Fourth of July publications that recorded and disseminated displays of both patriotism and protest, the 1855 *Leaves of Grass* joined with other antebellum Americans who saw in Independence Day an opportunity to question – as well as to pledge – their allegiance to the United States.

In recent years, scholars of antebellum history and culture have shown how Fourth of July celebrations provided Americans with as much opportunity to critique their nation as they did to celebrate it. Historian David Waldstreicher, for example, calls the Fourth of July "a site of creative meaning-making and political action" that allowed antebellum Americans not only to strengthen their commitment to the national community, but also to express their discontent with US policies (Waldstreicher 1997: 202). When abolitionist William Lloyd Garrison burned a copy of the Constitution on July 4, 1854 to protest the Fugitive Slave Law and Henry David Thoreau left behind what he considered to be a corrupt nation for the solitude of Walden Pond on July 4, 1845, both men demonstrated that Fourth of July celebrations were open to dissidents and patriots alike. In the years immediately following the July 4, 1776 signing of the Declaration of Independence Americans eagerly embraced the Fourth of July as a time to celebrate the things that united them as a nation, but before long the holiday became an opportunity to emphasize the differences that threatened to keep them apart. On the first Independence Day in 1776, Americans pulled down statues of England's King George; by the middle of the nineteenth century, however, Americans celebrated the Fourth of July by pulling their fellow citizens down in toasts and orations that lambasted their countrymen for their differing political beliefs.

During the nearly 80 years that passed between the first Independence Day in 1776 and the day in 1855 when Whitman published *Leaves of Grass,* the character of July Fourth activities evolved to reflect the conflicts that were raging in the antebellum United States. The earliest factional squabbles to alter the celebratory atmosphere of July Fourth festivities took place in the late eighteenth century between Federalists and Antifederalists, rival political camps who disagreed over the amount of power that should be granted to the central government. After years of holding separate Fourth of July celebrations – an irony given that the holiday was designed to cultivate national unity – in 1788 Federalist and Antifederalist factions in upstate New York agreed to celebrate Independence Day together in honor of the recently ratified Constitution. Despite their attempts at civility, however, the day degenerated into a violent conflict that left one person dead and many others wounded (Waldstreicher 1997: 97–9). By the turn of the century, Simon P. Newman writes, "more and more Americans were participating in ever more oppositional celebrations of the Fourth" as "celebration itself had become a venue for popular political conflict" (Newman 2000: 90, 99).

In the decades preceding the Civil War, antebellum activists made an art form of turning Independence Day celebrations into opportunities for political critique. Frederick Douglass's "What to the Slave is the Fourth of July?," the 1852 speech in which he decries the hypocrisy of a slaveholding nation that dares to celebrate a holiday devoted to liberty, is the best known of the texts in this tradition. But Douglass's speech was by no means unique in an era when reformers of every stripe made July Fourth a day for conflict and dissent. Women's rights supporters attending the Seneca Falls convention, for example, listened to a reading of Elizabeth Cady Stanton's gender-inclusive Declaration of Independence on the Fourth of July in 1848. Labor reformers in New York City also composed a "Working Man's Declaration of Independence" 20 years earlier, a document that was created with the same spirit as that of the New England textile workers whose planned strike on July 4, 1846 was hailed by supporters as "a second Independence Day" (quoted in Dennis 2002: 37). Similarly, African American insurrectionist Nat Turner planned a slave revolt for Independence Day in 1831, as did an earlier group of African American slaves in South Carolina who scheduled a rebellion for July 4, 1816.

Antebellum Americans began to realize, as Len Travers says, that "Independence Day increasingly revealed not so much what they held in common as what separated them"; the holiday, they feared, "had not only failed to promote American nationalism, but was in fact an annual opportunity for the social and political fabric to tear itself apart" (Travers 1997: 181, 222). Given this intimate link between social protest and the Fourth of July, Whitman's decision to publish his book in connection with Independence Day festivities seems less like an example of the "bumptious American nationalism" that Malcolm Cowley finds so disappointing in the 1855 *Leaves of Grass* (Cowley 1959: xxvii) and more like the political radicalism that a number of scholars have come to associate with Whitman's poetry.

Betsy Erkkila, for one, insists that the 1855 *Leaves of Grass* was not, "as is commonly assumed, a product of Whitman's unbounded faith in the democratic dream of America; on the contrary, [it was] an impassioned response to the signs of the death of republican traditions" (Erkkila 1989: 67). Other scholars have argued in a similar vein: Martin Klammer contends that Whitman's treatment of racial issues in the first *Leaves of Grass* contributed to debates over African American slavery (Klammer 1995); Michael Moon and William H. Shurr say that the sexually charged and homoerotic imagery of the 1855 poetry called into question prevalent beliefs about human sexuality (Moon 1992, Shurr 1991); and M. Wynn Thomas shows how Whitman's upbringing among the laborers and artisans of Long Island and New York influenced the perspective on social class that informs *Leaves of Grass* (Thomas 1987). Understanding how Whitman dovetailed the emergence of the first *Leaves of Grass* with antebellum Independence Day celebrations extends the arguments that these and other scholars have made about Whitman's investment in nineteenth-century political and social affairs. Specifically, it illuminates how Whitman thought of himself as a representative national poet and how he conceptualized the ongoing tension between individual freedom and national community.

In the 1855 edition of *Leaves of Grass* Whitman crafted a poetic persona that functioned equally as a representative national figure and as an outsider on the fringes of national society. This delicate balancing act between patriotism and dissent was particularly suited to the festivities associated with the Fourth of July. In the 10-page Preface that precedes the poems of the 1855 edition, Whitman presents himself (in the third-person) as the kind of representative American poet that antebellum literary nationalists had been searching for. Drawing upon the belief that a poet would emerge from the polity as an icon of national character, Whitman writes in his Preface that "a bard is to be commensurate with a people" because "His spirit responds to his country's spirit" (Whitman [1855] 1959: 6–7). Throughout the Preface, Whitman promises to fulfill the role of the representative national bard, understanding as he does that "The proof of a poet is that his country absorbs him as affectionately as he has absorbed it" (p. 24). While the Preface presents Whitman as someone qualified for the office of American bard because, in Whitman's words, he "is as superb as a nation [because] he has the qualities that make up a superb nation" (p. 24), elsewhere in the 1855 edition Whitman depicts himself as possessing qualities that would seem to invalidate his representative status.

Rather than include his name on the title page of the 1855 *Leaves of Grass,* Whitman identifies himself halfway through "Song of Myself" as "Walt Whitman, an American, one of the roughs, a kosmos" (Whitman [1855] 1959: 48). If Whitman deliberately misplaced his byline in order to attract attention to his self-identification as "one of the roughs," the strategy appears to have worked: numerous reviewers of the first edition of *Leaves of Grass* commented on Whitman's desire to affiliate himself with the lower-class "toughs" and "rowdies" whose criminal behavior had earned them a decidedly negative reputation in New York City's bestiary of urban types. As one mid-century commentator noted, "A more despicable, dangerous, and detestable character than the New-York rough does not exist. He is an epitome of all the meannesses and vices of humanity" (Browne 1869: 66). Whitman reinforced this image of himself as an urban outlaw by placing an engraved portrait of himself in working-class garb – his shirt open at the breast, his hands at his hips, his head arrogantly cocked to one side – opposite the title page of his book. Whitman would later refer to the portrait as "the street figure" (quoted in Traubel [1908] 1961: 412), while a reviewer of the 1855 *Leaves of Grass* said that the portrait "would answer equally well . . . as the true likeness of half a dozen celebrated criminals" (Notes on new books 1856: 37).

Much like the Fourth of July activists who opposed national policies in the midst of national celebrations, Whitman identified himself as "one of the roughs" in an effort to create a persona that was simultaneously common man and common criminal. Just as the figure of "the rough" epitomized the poverty and social disorder that was attributed to large cities like New York, it also resonated with the rhetoric about the centrality of ordinary citizens to American democracy. Invoking this rhetoric on behalf of the working classes, Whitman wrote in the Preface to the 1855 *Leaves of Grass* that "the genius of the United States is not best or most in its executives or legislatures . . . but always most in the common people" (Whitman [1855] 1969: 6). Whitman believed that the urban laborers who were often dismissed as unrefined "roughs" were, on the contrary, the best representatives of national character that the

United States had to offer. In an unpublished political tract from 1856, he asks, "Where is the real America?," and answers, "the laboring persons, ploughmen, men with axes, spades, scythes, flails. . . . carpenters, masons, machinists, drivers of horses, workmen in factories" (Whitman 1982: 1307, 1310).

By publishing the first edition of *Leaves of Grass* in conjunction with the Independence Day celebrations of 1855, Whitman put himself in an environment where he could experiment with notions of representative national identity. The Fourth of July publishing context allowed him to create a public persona who spoke to and for his nation while at the same time being at odds with that nation. As Matthew Dennis says, "Identity and the boundaries of American citizenship and public life are fundamentally at stake during the Fourth of July. The Fourth presents an opportunity to define, delimit, or expand – while celebrating – the American nation" (Dennis 2002: 14). Given, as Travers says, that "few, if any, 'ordinary citizens' actually performed the task" of directing Independence Day festivities (Travers 1997: 6), Whitman's persona of the American poet as "one of the roughs" tested the extent to which people in the United States were willing to embrace the reality behind their rhetorical love of the common man.

Whitman wrote in the Preface to the 1855 *Leaves of Grass* that his poetry was grounded in "the noble character of the young mechanics and of all free American workmen and workwomen" (Whitman [1855] 1959: 8). He similarly said later in his life that one of his goals for the first edition of *Leaves of Grass* was "to diagnose, recognize, state, the case of the mechanics, laborers, artisans, of America – to get into the stream with them – to give them a voice in literature" (quoted in Traubel [1908] 1961: 142–3). Despite Whitman's stated goal that *Leaves of Grass* would create a space for working Americans in national life and literature, it would be a stretch to say that the 1855 *Leaves of Grass* could carry the subtitle, "What to the Rough Is the Fourth of July?" While Whitman laments in the 1855 Preface that his nation has become a place where "it is better to be a bound booby and rogue in office at a high salary than the poorest free mechanic or farmer" (Whitman [1855] 1959: 16), the poetry of the first *Leaves of Grass* does not offer the kind of specific program for political change that many reform-minded Independence Day publications did.

Whitman's solution to the social ills he mentions in the first edition of *Leaves of Grass* was not the creation of a new political program, but the creation of stronger individuals. As he wrote in an 1856 notebook – and again in a more expanded form in his 1871 essay *Democratic Vistas* – "All I write I write to arouse in you a great personality" (*NUPM*, 1: 267). Rather than place the primary responsibility for social change on external political organizations (as other Fourth of July activists did), Whitman believed that the locus of social change lay in the individual. In "A Song for Occupations," a poem that venerates working-class Americans, Whitman wrote that political power does not flow from the top down, but that "All doctrines, all politics and civilizations exurge from you" (Whitman [1855] 1959: 92). This is not to say that Whitman's concern with issues of class and economic equality was merely a window-dressing for his more essential focus on "the individual" as an abstract concept. Rather, Whitman believed that there is an essential link between the private affairs of the individual and the public life of the nation, and that the key to both politics and poetry lies in a proper understanding of the relationship between the individual and the mass.

Antebellum Fourth of July celebrations enacted this tension between the individual and the mass in a number of different ways. As previously mentioned, the toastmakers and political dissidents who participated in Independence Day festivities were aware that attempts to make their individual voices heard involved negotiating with the collective voice of the nation as a whole. While the interplay between the individual and the mass was an implicit part of every nineteenth-century July Fourth celebration, on July 4, 1854 Whitman had the opportunity to hear an Independence Day orator explicitly say what the implications of this interplay were for both American politics and American poetry. Edwin Hubbell Chapin, a Unitarian minister from the Fourth Universalist Church of New York City, was the keynote speaker for the Fourth of July celebration held at Manhattan's Crystal Palace in 1854. The Crystal Palace was an ongoing exhibition of art, science, and culture that Whitman regularly attended during 1853 and 1854 – "I went a long time (nearly a year) – days and nights" (quoted in Cutler 1998: 72) – and there is a good chance that he would have celebrated the Fourth there the year before he published the first edition of *Leaves of Grass*.

While Ralph Waldo Emerson is the Unitarian minister whose name is most often connected with the first edition of *Leaves of Grass*, there are also strong affinities between Whitman's 1855 volume of poems and the Independence Day speech that Chapin delivered at the Crystal Palace in 1854. Whether Whitman's thinking was shaped by Chapin's oration or whether the two men merely shared a common set of concerns, there are instructive parallels between the message of the 1855 *Leaves of Grass* and the message preached at the Crystal Palace on the Fourth of July in 1854. Chapin begins his speech, "The American Idea, and What Grows Out of It," with an apology for presenting what may sound like "a bit of transcendental philosophy instead of historical fact" on a day when most orators devoted their speeches to recalling the events of the American Revolution (Chapin 1854: 6). He instead announces as his theme "the American Idea," an idea that he characterizes as an unflagging belief in "*the spiritual worth of every man*" (p. 6, italics in original). Prescient of Whitman's desire "to arouse in you a great personality" (*NUPM*, 1: 267), Chapin connects American nationalism with this belief in the infinite value of the individual, saying that "the truest patriotism co-exists with the truest development of personality" (Chapin 1854: 14).

Similar to Whitman's claim that each individual human being is "immortal and fathomless" (Whitman [1855] 1959: 31), Chapin encourages his listeners to accept "the great fact that a man is priceless" (Chapin 1854: 11). After making his case for "the worth of the individual, the spiritual dignity of man" (p. 6), Chapin then explains how national unity can exist in a society that places such a strong emphasis on the individual. He writes,

> [A] true individualism is not adverse but favorable to a true *nationality*. In developing the springs of personal worth and dignity, we develop the springs of all public greatness. Therefore, the doctrine involved in the American Idea is not a doctrine of disintegration, but of unity. For, in the first place, every man is two-fold in his nature. He is both individual and social. The necessity of a State is enfolded in and grows [out] of the very conditions of his being. On the other hand, the fulness and richness of his individual nature cannot be developed except through the organism of society. He never can be perfected in isolation – in solitary self-existence. (Chapin 1854: 13, italics in original)

On this Fourth of July in antebellum New York, amid revelers gathered to celebrate their unity as a nation while still retaining the right to express their individuality in a heterodox toast or dissident speech, Chapin explains how the ongoing tension between the individual and the mass that characterizes American Independence Day also defines the fundamental nature of the American nation.

Chapin further extends the implications of his discourse into the field of aesthetics, arguing that the reciprocal interaction between the individual and the mass in American culture lays the groundwork for a national literary tradition. Similar to Whitman's statement in the Preface to the 1855 edition of *Leaves of Grass* that "The United States themselves are essentially the greatest poem" (Whitman [1855] 1959: 5), Chapin says that the politics of individual freedom is poetry's kindest muse: "Despotism furnishes but a dull study," he writes,

> It is a lazy succession of dynasties. Out of its monotonous waste rise only the crowns of bloody and voluptuous kings. But pass into the area of a free land, and what variety and interest, in senate, and port, and citadel, to fill the pages of the annalist. [. . .] What inspiration from the springs of freedom, making the history of a nation finer than a poem. (Chapin 1854: 13–14)

Chapin's belief that there is enough "variety and interest" in a free society to "fill the pages" of a history greater than poetry stems from the same impulse as the poetic catalogues of the 1855 *Leaves of Grass*, with their detailed treatment of national diversity serving as a testament to the vibrancy of democracy and its faith in the absolute worth of the individual.

The Independence Day orations and toasts that, like Whitman's catalogues, allowed for individual voices to be expressed within a larger national context were an important part of July Fourth celebrations, but they were not the central focus of holiday activities. Public readings of the Declaration of Independence, which were a staple of antebellum Independence Day festivities, contributed more than anything else to the discussions of personal freedom that took place on the Fourth of July. As Chapin says, reminding his listeners that they had recently heard a reading of the Declaration of Independence, "this Idea of personal worth, of individual freedom, [has] culminated and blazed in that bold, distinct sentence which this day has been read in your ears: 'We hold these truths to be self-evident, that all men are created equal, and are endowed by their Creator with certain inalienable rights' " (Chapin 1854: 8).

Beginning with the first public readings of the Declaration of Independence in 1776, a tradition developed ascribing a performative power to the spoken words of the Declaration (Fliegelman 1993), a power that had the effect not only of creating a national community, but also, as Chapin indicates, of reminding Americans of the primary importance of their individual freedom. Whitman appears also to have thought of the 1855 *Leaves of Grass* as performing a similar function to that of the Declaration of Independence. While Michael Moon argues that the US Constitution, with its allowance for perpetual emendation, is "the single most significant political 'pre-text' for the revisionary qualities of *Leaves of Grass*" (Moon 1992: 16), the Fourth of July publishing context of the 1855 *Leaves of Grass* suggests that before Whitman ever considered applying a Constitutional precedent to amend his poems, he thought of *Leaves of Grass* as a text that, like the Declaration of Independence, could be read out loud at public gatherings.

A number of scholars have commented on the oral quality of the 1855 *Leaves of Grass*: Ezra Greenspan notes that the peculiar ellipses of the 1855 edition serve as verbal cues rather than grammatical organization, functioning in the poetry as "a kind of idiosyncratic caesura" (Greenspan 1990: 117); Ivan Marki says that the Preface in particular is "meant to be heard rather than read" (Marki 1976: 80); and C. Carroll Hollis observes that the 1855 *Leaves of Grass*, more so than later editions of the *Leaves*, exhibits a conscious desire to be audibly heard by its readers (Hollis 1983: 89). In the 1855 Preface, Whitman predicts that "gangs of kosmos and prophets en masse" will travel throughout the nation reading poems – from *Leaves of Grass*, presumably – and liberating their listeners from whatever dogma or ideology keeps them from giving full expression to the essence of individuality within them (Whitman [1855] 1959: 22).

The history of antebellum Independence Day celebrations indicates that many Americans were willing to revise and even rewrite the documents that underwrote the United States's political and cultural institutions. As David Reynolds attests, the 1855 *Leaves of Grass* was one such effort to reinvent texts like the Declaration of Independence: "In the turmoil of the 1850s," Reynolds writes, "the very idea of America was at stake. [. . .] With central texts of American democracy losing stable meaning, [Whitman] felt he had to create a new national text in which America was poetically reconstructed" (Reynolds 1995: 112). Whitman himself explains how he imagined his "new national text" through which the United States would be "poetically reconstructed" in the same way that the Declaration of Independence constructed a new nation on the first Independence Day in 1776: he writes in the 1855 Preface that great American poetry such as he deems his own to be "appears from the mouths of the people, it throbs a live interrogation in every freeman's and freewoman's heart" (Whitman [1855] 1969: 23). Lingering in "the mouths of the people" as they repeat its words every Fourth of July, the poems of *Leaves of Grass*, Whitman hopes, will stir the hearts of freemen and freewomen everywhere to make declarations of independence of their own and to have their first celebratory toast the next Independence Day be, "I celebrate myself."

References and Further Reading

Allen, Gay Wilson (1956). Regarding the "Publication" of the First *Leaves of Grass. American Literature*, 28: 78–9.

Bradley, Sculley and Blodgett, Harold W. (1965). Introduction. In Sculley Bradley and Harold W. Blodgett (eds.), *"Leaves of Grass": Comprehensive Reader's Edition*. New York: New York University Press, pp. xxix–lv.

Browne, Junius Henri (1869). *The Great Metropolis: A Mirror of New York*. Hartford, CT: American Publishing.

Chapin, Edwin Hubbell (1854). *The American Idea, and What Grows Out of It: An Oration, Delivered in The New York Crystal Palace July 4, 1854*. Boston: Abel Tompkins.

Cowley, Malcolm (1959). Introduction. In Malcolm Cowley (ed.), *"Leaves of Grass": The First (1855) Edition*. New York: Viking, pp. vii–xxxvii.

Cutler, Ed (1998). Passage to Modernity: *Leaves of Grass* and the 1853 Crystal Palace Exhibition in New York. *Walt Whitman Quarterly Review*, 16: 65–89.

Dennis, Matthew (2002). *Red, White, and Blue Letter Days: An American Calendar*. Ithaca, NY: Cornell University Press.

Erkkila, Betsy (1989). *Whitman the Political Poet*. New York: Oxford University Press.

Fliegelman, Jay (1993). *Declaring Independence: Jefferson, Natural Language, and the Culture of Performance*. Stanford, CA: Stanford University Press.

Goetsch, Paul and Hurm, Gerd (eds.) (1992). *The Fourth of July: Political Oratory and Literary Relations, 1776–1876*. Tübingen, Germany: Gunter Naar Verlag.

Greenspan, Ezra (1990). *Walt Whitman and the American Reader*. New York: Cambridge University Press.

Hollis, C. Carroll (1983). *Language and Style in "Leaves of Grass."* Baton Rouge: Louisiana State University Press.

Kaplan, Justin (1980). *Walt Whitman: A Life*. New York: Simon and Schuster.

Killingsworth, M. Jimmie (1993). *The Growth of "Leaves of Grass": The Organic Tradition in Whitman Studies*. Columbia, SC: Camden House.

Klammer, Martin (1995). *Whitman, Slavery, and the Emergence of "Leaves of Grass."* University Park: Pennsylvania State University Press.

Marki, Ivan (1976). *The Trial of the Poet: An Interpretation of the First Edition of "Leaves of Grass."* New York: Columbia University Press.

Marki, Ivan (1982). The Last Eleven Poems in the 1855 *Leaves of Grass. American Literature*, 54: 229–39.

Moon, Michael (1992). *Disseminating Whitman: Revision and Corporeality in "Leaves of Grass."* Cambridge, MA: Harvard University Press.

Newman, Simon P. (2000). *Parades and the Politics of the Street: Festive Culture in the Early American Republic*. Philadelphia: University of Pennsylvania Press.

Notes on New Books ([1856] 1996). In Kenneth M. Price (ed.), *Walt Whitman: The Contemporary Reviews*. New York: Cambridge University Press, pp. 36–8.

Pease, Donald (1987). *Visionary Compacts: American Renaissance Writers in Cultural Contexts*. Madison: University of Wisconsin Press.

Reynolds, David (1995). *Walt Whitman's America: A Cultural Biography*. New York: Alfred A. Knopf.

Shurr, William H. (1991). Walt Whitman's *Leaves of Grass*: The Making of a Sexual Revolution. *Soundings*, 74: 101–28.

Thomas, M. Wynn (1987). *The Lunar Light of Whitman's Poetry*. Cambridge, MA: Harvard University Press.

Traubel, Horace ([1908] 1961). *With Walt Whitman in Camden*, vol. 2. New York: Rowman and Littlefield.

Travers, Len (1997). *Celebrating the Fourth: Independence Day and the Rites of Nationalism in the Early Republic*. Amherst: University of Massachusetts Press.

Waldstreicher, David (1997). *In the Midst of Perpetual Fetes: The Making of American Nationalism, 1776–1820*. Chapel Hill: University of North Carolina Press.

White, William (1957). More About the "Publication" of the First *Leaves of Grass. American Literature*, 28: 516–17.

Whitman, Walt ([1855] 1959). *"Leaves of Grass": The First (1855) Edition*, ed. Malcolm Cowley. New York: Viking.

Whitman, Walt (1982). *Complete Poetry and Collected Prose*, ed. Justin Kaplan. New York: Library of America.

28
"Song of Myself"

Kerry C. Larson

> I shall be even with you and you shall be even with me.
> (Whitman, "Song of the Answerer")

In the second part of his *Democracy in America* (1840), Alexis de Tocqueville includes a chapter on "Literary Characteristics of Democratic Times." Like many commentators on both sides of the Atlantic, Tocqueville could not fail to notice the rather lackluster record of artistic accomplishment in the New World, though that does not deter him from predicting that America will generate a literature "peculiarly its own" and from speculating on the likely form it will take. As always, his analysis is guided by the fundamental contrast between aristocratic and democratic cultures.

> By and large the literature of a democracy will never exhibit the order, regularity, skill, and art characteristic of aristocratic literature; formal qualities will be neglected or actually despised. The style will often be strange, incorrect, overburdened, and loose, almost always strong and bold. Writers will be more anxious to work quickly than to perfect details. Short works will be commoner than long books, wit than erudition, imagination than depth. There will be a rude and untutored vigor of thought with great variety and singular fecundity. Authors will strive to astonish more than to please, and to stir passions rather than to charm taste. (Tocqueville 1969: 474)

Tocqueville's prophecy may be encountered in any number of surveys of American literature, and for good reason. His characterization of literature's "vehement and bold" style, to say nothing of its "untutored and rude vigor of thought," looks forward not only to Whitman, Dickinson, and Melville but also to many of their self-proclaimed heirs such as Crane, Moore, or Ashbery. Despite the occasional hint of caricature, his remarks, most commentators have agreed, have turned out to be uncannily prescient (Matthiessen 1941, Pearce 1961, Cushman 1991).

And yet Tocqueville's talents as a prophet, considerable though they are, do not begin to account for the full range and richness of his thinking. The better part of that thinking is devoted to what Tocqueville found to be the most important development in the New World, "equality of conditions." Tocqueville's great contribution was to see that equality was not simply an economic or political ideal but an ideological force that pervaded everyday life; as democracy's "generative fact," equality is for him best understood as a kind of Gestalt penetrating the values and beliefs of an entire population. As we are told on the first page of *Democracy in America*, "it creates opinions, gives birth to feelings, suggests customs, and modifies whatever it does not create" (Tocqueville 1969: 9). Unique among social theorists over the past two centuries, Tocqueville's interest was to discern and describe equality's social logic – the kinds of predispositions, preferences, and practices it is apt to encourage or discourage. Of course he is prepared to acknowledge the presence of inequality in antebellum America, but for all that his interest remains in equality as the decisive cultural influence. It is, for example, precisely because he believed that equality had so firmly established itself in the hearts and minds of Americans that he can so confidently predict the course of their literature before it had even emerged.

Whitman is famous for inventing poetic forms that would honor a truly democratic society. More keenly than any of his contemporaries, he understood that a society dedicated to egalitarian practices required "a readjustment of the whole theory and nature of poetry" (Whitman 1973: 566–7). True to his convictions, Whitman "readjusted" virtually every phase of the poetic process, from diction, punctuation, syntax, and meter to structure and theme. The result was, in the words of Angus Fletcher, "a new poetic expressive language whose grammar would reflect the different basis of speech and communication in the new political climate – a new grammar of status relations" (Fletcher 2004: 101). Naturally, opinions vary as to whether the poet fully succeeded in crafting what Fletcher calls "a new language of equality" (p. 112); for every critic who celebrates his accomplishment in this area there seem to be others who fault him for failing this ideal. Either way, though, there is little disagreement that equality is a central, if not dominant, concern in his verse.

My aim here is to take a fresh look at an old theme as it relates to "Song of Myself," Whitman's longest and perhaps best-known poem. It also remains one of his most elusive. Following Tocqueville's lead, I will be taking equality to signify a cultural and historical fact, as opposed to an ideal one might realize or fail to realize. Doing so should not only help to clarify some of the persistent critical debates that have grown up around the poem but also demonstrate the sheer *extremity* of its commitment to egalitarian norms. To appreciate this commitment in all its complexity, we do not need to excavate an imposing array of facts and figures; as Tocqueville recognized, a preoccupation with historical method narrowly understood runs the risk of missing out on those developments that are the most vital and central.

Democratic Reading

> The messages of great poets to each man and woman are, Come to us on equal terms, Only then can you understand us, We are no better than you, What we enclose you

> enclose, What we enjoy you may enjoy. Did you suppose there could be only one Supreme? We affirm there can be unnumbered Supremes and that one does not countervail another . . . (1855 Preface to *Leaves of Grass*, Whitman 1959: 13)

"Equality stimulates each man to want to judge everything for himself," Tocqueville remarks in *Democracy in America* (1969: 459). One year later, in 1841, Emerson published "Self-Reliance," which does not so much draw the same connection as make it a central article of faith. Emerson's essay is above all concerned to drive home two basic propositions. First, there is a "power" or "genius" that resides in each of us, the lowly and the great alike, a "power" or "genius" that derives from a greater whole (variously named the "Oversoul," "Universal Mind," or "aboriginal Self") of which each one of us is a part. Second, this fact of a fundamental likeness or spiritual equality should inspire self-reliance – "the conviction that envy is ignorance [and] that imitation is suicide" (Emerson 1990: 29). In other words, if I am in some sense just as good as Plato, then there's no reason why I should defer to Plato's opinion. I need to go out and create my own. Experiencing equality and striving for intellectual or mental independence go hand in hand. It's precisely because I'm your equal that makes me want to judge things for myself and therefore stand apart from you.

In "Song of Myself" this injunction to judge for oneself – to take nothing on faith, to look askance at tradition, to make up one's own mind – is most obviously reflected in Whitman's invocation of the reader, the ubiquitous "you, whoever you are" of his verse. We are introduced to this important protagonist in the second line of the poem ("And what I assume you shall assume"). As the poet explains in the 1855 Preface to *Leaves of Grass*, bringing the second person into the frame of the poem serves an explicit purpose. "A great poem is no finish to a man or woman but rather a beginning. Has anyone fancied he could sit at last under some due authority and rest satisfied with explanations and be content and full?" (Whitman 1959: 22). No more a hidden bystander than a passive consumer who, accustomed to "sheltered fatness and ease," complacently digests the meanings of the text, the self-reliant reader is constantly called out and challenged to strive for and work through those meanings until they are made his or her own. This basic proposition is sounded from the outset of "Song of Myself," whose second section concludes with these words:

> Have you reckon'd a thousand acres much? Have you reckon'd the earth much?
> Have you practis'd so long to read?
> Have you felt so proud to get at the meaning of poems?
> Stop this day and night with me and you shall possess the origin of all poems,
> You shall possess the good of the earth and sun, (there are millions of suns left,)
> You shall no longer take things at second or third hand, nor look through the eyes of the dead, nor feed on the spectres in books,
> You shall not look through my eyes either, nor take things from me,
> You shall listen to all sides and filter them from your self.
>
> (Whitman 1973: 30)

Casting aside the old division of labor, whereby the reader dutifully decodes the significances that the author transmits, represents a critical step in the quest to realize equality. To "take things at second or third hand" is to read aristocratically while to "filter them from your self" is to read democratically. In fact in "Song of Myself" we frequently witness a blurring of roles to the point where the reader is enlisted as a collaborator in the creation of meaning at the same time that the poet presents himself as another interpreter, scanning the natural world for tokens of a divine wholeness. ("To me the converging objects of the universe perpetually flow," Whitman writes at one point, "All are written to me, and I must get what the writing means," Whitman 1973: 47.)

To "possess the origin of all poems" is in this respect to come into contact with the primal materials out of which verse is forged. It is worth emphasizing how this effort to write a kind of ur-poetry serves not merely the poet's egalitarian ideals but, more pointedly, the goal of intellectual independence. One can only imagine the bafflement of anyone opening *Leaves of Grass* when it first appeared in 1855: 12 untitled texts ("songs"? "chants"? "poems"?) separated only by page breaks and preceded by a preface that also seemed to be neither prose nor poetry but a strange commingling of both. What we today call "Song of Myself" likewise carried no numbered sections nor any mention of an author other than what could be deduced from the copyright page or what could be gleaned from a passing reference in the poem itself. Epic in length, it featured no readily discernible principle of development, no overarching narrative, which would help readers connect one part to another. Without a story or a set of generic signals to fall back upon, the reader is thrown back on her or his own devices, which is of course precisely Whitman's intent. Dispensing with genre, Whitman dispenses with most of the standard features that serve to channel, frame, and guide the reader's response. We are on our own.

What organizes "Song of Myself" is in fact less a theme or even a cluster of themes than the ongoing pursuit by the reader of the poet, that elusive, shape-shifting, hectoring, seductive figure who issues his invitation "to stop this day and night with me" at the outset of the poem and who concludes it with the teasing assurance "I stop some where waiting for you" (Whitman 1973: 89). It is not, in other words, meaning that drives the poem forward and gives it coherence so much as it is the pursuit of a more basic encounter between "I" and "you" that comes before the formulation of meaning itself. "You will hardly know who I am or what I mean," Whitman remarks near the end of "Song of Myself," anticipating the terms of his legacy. Putting his reader on center stage, he at the same time works to downplay expectations about authorial mastery.

This last point relates directly to the theme of readerly freedom: the less we feel that the poet controls meaning the more apt we will feel that meaning is ours to make, a joint enterprise among us all, a collective effort. The most memorable illustration of this democratization of meaning may be found in Section 6, where the poet, abandoning himself to the drift of significances suggested by a simple word, invites the reader to do the same.

A child said, *What is the grass?* Fetching it to me with full hands;
How could I answer the child? I do not know what it is any more than he.
I guess it must be the flag of my disposition, out of hopeful green stuff woven.
Or I guess it is the handkerchief of the Lord,
A scented gift and remembrancer designedly dropt,
Bearing the owner's name someway in the corners, that we may see and remark, and say *Whose?*
Or I guess the grass is itself a child, the produced babe of the vegetation,
Or I guess it is a uniform hieroglyphic,
And it means, Sprouting alike in broad zones and narrow zones,
Growing among black folks as among white,
Kanuck, Tuckahoe, Congressman, Cuff, I give them the same, I receive them the same.
And now it seems to me the beautiful uncut hair of graves.
(Whitman 1973: 33–4)

In sampling different connotations of the term grass, the poet disarms the wish to settle upon or fix any one meaning. In guessing at its many possible significances, he places himself beside the reader, another interpreter of the mysteries of the text.

Here we can begin to see why a democratic poetics should privilege *indeterminacy* as a special virtue. Uncertainty can be inspiring. "The expression of the American poet," Whitman explains in the 1855 Preface, "is to be transcendent and new," which is to say that "it is to be indirect and not direct or descriptive or epic" (Whitman 1959: 8). If we come away from "Song of Myself" with a meaning, then we've failed the poem. Like his wish to distance his verse from generic conventions, Whitman's "indirection" is meant to move away from the presumption that the poet controls or owns meaning. His text resembles that "handkerchief of the Lord" which bears an "owner's name" ("Walt Whitman, an American, one of the roughs, a kosmos") even as it submits such attributions to fundamental questioning ("Whose?"). Since the very concept of ownership is empty without the notion of exclusivity (if everyone "owns" something then nobody really does) and since Whitman's egalitarianism above all embraces inclusiveness ("This is the meal equally set," he tells us, "I will not have a single person slighted or left away," Whitman 1973: 46), it becomes clear why the determinate should be linked to hierarchy and closure while the indeterminate is associated with equality and openness. The aristocratic poet stipulates; the democratic bard suggests. This is why it is vital for readers of "Song of Myself" to understand that "the indirect is always as great and as real as the direct" (Whitman 1959: 19).

Admiration for the poem's "indeterminate openness to experience" (Adams 1959: 181) has been a fixture in academic criticism for 50 years and more, although the logic connecting "indeterminate" to "openness" is more often assumed than analyzed. Thus in his very influential account of Whitman's sexual politics, Michael Moon adds a new twist to essentially the same logic by opposing the "more firmly grounded and determinate discourses of embodiment abroad in his culture" against the poet's vision of the body as embracing "a range of ungrounded possibilities standing in indeterminate relation" to these dominant discourses (Moon 1991: 11). Whereas Whitman's "cultural context," we are told, "overwhelmingly privilege[d] the solid, the stable, the fixed, the restricted, and the reserved," *Leaves of Grass* "asserts the primacy of 'fluidity' in the social, political, and 'natural' realms" (p. 60). The special distinction of his verse is to appropriate the fixed discourses of sexual embodiment of the time and "render the referents of those discourses indeterminate and fluid" (p. 14). A case in point is the famous vignette of the 29th bather (Section 11 of "Song of Myself"), in which a "lady," gazing upon "twenty-eight young men [who] bathe by the shore," is swept away by the force, it would seem, of her own erotic daydreaming:

> Dancing and laughing along the beach came the twenty-ninth bather,
> The rest did not see her, but she saw them and loved them.
> The beards of the young men glisten'd with wet, it ran from their long hair,
> Little streams pass'd all over their bodies.
> An unseen hand also passed over their bodies,
> It descended tremblingly from their temples and ribs.
> The young men float on their backs, their white bellies bulge to the sun, they do not ask who seizes fast to them,
> They do not know who puffs and declines with pendant and bending arch,
> They do not think whom they souse with spray.
>
> (Whitman 1973: 38–9)

Taking issue with past readings that view this scene as representing either a thwarted female sexuality that bears no connection to the rest of "Song of Myself" or a thinly disguised homoerotic fantasy that makes the lady a proxy for the poet's own longings, Moon argues that both accounts artificially divide what Whitman seeks to merge and complicate. On his account, male homoeroticism and feminine sexuality are much more blurred than distinct, the whole point of the vignette being to project "a utopian space" that "effectively destabilizes the genders" of both the lady and the young men. Properly interpreted, for example, the "unseen hand" no more belongs to the woman than to the men but is in fact "a figure of intense indeterminacy" (Moon 1991: 46) to the degree that it encompasses both and even extends to the "hand" of the poet himself. Just as the grass is a composite of many different meanings in one figure, so in the 29th bather we see Whitman "merging without excluding" (p. 45) a rich array of sexual identities.

Here again we see how the simple act of multiplying meaning is thought to go hand in hand with the project of realizing equality. Indeterminacy acquires a political significance because it *diffuses* authority so that the very idea of settling upon meaning begins to look like an arbitrary imposition. In contemplating the array of significances evoked by the text, the interpreter is free to choose not to choose. If the female is equal to the male, then it is indeed a mistake to choose – a mistake to think, that is, that Section 11 is "about" male or female sexuality when it is in fact about both and neither. And if the reader and poet are equals, then it is of course a mistake to think that the poet shall dictate what the reader shall think. In this respect, critics like Moon are surely right to view "the exemplary indeterminacy fundamental to Whitman's writing" (Moon 1991: 52) as a thoroughly political gesture responsive to the historical pressures of his time.

But putting the point this way also suggests a certain irony. If the poet wants us to see that there are many meanings to the grass, then that intention is every bit as clear and as determinate as any other. If he wishes to fuse and confuse male and female desire to the point where they are hard to tell apart, then that too is a stable, fixed, and certain intention. If, in other words, Whitman's writing were as indeterminate as his critics make it out to be, then there would be no grounds for thinking that the grass has many meanings and not just one, no reason to believe that male and female desire have been joined in order to create a "utopian space." Once indeterminacy acquires a politics, it isn't indeterminate any more. The idea that the reader is free to choose not to choose can only be described as a fiction. It is, to be sure, a powerful fiction, as the critical reception of *Leaves of Grass* attests, but it is a fiction all the same.

The real question concerning Whitman's interest in affirming an equality between author and reader is not how he pulls it off but why he should wish to do so in the first place. Although everyone can see the point of striving for political, social, or economic equality, the point of striving for epistemological equality is somewhat harder to see. Why is it so important for the poet to approach us "on equal terms?" The answer, presumably, is that the poet wishes to affirm a nonhierarchical relation between author and reader. But bringing the values of equality to bear on the interpretive process itself mixes apples and oranges. It threatens to make, as we have seen, the very idea of communicating a meaning start to look like an imposition of power, just as the mere act of understanding meaning may start to look like being enslaved to another's will. Instead of taking such assumptions at face value, we would do better, I think, to treat them as revealing mystifications – symptoms, as it were, of Whitman's democratic ideology.

The point here is not to find fault with "Song of Myself" or its readers. The point is to demonstrate just how far the poem is willing to go in honoring the call for intellectual independence. If Tocqueville was right in thinking that in times of equality the imperative to judge for oneself would not just be coveted but fetishized, "Song of Myself" exemplifies the insight perfectly in its drive to actualize an equality between author and reader. If, moreover, Angus Fletcher is right in thinking that during the Jacksonian period "the politics and political order defining the country shifted from a hierarchical top-down structuring . . . to an utterly different model" (Fletcher 2004: 97), then Whitman's appeals to "indirection" and his democratizing of meaning should not be viewed as esoteric preoccupations but on the contrary every bit as "historical" as his response to the slave crisis or his ties to the working class. It is, in other words, the very lengths to which the poem goes in its wish to *perform* equality that we can best measure equality's emergence as a cultural force.

Democratic Compassion

"I am he attesting sympathy" (Whitman 1973: 50).

For many interpreters of "Song of Myself," the connection between egalitarianism and indeterminacy applies not just to questions of meaning but to matters of identity as well. In his recent study of "Radical Abolitionists" of the antebellum period, for instance, John Stauffer finds that "a subjective notion of the self in a state of continuous flux" was instrumental in the "effort to dismantle ... dichotomies ... separating black from white, civilization from savagery, along with the racial divisions associated with these realms" (Stauffer 2002: 37). The Radical Abolitionists (more specifically, Gerrit Smith, Frederick Douglass, James McCune Smith, and John Brown) are in this way thought to have "approached Whitman's poetics" in seeing how an appreciation for the constructedness of identity could lead to radical change: "a fluid and subjective conception of the self," Stauffer writes, "greatly facilitated these men's efforts to break down racial hierarchies and envision an egalitarian and pluralist society" (2002: 38). Just as it is important for us to see that the people, places, and things of "Song of Myself" cannot be pinned down to one meaning, so is it important to see that the identity of its author likewise eludes a determinant form.

"I resist any thing better than my own diversity" (Whitman 1973: 45), announces the "kosmos" of "Song of Myself," and it is of course the sheer diversity of peoples and their experiences that the protean "I" of the poem is intent on projecting. Rather than expressing an identity, it would be better to say that this "I" is a site of identification that epitomizes the operations of a distinctively democratic empathy. The self of "Song of Myself" is many selves, the vessel through which old and young, foolish and wise, rich and poor, black and white, man and woman find expression. As the poet says, "In all people I see myself, none more and not one a barley-corn less" (1973: 47). As the great equalizer, he takes on or assumes the identities of all he can name, whether it is the wealthy lady of Section 11, the butcher-boy of Section 12, or the Negro dray-man of Section 13. (This series of impersonations culminate in the much longer catalogue of laborers and occupations in Section 15.) It is this sort of empathic connection that critics like Stauffer consider essential to Whitman's vision of a genuinely "pluralistic society" where "Southerners and Northerners, prostitutes and saints, blacks and whites, all liv[e] together in harmony" (Stauffer 2002: 39):

> I am of old and young, of the foolish as much as the wise,
> Regardless of others, ever regardful of others,
> Maternal as well as paternal, a child as well as a man,
> Stuff'd with the stuff that is coarse and stuff'd with the stuff that is fine,
> One of the Nation of many nations, the smallest the same and the largest the same,
> A Southerner soon as a Northerner, a planter nonchalant and hospitable down by the Oconee I live,
> A Yankee bound my own way ready for trade, my joints the limberest joints on earth and the sternest joints on earth,
> A Kentuckian walking the vale of the Elkhorn in my deer-skin leggings, a Louisianian or Georgian
>
> (Whitman 1973: 44–5)

And yet, stirring as all this sounds, many have nevertheless wondered if Whitman's democratic compassion is not stretched rather thin. When so many different constituencies are named, opportunities for empathic engagement become more remote. The vignette of the 29th bather, which has attracted so much critical commentary, is in fact uncharacteristic of the poem in the amount of attention it devotes to one object. More typically, we race from one reference to the next. D. H. Lawrence was one of the first, though certainly not the last, to be aggravated by this feature of the poem. Noticing that "as soon as Walt knew a thing, he assumed a One identity with it" (Lawrence [1923] 1969: 166), Lawrence takes him to task for indulging in a superficial and aggrandizing mode of sympathy. "This merging, en masse, One Identity" was not "true sympathy" but amounted to the democratic ego "forcing [itself] into other people's circumstances" (Lawrence [1923] 1969: 174). Ultimately, a welcoming of otherness turns out to harbor, on this reading, an impatience with it. Echoing Lawrence's complaint, Philip Fisher has more recently noted that Whitman's verse ultimately favors "transparency" over "difference," which is to say that it is less interested in recognizing real "experiential differences" between people than in affirming "a national harmony" where such differences are erased (Fisher 1999: 70). Likewise, it is precisely because the poet of "Song of Myself" is apt to identify with "the Negro" and not "a Negro" that moves Wai-Chee Dimock to maintain that the poem, in its ruthless abstraction of difference, closes off "access to a special world of loves and hates" (Dimock 1996: 124). Whitman's poetics of sympathy is, in short, formal, abstract, and mechanical.

Judging from this critique, the problem with multicultural readings of "Song of Myself" is that they fail to acknowledge how superficial Whitman's commitment to a truly "pluralistic society" is. What explains this apparent superficiality? Sticking for a moment to the critics just cited, we find a variety of answers. For Lawrence, it is tied to the decline of "the white race" and its tendency to "mentalize" primal attachments and therefore falsify what Lawrence calls "our blood-consciousness" (Lawrence [1923] 1969: 160). Fisher, on the other hand, sees the limited and perfunctory character of democratic compassion in "Song of Myself" as a necessary feature of its nationalist ambition to proclaim a distinctively American identity – "One of the Nation of many nations" – that overrides the particulars of place and history. Finally, Dimock points to the allegedly ahistorical and universalizing nature of liberalism, which, on her account, "Song of Myself" is taken to exemplify.

But if multicultural readings of "Song of Myself" err in taking Whitman's professions of sympathy for any and everyone too much at face value, these more skeptical responses may be said to err in the opposite direction by regarding these same professions as shallow and therefore a sign of bad faith. Perhaps there is an alternative, somewhat more expansive way to approach the question of democratic compassion that avoids the twin extremes of sentimentalizing or of stigmatizing it.

"When ranks are almost equal among a people," Tocqueville writes, when "all men think and feel in nearly the same manner, each instantaneously can judge the feelings of all the others; he just casts a rapid glance at himself" (Tocqueville 1969: 564). In effect, Tocqueville's democratic citizens presuppose as a matter of course that "what I assume, you shall assume." Compassion – the capacity to feel for and to feel with others – is not just made available to democratic society on an unprecedented scale. It is also made effortless. Where individuals consider themselves more or less equal to one another, the grounds for identification are already in place. To experience sympathy for others, all the citizen needs to do is look within himself – "that is enough." For "there is no misery that he cannot readily understand, and a secret instinct tells him its extent. It makes no difference if strangers or enemies are in question; his imagination at once puts him in their place" (Tocqueville 1969: 564).

But precisely because democratic compassion is so effortless, it is also bound to seem facile. "I was the man, I suffer'd, I was there," proclaims the bard of "Song of Myself," wearing his sympathy on his sleeve. Lawrence and others, balking at such expressions, find that they compromise the poem's democratic aspirations. True sympathy, Lawrence insists, "means feeling with, not feeling for"; Whitman's mistake was to think that merely affirming that he feels for "the Negro slave" was the same thing as genuinely feeling with the slave (Lawrence [1923] 1969: 175). But one advantage of Tocqueville's account is to suggest why the very thinness of compassion is better understood as a manifestation of egalitarianism than a betrayal of it. "In democratic ages men rarely sacrifice themselves for one another, but they show a general compassion for the human race" (Tocqueville 1969: 564). With an enlarged franchise that encompasses nothing less than humanity itself, democratic sympathy becomes more expansive even as it becomes less intense. Indeed, the two developments go together: the more objects sympathy touches the more abstract it is bound to be.

At bottom it is this general and generalizing compassion that Tocqueville identifies as endemic to democratic cultures that awakens the skepticism of critics like Lawrence, Fisher, or Dimock. Suspicious of the abstract nature of that compassion, they advance, as we have seen, various theories to account for its existence. But there is nothing anomalous about Whitman's democratic compassion that requires us to turn to hidden agendas (e.g., race, nation, liberalism). Making sympathy universal, equality makes it superficial. Interestingly, we tend to think of literature in opposite terms; from the briefest lyric to the lengthiest novel, its most distinctive feature is to recreate and enter into the beliefs and desires of others to a degree unmatched by other discourses. But, as we have seen, "Song of Myself" deliberately distances itself from literary norms in favor of egalitarian ones, and so the empathic intensity interpreters commonly expect from literature is notable for its absence here.

Democratic Constraints

The product of a long line of aristocrats, Tocqueville wrote as a conservative. Convinced that equality was an unstoppable force destined to rule the world, he worried that its very excesses might paradoxically lead to new forms of servitude. As readers of *Democracy in America* know, his reason for traveling to the New World was to study a society that had somehow avoided this fate, a society modeled on democratic principles that had nevertheless achieved a measure of stability and prosperity that had eluded Europe. The French Revolution had made it all too clear that a society overtaken by a mania for equality and nothing else could only result in disaster; Tocqueville's wish to explain why America succeeded where France failed therefore led him to ponder those features of American society that served to counter or offset the otherwise pervasive (and potentially pernicious) effects of equality. In studying democracy, he was especially anxious to understand its saving constraints.

Among these constraints the three that rank the highest in Tocqueville's estimation are religion, family, and political or civic engagement. The appeal of each of these domains is that they come equipped with their own norms and distinctive lines of authority. Whether it be interaction between God and worshiper, parent and child, or alderman and citizen, these are spheres where hierarchy is taken to be indispensable. Each retains nondemocratic elements in an otherwise democratic world. Each induces the democratic citizen to concede the salutary influence of inequality. Each serves as a counterweight to the leveling effects of equality and its irrational impatience with all forms of authority.

Whether or not we find Tocqueville's concerns on this subject compelling is beside the point, at least for our present purposes. Here I simply wish to note the curious fact that the checks and balances he recommends play virtually no role in "Song of Myself." For all its emphasis on inclusion, the poem shies away from each of Tocqueville's constraints. Consider, for example, the place of religion in the poem. References along these lines are scattered throughout "Song of Myself," albeit in a somewhat offhanded way, as in the passing image of "the handkerchief of the Lord" or a side glance at God as "the hugging and loving bed-fellow [who] sleeps at my side through the night." What direct mention of religion we do find generally adopts a resolutely pantheistic outlook. Section 48 is typical in this regard:

> I hear and behold God in every object, yet understand God not in the least,
> Nor do I understand who there can be more wonderful than myself.
> Why should I wish to see God better than this day?
> I see something of God each hour of the twenty-four, and each moment then,
> In the faces of men and women I see God, and in my own face in the glass
> (Whitman 1973: 86–7)

The passage is typical in that its primary aim is to remove any hint of inequality between worshiper and the worshiped. Rather than a Power that demands obedience, God is present in every object and in every subject. With divinity visible in every countenance, the idea of an external authority looking down upon us is made to seem outdated and quaint. God, if he can be said to embody anything, embodies the principle of equality – the spirit of likeness that resides in everyone everywhere. Instead of serving to check or offset equality, religion comes to epitomize it.

"The main business of religions," Tocqueville thought, "is to purify, control, and restrain that excessive and exclusive taste for well-being which men acquire in times of equality" (Tocqueville 1969: 448). Though steeped in biblical allusion, "Song of Myself" assigns no such function to religion – nor, for that matter, does it assign any such function to the family, likewise valorized by Tocqueville for "remaining studiously aloof from the daily turmoil of worldly business" (p. 448). In an age dominated by the so-called "cult" of domesticity, it is worth noting just how distant "Song of Myself" remains from familial themes. This is certainly not owing to a lack of familiarity with such themes, which dominate Whitman's early fiction, where angry fathers and forgiving mothers occupy center stage. And the same dynamic returns in many other texts such as "As I Ebb'd with the Ocean of Life" and "Out of the Cradle Endlessly Rocking" (to cite only two) where the fundamental dualism of paternal land and maternal ocean organizes the action. And yet, as with the example of religious authority, there really is no secure place for the family in "Song of Myself."

> I am the poet of the woman the same as the man,
> And I say it is as great to be a woman as to be a man,
> And I say there is nothing greater than the mother of men.
> (Whitman 1973: 48)

In telling us that men and women are equal but that mothers are greater than both, Whitman makes Tocqueville's point: to speak in terms of the family is already to drift away from the language of equality. Wishing above all to articulate this language, his poem is careful to make the presence of the family as oblique as possible.

Finally, it should be obvious to any reader of "Song of Myself" that the whole idea of a collective political activism is entirely foreign, if not expressly contrary to the poem's designs. Simply put, working to achieve change through traditional channels of political authority is not just absent from the poem but is antithetical to Whitman's conception of what poetry can and should do. We know from documents composed around the same time as the 1855 edition of *Leaves* that his disgust with politics was such that he called for the elimination of political parties altogether (Whitman 1928: 92–113). Reflecting the same anti-institutional bias, that first edition formally anoints the bard "the equalizer of his land and age" and informs the people that "their Presidents shall not be their common referee so much as their poets shall" (Whitman 1959: 8). With such substitutions Whitman makes it clear that, while hardly renouncing politics as such, he does renounce the kind of political association and group civic engagement so highly praised by Tocqueville.

"Never was justice so mighty amid injustice," Whitman wrote in the mid-1850s, "never did the idea of equality erect itself so haughty and uncompromising amid inequality, as to-day" (Whitman 1928: 113). "Song of Myself" was written to illustrate and prove this observation. This is why the sites of resistance to democratic excess named by Tocqueville – religious authority, the family, political institutions – are either altered, muted, or rejected by the poem. But this is also why many of

Tocqueville's other critical insights into life in times of equality can prove so helpful in getting us beyond a merely honorific or self-congratulatory approach to this crucial subject.

References and Further Reading

Adams, Robert Martin (1959). *Strains of Discord: Studies in Literary Openness*. Ithaca, NY: Cornell University Press.

Cushman, Stephen (1991). *Fictions of Form in American Poetry*. Princeton, NJ: Princeton University Press.

Dimock, Wai-Chee (1996). *Residues of Justice: Literature, Law, Philosophy*. Berkeley: University of California Press.

Emerson, Ralph Waldo (1990). *Essays First and Second Series*. New York: Library of America.

Fisher, Philip (1999). *Still the New World: American Literature in a Culture of Creative Destruction*. Cambridge, MA: Harvard University Press.

Fletcher, Angus (2004). *A New Theory for American Poetry: Democracy, the Environment and the Future of Imagination*. Cambridge, MA: Harvard University Press.

Lawrence, D. H. ([1923] 1969). *Studies in Classic American Literature*. New York: Viking.

Matthiessen, F. O. (1941). *American Renaissance: Art and Expression in the Age of Emerson and Whitman*. New York: Oxford University Press.

Moon, Michael (1991). *Disseminating Whitman: Revision and Corporeality in Leaves of Grass*. Cambridge, MA: Harvard University Press.

Pearce, Roy Harvey (1961). *The Continuity of American Poetry*. Princeton, NJ: Princeton University Press.

Stauffer, John (2002). *The Black Hearts of Men: Radical Abolitionists and the Transformation of Race*. Cambridge, MA: Harvard University Press.

Tocqueville, Alexis de (1969). *Democracy in America*, trans. George Lawrence. New York: Harper Perennial.

Whitman, Walt (1928). *Walt Whitman's Workshop: A Collection of Unpublished Manuscripts*, ed. Clifton Joseph Furness. Cambridge, MA: Harvard University Press.

Whitman, Walt (1959). *Walt Whitman's Leaves of Grass: The First (1855) Edition*, ed. Malcolm Cowley. New York: Viking.

Whitman, Walt (1973). *Leaves of Grass: Norton Critical Edition*, ed. Sculley Bradley and Harold W. Blodgett. New York: Norton.

29
"Crossing Brooklyn Ferry"

James Dougherty

"I am with you, you men and women of a generation hence, or ever so many generations hence" (Whitman 1856: 212). There is force in this annunciation. Whitman makes himself present to us, through the setting he depicts, through his "meditations" on it, and through the voice that speaks to us in "Crossing Brooklyn Ferry." Titled "Sun-Down Poem," it first appeared in the second (1856) edition of *Leaves of Grass*. Thoreau told a friend that it and "Song of Myself" were Whitman's two best poems. Indeed "Crossing Brooklyn Ferry" has come to figure almost as prominently as "Song of Myself" in discussions of Whitman's work. They complement each other, the latter being the more radically innovative, the former seeming more conventional but equally complex in its demands upon the reader's imagination.

Some early drafts of the poem survive in Whitman's manuscripts. After its first publication, he revised it in subsequent editions, retitling it, removing a few lines and passages, altering punctuation and capitalization, dividing it into sections and, over the years, altering those divisions. (The Textual Variorum of *Leaves of Grass*, *Var.*: 217–25, records these revisions, some of which are important to a full understanding of the poem.) The poem assumed its standard form in the 1881 edition of *Leaves of Grass*.

"Crossing Brooklyn Ferry" can be read as a poem in the Romantic tradition, a meditation on a landscape culminating in a deeper insight into the poet and his circumstances. It should also be taken as a reflection on urban life in America in the mid-nineteenth century. Again, because the poem meditates on how personal experience is conserved and communicated, it is a poem about poetry itself. And in recent years, the complex relationship between "I" and "You" has invited readers to reflect on how the poet uses language in his struggle to ensure that he is indeed with us, the men and women of another generation. These several accounts of "Crossing Brooklyn Ferry" complement one other, each furthering our understanding of the poem.

A Romantic Poem

"Flood-tide below me! I see you face to face!" (Whitman 1996: 307). The invocation recalls Wordsworth's apostrophe to the sylvan Wye and Shelley's to the Ravine of Arve and to the West Wind. A good point of entry into "Crossing Brooklyn Ferry" is to read it as a latter-day Romantic landscape poem, the kind that Meyer Abrams characterized as the Greater Romantic Lyric (Abrams 1965). Like the prototypical "Tintern Abbey," Whitman's poem begins by situating a speaker in a moment of powerful response to a landscape, describing that landscape in some detail, and searching for the ground of his response. The search deepens into meditation, arrives at an insight, and returns to the original setting, with which it has never completely lost touch. Typically poems in this genre acknowledge not only a spiritual "something" deeply interfused into the landscape but also another human presence, so that the poet's voice is not altogether soliloquy, the "overheard" speech postulated by John Stuart Mill (1981: 348), but dialogic, personal address.

However much Whitman may be associated with the "open road," in its themes and form "Crossing Brooklyn Ferry" is circular and repetitive, a ferry-like shuttling between alternatives. (Fulton Ferry was a double-ended craft plying a tidal waterway.) As the poem begins Whitman is struck with an overwhelming sense of presence, a "face to face" encounter, not only with the anonymous people around him on the ferry from Manhattan to Brooklyn but also with the harborscape, most especially the shipping, the moving waters and the waning sunlight. It is an encounter akin to what Sigmund Freud, in *Civilization and Its Discontents*, termed an "oceanic moment." That surge of at-one-ness immediately yields to a pang of loss, for the moment and the setting alike are in transition, moving not only through the water but also through time. To read the poem within its Romantic context is to follow a meditative process leading Whitman to recognize a spiritual presence pervading the landscape and incorporating the speaker-poet and his fellows into a common universal being. And it is to both the setting and the future passengers that he speaks.

As the ecstatic unity of the first few lines wanes, the poet thinks regretfully of the "disintegrated" solitude of each person's existence, and the brevity of those moments of "glory" – even if they may come again not only for him but also for the others and for "others that are to follow" (Whitman 1856: 212). What sustains one's sense of "I" through time, not just from visionary moment to quotidian interval, but from year to year, generation to generation? What makes the poet's experience, on this ferry at this sundown, similar enough to the experience of those around him, and those who will follow him, that they can share his experience, and he theirs? He divines a "simple, compact, well-join'd scheme" (p. 211) in which he and his fellow passengers are united, and they with others across time. Returning to the scene (section 3), and reaffirming his bond with future men and women (section 4) the poet declares that all share in a "float forever held in solution"(p. 216), a chemical metaphor for a universal substance, out of which individual souls are precipitated for a sojourn in time, and to which they return at death. Though this "float" has been identified with the Emersonian Oversoul (e.g., Miller 1992: 70–2), it is not Transcendental but Immanentist, that is, spiritual and material interfused. (In the Preface to the 1855 edition Whitman had mentioned a "sense of the oneness of nature" that is "called up of the float of the brain of the world" (Whitman 1996: 20). Theories of recurrence were widely diffused in Whitman's culture, from the literary fascination with Wordsworth's Immortality Ode, to the Egyptology movement (*NUPM*, 1: 198), to the "universal magnetic fluid" of the mesmerists (Reynolds 1995: 261).

In the course of his meditation Whitman also explores other, less speculative, bases of unity that transcend time. In section 6 he acknowledges that he too "[knew] what it was to be evil," cataloguing the "dark patches" of self-doubt and personal sin (Whitman 1856: 216). (It is on this passage that biographical and psychological readings of the poem have concentrated.) He likens human life to a play, in which the roles are forever fixed though the changing players may make more or less of their parts. And, early, middle, and late in the poem, he returns to New York's nexus of cities and waters, a "being than which none else is perhaps more spiritual" (p. 221). The poem's late movement, section 9, returns to the scene detailed in section 3 – but with an important syntactical change. In 3 its features were explicitly or implicitly the objects of "I saw," phenomena of consciousness. Now they are subjects, not objects: the seabirds fly, the light diverges, the cities thrive. The poet speaks no longer as a sustaining center of consciousness, but as one affirming what each thing characteristically does: his imperatives do not compel the river to flow or the masts to stand up, but rather recognize and applaud their autonomous being and doing.

In a brief, muted coda, however, Whitman reaffirms the idealist side of his visionary city, in a catalogue-become-litany invoking its features as "dumb [i.e., silent] beautiful ministers." Part of what things are and do is spiritual, serving as a ground of meditation, "furnish[ing] [their] parts toward eternity" (Whitman 1856: 222). The splendid physical scene from which the poem began is reaffirmed in its every detail as "the soul." Whitman may be thinking of a divine, universal soul, of which all individuals are temporary if god-like incarnations. But it is also characteristic of the Romantic mode, particularly as articulated by Emerson, to identify this "soul" with poetic consciousness, so that ship and factory, gulls and passengers, alike are absorbed into the poet's god-like vision. "Crossing Brooklyn Ferry" toys with the solipsism against which Emerson had struggled in *Nature* and in "Experience." Quentin Anderson reads the poem as a contest between Whitman's confidence in his omnivorous poetic powers and fear of imprisonment within his own sensorium: "instead of falling back on the utter solipsism of complete delusion, he faced about and carried his cosmic inward spectacle to the print-shop" (Anderson 1971: 136).

However, Anderson also points out that no Whitman poem is "more successful in offering us an apprehended world" (Anderson 1971: 121). Romanticist readings of "Crossing Brooklyn Ferry" frequently emphasize the mimetic power of Whitman's lengthy and reiterated description of the ferry passage. Like Coleridge in his Dejection Ode, Whitman takes pains to recreate the atmospherics of his passage, especially the senses of light and motion. He observes the spokes of light that surround his reflected image in the water; he sees the play of yellow and shadow on the bodies of the gulls; he detects the violet hue of the steam vapor: appropriately these effects have been termed Luminist (Thomas 1987) or impressionist (St Armand 1979), or linked with Ruskin's attention to the illusionist use of color in *Modern Painters* (Betsky-Zweig 1979). The harborscape is presented not objectively, but rather as it would be seen from a consciousness within it – Whitman's, the future travelers', the readers'. This element of subjectivity supports Whitman's claim to be with us, by reversing it: we are there with him, at the ferry's rail. Atmospheric detail likewise supports our sense that the ferry is moving through time and space. He prolongs the 10-minute journey, so that before it ends the sun is no longer "half an hour high," but has set, leaving the shores illuminated by the glare of foundry chimneys. Details of the harborscape are catalogued not at random but as they would successively pass before a person crossing from Manhattan to Brooklyn. And the scene itself is in flux, with a tide roiling the East River, harbor traffic coming and going from the sea and the Hudson, and sailors and passengers moving about the vessels. Detail and motion draw us into the scene, as they did in the nineteenth-century panorama (Dougherty 1992: 167–71).

Further, the Heraclitean setting fits with the poem's meditation on permanence and impermanence, multiplicity and unity. But unlike landscape poems in which the present flows into the irrecoverable past, here the motion is cyclic, the poet's thoughts shuttling between a future that becomes the present and a present that becomes the past as he imagines his relationship with those who will someday ride the ferry either in fact or by the proxy of his poem. This reciprocal motion renders change illusory, time timeless: it "avails not." The way forward, T. S. Eliot would later write, is the way back.

A City Poem

Thinking back on his youth in *Specimen Days* (1882), Whitman wrote that his life in Brooklyn and Manhattan "was curiously identified with Fulton ferry" (Whitman 1996: 724–5). Scholars following his suggestion have identified "Crossing Brooklyn Ferry" as a great poem of urban life. For Whitman the city was a vortex – or a spectacle – of dynamic forces. Almost always he presents himself in motion, walking Broadway, riding an omnibus, crossing Fulton ferry: part of the cities' endless flux, yet sufficiently detached to enjoy it as a "show." Alan Trachtenberg, seizing Whitman's term "procession," defines urban motion and the poet's relation to it as processional, a matter of ebb and flow, immersion and observation, through which Whitman discovered in the quotidian sights and events of city life an unnoticed "significance" or value. This empowered him to conflate city life with poetic inspiration, the ferry with the poem, and to address the city crowd as "ministers" of a harmony with the world, "a great trope for communal love, labor, and spirit" (Trachtenberg 1996: 164–5).

Whitman's encounter with the city was always sensuous, very often sexual. William Sharpe writes that the poet, like his contemporary Baudelaire, assumed in many poems the role of the *flâneur*, wandering the city's public places in search of a yet-unknown lover, perhaps one of those "young men" mentioned in section 6 (Sharpe 1990). The notebook where this poem began is also a store of the names of men, of addresses of specific businesses and descriptions of city sights. But there also Whitman reminds himself "put Manhattan for New York all through" (Whitman 1959: 5), thus linking "Crossing Brooklyn Ferry" with his poems about Mannahatta, his idealized city of casual but loving sexual adventure (Sharpe 1990: 82, Miller 1969: 202).

Sharpe notes, however, that many of Whitman's poems, "Crossing Brooklyn Ferry" among them, confess not requited desire but a profound loneliness (Sharpe 1990: 77). Trachtenberg says that Whitman's vision in "Crossing Brooklyn Ferry" is a fragile triumph over "forces of disintegration" (1996: 173). These forces, scarcely manifest in the poem, are social for some critics, psychological for others. Betsy Erkkila and M. Wynn Thomas argue that the "glories" celebrated in "Crossing Brooklyn Ferry" are fictions that Whitman created to gainsay the facts. Whitman, they write, lived in a time of social crisis, for which his city served as a microcosm. According to Thomas, "Crossing Brooklyn Ferry" masks two "historically specific" fissures beneath its luminist glow: the widening split between capital (mercantile Manhattan) and labor (residential Brooklyn); and the division within the poet's own "baffled" brain between his ideal America and the materialism that infected rich and poor alike. "The unilluminated, unresponsive reality of American society was . . . threatening to extinguish his creative faith" (Thomas 1987: 112). The poem's closing affirmations, then, appear to Thomas as the poetic reconstruction and reconsecration of a profaned world, accomplished by asserting his trust in the "sheer physical process of existence" (p. 114). Erkkila also sees the poem as "a response to the fact of fracture in self and world" (Erkkila 1989: 143), embracing not only the forces cited by Thomas and a worsening split between North and South, but also a personal crisis born of his alienation from a culture indifferent to his poetry and a society hostile to his sexual yearning for the "young men" glanced at in lines 79–80. It was in the face of all this evil that he designed his "simple, compact, well-join'd scheme," the poem itself, affirming the ideal city and citizen, over against the disjointed realities.

Whitman was among the first to describe the sensation of being immersed in the great urban crowd, linked only by chance with those sharing the same street corner or the same ferry boat. In "Crossing Brooklyn Ferry" the flood-tide may have a face, but the men and women about him do not. The great catalogue of section 3 notices only the faraway pilots and sailors. His rapture with the natural setting and the gross features of the cityscape is not the universal ecstasy depicted in section 5 of "Song of Myself," but rather an indirect acknowledgment of his disaffiliation from the crowd that surrounds him. He confesses later in the poem that he "saw many I loved . . . yet never told them a word" (Whitman 1856: 217). In Thomas's view, the commodification of labor has reduced them to a featureless mass. But, he says, Whitman evaded this conclusion, translating historically specific economic alienation into "evil," a universalized "human condition," to make it a basis for the mutuality he seeks to establish with those who share his experience (Thomas 1987: 112).

Whitman's alienation may indeed have some less specific ground, not the human condition perhaps but the urban condition, in which humans are increasingly separated from communities such as the family, the local church, or the stable neighborhood, mediators between the individual and the mass, that situate him in time and space. As Whitman begins his search for a spiritual "scheme" he acknowledges that he is himself "disintegrated," as is "everyone" (l. 7). The unmediated perspective of the *flâneur* is wholly a matter of individual perception. In one of Whitman's favorite city words, it is a "show" projected on the eye and mind of the lonely city-walker: "flashes and specks," as he called the city in "There Was a Child Went Forth" (Whitman 1996: 139). Seven decades later T. S. Eliot would call it simply "unreal."

In his extended descriptions of the city Whitman seeks to reintegrate himself with an urban community, through the medium of shared vision. The catalogues are not random but rather follow the natural rhythm of eyesight, shifting from objects near at hand (the waves, his own reflection) to those at or near the horizon (the hills of Brooklyn, the arriving ships) to orient the passenger in space. Further, the details selected include landmarks like the hills, storehouses and foundries – features that would draw the eye of a passenger, as familiar checkpoints of his daily journey, features which likewise become familiar to the reader as, moving through the poem, he or she encounters them again and again. The reader thus comes to share the city's (and the poem's) topology, dwelling in the poem as in a city, in a common visual and physiological space. Eyesight, as deployed in this poem, serves not to isolate the reader/viewer as a connoisseur of "shows," but to incorporate the reader into what the urbanist Christian Norberg-Schulz terms an existential space (1971: 11ff.). The ground of communion here is not a metaphysical "float," but an enveloping everyday landscape, in which the reader becomes an initiate, a citizen. "Appearances, . . . indicate what you are" (Whitman 1856: 221): flashes and specks, thus held in common, point the way to being, to incarnate reality (Sharpe 1990: 95–100, Dougherty 1992: 185–201).

A Poem about Poems

When Whitman invokes "you men and women of a generation, or ever so many generations hence" (l. 21), he is speaking not to his readers but directly to "you that shall cross from shore to shore years hence" (l. 5, Whitman 1856: 211). It is only near the poem's end that he acknowledges those who share his experience through the medium of print, "you who peruse me" (l. 112, p. 220). In between he has been gradually changing the terms of his relation to "you," eliding future passengers into future readers. So readers may be forgiven for supposing that, when we look back on Whitman because he looked forward to us, we are linked not by riding the Fulton ferry but by reading "Crossing Brooklyn Ferry."

Whitman's question, "What is it, then, between us?" (l. 54, Whitman 1856: 216) reads in more than one way. Taking "between" as a separator, it deprecates the barriers of time and distance; taking it as a connector, it also asks, What subtle knot ties me to you? What unmentioned instrument pours my meaning into you? (ll. 96–97: 219). The float of the oversoul and the dark patches of moral failure – the metaphysics – to be sure. The harborscape itself, for that is how Whitman answers his own question in part 5: "I too lived, Brooklyn of ample hills was mine" (l. 57, Whitman 1996: 310). Without naming it, he identifies the tie as the poem itself. For his fellow passengers, with whom he shares the commute between work and home, he has singled out landmarks: the warehouses on South Street, the foundries at Corlears Point, the Lower Bay. They share an existential space. For his readers also he proffers bonds of shared experience. The attentive descriptions of sundance on the water, gulls floating overhead, the coming on of dusk, depend on common reference points with his readers. We partake in his experience only insofar as our imaginations fuse the poem's powerful words with our own personal memory of comparable harbor crossings. "These and all else were to me the same as they are to you" (l. 49, 1856: 215). Arguing that Whitman advocated a "natural" reading that "repeat[s], on the reader's part, the same experience Whitman has when he interacts with nature," Mark Bauerlein says that "Crossing Brooklyn Ferry" is a "poem most clearly about reading." Those who read it sympathetically read not a text but through it "read" the tangible reality of the harborscape (Bauerlein 1991: 106–7), so that passenger and intuitive reader are, in truth, one and the same.

Whitman, like Wordsworth, endeavors to look steadily at his subject, but this includes more than his sensations and his reflections. Periodically he addresses – even harangues – his audience, adverting to the relationship between the poet and those who, through his words, are brought to share his experience. "Crossing Brooklyn Ferry" is a meditation on how writing negotiates with time. If indeed time "avails not," as he insists in the poem's first 20 lines, then future passengers might just look and think for themselves, and there would be no need for writing poems about the crossing. For Whitman as the author of this poem, though, time does avail. The currents are rushing him swiftly far away. The oceanic moment, like the experience of *déjà vu*, retreats and dissolves even as he tries to advert to it. His poem undertakes to record and perpetuate what is already past as his reflection begins – and still further past when the poem is written. From section 3 onward, Whitman changes his standpoint from his own moment to that of the future viewer or reader: "Just as you feel when you look on the river and sky, so I felt" (l. 22, Whitman 1856: 213). The time of experiencing the crossing is shifted from Whitman's time, forever in the past, to the present moment always unfolding as the poem is read: "Just as you stand and lean on the rail. . . . " (p. 213). Breasting the tide of the past, the ferry-as-poem moves always in the present. Hence the fitness of his trope of the play (ll. 83–5, 110–11), whose roles, unfolding in the play's own time, look back on a succession of actors and actresses who have enacted them.

The invocation of an absent person (the reader), and the speaker's poignant sense of separation both from that person and from the experience on which the poem is grounded, are in truth the condition in which all words are written. Imaginative retrieval of an absent person (the writer), and of the experience described (a harbor now different and yet the same), are the condition in which all words are read. And so "Crossing Brooklyn Ferry" is, among other things, a poem drawing attention to this sense of absence or distance: a poem that speaks for all poems. Looking forward, looking backward, looking at, it plies between poet, reader, and scene.

A Poem about Presence

But "Crossing Brooklyn Ferry" is not altogether an elegiac poem about absence. In the first (1856) version, Whitman's claim, "I am with you" (l. 21) was immediately followed by a proclamation of personal presence: "I project myself, also I return – I am with you, and know how it is" (Whitman 1856: 213). Again, immediately after the catalogue of the harbor, he said, "I project myself a moment to tell you – also I return" (p. 215). And, at the end of what would become section 8, his string of tantalizing rhetorical questions ends with an audacious claim:

> What I promised without mentioning it, have you not accepted?
> What the study could not teach – what the preaching could not accomplish is accomplished, is it not?
> What the push of reading could not start is started by me personally, is it not?
> (Whitman 1856: 219)

Thus Whitman's murmur to the reader "I am as good as looking at you now, for all you cannot see me" (l. 91, p. 218) exceeds his text-mediated descriptions and reflections: he asserts that he has "project[ed]" himself "personally" (if not physically) into "your" presence. Is this not to promise more than a poem can deliver?

Readers acquainted with Whitman may see it as a familiar gesture. Descrying steamers sailing through his poems, announcing that it is he, not his book, whom the reader holds, Whitman sought again and again to dissolve the barrier of print and to place in immediate contact his self, his reader, and his subject. Alternatively, the formulaic "project . . . return" may suggest that Whitman is echoing the Spiritualist or Swedenborgian thought so popular in his day, according to which an adept could travel, spiritually, to places remote in space and time (Reynolds 1995: 263–6). In the 1860 revision he removed these lines, proclaiming his "projection" into the passenger-reader's presence. Nonetheless their spirit lingers throughout the poem. Whitman is with us – not because he was sentimentally wistful about an intimacy with his reader, or because he believed in time travel, but because, while making these claims, he fashioned a poetic to support them.

As C. Carroll Hollis observed, Whitman uses the pronoun of presence, "You," far more frequently than any other poet of his time (Hollis 1983: 88–9). It is one of his devices for placing his reader in his presence, within earshot of his imagined voice. As a poem about the powers of the ego, "Song of Myself" relegates "you" to a lesser place as ratifying listener, alter ego, or "soul"; it can be read, as John Stuart Mill would have it, as an utterance overheard. On the other hand, "Crossing Brooklyn Ferry" is everywhere an invocation, "I" speaking to "you" face to face, demanding attention, inviting response, whether "you" is the scene, the passengers, or the reader. His address does not admit of distance or absence: "Closer yet I approach you" (l. 86, 1856: 218).

One may take Whitman's poem as a declamation, like "Song of Myself," by a speaker in a public assembly, whose appeal to "you" is an oratorical utterance, aimed at persuasion or exhortation. The early *Leaves of Grass* was designed as the script for an oration, an oral performance delivered by a prophet, for listeners rather than readers (Hollis 1983: 49). Kerry Larson has argued that "Crossing Brooklyn Ferry" seeks to construct, for an implicit audience, the grounds for a civil consensus (Larson 1988: 6). "You" is, in turn, his fellow passengers; or all those who have fallen out of the float into the identity of a body; or all those who know what it is to be evil. It becomes the "we" who appears first in the sixth and then the eighth sections, and who speaks as a single "soul" to ratify the "dumb, beautiful ministers" in the poem's coda.

But there is a flaw, or a gap, in the oration's rhetoric. For though the poem seems to be rising toward some persuasive insight in section 7, and to speak from the authority of that insight in sections 8–9, no compelling argument is proclaimed in between; rather it seems already behind us, assumed before the poem began. This gap occurs where Whitman canceled lines reiterating his ideas about the "float." But as Larson puts it, "The passage does not so much convey a meaning as tell us that a meaning has been conveyed" (1988: 11). Indeed Whitman taunts us, saying "preaching could not accomplish" the unity of I and You – and yet it "is accomplish'd, is it not?" (l. 100, Whitman 1856: 219).

This rhetorical sleight-of-hand has led scholars such as Hollis (1983: ch. III) and Tenney Nathanson (1992: 6–7) to invoke the "speech act" theory of J. L. Austin, according to which the poem's own declarations deliver You into the presence of I. Hollis notes Whitman's frequent use of "illocutionary acts" (Austin's term for speech acts that carry out what they are saying as they say it) to give his written words the immediacy and power of face-to-face communication. Nathanson adds to Austin's theory an emphasis on the role that voice plays in some of Whitman's poems, including "Crossing Brooklyn Ferry." "Whitman's appeal to voice," he writes, " . . . manage[s] to attain an uncanny immediacy" (Nathanson 1992: 7), for "the voice is no ordinary one: it traverses not only space, but also time; it conveys not only sound, but a personal presence " (Nathanson 1992: 12). This voice is "magical" (see Anderson 1971: 125, 132), for it claims immunity from the body's limitations and the constraints of culture, and seeks to re-enter a psychologically "archaic" world where, shaman-like, words have power to incarnate what they name (Nathanson 1992: 9).

But, Nathanson says, this they cannot do: we must indeed rely on "the push of reading" if we are to hear the voice; and whether written or spoken they are only the representation of presence: "[I]n Whitman's work it is not voice but the carefully orchestrated economy of voice and writing, a shell-game of presence and absence, that generates the illusion of such productive power" (Nathanson 1992: 14). That we sense the poet's presence is, finally, an illusion, a mark of how skillfully, if ruefully, Whitman has masked the fact that there is not a pea under any of his verbal walnut shells. Bauerlein writes: "[I]n the translation from sound to writing, the vocal presence, the immediacy of the speaker's soul, is left behind. A silence ensues, a voiceless vacuum . . . " (Bauerlein 1991: 46). To these late twentieth-century readers, "Crossing Brooklyn Ferry" shares not only the elegiac mode of "Tintern Abbey" but also the wordless impasses of Coleridge's Dejection Ode.

Having described the "oceanic moment," Freud dismissed it as a state unfamiliar to himself, and therefore an illusion, perhaps the survival of a primitive state of consciousness before the development of the ego – "limitless narcissism." A like skepticism pervades post-structuralist readings of "Crossing Brooklyn Ferry," according to which words cannot evoke presence. The poet is no longer even overheard, but made mute by linguistic self-consciousness. To an acutely literate age, as Walter Ong pointed out in *The Presence of the Word*, words have been silenced: they are read, but not heard, and so have lost much of their power to summon one person into the presence of another (Ong 1981: 63–74).

In a pioneering – if neglected – study of Whitman published in 1973, E. Fred Carlisle said:

> A poem is a word: one spoken between man and man; a word which embodies the voice and presence of the poet. The reader who encounters a Whitman poem with this in mind . . . begins to hear the voice of the poet; he begins to experience the presence of the man who may be dead, yet who lives in the spoken language of the poem. (Carlisle 1973: xiii)

If Carlisle's overarching purpose, to discern Whitman's personal identity through and within *Leaves of Grass*, may seem quaint today, his personalist approach to the poet's word remains a living alternative to the reduction of Whitman's language to a shell game. Grounded on Martin Buber's and Walter Ong's approaches to the dialogic word, Carlisle's reading of Whitman recognizes that the poem is the unfolding of the poet's dialogue with his persona and the reader's corresponding dialogue with that persona (Carlisle 1973: 29–30).

"Crossing Brooklyn Ferry" is neither an overheard monologue, Whitman mumbling to himself as he stands at the rail, nor the kind of public declamation he would roar from atop a Broadway omnibus (Whitman 1996: 727). Rather it is a voiced address to another person, the reader-become-hearer. Between them speaker and listener seek and create yet another ground of community: not the harbor, nor the metaphysics, nor the poem as a read "script," but rather in a sequence of words that are shared as they are uttered and shared as they are heard (Ong 1962: 51). In "Burnt Norton," another experimenter with "you" wrote, "My words echo /Thus, in your mind" (ll. 14–15). Though this could be said of any poem, such a verbal understanding is peculiarly at the heart of "Crossing Brooklyn Ferry" because this poem so self-consciously meditates on the grounds of human community and so insistently draws on the power of language to create that community. Not only through its use of the second person and its performative utterances, but also through the techniques of oral poetry – reiterating its phrases, drawing on formulaic epithets like "scallop-edg'd waves" – "Crossing Brooklyn Ferry" draws its reader into a shared aural space.

As Carlisle said, quoting Buber, the spoken word is uttered here and heard there, occupying "an oscillating sphere between the persons" (Carlisle 1973: 23). As an alternative for that oscillating sphere, the ferry once again is the apt image, a transitive space between the speaker hearing himself and the listener repeating the words as he understands them. "Face to face with the presence of offered meaning which we call a text," wrote George Steiner, "we seek to hear its language" (Steiner 1989: 156). Though "Crossing Brooklyn Ferry" may seem to depend on our visual imaginations cocreating its exterior spaces, New York harbor and its human communities, or upon our reading of a "text," it depends equally on the aural imagination, within whose interiors a voice speaks for those who can hear.

> Closer yet I approach you,
> What thought you have of me now, I had as much of you – I laid in my stores in advance,
> I consider'd long and seriously of you before you were born.
>
> (ll. 86–8, Whitman 1855: 218)

References and Further Reading

Abrams, Meyer (1965). Structure and Style in the Greater Romantic Lyric. In Frederick W. Hilles and Harold Bloom (eds.), *From Sensibility to Romanticism*. New York: Oxford University Press, pp. 527–60.

Anderson, Quentin (1971). *The Imperial Self*. New York: Knopf.

Bauerlein, Mark (1991). *Whitman and the American Idiom*. Baton Rouge: Louisiana State University Press.

Betsky-Zweig, S. (1979). An Uncommon Language: Crossing with Whitman. *Dutch Quarterly Review of Anglo-American Letters*, 10: 258–71.

Carlisle, E. Fred (1973). *The Uncertain Self: Whitman's Drama of Identity*. East Lansing: Michigan State University Press.

Cohen, Tom (1993). Only the Dead Know Brooklyn Ferry: The Inscription of the Reader in Whitman. *Arizona Quarterly*, 49 (2): 23–51.

Dougherty, James (1993). *Walt Whitman and the Citizen's Eye*. Baton Rouge: Louisiana State University Press.

Erkkila, Betsy (1989). *Whitman the Political Poet*. New York: Oxford University Press.

Hollis, C. Carroll (1983). *Language and Style in* Leaves of Grass. Baton Rouge: Louisiana State University Press.

Larson, Kerry (1988). *Whitman's Drama of Consensus*. Chicago: University of Chicago Press.

Mill, John Stuart (1981). Thoughts on Poetry and Its Varieties. In John M. Robson and Jack Stillinger (eds.), *The Collected Works of John Stuart Mill*, vol. 1: *Autobiography and Literary Essays*. Toronto: University of Toronto Press, pp. 341–65.

Miller, Edwin Haviland (1969). *Walt Whitman's Poetry: A Psychological Journey*. New York: New York University Press.

Miller, James E. Jr. (1992). Leaves of Grass: *America's Lyric-Epic of Self and Democracy*. New York: Twayne.

Nathanson, Tenney (1992). *Whitman's Presence: Body, Voice and Writing in* Leaves of Grass. New York: New York University Press.

Norberg-Schulz, Christian (1971). *Existence, Space and Architecture*. New York: Praeger.

Ong, Walter Jackson, SJ (1962). Voice as Summons for Belief. In *The Barbarian Within*. New York: Macmillan, pp. 49–67.

Ong, Walter Jackson, SJ (1981). *The Presence of the Word*. Minneapolis: University of Minnesota Press.

Reynolds, David S. (1995). *Walt Whitman's America: A Cultural Biography*. New York: Knopf.

Sharpe, William Chapman (1990). Walt Whitman's Urban Incarnation. In *Unreal Cities*. Baltimore: Johns Hopkins University Press, pp. 92–101.

St Armand, Barton (1979). Transcendence Through Technique: Whitman's "Crossing Brooklyn Ferry" and Impressionist Painting. In Harry R. Garvin and James M. Heath (eds.), *The Arts and their Interrelations*. Lewisburg, PA: Bucknell University Press, pp. 62–72.

Steiner, George (1989). *Real Presences*. Chicago: University of Chicago Press.

Stovall, Floyd (1974). *The Foreground of Leaves of Grass*. Charlottesville: University of Virginia Press.

Thomas, M. Wynn (1987). *The Lunar Light of Whitman's Poetry*. Cambridge, MA: Harvard University Press.

Trachtenberg, Alan (1996). Whitman's Lesson of the City. In Betsy Erkkila and Jay Grossman (eds.), *Breaking Bounds: Whitman and American Cultural Studies*. New York: Oxford University Press, pp. 163–73.

Whitman, Walt (1959). *An 1855–56 Notebook toward the Second Edition of* Leaves of Grass, ed. Harold W. Blodgett. Carbondale: Southern Illinois University Press.

Whitman, Walt (1856). "Sun-Down Poem." In *Leaves of Grass*. New York: Fowler & Wells, pp. 211–22. Available at Ed Folsom and Kenneth M. Price (eds.), *The Walt Whitman Archive*. < http:/ /www.whitmanarchive.org/works/>.

Whitman, Walt (1996). *Whitman: Poetry and Prose*, ed. Justin Kaplan. New York: Library of America.

30
"Out of the Cradle Endlessly Rocking"

Howard Nelson

Among the materials that Richard Maurice Bucke assembled in his early biographical volume *Walt Whitman* (1883) were sketches written by people who knew the poet in earlier days. Included in these was a reminiscence by Helen Price, the daughter of women's rights activist Abby Price. Whitman often visited the Price home in Brooklyn in the 1850s for socializing and discussion. During one visit Whitman mentioned that he had written a new poem "about a mocking bird . . . founded on a real incident." Mrs Price asked him to bring it along the next time he visited. A few days later he came back, but rather than read the poem himself, he asked that someone else read it instead. A man who lived with the Prices, a student of Swedenborgianism, read it first, "with great appreciation and feeling." Whitman then asked Mrs Price to read. After her reading, the others insisted that Whitman take his turn. Helen Price, writing 25 years later, said: "That evening comes before me now as one of the most enjoyable of my life. At each reading fresh beauties revealed themselves to me. I could not say whose reading I preferred; [Whitman] liked my mother's, and Mr. A liked his." She also says that after the readings Whitman asked for suggestions from the others, including herself, 17 years old at the time: "I can remember how taken aback and nonplussed I was when he turned and asked me also" (Myerson 1991: 27–8). This anecdote gives a nice glimpse of Whitman, one of relatively few first-hand descriptions of him from those prewar years; it is also the earliest recorded appearance of what would become one of his best-known and most admired poems, "Out of the Cradle Endlessly Rocking."

The poem was published in December 1859 in the *Saturday Press*, a weekly edited by Whitman's friend and advocate Henry Clapp, under the title "A Child's Reminiscence." It was identified as a "Christmas or New Year's present" to the journal's readers, and while the title could have announced a sentimental seasonal piece, the poem was something very different from that. Nearly two hundred lines, it begins with a very long, incantatory sentence that pulls together a bird, nipples and breasts, a barefoot boy, briers and blackberries, the moon "swollen as if with tears" (*LG*: 247, l.

10), references to "the thousand responses of my heart never to cease" (l. 12) and some word "stronger and more delicious than any" (l. 14), though what that word would be is not identified at this point in the poem. It then tells an odd story of a boy who becomes fixated on a mockingbird and experiences a revelation from listening to its song. The poem then concludes with stanzas that identify the mysterious word, Death, and praise it in lines that are a kind of sea-music.

The *Saturday Press* aimed for a sophisticated and bohemian audience, but whatever the general readership may have made of this Christmas present, the poem and its author were immediately attacked in the *Cincinnati Daily Commercial*, in one of the most enthusiastically negative reviews Whitman ever received. It is worth quoting from as a reminder of what Whitman was up against, and how truly outrageous and flat-out bad his work seemed to some contemporaries. The reviewer was familiar with Whitman from the first two editions of *Leaves of Grass* a few years earlier, and he wasn't happy to see him back: "The author of *Leaves of Grass* has perpetrated another 'poem.'... It is a shade less heavy and vulgar than the *Leaves of Grass*, whose unmitigated badness seemed to cap the climax of poetic nuisances. But the present performance has all the emptiness, without half the grossness, of the author's former efforts" (Price 1996: 71). The poem seemed especially weak to the reviewer in terms of meaning, and he referred to it as "stupid and meaningless twaddle," "irreclaimable drivel and inexplicable nonsense," without "the glimmering ghost of an idea" (p. 72).

Almost as if in response to this first reviewer's diatribe about meaning, "Out of the Cradle" has been one of the most extensively analyzed of Whitman's poems over the years. This, in turn, is ironic, as Whitman specifically advised against intellectualizing the poem. In fact, he said that to approach the poem, or his poetry in general, through the intellect was a fundamental error.

Whitman responded to the attack immediately. In its January 7 issue, the *Saturday Press* reprinted the hostile review, followed by an unsigned essay by Whitman titled "All about a Mocking-Bird." This is an interesting document not only for its display of Whitman's tough-spiritedness in the face of criticism, but also for his comments on what he had done and what he hoped to do in his poetry. Far from being daunted by "the tip-top cutting and slashing criticism," he forecast a burst of new work: "We are able to declare that there will... soon crop out the true LEAVES OF GRASS, the fuller-grown work of which the former two issues were the inchoates – this forthcoming one, far, very far ahead of them in quality, quantity, and in supple lyric exuberance" (Price 1996: 74). He had in mind what would be the 1860 edition, which would contain not only "Out of the Cradle" (under the title "A Word Out of the Sea"), but also the "Children of Adam" and "Calamus" sequences, the core of his poetry on sex and love – a book at least as extravagant, ground-breaking, and full of genius, not to mention likely to offend, as the first edition had been in 1855.

Whitman's willingness to write reviews of his own work is well known, but in addition to being a booster of himself, he can also be one of his own most interesting critics – a useful one too, though one needs to be careful to watch for distortions and self-interest, and to allow for inconsistencies. For example, "supple lyric exuberance" is a good succinct description of Whitman's poetry; hard to do better in three words. Whitman's response to the charge of incomprehensibility is especially pertinent as a statement of artistic purpose:

> Of course the ordinary critic, even of good eye, high intellectual calibre, and well accomplished, grasps not, sees not, any such ideal ensemble [i.e., the larger coherence and meaning of *Leaves of Grass*] – likely sees not the only valuable part of these mystic leaves, namely, not what they state, but what they infer – scornfully wants to know what the Mocking-Bird means, who can tell? – gives credit only for what is proved to the surface ear – and makes up a very fine criticism, not out of the soul, to which these poems altogether appeal, and by which only they can be interpreted, but out of the intellect, to which Walt Whitman has not, as far as we remember, addressed one single word in the whole course of his writings. (Price 1996: 74)

The remark about soul versus intellect is an overstatement, but one can understand Whitman's impulse, faced with such antagonism and incomprehension, to go all the way. (In another poem from the 1860 edition, "Says," Whitman would say, "I say nourish a great intellect, a great brain; /If I have said anything to the contrary, I hereby retract it," *LG*: 598.) Another bit of advice came in a note that accompanied the poem in the *Saturday Press*: "Like the *Leaves of Grass*, the purport of this wild and plaintive song, well enveloped, and eluding definition, is positive and unquestionable, like the effect of music. The piece will bear reading many times – perhaps, indeed, only comes forth, as from recesses, by many repetitions" (Price 1996: 73). Some critics have seemed to recognize the wisdom of Whitman's suggestions, even as they analyze the poem; for example, James E. Miller, Jr. saying that the poem's meaning "is not a fusion of logic in the intellect but rather a fusion of emotions in the soul" (Miller 1957: 107), or Edwin Haviland Miller saying: "Read aloud – and the poem, like music, refuses to remain silent on the printed page – without the intrusion of the rational mind decreeing sense or a critical intelligence attempting explication, 'Out of the Cradle Endlessly Rocking' interprets itself. The erotic sounds and movements, as in Wagner's music, evoke birth, love, loss, and death" (Miller 1968: 177).

One person who read Whitman aloud was Henry James. Edith Wharton described an evening they spent together as James read Whitman:

> . . . all that evening we sat rapt while he wandered from "The Song of Myself" [sic] to "When lilacs last in the door-yard bloomed" . . . to the mysterious music of "Out of the Cradle," reading, or rather crooning it in a mood of subdued ecstasy till the fivefold invocation to Death tolled out like the knocks in the opening bars of the Fifth Symphony. (quoted in Miller 1968: 171)

Edwin Haviland Miller says that James had the right tone until he shifted into melodrama with the tolling of the word *death*. Miller is no doubt right about this: Whitman's "lisp'd to me the low and delicious word death" (*LG*: 252, l. 169) doesn't seem to call for Beethoven. While oral readings of any poem will of course vary, when

Whitman said, "like the effect of music," he probably had a particular kind of music in mind. In his essay responding to the attack, he said, "Walt Whitman's method in the construction of his songs is strictly the method of the Italian opera" (Price 1996: 75). This does not necessarily mean that the poem should be read in the manner of opera at its most dramatic or soaring, yet a reader moving from the 1855 edition (e.g., "Song of Myself") to the 1860 edition (e.g., "Out of the Cradle") may notice differences, and one is that the former is more slangy and sharp while the latter is more operatic.

Whitman was sensitive to the charge that he lacked art, even while he cultivated his free-wheeling workingman image. Following his comment about the intellect, he immediately turned to the question of the poem's "art-statement": "Is this man really an artist at all? Or not plainly a sort of naked and hairy savage, come among us, with yelps and howls, disregarding all our lovely metrical laws?" (Price 1996: 74–5). In "Song of Myself" there is a sense of improvisation. He speaks musically, yes, but also as if pulling from his back pocket and reading from a notebook on which he has jotted dazzling, often disconnected descriptions of what he sees as he moves around Manhattan and rural Long Island, and other parts of the country. With "Out of the Cradle" there is a stronger sense of both concentration and performance – a man stepping forward to sing a prepared and formal song. In "Song of Myself" Whitman famously referred to his poetry as a "barbaric yawp" (*LG*: 89), and late in life he still liked the idea of "letting fly": ". . . *Leaves of Grass* are 400, 430 pages of *let-fly.* No art, no schemes, no fanciful, delicate, elegant constructiveness – but *let-fly*" (Schmidgall 2001: 77). This from the same man who said he had broken down and rebuilt his poetry several times before he hit on his true style, and who constantly revised his earlier work throughout his life – a very determined and self-conscious writer trying to get it right. We are definitely in the territory of "Do I contradict myself? /Very well then, I contradict myself" (*LG*: 88) here. Whitman's contradictions are really quite delicious. Perhaps a way to think of this one, art versus let-fly, is that the kind of letting-fly Whitman was after was something like the enormously artful soulful extravagance of opera.

In the 1855 edition, opera had already exerted its influence and helped transform Whitman's poetry, but by 1860 he had gone further, and "Out of the Cradle" seems an effort to emulate opera more specifically. In spite of a bias against European artistic models and influences, Whitman became a great lover of opera, which was flourishing in New York City in the 1840s and 1850s. Two books that deal with the subject in depth, written almost 50 years apart, are Robert Faner's *Walt Whitman and Opera* (1951) and Gary Schmidgall's *Walt Whitman: A Gay Life* (1997). Faner shows that "Out of the Cradle" is indebted to opera in many ways, including its basic structure, "with its opening song of ecstatic love, its central lyric of waiting, and its final outburst of passionate grief" (Faner 1951: 88). The poem's opening luxurious sentence seems a sort of grammatical equivalent of virtuoso singing. The poem itself refers to the song of the mockingbird at its center as an aria. Schmidgall devotes a chapter in his lively and unconventional biographical study to opera, and in particular to

Whitman's favorite singer, Marietta Alboni, calling her "a potent-voiced progenitor of that overwhelmingly affecting and liberating vocalist, the mocking-bird in the greatest of the new poems in the 1860 *Leaves of Grass*" (Schmidgall 2001: 14). Opera may well hold the answer, or at least a large part of it, to one of the great questions of Whitman biography: how did it happen that the unexceptional and conventional writer Whitman had been was transformed into a great, enormously expansive, enormously original poet? Many influences come together to make Whitman's poetry. Oratory, the Bible, his mother, the natural world, the Civil War, have all been credited, by Whitman and others. But Whitman's many nights listening to opera gave him a crucial model and transforming force, and it is in "Out of the Cradle" that this is most apparent.

"Out of the Cradle" has been one of the poems of Whitman most admired for its technical skill. For example, when Paul Fussell, Jr. and W. D. Snodgrass, both strong students of prosody, write on Whitman's greatness as an artist, "Out of the Cradle" is exhibit A. Fussell says of the last section of the poem, "It is a passage perhaps as stunning technically as any Whitman ever wrote; we will have to arrive at *Four Quartets* before we encounter in reflective American poetry anything so brilliant in meter, in figure, and in lithe idiomatic precision" (Fussell 1962: 48). Snodgrass, writing on the same section and noting the way it returns to the poem's opening cadence, says, " . . . just when it is almost forgotten, Whitman fetches that rhythm back for his closing . . . That rhythm's reprise is as hair-raising as anything in our poetry" (Snodgrass 2002: 165). At the same time, for all the poem's brilliant effects, its dramatic gestures and emotional outpouring can be off-putting. Even by Whitman's standards, it is liberal in its use of 'O's and exclamation marks, and some passages, read out of context ("*Loud! Loud! / Loud I call to you my love!*," (*LG*: 249, ll. 81–2, italics in original), are melodramatic. These aspects of the poem are palatable and effective only if we grant Whitman his operatic space and tone.

"Out of the Cradle" is a poem that says, "This is where I come from – this is what made me." In this it resembles the earlier, simpler "There Was a Child Went Forth," which enumerates early experiences in a flow of images, and then concludes, "These became part of that child who went forth every day, and who now goes, and will always go forth every day" (*LG*: 366). The poem also has something in common with the seemingly random catalogue in section 15 of "Song of Myself," where Whitman casts a wide net gathering sights and sounds of his time and place, and concludes, "And such as it is to be of these more or less I am, /And of these one and all I weave the song of myself" (*LG*: 44). Taking those two passages together, "These became part of that child . . . " and "of these . . . I weave the song of myself," one has a framework for understanding "Out of the Cradle." In it, the strands are fewer – the ocean shore, an early experience with mockingbirds, later experience of loss and grief and a new sense of self – and their weaving is more dramatic, elaborate, and anguished. But the basic process is the same: a weaving of elements into one self, one song.

The setting of "Out of the Cradle" is the Long Island (Paumanok) seashore. The poet returns to this place which was important to him in boyhood. After the opening long sentence of invocation, he focuses on a particular memory. A pair of mocking-birds had nested in the briers near the shore, and the boy visited them day after day, "never too close, never disturbing them, /Cautiously peering, absorbing, translating" (*LG*: 248, ll. 29–30). The poet then begins a remarkable act of translating: birdsong into human language, bird experience into human experience – any worries about anthropomorphism totally cast aside. The birds at first appear as the image of perfect happiness, but soon the female bird disappears, leaving the male to perch and fly about near the nest singing wildly. The boy continues to visit the nest, sometimes at night, listening to the bird's singing, now referring to him as "his brother." This leads into the poem's aria, italicized, an outpouring of grief for lost love. When the bird's song is over, we return to the boy, "ecstatic, with his bare feet the waves, with his hair the atmosphere dallying, /The love in the heart now loose, now at last tumultuously bursting" (p. 251, ll. 136–7). This is the moment of revelation, and also transformation: "Now in a moment I know what I am for, I awake, /And already a thousand singers, a thousand songs, clearer, louder and more sorrowful than yours, /A thousand warbling echoes have started to life within me, never to die" (p. 252, ll. 147–9).

The poem blends past and present in an extremely subtle way. Does this transformation take place when the poet is a boy or when he is a man? Whitman has it both ways. The boy may have been ecstatic, but "the love in the heart now loose" probably belongs to the man. The bird's loss becomes the boy's, the boy's becomes the man's. He is transformed into a poet, "an outsetting bard," and the compelling force behind his singing will be, like the bird's, love, loss, longing: "unsatisfied love," "the fire, the sweet hell within" (*LG*: 252, l. 156).

Strong as this climactic moment is, the poem continues, as the poet there on the beach (man or boy) wants more: "O give me the clew! (it lurks in the night here somewhere,) /O if I am to have so much, let me have more!" (*LG*: 252, ll. 158–9). What he receives comes from the sea, a word that the sea whispers – the word Death, repeated, within a few lines, 10 times. The poem then concludes with the rocking with which it began. The image of a crone is added, as the one rocking the cradle, and the poem ends with the phrase, "The sea whisper'd me" (p. 253), a wording that can be taken two ways: that the sea has whispered *to* him, or that its message has in a sense created him.

Whitman never said anything more about the "real incident" that he mentioned to the Prices. The Long Island shore was a place of indelible memories for him. In his late prose memoir *Specimen Days,* he says:

> I spent intervals many years, all seasons, sometimes riding, sometimes boating, but generally afoot (I was always then a good walker), absorbing fields, shores, marine incidents . . . always liked the bare sea beach, south side . . . As I write, the whole experience comes back to me after the lapse of forty or more years – the soothing rustle of the waves, and the saline smell – boyhood times, the clamdigging, barefoot, and with trousers rolled up . . . (Whitman 1971: 7)

He even mentions looking for birds' eggs, though those of seagulls, not mockingbirds; and he refers to a seashore memory turning up years later in a poem, but it is "The Sleepers," not "Out of the Cradle." Here it should be noted that for all its dramatic gestures and high emotion, the poem does not sacrifice Whitman's powers of sharp-eyed, startling description, as when he describes the nest with its "four light-green eggs, spotted with brown," and in its renderings of moon, shadows, and sea-sounds. His description of whitecaps seen from the beach as "The white arms out in the breakers tirelessly tossing" is one of the astonishing images in Whitman's poetry.

It is entirely probable that Whitman had some such boyhood experience with mockingbirds as described in the poem, but whether it was that experience that turned him into an "outsetting bard," making him conscious of "the sweet hell within," is doubtful. Is he describing something that happened to him, perhaps around puberty? Pretty clearly, this is projection backward of complex emotional experiences on an earlier, and simpler, outward one.

Some critics have said that the issue of biographical origins doesn't matter; that it is speculation at best, and possibly a distraction. Fussell took this attitude in his essay, a contribution to a Whitman colloquy in 1960, which became *The Presence of Walt Whitman* (Lewis 1962), a book that gives a good sampling of what mid-twentieth-century Whitman criticism was like, and which remains an excellent handbook on the poem. Fussell says, "The 'key' which the boy seeks and finds in the poem will not, I think, admit us into any of the dark, winding corridors of Whitman's actual life. But the key does do something perhaps even better. It unlocks both for Whitman and for us the front door of the palace of art" (Fussell 1962: 51).

Another critic who backed away from a specifically biographical approach to the poem was Gay Wilson Allen. This is a little ironic, as Allen was the most influential biographer of Whitman of the past half-century, and his book, *The Solitary Singer*, specifically takes its title from a line in "Out of the Cradle." In his commentary on the poem Allen says, "Nearly all critics have thought it a veiled allegory of a personal experience, though no one has discovered what experience" (Allen 1955: 233). When Allen mentions the "Calamus" poems and their lament for lost love, he says that "Out of the Cradle" "could be a symbolical treatment of that experience, though the sublimity of the poem seems out of proportion to such motivation. A more universal interpretation gives the poem greater depth of meaning and therefore seems more tenable" (p. 235).

This was 1955, and Allen's book was a product of its time. Still, such a statement does make it easy to understand the note of impatience in the work of some gay critics, as well as other scholars of gender and sexuality, who since that time have done so much revealing work on Whitman's biography and poetry. Schmidgall, for example, wants no more "universal interpretation." He calls "Out of the Cradle" Whitman's "greatest lovelorn poem" and says that it is "the emotional linchpin of the third edition," an edition of "brimming homosexual pathos" (Schmidgall 1997: 179). Schmidgall has been criticized for projecting twentieth-century experience too freely onto that of the nineteenth. But that "Out of the Cradle" is in such close chronological proximity to "Calamus," Whitman's cluster of poems celebrating love between men, which in turn contains within it the poems that he had earlier put together as the sequence "Live Oak, with Moss", which tells the story of a relationship, full of yearning, between men, makes it seem quite reasonable to see "Out of the Cradle" as reflective of an actual love loss suffered by Whitman. After decades of biography and criticism that either ignored, downplayed, or denied the depth or full dimensions of same-sex love in Whitman (the older, more cautious Whitman himself doing some of the original denying), more recent research has looked at Whitman's relationships with other men in detail, and the leading candidate for the lost love in the years leading up to "Out of the Cradle" is Fred Vaughan, a young man with whom Whitman had an intense relationship in the 1850s. Charley Shively designates Vaughan "Calamus Lover" and envisions in vivid detail their times together (Shively 1987: 36–41), while Jonathan Ned Katz says, "It is possible that a romantic and sexual relationship with Vaughan, then between nineteen and twenty-two years old, inspired some of Whitman's Calamus poems, though there is no direct evidence of this" (Katz 2001: 124).

Whitman did not place "Out of the Cradle" in the "Calamus" group, but the lines beginning, "Nevermore the cries of unsatisfied love be absent from me" (*LG*: 253, l. 153) seem enough to justify linking this poem to those others. Later, when Whitman was experiencing unhappiness in a relationship with another man, Peter Doyle, he wrote in his journal, "Depress the adhesive nature /It is in excess – making life a torment . . . Remember Fred Vaughan" (quoted in Katz 2001: 129), and "*It is* IMPERATIVE, that I obviate & remove myself (& my orbit) *at all hazards*, from this incessant *enormous & abnormal* PERTURBATION" (p. 171). Whether Fred Vaughan or someone else was behind "Out of the Cradle," it is in any case interesting to compare the language of notebook and the language of poem, both likely arising from similar affairs of the heart – "the adhesive nature . . . is in excess" to "nevermore the cries of unsatisfied love be absent from me" (p. 252, l. 153); "*enormous & abnormal* PERTURBATIONS" to "the fire, the sweet hell within, /the unknown want" (p. 252, ll. 156–7).

Other problems besides those connected to love and desire have been suggested as contributing to a crisis in Whitman's psychic life between the 1855 and 1860 editions. The approaching war and the splitting of the nation were very much on Whitman's mind and capable of cracking his philosophical and emotional optimism. Family difficulties, including the death of Whitman's father in 1855 and lack of support or comprehension of his poetry, have also been mentioned. Another possibility is a crisis in his self-concept as an artist. Another seashore poem which entered *Leaves of Grass* along with "Out of the Cradle" is "As I Ebb'd with the Ocean of Life." This is what Whitman's "supple lyric exuberance" sounds like there:

> O baffled, balk'd, bent to the very earth,
> Oppress'd with myself that I have dared to open my mouth,
> Aware now that amid all the blab whose echoes recoil upon me I have not once had the least idea who or what I am,

> But that before all my arrogant poems the real ME still stands untouch'd, untold, altogether unreach'd,
> Withdrawn far, mocking me with mock-congratulatory signs and bows,
> With peals of distant ironical laughter at every word I have written,
> Pointing in silence to these songs, and then to the sand beneath.
>
> (*LG*: 254)

This is one of the best descriptions in literature of the deflation and depression that sometimes come after great creative exertions and hopes. Emerson's letter greeting him "at the beginning of a great career" was as powerful a validation as any aspiring writer could dream of. Still, *Leaves of Grass* had been a self-published effort, sales were nonexistent, and such buoyant cosmic claims as he had made there could easily cave in to self-doubt – in fact, they almost ask for it. Whitman was tough, but he was not impervious to doubt and deflation. "As I Ebb'd with the Ocean" and "Out of the Cradle" make a complementary pairing. The phrase "mocking me with mock-congratulatory signs" in the one, and the key role of the mockingbird in the other, may be coincidental, yet they seem almost a cue to think of the two poems together. "Out of the Cradle" can be read as a response to the question of what to do in the face of being punctured or shattered. Whether it is unsatisfied love or other kinds of suffering, the only acceptable response, for Whitman, was to sing. In the initial burst of "Song of Myself" and the 1855 edition, Whitman proved himself as one of the great praisers. With the 1860 edition, he added lament to his repertoire, and *Leaves of Grass* became a darker, more complex, and greater book.

Whitman's growing, changing editions of what was purportedly the same book have provided a long and complicated project for scholarship, and they have provoked debate over the generations as to which version of the book, or of any individual poem, is to be preferred. The consensus seems to be that Whitman did some damage as he continued to revise and reorganize as his creative imagination became less vital and as he took some of the edge off his candor and boldness. Few would deny, however, that some changes were for the good as well, and the rolling, memorable title "Out of the Cradle Endlessly Rocking" is clearly one of these, replacing the bland "A Child's Reminiscence" and the static "A Word Out of the Sea." On the other hand, the deletion of the line "Out of the boy's mother's womb, and from the nipples of her breasts" from the opening of the poem is an instance of Whitman expurgating himself – much as he hated expurgation. "Damn the expurgated books! I say damn 'em! The dirtiest book in all the world is the expurgated book," he said in his old age (Schmidgall 2001: 113). Roy Harvey Pearce, an advocate for the 1860 edition and editor of a centennial facsimile, saw it as more than that: part of a drift from the naturalistic to the self-consciously prophetic. Pearce particularly disliked the poem's penultimate line, which did not appear until 1881: ("Or like some old crone rocking the cradle, swathed in sweet garments, bending aside,"). Pearce says, " . . . the sentimentality and bathos of this too-much celebrated line . . . is given away by the fact that it is the only simile, the only 'like' clause, in the poem. And, in relation to the total effect of the poem, the strategic withdrawal of the 'Or' which introduces the line is at least unfortunate, at most disastrous" (Lewis 1962: 104).

The most substantial revision, however, was the deletion of an entire nine-line stanza at a crucial moment in the poem's drama. Just after the poet receives his revelation, and as he is about to ask for more, "The word final, superior to all" (*LG*: 252, l. 161), the earlier versions contain these powerful transitional lines expressing the poet's anguish and confusion. Without them, the poet seems less wildly stirred and uncertain than they show him to be. The omission of those lines makes the shift to the closing more abrupt, and the necessity to "have more" less clear and impassioned. Here I should again mention Gary Schmidgall, who also believes that Whitman's earlier versions tend to be his best, and whose 1999 edition of Whitman's poetry is today probably the most readily available reprinting of "Out of the Cradle" in its original (1860) form.

The passage in which the sea speaks its word has proved extremely rich ground for interpretation, as has the whole question of death in Whitman. D. H. Lawrence, one of Whitman's most caustic critics and greatest advocates together in the same skin, can be said to have commenced the modern discussion: "Whitman would not have been the great poet he is if he had not taken the last steps and looked over into death. Death, the last merging, that was the goal of his manhood. . . . Whitman like a strange, modern, American Moses. Fearfully mistaken. And yet the great leader" (Lawrence [1923] 1964: 170–1). What did Whitman see when he looked over into death? Why did he see it as he did? Was he "fearfully mistaken"? Was there something pathological in his attitude toward death? Responses have included readings based in psychoanalysis (e.g., Edwin Haviland Miller, Stephen A. Black) and recent literary theory (e.g., Killingsworth, Bauerlein). Some are provocative and revealing, and some become ingenious or jargonized to the point where a basic truth may be obscured.

For death to enter at the end of this poem about his origin and identity as a poet is pure Whitman. If this strand weren't woven in, it wouldn't be an accurate account of him or his way of seeing the universe. In his late poem "A Clear Midnight," Whitman says:

> This is thy hour O soul, thy free flight into the wordless,
> Away from books, away from art, the day erased, the lesson done,
> Thee fully forth emerging, silent, gazing, pondering the themes thou lovest best,
> Night, sleep, death and the stars.
>
> (*LG*: 487)

His handling of this theme of death that he loved goes through many modulations and variations from one point in his work to another, but it is there all along, and for all the differences of mood and imagery, there is an underlying consistency. In the transcendental bravado of "Song of Myself" Whitman told death off: "And as to you Death, and you bitter hug of mortality, it is idle to try to alarm me" (*LG*: 87). But that poem is also marked by a tremendous sense of equanimity and acceptance of death, culminating in his own farewell: "I bequeath myself to the dirt to grow from the grass I love, /If you want me again look for me under your boot-soles" (p. 89). Later, in his Civil War poems, he showed death in painful details of torn bodies, glinting surgical instruments, and heart-breaking departures, but there was also the recognition that death was necessary and cleansing, as he expressed in his poem "Reconciliation":

> Word over all, beautiful as the sky,
> Beautiful that war and all its deeds of carnage must in time be utterly lost,
> That the hands of the sisters Death and Night incessantly softly wash again, and ever again, this soil'd world . . .
>
> (*LG*: 321)

Many other examples could be cited. Whether we are talking about the chaos of war or the "sweet hell within" of personal loss and longing, the awareness of death is the larger picture within which we see life truly. This was not for Whitman a morbid or pessimistic truth. While anguish has displaced bravado and Transcendental optimism in "Out of the Cradle," death is not the cause of that anguish; it is a completion rather than an anxiety. What the sea says is in tremendous contrast to the agitated virtuosity of the bird's aria. It has its own music, and it is a whispered music, "hissing melodious," "rustling at my feet," "laving me softly all over" (*LG*: 253, ll. 170, 171, 172). Even as it contains within it the insistent, monosyllabic "Death," the passage is very liquid and sibilant, and soothing. Once again, as Whitman suggested, listening to the music of the poem may be the best way to understand it.

Death, for Whitman, is that which soothes. Whether or not this justifies the added line about the old crone rocking the cradle, this is what he accented when he added it. Death is something real and present for him, not a negation. It is the great calm. It is the background, or simply the ground, for all the joys, longings, and sorrows of life, all unsatisfied loves, ecstatic songs, and laments. Even a poem as operatic, passionate, and powerfully written as "Out of the Cradle" is ultimately a small song, Whitman knew, like a bird's compared to the sound of the sea. But the singing of the bird or the poet is no less beautiful, moving, or necessary for that. "Out of the Cradle Endlessly Rocking" is one of Whitman's great expressions of this way of seeing life and death.

References and Further Reading

Allen, Gay Wilson (1955). *The Solitary Singer.* New York: Macmillan.

Bauerlein, Mark (1991). *Whitman and the American Idiom.* Baton Rouge: Louisiana State University Press.

Black, Stephen A. (1975). *Whitman's Journeys into Chaos.* Princeton, NJ: Princeton University Press.

Chase, Richard (1955). *Walt Whitman Reconsidered.* New York: William Sloane.

Faner, Robert D. (1951). *Walt Whitman and Opera*. Philadelphia: University of Pennsylvania Press.

Fussell, P. (1962). Whitman's Curious Warble: Reminiscence and Reconciliation. In R W. B. Lewis (ed.), *The Presence of Walt Whitman*. New York: Columbia University Press, pp. 28–51.

Katz, Jonathan Ned (2001). *Love Stories: Sex between Men before Homosexuality*. Chicago: University of Chicago Press.

Killingsworth, M. Jimmie (1989). *Whitman's Poetry of the Body*. Chapel Hill: University of North Carolina Press.

Lawrence, D. H. ([1923] 1964). *Studies in Classic American Literature*. New York: Viking.

Lewis, R. W. B. (ed.) (1962). *The Presence of Walt Whitman*. New York: Columbia University Press.

Miller, Edwin Haviland (1968). *Walt Whitman's Poetry: A Psychological Journey*. Boston: Houghton Mifflin.

Miller, James E., Jr. (1957). *A Critical Guide to Leaves of Grass*. Chicago: University of Chicago Press.

Myerson, Joel (ed.) (1991). *Whitman in His Own Time*. Iowa City: University of Iowa Press.

Pollak, Vivian R. (2000). *The Erotic Whitman*. Berkeley: University of California Press.

Price, Kenneth M. (ed.) (1996). *Walt Whitman: The Contemporary Reviews*. Cambridge, UK: Cambridge University Press.

Schmidgall, Gary (1997). *Walt Whitman: A Gay Life*. New York: Dutton.

Schmidgall, Gary (ed.) (2001). *Intimate with Walt: Selections from Whitman's Conversations with Horace Traubel 1888–1892*. Iowa City: University of Iowa Press.

Shively, Charley (1987). *Calamus Lovers: Walt Whitman's Working Class Camerados*. San Francisco: Gay Sunshine Press.

Snodgrass, W. D. (2002). *To Sound Like Yourself*. Rochester, NY: Boa Editions.

Whitman, Walt (1999). *Selected Poems 1855–1892: A New Edition*, ed. Gary Schmidgall. New York: St Martin's Press.

Whitman, Walt (1971). *Specimen Days*. Boston: David R. Godine.

Zweig, Paul (1984). *Walt Whitman: The Making of the Poet*. New York: Basic Books.

31
"Live Oak, with Moss," "Calamus," and "Children of Adam"

Steven Olsen-Smith

Composed in overlapping phases, and textually and conceptually related, Walt Whitman's "Live Oak, with Moss," "Calamus," and "Children of Adam" clusters represent the poet in his most intimate, most exposed, and most controversial postures. Whitman composed the 12-poem "Live Oak, with Moss" sequence in the late 1850s, apparently in response to a failed same-sex attachment, and not with the intent to publish it. Yet that act of private commemoration prompted a major creative impulse that produced the 45-poem "Calamus" cluster, thematically devoted to male comradeship, and his combination of old and new poems that would make up "Children of Adam" (originally "Enfans d'Adam"), devoted to sex, procreation, and love of men for women. Whereas both of the larger clusters were printed in the third (1860) edition of *Leaves of Grass*, "Live Oak, with Moss" was never published intact by Whitman, who instead dispersed and shuffled its 12 poems among the 33 other poems of "Calamus," eliminating its narrative of love, loss, and resolution. In dismantling the shorter sequence Whitman canceled the most complex and moving account of love and heartache that had yet emerged within American literature. But in sublimating his private passion Whitman produced two longer works that would contribute powerfully to his reputation as a poet and to the complexity of his artistic achievement.

The "Live Oak, with Moss" sequence was discovered and reassembled in the early 1950s by Fredson Bowers, who in examining Whitman's extant holograph drafts for "Calamus" recognized that 12 of the poems had originally formed a makeshift notebook and had constituted a shorter, separate Roman-numeraled sequence (Bowers 1955: lxiv–lxvii). Whitman's original intention for the notebook is indicated by his notation on the verso of a canceled draft of Poem II: "A Cluster of Poems, Sonnets expressing the thoughts, pictures, aspirations etc. Fit to be perused during the days of the approach of Death . . . that I have prepared myself for that purpose . . . Remember now – Remember then" (Bowers 1955: lxvii). The documentary connection of this note to the title poem of the sequence ("I saw in Louisiana a live-oak growing") makes it reasonably clear that the group of poems alluded to are those which make up "Live Oak, with Moss," which in its manuscript state holds enormous potential for our understanding of Whitman. But scholarship was slow to acknowledge the sequence, and it has yet to be satisfactorily edited.[1]

The neglect began with Bowers himself, who described the sequence as "Whitman's Manuscripts for the Original Calamus Poems" instead of as a discrete work written in its own right (as his research showed) before Whitman had adopted the calamus plant as a central image in his writing (Bowers 1953: 257). Bowers' conception of the sequence as an early draft for "Calamus" seems to have prompted subsequent judgments that in writing "Live Oak, with Moss" Whitman had merely made a trial arrangement of early "Calamus" poems (see Olsen-Smith and Parker 1997: 158–60). That the sequence in fact constituted a thoroughly formulated work in Whitman's own mind is revealed by Poem II, where, in discussing a live oak twig he has taken off a branch and entwined with moss, the speaker states: "it remains to me a curious token – I write these pieces, and name them after it" (Bowers 1955: 102). Whitman later replaced the second and third clauses of this line with an expression now holding iconic familiarity from the poem's published "Calamus" version: "it remains to me a curious token – it makes me think of manly love" (*LG Var.*, 2: 390). But the alteration followed Whitman's decision to cancel the sequence and include the individual poems within a different cluster newly entitled "Calamus-Leaves." Whereas the original line is missing from Bowers' edition and from reconstructive efforts of the early 1990s, its restoration is essential to any authentic edition of "Live Oak, with Moss," for it reveals Whitman's conception of the sequence as an integrated whole. That the sequence was finalized in its notebook form is indicated by the tone of closure in Whitman's note that he had "prepared" the cluster for perusal in old age and, most tellingly, by its fair-copy state (Bowers 1955: lxvi). Whereas the manuscripts now display cross-outs and revisions performed by Whitman after he detached the notebook, in its originally inscribed form "Live Oak, with Moss" is meticulously copied out in Whitman's best hand.

Apart from intermittent attention by critics, "Live Oak, with Moss" went unexplicated for almost 40 years after Bowers printed it. Editions and interpretations finally began to appear in prominent venues during the 1990s, but lingering imprecision about the state of the sequence and an increasingly politicized academic culture combined for an explosive debut. Alan Helms, reassembling the sequence from the revised "Calamus" versions of the 12 poems, interpreted it as a sad account of Whitman's submission to homophobic oppression (Helms 1992). In response, Hershel Parker attributed Helms's negative reading to his poor choice of copy-texts, and championed the sequence as a narrative of heartache followed by brave and heroic personal resolve (Parker 1996). Parker's argument that the sequence must be based on the manuscripts has been seconded by subsequent critics (Price 2001, Scholnick 2004). But the clashing interpretive views are symptomatic of a larger debate surrounding the question of gay consciousness in Whitman's writings, particularly

"Calamus," and about the purpose and legitimacy of his heterosexual cluster "Children of Adam." As we will see, their special relationship to "Live Oak, with Moss" is essential to the discussion. The sequence stands admirably well on its own, however, both as a stirring expression of emotional experience and a unique contribution to the Romantic literary tradition in America.

Poem I of the "Live Oak, with Moss" sequence, "Not the heat flames up and consumes," expresses the exhilaration of an expectant lover, with the speaker declaring that his passions surpass the intensity of earthly heat and sea waves, and of the air that "bears lightly along white down-balls of myriads of seeds, wafted, sailing gracefully, to drop where they may" (Bowers 1955: 92). The poem's subordination of natural phenomena to human emotional processes launches a major motif of the sequence. Its balanced rhetoric reveals an artful combination of diverse but harmonious emotional states, uniting burning desire ("the flames of me") with the delightful anticipation signified by the speaker's free-flowing "soul" which, in the poem's concluding image, is "borne through the open air, wafted in all directions, for friendship, for love" (pp. 92, 94). Commencing with passion, and ending with ecstasy, Poem I celebrates love's emotional profundity over and above the powerful forces of nature itself. Whitman's device for marking the disparity – parallel rhetoric – performs a variety of functions throughout the sequence and accounts in large part for the unity and coherence discerned but not hitherto elucidated in published criticism of "Live Oak, with Moss."

Whitman's version of the mind responding to nature illustrates qualities of the greater Romantic lyrical stance assumed by many nineteenth-century British and American writers. As described by M. H. Abrams, the greater Romantic lyric invokes aspects of the natural landscape, which in turn evoke a heightened psychological response on the part of the writer:

> In the course of this meditation the lyric speaker achieves an insight, faces up to a tragic loss, comes to a moral decision, or resolves an emotional problem. Often the poem rounds upon itself to end where it began, at the outer scene, but with an altered mood and deepened understanding which is the result of the intervening meditation. (Abrams 1984: 77)

What distinguishes "Live Oak, with Moss" as a variation on the mode is Whitman's outright subordination of nature to the uniqueness and majesty of the emotionally endowed Self. The sequence acknowledges human affinities with nature, but in every instance the correspondence is evoked only to be superseded by heightened qualities of the speaker's emotional life. The motif qualifies mainstream Romantic lyricism's more equivalent "interfusion of mind and nature," where the poet freely identifies with his object (Abrams 1984: 102). Behind this variation is Whitman's concern in the sequence with themes of love and companionship, for which the speaker looks to nature in vain.

Nowhere in "Live Oak, with Moss" is Whitman's variation on the greater Romantic lyric more pronounced than in Poem II. Here he acknowledges qualities of the live oak that seem analogous to personal characteristics he cherishes within himself, and in carrying away a twig that he has wrapped with moss he creates a "curious token" that inspires the sequence as a whole (Bowers 1955: 102). Yet the speaker concludes it cannot reflect his deepest emotional needs: "For all that, and though the tree glistens there in Louisiana, solitary in a wide flat space, uttering joyous leaves all its life, without a friend, a lover, near – I know very well I could not" (p. 102). The tree becomes Whitman's concentrated focus for the pattern of negation applied to various natural phenomena in Poem I, marking a notable break in Whitman's familiar bond with the natural world. In evidence throughout the 1855 and 1856 *Leaves of Grass*, that bond held special significance in the work that became "Song of Myself," where in a passage fusing mind, body, and nature Whitman described the live oak as a "loving lounger in my winding paths," its branches signifying the open arms of a sympathetic natural world poised for interfusion with the speaker-poet (*LG Var.*, 1: 34). From the detached perspective of Poem II, however, the live oak remains objectified. Whereas in "Calamus" the poet's break with nature will appear intermittently (and perhaps confusedly – in stark contradiction to separate avowals of natural solidarity), its original, concentrated development in "Live Oak, with Moss" makes the sequence unique among Whitman's writings.

To appreciate fully this quality of the sequence we must turn to Poem III in its original manuscript version. There the speaker derives joy not from being "praised in the Capitol" (signifying a hiatus in Whitman's desire for poetic fame, to be developed later in the sequence) nor from carousing, nor from accomplishing his plans, but from the arrival of his lover and the night they share together on a moonlit beach (Bowers 1955: 86). In revising this poem for "Calamus" Whitman created a sympathetic natural environment, with the landscape "whispering" in the sound of sand and surf "to congratulate me, – For the friend I love lay sleeping by my side" (p. 88). Readers of the "Calamus" version often invoke the poem's theme of natural sympathy while attributing contrary qualities of homophobic hostility to the image of the capitol (Cady 1978, Helms 1992). But the reference to nature's applause is part of a larger passage Whitman had pasted over an earlier manuscript version of Poem III, and in the opinion of Bowers it most likely dates to a period of revision following Whitman's detachment of the "Live Oak" notebook (1955: lxvi). That the revision consequently followed his reconception of the poem as part of a different work seems clear from the altogether different outlook of the original manuscript passage, which contains not the congratulatory attitude of a suddenly sympathetic natural world, but yet another declaration of the speaker's emotional primacy: "And that night O you happy waters, I heard you beating the shores – But my heart beat happier than you – for he I love is returned and sleeping by my side" (p. 88). Following in coherent fashion from the speaker's treatment of nature in Poems I and II, Poem III of "Live Oak, with Moss" creates an ideal context for Romantic interfusion, but only to subordinate the power of natural phenomena below the speaker's emotive capacities for love and affection.

In contrast to the traditional Romantic paradigm of seeing the self reflected in nature, Whitman has consistently employed parallel rhetoric to distinguish the speaker's feelings and needs from his natural environment. Now Whitman pursues the same rhetorical approach in subsequent poems with the quite different objective of establishing the speaker's sympathetic ties to other men. In Poem IV the speaker pauses to reflect on the emotional affinities that bind him to men across the world: "This moment as I sit alone, yearning and pensive, it seems to me there are other men, in other lands, yearning and pensive" (Bowers 1955: 106). Poem V renounces the poetic self-image Whitman had advanced in "Song of Myself" as America's representative poet, and the speaker devotes himself instead to private comradeship: "I am to go with him I love, and he is to go with me" (p. 82). Poem VI describes the parting of two men: "The one who remained hung on the other's neck and passionately kissed him – while the one who departed tightly prest the one who remained in his arms" (pp. 116–17). Poem VII reiterates the poet's new calling and asks that he be remembered by future bards not as national poet but as one who devoted himself to love: "Who ever, as he sauntered the streets, curved with his arm the manly shoulder of his friend – while the curving arm of his friend rested upon him also" (p. 86). The poem's frankness of expression and imagery of free movement reiterate thematic qualities that had opened the sequence; but now these themes appear alongside the speaker's first suspicions that his lover "might after all be indifferent to him" (p. 86). This hint of rejection introduces the rupture that will redirect the progress of the sequence, and in the following Poem VIII we find it confirmed: "For he, the one I cannot content myself without – soon I saw him content himself without me" (p. 82). Yet amidst the speaker's anguish in "Hours continuing long" we witness anew his impulse to identify with another who shares his emotional needs: "Is he too as I am now? . . . Does he see himself reflected in me? In these hours does he see the face of his hours reflected?" (p. 84). The natural world now functions merely as a back-drop to the intense drama of thwarted affection between men, and of the speaker's struggle to overcome his grief by visualizing one capable of understanding it.

In that act of sympathetic imagination (so instrumental throughout Whitman's writings) we see the assertion of a gay consciousness and identity that will enable the speaker to recover from his loss. In Poem IX he relates a dream-vision of male–male affection that seems to inspire him to continue seeking a lifelong lover: "I dreamed that was the city of robust friends – Nothing was greater there than the quality of manly love – it led the rest" (Bowers 1955: 114). The passage is reminiscent of other pivotal moments of perception in Whitman's extended lyrics, such as the correspondent "warbling echoes" experienced by the speaker in "Out of the Cradle Endlessly Rocking" and the "askant" vision of battlefield dead in "When Lilacs Last in the Dooryard Bloom'd." It is extremely significant, though, that the expression "manly love" was originally associated not directly with the live oak image of Poem II, but with an urban emotional stronghold that emblematizes Whitman's divergence in "Live Oak, with Moss" from the Romantic interfusion with nature informing those works.

The invocation of "manly love" at this climactic point of visionary experience would seem to mark the speaker's emergence from his suffering, as further illustrated in Poem X by the rekindled "electric fire" he feels for a new man (Bowers 1955: 120), and by a heightened understanding of the costs of love in Poem XI, where his inner turmoil is said to rival the volcanic powers of earth:

> Earth! My likeness! Though you look so impassive, ample and spheric there – I now suspect that is not all,
> I now suspect there is something terrible in you, ready to break forth,
> For an athlete loves me, and I him – But toward him there is something fierce and terrible in me,
> I dare not tell it in words – not even in these songs.
>
> (Bowers 1955: 114)

As we will see, the speaker's "fierce and terrible" feelings spring from the fear of unreturned affection, and here follow logically from his experience of a lover's "indifference" in previous poems. The address to Earth comes closer than previous poems to a solid identification with nature. But the identification is notably negative, conveying the lingering emotional costs of rejection and heartache, and the consequences of expressing same-sex affection where it may in the end prove unwelcome. As the product of an age that lacked a self-acknowledged culture of gay men, and that lacked even a name for homosexuality, "Live Oak, with Moss" derives in part from what was then the unstable character of same-sex emotional commitment.

The volatility of Poem XI is quickly checked, however, by the composure of the closing Poem XII, where the speaker's pledge to "engraft" the lessons of his experience is made only on the austere condition that the young male recipient be predisposed toward his teachings: "But if through him rolls not the blood of divine friendship, hot and red – If he be not silently selected by lovers, and do not silently select lovers – of what use were it for him to seek to become eleve of mine?" (Bowers 1955: 118–19). With its sequential phases of severance, reunification, and healing, the horticultural act of grafting returns the sequence to the image of the live oak twig broken off by the speaker in Poem II. In greater Romantic lyrical fashion, he has returned to the "token" that prompted the sequence with a changed mood and heightened understanding of himself and his experience. The speaker emerges as a prophet and teacher, resolute in his allegiance to love, who has withstood the tests of rejection and heartache.

That "Live Oak, with Moss" came into being as a private response to spurned same-sex attraction, and deals primarily with the successful struggle of coming to terms with rejection, seems clear from a poem Whitman recorded on one of the blank leaves of the dismantled "Live Oak" notebook (Bowers 1955: lxvii):

> Sometimes, with one I love I fill myself with rage for fear I effuse unreturned love.
> But now I think there is no unreturned love, – the pay is certain, one way or another,
> Doubtless I could not have perceived the universe or written one of my songs, if I had not freely given myself to comrades, to love. –
>
> (Bowers 1955: 116, 118)

This poem became number 39 in the "Calamus" cluster of 1860, and for the 1867 edition of *Leaves of Grass* Whitman altered the third line to read in part, "I loved a certain person ardently and my love was not return'd" (*LG Var.*, 2: 404). Along with clarifying the source of the speaker's "fierce and terrible" emotions in "Live Oak, with Moss," the poem illustrates a compensatory attitude that allows Whitman to convert private emotions into broader philosophical and religious concerns, namely the perception of universal truths and their expression through art.

Similar transmutative qualities are present in two other poems recorded on a remaining leaf of the "Live Oak" notebook:

> Here the frailest leaves of me, and yet the strongest-lasting, – the last to be fully understood.
> Here I shade down and hide my thoughts – I do not expose them,
> And yet they expose me more than all my other poems.
>
> ——
>
> Primeval my love for the woman I love!
> O bride! O wife! more resistless, more enduring than I can tell, the thought of you,
> Then, separate, as disembodied, ethereal, a further-born reality my consolation, I ascend to the regions of your love, O man, O friend.
>
> (Bowers 1955: 112)

These poems, too, found their way into "Calamus," as Nos. 44 and 38. All three new poems reflect common transitional tendencies – from rejection to attainment, from concealment to disclosure, and from corporeal to spiritual fulfillment – and suggest Whitman's drive to sublimate his recent struggle. The third of these, in fact, forecasts his matured conception of dividing existing and yet-to-be-written love poems among two separate clusters – one celebrating male comradeship, the other heterosexual love and sexuality. Whitman's fully formed intention appears in a notebook entry on a "Theory of a Cluster of Poems the same *to the Passion of Woman-Love* as the 'Calamus-Leaves' are to adhesiveness, manly love" (*NUPM*, 1: 413, emphasis in original). In borrowing the term "adhesiveness" from contemporary phrenological science (along with "amativeness," for heterosexual love), Whitman devised a vocabulary for channeling the sensations of recent private experience into "Calamus" and "Children of Adam."

As a work devoted to the promotion of "manly love" in America, "Calamus" to a degree embodies the vision of urban male sympathy first recorded in Poem IX of "Live Oak, with Moss," and in its position as "Calamus" No. 34 that poem constitutes Whitman's new rendition of the historically charged image of America as a great city and beacon of freedom. Whitman would later describe the cluster as fundamentally political in nature, and many of the "Calamus" poems (most prominently Nos. 5, 24, 30, and 35) support Whitman's pledge in No. 2 to "give an example to lovers, to take permanent shape and will through The States" (*LG Var.*, 2: 367). Many also have an urban setting and spotlight unabashed displays of public affection among men. According to Betsy Erkkila, "By interspersing the original twelve love poems of

'Live Oak with Moss' among poems of a more public nature, Whitman sought to reconnect his private homosexual feeling with the public culture of democracy" (Erkkila 1989: 179). Yet other "Calamus" poems (particularly the opening ones) depict private acts and expressions performed in isolated wilderness settings, creating a tension between the cluster's natural and urban environments. Beginning with 45 poems in 1860, and ending with 38 in the final 1881 edition of *Leaves of Grass*, "Calamus" remained unstable throughout much of Whitman's career and seems to involve an ongoing artistic preoccupation with the theme of "adhesiveness."

The exact nature of the strategy behind the 1860 "Calamus," and by extension Whitman's transmutation of private experience into published poetry, are among the most controversial subjects in Whitman studies. Much current criticism identifies Whitman as actively gay, and sees "Calamus" as the centerpiece of a homosexual aesthetic that pervades *Leaves of Grass*. This line of interpretation treats Poem 1 of "Calamus," "In paths untrodden," as depicting a retreat from the dominant heterosexual culture into an unprejudiced natural realm where the poet can declare and celebrate his homosexuality. Having "[e]scaped from the life that exhibits itself," the speaker embraces "the life that does not exhibit itself, yet contains all the rest," and he promises to disclose the great "secret" of his life: "the need of comrades" (*LG Var.*, 2: 364, 365). With homosexuality identified as the encompassing but unexhibited life, gay readings of "Calamus" have attributed to Whitman a strategy of veiled rhetoric that eluded detection by unsympathetic nineteenth-century readers while disclosing his sexual orientation to homosexual readers. With the calamus plant metaphorically identified as the male genitalia, the speaker's immersion of himself "in the growth by margins of pond waters" conveys an image of homosexual life and solidarity – a guarded reflection of behaviors and mindsets that connect identically constituted men in open society by surreptitious means (p. 364).

In "Calamus" No. 2, "Scented herbage of my breast," the speaker's poems are said to emerge from deep within himself as the calamus plant rises from the soil. As the speaker says of his poems: "I do not know whether many, passing by, will discover you, or inhale your faint odor – but I believe a few will" (*LG Var.*, 2: 366). A clear holdover from "Live Oak, with Moss," the idea of the predisposed lover is the central subject of No. 3, "Whoever you are holding me now in hand"; and in No. 4, "These I, singing in spring," the speaker gives to his friends a variety of gifts culled from the natural environment but offers his special "token of comrades," the calamus root, "only to them that love, as I myself am capable of loving" (p. 371). Additional poems that seem to illustrate intimate and at times secretive male–male love include Nos. 12, 29, 41, and most of the 12 poems that began as "Live Oak, with Moss," numbered in 1860: 14, 20, 11, 23, 8, 32, 10, 9, 34, 43, 36, and 42. Many are frequently treated as evidence not only that Whitman regularly engaged in sexual activity with other men, but that he promoted and celebrated his homosexuality in his writings.

While homosexual readings have become increasingly common in Whitman criticism, they have not eclipsed more traditional approaches identifying deeply spiritual intentions in "Calamus" that transcend earthly forms of fulfillment. According to this vein of criticism, the invocation in No. 1 of the "life that does not exhibit itself" reveals not a declaration of homosexual identity but the speaker's allegiance to the unseen, intuited divinity throughout and behind the material world – the compensatory universal perception gained from frustrated love in No. 39 above. Indeed, some poems suggest the "Calamus" speaker's love has never been physically consummated. In No. 6, particularly, the speaker's list of urges culminates in his avowal that "Not in any or all of them O adhesiveness! O pulse of my life! Need I that you exist and show yourself any more than in these songs" (*LG Var.*, 2: 376). Along these interpretive lines, sexual imagery in "Calamus" must be read metaphorically – not strictly to deny its homoerotic qualities, but to grasp the mainly noncorporeal, spiritual import of Whitman's intentions.

Nothing seems more relevant to the spiritual interpretation than Whitman's connection of the love theme developed in "Live Oak, with Moss" with themes of death and immortality in "Calamus." Whitman's "cluster" notation identifying his original poems of love as "Fit to be perused during the days of the approach of Death" would seem to suggest the two concepts were intertwined within the poet's mind from the beginning. In "Calamus" the theme dominates, with the speaker in No. 2 judging his poems are "to be perused best afterwards, / Tomb-leaves, body-leaves, growing up above me, above death" (*LG Var.*, 2: 365–6). As a conduit to the afterlife, "adhesive" love is fundamentally intended to provide evidence of experience beyond daily corporeal being rather than a means for fulfillment in the present. In "Calamus" No. 22, the speaker longingly addresses a passing stranger as if seeking an intimate relationship (p. 392). But their connection, we learn, has already been achieved in a pre-existent state, and the speaker declares their reunion must wait. Love-gratification here appears largely deferred to subsequent stages of existence, and while the poem is susceptible to a homosexual reading, its emphasis on pre- and postlife experiences suggests a much broader context than such readings tend to acknowledge.

Illustrating the profound differences between the homosexual and spiritual approaches are their contradictory interpretations of the brief "Calamus" No. 36, "Earth! My Likeness!" (originally Poem XI of "Live Oak, with Moss"). According to Robert K. Martin, the speaker's "fierce and terrible" feeling signifies his vexed awareness that the love he feels for the athlete is unsanctioned and punishable within a homophobic society. That he "dare not tell it in words" reveals the "terrible burden of the poet" to sing of homosexual love but still "feel constrained to self-censorship" (Martin 1979: 84). Subsequent critics have intensified the poem's alleged homoerotic element, including the assertion that "fierce and terrible" here signifies rough sex (Killingsworth 1989: 109–10). These readings clash dramatically with those of James E. Miller, Jr., and David Kuebrich, the first of whom describes the persona's unspoken feeling as "a deep and agitated spiritual love, . . . 'fierce and terrible' only in the sense that any spiritual passion could be when pent up for long without object on which to bestow its emotional intensity." Here the passion remains untold because of the "terror in alien [i.e. transcendent] spirituality, a spirituality so long foreign to man's experience" (Miller 1957: 67). Kuebrich, who makes an extended test case of the poem for determining Whitman's intentions, agrees that " 'Terrible' has the positive connotation of reverent fear before the mysterious and sublime." Citing evidence from antebellum religious discourse, he argues that Whitman's use of the term *athlete* conveys "his notion of this world as an arena for exercising and developing the soul" (Kuebrich 1989: 154, 159).

Without dismissing the strength and ingenuity of these readings, we should acknowledge that the unnamed inner turmoil of "Earth! My Likeness!" had originally followed rejection and heartache in "Live Oak, with Moss," and that it accords in spirit and conception with the "rage" of unreturned love in the poem that became "Calamus" No. 39. In its original context it does not convey a sense of homophobic censorship, though it does seem to illustrate a bottled insecurity of same-sex love – here attributed not to institutional proscription but to the possibility of indifference on the part of the one sought. While it might be argued that his indifference stems from societal pressures, neither the poem nor the original sequence addresses such connections. (Whitman altered Poem XI's "an athlete loves me" to "Calamus" No. 42's "an athlete is enamoured of me" [*LG Var.*, 2: 402], thus clarifying the poem's fundamental concern with unreliable affection.) On the other hand, it must also be observed that "Live Oak, with Moss" patently lacks the direct appeals to death, immortality, and transcendent consciousness that make a spiritual reading of "Calamus" possible, although its reference to "divine" friendship in Poem XII may well forecast the spiritual importance of the published cluster.

Can Whitman be said to have purged the "Live Oak" poems of their original meanings, and have infused them with new intentions for their appearance alongside other poems in "Calamus"? To a degree, and in certain situations, yes. But these matters reveal the importance of taking the original context of the poems into account when examining their revised versions in "Calamus." The transmission of "Live Oak, with Moss" into a scattering of "Calamus" poems presents a number of other significant opportunities for continued scholarship (see Olsen-Smith and Parker 1997), including issues related to the beleaguered legitimacy of "Children of Adam."

Whitman's anthem to heterosexuality is often read with distrust by critics who associate "Calamus" with a conscious gay agenda. Despite recent refutations (see Scholnick 2004: 125–6), the attitude lingers in M. Jimmie Killingsworth's description of "Children of Adam" as a "dumping ground for previously composed poems . . . an afterthought, [and] a record of the poet's intention to balance the intensity of 'Calamus' " (Killingsworth 2000: 131). But that position rests on the assumption that "Calamus" was at a well-advanced stage when Whitman conceived the idea for a parallel cluster. External evidence suggests otherwise, and documents Whitman's near-simultaneous conception of the ideas for "Calamus" and "Children of Adam." As noted above, Whitman expressed his intention for a work on "*the Passion of Woman-Love*" at a very early stage, while still referring to his cluster as "Calamus-Leaves." At an even earlier point, moreover – quite soon after dismantling the "Live Oak" sequence – Whitman alluded in his notes to "A string of Poems, (short, etc.) embodying the amative love of woman – the same as *Live Oak Leaves* do the passion of friendship for man" (*NUPM*, 1: 412). Since the manuscript of "Not the heat flames up and consumes" documents Whitman's direct substitution of "Calamus-Leaves" for "Live Oak, with Moss" (see Bowers 1955: 92), "*Live Oak Leaves*" should here be considered not an intermediate working title for the cluster but an inadvertent fusion of the two. Apparently both titles were still fresh in Whitman's mind when he conceived the idea for a work devoted to the love of women, and this indicates that his ideas for both "Calamus" and "Children of Adam" began to take shape at roughly the same time – the one prompting his detachment of the "Live Oak, with Moss" notebook, and the other following hard upon the event.

Not an afterthought, "Children of Adam" combines and concentrates themes that Whitman had been exploring since the first (1855) edition of *Leaves of Grass*. Its debut in the 1860 edition under the title "Enfans d'Adam" consisted of 15 poems, three of which had already been published. These were the poems that became "I Sing the Body Electric" (1855), "A Woman Waits for Me" (1856), and "Spontaneous Me" (1856). Of the 12 new poems that appeared in 1860, No. 11 ("In the new garden, in all the parts") was dropped by Whitman for subsequent editions of *Leaves*; and two others were added to "Children of Adam" for a final total of 16 poems. In the second of his two notebook references to the cluster, Whitman described the projected cluster on "*Woman-Love*" as

> Full of animal-fire, tender, burning, – the tremulous ache, delicious, yet such a torment,
> The swelling, elate and vehement, that will not be denied,
> Adam, as a central figure and type.
> one piece
> Presenting a vivid picture, (in connection with the spirit,) of a fully-complete, well-developed, man eld, bearded, swart, fiery – as a more than rival of the youthful type-hero of novels and love poems. (*NUPM*, 1: 413)

Whitman's three previously published poems had already laid the groundwork for these themes. By itself, "I Sing the Body Electric" (No. 3 in 1860) establishes the connection of body and soul, and delineates at length the human body in the persons of a common farmer (not unlike the heroic antitype described above), of male and female slaves at auction, and of the speaker himself. "A Woman Waits for Me" (No. 4) and "Spontaneous Me" (No. 5) both celebrate the human sex drive and procreation. All three seem to portray an Edenic natural environment. As James E. Miller, Jr., says of "Children of Adam": "Whitman exhorts a return to the Garden by recovering the sexual innocence of Adam and Eve before the Fall" (Miller 1998b: 115).

Whitman's "central figure and type" for the cluster appears most prominently in its opening and closing poems. Adam's "resurrection, after slumber," in No. 1 signifies Whitman's proclamation that a new and spiritually liberating view of sex is available to America, a nation long repressed (he felt) by institutionalized sexual prudery and denial (*LG Var.*, 2: 352). The poem is artfully crafted, bathing the material world of the present in a prelapsarian coloring, and supporting its reversal of the Fall with a version of history that combines revolving and linear concepts of time (see Schwiebert 1992: 121–3). At the end of the cluster, Whitman in No. 15 reiterates the opening motif of resurrection, with Adam emerging revitalized from eras of sleep and inviting readers to "Touch me – touch the palm of your hand to my body as I pass, Be not afraid of my body" (p. 364). Directed at a readership taught by orthodox Protestantism to see sexual pleasure as sinful, Adam's closing appeal carries the full weight of Whitman's religious radicalism.

Of all Whitman's published verse, "Children of Adam" most ran afoul of contemporary sensibility, resulting in the loss of his position as a clerk at the Bureau of Indian Affairs in 1865, and, in 1881, the suppression of *Leaves of Grass* by the Massachusetts District Attorney. Though well ahead of his time as a poet of sexual revolution, Whitman relied heavily in the cluster on well-known and respected medical and eugenic science, as Harold Aspiz has shown. Chief among these were popular opinions regarding the hereditary improvement of organisms and the ability of parents to transmit newly obtained physical characteristics immediately to their offspring. Often linked with a perfectionist faith in the perpetual improvement of the human race, these beliefs (inspired primarily by the work of French naturalist Jean-Baptiste Lamarck) were applied as well to theories of moral and intellectual evolution. As Aspiz explains, "Whitman's Adam-hero personifies the chaste, physically and morally flawless parent, obedient to the genetic laws, who possesses the perfect seed necessary to inaugurate a eugenic paradise" (Aspiz 1980: 195). References to clean, "uncorrupted" human bodies abound in the cluster, and sexual intercourse very frequently appears in association with the engendering of fit offspring.

Notwithstanding its reliance on then-respected eugenic theory, "Children of Adam" shows a frequent awareness of its own subversive character. No. 2 (later titled "From Pent-up Aching Rivers") opens with imagery connoting the unnatural suppression of sexual urges and moves quickly to the speaker's pledge to make sex "illustrious, even if I stand sole among men" (*LG Var.*, 2: 353). The poem presents us with sequential stages of assignation, withdrawal, and intercourse, with the enraptured speaker asking his lover, "what is it to us what the rest do or think?" (p. 355). Yet like so much of Whitman's verse, the poem's open treatment of sex finds justification in a natural and universalized sexual yearning: "Of the wet of woods, of the lapping of waves, Of the mad pushes of waves upon the land" (p. 354). Displaying what Miller has called the "omnisexual vision" of *Leaves of Grass* (Miller 1973), the poem intertwines human, natural, and cosmic sexual activity to convey Whitman's conviction of a pantheistic sexual demiurge.

After his break with nature in "Live Oak, with Moss," with its visionary city of "manly love," and the tension between natural and urban contexts in "Calamus," Whitman's Romantic faith in an interfusive natural world seems restored in "Children of Adam." In several poems Whitman employs natural imagery in association with human anatomical descriptions (at points in the form of his signature "catalogue" device). In Poem 6 (later titled "One Hour to Madness and Joy") the speaker aspires to "a new unthought-of nonchalance with the best of nature," and in Poem 7 (later "We

Two, How Long We Were Fool'd") he declares "We are Nature," and seamlessly associates himself and his lover with coupled manifestations of natural life and phenomena (*LG Var.*, 2: 357, 358). In addition, whereas both "Live Oak, with Moss" and "Calamus" alternate primarily between hushed modes of meditative expression and controlled declamatory pronouncements, "Children of Adam" at times borders on a level of delirium that parallels the explosive power of natural forces. As the speaker queries in the feverish No. 6, "What is this that frees me so in storms? What do my shouts amid lightnings and raging winds mean?" (p. 356). Yet it is the serene and self-composed image of the resurrected Adam that frames the cluster, and supplies a reverent decorum to Whitman's cluster on the theme of sexuality.

That theme of resurrection might well be discerned in the personal and aesthetic struggle from which "Live Oak, with Moss," "Calamus," and "Children of Adam" emerged as interconnected contributions to the Romantic tradition in America. In addition to the poet's severance from and reconciliation with nature, Whitman's familiar theme of social involvement can be seen to have undergone a similar crisis and resolution in the transmission from "Live Oak, with Moss" to "Calamus." Whereas the private sequence likewise documents Whitman's renunciation of his self-image as America's representative poet, that image too was subsequently restored in the two published clusters, as in the 1860 *Leaves* as a whole. The simultaneous evolution of these themes reveal their interdependency in Whitman's thought, and it is to be hoped that their related intricacies among the three clusters can be worked out by scholarship. As testaments to the inseparability of his private experience and aesthetic vision, Whitman's "Live Oak, with Moss," "Calamus," and "Children of Adam" illustrate the poet's emotional resilience and its role in his extraordinary poetic powers.

Note

1 Bowers' guiding principle of "final authorial intention" was ill-suited to the editorial challenges of "Live Oak, with Moss." Editions based on Bowers' transcription are available in Baym (2003: 2201–5); and Whitman (2002: 752–6). The present essay relies on the manuscripts of the poems housed in the Special Collections Division of Alderman Library, University of Virginia, with their Roman-numeral designations supplied for reference. Since I wish to quote the poems as closely as possible to their notebook states, I reconstruct Whitman's original black ink inscription (from Bowers 1955) and reject most of the poet's pencil and ink alterations. The manuscripts are available in digital photographic images through the *Walt Whitman Archive* directed by Ed Folsom and Kenneth M. Price (Whitman 1995–2005). All quotations from "Calamus" and "Children of Adam" refer to the 1860 versions, with the 1860 numberings supplied for reference, as reconstructed from volume 2 of *Leaves of Grass: A Textual Variorum of the Printed Poems*, ed. Sculley Bradley et al.

References and Further Reading

Abrams, M. H. (1984). Structure and Style in the Greater Romantic Lyric. In *The Correspondent Breeze: Essays on English Romanticism.* New York: W. W. Norton and Co, pp. 76–108.

Aspiz, Harold (1980). *Walt Whitman and the Body Beautiful*. Urbana: University of Illinois Press.

Aspiz, Harold (2004). *So Long!: Walt Whitman's Poetry of Death*. Tuscaloosa: University of Alabama Press.

Baym, Nina (ed.) (2003). *The Norton Anthology of American Literature: 1820–1865*. New York: W. W. Norton & Co.

Bowers, Fredson (1953). Whitman's Manuscripts for the Original "Calamus" Poems. *Studies in Bibliography*, 6: 257–65.

Bowers, Fredson (1955). *Whitman's Manuscripts: "Leaves of Grass" (1860): A Parallel Text*. Chicago: University of Chicago Press.

Cady, Joseph (1978). Not Happy in the Capitol: Homosexuality and the *Calamus* Poems. *American Studies* 19 (2): 5–22.

Erkkila, Betsy (1989). *Whitman the Political Poet*. Oxford: Oxford University Press.

Helms, Alan (1992). Whitman's "Live Oak with Moss." In Robert K. Martin (ed.), *The Continuing Presence of Walt Whitman*. Iowa City: University of Iowa Press, pp. 185–205.

Kearney, Martin F. (1987). Whitman's "Live Oak, with Moss": Stepping Back to See. *Innisfree*, 7: 40–9.

Killingsworth, M. Jimmie (1989). *Whitman's Poetry of the Body: Sexuality, Politics, and the Text*. Chapel Hill: University of North Carolina Press.

Killingsworth, M. Jimmie (2000). Whitman and the Gay American Ethos. In David S. Reynolds (ed.), *A Historical Guide to Walt Whitman*. New York: Oxford University Press, pp. 121–51.

Kuebrich, David (1989). *Minor Prophecy: Walt Whitman's New American Religion*. Bloomington and Indianapolis: Indiana University Press.

Kuebrich, David (1998a). Comradeship. In J. R. LeMaster and Donald D. Kummings (eds.), *Walt Whitman: An Encyclopedia*. New York and London: Garland Publishing, Inc, pp. 142–6.

Kuebrich, David (1998b). Religion. In J. R. LeMaster and Donald D. Kummings (eds.), *Walt Whitman: An Encyclopedia*. New York and London: Garland Publishing, Inc, pp. 580–4.

Loving, Jerome (1999). *Walt Whitman: The Song of Himself*. Berkeley: University of California Press.

Lynch, Michael (1985). "Here is Adhesiveness": From Friendship to Homosexuality. *Victorian Studies*, 29, 67–96.

Martin, Robert K. (1979). *The Homosexual Tradition in American Poetry*. Austin and London: University of Texas Press.

Miller, James E. Jr. (1957). *A Critical Guide to Leaves of Grass*. Chicago: University of Chicago Press.

Miller, James E. Jr. (1973). Walt Whitman's Omnisexual Vision. In Matthew J. Bruccoli (ed.), *The Chief Glory of Every People: Essays on Classic American Writers*. Carbondale and Edwardsville: Southern Illinois University Press, pp. 253–9.

Miller, James E. Jr. (1998a). Calamus (1860). In J. R. LeMaster and Donald D. Kummings (eds.), *Walt Whitman: An Encyclopedia*. New York and London: Garland Publishing, Inc., pp. 95–8.

Miller, James E. Jr. (1998b). Children of Adam (1860). In J. R. LeMaster and Donald D. Kummings (eds.). *Walt Whitman: An Encyclopedia*. New York and London: Garland Publishing, Inc., pp. 115–18.

Miller, James E. Jr. (1998c). Sex and Sexuality. In J. R. LeMaster and Donald D. Kummings (eds.). *Walt Whitman: An Encyclopedia*. New York and London: Garland Publishing, Inc., pp. 628–31.

Olsen-Smith, Steven and Parker, Hershel (1997). "Live Oak, with Moss" and "Calamus": Textual Inhibitions in Whitman Criticism. *Walt Whitman Quarterly Review*, 14: 153–65.

Parker, Hershel (1996). The Real "Live Oak, with Moss": Straight Talk About Whitman's "Gay Manifesto." *Nineteenth-Century Literature*, 51: 145–60.

Price, Kenneth (2001). Introduction. In *Sex, Politics, and "Live Oak, with Moss."* <http://www.iath.virginia.edu/fdw/volume3/price/lowm.php?inc=introduction>.

Scholnick, Robert J. (2004). The Texts and Contexts of "Calamus": Did Whitman Censor Himself in 1860? *Walt Whitman Quarterly Review*, 21: 109–30.

Schwiebert, John E. (1992). *The Frailest Leaves: Whitman's Poetic Technique and Style in the Short Poem*. New York: Peter Lang.

Shively, Charley (1987). *Calamus Lovers: Walt Whitman's Working Class Camerados*. San Francisco: Gay Sunshine Press.

Whitman, Walt (1995–2005). "Live Oak, with Moss." *The Walt Whitman Archive*, ed. Ed Folsom and Kenneth M. Price <http://www.whitmanarchive.org/manuscripts>.

Whitman, Walt (2002). *Leaves of Grass and Other Writings*, ed. Michael Moon. New York: W. W. Norton & Co.

32
Civil War Poems in "Drum-Taps" and "Memories of President Lincoln"

Ted Genoways

It was shortly after midnight on April 13, 1861. The performance of Verdi's *A Masked Ball* had just let out on Fourteenth Street in New York, and Walt Whitman was walking down Broadway toward his home in Brooklyn. Newsboys darted from one side of the street to the other, shouting out the headlines of the extras rushed from the presses. At Prince Street, Whitman stopped, bought a copy for a dime, and crossed over to the Metropolitan Hotel, where the gaslights still burned and people were gathered to read the news. As the crowd grew, one person read the telegram from Charleston aloud for all to hear. The dispatch in the *New York Times* began, "The ball has opened. War is inaugurated."

Within a matter of days after the firing on Fort Sumter, Lincoln issued a call for 75,000 troops, and the *Brooklyn Daily Eagle* reported that the war excitement was "daily increasing in Brooklyn." The following day, Whitman's brother George signed a hundred-day commitment with the 13th Regiment of the New York State Militia. The short enlistment period required at the beginning of the war seems foolishly optimistic now, but few on the Union side properly estimated the resolve of the breakaway Southern states. Fewer still would have thought it possible then that the war would eventually drag on for four long years, claiming more than three-quarters of a million lives on the battlefield, in makeshift military hospitals, in vast prison pens, and along the thousands of byroads and forgotten backwoods marched in between. Apart from the human toll, the destruction to the nation's infrastructure – its industry, agriculture, railroads, small businesses, and homes – would take more than a decade to repair, and the bitter period of reconstruction would be made still more rancorous by the bloody assassination of Whitman's beloved Abraham Lincoln.

But in April 1861, every Northern city crackled with an electric enthusiasm for war. Many years later, Whitman remembered talking with Martin Kalbfleisch, newly elected mayor of Brooklyn, on board the Fulton ferry in 1861. Kalbfleisch said he "hoped the Southern fire-eaters would commit some overt act of resistance, as they would then be at once so effectually squelch'd, we would never hear of secession again" (*PW*, 1: 26). This was a prevailing sentiment and – though tragically mistaken – its nationalistic passion pervades Whitman's early war poems.

The Recruiting Poems

Commonly referred to as the "recruiting poems," the first portion of "Drum-Taps" appears to have been written during these fervent early months of the war: the earliest version of "First O Songs for a Prelude," for example, exists as the manuscript draft "Broadway, 1861"; the poem "Eighteen Sixty-One" was submitted for publication by Whitman in October of that year; "Beat! Beat! Drums!" was published at the end of September 1861; "Virginia – The West" was first drafted (as the poem "Kentucky") on the reverse side of a letter written by Whitman 1861; and "The Centenarian's Story" was originally subtitled "Volunteer of 1861." By grouping these poems, Whitman was not creating a chronology of the war so much as providing a context and backdrop for the rest of the cluster. The poems serve to recreate the excitement of 1861 and admit Whitman's own early enthusiasm for the conflict, before initiating readers into the harsh realities to follow. In the 1871 and 1876 editions of *Leaves of Grass*, this structure was outlined in a simple, four-line epigraph to the cluster (later moved into the opening section of "The Wound-Dresser"):

> *Arous'd and angry,*
> *I thought to beat the alarum, and urge relentless war;*
> *But soon my fingers fail'd me, my face droop'd, and I resign'd myself,*
> *To sit by the wounded and soothe them, or silently watch the dead.*
> (*LG*: 280–1 n, italics in original)

The eagerness reflected in these early poems was hardly unique to Whitman. After only four days of drilling and training, George's unit, the 13th New York, marched down Broadway, past buildings hung with bunting and streamers, sidewalks jammed with well-wishers shouting encouragements. "First O Songs for a Prelude," the opening poem of "Drum-Taps," seems to draw from Whitman's brother's experience of inner turmoil as he left his worried mother but also thrilled to the excitement of the crowd:

> The tearful parting, the mother kisses her son, the son kisses his mother,
> (Loth is the mother to part, yet not a word does she speak to detain him,)
> The tumultuous escort, the ranks of policemen preceding, clearing the way,
> The unpent enthusiasm, the wild cheers of the crowd for their favorites . . .
> (ll. 36–9, *LG*: 281)

Yet the dominant feeling of the poem is not conflicted emotion, but rather unbridled eagerness for the coming battles.

Whitman later recalled that George and other members of the 13th were "provided with pieces of rope, conspicuously tied to their musket-barrels, with which to bring back each man a prisoner from the audacious South, to be led in a noose, on our men's early and triumphant return!" (*PW*, 1: 26). Similar boldness is reflected in Whitman's poem, as the poet swells with "pride and joy" at seeing:

> How you sprang – how you threw off the costumes of peace with indifferent hand,
> How your soft opera-music changed, and the drum and fife were heard in their stead,
> How you led to the war, (that shall serve for our prelude, songs of soldiers,)
> How Manhattan drums-taps led.
>
> (ll. 7–10, *LG*: 280)

After the termination of his hundred-day service, George was mustered out of the 13th New York State Militia on August 6, 1861, his military obligation complete – but the real war was only about to begin. The 13th left Virginia just before the beginning of the Battle of Bull Run – a disaster for the Union army that culminated with a panicked retreat back to Washington, DC. Many of George's former comrades were wounded or killed. When members of the 13th Regiment arrived in New York, they quickly joined new units then forming in the city. George re-enlisted in the Shepard Rifles (later the 51st New York) and the following day was promoted to sergeant major. The *New York Times* on September 20 announced that the regiment expected to leave for battle within the week. During those same few days, Whitman seems finally to have reckoned the protracted national struggle ahead and was finally moved to confront its potential threat to his democratic ideal in poetry.

While George was encamped at the Palace Gardens on Broadway, preparing to see his first real action in Virginia, Whitman began work on his poem "Beat! Beat! Drums!" – a rousing call to arms, rife with the martial rhythms of the recruiting drums and the fervor of the daily newspapers. When the poem appeared on Saturday morning, September 21, 1861, in the new issue of *Harper's Weekly*, "Beat! Beat! Drums!" was tucked unassumingly on the last text page of the issue. Nevertheless, the poem's popularity was instantaneous. Within a week it had been reprinted in the *New York Leader*, the *Boston Daily Evening Transcript*, and the *Brooklyn Daily Eagle*, making "Beat! Beat! Drums!" the most widely circulated poem of Whitman's career to date.

It's not hard to understand why the public embraced this poem more readily than any of those in Whitman's first three editions of *Leaves of Grass*. "Beat! Beat! Drums!" is comparatively conventional in structure. The poem is divided into three seven-line stanzas, each opening with the heavily accented refrain "Beat! beat! drums! – blow! bugles! blow!" and ending with a slightly modified second refrain. Furthermore, the closing refrain of each stanza is broken into two parts, each divided by a central dash to mark the caesura. In all three cases, the first part of the line is eight syllables, the second part six syllables. This structure roughly resembles the common measure used in church hymns and can be heard most clearly in the first iteration of the refrain: "So fierce you whirr and pound you drums – so shrill you bugles blow" (*LG*: 283). Here the meter follows a remarkably regular iambic rhythm that would have been familiar to the ears of Whitman's contemporary readers.

Such regular meters also mimic the harsh beat of the recruiting drum, calling the nation away from the humdrum of daily life to the common cause of defending the Union:

> No bargainers' bargains by day – no brokers or speculators – would they continue?
> Would the talkers be talking? Would the singer attempt to sing?
> Would the lawyer rise in the court to state his case before the judge?
> Then rattle quicker, heavier drums – you bugles wilder blow.
>
> (ll. 11–14, *LG*: 283)

By the poem's close, this pulsing rhythm drowns out all appeals for peace; old man, child, and mother alike are silenced by the snare drum's staccato taps and blasts from the wild bugles of war.

Despite these nods toward conventional versification, Whitman makes clear in "Eighteen Sixty-One" that he did not intend to turn to romanticized war verse: "No dainty rhymes or sentimental love verses for you terrible year, / Not you as some pale poetling seated at a desk lisping cadenzas piano" (ll. 2–3, *LG*: 282). Submitted to the *Atlantic Monthly* on October 1, only 10 days after "Beat! Beat! Drums!" had begun its remarkable string of appearances, "Eighteen Sixty-One" was rejected quickly by editor James T. Fields. In retrospect, this is not surprising. The poems published in the *Atlantic* during this period were usually inspiriting popular poems with regular rhythms and stock imagery that lent themselves easily to group singing on various occasions, such as Julia Ward Howe's "Battle Hymn of the Republic," or more traditionally literary poems, where themes of war were steeped in history or veiled in nature imagery, such as Whittier's "Mountain Pictures," in which the author begs, "let me hope the battle-storm that beats / the land" will leave "A greener earth and fairer sky behind, / Blown crystal-clear by Freedom's Northern wind!" (Whittier 1862).

Whitman, however, was not seeking to appeal to the patriotic public nor the literary establishment with these early war poems; his intention was to inspire young men, like his brother George, who were preparing for battle, and mobilize those men who were considering service. He depicted such men as the very spirit and voice of the year – not the "pale poetling" found in the pages of the *Atlantic Monthly* but:

> . . . as a strong man erect, clothed in blue clothes, advancing, carrying a rifle on your shoulder,
> With well-gristled body and sunburnt face and hands, with a knife in the belt at your side,
> As I heard you shouting loud, your sonorous voice ringing across the continent,
> Your masculine voice O year . . .
>
> (ll. 4–7, *LG*: 282)

The Journalistic Poems

After George's departure from New York, Whitman, like the rest of the divided nation, followed the war as he had on that night in April 1861 – by way of the comparatively new advance of telegraphic dispatches carried in newspapers. To Whitman's mind, the real history of the war lay in the impressions – the moods and moments – portrayed and created by these fragmentary dispatches, in the daily stream of information and misinformation that drove the anxiety of the period. Reports could arrive at any time and appear within hours in special extra editions of major newspapers, but the telegraph did more than create a constant stream of news; it also permanently altered the journalistic style of writing. Well into the Civil War, the cost of sending a typical 2,000-word story from Washington, DC to New York could easily exceed $100 – at a time when most New York newspapers sold for a nickel or even a penny (Harris 1999: 6). To fit more information into the limited space, reporters adopted a clipped, staccato style, free of the flowery description and elevated language of most literature of the period. Instead, the columns of newspapers were crammed with brutal realities rendered in frank, unstinting prose. As a former newspaper writer himself, Whitman recognized the power of this direct address and understood how this fractured narrative form could mimic and dramatize the anguish of the shattered nation.

Unlike most of his contemporaries, however, Whitman never composed poems to recount major historical events. In fact, Whitman's poems are startlingly ahistorical. Beginning with the poem "Cavalry Crossing a Ford," Whitman never provides details about time or place, or even whether the scenes described are of Union or Confederate soldiers. Such historical abstracting was too removed from the experience of common soldiers. Instead, Whitman used the direct, resolute style of the newspaper dispatch to create a sense of what army life *felt* like. Indeed, at least two of the four poems that mimic the journalistic style – "Cavalry Crossing a Ford" and "An Army Corps on the March" – were drawn directly from actual *New York Times* newspaper dispatches:

"Cavalry Crossing a Ford"	*New York Times* (August 3, 1864)
A line in long array where they wind betwixt green islands, They take a serpentine course, their arms flash in the sun – hark to the musical clank; Behold the silvery river, in it the splashing horses loitering stop to drink; Behold the brown-faced men, each group, each person a picture, the negligent rest on the saddles, Some emerge on the opposite bank – others are just entering the ford – while Scarlet and blue and snowy white,	The long array of horsemen winding between the green islands and taking a serpentine course across the ford – their arms flashing back the rays of the burning sun . . .
The guidon flags flutter gaily in the wind. (*LG*: 300, *New York Times* 1864a)	and guidons gaily fluttering along the columns.

Having access to this source material provides a unique opportunity to see Whitman at work, revising and improving for poetic effect. For example, Stephen Cushman has praised the "auditory effects" of "the constant assonance or rhymes" in the poem, several of which derive from the source material: "horse"-"ford," "green"-"serpentine," and "winding"-"island" (Cushman 1993: 39), but most of these patterns are heightened by Whitman's additions and revisions – "line" building on "winding"-"island," "hark" echoing "arms." Likewise, the suspended sentence of the original is considerably expanded in Whitman's version, underscoring the unity of the scene, and the off-rhyme of "silvery river," in a passage entirely Whitman's own, is a conscious echo of the assonance in the first two lines. Most importantly, the phrase "guidons gaily fluttering" is revised to "guidon flags flutter gaily." Examination of the source material lends considerable credence to Cushman's reading of the "phonemic chiasmus" of the phrase, in which the *g-fl* pattern ("guidon flags") is then inverted to an *fl-g* pattern ("flutter gaily") as the poem reaches closure. Of the three and a half wholly original lines, the new portion of line 3 begins with "Hark," the following two lines each start with "Behold," and in the second we are told of the soldiers that "each group, each person" constitutes "a picture." These cues are more than enough to recognize what appealed to Whitman in the original article; thus, he does not create the structure so much as select and intensify it.

Where the structure of "Cavalry Crossing a Ford" is merely suggested by the source material and greatly elaborated by Whitman, "An Army on the March" is a much closer gloss of the *New York Times* article:

"An Army Corps on the March"	*New York Times* (September 2, 1864)
With its cloud of skirmishers in advance,	Before the advance columns, a cloud of skirmishers moved out in a long, pencil-like line, now and then a single shot snapping like a whip, and again a running fire skipping along the line like a wave . . . Behind, the corps swept on,
With now the sound of a single shot snapping like a whip, and now an irregular volley,	
The swarming ranks press on and on, the dense brigades press on,	
Glittering dimly, toiling under the sun – the dust cover'd men,	in glittering columns,
Its columns rise and fall to the undulations of the ground,	the dark masses appearing and disappearing as they followed the undulations of the country;
With artillery interspers'd – the wheels rumble, the horses sweat,	and between them the different batteries of artillery slowly advanced, their measured pace evincing a deliberation in perfect keeping with the apparent dignity of the arm. Slowly, but steadily, they advanced.
As the army resistless advances.	
(*LG*: 301, *New York Times* 1864b)	

The length of the poem and the rhetorical structure are virtual copies of the source. Likewise, where "Cavalry" borrows mostly terminology and several key two-word phrases ("long array," "green islands," "serpentine course," "arms flash[-ing]"), "Army" directly appropriates two longer phrases: "cloud of skirmishers" and "a single shot snapping like a whip." Both phrases are also metaphorical rather than merely descriptive. Whitman is not simply appropriating terminology to build an aesthetic system, but in this case borrowing the images themselves. Here, Whitman found so much poetry in the original that he chose to make very few changes.

Just as importantly, Whitman's positioning of these poems – describing events of 1864 immediately following the 1861 poems – shows his regard for a personal, intuitive structure over a chronological narrative. Most poets who attempted to immortalize the events of the war followed the familiar tradition of epic poetry. Herman Melville's *Battle-Pieces and Aspects of the War* is typical of this unified, dramatic narrative. Though drawn from secondary sources – particularly the multi-volume set of newspaper articles collected in the *Rebellion Record* – *Battle-Pieces* begins with "The Portent," a poem of John Brown's execution in 1859, and proceeds chronologically through the major battles and events of the war (often invoking the names of God and Nature, and alluding to the myths of ancient Greece and Rome) leading up to "The Surrender at Appomattox" and the assassination of Lincoln in "The Martyr." Whitman refused to impose such traditional order on the chaos he perceived. Particularly in the 1865 version of *Drum-Taps*, he rejected the idea of the war as a single story.

It was impossible to construct a national narrative of the war, precisely because it was a *civil* war. For the preservation of the union to be complete, the prodigal sons of the South would have to be welcomed back, and the purgative value of those months of bloodshed would necessarily be called into question. Poets such as Melville – and even many of the soldier-poets themselves – would construct narratives of liberation for the slaves with Lincoln as the hero martyred for the cause of freedom. Whenever possible they avoided the realities of fratricidal warfare, but for Whitman, whose own brother was wounded and later imprisoned during the war, such simple stories negated the tension of the home front and the mass human suffering on the battlefield.

Yet, despite the potential Whitman saw in this kaleidoscopic structure and the precision of the telegraphic dispatch, he also was frustrated with newspaper accounts, which he believed focused too much on military maneuvers and not enough on the individual bravery of the common soldier. He sought a picture of the war that highlighted "not the official surface-courteousness of the Generals," but rather the "two or three millions of American young and middle-aged men, North and South, embodied in those armies" (*PW*, 1: 116).

The Soldier Poems

For Whitman, the project of writing about the common soldier began on December 16, 1862 – the day he recognized the misspelled name of his brother George in the *New York Herald* among the lists of wounded at Fredericksburg. Whitman rushed to the front, searching the hospitals in Falmouth, Virginia, across the Rappahannock River from the Fredericksburg battlefield. When he reached the Lacy House, he was directed outside to the dooryard to search amid a grisly scene of human carnage: "Out doors, at the foot of a tree, within ten yards of the front of the house, I notice a heap of amputated feet, legs, arms, hands, &c., a full load for a one-horse cart. Several dead bodies lie near, each cover'd with its brown woolen blanket" (*PW*, 1: 32). Whitman approached the three bodies lying on untended stretchers. In his notebook, he wrote, "Three dead men lying, each with a blanket spread over him – I lift one up and look at the young man's face, calm and yellow. 'Tis strange." Then, almost an afterthought, he added a parenthetical line directly addressing the young man: "I think this face of yours the face of my dead Christ" (*NUPM*, 2: 513). Nearly the entirety of the poem "A Sight in Camp in the Daybreak Gray and Dim" resided in that short entry. Whitman later added poetic touches and tropes – the persistent grays of the daybreak, the blanket, and the old man's hair, for example – but most of the poem is only a more elaborated version of that notebook jotting.

The moment of insight, the shocked recognition and direct address, however, underwent several significant changes. First, in the poem as published in 1865, the poet tells the young man "I think I know you," a momentary shock, especially for readers fresh from the war, still filled with the dread that this may be some friend or loved one. When Whitman lifted the woolen blankets to look into the faces of the dead, the fear of recognition was potent. But what he sees is not the face of his own brother, but rather "the face of the Christ himself, / Dead and divine and brother of all" (*LG*: 307).

By contrast, one of Whitman's best poems from *Drum-Taps* was significantly improved in revision. Drafted as "A battle. (Scenes, sounds, &c)" in the same notebook Whitman carried with him to Fredericksburg, many of the lines from this notebook version survive into the final form of "The Artilleryman's Vision," but this original version is composed as a straightforward description of the chaos of battle:

> The opening of the fight, when the skirmishers begin, the irregular snap, snap
> The varied sounds of the different missiles – the short s-s-t of the rifled ball
> Of the shells exploding, leaving a small white cloud,
> The hum and buzz of the great shells,
> The grape like the rushing whirr of wind hurtles through the trees, bursting like a fan
> The rattle of musketry from your own side never intermitted – from the other side, the short th-h-t, th-h-t, th-h-t, with irregular intervals between,
> The peculiar shriek of certain shells, – the thud of the round ball falling in the soft earth,

> The shouts and curses of men – the orders from the officers. –
> The wild cry of a regiment charging – (the colonel leads with his unsheathed sword)
> The gaps cut by the enemies batteries, (quickly fill'd up, no delay,)
> The groans of the wounded, the sight of blood,
> Sometimes the curious lull for a few seconds, awful quiet no firing on either side,
> Then resumed again, the noise worse than ever,
> All of a sudden from one part of the line, a cheer for a fine movement or charge, spirited attack
> The wild excitement and delight infernal,
> The scene at the batteries – what crashing and smoking! (how proud the men are of their pieces!)
> The chief gunner ranges and sights his piece, and selects a fuse of the right time,
> (After a shot, see how he leaning aside and looking eagerly off, to see the effect!)
> Then after the battle, what a scene! O my sick soul how the dead lie.
> Some lie on their backs with faces up & arms extended!
> Some lying curl'd on the ground – the dead in every position
> One reach'd forward, with finger extended, pointing – one in the position of firing
> (Some of the dead, how soon they turn black in the face and swollen!)
> O the hideous damned hell of war
> Were the preacher's preaching of hell?
> O there is no hell, more damned than this damned hell of war.
> O what is here? O my beautiful young men! O the beautiful hair, clotted! the faces!
>
> (Charles E. Feinberg Collection, #94)

As late as March 1865, Whitman still listed this version of the poem among his proposed table of contents for *Drum-Taps* (see Whitman 1959: xxxii-iii). However, when the war ended on April 9, Whitman appears to have hastily revised the poem from a present-tense description into a flashback from the war.

In the revised version, originally retitled "The Veteran's Vision" and later further revised to "The Artilleryman's Vision," Whitman turns the poem into a night-haunted memory. In setting and various formal aspects, the poem's new opening appears to rely heavily on the opening lines of Samuel Taylor Coleridge's "Frost at Midnight":

> The Frost performs its secret ministry,
> Unhelped by any wind. The owlet's cry
> Came loud – and hark, again! loud as before.
> The inmates of my cottage, all at rest,
> Have left me to that solitude, which suits
> Abstruser musings: save that at my side
> My cradled infant slumbers peacefully.
> 'Tis calm indeed! so calm, that it disturbs
> And vexes meditation with its strange
> And extreme silentness. . . .
>
> (Coleridge 1950: 128)

From this poem, Whitman borrows not only the time ("vacant midnight") and the setting of the silent home, but also such important details as the sleeping infant and the self-interruption of the speaker ("Came loud – and hark, again!" in Coleridge; "I hear, just hear, the breath of my infant" in Whitman, *LG*: 317). Also, the lines are some of the most nearly metrical in all of Whitman's free verse. Each of the first four lines begins with an iambic pentameter phrase before reaching a natural caesura; the continuation of each line varies between seven and eight syllables, but each is accented three times. The effect is especially potent, because the metrical feel of these lines creates a sense of order in the peacetime household, before we are transported back to the bedlam of the free-verse descriptions of battle.

The final lines, also heavily revised at the last minute, show that Whitman was not merely revising the experience of battle into a postwar flashback, but was also overlaying an allusive commentary: "With the patter of small arms, the warning *s-s-t* of the rifles, (these in my vision I hear or see,) / And bombs bursting in air, and at night the vari-color'd rockets" (*LG*: 318). Francis Scott Key's "The Star Spangled Banner" first became popular in 1814, after Key penned the famous lines describing the bombardment of Ft. McHenry to the tune of the popular drinking song "To Anacreon in Heaven." It was not until the Civil War, however, that the song began to be referred to as the "national song" or "national anthem." During the war, a number of Southern composers published Southern national songs, such as "Farewell to the Star Spangled Banner" and "Adieu to the Star Spangled Banner Forever," in response to which Northern composers offered songs such as "Stars and Bars": "O say, does that Bar-Spangled Banner still wave / O'er the land of the thief and the home of the slave?" Whitman is operating within this same tradition when he echoes and rewrites Key's famous line, "And the rockets' red glare, the bombs bursting in air," but imagines a soldier who has fought for the Union awakened by grisly dreams of battle, returning these oft-sung words to their original meaning. Whitman clearly expects his readers to recognize his allusion to "The Star Spangled Banner" and hopes to draw power by upturning its popular sentiments.

The Hospital Poems

After finding George alive and well, having suffered only a superficial facial wound at Fredericksburg, Whitman was nevertheless determined to return with him to Washington, DC to find work in the government and volunteer in the military hospitals. Eventually, he found a part-time job as a copyist in the army paymaster's office, and cut his expenses by moving in with an abolitionist couple who supported his work. Visiting the hospitals almost every day for all of 1863 and for months at a time in 1864 and 1865 gave Whitman the intimate understanding of the common soldier that he so craved.

The poem that came most directly from his hospital experiences is undoubtedly "The Wound-Dresser." However, many early biographers tended to read the poem incorrectly as a piece of direct autobiography. While the poem has the ring of authenticity, there are numerous clues that this is a dramatic monologue. First, the poem opens with an imagined scene in the future, in which children gather around the speaker, by then an old man, and beg him to describe his service during the war. The frame itself establishes a fanciful setting, but more importantly, the second section begins with the veteran's memory of combat:

> Soldier alert I arrive after a long march cover'd with sweat and dust,
> In the nick of time I come, plunge in the fight, loudly shout in the rush of successful charge,
> Enter the captur'd works – yet lo, like a swift-running river they fade,
> Pass and are gone they fade . . .
>
> (ll. 15–18, *LG*: 309)

The veteran insists that it is not memory of the combat itself that still troubles his sleep, but the lingering images of the human toll. In this reverie, "this dreams' projection," the speaker returns to the hospitals to tend to the wounded. In these unexpectedly gory war memories, the veteran further surprises his audience – both the imagined children and ourselves as readers – by recounting not his own heroism, but rather his helplessness. He lowers to his knees in reverence and supplication to clean and dress the wounds of the soldiers in their cots and, in a moment of radical identification, declares, "poor boy! I never knew you, / Yet I think I could not refuse this moment to die for you, if that would save you" (ll. 37–8, *LG*: 310).

From that moment of deep intimacy, Whitman moves to one of his signature catalogues, listing the amputations, the bullet wounds, and "the gnawing and putrid gangrene" (l. 54). Though this section draws from Whitman's notebooks of his hospital period, the images are not meant as autobiography but rather as an extension and elaboration of section 2. Just as he would have traded places with the "poor boy" in section 2, so the veteran recalls the countless other soldiers with whom he would have gladly traded places, if it would have eased their suffering. Then, in section 4, this connection is made overt, as the veteran recalls, "The hurt and wounded I pacify with soothing hand, / I sit by the restless all the dark night" (ll. 61–2). In the end, however, it is not the wound-dresser's healing touch that lingers; instead, the speaker concludes: "Many a soldier's kiss dwells on these bearded lips" (l. 65, *LG*: 311). The essential word here is "dwells" – because it is present tense, not a past and completed action, and because "dwells" implies that after so many years those kisses still live, the most basic act of survival. Thus, no matter the fate of the individual soldier, he lives on the lips of the poet and is spoken – through the language of the poem – back into life.

Among the other comforts Whitman provided to the sick and wounded soldiers was something simpler, but just as intimate: writing letters home on their behalf. In one such surviving letter, Whitman wrote for David Ferguson to his wife, on April 29, 1863, to inform her that "the doctor does not call my disease by any particular name – I have considerable cough – but I think I shall be up all right before a great while" (*Corr*, 1: 244–5). Whitman could imagine, however, the shock and fear at seeing another person's handwriting, so he attached the postscript: "The above letter is written by Walt Whitman, a visitor to the hospitals." This was but one of dozens of such letters Whitman wrote in the Washington hospitals – and most reported far worse news: a serious wound, an amputation, a dead son or husband. On June 30 of the same year, he wrote despairingly to his mother, "Alas, how many of these healthy handsome rollicking young men will lie cold in death, before the apples ripe in the orchards – " (*Corr*, 1: 114).

These thoughts seem to have combined to create the setting of "Come Up from the Fields Father," where a letter "from thy dear son" (l. 2) arrives in Ohio "where apples ripe in the orchards hang" (l. 6). But immediately the mother recognizes: "O this is not our son's writing, yet his name is sign'd, / O a strange hand writes for our dear son, O stricken mother's soul!" (ll. 17–18). Whitman describes movingly how the shocked mother is unable to take in the whole linear narrative of the letter, only bits and pieces as her eyes skitter frantically down the page:

> All swims before her eyes – flashes with black – she catches the main words only;
> Sentences broken – *gun-shot wound in the breast, cavalry skirmish, taken to hospital,*
> At present low, but will soon be better.
>
> (ll. 20–2, italics in original)

The language of the poem itself breaks down into fragments and "flashes," effectively mimicking the mother's panic.

The last phrase – "*will soon be better*" – offers hope, but at that moment the poet steps forward. He pauses to frame the portrait of grief: the mother "[s]ickly white in the face, and dull in the head," the sisters sobbing and insisting that "*Pete will soon be better,*" then reveals:

> Alas, poor boy, he will never be better, (nor may-be needs to be better, that brave and simple soul;)
> While they stand at home at the door, he is dead already;
> The only son is dead.
>
> (ll. 29–31, *LG*: 302–3)

The shock is real, and Whitman allows it to echo through the end of the poem, as he flashes forward to the mother, dressed in black, sleepless and unable to eat, so consumed is she with "one deep longing" (l. 35). In the final lines, Whitman writes of the dead soldier's mother: "O that she might withdraw unnoticed – silent from life, escape and withdraw, / To follow, to seek, to be with her dear dead son." No contemporary reader of Whitman could have been expected to read those lines without hearing an echo of Tennyson's "Ulysses," which concludes: "that which we are, we are – / One equal temper of heroic hearts, / Made weak by time and fate, but strong in will / To strive, to seek, to find, and not to yield." Clearly, Whitman wishes us to hear Tennyson's lines behind his own and to contrast Ulysses, the returning soldier remembering his past glories, with the grieving mother who will never see her soldier son again.

Scenes of similar loss pervade *Drum-Taps*. Whether it is the visceral carnage of a makeshift hospital in the woods in "A March in the Ranks Hard-prest, and the Road Unknown" or the tender quiet of one soldier sitting by his comrade's side on the battlefield waiting all night for him to die before burying him at sunrise in "A Vigil Strange I Kept on the Field One Night," Whitman focuses our attention unflinchingly on the impact of the war. As he completed writing the first edition of *Drum-Taps* in March and early April 1865, however, Whitman could not have known that the Union soon to be secured by the bloodshed of soldiers was also about to have its national martyr.

Memories of President Lincoln

Whitman completed the typesetting for *Drum-Taps* at Peter Eckler's print shop in New York City on April 14, 1865, and must have gone to sleep believing that his book of war poetry was complete. Little did he know that that very night Abraham Lincoln was shot at Ford's Theatre in Washington, DC and died the following morning. When word of Lincoln's death reached New York by wire, everything halted. In his notebook, Whitman recorded, "business public & private all suspended, & shops closed – strange mixture of horror, fury, tenderness, & a stirring wonder brewing" (*NUPM*, 2: 762). He spent the morning with his mother passing the newspapers back and forth in silence, and in the afternoon ventured into the rain to join the crowds around the bulletin boards, where the evening editions were posted (p. 764).

Whitman quickly set to writing a poem for the funeral of Abraham Lincoln. All the newspapers announced that the funeral would be held in Washington, DC on April 19. Manuscript drafts of "Hush'd be the camps to-day" indicate that Whitman was working on the poem on or before that date, for the poem refers to "the lower'd coffin" and "the shovel'd clods that fill the grave" (Whitman 1959: 69) apparently unaware that Lincoln was merely to lie in state in the Capitol before being placed on the funeral train. He was able to insert it into *Drum-Taps* before printing began, but the poem with its inaccuracies and stock memorialization clearly did not satisfy Whitman; he soon began drafting two very different poems that have endured as more lasting memorials to Lincoln.

For the poem "O Captain! My Captain!" (*LG*: 337–8) Whitman wanted to compose a simple elegy that would reach the masses. And though the poem has a nearly regular meter, with an *aabbcded* rhyme scheme and fixed stanza form – as opposed to his more familiar free verse – the poem is still recognizably Whitman's style. The line lengths vary greatly and stretch across the page, but here his syntactical inversions, heightened "poetic" language, and falsely elegiac form, hamper the voice we associate with Whitman. As early as 1881, Edward P. Mitchell leveled similar criticism, when he wrote: "Fancy the untamable, untranslatable Walt pottering over rondeaux, or elaborating canzonets, or measuring off fourteen lines to the idea! In the three or four poems which have rhyme and the stanza, the rhymes are of the crudest and the stanzas are fetters" (Mitchell 1881). Nevertheless, the poem remains one of Whitman's most popular works.

The fallen "captain" of the poem is Lincoln, come to the end of his "fearful trip" (l. 1). Imagery of the sea, introduced by the title, carries throughout the poem – from the "ship" (l. 2) to the "port" (l. 3), "steady keel" (l. 4) and "vessel grim" (l. 4). In the second stanza, this imagery turns toward the more literal setting of Lincoln's funeral bier, as around him people crowd with "bouquets and ribboned wreaths" (l. 11). In line 12, the best turn of phrase in the poem is executed, as Whitman refers to the crowd as "the swaying mass" – at once evoking the thronged streets and the keening of people in a religious service. But the third stanza quickly returns to more conventionally poetic language and images of the sea. Though the two references to "the father" in stanza two and three are moving – especially in light of Lincoln's nickname of "Father Abraham" – even Whitman himself came to regret having written a poem so uncharacteristic and so overtly public. Though "O Captain, My Captain!" successfully captured the inarticulate grief of an entire nation, there is nothing in this poem to approach the sustained elegiac force of "When Lilacs Last in the Dooryard Bloom'd."

Nevertheless, "Lilacs" is, in many ways, more conventional than the majority of Whitman's work. The imagery, in particular, relies heavily on images of death and rebirth that are typical of the elegy. In constructing the poem, Whitman connects and counterpoints three central images: the lilacs of spring (a symbol of eternal rebirth), the evening star sinking in the west (the fallen president), and the song of the hermit thrush (the poet's death chant). The first two images were drawn from literal details around Washington in the spring of 1865. The lilacs were, in fact, in full bloom, and Venus, the western star, was sinking in the night sky. The addition of the hermit thrush harkens back to Whitman's great prewar song of death, "Out of the Cradle Endlessly Rocking," but, unlike the mockingbird of that poem, "singing yourself, projecting me," the hermit thrush is "withdrawn to himself" (l. 20, *LG*: 330) and only sings at the poet's urging.

Whitman watches the disappearance of the western star and with it the memory of a night before Lincoln's assassination, when the poet, filled with woe over the war, found some consolation in the "sad orb" (l. 65, *LG*: 331). The star's direction parallels the westward progress of Lincoln's funeral train, "[c]arrying a corpse to where it shall rest in the grave" (l. 31, p. 330), creating a backdrop for the alternating sections describing the lilacs and following the poet's journey further into the swamp in search of the hermit thrush whose song he believes will help him to elegize the fallen Lincoln. When the poet finally finds the hermit thrush and records his song, "*joyously sing{ing} the dead*" (l. 148, p. 331), it does not provide him merely with the words to memorialize Lincoln. Instead, the four long years of national anguish come pouring out:

And I saw askant the armies,
And I saw as in noiseless dreams hundreds of battle-flags,
Borne through the smoke of the battles and pierc'd with missiles I saw them,
And carried hither and yon through the smoke, and torn and bloody,
And at last but a few shreds left on the staffs, (and all in silence,)
And the staffs all splinter'd and broken.
I saw battle-corpses, myriads of them,
And the white skeletons of young men, I saw them,
I saw the debris and debris of all the dead soldiers of the war...
(ll. 169–78, *LG*: 336)

But, despite the visionary depiction of mass death, the poet finds a shred of reassurance in the notion that, "They themselves were fully at rest, they suffer'd not" (l. 181, *LG*: 336). It is not the dead who suffer but the living who "remain'd and suffer'd, the mother suffer'd, / And the wife and the child, and the musing comrade suffer'd, / And the armies that remain'd suffer'd" (ll. 182–4). And with this odd consolation, the poet at last leaves aside the lilac with its heart-shaped leaves and the western star sinking on the horizon, but charges the reader to remember the song of the hermit thrush and "the tallying chant, the echo arous'd in my soul" (l. 200, *LG*: 337). In this way, the reader is asked to permanently pair, as the poet does, the fallen soldiers – "the dead I loved so well" (l. 203) – with the slain president – "the sweetest, wisest soul of all my days and lands" (l. 204).

Conclusion

A decade after the guns had fallen silent at Appomattox, Whitman still rued that "the real war will never get in the books," not because "the seething hell" of the war was fading from memory, but because history tended to focus on "the few great battles," rather than the daily realities of war for common soldiers (*PW*, 1: 116):

> Its interior history will not only never be written – its practicality, minutia of deeds and passions, will never even be suggested. The actual soldier of 1862–'65, North and South, with all his ways, his incredible dauntlessness, habits, practices, tastes, language, his appetite, rankness, his superb strength and animality, lawless gait, and a hundred unnamed lights and shades of camp, I say, will never be written – perhaps must not and should not be. (*PW*, 2: 116 n, 117)

But Whitman did not see these common soldiers as mere poetic subjects; to him, they *were* the poetry of the war. Early in the war, walking the rows of wounded soldiers in Brooklyn's hospitals, he marveled at "What a volume of meaning, what a tragic poem there is in every one of those sick wards!" (Glicksberg 1933: 29). On December 26,

1864, reading his brother's diary of the war, he declared that "it would outvie all the romances in the world, & most of the famous histories & biographies to boot. It does not need calling in play the imagination to see that in such a record as this, lies folded a perfect poem of the war" (*NUPM*, 2:745–6). Barely a month from the war's end, Whitman heard the story of a brave Confederate flagbearer killed in battle and mused: "Perhaps, in that boy of seventeen, untold in history, unsung in poems, altogether unnamed, fell as strong a spirit, and as sweet, as any in this war" (Whitman 1865). Thus it became Whitman's project to document this untold history, to write this unsung poetry.

It was a project he never fully completed, as he continually added new poems about the war and moved them ever more pervasively into the body of *Leaves of Grass*, at one point writing that, "[M]y book and the war are one, / Merged in its spirit I and mine . . . / As a wheel on its axis turns" (*LG*: 5). The seeming contradiction between asserting on the one hand that "the real war will never get in the books" and on the other hand declaring that "my book and the war are one," is at the very heart of Whitman's lasting ambivalence about the war. In many ways, he came to regard the war as a necessary purgative act, a trial by fire from which the disparate states were forged into a national whole, and yet this unity came at a cost that Whitman had difficulty accepting. He had seen too many soldiers endure amputation, suffer fever and gangrene, and die alone in large hospitals far from their homes and families. As Susan Stewart writes, Whitman "shows how fratricide blocks the enthusiasm of epic" (2002:300). The only solution – as outlined in the final section of "Lilacs" – was to remember the human tally, the sacrifice of each common, brave soldier. Their sacrifice, for Whitman, became central to the survival of the democratic experiment and, thus, became central to Whitman's chants of democracy.

References and Further Reading

Brooklyn Daily Eagle (1861). The War Excitement. The Feeling in the City. *Brooklyn Daily Eagle*, April 19: 2. Available at <http://eagle.brooklynpubliclibrary.org/Default/scripting/articlewin.asp?From=Archive&Source =Collection&Skin =Be &BaseHref=BEG/1861/04/19&ViewMode=GIF & EntityId=Ar00201>.

Charles E. Feinberg Collection. The Papers of Walt Whitman. Washington, DC: Library of Congress.

Coleridge, Samuel Taylor (1950). *The Portable Coleridge*, ed. I. A. Richards. New York: Viking.

Curtis, George William (1861). The Editor's Easy Chair. *Harper's Monthly*, September.

Cushman, Stephen (1993). *Fictions of Form in American Poetry*. Princeton, NJ: Princeton University Press.

Glicksberg, Charles I. (ed.) (1933). *Walt Whitman and the Civil War*. Philadelphia: University of Pennsylvania Press.

Harris, Brayton (1999). *Blue & Gray in Black & White: Newspapers in the Civil War*. Washington, DC: Brassey's.

Mitchell, Edward P. (1881). Walt Whitman and the Poetry of the Future. *New York Sun*, 19 November: 2.

New York Times (1861). The First Gun Fired by Fort Moultrie Against Fort Sumpter. *New York Times*, April 13: 1.

New York Times (1864a). Gen. Rousseau's Raid. *New York Times*, August 3: 8.

New York Times (1864b). Gen. Sheridan's Army. *New York Times*, September 2: 8.

Stewart, Susan (2002). *Poetry and the Fate of the Senses*. Chicago: University of Chicago Press.

Whitman, Walt (1865). The Soldiers. *New York Times*, March 6: 2.

Whitman, Walt (1959). *Drum-Taps (1865) and Sequel to Drum-Taps (1865–6)*, ed. F. DeWolfe Miller. Gainesville, FL: Scholars' Facsimiles & Reprints.

Whittier, John Greenleaf (1862). Mountain Pictures. *Atlantic Monthly*, March: 299.

PROSE WORKS

Inspired by a Thomas Eakins Photograph (1891). Tonal graphite drawing by Doug DeVinny.

33
Democratic Vistas

Robert Leigh Davis

The Civil War was the defining event of Whitman's life. The first drumbeats in 1861 had pulled him from a "slough" of artistic despond and inspired what he considered the best writing of his career. The Civil War *proved* democracy for Whitman and revealed what he liked to call "the primal hard-pan" of America's national character (*PW*, 2: 707) – the dignity, courage, and basic human goodness he saw in common soldiers like Lewis K. Brown, Oscar Cunningham, Erastus Haskell, and Thomas Sawyer. In the canvas hospital tents in Washington he watched soldiers endure terrible suffering without a word of bitterness or complaint. Lewy Brown told him battlefield stories of astonishing courage and mercy. It deeply moved Whitman that average Americans had taken up arms for an idea – the concept of Union – rather than the ancient motivations for war: territory, pillage, self-defense.

As the memory of the war began to fade, however, Whitman saw mounting evidence of moral depravity in postwar America that dishonored the memory of the dead. Ku Klux Klan lynchings were reported in the Washington newspapers. The Boss Tweed Ring had virtually eliminated democratic process in New York. Andrew Johnson had become the first American president subject to an impeachment trial. And worse: Whitman saw the emergence of a new style of American character – smarter, hipper, more cynical, more in love with money. There is a profound sense of moral gravity in Whitman's Civil War writings, a sense of life compressed to moments of great clarity and reverence. Nothing in the war quite prepared Whitman for the cultural mood emerging just a few years later, a moral breeziness or indifference he calls a "pervading flippancy":

> Confess that to severe eyes, using the moral microscope upon humanity, a sort of dry and flat Sahara appears, these cities, crowded with petty grotesques, malformations, phantoms, playing meaningless antics. Confess that everywhere, in shop, street, church, theatre, barroom, official chair, are pervading flippancy and vulgarity, low cunning, infidelity – everywhere the youth puny, impudent, foppish, prematurely ripe. (*PW*, 2: 371–2)

He can barely contain his contempt. Rather than proving America, the aftermath of war revealed a confederacy of Gilded-Age dunces falling over one another in a mad scramble for loot: thieves, conspirators, jobbers, swindlers. It was like looking under a rock. These doubts had occurred to Whitman before. "[T]hen comes the terrible query and will not be denied," he wrote in an 1863 notebook. Is "faith [in] Democracy [and] this thing of human rights humbug after all – are these flippant people with hearts of rags & souls of chalk, are these worth preaching for & dying for"? (*NUPM*, 2: 542). Rather than restraining "these flippant people with hearts of rags," the war, Whitman felt, had handed them the country.

To make matters worse, this was the moment Thomas Carlyle decided to weigh in with his "dismal prediction" on the future of democracy in an essay called, "Shooting Niagara: And After?" – originally published in *Macmillan's Magazine* and reprinted in August 1867 in Horace Greeley's *New York Tribune*. In general, Whitman paid little attention to the hand-wringing jeremiads of British intellectuals. Mathew Arnold's *Culture and Anarchy*, published in 1869, was easily dismissed as the knee-jerk response of a sheltered dilettante – "one of the dudes of literature," Whitman called him (quoted in Kaplan 1980: 335). But Carlyle was harder to ignore. Whitman had been reading Carlyle carefully since the 1840s. The prophet-hero of Carlyle's *On Heroes, Hero-Worship and the Heroic in History* (which Whitman reviewed for the *Brooklyn Daily Eagle* in 1846) was an important source for the bardic voice of *Leaves of Grass*. And Carlyle's theories of free verse had helped pry open Whitman's poetic line in 1855 (Peach 1982: 163, 165). Beyond that, Whitman relished the sharp-edged flintiness of the Scottish writer, his sheer "cussedness" and nonconformity. And he mused in a later essay that Carlyle would have been a great democratic writer if a long life in the States had bled the aristocratic toxins out of him (*PW*, 2: 891).

Carlyle's flintiness cut deep in "Shooting Niagara" – a furious assault on the idea of democratic self-government prompted by Benjamin Disraeli's Reform Bill. Punning on the word, *Schwärmerei*, German for *enthusiasm*, Carlyle views democracy not as the highest expression of human spirit but as the *worst* that can be thought and said, a human "Swarmery" of balderdash and beer (Carlyle 1915: 301). Led astray by a seductive and misleading rhetoric of equal rights, the human swarms let loose by democracy decide everything by a show of hands and so scale life down to the lowest common denominator: whatever plays in Cheapside, whatever sells on the street. The great danger of human Swarmery is that the really interesting people will get voted off the island. Swarmery threatens to wrest political control from Britain's "Real-Superiors" – the aristocratic heroes who rise in Carlyle's imagination to stand in the breach against lawlessness and mass-rule – the same barbarians at the gates of *Culture and Anarchy*. True emancipation, Carlyle believed, comes from finding and fulfilling one's place in a social hierarchy and paying honorable allegiance to the cultural elite best suited by birth, training, precedent, and disposition to fulfill humankind's "instinctive desire of Guidance." Without that guidance, human society devolves into brutal and beastlike forms of existence, no better than cattle, beavers, and bees.

Whitman had a word for this sort of thing: *feudalism*. Deeply aversive to the self-governing spirit of democracy, feudalism imposes a finely calibrated militaristic control. (The culture hero of "Shooting Niagara" is the Drill-Sergeant.) Whitman uses the word "feudalism" not only to announce the foreignness of Carlyle's ideas but also to suggest their cultural obsolescence. As several critics have argued, the problems America faced in 1871 – industrialization, universal suffrage, an inflationary economy, the rise of corporate capitalism, urban poverty, the empowerment of women, a multiracial democracy – are the problems of modernism itself (Erkkila 1989: 250–1, Mack 2002: 139, Jay 1997: 49). Whitman's response to industrial modernity – the central topic of *Democratic Vistas* – involves rethinking the role of the arts in American public life. In particular, Whitman calls for the emergence of a new class of native writers – divine "literatuses" (*PW*, 2: 365) – who will provide the myths, plots, symbols, poetry, and narrative through which modern culture comes to consciousness, the "literature" (in the most expanded sense) Americans will use to articulate and organize their lives:

> Our fundamental want to-day in the United States, with closest, amplest reference to present conditions, and to the future, is of a class . . . of native authors, literatuses, far different, far higher in grade than any yet known, sacerdotal, modern, . . . permeating the whole mass of American mentality, taste, belief, breathing into it a new breath of life, giving it decision, affecting politics far more than the superficial suffrage. (*PW*, 2: 365)

In Whitman's view, such writers are more important in forming what we might now call the political unconscious of the nation – its "primal hard-pan" – than any of the more flamboyant expressions of American public life, from civil elections to civil war. Rather than standing on the margins as a diversion from the real, the arts produce and organize the real, Whitman believed, blueprinting in people the deep pattern of feelings and fears that constitute humanness in a particular time and place. And up until now that cultural blueprint has ignored the needs and dignity of common people. Indeed the arts have insulted common people in ways so grooved into the national mind that they do not seem like insults at all, just passive descriptions of the way things are. The story genteel literature tells is that ordinary people are not worth very much, that their lives are puny and wretched, and that power should remain in the hands of those best suited to guide them. It did not help that the Civil War was a four-year lesson in subordination and social discipline that ushered in a particularly ruthless capitalist economy. It also did not help that common people seemed pretty wretched to Whitman just then – "puny, impudent, foppish, prematurely ripe" – especially compared to the Lewy Browns and Oscar Cunninghams he had known during the war.

But the solution is not to leash that impudence with more rigid and permeating forms of control – Carlyle's solution. In line with his idealism, Whitman attacks the problem from the other direction: from the *ideas* that produced Gilded Age depravity, the ensemble of cultural texts playing through the minds of those foppish kids and providing the scripts they use to understand themselves – the scripts that tell them greed is good, flippant is *cool*. Change those scripts, Whitman believes, and you change everything: "Causes, original things, being attended to, the right manners unerringly follow" (*PW*, 2: 397). This is exactly what Whitman expects the literatuses to do: rewrite the cultural scripts of the nation from an explicitly modern and democratic point of view, provide a new set of cultural blueprints that honors the complexity of common people and calls forth from them the latent promise of their lives. No wonder these writers are "divine." The scope of Whitman's culture "programme" in *Democratic Vistas* is stunning in its ambition: nothing less than a "mental-educational" revolution of consciousness, the opening of the American mind (*PW*, 2: 396–7).

I Hear America Screaming

"[R]oused to much anger and abuse" by "Shooting Niagara" (*PW*, 2: 375), Whitman set about describing this cultural revolution in three linked essays – "Democracy," "Personalism," and "Orbic Literature." The first two appeared in the *Galaxy* (December 1867 and May 1868), and the three were published together in 1871 as *Democratic Vistas*, an 84–page pamphlet printed privately in Washington, then reissued with *Passage to India* as *Two Rivulets* (1876) and finally incorporated into *Specimen Days and Collect* (1882). The original "Democracy" essay included a passage mocking Carlyle's antidemocratic rant as so much "comic-painful hullabaloo and vituperative cat-squalling" (*PW*, 2: 750). Whitman later deleted that passage, softened the references to Carlyle, and conceded in a long footnote that he had himself endured similar moods. In fact the unleashed swarms of "Shooting Niagara" look very much like the confederacy of dunces in *Democratic Vistas* – the same jobbers, the same low cunning – and Whitman's cultural jeremiad includes some of his most enraged cat-squalling. We are a long way from the eerie quiet of the Civil War hospital. If *Democratic Vistas* were a poem, Whitman might have called it, "I Hear America Screaming":

> I say we had best look our times and lands searchingly in the face, like a physician diagnosing some deep disease. Never was there, perhaps, more hollowness at heart than at present, and here in the United States. Genuine belief seems to have left us. The underlying principles of the States are not honestly believ'd in, (for all this hectic glow, and these melodramatic screamings,) nor is humanity itself believed in. What penetrating eye does not everywhere see through the mask? The spectacle is appaling [sic]. . . . It is as if we were somehow being endow'd with a vast and more and more thoroughly-appointed body, and then left with little or no soul. (*PW*, 2: 369–70)

Whitman had not written anything quite like this since the bare-knuckle journalism of "The Eighteenth Presidency!" and its companion poem "Respondez!" (1856). Carlyle had clearly hit a nerve. However, Whitman does not look postwar America all that "searchingly in the face." Or at least not for long. Many scholars have noted Whitman's tendency to deny the hard facts of American life in *Democratic Vistas* in order to preserve an imperiled idealism, whistling past the graveyard of his American dream (Golden 1994: 94–8, Chase 1955: 153–65, Erkkila 1989: 253, Thomas 1987: 266, 292). Thus Whitman speaks in general of universal suffrage and the "widest opening of the doors" (*PW*, 2: 364) but does not mention the Black Codes restricting voting rights in the South or the ratification of the 15th Amendment or the full integration of African Americans into a genuinely multiracial democracy – this despite the fact that Carlyle had zeroed in on the "Settlement of the Nigger Question" as exactly the kind of democratic balderdash that was sending America and Britain over the falls in a barrel (Carlyle 1915: 302). Similarly, Whitman identifies the "depletion" of women (*PW*, 2: 372) as a principle source of moral corruption in America but says nothing about the 1848 Seneca Falls Convention or women's suffrage or any of a dozen practical efforts of feminist reform aimed at challenging that depletion. At one point in *Democratic Vistas*, Whitman urges young men to pursue a career in American politics while remaining aloof from particular parties, leaders, elections, or platforms (*PW*, 2: 399). Heeding that advice, Whitman writes an 84–page political essay that has very little to say about the actual *stuff* of nineteenth-century politics – which is to say, particular parties, leaders, elections, and platforms.

The perspective he assumes instead is the hilltop view of distant horizons – not *this* America soulless and screaming, but that *other* America we glimpse up ahead, the *real* America future "realizers" and "comprehenders" will recognize as their own (*PW*, 2: 390, 362). This is what Richard Chase calls the view from "Pisgah" (1955: 153) – the Moses-on-the-mountaintop stance Whitman assumes in *Democratic Vistas* both to admit Carlyle's critique – the chosen people are still wandering in the desert: a "dry and flat Sahara" (*PW*, 2: 372) – and to challenge the finality of his claims. This desert, after all, is not our home. Like Moses, Whitman points the way to a promised land he will not be permitted to enter:

> Though not for us . . . the chance ever to see with our own eyes the peerless power and splendid *eclat* [sic] of the democratic principle, arriv'd at meridian, filling the world with effulgence and majesty . . . there is yet . . . the prophetic vision, the joy of being toss'd in the brave turmoil of these times – the promulgation and the path. (*PW*, 2: 391)

The Pisgah perspective allowed Whitman to concede (and indeed emphasize) the inadequacy of contemporary American life while at the same time making room for a future America different from the present age, an elusive future "Something" we catch glimpses of from time to time but have not yet fully realized (*PW*, 2: 374). This is a subtle but crucial issue in *Democratic Vistas*. It relies on a distinction between a real-world materialism of the present moment – what a cultural diagnostician might see through a moral microscope – and a latent democratic "spirit" or "principle" or "being" or "idea" that outgrows its cultural formulations, remains *greater* than those formulations, and so provides the grounds for historical change. In this way the real "America" remains just out of reach in Whitman, its dreams still deferred, its "reconstruction . . . still in abeyance" (*PW*, 2: 384), because any particular manifestation of democracy – the Gilded Age mess he sees in 1867, for instance – does not exhaust the latent potential of this ideal.

The Caller-forth of Persons

The purpose of democracy is to draw out and strengthen that potential: "[T]he ulterior object of political and all other government [is] not merely to rule, to repress disorder, &c., but to develop, to open up to cultivation, to encourage the possibilities of all" (*PW*, 2: 379). This is the political credo of *Democratic Vistas*. Democracy exists not to maintain order or secure prosperity, Whitman argues, not to preserve and pass along the best that has been thought and said, not to ensure that Carlyle's "Real-Superiors" are always at the helm. The purpose of democracy is to inspire and train its citizens, bringing to full flower the latent promise of their lives. Democracy is the "formulater, general caller-forth, trainer" of human excellence (*PW*, 2: 380). It provides the language, mythology, material security, and social relationships people need to discover and realize the best in themselves – as a child might formulate a gift for drawing by turning the pages of a book in a library or a gift for dance by standing in the doorway of a studio and realizing that the spontaneous play of the body can be organized into shared and named expressions of beauty. To the extent that sexism or racism or poverty close the studio or forbid some children from standing in its doorway or convince others that what they see there is degrading or immoral, the gift remains unformulated, that thing which is not named. Democracy calls forth that unnamed excellence. It is the open studio, the open training-school, a "gymnasium, not of good only, but of all":

> Political democracy, as it exists and practically works in America, . . . supplies a training-school for making first-class men. It is life's gymnasium, not of good only, but of all. We try often, though we fall back often. A brave delight, fit for freedom's athletes, fills these arenas, and fully satisfies, out of the action in them, irrespective of success. (*PW*, 2: 385)

This talk of athletes and arenas may remind us that Whitman's thinking about civil society threads back to the social contract theorists of ancient Greece. As Elaine Scarry has recently argued, the concern for what kind of society will produce the most noble and compassionate people is the central question not only of classical political theory but also of the *Federalist Papers* and Marx's *Grundrisse* (Scarry 2002: 109). The proof of a civil society is not its wealth or longevity. The proof is the moral excellence of the citizens it produces – a point Whitman makes again and again in *Democratic Vistas*. Democracy is many things to Whitman – a body of civil law, a poetics of plenitude, an open-ended cosmology – but in *Democratic Vistas* it is an instrument of self-making, a tool we use to create and recreate ourselves.

This transformation happens in several ways. The break-up of social hierarchies taking place in cities like New York and Washington releases people from stratified circles, putting Americans elbow-to-elbow with people from different classes, dispositions, and ethnicities. Looking out over the urban swarms of New York in *Democratic Vistas*, Whitman discovers aspects of his nature he might otherwise ignore and experiences social diversity as an incentive to change, a caller-forth of his own potential. The economic and social variety of New World democracy – "these interminable swarms of alert, turbulent, good-natured, independent citizens" (*PW*, 2: 388) – stir the individual to a richer vision of his or her own potential. The speaker of *Democratic Vistas* models this mobility by cycling through various guises – urban *flâneur*, Old Testament prophet, Civil War healer, moral diagnostician, orbic literatus – that do not fully capture or reveal his range.

The "interminable swarms" released by modernity *annihilate* the self in Carlyle. They bleach out valuable social difference and produce the standard-issue gray of mass conformity. The same swarms *release* the self in Whitman. They externalize a human variety to which he too is eligible and provide a powerful emblem for the latent possibilities swarming within. Whitman enters the crowd to experience the now visible resources of his inner life, to be refreshed by their ingenuities and redeemed from isolation. The rough-and-tumble negotiations growing out of such encounters are training grounds in democratic citizenship. Mixing it up with people who do not look, think, or live their lives as we do forces us to develop unexpected capacities for compromise, flexibility, and self-revision – an idea in *Democratic Vistas* virtually identical to contemporary defenses of democratic multiculturalism (Mack 2002: 151).

We cannot accomplish this transformation alone. We need the elbow-to-elbow turmoil of the democratic swarm to provoke new growth. The excellence Whitman imagines requires the presence of others, as Hannah Arendt would say, requires that our lives and values be street-tested in the open arenas of public life. The democracy Whitman describes in *Democratic Vistas* resembles the culture theory of transcendentalism in its declaration of independence from feudal mentalities. But democratic independence is met at every turn by social communities that temper individualism with social responsibility and love, the adhesive "comradeship" Whitman experienced intensely during the war (*PW*, 2: 414).

Whitman's decision to turn to prose in *Democratic Vistas* is a version of the practical engagement he has in mind. It would have been easy enough for Whitman to strip out the Carlyle allusions and publish something less conspicuously marked by the local circumstances of its composition. Instead, Whitman announces those circumstances not only in explicit references to "Shooting Niagara" but in parenthetical time- and place-stamps scattered across *Democratic Vistas* like a journalist's byline: "After an absence, I am now again (September, 1870) in New York city"; "As I write this particular passage, (November, 1868,) the din of disputation rages around me. Acrid the temper of the parties, vital the pending questions" (*PW*, 2: 371, 384).

Whitman's emphasis on the shaping influence of milieu is one of the ways he imagines and accurately predicts modern theories of literature. Rejecting the notion of an autonomous text, Whitman insists that modern literature emerges from and answers the "din of disputation" raging at the scene of writing – a point he would make again in "A Backward Glance O'er Traveled Roads" (Thomas 1987: 1). Whether or not Whitman effectively answers "Shooting Niagara" is an open question. Ed Folsom's discussion of Whitman's "stunning avoidance" of black suffrage in *Democratic Vistas* is headed "Forgetting to Answer Carlyle" (2000: 79). But Carlyle's presence in *Democratic Vistas* helps Whitman demonstrate a larger claim: modern literature is not a museum piece dust-sealed for all time. It does not transcend local milieu as the best that has been thought and said but is closer to what Gerald Graff calls a local "*rejoinder* in a conversation or dialogue" (1987: 10, emphasis added) – the very word Whitman initially used to describe *Democratic Vistas:* "some sort of counterblast or rejoinder to Carlyle's late piece" (*Corr.*, I: 342).

More local rejoinder than verbal icon, modern literature for Whitman is contextual, dialogic, marked by the time- and place-stamps of milieu. It is crowded with the voices and ideas of others – just as Whitman's page is uncharacteristically busy with citations: "Walter Scott's Border Minstrelsy, Percy's collection, Ellis's early English Metrical Romances, the European continental poems of Walter of Aquitania" (*PW*, 2: 366). This is "Personalism" – Whitman's word for the complex interaction of self and community – as literary theory. The elbow-to-elbow jostling of the modern city parallels the intertextual "jostling of competing representations" that historically minded critics like Stephen Greenblatt substitute for the isolated genius of the romantic author: "In place of a blazing genius," Greenblatt writes in *Shakespearean Negotiations*, "one begins to glimpse something that seems at first far less spectacular: a subtle, elusive set of exchanges, a network of trades and trade-offs, a jostling of competing representations, a negotiation between joint-stock companies" (1988: 7).

Attacking the myth of the self-contained text, Whitman views modern writing as a dynamic set of intellectual and stylistic negotiations with prior texts and authors – with Carlyle and Arnold and John Stuart Mill, but also with the stories Lewy Brown told him in the Armory Square Hospital, with the stories his mother told him about Thomas Jefferson and Andrew Jackson, with the articles he read in the London *Times*. The "din of disputation" rages at the scene of Whitman's writing, as it does for all writing, but *Democratic Vistas* lets us hear that din like the roar of a waterfall. Whitman uses "Shooting Niagara" to make the intertextual origins of modern literature as high profile as possible and so challenge the elitist myth of a writer detached from contexts, gazing down on the world like an aloof God. Milieu is the caller-forth of modern literature, and a democratic milieu – in which access to Carlyle and Arnold and *The Times* is not limited to a privileged few – is the caller-forth of a greater excellence.

An Ensemble of Texts

But the negotiation between writer and culture goes both ways. If culture time-stamps literature with the shaping pressures of milieu, literature in a democratic society re-enters and transforms milieu as a powerful instrument of acculturation. From one point of view, art in America could not be more trivial – "a parcel of dandies and ennuyees" entertaining audiences with "their thin sentiment of parlors, parasols, piano-songs" (*PW*, 2: 408). Just more of "the dudes of literature." But Whitman has a much larger notion of art and culture in mind in *Democratic Vistas*, one that includes the High Culture world of parasols and piano-songs but extends out and down from the Victorian parlor to touch all sorts of things not usually considered artistic, literary, or even all that cultural: "the questions of food, drink, air, exercise, assimilation, digestion" (*PW*, 2: 397). The literatuses have a hand in these things too, Whitman argues, coming down from the heights of epic poetry to provide cultural blueprints for the way Americans cook, dress, dream, eat, and exercise, the way they care for their children, the way they care for their bodies. "By describing the totalizing . . . influence of literature on the 'conscious and unconscious' beliefs and even 'intuitions' of an entire people," Stephen John Mack argues, "Whitman has described something like the modern conception of culture. Or more precisely, he has conflated culture with the rhetorical forms by which culture is manifested and perpetuated" (Mack 2002: 140). Culture, in this modern sense, is woven into the everyday fabric of American life – shaping not only conscious habits of thought and speech but also "dreams," "intuitions," "fondnesses," "aversions" (*PW*, 2: 366, 411).

As a modern instance of the conflation of culture and text Mack describes, consider Clifford Geertz's famous essay, "Deep Play: Notes on the Balinese Cockfight." "The culture of a people is an ensemble of texts, themselves ensembles, which the anthropologist strains to read," Geertz argues (1973: 452) – a formulation close to the spirit of *Democratic Vistas*. Read and internalized over long periods of time, these texts rehearse a specific kind of citizenship. One learns how to be British by reading Shakespeare (among other things) or how to be German by listening to Wagner, or how to be Balinese, Geertz suggests, by watching cockfights. Not "reading" or "listening" or "watching" exactly – which seem too passive for both Whitman and Geertz – but *absorbing* those texts (Whitman's word), drinking them in, learning them by heart, indeed acquiring a "heart" as a consequence of this pedagogy. For the cultural text absorbed in deep play (again thinking of "text" in the broadest sense) produces and organizes the subjectivity it appears only to exhibit (Geertz 1973: 451). It may look like "play" from the outside, but this is serious business, a *schooling* of minds and hearts in what it means to be and feel Balinese. The "nation" enters people in just this way: not as abstraction, "The Nation of Bali," but as a shiver of revulsion at a spray of blood in the cockfight or the belly-thrill of outbetting a rival. The symbolic structures of Balinese life – especially its caste hierarchies – are played out in a blood-language of revulsion and thrill that touches the heart and *sticks* there – down in the primal hard-pan where it is not easily unlearned or discarded.

Whitman would have been repulsed by the violence of the cockfight and by the way it rehearses status hierarchies – a sure sign of feudalism. But he would have recognized this deep play as a version of his "programme of culture" in *Democratic*

Vistas – especially in its redefinition of culture as "an ensemble of texts" and in the way these texts inculcate a citizenship not easily disowned. For this is the opposite of the moral "flippancy" Whitman saw in postwar America – the utterly shallow play of citizens for whom "democracy" or "America" were pure abstractions. Phrases like "culture theory" or culture "programme" or "mental-educational" revolution do not fully convey the urgency Whitman felt about a citizenship of the body, an American democracy absorbed into the deepest recesses of the self: "it is clear to me that, unless [democracy] goes deeper, gets at least as firm and as warm a hold in men's hearts, emotions and belief, as, in their days, feudalism or ecclesiasticism . . . its strength will be defective, its growth doubtful" (*PW*, 2: 368).

Getting down to details, Whitman tries his hand at describing this kind of embodied citizenship in a passage Gay Wilson Allen compares to a Renaissance conduct manual (1970: 96). Presenting "a basic model . . . of personality for general use for the manliness of the States," Whitman describes how an American man should stand, breathe, gesture, and speak (*PW*, 2: 397). We are told that in his youth he is "fresh, ardent, emotional, aspiring" and that as he grows older he becomes "brave, perceptive, under control, neither too talkative nor too reticent" (p. 397). We learn that the proper position of his chest is "expanded," the proper color of his face "somewhat flush'd," the proper way to hold the eyes is "calm and steady, yet capable also of flashing" (p. 397). It may be worth remembering that one of Whitman's journalistic pieces in the 1850s was on the proper size and shape of a man's legs.

There is more than a hint of Whitman's lifelong fascination with eugenics here. But Whitman's "basic model" of American masculinity is part of a larger argument about the political identity of the body in *Democratic Vistas* – Whitman's awareness of the way culture enters the body through barely visible habits of appetite, disposition, and posture: a certain way of holding one's chest or eyes, a fondness for certain kinds of food or music or reading (and a distaste for others), a learned repertoire of physical gestures and expressions. These are forms of microcitizenship by which the nation "permeat[es] the whole mass of American mentality, taste, belief" (*PW*, 2: 365). Permeates and sticks there. *Americanness* for Whitman has as much to do with these learned habits of the everyday – "questions of food, drink, air, exercise, assimilation, digestion" – as with saluting a flag or reciting a pledge.

This is a remarkable insight into what Paul Jay calls the role of ideology in the formation of the self (1997: 47). The culture of the everyday is so thoroughly a part of us that we cannot easily separate "us" from "it" and so acquire the distance necessary to see culture for what it is: an artificial (and thus changeable) ensemble of texts. And that of course is the problem. For up until now, the deep-culture texts blueprinting American life have never recognized common people with anything like the dignity and complexity they deserve, either writing them out of the script altogether as faceless rustics in the background of a Shakespeare play or actively mocking their pretensions to gentility in the foreground of a Gilded Age comedy. What's worse, this particular ensemble of texts has been more or less invisible to American readers, just part of a cultural atmosphere they breathe in like air:

> The great poems, Shakspere included, are poisonous to the idea of the pride and dignity of the common people, the lifeblood of democracy. The models of our literature, as we get it from other lands, ultramarine, have had their birth in courts, and bask'd and grown in castle sunshine; all smells of princes' favors. (*PW*, 2: 388)

Whitman challenges his readers to smell the stink of princely favor in genteel literature, to notice and reject a cultural surround that is both toxic and invisible. For what we are absorbing in Shakespeare – or the hundred other cultural texts we learn by heart – is fundamentally opposed to the democratic identity Whitman has in mind.

As far as we can tell no one wrote the script for the Balinese cockfight. It is a "text" – at least in the way Geertz writes about it – but a text without an author. Which is one reason it seems so modern. The cultural scripts that produce and organize modern subjectivity do not seem to be authored by anyone. We certainly have our own codes of maleness or femaleness, a cultural pedagogy schooling us in a thousand postures and manners far more sophisticated than the "basic model" Whitman offers in *Democratic Vistas*. But we cannot really say where those scripts come from: power? capitalism? ideology? language? Does this make Whitman's culture theory less relevant to contemporary readers? Is *Democratic Vistas* too rooted in "the din of disputation" of Whitman's milieu to be of much use in our own?

Maybe. But Whitman's emphasis on the *authored* nature of modern culture is a particularly intriguing idea. It may help to think of a literatus or two lurking behind the conduct manuals of contemporary American life if that way of thinking calls attention to our role as readers of culture and encourages us to do the resistant, athletic things self-conscious readers do: judging, questioning, evaluating, reading between the lines, reading against the lines, jostling with authors, cat-squalling with them. The divine literatuses may turn out to be particularly useful for modern America if they intensify our role as interpreters of culture rather than robotic followers of the latest foppish fad.

The Civil War seemed to pry up the ordinarily invisible scripts of American citizenship. It put in question the taken-for-grantedness of American life and showed people that the fundamental values they use to organize the real – what it means to be a citizen, a person, a man, a woman – are not given once and for all but manufactured in a particular time and place, *authored*, and up for grabs for a while. Most of the time, those scripts are so naturally and inevitably a part of our identity – so *us* – that we do not think of them as cultural at all. Not something we learn but something we are – and thus beyond the reach of conscious thought and revision. The Civil War changed all that. It wrenched America's cultural scripts out into the open where we could get a good look at them, see them as "an ensemble of texts" rather than self-evident truths, and so read and judge them for ourselves.

Whitman wants to bed those scripts back down into the unconscious hard-pan of the nation's life as quickly as possible – so that democracy can become natural and effortless, and we won't have to think about the humanness of common people as a deliberate discipline or keep asking ourselves every two minutes whether "this thing of human rights" is "humbug after all" (*NUPM*, 2: 542). Whitman was fascinated by the idea that democracy could become a *reflex*, a set of ideas and responses schooled so far down that no other culture "programme" – fascist, feudal, ecclesiastical – could come along and dislodge them. But that promised land is still far off. For now, Whitman suggests, it helps to think of America as an ensemble of texts, and the citizen, then, as an empowered and self-conscious reader. Which is the image Whitman turns to at the end:

> Books are to be call'd for, and supplied, on the assumption that the process of reading is not a half-sleep, but, in highest sense, an exercise, a gymnast's struggle; that the reader is to do something for himself, must be on the alert, must himself or herself construct indeed the poem, argument, history, metaphysical essay – the text furnishing the hints, the clue, the start or frame-work. Not the book needs so much to be the complete thing, but the reader of the book does. That were to make a nation of supple and athletic minds, well-train'd, intuitive, used to depend on themselves, not on a few coteries of writers. (*PW*, 2: 424–5)

Democracy calls forth this supple and self-conscious reader. It schools its citizens in habits of intellectual self-reliance and teaches them how to hold their own in the athletic give-and-take of reading, not backing down from the divine literatuses, not taking their word on faith. *Democratic Vistas* begins with a view of authors as legislating gods hardwiring the political unconscious of the nation. It ends with a view of readers challenging those gods, wrestling with them, and in that democratic gymnasium finding the true measure of their strength.

References and Further Reading

Allen, G. W. (1970). *A Reader's Guide to Walt Whitman*. New York: Farrar, Straus, and Giroux.

Aspiz, H. (1994). The Body Politic in *Democratic Vistas*. In Ed Folsom (ed.), *Walt Whitman: The Centennial Essays*. Iowa City: University of Iowa Press, pp. 105–19.

Carlyle, T. (1915). Shooting Niagara: And After? In *Scottish and Other Miscellanies*. London: J. M. Dent, pp. 299–339.

Chase, R. (1955). *Walt Whitman Reconsidered*. New York: William Sloane.

Erkkila, B. (1989). *Whitman the Political Poet*. New York: Oxford University Press.

Folsom, E. (2000). Lucifer and Ethiopia: Whitman, Race, and Poetics before the Civil War and After. In David S. Reynolds (ed.), *A Historical Guide to Walt Whitman*. New York: Oxford University Press, pp. 45–96.

Geertz, C. (1973). Deep Play: Notes on the Balinese Cockfight. In *The Interpretation of Culture*. New York: Basic Books, pp. 412–53.

Golden, A. (1994). The Obfuscations of Rhetoric: Whitman and Visionary Experience. In Ed Folsom (ed.), *Walt Whitman: The Centennial Essays*. Iowa City: University of Iowa Press, pp. 88–102.

Graff, G. (1987). *Professing Literature: An Institutional History*. Chicago: University of Chicago Press.

Greenblatt, S. (1988). *Shakespearean Negotiations: The Circulation of Social Energy in Renaissance England*. Berkeley: University of California Press.

Grier, E. F. (1951). Walt Whitman, the *Galaxy*, and *Democratic Vistas*. *American Literature*, 23: 332–50.

Jay, P. (1997). Emerson, Whitman, and the Problem of Culture. In *Contingency Blues: The Search for Foundations in American Criticism*. Madison, Wisconsin: University of Wisconsin Press, pp. 42–56.

Kaplan, Justin (1980). *Walt Whitman: A Life*. New York: Simon & Schuster.

Mack, S. J. (2002). *The Pragmatic Whitman: Reimagining American Democracy*. Iowa City: University of Iowa Press.

Peach, L. (1982). The True Face of Democracy?: Carlyle's Challenge to Whitman's Idealism. In *British Influence on the Birth of American Literature*. New York: St Martins Press, pp. 162–93.

Scarry, E. (2002). The Difficulty of Imagining Other People. In Martha Nussbaum (ed.), *For Love of Country*. Boston: Beacon Press, pp. 99–110.

Thomas, M. (1987). *The Lunar Light of Whitman's Poetry*. Cambridge, MA: Harvard University Press.

Trachtenberg, A. (1994). Whitman's Visionary Politics. In Geoffrey M. Sill (ed.), *Walt Whitman of Mickle Street*. Knoxville: University of Tennessee Press, pp. 94–108.

Whitman, W. (1982). *Specimen Days*, in *Walt Whitman: Complete Poetry and Collected Prose*, ed. Justin Kaplan. New York: Literary Classics of the United States.

34
Specimen Days
Martin G. Murray

Walt Whitman admitted up front that *Specimen Days* was the "most wayward, spontaneous, fragmentary book ever printed," and readers will no doubt agree (*PW*, 1: 1). Published by Rees Welsh and Company in 1882 as part of the larger *Specimen Days and Collect*, the autobiography of sorts consists of nearly 250 chapters, few longer than a page in length, of "diary-jottings, war-memoranda of 1862–'65, Nature-notes of 1877–'81, with Western and Canadian observations afterwards, all bundled up and tied by a big string" (*PW*, 1: 1). As impromptu as it was, the book was Whitman's last sustained treatment of the major themes that had animated his lifework – comradeship, nationhood, spirituality, immortality. Whitman's use of prose to express these themes was also a type of homecoming, the poet having begun his long sojourn as a journalist determined to record that "strange, unloosen'd, wondrous time," mid-nineteenth-century America, as experienced by one Walt Whitman who felt graced to be a part of it (*PW*, 1: 3). Indeed, a large portion of *Specimen Days* was originally printed as journalism, from Whitman's poignant Civil War reports for the *New York Times*, to his Delaware ferry crossings for the *Philadelphia Progress*, and his observations on America's literati for the *Critic*.

Whitman remarks that his work came about in response to the queries of "an insisting friend," that being Richard Maurice Bucke, the Canadian physician who was preparing a biography of the poet (*PW*, 1: 3). Although Bucke eventually published his own study (1883), Whitman arranged to have *Specimen Days* published first, and as a result largely pre-empted Bucke's work. This was in keeping with Whitman's dual desire to receive the imprimatur of the cultivated, while safeguarding his own role of chief publicist, which he had sharpened through years of newspaper work. *Specimen Days* was a hit, quickly selling an initial run of 1,000 copies by piggy-backing on the notoriety that attended the banning in Boston of Whitman's 1881 Osgood edition of *Leaves of Grass*, which itself had proven a great success after it was picked up and published by Rees Welsh earlier in 1882.

Accustomed as we are to the self-aggrandizing properties of today's popular autobiographies, *Specimen Days* seems quaintly modest. Indicative is Whitman's casual mention, 15 chapters into the book, that in the year 1855, he "commenced putting *Leaves of Grass* to press for good, at the job printing office of my friends, the brothers Rome, in Brooklyn, after many MS. doings and undoings – (I had great trouble in leaving out the stock 'poetical' touches, but succeeded at last)" (*PW*, 1: 22). Nothing more is said of the event that Whitman, more than anyone, knew constituted the birth of modern American poetry.

Even here, however, Whitman is being coy, since the preceding chapters were specifically written to cast light upon "the go-befores and embryos of *Leaves of Grass*" (*PW*, 1: 4). The "long foreground," as Emerson famously put it, included Whitman's own family genealogy, which in his telling was inextricably linked with the land he claimed to speak for, traced back on his father's side to the earliest English settlers who arrived on the *True Love* in 1640 in Weymouth, Massachusetts, and on his mother's to "the old race of the Netherlands, so deeply grafted on Manhattan island and in Kings and Queens counties" (*PW*, 1: 8). Whitman was born on Long Island, and his early boyhood was spent spearing eels in Hampton Bay, or underfoot at the rambling farm house of his grandparents, Quaker Amy and Major Cornelius Van Velsor, a "mark'd and full Americanized specimen" (*PW*, 1: 8). In Brooklyn, Whitman claimed a prescient blessing from the French Revolutionary War hero Lafayette, who took the boy Walter to his breast during his acclaimed tour of the States in 1824. The poet recounts his visceral acquaintance with words as a printer's apprentice, and their power to entrance when spoken by such talented actors as "old Booth in *Richard Third*, or *Lear*" or "Charlotte Cushman [as] Lady Gay Spanker in *London Assurance*," or sung by the prima contralto Marietta Alboni or "the baritone Badiali, the finest in the world" (*PW*, 1: 20, 21). Whitman's delight in the common people was stoked by contact with that "strange, natural, quick-eyed and wondrous race," the Broadway omnibus drivers, with whom he would ride for hours "the whole length of Broadway listening to some yarn, (and the most vivid yarns ever spun, and the rarest mimicry)" and whose recollected names suggest their piquant attraction – "Broadway Jack, Dressmaker, Balky Bill, George Storms, Old Elephant, his brother Young Elephant (who came afterward,) Tippy, Pop Rice, Big Frank, Yellow Joe, Pete Callahan, Patsy Dee" (*PW*, 1: 18–19).

The heart of Whitman's autobiography recounts his wartime ministrations in the nation's capital from December 1862 through the end of the Civil War. In fact, the two and a half years Whitman spent tending the wounded encompass nearly a third of the 63 year old's memoir. Drawn from his published journalism, private correspondence, and notebook jottings, the Civil War memoranda have proven to be some of the poet's more curious and endearing prose works. At a time when the public was gobbling up regimental histories and heroic personal narratives of "shoulder-straps" (i.e., officers) leading men into glorious battle, Whitman invited the reader to revisit the war from the unique perspective of the Army hospital, "that little town ... of wounds, sickness, and death" and, more particularly, at the bedside of its "rank and file" residents (*PW*, 1: 28, 66, 74).

Shortly after arriving in Washington, Whitman confided to Emerson that, "I desire and intend to write a little book out of this phase of America . . . already brought to Hospital in her fair youth" (*Corr.*, I: 69). Although Whitman proposed such a book in 1863 to James Redpath, whose publication of Louisa May Alcott's *Hospital Sketches* was then a popular sensation, it wasn't until 1876 that *Memoranda During the War*, from which *Specimen Days* is drawn, was published. *Memoranda*, in turn, was a tapestry of previously published essays written in two separate periods roughly 10 years apart. The first group includes five articles written by Whitman as a special Washington correspondent for the *New York Times*, between February 1863 and March 1865. The second group includes six articles published in the *New York Weekly Graphic* between January and March 1874.

Whitman printed *Memoranda* himself, at a neighbor's print shop in Camden in an edition of roughly one thousand copies. Apparently it did not prove a commercial success: only about 100 copies seem to have been issued and many of them were given to special friends as a "Remembrance." Yet like most of Whitman's curiosities, his Civil War musings have shown remarkable staying power. Eventually melded with other personal reflections and repackaged as *Specimen Days*, the war narrative is among Whitman's most popular works. In our own day, we may encounter it in such diverse settings as Ned Rorem's musical settings, Ken Burns's television documentary, and Chris Adrian's fiction.

Whitman claimed that "[M]ost of its pages are *verbatim* renderings" of his "impromptu jottings in pencil" made "on the spot" and put in his hospital journals during the war (*PW*, 1: 2). In an era made cynical by the journalistic fabrications of Stephen Glass and Jayson Blair, it is reassuring to pick up Whitman's surviving notebooks and encounter there the same soldiers who populate the pages of *Specimen Days*. We see, for example, that Whitman drew the following sketch, of a patient he met on January 21, 1863 in Armory Square Hospital, directly from his notebook: "Interesting cases in Ward I; Charles Miller, bed No. 19, Company D, Fifty-third Pennsylvania, is only sixteen years of age, very bright, courageous boy, left leg amputated below the knee; next bed to him, another young lad very sick; gave each appropriate gifts" (*PW*, 1: 36). The corresponding hospital notebook entries read:

> Chas Miller bed 19, Ward I some apples also tobacco – (also one to each of the boys each side)/bed 19 Ward I Armory Hospital Chas Miller, (only 16) co D. 53 Penn. left leg amputated – father living – mother dead – no relatives or friends been to see him – gave him 20 cts – Eugene Kelsey, co B. 64th N Y Vol. . . . (side of Charly Miller)/(*NUPM*, 2: 600, 604, 787)

Further, in cases where Whitman's notebooks have not survived, we can verify his accounts of soldiers through extant military records. Although Whitman's vignette,

"Death of a Wisconsin Officer" (*PW*, 1: 64), does not identify the young lieutenant dying from wounds received at Chancellorsville, an examination of the Armory Square Hospital register reveals him as John McMurtrey, First Lieutenant, Company H, Fifth Wisconsin Infantry (see Price, Murray, and Nelson 2001). Admitted to the hospital on May 8 with a gunshot wound to the spine, McMurtrey began hemorrhaging on the morning of May 30, 1863 ("vomiting dark brown matter incessantly," according to his attending physician Charles Bowen), and died that same afternoon.

Nevertheless, Whitman did take some liberties regarding the chronological placement of a few sketches. For example, in "A Yankee Soldier," Whitman describes an encounter on Washington's streets with Charles Carroll of a Massachusetts regiment "one cool October evening," in 1864 (*PW*, 1: 77). In fact, Whitman was at that time recuperating in his mother's Brooklyn home from emotional and physical exhaustion brought on by his hospital work. Introducing his own debilitation at this point in the hospital narrative would have undermined his projection of "ordinary cheer and magnetism," which Whitman believed "succeeded and help'd more than . . . medical nursing, or delicacies, or gifts of money, or anything else" (*PW*, 1: 51–2). Carroll, however, was a real soldier of the Fourth Massachusetts Heavy Artillery, who was stationed in Washington in the early months of 1865 when Whitman would have met him, and his soldier brothers Obediah and Grant died all too real deaths within hours of one another while prisoners at Andersonville, as Whitman records in *Specimen Days* (see Price et al. 2001).

It is natural that Whitman was drawn to serve the Union cause as a hospital visitor given his nature – "a great tender mother-man," in his friend John Burroughs' apt description (Burroughs 1928: 237). Following the war, some accused Whitman of shirking his responsibilities by not enlisting as a soldier. However, a man of Whitman's age (he was 41 when the war began) was a rarity among enlistees. Only 5.6 percent of all Union enlistments during the war's first two years were Whitman's age or older; the average age was 25, and the age of the largest number of enlistees was only 18, according to a statistical analysis by the US Sanitary Commission (Gould [1869] 1979: 34–5). Once the draft was initiated in 1863, Whitman stood ready to be called (as a single man, he was eligible through age 45). He did not avail himself of the option to purchase commutation or a substitute, unlike 42 percent of his fellow enrollees who did so (Murdock 1971: 198), including Whitman's younger brother Jeff.

As a wartime journalist, Whitman hoped to convey the essence of a wounded soldier's experience to a Northern audience who warily scanned the dry but nevertheless alarming lists of casualties, which were a common feature of the daily newspaper. (Whitman himself had experienced the shock of finding his own brother George listed in the New York *Herald* among the wounded from the battle of Fredericksburg.) While some of his reports may strike us as brutally frank, Whitman understood the reassurance that came from hard but truthful information. He also hoped to rally support for reforms in the medical treatment of the wounded and sick, as well as to encourage, through his own example, the application of tender mercies to scarred psyches.

M. Wynn Thomas notes that "One of the deepest compulsions behind Whitman's wartime activities . . . [was] his passionate determination to record the achievements and sufferings of the 'unknown' soldier and, wherever possible, to restore to those soldiers at least a trace of that personal identity that had almost been obliterated by . . . mass warfare" (Thomas 1995: 35–6). Whitman recovers the memory of Thomas Haley, a "regular Irish boy, a fine specimen of youthful physical manliness," who was recruited in Ireland to fight for a New York regiment, and lay dying at Armory Square, alone save for the "heart of a stranger that hover'd near" (*PW*, 1: 49, 50). And John Mahay, whose gunshot wound to the bladder caused him to "lay almost constantly in a sort of puddle," and whose hospital friends marked his death with a grand funeral (*PW*, 1: 39).

Whitman was an early adversary of "rankism," to use Robert Fuller's recently coined term to describe the devaluing of those who lack social rank or status. In Whitman's Civil War memoir, we mainly encounter not generals or statesmen, but "the Common People, emblemised in thousands of specimens of first-class Heroism, steadily accumulating, (no regiment, no company, hardly a file of men, North or South, the last three years, without such first-class specimens)" (*PW*, 1: 322). There is Calvin Harlowe, the 24-year-old Massachusetts Veteran Volunteer who, "disdaining to surrender," was killed while defending Fort Stedman at Petersburg (*PW*, 1: 97), as well as the anonymous 17-year-old "Secesh brave," who died while planting his company's battle-flag in the mouth of a Union cannon at Franklin, Tennessee (*PW*, 1: 43).

As in his poetic enumerations, Whitman's tally of soldiers in *Specimen Days* strives for inclusiveness. The 50 individual and identifiable soldiers hail from 11 different loyal states (Connecticut, Massachusetts, Maine, Michigan, New Hampshire, New Jersey, New York, Ohio, Pennsylvania, Wisconsin, and West Virginia), five rebellious ones (Alabama, Georgia, Louisiana, Mississippi, and North Carolina), as well as Maryland of divided loyalty (see Price et al. 2001). Whitman took pride in the fact that the bulk of the soldiers were US-born, but his list also registers several Europeans, including French-born Maximilian de Fisheur, "an intelligent looking man, has a foreign accent, black-eyed and hair'd, a Hebraic appearance" (*PW*, 1: 38). Catholics and Quakers inhabit his Army of wounded and sick, as well as the pious Oscar Wilber, whom Whitman comforted with a reading from the dying soldier's "chief reliance," the New Testament (*PW*, 1: 56).

Although relishing diversity, Whitman nevertheless showed some partiality in his presentation of soldiers in *Specimen Days*. Not surprisingly, nearly 40 percent of the Union soldiers whose specific identities have been recovered served Whitman's home state of New York (see Price et al. 2001). Also, while intent on including Rebels in his story, Whitman's treatment of them reflects his strong Union bias. In "Two Brothers, One South, One North," for example, there is a sense of shame attached to the Southerner. Though listed first in the narrative, only his initials, "W.S.P.," identify him and he proffers apology to his caregiver. The Union brother, by contrast, is introduced proudly as "an officer of rank, a Union soldier, a brave and religious man," and identified fully by name, rank, and regiment, "Col. Clifton K. Prentiss, Sixth Md. Infantry, Sixth Corps" (*PW*, 1: 107).

Similarly, the "Secesh brave" who faced down Union cannonballs mentioned above, is not identified by name, but the heroic Union soldier, Calvin Harlowe, is. Indeed only two Southern soldiers are identified by their surnames, David Irving of the Eighth Louisiana and John Wormley of the Ninth Alabama, the latter an "escapee" from the Rebel Army (Whitman refused to call such men deserters) (*PW*, 1: 76, 89, 91). Another soldier who is sometimes mistaken as a Rebel, "James H. Williams, aged 21, 3d Va. Cavalry," is actually a Union soldier serving from the loyal Western region (*PW*, 1: 108). By listing Williams's regiment in this manner, Whitman implicitly endorses West Virginia's claim to represent the legitimate Virginia state government in opposition to the secession.

Also telling is Whitman's mere passing reference in *Specimen Days* to an unidentified "Mississippian, a captain" whom he met as a patient in the Lacy mansion opposite Fredericksburg (*PW*, 1: 32). Unlike his other narratives that were drawn from personal observation, Whitman's private notation that the soldier "wears his confederate uniform, proud as a devil" did not find its way into the published prose (*Corr.*, 1: 81). Nor did the Mississippi Infantry's successful guerilla defense of Fredericksburg, which slowed the Union advance sufficiently to allow Rebel forces to strengthen their position on Marye's Heights and thus ensure a Confederate victory. That Whitman and this soldier-patient (now known to be Thomas Thurman of the Thirteenth Mississippi Infantry, *see* Price, Murray and Nelson) also shared "a tremendous friendship . . . our affection is quite an affair, quite romantic," would otherwise have argued for memorializing him (*Corr.*, 1: 81). Likewise, Whitman's Washington lover, Peter Doyle, appears in the Civil War section, but no mention is made of his status as a former Rebel.

Whitman's rebuff reflects not only his political disagreement with Secession, but also his deep anger and disgust with the South's conduct of one particular aspect of the war: its treatment of Union prisoners. In *Specimen Days*, Whitman records his shock at the sight in Annapolis, Maryland, of returning prisoners:

> Can those be *men* – those little livid-brown, ash-streak'd, monkey-looking dwarfs? – are they really not mummied, dwindled corpses? They lay there, most of them, quite still, but with a horrible look in their eyes and skinny lips, often with not enough flesh on the lips to cover their teeth. Probably no more appaling [*sic*] sight was ever seen on this earth. (There are deeds, crimes, that may be forgiven; but this is not among them. It steeps its perpetrators in blackest, escapeless, endless damnation. . . .) (*PW*, 1: 100)

Whitman believed the Southern prisons were indicative of an underlying Southern character flaw. In recalling the war with his secretary Horace Traubel, Whitman claimed:

> [Y]ou have no idea, Horace, how really fiendish the disposition of the South towards a foe is likely to be . . . [O]ur Southern people would go to a length of animosity not even manifested by the animals. It was long ago said by naturalists, believed by them, that some of the animals, smelling a body, finding it dead, would pass away, leaving it

untouched. Some naturalists believe this yet: think, then, of the prisons South. (Traubel 1906, 4: 331–2)

Whitman's anger was personal: his brother George had been a prisoner of war. Captured at Poplar Grove Church near Petersburg in September 1864, George Whitman was imprisoned for six months successively in Richmond, Salisbury, and Danville. When Whitman describes in *Memoranda* "the scrawl'd, worn slips of paper that came up by bushels from the Southern prisons, Salisbury or Andersonville, by the hands of exchanged prisoners" (*PW*, 1: 321), he is literally depicting how his own family received word from George (Murray 2000: 65).

African Americans also do not figure prominently in Whitman's Civil War. Although Whitman claimed, "Among the black soldiers, wounded or sick, and in the contraband camps, I also took my way whenever in their neighborhood, and did what I could for them" (*PW*, 1: 113–14), the fact remains that each individual, identifiable soldier who appears in *Specimen Days* is white (Price et al. 2001). This absence was typical of memoirs revolving around the Civil War, according to Ann C. Rose. Having analyzed the published and private reminiscences of 75 American Victorians, Rose observes, "[W]ithin [Victorians'] voluminous personal writings on wartime, blacks were scarcely mentioned, as if the freedmen's dilemma failed to grip the Victorians' consciousness in an affecting way" (Rose 1992: 242). George Hutchinson attributes Whitman's neglect to "his view of the war as a 'family' drama; the ideology of race as 'family' made it impossible for Whitman to conceive of the Civil War as centrally involving African Americans" (Hutchinson 2003: 145). Whitman also subscribed to prevailing racial stereotypes. His conversations with Traubel are speckled with racially charged comments such as his description of Africans as "a superstitious, ignorant, thievish race," but also, "full of good nature, good heart" (Traubel 1906, 9: 48). Since Whitman's memorializing project involved the recovery of individual identities, his inability to view blacks as individuals precluded their meaningful inclusion in *Specimen Days*.

With respect to Southerners and African Americans, however, Whitman's sins were acts of omission rather than commission. Whatever his privately expressed feelings, Whitman was ever mindful not to express in his published writings hateful attitudes towards either group.

"What shall I hang on the chamber walls . . . to adorn the burial-house of him I love?" Whitman pondered in his "Lilacs" memorial to Lincoln (*LG*: 332). Whitman adorns his Civil War memorial with tableaux of war from the perspective of the common soldiers he seeks to honor. There are soldiers writing letters home, or gathered singing hymns with their nurses. A mother keeps watch over the bedside of her wounded youngest. Soldiers slump exhausted in city doorways following the retreat from Bull Run. A cavalry troop is setting up camp on a hillside, and drovers are herding cattle in the shadow of Washington's monument. The President solemnly nods as he passes by on the street. A visitor distributes ice cream at Carver Hospital. The Patent Office is furnished with cots of wounded, then filled with perfumed waltzers at an Inaugural ball. Veterans are receiving their re-enlistment bounties. Crutches clank down office corridors and returning armies march along Pennsylvania Avenue.

Fearful that future generations might think the war merely a "quadrille in a ballroom," Whitman's memorial also depicts war's hellish fantasia (*PW*, 1: 117). A Rebel lies on the battlefield with his head blown open, while his foot rhythmically digs a hole in the ground. Soldiers writhe as the woods take fire at Chancellorsville. Corpses float down the Potomac and catch and lodge. Mosby's guerrillas massacre a trainload of wounded, and Union soldiers kill unarmed captives. Prisoners starve in Andersonville.

Whitman was never quite satisfied, however, that he had truly captured the soldier's experience of war. The shifting chronological structure of his memorial, as Whitman refashioned the 1876 *Memoranda* into the 1882 *Specimen Days*, reflects his wrestling with this failure.

Memoranda begins its war chronology in December 1862, with news of George Whitman's wounding at Fredericksburg. It moves forward in time to the war's culmination, but in an addendum shifts back to the conflict's opening with a description of Lincoln's election, the attack on Ft. Sumter, and the defeat at First Bull Run. In structure it bears some resemblance to Maya Ying Lin's Vietnam Veterans memorial, in which the visitor enters along the eastern wall, encountering the first listed casualty, dating to mid-war 1968. As the visitor follows the plunging wall, the list of dead progresses chronologically to the last soldier killed in 1975. The list doesn't end at the vortex, however, but begins again in 1959 with the name of the war's first dead soldier immediately following, and thereafter as the western wall ascends and stops abruptly in mid-war 1968 again. Both the wall and *Memoranda* create a sensation of unending – "the strange sad war revolving" (*LG Var.*, 3: 628 n.), as Whitman described it in "To Thee, Old Cause" in his 1872 *Leaves* – reflecting their society's inability to fully grasp the import of the conflict.

With *Specimen Days*, Whitman straightened the war chronology, starting his diary with Ft. Sumter in April 1861 and ending with the Grand Review of troops in May 1865. While retaining virtually all of *Memoranda*, Whitman did add two significant phrases, which follow one another in his closing section: "The real war will never get in the books. And so good-bye to the war" (*PW*, 1: 115). In doing so, Whitman conceded his inability to grasp the incomprehensible and made peace with it. He was now ready to move on and minister to his own wounding.

Whitman fast-forwards a decade to continue his autobiography in the New Jersey countryside, where he had retreated after suffering a debilitating stroke in 1873 that left him a "half-Paralytic" (*PW*, 1: 248). The "interregnum" years spent in Washington Whitman summarizes with the terse observation, "I continued at Washington working in the Attorney-General's department through '66 and '67, and some time afterward" (*PW*, 1: 118). Those years had been remarkably rich ones personally and professionally, and Whitman's decision to overlook them is pregnant with meaning. Whitman published nearly 100 new poems during this period, including "Drum-

Taps," the Lincoln elegies, and *Passage to India. Leaves of Grass* was reissued in two new domestic editions, and a British selection of his poems edited by William Michael Rossetti gained the poet an appreciative and influential foreign audience. He fell in love with Peter Doyle, and through his friendship with William and Ellen O'Connor, Charles Eldridge, and John Burroughs, Whitman was introduced to the capital's political and literary cognoscenti. Whitman experienced a modestly successful government career, eventually rising to a mid-level clerkship in the Attorney General's Office, where he had cordial relationships with office holders J. Hubley Ashton, Henry Stanbery, and William Evart. Whitman also refrains from telling a tale that has become standard in his biographical canon – the poet's dismissal from a government job by Interior Secretary James Harlan for authoring "that book" as the Secretary disdainfully called Whitman's life work. (Imagine Clinton's *My Life* without a mention of Kenneth Starr!)

Such highfalutin accomplishments were not in keeping with Whitman's attempt to present a more approachable character, with whom a reader might identify and who might emulate the essential verities that Whitman's autobiography seeks to promote. Indeed, in his introduction to his next principal section, the Nature notes, Whitman advises,

> After you have exhausted what there is in business, politics, conviviality, love, and so on – have found that none of these finally satisfy, or permanently wear – what remains? Nature remains; to bring out from their torpid recesses, the affinities of a man or woman with the open air, the trees, fields, the changes of seasons – the sun by day and the stars of heaven by night. We will begin from these convictions. Literature flies so high and is so hotly spiced, that our notes may seem hardly more than breaths of common air, or draughts of water to drink. But that is part of our lesson. (*PW*, 1: 119–20)

Like his Civil War memoranda, the Nature chapters in *Specimen Days* are a pastiche of previously published newspaper prose, gleanings from his private correspondence, and a smattering of original manuscripts. Before he had ever conceived of his autobiography, Whitman had told Anne Gilchrist in an August 18, 1879, letter of his intention to write "a smallish 100 page book of my accumulated memoranda down at the Creek, & across the Ferry, days & nights, under the title of *Idle Days & Nights of a half-Paralytic*" consisting of "free gossip mostly" (*Corr.*, 3: 169). Organizing them for *Specimen Days* as a diary that generally follows the seasons roughly from spring 1876 through spring 1879, Whitman mimics Thoreau whose *Walden* (1854) was one of the nation's earliest and most acclaimed autobiographies (Aarnes 1982b: 405–6). Like Thoreau, Whitman presents this period as one of relative isolation, although both writers were actually in fairly constant communication with the outside world. Whitman, in particular, lived in Camden with his brother George, his sister-in-law Louisa, and his younger, retarded brother Eddie, and the poet was frequently accompanied to Timber Creek (in Laurel Springs, New Jersey) by members of the Stafford farm family, especially Harry who served as the last of Whitman's "Calamus" lovers.

Whitman's retreat to Nature was in part scientifically based. As Harold Aspiz remarks, "the regimen of temperance, fresh air, water, massage, nakedness, and good cheer which helped the poet to achieve periods of respite from the rigors of paralysis . . . was grounded in the concept of the air cure and was a variant of conventional and hydropathic medical practice" (Aspiz 1983: 49). Whitman was influenced by a leading practitioner, Dr Russell Thatcher Trall, with whom Whitman had been acquainted when both were associated with Fowler and Wells' publishing house in 1855–56. "A Sun-Bath – Nakedness" chapter, for example, describes Whitman's immersion in an "Adamic air-bath and flesh-brushing," along with abstention from medicine, which Trall had specifically prescribed in his writings as a treatment for paralysis (*PW*, 1: 150–1).

Whitman, of course, was interested not just in his own healing, but that of his countrymen, who like him were in need of "soothing, healthy, restoration-hours. . . . after the long strain of the war, and its wounds and death" (*PW*, 1: 120). As we have suggested, Whitman's *Memoranda During the War* has its corollary in the Vietnam Veteran's Memorial as a perpetual and unresolved act of mourning. Perhaps the reconstituted War/Nature chapters in *Specimen Days* are analogous to a more recent public memorial, "Reflecting Absence," which commemorates our own time's singular trauma on September 11, 2001. As envisioned by its designers Michael Arad and Peter Walker, the memorial to the victims of the World Trade Center attacks incorporates the names of the dead within a healing landscape of vegetation and water. Visitors to this site, as to Whitman's prose, are invited to honor those absent but also to find balm and rejuvenation.

Nature is a predominant theme throughout Whitman's work, and he exhibits an appreciation for it both literally and figuratively. Extending his democratic principles to material objects, Whitman focuses on the commonplace in *Specimen Days* – bumble-bees, crows, oaks and elm trees, the cedar-apple, locusts, and katydids – just as his poetic enumerations gloried in "[L]eaves stiff or drooping in the fields, / And brown ants in the little wells beneath them, / And mossy scabs of the worm fence, heap'd stones, elder, mullein and poke-weed" (*LG*: 33). Nature also possesses spiritual significance, intimating an immortality that Whitman increasingly sought as he aged. Stephen Tanner observes that the night sky, in particular, "was for Whitman . . . the brink of the unknown, the frontier for the spiritual pioneer, and opening into the eternal" (Tanner 1973: 158). Whitman discerned in "The Milky Way, as if some superhuman symphony, some ode of universal vagueness, disdaining syllable and sound – a flashing glance of Deity, address'd to the soul" (*PW*, 1: 174–5).

Again taking a leaf from Thoreau, Whitman's Nature notes were also political in their effort to get readers to think about and challenge the ubiquitous commercial culture and "the mania of owning things," which had become even more pronounced during the Gilded Age than in the ante-bellum period when Whitman, in the very first edition of *Leaves*, had originally denounced it (*LG*: 60). Whitman seductively invites his "reader dear" to come

> Away, from curtain, carpet, sofa, book – from "society" – from city house, street, and modern improvements and luxuries – away to the primitive winding . . . wooded creek, with its untrimm'd brushes and turfy banks . . . away from ligatures, tight boots, buttons, and the whole cast-iron civilized life . . . from tailordom and fashion's clothes – from any clothes, perhaps, for the nonce, the summer heats advancing, there in those watery, shaded solitudes. . . . returning to the naked source-life of us all – to the breast of the great silent savage all-acceptive Mother. (*PW*, 1: 121–2)

Replenished by this intimate contact with Nature, Whitman was prepared, as William Aarnes notes, to "resum[e] involvement in society. In the notes following the nature notes Whitman records not a life of seclusion but one of social activity" (Aarnes 1982b: 415). Appropriately, Whitman's homecoming occurs in his beloved Manhattan.

> After an absence of many years . . . again I resume with curiosity the crowds, the streets I knew so well, Broadway, the ferries, the west side of the city, democratic Bowery – human appearances and manners as seen in all these, and along the wharves, and in the perpetual travel of the horse-cars, or the crowded excursion steamers, or in Wall and Nassau streets by day – in the places of amusement at night – bubbling and whirling and moving like its own environment of waters – endless humanity in all phases. (*PW*, 1: 171)

Much of the remainder of *Specimen Days* constitutes a travelogue extending from Massachusetts to the Rockies, with a visit to Bucke's Canada thrown in for good measure. Of particular significance to Whitman was his "long jaunt west," an excursion he took in the fall of 1879 as a guest of Colonel John W. Forney, editor of the *Philadelphia Progress* and a former leader of the Free-Soil movement, who partook a speaking tour of Kansas to mark the 25th anniversary of the state's organization (*PW*, 1: 205). Although the poet-in-residence was frequently asked to versify, Whitman felt that "a poem would be almost an impertinence," amidst the prairie's "vast Something, stretching out on its own unbounded scale, unconfined . . . combining the real and ideal, and beautiful as dreams" (*PW*, 1: 208). Whitman was taken by every aspect of the West: "the grandeur and superb monotony of the skies," or "the cactuses, pinks, buffalo grass, wild sage" of the plains; he found the cowboys "a strangely interesting class, bright-eyed as hawks, with their swarthy complexions and their broad-brimm'd hats," and even the businessmen had "a certain racy wild smack," all of their own (*PW*, 1: 208, 215, 219). Extending his visit to encompass Colorado and the Rocky Mountains, Whitman felt justified not only in this journey but also uniquely in his life's mission. In the "joyous elemental abandon" of the mountains' canons, streams and gorges, its towering, varicolored rocks, the "entire absence of art, untrammel'd play of primitive Nature," Whitman had at last "found the law of my own poems" (*PW*, 1: 210).

One might expect Whitman to end his reminiscences at such a natural high. Instead, they continue for another 66 chapters, whose range of topics may prove daunting to the most enthusiastic reader. There's "Sunday with the Insane" at Dr Bucke's Canadian clinic, and "Cedar-Plums Like-Names," a list of rejected titles for *Specimen Days*; "Edgar Poe's Significance" provides an image of the Gothic author at the mast of a storm-toss'd ship (which served as the impetus for Dominick Argento's 1976 opera), along with "Carlyle from American Points of View," and "My Tribute to Four Poets," containing comments on Emerson, Longfellow, Bryant, and Whittier. Perhaps it is best to regard Whitman's autobiography as we would his poetical catalogues and keep Edward Dowden's useful caution in mind:

> His catalogues are for the poet always, if not always for the reader, *visions* – they are delighted – not perhaps delightful – enumerations; when his desire for the perception of greatness and variety is satisfied, not when a really complete catalogue is made out, Whitman's enumeration ends; we may murmur, but Whitman has been happy; what has failed to interest our imaginations has deeply interested his; and even for us the impression of multitude, of variety, of equality is produced, as perhaps it could be in no other way. Whether Whitman's habit of cataloguing be justified by what has been said, or is in any way justifiable, such at least is its true interpretation and significance. (Dowden [1871] 1996: 194)

As Whitman is satisfied, then so must we be.

References and Further Reading

Aarnes, William (1982a). Free Margins: Identity and Silence in Whitman's *Specimen Days*. *Emerson Society Quarterly*, 28 (4): 243–60.

Aarnes, William (1982b). Withdrawal and Resumption: Whitman and Society in the Last Two Parts of *Specimen Days*. In Joel Myerson (ed.), *Studies in the American Renaissance*. Boston: Twayne, pp. 401–32.

Aspiz, Harold (1983). Specimen Days: The Therapeutics of Sun-Bathing. *Walt Whitman Quarterly Review*, 1: 48–50.

Burroughs, John (1928). *The Heart of Burroughs' Journals*. Boston: Houghton Mifflin.

Chielens, Edward E. (1975). Whitman's Specimen Days and the Familiar Essay Genre. *Genre*, 8: 366–78.

Cummings, Glenn N. (1992). Whitman's *Specimen Days* and the Theatricality of "Semirenewal." *American Transcendental Quarterly*, 6 (3): 177–87.

Dowden, Edward ([1871] 1996). Review in *Westminster Review*, 96, July. In Kenneth M. Price (ed.), *Walt Whitman: The Contemporary Reviews*. New York: Cambridge University Press, pp. 181–208.

Eitner, Walter H. (1981). *Walt Whitman's Western Jaunt*. Lawrence: The Regents Press of Kansas.

Everett, Nicholas (1996). Autobiography as Prophecy: Walt Whitman's *Specimen Days*. In Vincent Newey and Philip Shaw (eds.), *Mortal Pages, Literary Lives: Studies in Nineteenth-Century Autobiography*. Brookfield, VT: Ashgate, pp. 217–34.

Fichtelberg, Joseph (1989). The American Voice: Walt Whitman. In *The Complex Image: Faith and Method in American Autobiography*. Philadelphia: University of Pennsylvania Press, pp. 22–52.

Gould, Benjamin Apthorp ([1869] 1979). *Investigations in the Military and Anthropological Statistics of American Soldiers*. New York: Arno Press.

Hutchinson, George (2003). Race and the Family Romance: Whitman's Civil War. *Walt Whitman Quarterly Review*, 20 (3/4): 134–50.

Johnson, Linck C. (1975). The Design of Walt Whitman's *Specimen Days*. *Walt Whitman Review*, 21 (March): 3–14.

Major, William (2001). "Some Vital Unseen Presence": The Practice of Nature in Walt Whitman's Specimen Days. *ISLE*, 7 (1): 79–96.

Mullin, Joseph Eugene (1994). The Whitman of *Specimen Days. Iowa Review,* 24 (Winter): 148–61.

Murdock, Eugene C. (1971). *One Million Men; The Civil War Draft in the North.* Madison, WI: The State Historical Society of Wisconsin.

Murray, Martin G. (2000). Walt Whitman on Brother George and his Fifty-First New York Volunteers: An Uncollected New York Times Article. *Walt Whitman Quarterly Review,* 18 (Summer/Fall): 65–70.

Myerson, Joel (1993). *Walt Whitman: A Descriptive Bibliography.* Pittsburgh: University of Pittsburgh Press.

Philippon, Daniel J. (1998). "I Only Seek to Put You in Rapport": Message and Method in Walt Whitman's *Specimen Days.* In Michael P. Branch (ed.), *Reading the Earth: New Directions in the Study of Literature and Environment.* Moscow, ID: University of Idaho Press, pp.179–93.

Price, Kenneth M. (1980). Whitman on Other Writers: Controlled "Graciousness" in *Specimen Days. Emerson Society Quarterly,* 26 (2): 79–87.

Price, Kenneth M., Murray, Martin G., and Nelson, Robert K. (2001). Whitman's Memory. *The Classroom Electric; Whitman, Dickinson and American Culture,* <http://www.iath.virginia.edu/fdw/volume2/price/memoranda/index.htm>.

Rose, Anne C. (1992). *Victorian America and the Civil War.* Cambridge, UK: Cambridge University Press.

Tanner, Stephen (1973). Star-gazing in Whitman's *Specimen Days. Walt Whitman Review,* 19 (December): 158–61.

Thomas, M. Wynn (1995). Fratricide and Brotherly Love: Whitman and the Civil War. In Ezra Greenspan (ed.), *The Cambridge Companion to Walt Whitman.* Cambridge, UK: Cambridge University Press, pp. 27–44.

Traubel, Horace (1906). *With Walt Whitman in Camden,* vol. 1. Boston: Small, Maynard.

35
The Prose Writings: Selected Secondary Sources

Donald D. Kummings

Because space is limited, items of marginal value or of historical interest only have been excluded from this compilation.

Short Stories

Abrams, Robert E. (1976). An Early Precursor of "The Sleepers": Whitman's "The Last of the Sacred Army." *Walt Whitman Review*, 22: 122–5.

Asselineau, Roger (1980). The Katinka Mystery: or, Who Will Unknot "Abbie Nott and Other Knots"? *Leaves of Grass* at 125, Supplement to *Walt Whitman Review*, 26: 15–19.

On a collection of tales and sketches that may have been authored (but probably not) by Whitman.

Bergman, Herbert (1982). A Hitherto Unknown Whitman Story and a Possible Early Poem. *Walt Whitman Review*, 28: 3–15.

Black, John (1920). Walt Whitman: Fiction-Writer and Poets' Friend. *Bookman* 51 (April): 172–4.

On Whitman's editorials and prose sketches in the Brooklyn *Eagle*.

Brasher, Thomas L. (1963). Introduction. *The Early Poems and the Fiction*, by Walt Whitman, ed. Thomas L. Brasher. New York: New York University Press, pp. xv–xviii.

Cohen, Matt (1998). Whitman's Short Fiction. In J. R. LeMaster and Donald D. Kummings (eds.), *Walt Whitman: An Encyclopedia*. New York and London: Garland, pp. 635–6.

Gannon, Thomas C. (2004/2005). Reading Boddo's Body: Crossing the Borders of Race and Sexuality in Whitman's "Half-Breed." *Walt Whitman Quarterly Review*, 22 (Fall/Winter): 87–107.

Katz, Jonathan Ned (2001). A Gentle Angel Entered. In *Love Stories: Sex Between Men Before Homosexuality*. Chicago: University of Chicago Press, pp. 33–41.

On "The Child's Champion."

Knapp, Bettina L. (1993). Fiction. In *Walt Whitman*. New York: Continuum, pp. 203–9.

Mabbott, Thomas Ollive (1927). Introduction. *The Half-Breed and Other Stories by Walt Whitman*, ed. Thomas O. Mabbott. New York: Columbia University Press, pp. 11–19.

McGuire, Patrick (1998). "The Angel of Tears," "Bervance; or, Father and Son," "The Boy Lover," "The Child and the Profligate," "Death in the School-Room (A Fact)," "The Death of Wind-Foot," "Dumb Kate," "The Fireman's Dream," "The Half-Breed," "The Last Loyalist," "The Last of the Sacred Army," "A Legend of Life and Love," "Lingave's Temptation," "Little Jane," "The Little Sleighers," "The Love of Eris: A Spirit Record," "The Madman," "My Boys and Girls," "One Wicked Impulse!" "Reuben's Last Wish," "Richard Parker's Widow," "The Shadow and the Light of a Young Man's Soul," "Shirval:

A Tale of Jerusalem," "Some Fact-Romances," "The Tomb Blossoms," and "Wild Frank's Return." In J. R. LeMaster and Donald D. Kummings (eds.), *Walt Whitman: An Encyclopedia*. New York and London: Garland, pp. 21–2, 54–5, 71–2, 114–15, 169, 170–1, 194–5, 224–5, 264, 350–1, 388–9, 396, 399–400, 412, 416, 442, 482–3, 586–7, 590, 632, 634–5, 650–1, 735–6, 789–90.

Moon, Michael (1989). Disseminating Whitman. *South Atlantic Quarterly*, 88 (Winter): 247–65.

On Whitman's "The Child's Champion" and other homoerotic texts.

Moon, Michael (1991). Rendering the Text and the Body Fluid: The Cases of "The Child's Champion" and the 1855 *Leaves of Grass*. In *Disseminating Whitman: Revision and Corporeality in* Leaves of Grass. Cambridge, MA, and London: Harvard University Press, pp. 26–58.

Rachman, Stephen (1998). *American Whig Review*. In J. R. LeMaster and Donald D. Kummings (eds.), *Walt Whitman: An Encyclopedia*. New York and London: Garland, p. 20.

This journal published one of Whitman's early stories, "The Boy Lover."

Reynolds, David S. (1995). From Periodical Writer to Poet: Whitman's Journey Through Popular Culture. In Kenneth M. Price and Susan Belasco Smith (eds.), *Periodical Literature in Nineteenth-Century America*. Charlottesville: University Press of Virginia, pp. 35–50.

Rubin, Joseph Jay (1938). Whitman and the Boy-Forger. *American Literature*, 10 (May): 214–15.

Comments on the story "Fact-Romances."

Scheick, William J. (1977). Whitman's Grotesque Half-Breed. *Walt Whitman Review*, 23: 133–6.

Smith, Susan Belasco (1998). *Democratic Review*. In J. R. LeMaster and Donald D. Kummings (eds.), *Walt Whitman: An Encyclopedia*. New York and London: Garland, pp. 175–6.

Tanselle, G. Thomas (1962). Whitman's Short Stories: Another Reprint. *Papers of the Bibliographical Society of America*, 56 (First Quarter): 115.

Thompson, George A., Jr. (1984). Katinka Unveiled: The Authorship of *Abbie Nott and Other Knots*. *Papers of the Bibliographical Society of America*, 78: 71–4.

The author of *Abbie Nott* is not Whitman but Catherine Brooks (Mrs Linus) Yale.

Thompson, G. R. (1973). An Early Unrecorded Printing of Walt Whitman's "Death in the School-Room." *Papers of the Bibliographical Society of America*, 67 (January–March): 64–5.

Unsigned (1927). Review of Thomas Ollive Mabbott, ed. *The Half-Breed and Other Stories by Walt Whitman*. *Saturday Review of Literature*, 3 (28 May): 869.

White, William (1958). Walt Whitman's Short Stories: Some Comments and a Bibliography. *Papers of the Bibliographical Society of America*, 52 (Fourth Quarter): 300–6.

White, William (1960). Walt Whitman's Short Stories: Two Addenda. *Papers of the Bibliographical Society of America*, 54 (Third Quarter): 126.

White, William (1962). Whitman as Short Story Writer: Two Unpublished Manuscripts. *Notes and Queries*, 9 (March): 87–9.

White, William (1963). Addenda to Whitman's Short Stories. *Papers of the Bibliographical Society of America*, 57 (Second Quarter): 22.

White, William (1975). Whitman's Short Stories: More Addenda. *Papers of the Bibliographical Society of America*, 69 (Third Quarter): 402–3.

White, William (1987). Two Citations: An Early Whitman Article and an Early Reprinting of "Death in the School-Room." *Walt Whitman Quarterly Review*, 5 (Summer): 36–7.

Yoshizaki, Kuniko (1985). The Journalistic Aspect of Walt Whitman's Fiction. *Kyushu American Literature*, 26: 1–10.

In his journalistic writings Whitman acquired a didactic bent that he sustained in his fiction and, later on, in his poetry.

Franklin Evans

Cowie, Alexander (1948). Walt Whitman (1819–1892): Temperance Tractarian. In *The Rise of the American Novel*. New York: American Book Co., pp. 306–9.

Dalke, Anne (1985). "Whitman's Literary Intemperance": *Franklin Evans*, or The Power of Love. *Walt Whitman Quarterly Review*, 2 (3): 17–22.

Downey, Jean (1967). Introduction. *Franklin Evans or The Inebriate: A Tale of the Times*, by Walt Whitman, ed. Jean Downey. New Haven, CT: College and University Press, pp. 7–27.

Hendler, Glenn (1999). Bloated Bodies and Sober Sentiments: Masculinity in 1840s Temperance Narratives. In Mary Chapman and Glenn Hendler (eds.), *Sentimental Men: Masculinity and the Politics of Affect in American Culture*. Berkeley: University of California Press, pp. 124–48.

Hollingsworth, Marian (1962). Americanism in *Franklin Evans. Walt Whitman Review*, 8 (December): 88–9.

Holloway, Emory (1929). Introduction. *Franklin Evans*, by Walter Whitman, ed. Emory Holloway. New York: Random House, pp. v–xxiv.

Holloway, Emory (1956). More Temperance Tales by Whitman. *American Literature*, 27 (January): 577–8.

In addition to writing *Franklin Evans*, Whitman began a second temperance novel – called *The Madman*.

Hynes, Jennifer A. (1998). Temperance Movement. In J. R. LeMaster and Donald D. Kummings (eds.), *Walt Whitman: An Encyclopedia*. New York and London: Garland, pp. 709–11.

Ifkovic, Edward (1968). "I Took a Jaunt": Dickens's *American Notes* and Whitman's *Franklin Evans. Walt Whitman Review*, 14 (December): 171–4.

Karp, David Lawrence (1991). Death at the Birth of *Leaves of Grass*: Domestic and Morbid Imaginings in Walt Whitman's Writing, 1839–1856. PhD Dissertation, University of Washington, 1991. *Dissertations Abstracts International*, 52 (November 1991), 1747A.

Chapter 4 discusses *Franklin Evans*.

Lulloff, William G. (1998). *Franklin Evans*. In J. R. LeMaster and Donald D. Kummings (eds.), *Walt Whitman: An Encyclopedia*. New York and London: Garland, pp. 234–6.

Mabbott, Thomas Ollive (1925). Notes on Walt Whitman's "Franklin Evans." *Notes and Queries*, 149 (12 December): 419–20.

Murphy, Gretchen (1995). Enslaved Bodies: Figurative Slavery in the Temperance Fiction of Harriet Beecher Stowe and Walt Whitman. *Genre*, 28 (Spring/Summer): 95–118.

O'Reilly, Edmund Bernard (1988). Toward Rhetorical Immunity: Narratives of Alcoholism and Recovery. PhD Dissertation, University of Pennsylvania, *Dissertations Abstracts International*, 49/09–A, 2771.

Discusses Whitman's *Franklin Evans,* Jack London's *John Barleycorn*, and other "literary fictions" of alcoholism.

Reynolds, David S. (1997). Black Cats and Delirium Tremens: Temperance and the American Renaissance. In David S. Reynolds and Debra J. Rosenthal (eds.), *The Serpent in the Cup: Temperance in American Literature*. Amherst: University of Massachusetts Press, pp. 22–59.

See pages 47–53.

Sanchez-Eppler, Karen (1989). To Stand Between: A Political Perspective on Whitman's Poetics of Merger and Embodiment. *ELH*, 56 (Winter): 923–49.

Pages 928–34 are on *Franklin Evans*.

Shirakawa, Keiko (2002). The Paradox of Independence in Whitman's *Franklin Evans. Studies in English Literature*, 79: 37–57.

St Armand, Barton Levi (1971). *Franklin Evans*: A Sportive Temperance Novel. *Books at Brown*, 24: 134–47.

Warner, Michael (1996). Whitman Drunk. In Betsy Erkkila and Jay Grossman (eds.), *Breaking Bounds: Whitman and American Cultural Studies*. New York: Oxford University Press, pp. 30–43.

White, William (1971). A Unique *Franklin Evans? Walt Whitman Review*, 17 (March): 31–2.

Journalism

Asselineau, Roger (1999). Review of Walt Whitman, *The Journalism*, Volume 1, ed. Herbert Bergman, Douglas A. Noverr, and Edward J. Recchia. *Etudes Anglaises*, 52 (January–March): 110–11.

In French.

Bawcom, Amy M. (1998). *Evening Tattler* (New York) and *Saturday Press*. In J. R. LeMaster and Donald D. Kummings (eds.), *Walt Whitman: An Encyclopedia*. New York and London: Garland, pp. 213, 609–10.

Beach, Christopher (2000). Review of Walt Whitman, *The Journalism*, Volume 1, ed. Herbert Bergman, Douglas A. Noverr, and Edward J. Recchia. *American Literature*, 72 (March): 193–4.

Bergman, Herbert (1970). The Influence of Whitman's Journalism on *Leaves of Grass*. *American Literary Realism, 1870–1910*, 3 (Fall): 399–404.

Bergman, Herbert (1970). On Editing Whitman's Journalism. *Walt Whitman Review*, 16 (December): 104–9.

Bergman, Herbert (1971). Walt Whitman as a Journalist, 1831–January, 1848. *Journalism Quarterly*, 48 (Summer): 195–204.

Bergman, Herbert (1971). Walt Whitman as a Journalist, March, 1848–1892. *Journalism Quarterly*, 48 (Autumn): 431–37.

Bergman, Herbert (1971). Whitman on Editing, Newspapers and Journalism. *Journalism Quarterly*, 48 (Summer): 345–8.

Bergman, Herbert (1983). Walt Whitman's Journalism: Missing Files. *Walt Whitman Quarterly, Review*, 1 (1): 45–6.

Bergman, Herbert (1998). Preface and Introduction: Walt Whitman as a Journalist, 1831–January 1848. In Walt Whitman, *The Journalism*. Volume 1: 1834–1846, ed. Herbert Bergman, Douglas A. Noverr, and Edward J. Recchia. New York: Peter Lang, pp. xxv–xxxii, xliii–lxx.

Bergman, Herbert (2003). Preface and Editorial Principles. In Walt Whitman, *The Journalism*. Volume 2: 1846–1848, ed. Herbert Bergman, Douglas A. Noverr, and Edward J. Recchia. New York: Peter Lang, pp. xxv, xxvii–xxviii.

Bergman, Herbert and White, William (1970). Walt Whitman's Lost "Sun-Down Papers," Nos. 1–3. *American Book Collector*, 20 (January): 17–20.

Bergmann, Hans (1995). Walt Whitman: Over the Roofs of the World. In *God in the Streets: New York Writing from the Penny Press to Melville*. Philadelphia: Temple University Press, pp. 69–90.

Brasher, Thomas L. (1970). *Whitman as Editor of The Brooklyn Daily Eagle*. Detroit: Wayne State University Press.

Brown, Charles H. (1950). Young Editor Whitman: An Individualist in Journalism. *Journalism Quarterly*, 27 (Spring): 141–8.

Christman, Henry M. (1963). Introduction. *Walt Whitman's New York: From Manhattan to Montauk*, ed. Henry M. Christman. New York: Macmillan, pp. ix–xiv.

On a series of Whitman articles entitled "Brooklyniana."

Duban, James (1979). Satiric Precedents for Melville's "The Two Temples." *American Transcendental Quarterly*, 42 (Spring): 137–46.

On Whitman's Brooklyn *Daily Eagle* pieces as possible sources for Melville's satire on stylish worship in New York City.

Erkkila, Betsy (1998). *The New World* (New York). In J. R. LeMaster and Donald D. Kummings (eds.), *Walt Whitman: An Encyclopedia*. New York and London: Garland, pp. 457–8.

Fishkin, Shelley Fisher (1985). Walt Whitman. In *From Fact to Fiction: Journalism and Imaginative Writing in America*. Baltimore, MD: Johns Hopkins University Press, pp. 11–51.

Genoways, Ted (2000). Notes on Whitman: "Fish, Fishermen, and Fishing, on the East End of Long Island": An Excerpt from Walt Whitman's Uncollected Serial "Letters from a Travelling Young Bachelor." *Shenandoah*, 50 (Winter): 49–56.

Glicksberg, Charles I. (1936). Walt Whitman, the Journalist. *Americana*, 30 (July): 474–90.

Graffin, Walter (1998). New York *Times*. In J. R. LeMaster and Donald D. Kummings (eds.), *Walt Whitman: An Encyclopedia*. New York and London: Garland, p. 463.

Gruesz, Kirsten Silva (2001). The Fertile Crescent: Whitman's Immersion in the "Spanish Element." In *Ambassadors of Culture: The Transamerican Origins of Latino Writing*. Princeton, NJ: Princeton University Press, pp. 121–36.

Discusses Whitman's New Orleans *Crescent* piece, "A Walk about Town."

Harris, Maverick Marvin (1998). New Orleans *Crescent* and New Orleans *Picayune*. In J. R. LeMaster and Donald D. Kummings (eds.), *Walt Whitman: An Encyclopedia*. New York and London: Garland, pp. 455–6, 457.

Holloway, Emory (1924). More Light on Whitman. *American Mercury*, 1 (February): 183–9.

On Whitman's work for the Brooklyn *Evening Star*.

Holloway, Emory (1932). Whitman as Journalist. *Saturday Review of Literature*, 8 (23 April): 679–80.

Holloway, Emory (1932). Introduction. *I Sit and Look Out: Editorials from the Brooklyn Daily Times by Walt Whitman*, ed. Emory Holloway and Vernolian Schwarz. New York: Columbia University Press, pp. 3–30.

Holloway, Emory and Adimari, Ralph (1936). Introduction: Life Begins at Thirty-Five. *New York Dissected By Walt Whitman: A Sheaf of Recently Discovered Newspaper Articles by the Author of Leaves of Grass*, ed. Emory Holloway and Ralph Adimari. New York: Rufus Rockwell Wilson, pp. 1–14.

Jaffe, Steven H. (1992). "... the history of the future": Whitman and the New Journalism. *Seaport*, 26 (Spring): 26–31.

Karbiener, Karen (1998). *Long Island Democrat*, *Long Island Patriot*, *Long Island Star*, and *Long Islander*. In J. R. LeMaster and Donald D. Kummings (eds.), *Walt Whitman: An Encyclopedia*. New York and London: Garland, pp. 404, 406–8.

Killingsworth, M. Jimmie (1998). Whitman's Journalism. In J. R. LeMaster and Donald D. Kummings (eds.), *Walt Whitman: An Encyclopedia*. New York and London: Garland, pp. 333–6.

Killingsworth, M. Jimmie (1999–2000). Review of Walt Whitman, *The Journalism*, Volume 1, ed. Herbert Bergman, Douglas A. Noverr, and Edward J. Recchia. *Walt Whitman Quarterly Review*, 16 (3/4): 222–5.

Loving, Jerome M. (1974). "A Brooklyn Soldier, and a Noble One": A Brooklyn *Daily Union* Article by Whitman. *Walt Whitman Review*, 20 (March): 27–30.

Loving, Jerome M. (1974). "Our Veterans Mustering Out" – Another Newspaper Article by Whitman about His Soldier-Brother. *Yale University Library Gazette*, 49 (October): 217–24.

Loving, Jerome M. (2000). The Political Roots of *Leaves of Grass*. In David S. Reynolds (ed.), *A Historical Guide to Walt Whitman*. New York: Oxford University Press, pp. 97–119.

Loving, Jerome M. (2004). "Going to Bed": A Recovered Whitman Article from the Brooklyn *Daily Eagle*. *Walt Whitman Quarterly Review*, 22 (Summer): 28–30.

Loving, Jerome M. (2004). Review of Walt Whitman, *The Journalism*, Volume 2, ed. Herbert Bergman. *Walt Whitman Quarterly Review*, 22 (Summer): 31–6.

Mabbott, Thomas Ollive (1967). Walt Whitman Edits the *Sunday Times*, July, 1842–June, 1843. *American Literature*, 39 (March): 99–102.

MacLachlan, C. H. (1960). Walt Whitman as a Country Editor. *Grassroots Editor*, 1 (January): 15–16.

On Whitman's one-year editorship of *The Long-Islander* (1838–39).

MacLachlan, C. H. (1963). Whitman as a Newspaper Editor. *Long Island Forum*, 26 (November): 249–50, 266.

Murray, Martin G. (2000). Walt Whitman on Brother George and His Fifty-First New York Volunteers: An Uncollected *New York Times* Article. *Walt Whitman Quarterly Review*, 18 (Summer/Fall): 65–70.

Murray, Martin G. (2003). Two Pieces of Uncollected Whitman Journalism: "Washington as a Central Winter Residence" and "The Authors of Washington." *Walt Whitman Quarterly Review*, 20 (Winter/Spring): 151–76.

Murray, Martin G. (2004). "Yesterday's Military Show": An Uncollected Piece of Whitman Journalism. *Walt Whitman Quarterly Review*, 21 (Winter/Spring): 166–72.

Panish, Jon (1998). Brooklyn *Freeman*. In J. R. LeMaster and Donald D. Kummings (eds.), *Walt Whitman: An Encyclopedia*. New York and London: Garland, pp. 82–3.

Pannapacker, William A. (1998). *Life Illustrated* and *The North American Review*. In J. R. LeMaster and Donald D. Kummings (eds.), *Walt Whitman: An Encyclopedia*. New York and London: Garland, pp. 392–3, 465–6.

Parker, Simon (1999). Unrhymed Modernity: New York City, the Popular Newspaper Page, and the Forms of Whitman's Poetry. *Walt Whitman Quarterly Review*, 16 (3, 4): 161–71.

Pollin, Burton R. (1969). "Delightful Sights": A Possible Whitman Article in Poe's *Broadway Journal. Walt Whitman Review*, 15 (September): 180–7.

An article on Manhattan "tableaux."

Price, Kenneth M. (1998). Review of Walt Whitman, *The Journalism*, Volume 1, ed. Herbert Bergman, Douglas Noverr, and Edward J. Recchia. *The Book*, 46 (November): 3–4.

Renner, Dennis K. (1998). Brooklyn *Daily Eagle*, Brooklyn *Daily Times*, and New York *Aurora*. In J. R. LeMaster and Donald D. Kummings (eds.), *Walt Whitman: An Encyclopedia*. New York and London: Garland, pp. 79–81, 81–2, 458–9.

Rodgers, Cleveland (1920). Walt Whitman's Prose Issued as a New Book – Poet as Editor Before Civil War. *New York Herald Magazine and Books*, 9 (19 December): 2–5.

Rodgers, Cleveland (1920). Whitman's Life and Work 1846–1847. In *The Gathering of the Forces*, by Walt Whitman, 2 vols., ed. Cleveland Rodgers and John Black. New York: Putnam, vol. 1, pp. xi–liii.

Rosenthal, Bernard (1993). Whitman and Slavery. *Concourse*, 6: 17–24.

Examines Whitman's views as expressed in his newspaper pieces.

Rubin, Joseph Jay (1937). Whitman in 1840: A Discovery. *American Literature*, 9 (May): 239–42.

Newspaper items by and about Whitman.

Rubin, Joseph Jay (1939). Whitman's *New York Aurora*. *American Literature*, 11 (May): 214–17.

A complete file of the *New York Aurora* during Whitman's editorship has been found.

Rubin, Joseph Jay and Brown, Charles H. (1950). Introduction. *Walt Whitman of the New York "Aurora," Editor at Twenty-two: A Collection of Recently Discovered Writings*, ed. J. J. Rubin and C. H. Brown. State College, PA: Bald Eagle Press, pp. 1–13.

Schroth, Raymond A., S.J. (1974). Walt Whitman. *The Eagle and Brooklyn: A Community Newspaper, 1841–1955*, ed. Raymond Schroth. *Contributions in American Studies*, 13. Westport, CT: Greenwood Press, pp. 39–58.

Skinner, Charles M. (1903). Walt Whitman as an Editor. *Atlantic Monthly*, 92 (November): 679–86.

Stacy, Jason (2005). Review of Walt Whitman, *The Journalism*, Volume 1, ed. Herbert Bergman, Douglas A. Noverr, and Edward Recchia. *American Literature*, 77 (March): 183–4.

Thomas, M. Wynn. (1994). Whitman's Tale of Two Cities. *American Literary History*, 6 (Winter): 633–57.

Compares Whitman's poetic New York and his journalistic New York.

White, William (1962). Walt Whitman: Journalist. *Journalism Quarterly*, 39 (Summer): 339–46.

White, William (1963). Some Uncollected Whitman Journalism. *Emerson Society Quarterly*, 33 (Fourth Quarter): 84–90.

White, William (1967). Walt Whitman, The Newspaperman. *Grassroots Editor*, 8 (March–April): 14–16, 27.

White, William (1968). Walt Whitman Reports a Murder. *Quarterly Journal of the Book Club of Detroit*, 1 (Summer): 14–17.

White, William (1968). Whitman's Earliest Extant Prose. *Walt Whitman Review*, 14 (September): 142.

About a brief piece entitled "Effects of Lightning." It originally appeared in *The Long-Islander*.

White, William (1969). *Walt Whitman's Journalism: A Bibliography*. Detroit: Wayne State University Press.

First published in *Walt Whitman Review*, September 1968.

White, William (1971). A Tribute to William Hartshorne: Unrecorded Whitman. *American Literature*, 42 (January): 554–8.

Hartshorne was a veteran Brooklyn printer from whom Whitman learned the printing and newspaper business.

White, William (1971). Walter Whitman: Kings County Democratic Party Secretary. *Walt Whitman Review*, 17 (September): 92–8.

Reprints a long piece of Whitman's journalism.

White, William (1984). Whitman's Years with the *Daily Eagle*, Before and After. *Calamus*, 25: 5–33.

Widmer, Edward L. (1999). Whitman. In *Young America: The Flowering of Democracy in New York City*. New York: Oxford University Press, pp. 81–5.

Widmer, Ted (1998). New York *Evening Post*. In J. R. LeMaster and Donald D. Kummings (eds.), *Walt Whitman: An Encyclopedia*. New York and London: Garland, pp. 462.

Winne, Judith W. (2000). Poet Walt Whitman Once Wrote for the "Courier-Post." *Courier-Post Online* [electronic version of *Camden Courier-Post*] (2000), <http:// www.courierpostonline.com/125anniversary/ whitman.html>.

Celebrates Whitman's associations with Camden, New Jersey and with the *Camden Courier-Post*; reprints a three-part article that originally appeared in the *Camden Daily Post* in 1879.

Wortham, Thomas (1999). Brief review of Walt Whitman, *The Journalism*, Volume 1, ed. Herbert Bergman, Douglas A. Noverr, and Edward J. Recchia. *Nineteenth-Century Literature*, 53 (March): 564.

"The Eighteenth Presidency!"

Blake, David Haven (1998). "The Eighteenth Presidency!" In J. R. LeMaster and Donald D. Kummings (eds.), *Walt Whitman: An Encyclopedia*. New York and London: Garland, pp. 201–3.

Fitch, Noel Riley (1983). Walt Whitman in Paris: American Rhythms, 1925–1926. In *Sylvia Beach and the Lost Generation: A History of Literary Paris in the Twenties and Thirties*. New York and London: Norton, pp. 221–40.

Discusses Beach's exhibition on Whitman and her translation of *The Eighteenth Presidency*!

Grier, Edward F. (1956). Introduction. Walt Whitman, *The Eighteenth Presidency!*, ed. Edward F. Grier. Lawrence: University of Kansas Press, pp. 1–18.

Hunzicker, Karen Dell (1978). *Whitman the Teacher: The Poet in a Democratic Society*. Dissertation, Yale University, 1977. Ann Arbor: UMI, 7815919.

Warren, James Perrin (1999). Whitman's Agonistic Arena. In *Culture of Eloquence: Oratory and Reform in Antebellum America*. University Park: Pennsylvania State University Press, pp. 169–95.

Wilson, Ivy Glenn (2002). "I give the sign of democracy": Race, Labor, and the Aesthetics of Nationalism. PhD Dissertation, Yale University, *Dissertations Abstracts International*, 63 (September), 950A.

This dissertation focuses chiefly on Herman Melville and Walt Whitman. Chapter 4 is devoted to a discussion of Whitman's *The Eighteenth Presidency!*

Preface to 1855 Edition of *Leaves of Grass*, "Letter to Ralph Waldo Emerson" (1856), Preface to *As a Strong Bird on Pinions Free* (1872), Preface to *Two Rivulets* (1876), and "A Backward Glance O'er Travel'd Roads" (1888)

Adolph, Robert (1995). Whitman, Tocqueville, and the Language of Democracy. In Donald E. Morse (ed.), *The Delegated Intellect: Emersonian Essays on Literature, Science, and Art in Honor of Don Gifford*. New York: Peter Lang, pp. 65–88.

Includes discussion of 1855 Preface to *Leaves of Grass*.

Ahluwalia, Harsharan Singh (1974). *Whitman's Idea of the Poet in His Preface 1855 and Democratic Vistas*. Amritsar, India: Guru Nanak University.

Bradley, Sculley and Stevenson, John A. (1947). Introduction. *Walt Whitman's Backward Glances*, ed. Sculley Bradley and John A. Stevenson. Philadelphia: University of Pennsylvania Press, pp. 1–13.

Duerksen, Roland A. (1964). Shelley's "Defence" and Whitman's 1855 "Preface": A Comparison. *Walt Whitman Review*, 10 (September): 51–60.

Folsom, Ed (2000). "till the simple religious idea": An Unpublished Whitman Manuscript Fragment. *Walt Whitman Quarterly Review*, 18 (Summer/Fall): 63–4.

Pertains to the 1855 Preface to *Leaves*.

Folsom, Ed (2001). A Manuscript Draft of Whitman's Preface, 1876. *Walt Whitman Quarterly Review*, 19 (Summer): 63.

French, R. W. (1998). Preface to *Leaves of Grass*, 1855 Edition. In J. R. LeMaster and Donald D. Kummings (eds.), *Walt Whitman: An Encyclopedia*. New York and London: Garland, pp. 542–4.

Greenberg, Wendy (1978). Hugo and Whitman: Poets of Totality. *Walt Whitman Review*, 24: 32–6.

Compares Preface to Victor Hugo's *Les Rayons et les ombres* to Whitman's Preface to the 1855 *Leaves of Grass*.

Hart, James D. (1982). Foreword. Walt Whitman, *American Bard: The Original Preface to Leaves of Grass*, arranged in verse, with woodcuts by William Everson. New York: Viking Press, pp. 3–4.

Hoffman, Michael J. (1972). Whitman's [1855] Preface: Every Man His Own Priest. In *The Subversive Vision: American Romanticism in Literature*. Port Washington, New York, and London: Kennikat Press, pp. 58–68.

Hollis, C. Carroll (1990). Whitman on "Periphrastic" Literature. *Walt Whitman Quarterly Review*, 7 (Winter): 131–40.

A Whitman passage that may have been written for inclusion in the 1855 Preface to *Leaves*.

Hasek, Chaviva M. (1979). The Rhetoric of Whitman's 1855 Preface to *Leaves of Grass*. *Walt Whitman Review*, 25: 163–73.

Keuling-Stout, Frances E. (1998). Preface to *Two Rivulets* and *Two Rivulets*, Author's Edition. In J. R. LeMaster and Donald D. Kummings (eds.), *Walt Whitman: An Encyclopedia*. New York and London: Garland, pp. 544–5, 748–9.

Mancuso, Luke (1998). Preface to *As a Strong Bird on Pinions Free*. In J. R. LeMaster and Donald D. Kummings (eds.), *Walt Whitman: An Encyclopedia*. New York and London: Garland, pp. 540–1.

Miller, James E., Jr. (1962). "Attributes of the Poet" and "The Making of Poems." In *Walt Whitman*. New York: Twayne, pp. 64–71.

On the Preface to the 1855 *Leaves*.

Morley, Christopher (1928). The 1855 Preface. In *Essays*. Garden City, NY: Doubleday, Doran, pp. 694–707.

Niemeyer, Mark (2000). Literary-Manifest-Destiny, or Manifest Destiny and the Literary Manifests of Herman Melville and Walt Whitman. In Françoise Clary (ed.), *La Destinee Manifeste des Etat-Unis au xixe Siècle: Aspects culturels geopolitiques et idéologigues*. Rouen: Publications de Université de Rouen, pp. 19–33.

Discusses Melville's "Hawthorne and His Mosses" and Whitman's 1855 Preface to *Leaves of Grass*.

Pascal, Richard (1989). "Dimes on the Eyes": Walt Whitman and the Pursuit of Wealth in America. *Nineteenth-Century Literature*, 44 (September): 141–72.

See pp. 147–53 for comments on the Preface to the 1855 *Leaves*.

Powell, David Glenn (2001). Prophetic Voices, Proper Histories: Walt Whitman's Preface to the 1855 Edition of *Leaves of Grass* and Galway Kinnell's *The Book of Nightmares*. PhD Dissertation, University of Mississippi, 2000, *Dissertations Abstracts International*, 61 (February), 3175A.

Price, Kenneth M. (1984). Whitman on Emerson: New Light on the 1856 Open Letter. *American Literature*, 56: 83–7.

Raleigh, Richard (1998). "Letter to Ralph Waldo Emerson." In J. R. LeMaster and Donald D. Kummings (eds.), *Walt Whitman: An Encyclopedia*. New York and London: Garland, pp. 390–1.

Richards, Page (2003). Whitman's Frames. *Dalhousie Review*, 83 (Autumn): 355–68.

Mainly on the 1855 Preface.

Shucard, Alan (1998). "A Backward Glance O'er Travel'd Roads." In J. R. LeMaster and Donald D. Kummings (eds.), *Walt Whitman: An Encyclopedia*. New York and London: Garland, pp. 47–8.

Snyder, John (1975). *The Dear Love of Man: Tragic and Lyric Communion in Walt Whitman*. Studies in American Literature, vol. 28. The Hague: Mouton, pp. 25–34.

On the 1855 Preface to *Leaves of Grass*.

Weathers, Willie T. (1947). Whitman's Poetic Translations of His 1855 Preface. *American Literature*, 19 (March): 21–40.

White, William (1982). Preface to 1855 *Leaves* in Verse Form: Review. *Walt Whitman Review*, 28 (March): 36–7.

Review of Walt Whitman, *American Bard: The Original Preface to Leaves of Grass*, arranged in verse by William Everson.

Whitley, Edward (2001). Presenting Walt Whitman: "Leaves-Droppings" as Paratext. *Walt Whitman Quarterly Review*, 19 (Summer): 1–17.

Includes many comments on Whitman's 1856 letter to Emerson.

Xiques, Sister Donez Mary, C.N.D. (1972). A Descriptive Analysis of Selected Elements of Walt Whitman's Prose Style in the 1855 Preface to *Leaves of Grass*. PhD dissertation, Fordham University, New York.

Xiques, Sister Donez Mary, C.N.D. (1977). Whitman's Catalogues and the Preface to *Leaves of Grass*, 1855. *Walt Whitman Review*, 23: 68–76.

An American Primer, "America's Mightiest Inheritance," "Slang in America," and Other Works on Language

Adolph, Robert (1995). Whitman, Tocqueville, and the Language of Democracy. In Donald E. Morse (ed.), *The Delegated Intellect: Emersonian Essays on Literature, Science, and Art in Honor of Don Gifford*. New York: Peter Lang, pp. 65–88.

Includes commentary on *An American Primer*.

Allen, Gay Wilson (1987). Afterword. In *An American Primer by Walt Whitman, With Facsimiles of the Original Manuscript*, ed. Horace Traubel. Stevens Point, WI: Holy Cow! Press, pp. 37–44.

Allen, Irving Lewis (1993). *The City in Slang: New York Life and Popular Speech*. New York and Oxford: Oxford University Press, pp. 189–96.

Bauerlein, Mark (1991). Theory. In *Whitman and the American Idiom*. Baton Rouge and London: Louisiana State University Press, pp. 17–52.

Bell, Ian F. A. (1986). Lockean Sensationalism and American Literary Language. *Journal of American Studies*, 20 (August): 291–3.

Deals with "Slang in America."

Birss, John Howard (1932). Nicknames of the States – a Note on Walt Whitman. *American Speech*, 7 (June): 389.

On "Slang in America."

Camboni, Marina (1994). Walt's New World Language. In Marina Camboni (ed.), *Utopia in the Present Tense: Walt Whitman and the Language of the New World*. Rome: Il Calamo, pp. 71–88.

Focuses on "America's Mightiest Inheritance" and the first three editions of *Leaves of Grass*.

Camboni, Marina (2004). Walt Whitman e la lingua inglese d'America. In *Walt Whitman e La Lingua Del Mondo Nuovo*. Roma: Edizioni di Storia e Letteratura, pp. 1–65.

Includes two chapters in Italian and one in English, the latter reprinted from *Utopia in the Present Tense* (1994).

Cmiel, Kenneth (1992). "A Broad Fluid Language of Democracy": Discovering the American Idiom. *Journal of American History*, 79 (December): 913–36.

Dressman, Michael R. (1974). Walt Whitman's Study of the English Language. PhD dissertation, University of North Carolina.

Dressman, Michael R. (1979). Another Whitman Debt to Emerson. *Notes and Queries*, NS 26: 305–6.

On "Slang in America."

Dressman, Michael R. (1979). Walt Whitman's Plans for the Perfect Dictionary. *Studies in the American Renaissance 1979*, ed. Joel Myerson. Boston: Twayne, pp. 457–74.

Dressman, Michael R. (1998). *An American Primer* and "Slang in America." In J. R. LeMaster and Donald D. Kummings (eds.), *Walt Whitman: An Encyclopedia*. New York and London: Garland, pp. 16–18, 639–40.

Erkkila, Betsy (1989). Aesthetics and Politics. In *Whitman the Political Poet*. New York and Oxford: Oxford University Press, pp. 68–91.

Folsom, Ed (1994). Whitman and Dictionaries. In *Walt Whitman's Native Representations*. Cambridge, UK: Cambridge University Press, pp. 12–26.

Hollis, C. Carroll (1957). Whitman and the American Idiom. *Quarterly Journal of Speech*, 43 (December): 408–20.

Concentrates on a homemade book entitled *Words*.

Hollis, C. Carroll (1959). Whitman and Swinton: A Co-operative Friendship. *American Literature*, 30: 425–49.

Hollis, C. Carroll (1983). *Language and Style in "Leaves of Grass."* Baton Rouge: Louisiana State University Press.

Howard, Leon (1930). Walt Whitman and the American Language. *American Speech*, 5 (August): 441–51.

Mainly on *An American Primer*.

Kramer, Michael P. (1992). *Imagining Language in America: From the Revolution to the Civil War*. Princeton, NJ: Princeton University Press, pp. 90–115.

See Chapter 3: "A Tongue According": Whitman and the Literature of Language Study.

Kummings, Donald D. (1988). Review of Whitman, *An American Primer* [Holy Cow! Press reprint]. *The Mickle Street Review*, 10: 99–102.

Kummings, Donald D. (1998). "America's Mightiest Inheritance." In J. R. LeMaster and Donald D. Kummings (eds.), *Walt Whitman: An Encyclopedia*. New York and London: Garland, pp. 20–1.

Lewis, Robert W. (1987). Review of Whitman, *An American Primer* [Holy Cow! Press reprint]. *North Dakota Quarterly*, 55 (Summer): 239–40.

Morillas Sanchez, Rosa, and Aguilera Linde, Mauricio D. (1992). Sinewy Words: Whitman's Proposal for a New American Language. In Manuel Villar Raso, Miguel Martinez Lopez, and Rosa Morillas Sanchez (eds.), *Walt Whitman Centennial International Symposium*. Granada: Instituto de Ciencias de la Educación, Universidad de Granada, pp. 167–78.

Mainly on *An American Primer*.

Nathanson, Tenney (1992). Expression and Indication: Organic and Arbitrary Signs. In *Whitman's Presence: Body, Voice, and Writing in "Leaves of Grass."* New York and London: New York University Press, 1992, pp. 183–245.

Southard, Sherry G. (1984). Whitman and Language: An Annotated Bibliography. *Walt Whitman Quarterly Review*, 2: 31–49.

Traubel, Horace (1904). Foreword. *An American Primer by Walt Whitman*, ed. Horace Traubel. Boston: Small, Maynard, pp. v–ix.

Warren, James Perrin (1983). Dating Whitman's Language Studies. *Walt Whitman Quarterly Review*, 1 (2): 1–7.

On *Words*, *The Primer of Words*, "America's Mightiest Inheritance," and other works on language.

Warren, James Perrin (1984). Whitman as Ghostwriter: The Case of *Rambles Among Words*. *Walt Whitman Quarterly Review*, 2 (2): 22–30.

Warren, James Perrin (1990). *Walt Whitman's Language Experiment*. University Park and London: Pennsylvania State University Press.

West, Michael (2000). Copyrighting Etymological Ecstasy and Whitman's Experiments with Language. In *Transcendental Wordplay: America's Romantic Punsters and the Search for the Language of Nature*. Athens: Ohio University Press, pp. 171–82, 370–401.

On Whitman's writings on language, including *Rambles Among Words*.

White, William (1961). Walt Whitman, "Western Nicknames": An Unpublished Note. *American Speech*, 36 (December): 296–8.

Concerns "Slang in America."

White, William (1967). "Words": Whitman's Dictionary Notebook. *Walt Whitman Review*, 13 (September): 103–4.

Democratic Vistas

Allen, Gay Wilson (1946). *Democratic Vistas*, 1871. In *Walt Whitman Handbook*. Chicago: Packard, pp. 186–92.

Allen, Gay Wilson (1970). *A Reader's Guide to Walt Whitman*. New York: Farrar, Straus & Giroux.

See pp. 92–8 on *Democratic Vistas*.

Aspiz, Harold (1985). Another Early Review of *Democratic Vistas*. *Walt Whitman Quarterly Review*, 2(4): 31–5.

Aspiz, Harold (1994). The Body Politic in *Democratic Vistas*. In Ed Folsom (ed.), *Walt Whitman: The Centennial Essays*. Iowa City: University of Iowa Press, pp. 105–19.

Asselineau, Roger (1965). Whitman, The Doubter. *American Dialog*, 2 (October–November): 3–6.

Asselineau, Roger (1992). Walt Whitman's Democracy Yesterday and Today. In Paul A. Isbell (ed.), *Homenaje a Walt Whitman en el Centenario de Muerte*. Madrid: Casa de America, United States Information Service, pp. 21–3.

Contrasts the idealized poetry of Democracy in *Leaves of Grass* with the more realistic "prose of Democracy" in *Democratic Vistas*.

Balakian, Peter (1994). Whitman as Jeremiah. In Geoffrey Sill (ed.), *Walt Whitman of Mickle Street: A Centennial Collection*. Knoxville: University of Tennessee Press, pp. 70–9.

Analysis of *Democratic Vistas* as a bleak American jeremiad. Originally published in *The Mickle Street Review*, 10 (1988): 71–80.

Blodgett, Harold W. (1975). *Democratic Vistas* – 100 Years After. In Karl Schubert and Ursula Müller-Richter (eds.), *Geschichte und Gesellschaft in der amerikanischen Literatur*. Heidelberg: Quelle and Meyer, pp. 114–31.

Brasher, Thomas L. (1971). Walt Whitman in League with Women. *Walt Whitman Review*, 17 (June): 62–3.

Brooks, David (2003). What Whitman Knew. *Atlantic Monthly*, 291 (May): 32–3.

Cmiel, Kenneth (2000). Whitman the Democrat. In David S. Reynolds (ed.), *A Historical Guide to Walt Whitman*. New York: Oxford University Press, pp. 205–33.

Cooke, Alice L. (1958). Whitman as a Critic: *Democratic Vistas* with Special Reference to Carlyle. *Walt Whitman Newsletter*, 4 (June): 91–5.

Detweiler, Robert (1963). The Concrete Universal in *Democratic Vistas*. *Walt Whitman Review*, 9 (June): 40–1.

Folsom, Ed (2000). Lucifer and Ethiopia: Whitman, Race, and Poetics before the Civil War and After. In David S. Reynolds (ed.), *A Historical Guide to Walt Whitman*. New York: Oxford University Press, pp. 45–95.

Frank, Waldo (1919). The Multitudes in Whitman. In *Our America*. New York: Boni & Liveright, pp. 202–21.

Freedman, William A. (1961). Whitman and Morality in the Democratic *Republic*. *Walt Whitman Review*, 7 (September): 53–6.

Golden, Arthur (1994). The Obfuscations of Rhetoric: Whitman and the Visionary Experience. In Ed Folsom (ed.), *Walt Whitman: The Centennial Essays*. Iowa City: University of Iowa Press, pp. 88–102.

Grier, Edward F. (1951). Walt Whitman, the *Galaxy*, and *Democratic Vistas*. *American Literature*, 23 (November): 332–50.

Grünzweig, Walter (1997). The New Empire Grander Than Any Before: Nineteenth-Century American Versions of a Democratic Imperialism. In John G. Blair and Reinhold Wagnleitner (eds.), *Empire: American Studies*. Tübingen: Gunter Narr; Swiss Papers in English Language and Literature, 10, pp. 243–50.

Haddox, Thomas F. (2004). Whitman's End of History: "As I Sat By Blue Ontario's Shore," *Democratic Vistas*, and the Postbellum Politics of Nostalgia. *Walt Whitman Quarterly Review*, 22 (Summer): 1–22.

Holloway, Emory (1923). Whitman as Critic of America. *Studies in Philology*, 20 (July): 345–69.

Holloway calls *Democratic Vistas* "the most searching examination ever made of the state of American literature by a contemporary."

Jay, Paul (1997). Emerson, Whitman, and the Problem of Culture. In his *Contingency Blues: The Search for Foundations in American Criticism*. Madison: University of Wisconsin Press, pp. 42–56.

Jones, Joseph (1960). Carlyle, Whitman, and the Democratic Dilemma. *English Studies in Africa*, 3 (September): 179–97.

Whitman's *Democratic Vistas* resulted from his effort to answer tough questions about democracy posed by Thomas Carlyle.

Kazin, Alfred (1976). Democracy According to Whitman. *Commentary*, June: 52–8.

Knapp, Bettina L. (1993). *Democratic Vistas* (1870). In *Walt Whitman*. New York: Continuum, pp. 209–13.

Lenhart, Gary (1991). Whitman's Informal History of His Times: *Democratic Vistas* & *Specimen Days*. In Ron Padgett (ed.), *The Teachers and Writers Guide to Walt Whitman*. New York: Teachers & Writers Collaborative, pp. 130–50.

Lessing, O. E. (1919). Walt Whitman's Message. *Open Court*, 33 (August): 449–62.

Long, Mark C. (1996). The Measure of Inquiry: Whitman, Peirce, Williams and the Claims of Reading in Literary Theory and Criticism. PhD Dissertation, University of Washington, *Dissertations Abstracts International*, 57 (November), 2040A.

Chapter 2 focuses on *Democratic Vistas*.

Mack, Stephen John (2002). "The Divine Literatus Comes": Religion and Poetry in the Cultivation of Democratic Selfhood. In *The Pragmatic Whitman: Reimagining American Democracy*. Iowa City: University of Iowa Press, pp. 135–59.

Mancuso, Luke (1994). "Reconstruction is Still in Abeyance": Walt Whitman's *Democratic Vistas* and the Federalizing of National Identity. *American Transcendental Quarterly*, 8 (September): 229–50.

Mancuso, Luke (1997). *The Strange Sad War Revolving: Walt Whitman, Reconstruction, and the Emergence of Black Citizenship*. Columbia, SC: Camden House.

Contains a chapter on *Democratic Vistas*.

Marcell, David W. (1970). The Two Whitmans and *Democracy in America*. In Ray B. Browne, Larry N. Landrum, and William K. Bottorff (eds.), *Challenges in American Culture*. Bowling Green, OH: Bowling Green University Popular Press, pp. 178–89.

On Whitman's pre-Civil War vs. his post-Civil War views of democracy.

Marr, David M. (1988). "Come Forth, Sweet Democratic Despots of the West!": Whitman's *Democratic Vistas*. In *American Worlds Since Emerson*. Amherst: University of Massachusetts Press, pp. 73–91.

Martinez Lopez, Miguel (1992). Walt Whitman and the American Utopian Tradition: *Democratic Vistas*. In Manuel Villar Raso, Miguel Martinez Lopez, and Rosa Morillas Sanchez (eds.), *Walt Whitman Centennial International Symposium*. Granada: Instituto de Ciencias de la Education, Universidad de Granada, pp. 129–38.

Marx, Leo (1961). *Democratic Vistas*: Notes for a Discussion. *Emerson Society Quarterly* (First Quarter): 12–15.

Mazzaro, Jerome L. (1962). Whitman's *Democratic Vistas*: The Vast General Principle and Underlying Unity. *Walt Whitman Review*, 8 (December): 89–90.

McCarthy, Harold T. (1971). Henry Miller's Democratic Vistas. *American Quarterly*, 23 (May): 221–35.

Henry Miller expressed ideas similar to those espoused by Whitman in *Democratic Vistas*.

McGuire, Ian (2001). Culture and Antipathy: Arnold, Emerson and *Democratic Vistas*. *Symbiosis*, 5 (April): 77–84.

Paine, Gregory (1939). The Literary Relations of Whitman and Carlyle with Especial Reference to Their Contrasting Views on Democracy. *Studies in Philology*, 36 (July): 550–63.

On Whitman's revisions of *Democratic Vistas*.

Pascal, Richard (1989). "Dimes on the Eyes": Walt Whitman and the Pursuit of Wealth in America. *Nineteenth-Century Literature*, 44 (September): 141–72.

See pp. 165–9 for comments on *Democratic Vistas*.

Peach, Linden (1982). The True Face of Democracy?: Carlyle's Challenge to Whitman's Idealism. In *British Influence on the Birth of American Literature*. New York: St Martin's Press, pp. 162–93.

Piasecki, Bruce (1981). Whitman's "Estimate of Nature" in *Democratic Vistas*. *Walt Whitman Review*, 27: 101–12.

Pincus, Robert L. (1984). A Mediated Vision, a Measured Voice: Culture and Criticism in Whitman's Prose. *Walt Whitman Quarterly Review*, 2(1): 22–31.

Prettyman III, Charles Gibbons (1994). The Great Trust: Idealizations of Industry in American Middle-class Literature. PhD Dissertation, University of California, Irvine, 1993. *Dissertations Abstracts International*, 54 (February), 3034A.

Prettyman discusses Ralph Waldo Emerson, Walt Whitman, Edward Bellamy, and Booker T. Washington. The chapter on Whitman discusses "industrial methods" as embodied in *Democratic Vistas*.

Reeves, Paschal (1962). The Silhouette of the State in *Democratic Vistas* – Hegelian or Whitmanian? *Personalist*, 43 (Summer): 374–82.

Riese, Utz (1971). Walt Whitmans demokratische Vision. *Wissenschaftliche Zeitschrift Pädagogische Hochschule Potsdam*, 15 (2): 345–51.

In German.

Rising, Clara (1961). Vistas of a Disillusioned Realist. *Walt Whitman Review*, 7 (December): 63–71.

Rosenblatt, Louise M. (1978). Whitman's *Democratic Vistas* and the New "Ethnicity." *Yale Review*, 67: 187–204.

Santayana, George (1898). Whitman. In George Rice Carpenter (ed.), *American Prose: Selections with Critical Introductions by Various Writers and a General Introduction*. New York and London: Macmillan, pp. 383–8.

Scarry, Elaine (1996). The Difficulty of Imagining Other People. In Martha Nussbaum (ed.), *For Love of Country*. Boston: Beacon Press, pp. 99–110.

Scholnick, Robert J. (1979). Individual Identity and Democratic Culture: The Problem of Whitman's *Democratic Vistas*. In Don Harkness (ed.), *SEASA 79 Proceedings: Southeastern American Studies Association*. Papers Presented at the Biennial Conference, Tampa, Florida, April 5–7. Tampa: American Studies Press, pp. 17–23.

Scholnick, Robert J. (1981). Toward a "Wider Democratizing of Institutions": Whitman's *Democratic Vistas*. *American Transcendental Quarterly*, 52: 287–302.

Scholnick, Robert J. (1982). *The Galaxy* and American Democratic Culture, 1866–1878. *Journal of American Studies*, 16 (April): 69–80.

Scholnick, Robert J. (1985). The American Context of *Democratic Vistas*. In Joann P. Krieg (ed.), *Walt Whitman: Here and Now*. Westport, CT: Greenwood, pp. 147–56.

Scholnick, Robert J. (1996). "Culture" or Democracy: Whitman, Eugene Benson, and *The Galaxy*. *Walt Whitman Quarterly Review*, 13 (Spring): 189–98.

On publications that were absorbed by *Democratic Vistas*.

Schultz, Susan M. (1989). The Success of Failure: Hart Crane's Revisions of Whitman and Eliot in *The Bridge*. *South Atlantic Quarterly*, 54 (January): 55–70.

Contains references to *Democratic Vistas*.

Shreiber, Maeera (1997). "Where Are We Moored?" Adrienne Rich, Women's Mourning, and the Limits of Lament. In Yopie Prins and Maeera Shreiber (eds.), *Dwelling in Possibility: Women Poets and Critics on Poetry*. Ithaca, NY: Cornell University Press, pp. 301–17.

Pages 312–14 discuss Rich's work in relation to *Democratic Vistas*.

Smith, Bernard (1939). Democracy and Realism, II. The Romance of Reality: Whitman. In *Forces in American Criticism: A Study in the History of American Literary Thought*. New York: Harcourt, Brace, pp. 143–57.

Snyder, John (1975). *The Dear Love of Man: Tragic and Lyric Communion in Walt Whitman*. Studies in American Literature, vol. 28. The Hague: Mouton.

See pp. 205–28 on *Democratic Vistas*.

Sørensen, Villy (1991). Foreword. *Demokratiske Visioner*. Copenhagen: Gyldendals Kulturbibliotek, pp. 5–13.
Danish translation of *Democratic Vistas* by Annette Mester; foreword is in Danish.
Teichgraeber III, Richard F. (1999). "Culture" in Industrializing America. *Intellectual History Newsletter*, 21: 11–23.
Trachtenberg, Alan (1994). Whitman's Visionary Politics. In Geoffrey M. Sill (ed.), *Walt Whitman of Mickle Street*. Knoxville: University of Tennessee Press, pp. 94–108.
Warren, James Perrin (1994). Reconstructing Language in *Democratic Vistas*. In Ed Folsom (ed.), *Walt Whitman: The Centennial Essays*. Iowa City: University of Iowa Press, pp. 79–87.
Warren, James Perrin (1999). Whitman's Agonistic Arena. In *Culture of Eloquence: Oratory and Reform in Antebellum America*. University Park: Pennsylvania State University Press, pp. 169–95.
Watts, Emily Stipes (1982). "The American" and the Artist. In *The Businessman in American Literature*. Athens: University of Georgia Press, pp. 45–54.
White, William (1963). Preface to *Democratic Vistas*. *Walt Whitman Review*, 9 (September): 71–2.
White, William (1965). Whitman's *Democratic Vistas*: An Unpublished Self-Review? *American Book Collector*, 16 (December): 21.
Wrobel, Arthur (1998). *Democratic Vistas*. In J. R. LeMaster and Donald D. Kummings (eds.), *Walt Whitman: An Encyclopedia*. New York and London: Garland, pp. 176–9.

Memoranda During the War

Bandy, W. T. (1985). An Unknown "Washington Letter" by Walt Whitman. *Walt Whitman Quarterly Review*, 2 (3): 23–7.
On a *New York Times* article that was reprinted in *Memoranda During the War* and in *Specimen Days*.
Basler, Roy P. (1962). Introduction. *Walt Whitman's Memoranda During the War & Death of Abraham Lincoln*, ed. Roy Basler. Bloomington: Indiana University Press, pp. 1–46.
Bouziotis, Christy Lynn (2002). The "mysteries dimly sealed": Walt Whitman, Herman Melville, and the Civil War. PhD Dissertation, Drew University, Madison, NY. *Dissertations Abstracts* International, 63 (September), 941A.
Focuses on Melville's poetry and Whitman's "prose accounts of his experience as a Civil War hospital volunteer."
Coviello, Peter (2004). Introduction: Whitman at War. *Memoranda During the War*, by Walt Whitman, ed. Peter Coviello. New York: Oxford University Press, pp. ix–liv.
Cushman, Stephen (1999). Eyewitness. In *Bloody Promenade: Reflections on a Civil War Battle*. Charlottesville: University Press of Virginia, pp. 76–80.
Davis, Robert Leigh (1997). *Whitman and the Romance of Medicine*. Berkeley: University of California Press.
Analyzes Whitman's Civil War hospital writings and related texts. One whole chapter (pp. 95–117) is on *Memoranda During the War*.
Davis, Robert Leigh (1998). *Memoranda During the War*. In J. R. LeMaster and Donald D. Kummings (eds.), *Walt Whitman: An Encyclopedia*. New York and London: Garland, pp. 423–4.
Glicksberg, Charles I. (1933). Introduction. *Walt Whitman and the Civil War: A Collection of Original Articles and Manuscripts*, ed. Charles Glicksberg. Philadelphia: University of Pennsylvania Press, pp. 1–11.
Hanson, Russell Galen (1968). Reflections on Whitman's Role as Tragic Poet of the American Civil War. *Walt Whitman Review*, 14 (June): 50–4.
Kinney, Katherine (1996). Making Capital: War, Labor, and Whitman in Washington, D.C. In Betsy Erkkila and Jay Grossman (eds.), *Breaking Bounds: Whitman and American Cultural Studies*. New York: Oxford University Press, pp. 174–89.

Luria, Sarah de Lima (1995). Capital Speculations: Architecture and Letters in Washington, D.C., 1860–1900. PhD Dissertation, Stanford University. *Dissertations Abstracts International*, 56 (December), 2238A.

Chapter 2 discusses Whitman's "war journalism."

McElroy, John Harmon (1999). Introduction. In John Harmon McElroy (ed.), *The Sacrificial Years: A Chronicle of Walt Whitman's Experiences in the Civil War*. Boston: David R. Godine, pp. xi–xix.

On Whitman's wartime letters and "memoranda."

Miller, F. DeWolfe (1963). A Note on *Memoranda. Walt Whitman Review*, 9 (September): 67–8.

Rietz, John (1993). A Sense of the Past: Memory and History in Whitman's Poetry and Prose. PhD Dissertation, University of Michigan. *Dissertations Abstracts International*, 54 (July), 180A.

"The Death of Abraham Lincoln"

Angle, Paul M. (1962). A Note. *Death of Abraham Lincoln*, ed. Paul M. Angle. Chicago: Black Cat Press, pp. vii–xiv.

Barton, William E. (1928). Whitman's Lecture on Lincoln. *Abraham Lincoln and Walt Whitman*. Indianapolis: Bobbs-Merrill, pp. 187–229.

Basler, Roy P. (1962). Introduction. *Walt Whitman's Memoranda During the War & Death of Abraham Lincoln*, ed. Roy P. Basler. Bloomington: Indiana University Press, pp. 1–46.

Epstein, Daniel Mark (2004). Madison Square Theater: New York, April 14, 1887. *Lincoln and Whitman: Parallel Lives in Civil War Washington*. New York: Ballantine Books, pp. 309–39.

Golden, Arthur (1988). The Text of a Whitman Lincoln Lecture Reading: Anacreon's "The Midnight Visitor." *Walt Whitman Quarterly Review*, 6 (Fall): 91–4.

Griffin, Larry D. (1998). "Death of Abraham Lincoln." In J. R. LeMaster and Donald D. Kummings (eds.), *Walt Whitman: An Encyclopedia*. New York and London: Garland, pp. 169–70.

Hutchinson, George (1990). Whitman's Confidence Game: The "Good Gray Poet" and the Civil War. *South Central Review*, 7 (Spring): 20–35.

Peterson, Merrill D. (1994). *Lincoln in American Memory*. New York: Oxford University Press.

Unsigned (1993). The Great American Poet on the Great American Statesman. *Rare Americana*. New Haven: William Reese Co. Catalogue 120, item 74.

Describes Whitman's autograph manuscript of his "Death of Abraham Lincoln" lecture, dated February 1879; 17 leaves, "heavily worked and corrected," with attached newspaper and book clippings and portraits of Whitman and Lincoln; to be sold.

Warren, James Perrin (1999). Whitman's Agonistic Arena. In *Culture of Eloquence: Oratory and Reform in Antebellum America*. University Park: Pennsylvania State University Press, pp. 169–95.

Literary Criticism

Allen, Gay Wilson (1965). Critical Comment on M. Asselineau's Paper. In Leon Edel et al. (eds.), *Literary History & Literary Criticism: ACTA of the Ninth Congress International Federation for Modern Languages & Literature, Held at New York University, August 25 to 31, 1963*. New York: New York University Press, pp. 61–4.

See Asselineau's "A Poet's Dilemma."

Asselineau, Roger (1965). A Poet's Dilemma: Walt Whitman's Attitude to Literary History and Literary Criticism. In Leon Edel et al. (eds.), *Literary History & Literary Criticism: ACTA of the Ninth Congress International Federation for Modern Languages & Literature, Held at New York University, August 25 to 31, 1963*. New York: New York University Press, pp. 50–61.

On the theory behind the criticism written by Walt Whitman.

Asselineau, Roger (1996). Whitman on Robert Burns: A Footnote. *Walt Whitman Quarterly Review*, 14 (Summer): 39.

Bandy, W. T. (1984). A Source of Whitman's "Poetry of the Future." *Walt Whitman Quarterly Review*, 1 (4): 31.

Barnett, Robert W. (1998). "Poetry To-day in America – Shakspere – The Future." In J. R. LeMaster and Donald D. Kummings (eds.), *Walt Whitman: An Encyclopedia*. New York and London: Garland, pp. 528–9.

Boor, Jan (1978). Walt Whitman and the Theater. *Calamus*, 16: 15–17.

Discusses several Whitman essays: "Plays and Operas Too" in *Specimen Days* and "The Old Bowery" and "Miserable State of the Stage" – his "two most important articles" on the theatre.

Bristol, James (1966). Literary Criticism in *Specimen Days. Walt Whitman Review*, 12 (March): 16–19.

Cohen, Sarah Blacher (1972). Walt Whitman's Literary Criticism. *Walt Whitman Review*, 18 (June): 39–50.

Foerster, Norman (1928). Whitman. In *American Criticism: A Study in Literary Theory from Poe to the Present*. Boston and New York: Houghton Mifflin, pp. 157–222.

Folsom, Ed (2000). Whitman's Notes on Emerson: An Unpublished Manuscript. *Walt Whitman Quarterly Review*, 18 (Summer/Fall): 60–2.

Golden, Arthur (1985). Uncollected Whitman Material in the Folger Shakespeare Library. *Papers of the Bibliographic Society of America*, 79: 529–39.

Eight Whitman items, all with Shakespeare connections. One manuscript includes handwritten emendations to a printed version of "Poetry To-day in America – Shakspere – The Future."

Harris, Natalie (1985). Whitman's Kinetic Criticism. *American Poetry*, 2(3): 19–33.

Johnson, Maurice O. (1938) Walt Whitman as a Critic of Literature. *University of Nebraska Studies in Language, Literature, and Criticism*, 16: 1–73.

Mabbott, Thomas Ollive and Silver, Rollo G. (1932). Mr. Whitman Reconsiders. *Colophon*, 9 (February): 1–8.

On "An Interviewer's Item."

Moore, John B. (1926). The Master of Whitman." *Studies in Philology*, 23 (January): 77–89.

Claims that Whitman's essay "Emerson's Books, (The Shadows of Them)" is one of "most indispensable ever written upon Emerson."

Rathbun, John W. and Clark, Harry H. (1979). Walt Whitman (1819–1892). In *American Literary Criticism, 1860–1905*. Boston: Twayne, pp. 38–40.

Scharnhorst, Gary (1996). Whitman on Robert Burns: An Early Essay Recovered. *Walt Whitman Quarterly Review*, 13 (Spring): 217–20.

Silver, Rollo G. (1935). A Note About Whitman's Essay on Poe. *American Literature*, 6 (January): 435–6.

On Whitman's essay "Edgar Poe's Significance."

Wells, Carolyn and Goldsmith, Alfred F. (1928). Introduction. *Rivulets of Prose: Critical Essays by Walt Whitman*, ed. C. Wells and A. F. Goldsmith. New York: Greenberg, pp. vii–xviii.

Yamauchi, Hisako (1988). Walt Whitman. In John W. Rathbun and Monica M. Grecu (eds.), *American Literary Critics and Scholars, 1850–1880*. Detroit: Gale Research, pp. 274–87.

Specimen Days

Aarnes, William (1979). *Scraps: A Study of Walt Whitman's* Specimen Days. Dissertation, Johns Hopkins University. Ann Arbor: UMI, 7924600.

Aarnes, William (1981). "Cut This Out": Whitman Liberating the Reader in *Specimen Days. Walt Whitman Review*, 27: 25–32.

Aarnes, William (1982). "Almost Discover": The Spiritual Significance of Soldier Talk in Whitman's *Specimen Days. Walt Whitman Quarterly Review*, 28: 84–91.

Aarnes, William (1982). "Free Margins": Identity and Silence in Whitman's *Specimen Days. ESQ: A Journal of the American Renaissance*, 28: 243–60.

Aarnes, William (1982). Withdrawal and Resumption: Whitman and Society in the Last Two Parts of *Specimen Days*. In Joel Myerson (ed.), *Studies in the American Renaissance*. Boston: Twayne, pp. 401–32.

Allen, Gay Wilson (1946). *Specimen Days*, 1882. In *Walt Whitman Handbook*. Chicago: Packard, pp. 220–2.

Aspiz, Harold (1983). *Specimen Days*: The Therapeutics of Sun-Bathing. *Walt Whitman Quarterly Review*, 1 (3): 48–50.

Balkun, Mary McAleer (1999). Whitman's *Specimen Days* and the Culture of Authenticity. *Walt Whitman Quarterly Review*, 17 (Summer/Fall): 15–24.

Boggs, Colleen Glenney (2002). Specimens of Translation in Walt Whitman's Poetry. *Arizona Quarterly*, 58 (Autumn): 33–56.

Bradley, Sculley (1933). Walt Whitman on Timber Creek. *American Literature*, 5 (November): 235–46.

Bristol, James (1966). Literary Criticism in *Specimen Days. Walt Whitman Review*, 12 (March): 16–19.

Chase, Richard (1961). Foreword. Walt Whitman, *Specimen Days*, ed. Richard Chase. New York: New American Library, Signet Classic, pp. ix–xvi.

Chielens, Edward E. (1975). Whitman's *Specimen Days* and the Familiar Essay Genre. *Genre*, 8 (December): 366–78.

Chukovsky, Kornei (1967). Walt Whitman's Greetings to the Russian People. *Sputnik*, 6: 88–93.

Couser, G. Thomas (1976). Of Time and Identity: Walt Whitman and Gertrude Stein as Autobiographers. *Texas Studies in Literature and Language*, 17: 787–804.

Couser, G. Thomas (1979). Walt Whitman: Vision and Revision. *American Autobiography: The Prophetic Mode*. Amherst: University of Massachusetts Press, pp. 80–100.

On "Song of Myself" and *Specimen Days*.

Cravens, Gwyneth (1991). "Past Present." *Nation*, 252 (April 15): 497–8.

Review of Walt Whitman, *Complete Poetry and Collected Prose* (Library of America), with extended comments on *Specimen Days*.

Cummings, Glenn N. (1992). Whitman's *Specimen Days* and the Theatricality of "Semi-renewal." *American Transcendental Quarterly*, 6 (September): 177–87.

Deleuze, Gilles (1997). "Whitman." In *Essays: Critical and Clinical*, trans. Daniel W. Smith and Michael A. Greco. Minneapolis: University of Minnesota Press, pp. 56–60.

The book was originally published in French in 1993; essay focuses on Whitman's *Specimen Days*.

Dowden, Edward (1882). *Specimen Days and Collect. Academy*, 22 (18 November): 357–9. Available online at <http://www.whitmanarchive.org/criticism/ >.

Eitner, Walter H. (1981). *Walt Whitman's Western Jaunt*. Lawrence: Regents Press of Kansas.

Ely, M. Lynda (1997). Memorializing Lincoln: Whitman's "Revision" of James Speed's *Oration Upon the Inauguration of the Bust of Abraham Lincoln. Walt Whitman Quarterly Review*, 14 (Spring): 176–80.

Everett, Nicholas (1996). Autobiography as Prophecy: Walt Whitman's *Specimen Days*. In Vincent Newey and Philip Shaw (eds.), *Mortal Pages, Literary Lives: Studies in Nineteenth-Century Autobiography*. Aldershot, UK: Scolar, pp. 217–34.

Ewart, Gavin (1979). Introduction. *Specimen Days in America*, by Walt Whitman. London: The Folio Society, pp. 11–17.

Fichtelberg, Joseph (1989). *The Complex Image: Faith and Method in American Autobiography*. Philadelphia: University of Pennsylvania Press, pp. 22–52.

Compares Whitman's *Specimen Days* and John Stuart Mill's *Autobiography*.

Folsom, Ed, and Reed, Kendall (2000). An Unpublished *Specimen Days* Manuscript Fragment. *Walt Whitman Quarterly Review*, 18 (Summer/Fall): 71–2.

Prints an early draft of "A Week's Visit in Boston," an essay published in *Specimen Days*.

Grünzweig, Walter (1987). Review of Eva Manske, ed. *Tagebuch {Specimen Days}. Walt Whitman Quarterly Review*, 5 (Fall): 39–40.

Harrison, Henry Leslie (2002). The Temple and the Forum: The American Museum and Cultural Authority in Hawthorne, Melville, Stowe, and Whitman. PhD Dissertation, Texas A & M University. *Dissertations Abstracts International*, 63 (October), 1338A.

Hutchinson, George B. (1987). Life Review and the Common World in Whitman's *Specimen Days*. *South Atlantic Review*, 52 (Autumn): 3–23.

Hutchinson, George B. (1998). *Specimen Days*. In J. R. LeMaster and Donald D. Kummings (eds.), *Walt Whitman: An Encyclopedia*. New York and London: Garland, pp. 678–81.

Jaworski, Philippe (1993). Préface à Walt Whitman, *Comme des baies de genévrier – Feuilles de carnets*, trans. Julien Deleuze. Paris: Mercure de France, pp. I–VII.

French translation of extracts from *Specimen Days*.

Johnson, Linck C. (1975). The Design of Walt Whitman's *Specimen Days*. *Walt Whitman Review*, 21 (March): 3–14.

Kazin, Alfred (1970). The Great American Poet. *New York Review of Books*, 15 (22 October): 42–6.

Reprinted as the Introduction to an edition of Whitman's *Specimen Days* published in Boston in 1971 by David R. Godine.

Knapp, Bettina L. (1993). *Specimen Days and Collect*. In *Walt Whitman*. New York: Continuum, pp. 213–25.

Lehmberg, P. S. (1978). "That Vast Something": A Note on Whitman and the American West. *Studies in the Humanities*, 6 (2): 50–3.

Lenhart, Gary (1991). Whitman's Informal History of His Times: *Democratic Vistas* & *Specimen Days*. In Ron Padgett (ed.), *The Teachers and Writers Guide to Walt Whitman*. New York: Teachers & Writers Collaborative, pp. 130–50.

Lewin, Walter (1887). Review of *Specimen Days*. *Academy*, 31 (4 June): 390–1. Available online at <http://www.whitmanarchive.org/criticism/ >.

Major, William (2000). "Some Vital Unseen Presence": The Practice of Nature in Walt Whitman's *Specimen Days*. *Interdisciplinary Studies in Literature and Environment*, 7 (Winter): 79–96.

Manson, Matthew Jack (2003). Unmaking History: Modern American Literary Autobiography and the Limits of Nineteenth Century Life-Writing. PhD Dissertation, University of Southern California, 2002. *Dissertations Abstracts International*, 63 (June), 4315A.

Marx, Leo (1971). Some Sources of Walt Whitman's Art, Self-reported in *Specimen Days*. *New York Times Book Review*, 21 November: 6–7, 82.

Meehan, Sean Ross (1999). Specimen Daze: Whitman's Photobiography. *Biography*, 22 (Fall): 477–516.

Mishra, R. S. (1983). *Specimen Days*: "An Immensely Negative Book." *Delta*, 16: 95–110.

Morley, Christopher (1936). Notes on Walt. *Saturday Review of Literature*, 14 (30 May): 12, 16.

Mullin, Joseph Eugene (1994). The Whitman of *Specimen Days*. *Iowa Review*, 24 (Winter): 148–61.

Pétillon, Pierre-Yves (1993). Herbier d'automne. *Quinzaine Littéraire*, 633 (October 16): 5–6.

Review of Julien Deleuze, trans., *Comme des baies de genevrier* (French translation of *Specimen Days*).

Philippon, Daniel J. (1998). "I only seek to put you in rapport": Message and Method in Walt Whitman's *Specimen Days*. In Michael P. Branch, Rochelle Johnson, Daniel Patterson, and Scott Slovic (eds.), *Reading the Earth: New Directions in the Study of Literature and Environment*. Moscow: University of Idaho Press, pp. 179–93.

Price, Kenneth M. (1980). Whitman on Other Writers: Controlled "Graciousness" in *Specimen Days*. *ESQ: A Journal of the American Renaissance*, 26: 79–87.

Rubenfeld, Andrew (1984). Walt Whitman's New Jersey Birds. *New Jersey Audubon*, 10 (2): 10–15.

Spector, Robert Donald (1951). The Reality of War in Whitman's *Specimen Days*. *Notes and Queries*, 196 (9 June): 254–5.

Tanner, Stephen L. (1973). Star-gazing in Whitman's *Specimen Days*. *Walt Whitman Review*, 19 (December): 158–61.

Teller, Walter (1966). Speaking of Books: Whitman at Timber Creek. *New York Times Book Review*, 10 April: 2, 31.

Comments on the "nature writing" published in *Specimen Days*.

Unsigned (1908). New England Nature Studies: Thoreau, Burroughs, Whitman. *Edinburgh Review*, 208 (October): 343–66.

Unsigned (1883). Review of *Specimen Days. Westminster Review* n.s., 64 (July): 287–91. Available online at <http://www.whitmanarchive.org/criticism/ >.

White, William (1964). MS of "How I Get Around." *Walt Whitman Review*, 10 (December): 103–4.

White, William (1966). Author at Work: Whitman's *Specimen Days. Manuscripts*, 18 (Summer): 26–8.

White, William (1970). Whitman Writes About Huntington. *Long-Islander*, 28 May, Section I: 9, 12.

Puffs, Self-Reviews, and Other Writings Anonymously Authored by Whitman

Bergman, Herbert (1970). Walt Whitman: Self Advertiser. *Bulletin of the New York Public Library*, 74 (December): 634–9.

On Whitman's many anonymous reviews and notices of his own poetry.

Glicksberg, Charles I. (1937). Walt Whitman in New Jersey, Some Unpublished Manuscripts. *Proceedings of the New Jersey Historical Society*, 55 (January): 42–6.

Describes Whitman's 19 years in Camden and his publishings in local papers, including possibly some anonymous articles which have not been discovered.

Holloway, Emory (1929). Whitman As His Own Press Agent. *American Mercury*, 18 (December): 482–8.

On "puffs" written by Whitman himself. Examines many pieces from Washington papers.

Jaffe, Harold (1969). Bucke's *Walt Whitman*: A Collaboration. *Walt Whitman Review*, 15 (September): 190–4.

Whitman wrote or revised more than half of Bucke's biography. Whitman's contribution is perhaps his most significant self-advertisement.

Killingsworth, M. Jimmie (1998). Whitman's Anonymous Self-Reviews of the 1855 *Leaves*. In J. R. LeMaster and Donald D. Kummings (eds.), *Walt Whitman: An Encyclopedia*. New York and London: Garland, pp. 624–5.

Maggin, Daniel (1974). Foreword. *Walt Whitman's Autograph Revision of the Analysis of Leaves of Grass (For Dr. R. M. Bucke's Walt Whitman)*, ed. Stephen Railton. New York: New York University Press, pp. 7–9.

Scholnick, Robert (1977). The Selling of the "Author's Edition": Whitman, O'Connor, and the *West Jersey Press* Affair. *Walt Whitman Review*, 23: 3–23.

On Whitman's anonymous article in the *West Jersey Press* – at least in part.

White, William (1970). Whitman on Himself: An Unrecorded Piece. *Papers on Language and Literature*, 6 (Spring): 202–5.

An essay entitled "Foreign Criticism of an American Poet" was found among Whitman's papers at his death. Whitman himself seems to have authored the essay.

General and Miscellaneous Studies

Andriano, Joseph (1998). *Notebooks and Unpublished Prose Manuscripts*. In J. R. LeMaster and Donald D. Kummings (eds.), *Walt Whitman: An Encyclopedia*. New York and London: Garland, pp. 468–9.

Asselineau, Roger (1979). Review of Walt Whitman, *Daybooks and Notebooks. Etudes Anglaises*, 32 (Janvier–Mars): 106.

Atwan, Robert (1990). ". . . observing a spear of summer grass." *Kenyon Review*, 12 (Spring): 17–25.

Whitman's poetry strongly resembles the "philosophical verse essay, one of the most popular poetic forms of the 18th century."

Barcus, Jr., James E. (1998). *November Boughs*. In J. R. LeMaster and Donald D. Kummings (eds.), *Walt Whitman: An Encyclopedia*. New York and London: Garland, pp. 469–72.

Berry, Faith (2001). Walt Whitman. In Faith Berry (ed.), *From Bondage to Liberation: Writings by and about Afro-Americans from 1700 to 1918*. New York: Continuum, pp. 200–2.

Briefly discusses the "racist Whitman who emerges in his diaries, letters, sketches, fiction, essays, and journalism."

Black, Stephen A. (1978). Review of Walt Whitman, *Daybooks and Notebooks* and Randall A. Waldron (ed.), *Mattie: The Letters of Martha Mitchell Whitman. West Coast Review*, 13 (October): 62–3.

Blodgett, Harold W. (1959). Introduction. *An 1855–56 Notebook Toward the Second Edition of* Leaves of Grass, ed. Harold W. Blodgett, foreword by Charles E. Feinberg, additional notes by William White. Carbondale: Southern Illinois University Press, pp. vii–x.

Brooks, Van Wyck (1921). A Reviewer's Notebook. *Freeman*, 4 (14 December): 334–5.

Brief review of several books, including *The Uncollected Poetry and Prose of Walt Whitman*, ed. Emory Holloway.

Burnes, Brian (1985). A Poet's Scribbles on *Leaves of Grass. Kansas City Star* (February 25): pp. 1B, 4B. Reprinted in *Newsbank Electronic Index*, Literature Index 92 (1984–1985), B6–7.

Review of Walt Whitman, *Notebooks and Unpublished Prose Manuscripts*, ed. Edward F. Grier.

Campbell, Killis (1929). Review of *A Leaf of Grass from Shady Hill*, edited by Kenneth B. Murdock, and *Walt Whitman's Workshop*, edited by Clifton Joseph Furness. *American Literature*, 1 (May): 204–6.

Dean, Susan Day (1990). The Poetic Uses of Whitman's Prose. In Donald D. Kummings (ed.), *Approaches to Teaching Whitman's "Leaves of Grass."* New York: Modern Language Association, pp. 112–19.

Doyle, James (1983). Whitman's Canadian Diary. *University of Toronto Quarterly*, 52: 277–87.

Eitner, Walter H. (1980). Whitman's *Daybooks*: Further Identifications. *Walt Whitman Review*, 26 (June): 72–4.

Erkkila, Betsy (1988). Review of Whitman, *Notebooks and Unpublished Prose Manuscripts*, ed. Edward F. Grier. *The Mickle Street Review*, 10: 102–15.

Folsom, Ed (1986). Review of Walt Whitman, *Notebooks and Unpublished Prose Manuscripts*, ed. Edward Grier. *Philological Quarterly*, 65 (Spring): 287–91.

Folsom, Ed (1993). An Uncollected Whitman Prose Manuscript. *Walt Whitman Quarterly Review*, 11 (Fall): 103.

Furness, Clifton Joseph (1928). Introduction. *Walt Whitman's Workshop: A Collection of Unpublished Manuscripts*. Cambridge, MA: Harvard University Press, pp. 1–24.

Golden, Arthur (1978). Whitman Day by Day, 1876–1891. *Walt Whitman Review*, 24 (June): 84–9.

Review of Walt Whitman, *Daybooks and Notebooks*.

Gosse, Edmund W. (1876). Walt Whitman's New Book. *Academy*, 9 (24 June): 602–3.

Review of *Two Rivulets*. Available online at <http://www.whitmanarchive.org/criticism/ >.

Graham, Rosemary (1998). *The Collected Writings of Walt Whitman* and *The Complete Writings of Walt Whitman*. In J. R. LeMaster and Donald D. Kummings (eds.), *Walt Whitman: An Encyclopedia*. New York and London: Garland, pp. 133–6, 140–1.

Green, Charles B. (1998). "Missing Me One Place Search Another": Three Previously Unpublished Walt Whitman Notebooks. *Walt Whitman Quarterly Review*, 15 (Spring): 147–60.

Grier, Edward F. (1984). Introduction. Walt Whitman, *Notebooks and Unpublished Prose Manuscripts*, ed. Edward Grier, 6 vols. New York: New York University Press, pp. xiii–xx.

Hollis, C. Carroll (1984). Emerson, Whitman, and Poetic Prose. *The Long-Islander*, 147 (21 June): 15.

Holloway, Emory (1921). Introduction: Critical: I. Whitman's Prose. *The Uncollected Poetry and Prose of Walt Whitman*, ed. Emory Holloway, 2 vols. Garden City, NY, and Toronto: Doubleday, Page, vol. 1, pp. lxi–lxxxiv.

Kaplan, Justin (1978). Specimen Days. *Book World: The Washington Post*, 23 April: E5.

Review of Walt Whitman, *Daybooks and Notebooks*.

Krieg, Joann P. (1999). *Two Rivulets. Starting from Paumanok*, 13 (Spring/Summer): 2–3.

LeMaster, J. R. (1998). *Collect*. In J. R. LeMaster and Donald D. Kummings (eds.), *Walt Whitman: An Encyclopedia*. New York and London: Garland, pp. 132–33.

'Loving, Jerome (1979). Review of Walt Whitman, *Daybooks and Notebooks. Modern Philology*, 76 (May): 420–4.

Loving, Jerome (1985). Review of Edward F. Grier, editor. Walt Whitman, *Notebooks and Unpublished Prose Manuscripts. American Literature*, 57 (October): 498–500.

Loving, Jerome (1995). "Broadway, the Magnificent!": A Newly Discovered Whitman Essay. *Walt Whitman Quarterly Review*, 12 (Spring): 209–16.

Martin, Roger (1984). Whitman's Leavings: From Lecture Notes to Love Agonies. *Explore*, 4: 2–4.

A review of Whitman's *Notebooks and Unpublished Prose Manuscripts*, ed. Edward F. Grier.

Matteson, John T. (1998). *The Galaxy* and *West Jersey Press*. In J. R. LeMaster and Donald D. Kummings (eds.), *Walt Whitman: An Encyclopedia*. New York and London: Garland, pp. 245, 764–5.

McLeod, Colin (1978). Review of Walt Whitman, *Daybooks and Notebooks. Library Journal*, 103 (1 June): 1178.

Moore, William L. (1984). An Appreciation to Edward Grier. *Calamus*, 26: 30–5.

Whitman's six-volume *Notes and Unpublished Prose Manuscripts*, edited by Grier, reveals a writer who is less mystical than was previously thought.

Murray, Martin G. (1999). The Poet-Chief Greets the Sioux. *Walt Whitman Quarterly Review*, 17 (Summer/ Fall): 25–37.

On Whitman's prose essay "Real American Red Men."

Nelson, Raymond (1979). Stalking Whitman with Shotgun and Bludgeon. *The Virginia Quarterly Review*, 55 (Summer): 536–7.

Review of Whitman, *Daybooks and Notebooks*.

Pound, Louise (1935). Introduction. Walt Whitman, *Specimen Days*, *Democratic Vistas and Other Prose*. Garden City, NY: Doubleday, Doran, pp. ix–xlvi, xlvii–lii.

Price, Kenneth M. (1985). Trivia and Poetry: The Range of Whitman's Private Writings. *American Literary Realism, 1870–1910*, 18 (Spring/Autumn): 271–7.

Review of Walt Whitman, *Notebooks and Unpublished Prose Manuscripts*, ed. Edward F. Grier.

Price, Kenneth M. (2002). An Unknown Whitman Prose Manuscript on the Principle of Aggregation. *Walt Whitman Quarterly Review*, 19 (Winter/Spring): 182–3.

Rachman, Stephen (1998). *Broadway Journal*. In J. R. LeMaster and Donald D. Kummings (eds.), *Walt Whitman: An Encyclopedia*. New York and London: Garland, p. 78.

Broadway Journal, edited by Poe, published Whitman's brief article, "Art-Singing and Heart-Singing," in 1845.

Rachman, Stephen (1998). "The Tramp and Strike Questions." In J. R. LeMaster and Donald D. Kummings (eds.), *Walt Whitman: An Encyclopedia*. New York and London: Garland, pp. 736–7.

Renner, Dennis K. (1998). *Daybooks and Notebooks*. In J. R. LeMaster and Donald D. Kummings (eds.), *Walt Whitman: An Encyclopedia*. New York and London: Garland, pp. 164–5.

Sayre, Robert F. (1965). Review of Walt Whitman, *Prose Works 1892*. Vol. 1, *Specimen Days*; Vol. 2, *Collect and Other Prose*, edited by Floyd Stovall; and *The Correspondence of Walt Whitman*. Vol. 3, 1876–1885, edited by Edwin Haviland Miller. *Journal of English and Germanic Philology*, 64 (April): 339–42.

Silver, Rollo G. (1938). Whitman's Earliest Signed Prose: A Correction. *American Literature*, 9 (January): 458.

Whitman's earliest signed prose, it turns out, were the minutes he wrote for the Smithtown Debating Society.

Stovall, Floyd (1971). Dating Whitman's Early Notebooks. *Studies in Bibliography*, 24: 197–204.

Whitman's preparations for *Leaves* began not in the 1840s but in 1853, 1854, even 1855 – as revealed by six notebooks in the Harned Collection.

Unsigned (1979). Review of Walt Whitman, *Daybooks and Notebooks. Choice*, 15 (January): 1523.

Versluys, K. (1981). Walt Whitman's *Daybooks and Notebooks. English Studies* (Lisse, Holland), 62 (April): 198.

Wertheimer, Eric (1999). Passage: Two Rivulets and the Obscurity of American Maps. In *Imagined Empires: Incas, Aztecs, and the New World of American Literature, 1771–1876*. Cambridge, UK: Cambridge University Press, pp. 160–90.

On *Two Rivulets* and especially on "Passage to India." There are also references to *Democratic Vistas* and to "The Spanish Element in Our Nationality."

White, William (1962). An Unpublished Notebook: Walt Whitman in Washington in 1863. *American Book Collector*, 12 (January): 8–13.

In this 8" x 5" notebook Whitman recorded various impressions of Washington, DC.

White, William (1967) "Ned – A Phantasy" – Uncollected Whitman. *Emerson Society Quarterly*, 47 (Second Quarter), Part 2: 100–1.

An unpublished, descriptive sketch (255 words) about Whitman's horse.

White, William (1978). *Daybook* Notes Left Over. *Walt Whitman Review*, 24 (June): 91, 92.

White, William (1978). Introduction. Walt Whitman, *Daybooks and Notebooks*, 3 vols., ed. William White. New York: New York University Press, vol. 1, pp. xi–xix.

White, William (1980). "Some Late Occurrences, Facts, in Boston": Unpublished Whitman Prose. *Leaves of Grass* at 125, Supplement to *Walt Whitman Review*, 26: 75–7.

A manuscript regarding a preacher who spoke out against the suppression of *Leaves of Grass*.

White, William (1980). Whitman's *Daybooks*: Corrections Re Morse, McWatters, Colles, Hunter. *Walt Whitman Review*, 26 (June): 71–2.

White, William (1981). "The Body at Its Best": A Whitman Fragment. *Walt Whitman Review*, 27: 48.

A prose fragment that was pasted into the front of an issue of the *Complete Prose Works*.

White, William (1981). Walt Whitman: An Unknown Piece by "Paumanok." In Vince Clemente and Graham Everett (eds.), *Paumanok Rising: An Anthology of Eastern Long Island Aesthetics*. Port Jefferson, NY: Street Press, pp. 31–5.

A short piece by Whitman concerning the history of the Indians of Long Island.

White, William (1985). Review of Edward F. Grier, editor. Walt Whitman, *Notebooks and Unpublished Prose Manuscripts. Walt Whitman Quarterly Review*, 3 (Summer): 25–7.

Wihl, Gary (2001). The Manuscript of Walt Whitman's "Sunday Evening Lectures." *Walt Whitman Quarterly Review*, 18 (Winter): 107–33.

Zhang, Yujiu (1988). Reading Whitman's Prose. *Foreign Literature Studies* [China], 39 (March): 39–44.

Analyzes *Specimen Days*, *Democratic Vistas*, and "A Backward Glance," concluding that Whitman's prose reflects his poetry; in Chinese.

Zweig, Paul (1978). Spontaneity Imitator. *The New York Times Book Review*, April 16: 9, 28–9.

Review of Whitman, *Daybooks and Notebooks*.

Index

Note: Page references in bold type indicate major chapter-length references